D0084646

THE PAPERS OF WILL ROGERS

From Vaudeville to Broadway

Volume Three

September 1908–August 1915

Will Rogers posing as The Oklahoma Cowboy in vaudeville. *(OkClaW)*

The Papers of Will Rogers

From Vaudeville to Broadway

Volume Three

September 1908–August 1915

EDITED BY

Arthur Frank Wertheim

AND

Barbara Bair

CALVIN T. RYAN LIBRARY
U. OF NEBRASKA AT KEARNEY

UNIVERSITY OF OKLAHOMA PRESS : NORMAN

OTHER BOOKS BY ARTHUR FRANK WERTHEIM

The New York Little Renaissance: Iconoclasm, Modernism,
and Nationalism in American Culture (New York, 1976)
Radio Comedy (New York, 1979)
(ed.) *American Popular Culture: A Historical Bibliography*
(Santa Barbara, Calif., 1984)
(ed.) *Will Rogers at the Ziegfeld Follies* (Norman, 1992)
(ed. with Barbara Bair) *The Papers of Will Rogers,* vol. 1: *The Early Years;*
vol. 2: *Wild West and Vaudeville* (Norman, 1996, 2000)

OTHER BOOKS BY BARBARA BAIR

(ed. with Robert A. Hill) *Marcus Garvey: Life and Lessons* (Berkeley, 1987)
(ed. with Robert A. Hill) *The Marcus Garvey and Universal Negro Improvement*
Association Papers, vols. 6 and 7 (Berkeley, 1989, 1990)
(ed. with Susan E. Cayleff) *Wings of Gauze: Women of Color and the Experience of*
Health and Illness (Detroit, 1993)
(ed. with Arthur Wertheim) *The Papers of Will Rogers,* vol. 1: *The Early Years;*
vol. 2: *Wild West and Vaudeville* (Norman, 1996, 2000)
Though Justice Sleeps: African Americans 1880–1900 (New York, 1997)

Library of Congress Cataloguing-in-Publication Data
Rogers, Will, 1879–1935.
  The papers of Will Rogers / edited by Arthur Frank Wertheim and Barbara Bair.
    p.   cm.
  Contents: v.   3. From Vaudeville to Broadway, September 1908–August 1915.
  ISBN 0-8061-3315-5
    1. Rogers, Will, 1879–1935—Archives.   2. Rogers, Will, 1879–1935—Corre-
spondence.   3. Performing arts—United States—History—20th century—Sources.
I. Wertheim, Arthur Frank, 1935–   .   II. Bair, Barbara, 1955–   .   III. Title.
PN2287.R74A25   1995, vol. 3
792.7´028´092—dc20   94-24165
                                                                              CIP

Book and series design by Bill Cason.

The paper in this book meets the guidelines for permanence and durability of the
Committee on Production Guidelines for Book Longevity of the Council on Library
Resources, Inc. ∞

Copyright © 2001 by Will Rogers Heritage Trust, Inc., Claremore, Oklahoma.
Published by the University of Oklahoma Press, Norman, Publishing Division of the
University. All rights reserved. Manufactured in the U.S.A.

2 3 4 5 6 7 8 9 10

THE WILL ROGERS PAPERS PROJECT IS A DOCUMENTARY HISTORY PROJECT OF THE WILL ROGERS MEMORIAL COMMISSION, CLAREMORE, OKLAHOMA. JOSEPH H. CARTER IS PROJECT DIRECTOR AND DIRECTOR OF THE MEMORIAL. FUNDING FOR THE PROJECT HAS COME FROM THE SARKEYS FOUNDATION, THE WILL ROGERS HERITAGE TRUST, INC., AND THE STATE OF OKLAHOMA.

THIS BOOK IS ALSO PUBLISHED WITH THE ASSISTANCE OF THE NATIONAL ENDOWMENT FOR THE HUMANITIES, A FEDERAL AGENCY WHICH SUPPORTS THE STUDY OF SUCH FIELDS AS HISTORY, PHILOSOPHY, LITERATURE AND LANGUAGE.

Contents

Documents

1. WITH ALL MY HEART

5. BROADWAY FOOTLIGHTS

Illustrations

Acknowledgments

THE WILL ROGERS PAPERS PROJECT IS ESPECIALLY INDEBTED TO THE BOARD of Trustees and officers of the Sarkeys Foundation for funding that established crucial underwriting for the volumes. The start-up grant provided funds for staffing, equipment, travel, and other necessary expenses to carry out research and publication. We are very grateful to the trustees of the Foundation for supporting the legacy of Will Rogers: Richard D. Bell, Jane A. Jayroe, Joseph W. Morris, Robert T. Rennie, Robert S. Rizley, Paul F. Sharp, and Lee Anne Wilson. We also thank Cheri D. Cartwright, the director of grants for the Sarkeys Foundation.

State Senator Stratton Taylor and Representative Dwayne Steidley, with the backing of the Oklahoma legislature, helped provide public means to match private funds. We thank the citizens of Oklahoma for their support of our tribute to their native son.

This project would never have been possible without the endorsement of several other key individuals. We are especially thankful for the encouragement of Will Rogers, Jr., and Jim Rogers, both of whom strongly believed in the project's mission. Dean Robert H. Henry of the School of Law, Oklahoma City University, also deserves our gratitude for his support, which helped launch the project in its early phase.

We are also very grateful to the members of the Will Rogers Memorial Commission for their endorsement of the project: commissioners Patricia Crume, John Denbo, James L. Hartz, J. Kevin Hayes, Hunt Lowry, James B. Rogers, and Charles Ward.

We appreciate the time and effort the staff at the Will Rogers Memorial have devoted to the project. Joseph H. Carter, director of the Memorial and the Will Rogers Papers Project, first conceived of the project. Patricia Lowe, Memorial librarian and archivist and the project's editorial assistant, provided an enormous amount of time and energy in the initial research on and transcription of Rogers's correspondence. Most important, she lent her incomparable archival expertise, serving as an indispensable guide to the entire Will Rogers collection at the Memorial.

We thank the Will Rogers Cooperative Association and the state park rangers and staff for their support. Nancy Mendez, curator, helped us gain access to Rogers's documents housed at the park, and Randy Young shared his enthusiasm and assisted us in making photographs from Rogers's scrapbooks. Steven Leikin served as an editorial assistant with the Will Rogers Papers Project. He transcribed and proofread many new, noncorrespondence documents that were selected by the editors to appear in the volume, including playbills, newspaper articles, and reviews. He also conducted background research and drafted selective annotations for the volume. Jane Collings, the assistant editor of the volume, contributed to every phase of the research on the selected documents. She conducted archival searches and contacted special collections across the country to identify obscure individuals and events that figure in the history of Rogers's early career. She also helped draft selective annotations and Biographical Appendix entries on cinematic history, theaters, and individuals who appear in the volume, and helped the editors with basic editorial tasks in the production of the manuscript. Her contribution was essential to the success of the project.

The Interlibrary Loan Office of the UCLA Libraries, headed by Ian Dacosta, ordered many critical documents for the project from other repositories. Librarians at the McHenry Library, University of California, Santa Cruz, also contributed to the project's research.

Extensive document collection and annotation research in primary materials were conducted by the editors, who traveled to university and public libraries, research centers, museum and theater archives, and special collections around the country and in London in pursuit of materials. Among the collections that were indispensable to our task of compiling information about the many individuals with whom Rogers performed in vaudeville were the Billy Rose Theatre Collection and Robinson Locke Collection of the New York Public Library for the Performing Arts, Lincoln Center, New York; the Theater Arts Collection of the Harry Ransom Humanities Research Center at the University of Texas at Austin; the Buck McKee Collection, California Section, California State Library, Sacramento; and the Theater Collection of the Philadelphia Free Library. We would like to offer very special thanks to Bob Taylor, curator of the Billy Rose Theatre Collection, and to the following librarians who serve on the staff of the New York Public Library for the Performing Arts: David Bartholomew, Roderick Bladel, Christopher Frith, Don Glenn, Christine Karatnytsky, Brian O'Connell, Daniel D. Patri, Louis Paul, Edward J. Sager, and Kevin Winkler. Melissa Miller, curator of the Theater Arts Collection at the Harry Ransom Humanities Research Center;

Jeanette Rustan and John R. Gonzales, librarians, of the California State Library; and Geraldine Duclow, archivist, and Elaine Ebo, assistant archivist, of the Theater Collection at the Philadelphia Free Library were all of special help in guiding our on-site research and arranging for the copying of photographs or primary materials.

We are also indebted to the following librarians and archivists who greatly helped with research or with the location of photographs of the vaudeville and Wild West era: Annette Fern, reference and research librarian, Harvard Theatre Collection, Harvard College Library, Cambridge, Mass.; Kristen Tanaka, head librarian, San Francisco Performing Arts Library and Museum; Giuseppe Bisaccia, curator of manuscripts, Division of Rare Books and Manuscripts, Boston Public Library; Cathy Wright, director, Taylor Museum for Southwestern Studies of the Colorado Springs Fine Arts Center; Maryann Chach, archivist, and Mark Swartz, assistant archivist, Shubert Archive, New York; Fred Dahlinger, Jr., director, Robert L. Parkinson Library and Research Center, Circus World Museum, Baraboo, Wis.; Marty Jacobs, special consultant, Theatre Collection, and Marguerite Lavin, Museum of the City of New York; Marie Demeroukas, registrar, Rogers Historical Museum, Rogers, Ark.; Raymond Wemmlinger, curator and librarian, Hampden-Booth Theatre Library, New York; Mylon Houston, head librarian, and Paula Stewart, archivist, Amon Carter Museum Library, Fort Worth, Tex.; Cathy Henderson, research librarian, Charles Bell, curator, and Andrea Inselmann, archivist, Film and Photograph Division, Harry Ransom Humanities Research Center, University of Texas, Austin; Nathan E. Bender, head, Special Collections and Archives, Montana State University, Bozeman; Kathy Dickson, director of museums, Oklahoma Historical Society, Oklahoma City; Susan M. Kooyman, archivist, Glenbow Museum Library and Archives, Calgary, Alberta, Canada; Anne B. Wheeler, National Cowboy Hall of Fame, Oklahoma City; Virginia Artho, assistant director, National Cowgirl Hall of Fame and Western Heritage Center, Hereford, Tex.; Patricia Florence, assistant director and curator, ProRodeo Hall of Fame and Museum of the American Cowboy, Colorado Springs; Steve Gossard, curator of circus collections, Milner Library Special Collections, Illinois State University, Normal; Robert A. McCown, head, Special Collections and Manuscripts, University Libraries, University of Iowa, Iowa City; Bill Benedict, archive consultant, Theatre Historical Society of America, Elmhurst, Ill.; Eleanor J. Mish, registrar and manager, American Museum of the Moving Image, Astoria, N.Y.; Patricia Michaelis, Manuscripts Collection, Kansas State Historical Society, Topeka; Samuel Gill, archivist emeritus, Margaret Herrick Library, the Academy of Motion Picture Arts and

Sciences, Beverly Hills, Calif.; Dace Taube, librarian, Regional History Collection, Special Collections, and Ned Comstock, archivist, Special Collections, University of Southern California, Los Angeles; Frances B. Clymer, associate librarian, Buffalo Bill Historical Center, Cody, Wyo.; Jerry Hatfield, librarian, Library of Congress, Washington, D.C.; William H. Richter, reference archivist, Center for American History, University of Texas, Austin; and Don Bell, of Byron, Wyo.

We are grateful for the assistance of the following archivists, librarians, curators, and scholars who provided information and material for the Rogers volumes: William D. Welge, director, Archives and Manuscript Division, Oklahoma Historical Society, Oklahoma City; Bradford Koplowitz, curator, Western History Collections, University of Oklahoma Libraries, Norman; Betty Bustes, Panhandle-Plains Historical Museum, Canyon, Tex.; Victoria Sheffler, university archivist, Northeastern State University, Tahlequah, Okla.; Annabell Southern, librarian, Vinita Public Library, Vinita, Okla.; Derrick Austin and Lance Vanzant, archival assistants, Southwest Collection, Texas Tech University, Lubbock; Richard Fusick, archivist, Civil Reference Branch, National Archives, Washington, D.C.; Joy Dodson, public services assistant, Central Methodist College, Fayette, Mo.; Robin Courtney, librarian, City County Library, Neosho, Mo.; Devon Mahesuah, professor, Department of History, Northern Arizona University, Flagstaff; Glenn Colliver, assistant archivist, Department of History, Presbyterian Church (USA), Philadelphia; Joan McCullough, librarian, Oklahoma United Methodist Archives, Dulaney-Browne Library, Oklahoma City University; Jim Gatewood, director of public affairs, Kemper Military School, Boonville, Mo.; Twila D. McClure, librarian, Chelsea Public Library, Chelsea, Okla.; Joan Singleton, public services librarian, Bartlesville Public Library and History Museum, Bartlesville, Okla.; Peter Stark, map librarian, University of Oregon, Eugene; Diane Boucher Ayotte, manuscript specialist, Western Historical Manuscript Collection, Ellis Library, University of Missouri, Columbia; Heather Lloyd, head, Special Collections, Oklahoma State University, Stillwater; Jennie Terrapin, history coordinator, Official Web Site of the Cherokee Nation; Valerie Helson, acting manuscript librarian, Australian Collections and Services, National Library of Australia, Canberra; Jo Peoples, curator, Performing Arts Collection of South Australia, Theatre Museum, Adelaide; Mark Valentine St. Leon, writer/researcher, Gleble, New South Wales, Australia; archivists of the Cape Archives Depot, Cape Town, the Free State Archives Depot, Bloemfontein, the Natal Archives Depot, Pietermaritzburg, and the Transvaal Archives Depot, Pretoria, South Africa; Rooksana Omar of the Local History Museum and Chantelle Wyley, history subject librarian, University of Natal Library, Durban, Natal, South Africa. Other individuals who answered inquiries and provided material were E. Paul Alworth, Jack D. Baker, Genny Mae Bard, Dr. Robert Henderson, Kathryn Jenkins, Harold Keith, Howard Meredith, Peter Rollins, Emil Sandmeier, and John and Faith Wylie.

Librarians, archivists, or curators at the following institutions have provided important help to the project in document collection and research: the Library of Congress, the National Archives, and the Smithsonian National Air and Space Museum Library, Washington, D.C.; the California Section, California State Library, Sacramento; the Oral History Project and the Rare Book and Manuscript Library, Columbia University, New York; the Missouri Historical Society, St. Louis; the Bancroft Library, University of California, Berkeley; the Hoover Institute, Stanford University, Palo Alto, Calif.; the American Film Institute, Charles Feldman Library, Los Angeles; the Keith-Albee Collection, University of Iowa, Iowa City; the Museum of Modern Art Film Center, New York; the Western History Collection, Denver Public Library; the Circus Collection, San Antonio Public Library; the Rodeo Historical Society and National Cowboy Hall of Fame's Rodeo Division, Oklahoma City; the Charles Lummis Collection, Southwest Museum, Pasadena, Calif.; the Montana Historical Society, Helena; the Tulsa Historical Society, Tulsa, Okla.; the Oologah Historical Society, Oologah, Okla.; the Newport Historical Society, Newport, R.I.; the New-York Historical Society; the Glenbow Museum and Archives, Calgary, Alberta, Canada; and the Victoria and Albert Theatre Museum, National Museum of the Performing Arts, Theatre Collection, Covent Garden, London, England.

We would especially like to thank Rogers biographer Ben Yagoda, who shared with us his typescript copy of the unpublished autobiographical notes that Rogers wrote for Sime Silverman, making it possible for us to print an excerpt from those notes in our documentary edition. Laurie Weltz and Martha Fisch also generously shared with us their private collections of scrapbooks and photographs chronicling the experiences of family members who were Will Rogers's friends and colleagues.

A special note of thanks is due Carol Wertheim and Jason Wertheim, both for their archival research and their support and encouragement. Personal thanks also go to Martha Fisch, Dana Frank, Mari Jo and Paul Buhle, Sylvia Tidwell and William Brice, Richard Taskin, and Michael Wreszin for their interest and kindness during the production of the Rogers Papers volumes.

We are grateful to our many fine colleagues at the University of Oklahoma Press. Sarah Iselin, former associate editor, guided the manuscript in its early stages. Our special thanks go to director John Drayton for his ongoing support of our project, and to managing editor Alice Stanton for her expert and friendly guidance of the Rogers volumes through the editorial process. This volume was copyedited and computer-coded for the press by Lys Ann Shore, of Shore Editorial Services, South Bend, Ind., and we thank her for the high quality of her work.

THE PAPERS OF WILL ROGERS

From Vaudeville to Broadway

Volume Three

September 1908–August 1915

Introduction

THERE IS A FIXED IMAGE OF WILL ROGERS IN THE PUBLIC HEART. THAT IMAGE, based on familiarity with Rogers's friendly face and the knowledge that one could rely on having a chuckle over his newest witticism about current events or the foibles of being human, stems from the fame that Rogers garnered in the 1920s and early 1930s. Before that time in which Rogers's self-presentation fell into place, there was a long process of uneven development. The earlier off-stage personality and on-stage character of Will Rogers were both continually evolving, in a process of repeated renewal and staggered maturation. The first half of his life was marked by transformation. First he evolved from a reluctant schoolboy and enthusiastic steer roper in the Cherokee Nation to an itinerant wanderer in the Southern Hemisphere. Then he went from life as a Wild West performer and vaudeville trouper with several romantic attachments to the more settled life of a loyal husband and family man. He worked through a relationship of conflict with his father to one of reconciliation. He converted himself from bashful boy to international speechmaker, and he went from a youth of obscurity and rebellion to an adulthood of celebrity and public accolades.

As Rogers matured, so did the nation. Part of the appeal of his public persona was recognition on the part of common people that he somehow had managed to represent through his career the major trends in the mainstream culture of the United States, all the while remaining, despite his celebrity status, a voice for people like themselves. He represented how things had changed. He also preserved a kind of fundamental humility. Rogers's show-business career, as documented in these volumes, can be seen as a mirror reflecting the evolution of American culture as it was manifested in popular modes of expression—in the likes of dime novels, jokes, stories, and songs—and in the theater arts, from the elaborate pantomimes of western conflicts staged in Wild West arenas to the ethnic jokes and wonderments of vaudeville performances, to the humor and commentary on gender roles embedded in musical comedies, farces, and sketches on the vaudeville and legitimate stage. Each of these forms of performance dealt with things that had been lost or were in the process of being reworked—the unsettled West, the cowboy cul-

ture of the cattle drive, the ways of Europe left behind in immigration, the perceived homogeneity of American urban life, the seemingly fixed roles of men
and women, hierarchies of race and ethnicity. Rogers's performance art exemplified how modes of popular culture and mass entertainment developed in
the early twentieth century, as he moved from one genre to another: from Wild
West shows to vaudeville, from the variety stage to the Broadway musical and
revue, from Broadway to front-page newspaper columnist, from print communication to visual communication, and from film media to network radio.

Rogers possessed the determination and talent to master each of these
popular culture forms and to repeatedly revitalize his public self in new medi-
ums. The lariat tricks he learned as a youngster in the Indian Territory were
transferred from the range to the steer-roping arena, from the Wild West show
to the vaudeville stage, and from the *Ziegfeld Follies* to the film *The Roping Fool*
(1922). The humorous patter in vaudeville evolved into the timely political
and topical humor in the *Ziegfeld Follies*. His wry crackerbarrel comedic style
migrated from the stage to film and radio performances that captivated a mass
audience.

Documents in the first two volumes of *The Papers of Will Rogers* illustrate
the changes and events in Rogers's life and career from 1879 to 1908. Volume
one covers the years from Rogers's birth in 1879 to 1904. It relates his
upbringing and his Cherokee heritage; his early friendships and his family history; the vast political, social, and economic upheavals in the Indian Territory
that took place in his father's lifetime; and the urbanization and commercial-
ization of the West. The volume also recounts Rogers's initial experiences as a
performer in steer-roping events, Wild West shows, and the circus. The years
from 1904 to 1908 are covered in volume two, which depicts Rogers's transformation from Wild West performer to vaudeville entertainer. The volume
relates Rogers's stage career to turmoil in the vaudeville industry and the
growth of vaudeville theater circuits, and reveals the impact of the popularity
of mythic images of the West on Rogers's carefully crafted public persona.
Correspondence from Rogers to Betty Blake in volume two describes their
mercurial relationship, from expressions of deep love to arguments over petty
jealousies. In volume three, which documents the years from 1908 to 1915,
Rogers's dabbling in show business matures into a career, and his roaming
personal life becomes centered in a commitment to Betty Blake that would
similarly last his lifetime.

Rogers in the late summer of 1908 was an unhappy man. Finding work in
vaudeville was a constant struggle, and he was tiring of life on the road.
Vaudeville, in his mind, was still a temporary lark, and his correspondence

home to his father is filled with plans to consolidate property in the Oologah area and return in the near future to Oklahoma to ranch and farm, leaving the show-business life behind him. Some soul searching in the early fall of 1908 led Rogers to lay his personal transgressions at the feet of Betty Blake, who had herself long refrained from giving Rogers the commitment he wanted. She responded to this risk taking by Rogers in a generous way. The turning point in Rogers's personal life came in October 1908, when Betty Blake agreed to marry him. Happiness and certainty rushed in where doubt and indiscretion had formerly ruled. Rogers was thrilled about the impending marriage, and shared his exuberance with everyone who would listen. His family were surprised and pleased at his big news. Rogers himself went into the backyard of his sister's home and burned two bushels of mementos from his former love life, purging himself of the past and committing himself with a clean slate to the future. The wedding took place on 25 November 1908, the day before Thanksgiving, in a small ceremony in Betty Blake's mother's home in Rogers, Ark. The newlyweds were pelted with rice and good wishes by rejoicing residents of Rogers as they took a wagon from the Blake residence to the railway station and entered into their new life together. For Betty Blake, marriage to Rogers meant a sudden immersion in the vaudeville life. It called for her to dispense with some of the negative prejudices she held about actors and their way of life. She found a new freedom on the vaudeville tour, which opened up new realities for her. She went on the road with Rogers and saw places she had never seen before, and met many new and different people. For Rogers, who remained an essentially shy person even while becoming a favorite among his friends on the circuit, Betty was a true partner and companion who filled the emptiness that had previously been gnawing at him as he traveled from town to town. Buck McKee, his assistant in the vaudeville act, soon began feeling like a third wheel, for Rogers had eyes only for Betty.

Meanwhile, the envisioned home and ranch in Oklahoma became more remote in both Will and Betty Blake Rogers's minds. They continued to postpone going home to Oklahoma, until by 1911 New York had effectively become their home. It would remain so until 1919, when they would make their way to Hollywood. The temporary life Rogers thought he had made in vaudeville became—by virtue of its success—a lifelong career. It led Rogers not back to Oklahoma but onward to stage work and a beckoning fame. While this important professional evolution was occurring, major family transitions also took place.

One of the first shocks that the Rogerses' new marriage had to absorb was the news, which came to them in July 1909, that Rogers's sister May Stine had died at Sallie McSpadden's home in Chelsea, Okla. The severity of her illness had been underestimated, and there was not sufficient time, once the truth was realized, for the Rogerses to be notified in New York and get to Oklahoma in time to see Stine before her death. They missed the funeral also. But they were nevertheless drawn ever more closely into the family circle by the web of empathetic correspondence that circulated among the family members over their loss. Betty became more truly a sister to the remaining Rogers girls, and she was a dutiful daughter-in-law to Clement Vann Rogers, the family patriarch. It is through her letters to her father-in-law that we know much about her early married life with Rogers, his work, and their situations in New York City. Happiness and loss would continue to be closely entwined. In 1911 the Rogers's first child, William Vann Rogers, was born, and one week later Clement Vann Rogers died. Thus Rogers became a father himself only days before losing his own father, one who had figured very large in his life. Over the next few years the Rogers family continued to grow, with the birth of Mary Amelia (named for her paternal and maternal grandmothers) in 1913, and of James Blake in 1915. In each case, the father would joyfully announce the birth from behind the footlights where he was playing.

This evolution of Rogers from gallivanting bachelor to adoring husband and father, from young wayward son in his birth family to head of a family of his own, was the personal backdrop to similar transformations in his show-business career. In 1910 Rogers reached back to his roots in Oklahoma, Indian Territory, and Texas. He renewed old ties to Wild West and roping-contest performers. His notorious falling out with Zack Mulhall back in the summer of 1905 was healed with an agreement, signed between the two men in March 1910, for the return of Rogers's boyhood cow pony, Comanche, who had ended up through somewhat shady circumstances in Mulhall's hands five years before. Rogers went to St. Louis in April 1910 and appeared in a Wild West show with his old friends, Lucille Mulhall, J. Ellison Carroll, and Tom Mix. A few weeks later he was doing rope tricks as a feature in Buffalo Bill's Wild West and Pawnee Bill's Far East show at Madison Square Garden in New York City. He mounted his own Will Rogers Wild West show for one week with western performers and vaudevillians at the Big Hip in Philadelphia, and in September he did a trick rope exhibition during a roping contest organized by Carroll in Tulsa. He had re-immersed himself in his old network of friends.

Rogers was also searching for a way to change and broaden his act. For five years he had traveled with Buck Mckee and his bay pony Teddy, wowing audiences with his skill with a lariat. In the summer of 1910 he retired Teddy to a pasture in Oologah. Rogers and McKee then broke in a new horse for the act. In the meantime Rogers developed a new group act, bringing Wild West equestrienne feats to the stage. He hired from among the best of female talent in Wild West and rodeo circuits—bronc rider Goldie St. Clair, champion trick roper Tillie Baldwin, high-school horse rider and western-style roper Florence LaDue—and put together a smash-bang act with the women and horses on center stage, himself on the sidelines as narrator. The act proved too unwieldy and too far removed from what theater managers expected from Rogers. By the spring of 1911 he had pared it down, performing himself with Buck McKee and his close friends Charles and Mabel Hackney Tompkins. It was the last gasp of his Wild West years. By May of 1911 horses, McKee, and bronc riders were gone. Rogers had a new agent, Max Hart, and he went on the road as a single act—Will Rogers, No Horse. Hart marketed Rogers as the Oklahoma Cowboy, and sent him off on a career path that would lead through stage work and the Orpheum Circuit direct to the *Ziegfeld Follies*. No longer alone in his personal life, Rogers finally was standing on his own on stage.

By working regularly on the Orpheum Circuit, Rogers joined in the most successful vaudeville chain west of Chicago, and was also involved directly in the rivalry between the Western Vaudeville Managers Association, headed by Martin Beck and Morris Meyerfield, and the Eastern Vaudeville Managers Association, headed by B. F. Keith and Edward Albee. In between the warring managers and theater owners were the actors' rights organizations, like the White Rats union, which included some of Rogers's close friends, such as entertainer Fred Stone. Rogers threaded his way through the controversies and takeovers in the business, working all over the United States. In 1914 he traveled to London, where he appeared in the *Merry-Go-Round* revue. The revue work came on the heels of his successful run in *The Wall Street Girl*, a western musical comedy starring the popular Blanche Ring, in which Rogers appeared as a cowboy character. The show ran first at the George M. Cohan Theatre in New York (April—June 1912) and then on the road from September 1912 to March 1913. Stage work was interspersed with vaudeville engagements, and Rogers appeared on vaudeville playbills and in benefit programs with friends like Winona Winter, Harry Houdini, and Pat Rooney and Marion Bent. When his daughter Mary was an infant, he was on stage with Eddie Cantor and George Jessel. It was a rich time in Rogers's life, and the heyday of his vaudeville career, peaking with his appearances at New York's grand Palace Theatre.

In late 1910 Rogers wrote out a version of his life for Sime Silverman, founder of *Variety* and champion of actors' rights within the vaudeville managers' wars. Though it was not published, the draft essay contained a kernel of what was to come in Rogers's journalistic career, showing early evidence of his trademark modes of expression and his use of autobiography as social commentary. In August 1913, in the midst of stage and vaudeville appearances, Rogers produced his first article for publication, a piece about roping that he wrote for his friend J. Ellison Carroll. It was printed in *The Stampede,* the program of the 1913 Winnipeg Stampede in Manitoba, Canada. In May 1915 Rogers performed at the Victoria Theatre in its last week of offering vaudeville entertainment. Rogers too would eventually make the transition from the genre of vaudeville to film. In July 1915 he signed with Lee Shubert for a role in *Hands Up.* Though not a successful show, the engagement was a stepping-stone to an August 1915 contract for the *Just Girls* revue, a segment of Ziegfeld's *Midnight Frolic.* Volume three ends with this successful transition through vaudeville to Broadway, on the brink of Rogers's breakthrough as a star of the *Ziegfeld Follies.*

Chronology, 1908–1915

1908

14–19 September	Rogers performs at the Cook Opera House, Rochester, N.Y.
21–26 September	Grand Opera House, Pittsburgh.
23 September	Rogers admits to Betty Blake that he has been seeing another woman, and apologizes to her for his unfaithful behavior.
28 September–3 October	Armory Theater, Binghamton, N.Y.
5–10 October	Grand Opera House, Syracuse, N.Y.
ca. 8 October	Rogers and Betty Blake come to an agreement to be married. He plans a trip home to his family.
12–17 October	Princess Theater, Montreal, Quebec.
19–24 October	Grand Theater, Auburn, N.Y.
26–31 October	Poli's Theater, Wilkes-Barre, Pa.
27 October	Rogers sees Robert Edison in *Call of the North*.
11 November	Arrives in Chelsea, Okla., after traveling through Rogers, Ark., on the train.
12 November	Informs his family that he intends to marry Betty Blake.
19 November	Sallie McSpadden's daughter, Irene, is ill with scarlet fever and the entire McSpadden family is quarantined. They will be unable to attend Rogers's wedding.
25 November	Rogers and Betty Blake are married in a small private ceremony at her mother's home in Rogers, Ark.
26 November	On a brief honeymoon in St. Louis, Will and Betty Blake Rogers see the Carlisle Indians defeat St. Louis University in a Thanksgiving football game.

7–12 December	Betty Blake Rogers, for the first time, sees her husband perform his act, at Proctor's Theatre, Newark, N.J.
14–19 December	Colonial Theatre, New York City.
14 and 15 December	Rogers signs Orpheum Circuit contracts to tour cities in the South, Midwest, and West with his act including horse Teddy and friend Buck McKee. Betty Blake Rogers accompanies him on the circuit.
28–31 December	American Theatre, St. Louis.

1909

1 January	Rogerses visit Chelsea, Okla., for New Year's Day.
4–9 January	Orpheum, Memphis.
11–16 January	Orpheum, New Orleans.
22 January	Rogerses visit Chelsea and Claremore, Okla.
25–30 January	Rogers plays the Orpheum, Kansas City, Mo.
1–6 February	Orpheum, Omaha.
8–13 February	Orpheum, St. Paul, Minn.
15–20 February	Orpheum, Minneapolis.
25 February	Rogerses are robbed when their trunk is broken into in their hotel room in Butte, Mont.
27 February–6 March	Orpheum, Butte.
8–13 March	Orpheum, Spokane.
15–20 March	Orpheum, Seattle.
22–27 March	Orpheum, Portland, Ore.
29 March–3 April	Orpheum, San Francisco.
5–10 April	Orpheum, Salt Lake City.
12–17 April	Orpheum, Denver.
20 April	Rogerses visit friends and family in Claremore. Betty Blake Rogers goes on to visit her family in Rogers, Ark., while Will Rogers goes back to work for a month without her on the circuit.
25 April	En route to Louisville, Ky., Rogers sees the Chicago Cubs play the St. Louis Cardinals in St. Louis.

26 April–1 May	Mary Anderson Theatre, Louisville, Ky.
3–8 May	Columbia Theatre, Cincinnati.
10–15 May	Forest Park Highlands, St. Louis.
17–22 May	Grand Theater, Indianapolis.
24–29 May	Ramona Theatre, Reed's Lake, Grand Rapids, Mich. Betty Blake Rogers rejoins her husband on the road.
30 May–5 June	Rogers's father Clement Vann Rogers, niece Estelle Lane, and cousin Mary Gulager travel to Chicago to see Rogers play at the Majestic Theatre.
most of June	Rogerses vacation in Atlantic City, N.J.
26 June	Rogers plays at Young's Pier Theatre, Atlantic City, N.J.
14 July	Rogerses return to New York City, where they reside at the Preston Hotel, across from Madison Square Garden.
19 July	Betty Blake Rogers reports to Clement Vann Rogers that Will Rogers has lined up work in Newport, R.I., and Brighton Beach and Rockaway Beach, N.Y., and that the two of them may take the next week off to go to the mountains.
25 July	After a brief illness, Rogers's sister, May Rogers Yocum Stine, dies at Sallie McSpadden's home in Chelsea, Okla. Will and Betty Blake Rogers are unable to travel to Oologah in time for the funeral.
26 July	May Stine's funeral is conducted in the Southern Methodist Episcopal Church of Oologah, and she is laid to rest in the Oak Hill Cemetery.
9–14 August	Keith's Theatre, Philadelphia. Rogers appears with Al Jolson.
10 August	Rogers sets up vaudeville work for the fall of 1909 and the first months of 1910. He signs contracts with F. F. Proctor's Amusement

Enterprises and with Percy G. Williams Circuit through United Booking Offices of America (UBO) for work in New York area, with B. F. Keith Theatre Co. for work in Boston, with B. F. Keith Hippodrome Co. for work in Cleveland, and with B. F. Keith Amusement Enterprises for work in Philadelphia.

16–21 August	Sheedy's Theatre, Freebody Park, Newport, R.I. Betty Blake Rogers accompanies Rogers to Newport, and they enjoy sightseeing in the resort town. The two continue to travel together on the circuit.
30 August–4 September	Alhambra Theatre, New York City.
6–11 September	Poli's Theatre, Waterbury, Conn.
27 September–2 October	Hudson Theatre, Union Hill, N.J.
4 October	Shubert Theatre, Utica, N.Y.
11–16 October	Shea's Theatre, Buffalo, N.Y.
18–23 October	Toronto, Ontario, Canada.
25–30 October	Ottawa, Quebec, Canada.
1–6 November	Orpheum, Harrisburg, Pa.
7 November	Rogerses return to New York City.
8–13 November	Proctor's Theatre, Newark, N.J.
ca. 14 November	Rogerses move into an apartment at 560 West 113th Street, New York City. They board with a couple from Muskogee, Okla.
15–20 November	Loew's Theatre, New Rochelle, N.Y.
ca. 22 November	Rogers finds himself caught in the middle of a power dispute between UBO and the Joe Wood Agency (representing Loew Enterprises), over control of performers and bookings for Proctor's chain of theaters.
22–27 November	Proctor's Theatre, Albany, N.Y.
29 November–4 December	Keith's Theatre, Boston.
6–11 December	Star Theatre, Brooklyn, N.Y.
13–18 December	Gaiety Theatre, Brooklyn, N.Y.
20–25 December	Hammerstein's Victoria Theatre, New York City.

1910

3–8 January	Colonial Theatre, Norfolk, Va.
10–15 January	Bronx Theatre, New York City.
17–22 January	Greenpoint Theatre, New York City.
24–29 January	Young's Pier Theatre, Atlantic City, N.J.
31 January–5 February	Temple Theatre, Detroit.
7–12 February	Temple Theatre, Rochester, N.Y.
14–19 February	Rogers's vaudeville calendar indicates an (unconfirmed) engagement in Johnstown (Pa. or N.Y.).
21–26 February	Keith's Hippodrome, Cleveland.
28 February–5 March	Keith's Theatre, Philadelphia.
14–19 March	Poli's Theatre, Springfield, Mass.
21–26 March	Poli's Theatre, New Haven, Conn.
22 March 1910	Zack Mulhall and Rogers come to an agreement regarding the return of Rogers's horse Comanche.
28 March–2 April	Poli's Theatre, Meriden, Conn.
7 April	Rogers appears in Mulhall's Wild West show directed by Jim Gabriel at the St. Louis Coliseum. Fellow performers include old friends Lucille Mulhall, J. Ellison Carroll, and Tom Mix.
11–16 April	Keith and Proctor's Fifth Avenue Theater, New York City. Rogers appears with W. C. Fields.
18–23 April	Orpheum's Alhambra Theatre, New York City. Appears with Pat Rooney and Marion Bent.
23–30 April	Rogers appears in vaudeville at the Colonial Theatre, New York City. Lew Dockstader is also on the bill.
26–30 April	While he is on the bill at the Colonial, Rogers also appears with Buffalo Bill's Wild West and Pawnee Bill's Far East combined show at Madison Square Garden, New York City.
2–14 May	Performs in Buffalo, N.Y.
16–21 May	Warburton Theatre, Yonkers, N.Y.

30 May–4 June	William Penn Theatre, Philadelphia.
6–11 June	Murray Hill Theatre, New York City.
13–18 June	Rogers mounts Will Rogers's Wild West show at the Big Hip arena and ball park, Philadelphia, combining Wild West and vaudeville acts in an outdoor setting.
20–25 June	Rogers does his rope act in a group show at the Airdome arena and ball park, Boston.
18–23 July	Casino Theatre, Ponce de Leon Park, Atlanta.
25–30 July	Rogers plays in Chattanooga, Tenn. He and McKee give their last performance using Teddy.
August	Rogerses visit family in Rogers, Ark., and the Claremore-Chelsea area. Teddy is retired to pasture at the Rogers ranch.
ca. 18 August	Teddy and another horse disappear from their Oologah pasture.
21 September	Rogers appears at a roping contest at the Tulsa fairgrounds organized by J. Ellison Carroll.
mid-October	On a quick trip home, Rogers purchases two ponies and a filly in Oklahoma. He seeks a replacement for Teddy in his vaudeville act and also mounts for his equestrians to use in the new "Big Act," a group Wild West act he has decided to develop for the stage.
24–29 October	Casino Theatre, Brooklyn, N.Y.
31 October–5 November	Empire Theatre, Brooklyn, N.Y.
ca. 1 November	Rogers recruits top female riders from Wild West shows to appear in his new group act, including Goldie St. Clair, Mabel Hackney Tompkins, and Florence LaDue. He spends his free time training the new horses for the act.
7–12 November	Miners Theatre, New York City.
14–19 November	Performs in Orange and Bayonne, N.J.
21–26 November	Performs in New Brunswick and Patterson, N.J.
25 November	Rogerses celebrate their second wedding anniversary, in New York City, while he is commuting to work in New Jersey.

ca. 1 December	New Wild West act goes into rehearsal with the women riders in preparation for planned 5 December opening.
5–10 December	In Bayonne, N.J. Probably the trial run of the new big Wild West act.
12 December	Betty Blake Rogers reports to Clement Vann Rogers that Will Rogers plans to bring the new act into New York City the next day, and that he is worried that it may have too many horses to fit well on the stage.
12–17 December	Third Avenue Theatre and Prospect Theatre, Bronx, N.Y.
18 December	Will Rogers and His Broncos act appears at the *New York American's* Christmas Fund Benefit at the Hippodrome.
19–24 December	Empire Theatre, Pittsfield, Mass.

1911

2–7 January	Plays in Lawrence, Kans.
5 January	Rogers proposes to his father that Clement Vann Rogers, Sallie McSpadden, and Maud Lane join him and Betty Blake Rogers on a trip to Europe.
9—14 January	Plays in Columbia, N.Y.
11 January	Clement Vann Rogers celebrates his seventy-second birthday at a big party given in his honor at the home of Sallie McSpadden in Chelsea, Okla.
16—21 January	Rogers plays in Albany and Schenectady, N.Y.
23—28 January	Star Theatre, Brooklyn, N.Y.
30 January—4 February	Prospect Theatre, Cleveland.
6—11 February	Performs in Detroit.
13—18 February	Performs in Rochester, N.Y.
17 February	Rogers signs contract for Will Rogers and Co., listed as a specialty "Bronco Busters" act (streamlined to four performers), to appear in Philadelphia.
20–25 February	Performs in Barrington, R.I.

6–11 March	Keith and Proctor's Fifth Avenue Theatre, New York City.
13–18 March	Performs in Providence, R.I.
27 March–1 April	Keith's Theatre, Philadelphia.
1–6 May	Begins his single act at the Victoria Theatre, New York City.
8–13 May	Orpheum Theatre, Brooklyn, N.Y.
24 May	Visits Clement Vann Rogers in Claremore, Okla.
31 May–5 June	Lake Cliff's Casino Theatre, Dallas.
7 June	In Claremore and Chelsea, Okla., visiting his father and sisters.
12–25 June	Majestic Theatre, Chicago. Rogers is held over for a second week. Max Hart is now his agent.
28 July–3 August	Visits Clement Vann Rogers in Claremore, Okla. Buys 20-acre tract of land in Claremore, the future site of the Will Rogers Memorial.
7–12 August	Performs at Victoria Theatre's Paradise Roof Garden, New York City.
14–19 August	Keith's Theatre, Boston.
21–26 August	Orpheum, Montreal, Quebec, Canada.
23 August	The Rogerses begin to reside at the St. Francis Hotel on West Forty-seventh Street, New York City.
2 September	Shea's Theatre, Buffalo, N.Y.
4–9 September	Shea's Theatre, Toronto, Ontario, Canada.
9 September	The Rogerses are living in a five-room apartment at 203 West 94th Street, New York City.
11–16 September	Grand Opera House, Syracuse, N.Y.
18–23 September	Rogers performs in Erie, Pa.
25–30 September	Keith's Hippodrome, Cleveland.
2–7 October	Keith's Theatre, Columbus, Ohio.
7 October	The Rogerses move to 551 West 113th Street, New York City.
9–14 October	Alhambra Theatre, New York City.
16–21 October	Hudson Theatre, Union Hill, N.J.

17 October	Rogers attends World Series baseball game at the New York Giants' Polo Grounds. The Philadelphia Athletics beat the Giants two to one in eleven innings.
20 October	William Vann Rogers is born.
23–29 October	Victoria Theatre, New York City.
28 October	Clement Vann Rogers dies at the home of his daughter, Maud Lane, in Chelsea, Okla.
31 October	Rogers attends his father's funeral at Chelsea. He cancels his engagements at the Victoria Theatre and Keith and Proctor's Fifth Avenue Theatre, New York City.
6–11 November	Returning to New York City, Rogers performs in Newark, N.J.
13–18 November	Greenpoint Theatre, Brooklyn, N.Y.
20–25 November	Orpheum Theatre, Brooklyn, N.Y.
27 November–2 December	Bushwick Theatre, Brooklyn, N.Y.
30 November	Rogers and other vaudevillians perform for prisoners on Blackwell Island.
4–9 December	Performs in Trenton.
11–16 December	Maryland Theatre, Baltimore.
18–23 December	Forsyth Theatre, Atlanta.
25–30 December	Keith's Theatre, Philadelphia.

1912

1–6 January	Poli's Theatre, Scranton, Pa.
8–13 January	Colonial Theatre, New York City.
15–20 January	Orange Theatre, Bayonne, N.J., or Orpheum Theatre, Brooklyn, N.Y.
22–27 January	Keith's Bijou Theatre, Philadelphia, or Alhambra Theatre, New York City.
29 January–3 February	Victoria Theatre, New York City.
5–10 February	Keith's Theatre, Providence, R.I.
12–17 February	Poli's Theatre, Bridgeport, Conn.
12 February	Herb McSpadden locates Teddy, who was being used as a plowhorse on a sharecropper's farm,

	and returns him to pasture at the Rogers ranch near Oologah.
19–24 February	Poli's Theatre, New Haven, Conn.
26 February–2 March	Poli's Theatre, Worcester, Mass.
4–9 March	Poli's Theatre, Springfield, Mass.
11–16 March	Poli's Theatre, Hartford, Conn.
13–23 March	Possibly Orpheum Theatre, Utica, N.Y.
25–30 March	Possibly Orpheum Theatre, Harrisburg, Pa.
1–6 April	Possibly Grand Opera House, Pittsburgh.
8–13 April	Possibly either Detroit's Temple Theatre, Rochester's Cook Opera House, or Keith and Proctor's Fifth Avenue Theatre, New York City.
15 April–June 1	Rogers performs in *The Wall Street Girl,* George M. Cohan Theatre, New York City.
21 April	Participates in a *Titanic* relief benefit, George M. Cohan Theatre, New York City.
5 June	The Rogerses and their young son arrive in Claremore and Chelsea, Okla., to visit relatives.
17–30 June	Rogers performs on the Orpheum Circuit at the Orpheum Theatre, Seattle, and Orpheum Theatre, Spokane.
1–7 July	Orpheum Theatre, Portland, Ore.
8 July	Leaves Portland by train, returns to Oklahoma via Kansas City.
15–21 July	Majestic Theatre, Chicago.
21 July	Performs in the Memorial to Hugh E. Keough, Colonial Theatre, Chicago.
22–27 July	Possibly Majestic Theatre, Milwaukee.
29 July–3 August	Temple Theatre, Detroit.
5–10 August	Possibly Ramona Theatre, Grand Rapids, Mich.
17 August	Rogers is in Claremore, Okla., visiting relatives and attending to business matters.
29 August	Attends Clem McSpadden's funeral in Chelsea, Okla.
4 September	Leaves Claremore, Okla., and travels to New York City.

19 September	Begins tour of *The Wall Street Girl*, Collingwood Theatre, Poughkeepsie, N.Y.
21 September	Rogers's two sisters, Maud Lane and Sallie McSpadden, sell him the real estate holdings they had inherited from Clement Vann Rogers.
23–28 September	Performs in *The Wall Street Girl*, Nixon's Apollo Theatre, Atlantic City, N.J.
30 September–12 October	*The Wall Street Girl*, Lyric Theatre, Philadelphia.
14–16 October	*The Wall Street Girl*, Parsons Theatre, Hartford, Conn.
17 October	*The Wall Street Girl*, Poli's Theatre, Waterbury, Conn.
18–19 October	*The Wall Street Girl*, Court Square Theatre, Springfield, Mass.
21 October–2 November	*The Wall Street Girl*, Tremont Theatre, Boston.
29 October	Rogers and other *Wall Street Girl* cast members perform at an afternoon benefit for the Henry B. Harris Rest Home for Stage Children, Colonial Theatre, Boston.
4 November	*The Wall Street Girl*, Empire Theatre, Salem, Mass.
5 November	*The Wall Street Girl*, Lowell Opera House, Lowell, Mass.
6 November	*The Wall Street Girl*, City Theatre, Brockton, Mass.
7 November	*The Wall Street Girl*, New Bedford Theatre, New Bedford, Mass.
8 November	*The Wall Street Girl*, Savoy Theatre, Fall River, Mass.
9 November	*The Wall Street Girl*, Opera House, Newport, R.I.
11–12 November	*The Wall Street Girl*, Worcester Theatre, Worcester, Mass.
13 November	*The Wall Street Girl*, Empire Theatre, North Adams, Mass.
14 November	*The Wall Street Girl*, Colonial Theatre, Pittsfield, Mass.

15 November	*The Wall Street Girl*, Rand's Opera House, Troy, N.Y.
16 November	*The Wall Street Girl*, Opera House, Kingston, N.Y.
18–23 November	*The Wall Street Girl*, Grand Opera House, New York City.
25 November	*The Wall Street Girl*, Majestic Theatre, Utica, N.Y.
26–27 November	*The Wall Street Girl*, Empire Theatre, Syracuse, N.Y.
28–30 November	*The Wall Street Girl*, Lyceum Theatre, Rochester, N.Y.
1–14 December	*The Wall Street Girl*, Illinois Theatre, Chicago.
17–21 December	Rogers and his wife visit relatives in Chelsea and Claremore, Okla.
22–28 December	*The Wall Street Girl*, Willis Wood Theatre, Kansas City, Mo.
30 December	*The Wall Street Girl*, Berchel Theatre, Des Moines.
31 December	*The Wall Street Girl*, Waterloo Theatre, Waterloo, Iowa.

1913

1 January	*The Wall Street Girl*, Grand Opera House, Dubuque, Iowa.
2–4 January	*The Wall Street Girl*, Davidson Theatre, Milwaukee.
5–8 January	*The Wall Street Girl*, Metropolitan Opera House, St. Paul, Minn.
9–11 January	*The Wall Street Girl*, Metropolitan Opera House, Minneapolis.
12–13 January	*The Wall Street Girl*, Lyceum Theatre, Duluth, Minn.
14 January	*The Wall Street Girl*, La Crosse Theatre, La Crosse, Wis.
15 January	*The Wall Street Girl*, Fuller Opera House, Madison, Wis.

16 January	*The Wall Street Girl*, Oliver Theatre, South Bend, Ind.
17–18 January	*The Wall Street Girl*, Valentine Theatre, Toledo, Ohio.
20–25 January	*The Wall Street Girl*, Euclid Opera House, Cleveland.
27–29 January	*The Wall Street Girl*, Detroit Opera House, Detroit.
30 January	*The Wall Street Girl*, New Whitney Theatre, Ann Arbor, Mich.
31 January	*The Wall Street Girl*, Athenaeum Theatre, Jackson, Mich.
1 February	*The Wall Street Girl*, Majestic Theatre, Fort Wayne, Ind.
3–8 February	*The Wall Street Girl*, Grand Opera House, Cincinnati.
10 February	*The Wall Street Girl*, Opera House, Lexington, Ky.
11 February	*The Wall Street Girl*, Grand Theatre, Owensboro, Ky.
12 February	*The Wall Street Girl*, Well's Bijou Theatre, Evansville, Ind.
13 February	*The Wall Street Girl*, Kentucky Theatre, Paducah, Ky.
14–15 February	*The Wall Street Girl*, Vendome Theatre, Nashville, Tenn.
17—18 February	*The Wall Street Girl*, Lyceum Theatre, Memphis.
19 February	*The Wall Street Girl*, Jefferson Theatre, Birmingham, Ala.
20—22 February	*The Wall Street Girl*, Atlanta Theatre, Atlanta.
24 February	*The Wall Street Girl*, Grand Theatre, Macon, Ga.
25 February	*The Wall Street Girl*, Grand Theatre, Augusta, Ga.
26 February	*The Wall Street Girl*, Columbia Theatre, Columbia, S.C.
27 February	*The Wall Street Girl*, Academy of Music, Wilmington, N.C.

28 February	*The Wall Street Girl,* Academy of Music, Raleigh, N.C.
1 March	*The Wall Street Girl,* Academy of Music, Newport News, Va.
3 March	*The Wall Street Girl,* Academy of Music, Norfolk, Va.
4 March	*The Wall Street Girl,* Academy of Music, Roanoke, Va.
5 March	*The Wall Street Girl,* Academy of Music, Lynchburg, Va.
6 March	*The Wall Street Girl,* Huntington Theatre, Huntington, W.Va.
7 March	*The Wall Street Girl,* Camden Theatre, Parkersburg, W.Va.
8 March	*The Wall Street Girl,* New Theatre, Clarksburg, W.Va.
10–15 March	*The Wall Street Girl,* Nixon Theatre, Pittsburgh.
17–22 March	Rogers returns to vaudeville at the Majestic Theatre, Chicago.
24–26 March	Majestic Theatre, Milwaukee.
27–30 March	Majestic Theatre, Chicago.
31 March–2 April	Orpheum Theatre, Madison, Wis.
3–5 April	Majestic Theatre, LaCrosse, Wis.
6–9 April	Lincoln Theatre, Chicago.
10–12 April	Majestic Theatre, Springfield, Ill.
13–16 April	Orpheum Theatre, South Bend, Ind.
17–19 April	Walker Opera House, Champaign, Ill.
20–23 April	Rogers performs in Alton, Ill.
24–27 April	New Grand Theatre, Evansville, Ind.
30 April	Rogers buys the property of his father inherited by the children of his deceased sister, May Rogers Yocum Stine, and Frank Stine, guardian.
5–10 May	Majestic Theatre, Fort Worth, Tex.
12 May	Rogers buys his father's property inherited by Johnny Yocum, son of his sister May Rogers

Yocum Stine and MatthewYocum, both deceased (John T. McSpadden acting as guardian).

12–17 May	Majestic Theatre, Dallas. Performs in a Wild West show in Dallas organized by the Shriners.
18 May	Mary Amelia Rogers is born in Rogers, Ark.
19–24 May	Majestic Theatre, Houston.
26 May–1 June	Plaza Theatre, San Antonio.
10–15 June	Begins Orpheum Circuit tour; performs at Orpheum Theatre, Winnipeg, Manitoba, Canada. On the program is Gus Edwards's Kid Kabaret with Eddie Cantor and George Jessel.
17–29 June	Performs on Orpheum Circuit in Edmonton and Calgary, Alberta, Canada.
1–13 July	Performs in Spokane, Wash., during this time and possibly also in Vancouver, B.C., Canada.
14–19 July	Orpheum Theatre, Seattle.
21–26 July	Orpheum Theatre, Portland, Ore.
28 July	Arrives in Chelsea, Okla., to see relatives.
29 July	Rogers visits his ranch in Oologah, Okla.
31 July	Rogers is in Claremore, Okla.
6 August	Rogers leaves by train for San Francisco to continue his Orpheum Circuit tour.
7–8 August	During his train trip Rogers writes postcards to Betty Blake Rogers and Will Rogers, Jr., from Amarillo, Tex., Albuquerque, N.Mex., Winslow, Ariz., and Barstow, Calif.
9 August	Arrives San Francisco.
9–16 August	Rogers's first published article appears in *The Stampede,* program of the 1913 Winnipeg Stampede, Manitoba, Canada.
11–23 August	Orpheum Theatre, San Francisco.
24–30 August	Orpheum Theatre, Oakland, Calif.
31 August–6 September	Orpheum Theatre, Los Angeles.
10 September	Photograph taken of Rogers on horseback and friends taken on the Bright Angel Trail at the Grand Canyon, Ariz.

15–20 September	Orpheum Theatre, Ogden, Utah.
21–27 September	Orpheum Theatre, Salt Lake City.
28 September–4 October	Orpheum Theatre, Denver.
5–11 October	Orpheum Theatre, Lincoln, Nebr.
12–18 October	Orpheum Theatre, Sioux City, Iowa.
19–25 October	Orpheum Theatre, Omaha.
26 October–1 November	Orpheum Theatre, Kansas City, Mo. Nieces Helen and Irene McSpadden attend a performance.
2–8 November	Orpheum Theatre, Des Moines.
9–15 November	Orpheum Theatre, Minneapolis.
16–22 November	Orpheum Theatre, Duluth, Minn.
23 November–6 December	Palace Theatre, Chicago.
9 December	Contract with B. F. Keith's Circuit to perform at New York's Alhambra Theatre the week of 12 January 1914 at $350 weekly.
7–13 December	Columbia Theatre, St. Louis.
13 December	Contract signed to play at Hammerstein's Victoria Theatre, New York City, the week of 19 January 1914 at $350 weekly.
14–20 December	Orpheum Theatre, Memphis.
21–27 December	Orpheum Theatre, New Orleans.
28 December	Finishing the Orpheum Circuit, Rogers travels back to New York City.
31 December	Contract with B. F. Keith's Circuit to perform at Keith's Theatre, Philadelphia, the week of 9 February 1914 at $350 weekly.

1914

2 January	Contract signed to appear at Keith's Colonial Theatre, New York city, the week of 12 January, for $350.
4–10 January	Rogers makes his first performance at the famous Palace Theatre, New York City.

8 January	Contract to perform at Keith's Orpheum Theatre in Brooklyn, N.Y., the week of 19 January, for $350.
9 January	Contract to appear at Keith's Alhambra Theatre, New York City, the week of 25 January, for $350.
12–17 January	Colonial Theatre, New York City.
16 January	Contracts approved at $350 weekly for Keith's Theatre, Columbus, Ohio (week of 16 February); Keith's Theatre, Cincinnati (week of 22 February); Keith's Grand Theatre, Syracuse, N.Y. (week of 2 March); Opera House, Pittsburgh (week of 9 March); Keith's Hippodrome, Cleveland (week of 16 March); and Keith's Theatre, Louisville, Ky. (week of 19 April).
19–24 January	Performs at Hammerstein's Victoria Theatre, New York City, on the occasion of the theater's nineteenth anniversary. Also appears at the Orpheum Theatre, Brooklyn, N.Y.
25 January–1 February	Rogers appears at three New York theaters: Hammerstein's Victoria, Keith's Union Square Theatre, and the Alhambra. He does forty-two shows, and publicity claims that he set a record. Also performs at the Vaudeville Comedy Club and possibly in his first film with Reine Davies.
28 January	Participates in benefit for the Home for Incurables, New York City.
2–7 February	Performs at Keith's Bronx Theatre, New York City.
9–14 February	Chestnut Street Theatre, Philadelphia. Performs on the same program with Pat Rooney and Marion Bent.
16–21 February	Keith's Theatre, Columbus, Ohio.
23–28 February	Keith's Theatre, Cincinnati.
2–7 March	Grand Opera House, Syracuse, N.Y.
9–14 March	Grand Opera House, Pittsburgh.
16–21 March	Hippodrome, Cleveland.
23–28 March	Columbia Theatre, Grand Rapids, Mich.

30 March–4 April	Keith's Theatre, Toledo, Ohio.
6–11 April	Keith's Theatre, Indianapolis.
20–25 April	Keith's Theatre, Louisville, Ky.
27 April–2 May	Temple Theatre, Detroit.
4–9 May	Temple Theatre, Rochester, N.Y.
11–23 May	Rogers performs at Keith's Theatre, Atlantic City, N.J.
26 May	Leaves New York on the *Vaterline* bound for London.
11 June–ca. 9 July	Performs in *The Merry-Go-Round* revue at the Empire Theatre, London.
15 July	Arrives back in New York City on board the *Imperator.*
25 July–12 August	Arrives in Claremore, Okla., to see relatives and to look after his property. Visits his wife and family in Rogers, Ark.
13 August	Leaves by train for San Francisco where he begins Orpheum Circuit tour.
16 August	Arrives in San Francisco.
16–21 August	Orpheum Theatre, San Francisco.
22–29 August	Orpheum Theatre, Oakland, Calif.
31 August–1 September	Clunie-Orpheum Theatre, Sacramento, Calif.
2–3 September	Orpheum Theatre, Stockton, Calif.
4–5 September	Orpheum Theatre, San Jose, Calif.
6–19 September	Orpheum Theatre, Los Angeles.
20–25 September	Spreckels Theatre, San Diego.
23 September	Visits Tijuana, Mexico.
27 September–3 October	Orpheum Theatre, Salt Lake City.
4–10 October	Orpheum Theatre, Denver.
11–17 October	Orpheum Theatre, Lincoln, Nebr.
18–24 October	Orpheum Theatre, Omaha.
26–31 October	Orpheum Theatre, Kansas City, Mo.
1–7 November	Orpheum Theatre, Sioux City, Iowa.
8–14 November	Orpheum Theatre, Minneapolis.
16–21 November	Orpheum Theatre, Duluth, Minn.

22–28 November	Orpheum Theatre, Winnipeg, Manitoba, Canada.
29 November– 5 December	Majestic Theatre, Milwaukee.
6–12 December	Majestic Theatre, Chicago.
13–19 December	Majestic Theatre, Cedar Rapids, Iowa.
21–26 December	Columbia Theatre, Davenport, Iowa.
27 December–2 January	Majestic Theatre, Peoria, Ill.

1915

3–9 January	Empress Theatre, Decatur, Ill.
11–16 January	Forsyth Theatre, Atlanta.
18–23 January	Lyric Theatre, Birmingham, Ala.
25–27 January	Bijou Theatre, Savannah, Ga.
28–30 January	Victoria Theatre, Charleston.
1–3 February	Colonial Theatre, Norfolk, Va.
4–6 February	Lyric Theatre, Richmond, Va.
7–13 February	Palace Theatre, N.Y. Performs with Alla Nazimova, Ina Claire, and Rooney and Bent.
15–20 February	Grand Opera House, Rochester, N.Y.
22–27 February	Keith's Theatre, Toledo, Ohio.
1–6 March	Hippodrome Theatre, Cleveland.
8–13 March	Keith's Theatre, Columbus, Ohio.
15–20 March	Keith's Theatre, Indianapolis.
21–27 March	Keith's Theatre, Louisville, Ky. Performs with Houdini.
29 March–3 April	Grand Opera House, Pittsburgh.
5–10 April	Keith's Theatre, Cincinnati.
12–17 April	Keith's Theatre, Washington, D.C.
19–24 April	Maryland Theatre, Baltimore.
26 April–1 May	Victoria Theatre, New York City. Performs on a gala bill comprising the favorite acts of the late Willie Hammerstein. It is the last week of vaudeville at the Victoria.
3–8 May	Bushwick Theatre, Brooklyn, N.Y.

10–15 May	Keith's Theatre, Philadelphia.
17–22 May	Keith's Theatre, Boston.
24–29 May	Prospect Theatre, Brooklyn, N.Y.
20 June	Sunday Concert, Proctor's Fifth Avenue Theatre, New York City.
18–22 July	Palace Theatre, New York City.
20 July	Letter from Lee Shubert offering Rogers a role in *Hands Up*.
22 July	Opening of *Hands Up*. Rogers's remaining two days at the Palace Theatre are canceled.
25 July	James Blake Rogers is born in New York City.
23 August	Rogers appears in *Just Girls,* a revue at Florenz Ziegfeld's *Midnight Frolic*. Beginning of his association with Ziegfeld.

Editorial Principles and Practices

DOCUMENT SELECTION FOR VOLUME THREE

VOLUME THREE OF *The Papers of Will Rogers* PRESENTS THE READER WITH printed transcriptions of documents of various types. These include handwritten personal correspondence; correspondence printed in newspapers; published newspaper articles, interviews, birth notices, and reviews; typescript performance reviews by theater managers; theater and Wild West programs; vaudeville playbills and advertisements; and legal documents, including passports and a last will and testament. Emphasis is placed on personal correspondence, especially that of Will Rogers himself, and on documentation of Rogers's performance schedule. This collection includes about one out of fifteen noncorrespondence documents collected by the Will Rogers Papers Project for the 1908–15 period and about one out of three extant pieces of correspondence written by Rogers in those years, along with a sampling of letters written to or about Rogers by family members and friends. The personal correspondence, records, newspaper reports, performance reviews, and other documents have not been previously published in comprehensive form in a scholarly edition.

In the selection of documents for this volume, emphasis was placed on capturing both the development of Rogers's private life, as he married and had a young family, and the changes in his vaudeville career that brought him from circuit work to Broadway. Correspondence was selected to elucidate his personal life and relationships. His own letters and postcards, and those written to him, help describe his connections with his family and the nature of his work in different places. Correspondence, reviews, and playbills help the reader trace Rogers's travels from performance to performance. We are fortunate that Rogers maintained careful scrapbooks of his vaudeville engagements, as well as some performance notes and handwritten schedules of his itineraries. The various scrapbooks of vaudeville materials have been mined for both document and annotation materials. They include playbills and programs, clippings of reviews, notes, photographs, and business cards. The vaudeville and stage materials drawn from the scrapbooks have been selected and combined with other types of documents—such as theater managers' reports, reviews and articles gathered from local newspapers in the towns and cities where Rogers appeared, and vaudeville contracts—so as to re-create for the reader Rogers's complete performance schedule, the details of his itinerary, the critical reactions to his act, and the ways in which he modified his performance as his career proceeded. Effort has been made to identify every location and venue where Rogers appeared in this time period, and to make available to the reader—either through the documents themselves or in the annotations that link the documents—both the details of his personal experience and the larger cultural context. The volume is replete with coverage of both the performance and business ends of vaudeville. It provides capsule histories of theaters, managers, and agents. It profiles the performers and acts featured in the playbills, programs, and reviews. In conjunction with volume two, it traces the history of the development of different circuits, and explains the conflicts that existed between the major booking agencies and circuit operators. It contains names and, when possible, profiles of those both famous and obscure who made vaudeville into one of the primary forms of middle-class entertainment in the first two decades of the twentieth century. In many cases, information on performers and acts has been gathered from oral interviews with family members and from primary archival materials, and has never before been published in book form. Attention has been given to the private as well as the public side of vaudevillians' lives. The correspondence of Rogers and Betty Blake—the woman who, in the time period covered by this volume, became his wife, his companion on the vaudeville trail, and the mother of his children—provides insight into the personal side of Rogers's vaudeville career, just as Betty Blake Rogers's letters to her father-in-law, Clement Vann Rogers, offer glimpses into the Rogers family dynamic and the early married life of the Rogerses. Family life is a major theme of this volume, which also chronicles the deaths of Rogers's sister, May Stine, and his father, and the births of three of his children: William Vann Rogers, Mary Amelia Rogers, and James Blake Rogers. Photographs have been selected to show Rogers in the different phases of his vaudeville career, and to illustrate him in his relationships with his wife and children, and with friends and actors and actresses with whom he shared his life in the entertainment industry.

PLACEMENT OF DOCUMENTS

Documents are presented in chronological order, determined by date of authorship or period of performance. In cases where the date of creation is not known and a document appeared in published form, the date of publication is used to determine placement. Incompletely dated documents are placed at the end of a given time frame (e.g., a document dated September 1913, with no specific day given, would appear following all other documents for September 1913); similarly, a document dated with only a year or season (e.g., 1910 or summer 1914) is placed at the end of that year, or in context within the seasonal period of time. Dates construed by the editors are indicated as "circa" (ca.) a given date in document headings, usually with some explanation in annotations of the choice of date. Questionable dates or errors in dating in place and date lines are corrected within brackets. Dates have been construed either from the content of the document (e.g., mention within the document of a particular event or date or allusion to a stage in Rogers's itinerary) or from other material (e.g., a hotel letterhead that indicates context with other similar letters or a postmark on an envelope in which an original undated letter was received). The date designation of documents created on more than one day (e.g., a letter written over the course of several days or a composite document containing a series of reviews from a particular time period) indicates a time span (e.g., 7 August 1911–March 1912), and the document is placed according to the first date in that span. Two or more documents of the same date are arranged according to historical sequence or in the best contextual relationship to documents that directly precede or follow.

Volume three has been broken into five thematic sections, each with its own introduction. Sections are based on discrete stages in Rogers's personal life or career. Part one, "With All My Heart," documents the culmination of Rogers's and Betty Blake's long courtship in engagement and marriage. It follows them through their decision to marry, in the fall of 1908, their wedding ceremony and brief honeymoon in November 1908, and on to married life together in New York City and on the road. Part two, "Will Rogers and Co.," charts Rogers's efforts to revamp his vaudeville act, first by retiring Teddy, the pony he had been using in the act since its inception, and then by developing a new big group act with Wild West and rodeo performers riding horses on the stage. Part three, "The Oklahoma Cowboy and The Wall Street Girl," traces the period following the financial failure of the big act, when Rogers streamlined his act down to the single format for which he would become famous. He began appearing as a man alone on stage, chewing gum, doing a monologue, and swinging a lariat. This section also documents his taking the cowboy character he had perfected in vaudeville onto the legitimate stage, with a part in Blanche Ring's musical with a western theme, *The Wall Street Girl*. Part four brings Rogers back to the vaudeville stage, on tours that find him near the height of his vaudeville career, and headed, as the part title puts it, "On the Road to the Palace." Finally, part five, "Broadway Footlights," shows

Rogers, through his business relationship with the Shuberts, making the transition into stage work that would lead to his being cast in the *Ziegfeld Follies.* The volume ends with Rogers on the brink of his break into superstardom.

In each section, introductions are used to set the context and identify some of the major themes that appear in the documents that follow. Headnotes introduce particular documents, further establishing their context and supplying brief, pertinent information.

PRESENTATION OF DOCUMENTS AND EDITORIAL ELEMENTS

All documents are presented with a caption or document heading, a place and date line, a descriptive source note, and, if appropriate, annotations.

Captions of correspondence assume that Will Rogers is either the author or the recipient of the letter and indicate only the other party in the correspondence (e.g., "To Betty Blake" or "From Clement Vann Rogers"). Noncorrespondence primary documents and published third-party documents are given descriptive titles (e.g., "Manager's Report, Keith's Philadelphia Theatre" or "Review from *Variety*"). Document headings also include the date of the document and the place where it originated. The day-month-year dating style is used in the captions, and the abbreviation *ca.* (for *circa*) is used to prefix editorially construed dates. Documents that are printed as enclosures to other documents are labeled as enclosures, followed by a full descriptive heading in the same style as any other document.

Place and date lines are printed flush right at the beginning of the documentary text, regardless of where this information may have been presented in the original document. Lines breaks of the place and date information are structured in accordance with the original, unless they are of such length as to demand alteration. When no place or date appears on the original document, the place and date line is left blank.

For letters where a recipient's address is given on the original document, the address is set flush left above the salutation, regardless of where the information may have been given in the original. Salutations are similarly set flush left no matter how they appear in original correspondence. Headlines of printed documents taken from newspapers are centered and, if abridged, are so described in the descriptive source note.

Documents are presented with as little editorial intervention as possible. Texts are reproduced as written, with irregularities in grammar, punctuation, and spelling left intact. Paragraphs are indented. Rogers often wrote without punctuation and with irregular use of capitalization. In transcriptions of his handwritten letters, extra spaces have been added at the end of a sentence or phrase break where no period or other punctuation was supplied in the original, in order to make his correspondence easier to read. Italics are used to render single-underlined words in autograph texts and italicized text in printed documents. Double-underlined words in autograph texts are rendered in italics with underline. Documents such as letterheads with printed place and date lines or application forms that include blanks filled out by hand are presented with the filled-in words in roman type and the blanks indicated by underlining. Minor typographical errors in published documents have been silently corrected. Typescript managers' reports from Keith theaters have been regularized to paragraph format. Misspellings or abbreviations that occur in original documents are sometimes clarified in notes or with the use of square brackets. Illegible words or missing or mutilated text are indicated by an editorial message in italics and square brackets (e.g., [*word illegible*] or [*page torn*]). Interlineations are indicated by the use of the ▲ or ▼ symbol at the beginning and end of the superscript or subscript text. Marginal notes are quoted in annotations. Some documents that were not written by Rogers have been abridged. Abridgments are indicated by unbracketed ellipses. If ellipses occurred in the original documents, this is indicated either in the descriptive source note or by an annotation.

Closings of letters are set flush right or are run into the last paragraph of the letter, as they are in the original document. Signatures are set flush right, no matter how they were rendered in the original. Postscripts follow signatures, and mailing addresses, endorsements, or docketing are set flush left above the source note.

Descriptive source notes contain the following information: the type of document, given in abbreviated form (e.g., ALS for "autograph letter signed"); a brief indication of the nature of the document (e.g., rc for "recipient's copy"); the source of the document (repository, manuscript collection, or printed source), and any further information pertaining to the physical nature of the document or its content and presentation, including letterhead data. Facts printed, stamped, or written on an envelope are given if pertinent. All abbreviations used in the source notes are explained in the list of symbols and abbreviations that follows this section.

Annotations are used to clarify the text, to provide cross-references, or to identify people, places, and events. The full contents of playbills have been presented, whenever possible, with the acts listed in the order in which they appeared on stage. Descriptions of the acts have been repeated from the original bills or programs and presented in parentheses. Capitalization of these listings has been retained as it is in the original documents, but the descriptions are given in capital and lower-case letters, even if they appear in all capital letters or another form in the originals. Cross-references to other documents in the volume are given by description and date of the document, with a designation of whether the document is printed above or below (preceding or following) the cross-reference. Cross-references to the Biographical Appendix are given by the name of the person profiled. Places, events, organizations, and institutions are identified when they are significant to Rogers's life and career or are not widely known. Annotations fully identify individuals who are referred to in the text by initials only or by first or last names (unless an individual appears frequently). Biographical annotations of individuals are presented at first appearance. Research has been conducted to identify individuals important to Will Rogers's life. In some cases, however, biographical searches either revealed no data or were limited by the obscurity of the individual and lack of public information.

Rogers's close friends or colleagues, and people of particular significance to his career or personal life, are profiled in the Biographical Appendix. The annotation at the first appearance of such an individual's name in the text is a cross-reference to the appropriate appendix entry. A comprehensive name index also appears at the beginning of the appendix as a guide to the reader. Additional information about individuals included in the appendix may also appear in annotations specific to documents in the volume. All other individuals named in the text whom we could identify are described in annotations, unless already annotated in a previous volume. An effort was made (through extensive archival research in Wild West, circus, theater, and film collections and through reviews of entertainment-trade periodicals and newspapers) to identify every individual or act with which Rogers performed that is named in the documents. Bibliographic source citations are given in annotations and in all Biographical Appendix entries in either abbreviated or short-title form. Complete listings of all sources appear either in Symbols and Abbreviations or in the Bibliography.

Symbols and Abbreviations

TEXTUAL DEVICES

[roman]	Editorial clarification or addition to text.
[roman?]	Conjectural reading for missing, mutilated, or illegible text.
[*italic*]	Editorial message regarding the nature of the original text (e.g., [*line missing*], [*page mutilated*], or [*word illegible*]).
. . .	Text editorially abridged.
~~canceled~~	Word deleted in original.
▲ ▲	Text that appears between markers is written above the line in original document.
▼ ▼	Text that appears between markers is written below the line in original document.

DESCRIPTIVE SYMBOLS

AD	Autograph Document
ADS	Autograph Document Signed
AL	Autograph Letter
ALS	Autograph Letter Signed
AMS	Autograph Manuscript
AN	Autograph Note
ANS	Autograph Note Signed
APC	Autograph Postcard
APCS	Autograph Postcard Signed
PD	Printed Document
TD	Typed Document
TDS	Typed Document Signed
TG	Telegram
TL	Typed Letter
TLS	Typed Letter Signed
TMS	Typed Manuscript
cc	Carbon Copy
cy	Copy Other than Carbon (Correspondence)

dc   Draft Copy (of Printed Article)
rc   Recipient's Copy (Correspondence)

MANUSCRIPT COLLECTION AND REPOSITORY SYMBOLS

BBC-RHM   Betty Blake Rogers Collection, Rogers Historical Museum, Rogers, Ark.
BMc-C   Buck McKee Collection, California State Library, Sacramento
BMC-OkClaW   Buck McKee Collection, Will Rogers Memorial, Claremore, Okla.
CBevA   American Film Institute, Louis B. Mayer Library, Los Angeles
CLAc   Academy of Motion Picture Arts and Sciences, Margaret Herrick Library. Beverly Hills, Calif.
CLSU   University of Southern California, Los Angeles
CPpR   Will Rogers State Historic Park, Pacific Palisades, Calif.
CSf-PALM   San Francisco Performing Arts Library and Museum
GWP-GA   Guy Weadick Papers, Glenbow Archives, Calgary, Alberta, Canada
HCP-MoU   Homer Croy Papers, Western Historical Manuscript Collection, University of Missouri, Columbia
HTC-MH   Harvard Theatre Collection, Harvard College Library, Harvard University, Cambridge, Mass.
JLC-OkClaW   Joseph Levy, Jr., Collection, Will Rogers Memorial, Claremore, Okla.
KAC-IaU   Keith-Albee Collection, University of Iowa, University Libraries, Special Collections, Iowa City
LHM-LHP   Louise Henry Memoir, Louise Henry Papers, Laurie Weltz Private Collection, New York
LHS-LHP   "L. H. The Sal Skinner Gal Album," Louise Henry Scrapbook, Louise Henry Papers, Laurie Weltz Private Collection, New York
MFC   Mulhall Family Collection, Martha Fisch Private Collection, Guthrie, Okla.
NN   New York Public Library
NNC   Columbia University, Butler Library, New York
NNHi   New-York Historical Society
NN-L-BRTC   New York Public Library, Research Library for the Performing Arts at Lincoln Center, Billy Rose Theatre Collection

NN-L-RLC	New York Public Library, Research Library for the Performing Arts at Lincoln Center, Robinson-Locke Collection
NNMoMA-FC	Museum of Modern Art, Film Study Center, New York
NNMuS	Museum of the City of New York, Theatre Collection
NNSA	Shubert Archive, New York
OkClaW	Will Rogers Memorial, Claremore, Okla.
OkHi	Oklahoma Historical Society, Oklahoma City
OkNCHOF	National Cowboy Hall of Fame and Western Heritage Center, Oklahoma City, Okla.
PP	Free Library of Philadelphia, Theatre Collection
PR-TxU	Pat Rooney Collection, Theatre Arts Collection, Harry Ransom Humanities Research Center, University of Texas, Austin
RHM	Rogers Historical Museum, Rogers, Ark.
THS	Theatre Historical Society of America, Elmurst, Ill.
TMC-RHM	Tom Morgan Collection, Rogers Historical Museum, Rogers, Ark.
TxFACM	Amon Carter Papers, Amon Carter Museum, Ft. Worth, Tex.
TxU-HRHRC	Theatre Arts Collection, Hobilitzelle Theatre Arts Library, Harry Ransom Humanities Research Center, University of Texas, Austin
TxNCMHOF	National Cowgirl Museum and Hall of Fame, Fort Worth, Tex.
URL-CLU	Department of Special Collections, University Research Library, University of California, Los Angeles
VATM	Victoria and Albert Theatre Museum, National Museum of the Performing Arts, Theatre Collection (Study Room), Covent Garden, London
WBaraC	Circus World Museum, Robert L. Parkinson Library and Research Center, Baraboo, Wis.
WHC-OKU	Western History Collection, University of Oklahoma, Norman, Okla.
WRPP	Will Rogers Papers Project, Los Angeles

GUIDE TO ABBREVIATED CITATIONS FOR PUBLISHED SOURCES

NEWSPAPERS

CC	*Chelsea Commercial,* Chelsea, Okla.
CDP	*Claremore Daily Progress,* Claremore, Okla.
CM	*Claremore Messenger,* Claremore, Okla.

CP	*Claremore Progress,* Claremore, Okla.
CR	*Chelsea Reporter,* Chelsea, Okla.
CWP	*Claremore Weekly Progress,* Claremore, Okla.
LAHE	*Los Angeles Herald Express*
LAT	*Los Angeles Times*
ME	*Mulhall Enterprise,* Mulhall, Okla.
NYA	*New York American*
NYC	*New York Clipper*
NYDM	*New York Dramatic Mirror*
NYHT	*New York Herald Tribune*
NYT	*New York Times*
SFC	*San Francisco Chronicle*
StLGD	*St. Louis Globe-Democrat*
StLPD	*St. Louis Post-Dispatch*
StLR	*St. Louis Republic*
TDW	*Tulsa Daily World,* Tulsa, Okla.
WRB	*White Rats Bulletin,* New York
WP	*Washington Post,* Washington, D.C.

REFERENCE WORKS

ABTB	*American and British Theatrical Biography.* Edited by J. P. Wearing. Metuchen, N.J.: Scarecrow Press, 1979.
BE	*The Baseball Encyclopedia.* Edited by Joseph L. Reichler. 6th ed. New York: Macmillan Publishing, 1985.
BEWHAT	*The Biographical Encyclopaedia and Who's Who of the American Theatre.* Edited by Walter Rigdon. New York: James H. Heineman, 1966.
CmpEnc	*Complete Encyclopedia of Popular Music and Jazz, 1900–1950.* Edited by Roger D. Kinkle. 4 vols. New Rochelle, N.Y.: Arlington House Publishers, 1974.
DAB	*Dictionary of American Biography.* Edited by Allen Johnson, Dumas Malone, et al. 22 vols. New York: Charles Scribner's Sons, 1928–80.
DE	*The Dance Encyclopedia.* Compiled and edited by Anatole Chujoy. New York: A. S. Barnes, 1949.
EAB	*Encyclopedia of American Biography.* Edited by Winfield Scott Downs. New York: American Historical, 1942.
EAM	*The Encyclopedia of American Music.* Edited by Edward Jablonski. Garden City, N.Y.: Doubleday, 1981.

ENYC	*The Encyclopedia of New York City.* Edited by Kenneth T. Jackson. New Haven, Conn.: Yale University Press, 1995.
GRB	*The Green Room Book or Who's Who on the Stage.* Edited by John Parker. 3 vols. London: T. Sealey Clark, 1907–9.
NotNAT	*Notable Names in the American Theatre.* Clifton, N.J.: James T. White, 1976.
NYTheRe	*New York Times Theater Reviews.* 20 vols. New York: New York Times and Arno Press, 1975.
NYTheReI	*The New York Times Theater Reviews Index, 1870–1919.* New York: New York Times and Arno Press, 1975.
OCF	*Old Cherokee Families, Notes of Dr. Emmet Starr.* Vol. 1, *Letter Books A–F.* Vol. 2, *Letter Books G–L, Index to Letter Books.* Edited by Jack D. Baker and David Keith Hampton. Oklahoma City: Baker Publishing, 1988.
OF	*Obituaries on File.* Edited by Felice Levy. 2 vols. New York: Facts on File, 1979.
WhMuDr	*Who's Who in Music and Drama: An Encyclopaedia of Biography of Notable Men and Women in Music and the Drama.* Edited by Dixie Hines and Harry Prescott Hanaford. New York: H. P. Hanaford, 1914.
WhoHol	*Who's Who in Hollywood: The Largest Cast of International Personalities Ever Assembled.* Edited by David Ragan. 2 vols. New York: Facts on File, 1992.
WhoHolly	*Who's Who in Hollywood, 1900–1976.* Edited by David Ragan. New Rochelle, N.Y.: Arlington House Publishers, 1976.
WhoStg	*Who's Who on the Stage, 1908.* Edited by Walter Browne and E. De Roy Koch. New York: B. W. Dodge, 1908.
WhoThe	*Who's Who in the Theatre.* Edited by John Parker. London: Isaac Pitman and Sons, 1914, 1916.
WhScrn 1	*Who Was Who on the Screen.* Edited by Evelyn Mack Truitt. 3d ed. New York: R. R. Bowker, 1983.
WhScrn 2	*Who Was Who on the Screen.* Edited by Evelyn Mack Truitt. 2d ed. New York: R. R. Bowker Co., 1977.
WhThe	*Who Was Who in the Theatre: 1912–76: A Biographical Dictionary of Actors, Actresses, Directors, Playwrights, and Producers of the English-speaking Theatre.* 4 vols. Gale Composite Biographical Dictionary Series 3. Detroit: Gale Research, 1978.

WNBD	*Webster's New Biographical Dictionary.* Springfield, Mass.: Merriam-Webster, 1988.
WNGD	*Webster's New Geographical Dictionary.* Springfield, Mass.: Merriam-Webster, 1988.

FREQUENTLY CITED SOURCES

AmSCAP	*The ASCAP Biographical Dictionary of Composers, Authors and Publishers.* Compiled and edited by the Lynn Farnol Group. New York: American Society of Composers, Authors and Publishers, 1966.
EV	*The Encyclopedia of Vaudeville.* Edited by Anthony Slide. Westport, Conn.: Greenwood Press, 1994.
FILM	*Filmarama.* Vol. 1, *The Formidable Years, 1893–1919.* Vol. 2, *The Flaming Years, 1920–1929.* Compiled by John Stewart. Metuchen, N.J.: Scarecrow Press, 1975, 1977.
FilmEnc	*The Film Encyclopedia.* By Ephraim Katz. 2d ed. New York: Harper Perennial, 1994.
GHNTD	*Gus Hill's National Theatrical Directory.* New York: Hill's National Theatrical Directory, 1914–15.
HRC	*History of Rogers County, Oklahoma.* Claremore, Okla.: Claremore College Foundation, 1979.
JCGHTG	*The Julius Cahn—Gus Hill Theatrical Guide and Moving Picture Directory, Containing Authentic Information of Theatres in Cities, Towns, and Villages of the United States and Canada, also Details of All Moving Picture Theatres Giving the Name of the City, Population, Manager and Seating Capacity.* Vol 20. New York: Longacre Building, 1921.
JCOTG	*Julius Cahn's Official Theatrical Guide, 1906–1907, Containing Authentic Information of the Theatres and Attractions in the United States, Canada, Mexico and Cuba.* New York: Empire Theatre Building, 1906.
OCAT	*The Oxford Companion to the American Theatre.* Edited by Gerald Bordman. 2d ed. New York and Oxford: Oxford University Press, 1992.
PWR	*The Papers of Will Rogers.* Edited by Arthur Frank Wertheim and Barbara Bair. Norman: University of Oklahoma Press.
VO	*Variety Obituaries.* 14 vols. New York: Garland Publishing, 1988.

1. WITH ALL MY HEART
September 1908–July 1909

Betty Blake's engagement photograph, 1908. *(OkClaW)*

"ONCE IN A WHILE A REAL COWBOY EMERGES FROM FICTION AND SONG INTO real life. Such is Will Rogers from Oklahoma, who performs a series of astonishing maneuvers with a lariat." So wrote a reporter for the *Minneapolis Journal* in February 1909.[1] The article was one of many that demonstrated journalists' vision of Rogers as a bridge between real-life and mythic cowboy experience. These writers, along with the agents and theater managers who booked his act, were aware that Rogers was an exemplary embodiment of the cult of the West that had swept the nation during the Progressive Era. The merging of the working cowboy with the pop-culture cowboy had become a common twist used by reporters to describe Rogers's vaudeville act. Earlier reviews, which had portrayed Rogers as the Cherokee Kid rather than the Oklahoma Cowboy and had emphasized his Native American heritage, had gone by the wayside. Rogers's ethnicity was marginalized in the new image, and his sexuality emphasized. The Indian was transformed into the all-American cowboy, lithe, wise-cracking, and handsome. The cowboy image encapsulated the virility that Theodore Roosevelt and his cohort—purveyors of the Eastern cult of masculinity—heralded as arising from the experiential contact between man and wilderness. The most popular exemplar of this image in the years when Rogers was developing his career on the vaudeville stage was the character created by Owen Wister in his novel *The Virginian*. The 1908 *Detroit Free Press* interview by Bertha O'Brien that opens this section of documents emphasizes the repeated comparison drawn by performance reviewers between Rogers and Wister's somewhat mysterious protagonist. The comparison was apt, not just because of the cult attributes that Rogers shared with the fictional cowboy hero, but because of the romantic theme of Wister's novel, in which the western protagonist, born in the South, is "civilized" through the influence of a woman. Wister's story of the roughhewn cowboy bachelor ends happily with his marriage to a woman of greater refinement, who has learned, in turn, to adapt herself to and admire his uncultivated but free outdoor ways. So with Will Rogers and his longtime on-again, off-again girlfriend, Betty Blake.[2]

The fall of 1908 was a watershed time for Will Rogers, both in his career and in his personal life. After three years on the road with his act including

Buck McKee and his pony Teddy, Rogers had proven something to himself and his family about his ability to make a living in entertainment. He was almost thirty years old, and he still had a mind to give up performing at some point and return home to the Claremore and Oologah area as a farmer. As autumn of 1908 arrived, he felt adrift in his traveling from town to town, but more important, he felt morally adrift and straying. He had begun to feel acutely the instability of vaudeville life and the strain of constantly having to scramble to arrange for work. Never quite sure where he would be from week to week and feeling the pinch of erratic payment, he told his sisters that "things are none too good in this business this year still I will be all right if I can keep working."[3] He sent money home and gave a lot of thought to the question of when he should call it quits and return to a ranching life in Oklahoma.

He also decided to clean up his personal life. He and Betty Blake had both had other relationships, and Blake had rebuffed Rogers's attempt to form a more committed relationship in the past. While Blake's relationships took the form of dating and the occasional steady beau, Rogers was indulging in affairs with other vaudeville performers that went beyond flirtation. Buck McKee hinted at the widespread culture of promiscuity on the vaudeville circuits in his letters home to his wife, and expressed to her his own discomfort with this practice among those who had wives and girlfriends at home. Rogers had not been entirely open with Betty Blake about his own behavior. Nearly two years before he had gone so far as to forward to Blake a letter he had received from another woman. A fellow vaudevillian named Nina, she cordially acknowledged in the note that he had broken off a relationship with her and stated her belief that whoever ended up with him would be a lucky woman. Rogers's tactic of sharing the letter apparently did not encourage Blake toward more of a commitment to him than the long-distance one they already had in place. On 23 September 1908 he decided to throw himself completely on Blake's mercy. He confessed to her his ongoing infidelity and his disappointment with his own behavior and lifestyle. "I done the greatest wrong that any one could do and I have wished and prayed a thousand times since that I had not done it . . . I just drift and drift. God knows where too," he wrote her.[4] After laying his transgressions at her feet, he told her, "Dont you think of deserting me in this."[5] She did not.

In the last months of 1908 Rogers found in Betty Blake a sure anchor for his drifting lifestyle. His letter confessing his waywardness was a turning point in their relationship. Not only did she forgive him, the frank discussion of his behavior and their feelings for one another led, finally, to a commitment to marriage. The two planned to marry during a break in his vaudeville schedule in November—a time that happened to coincide with the Thanksgiving holiday.

The correspondence from Rogers to Blake in the fall of 1908 grows increasingly ardent in anticipation of the event. Far from the questioning, dabbling, wandering young man of the past, Rogers shifted into a true and focused direction in his private life. He approached his marriage with surety and without doubts. "Are you scared, *hon*," he wrote Betty Blake the day before their wedding. "I am not."[6] He had already confessed, in a 20 November 1908 letter to Betty's brother Sandy Blake, that deep down, this commitment he was voicing to everyone now was nothing new. He had always loved Betty from the moment he met her on a dusty day at the Oologah train station. With further acquaintance, he found that her education, her hard work, and her stability, with strong ties to family and friends, were part of what attracted him. "I want someone that I can look up to and not a *bum* like myself," he wrote to her, explaining his own view of the class contrast between the two of them and his vaudevillian versus her settled life style.[7] Despite her middle-class behavior and grammar, she was down-to-earth, with no pretense about her. As Rogers wrote to Sandy, she was to him "the only *real* girl I ever saw."[8] Two months after his confession of waywardness, they were married. For Rogers, the self-castigation and disillusionment that had plagued him in September were replaced with constancy and purpose. He greeted the change with euphoria. Two weeks before his wedding he wrote, "Oh, Betty I am so Happy and So Glad," and a week before the ceremony he told her exuberantly, "You are just the grandest girl in all the world. Oh I love love Love you with all my heart."[9]

Historians cringe at the news, conveyed in a letter from Rogers's brother-in-law, C. L. (Cap) Lane, to Betty Blake near the eve of her wedding, that Rogers purged himself of his rather busy past with other women by burning letters and photographs that he had formerly cherished but "now thinks very little of as he has torn and burned up two & one half bushels."[10] Whoever the individual women were whom Rogers had been close to in his youth or in the first years of vaudeville, they were largely consigned to historical oblivion when he set fire to the bushels of documentation of their connection to him, symbolically purging those old ties from his heart.

His relationship with his wife proved to be long lasting and solid. They weathered early years of life on the road and separations, as well as the birth, raising, and illness of young children in circumstances where parenting duties fell mainly to Betty Blake Rogers. They then shared the rewards and burdens of fame and wealth that followed the years of struggle and adventure that had characterized the first part of their marriage. The perception of this bedrock quality of the marriage is reinforced by the absence of documentation of other earlier relationships and by every indication of complete steadfastness after the marriage. Although Betty Blake Rogers saved the letters she received from her husband, she destroyed her own correspondence to him, including all record of her own reactions during their courtship and the period of their wedding. Aside from her published memoirs, we thus have only his half of the story—no doubts, worries, or complaints of hers, no documentation of her own preparations for the ceremony, and no account of her own feelings in the matter.

It is clear that the Rogers family were extremely happy—or, as Rogers put it himself, relieved—that Rogers was finally marrying, and marrying someone they all knew, from a family of good reputation and of similar southern background. Rather than an actress or a chorus girl—the women whom Rogers worked with, became friendly with, and had affairs with—it was the girl next door (in neighboring Arkansas), whom Rogers had met on a fateful day in the local Oologah train station when she came to town to recover from an illness and have an extended visit with her sister. The wholesomeness of their connection seemed (to everyone involved) in sharp contrast to the fast life of the theater. She was someone with whom he, as a young man, had pulled taffy at a local friend's house. He had done silly antics on his bicycle in an effort to impress her, had played the banjo for her, and had resented it when she danced with other fellows at an Indian Territory party. Instead of a woman who wore makeup and costumes and made a living in the public eye on stage—or one, like his friend Lucille Mulhall, who could ride a horse or lasso as well as he could himself in public exhibition—he chose a woman who, as it would turn out, would live a very private life centered on husband and family. Betty Blake was like one of the girls from Claremore and Oologah whom Rogers joined on Pocahontas Club hayrides and picnics when he was a teenager and young man.

Will Rogers and Betty Blake were a study in contrasts and similarities in terms of culture, class, and family. Although Rogers had made his own way in the past decade, he had grown up surrounded by comparative wealth, with a father who owned and operated a large ranch and who was an important politician and leader in the circle of influential mixed-blood Cherokee families in the region where he was raised. Two of his three sisters had married well-to-do businessmen in the town of Chelsea. Blake, by contrast, had grown up in less prosperous circumstances. Her mother was a widow who raised her large family by her own means, working as a dressmaker, and shaped her children into a highly respected set of individuals in Rogers, Arkansas. While Rogers was rebellious in his youth, Betty Blake was a hard-working young woman. She was employed as a railroad clerk and in other jobs from young adulthood. But she and Rogers had much in common in their family history and the kind of close neighborly associations they were used to in their respective small towns. They both had a brother who died when they were young. They both also knew what it was to lose a parent to death. Blake's father had died when she was a child; Rogers, the baby of his family, had similarly lost his mother. Blake's brother James K. (Sandy) Blake compensated in her family's life for the loss of her father and eldest brother, taking seriously his responsibility for the welfare of his mother and sisters. And, as Rogers's sister Maud Lane reminded Betty Blake shortly before the wedding, Rogers had been raised by his older sisters who stepped in to help their mother when he was small and who continued to watch over him in the years after her death, though they soon had families of their own. The family dynamic of several sisters—he had three, she had six (one a half-sister)—were another thing that Rogers and Blake had in common.

For Rogers, there was also an element of resolution between father and son that came along with the elder Rogers's deep approval of his son's marriage. For Clement Vann Rogers, with whom Rogers had had his differences growing up, Betty Blake did well as another daughter. And she, who had no father, gained in the Rogers patriarch a devoted father-in-law. On the Blake family side, some wondered about the wisdom of Betty's choice, since she had had other offers from wealthier and better established men in her own hometown. Her friend Mary Quisenberry, however—after very honestly confessing her initial shock at the news of Betty's plans—went on to express her liking for Rogers and her good wishes for the marriage.

The wedding ceremony itself was understated. Put together without much advance notice, it took place on 25 November 1908 in Betty Blake's mother's home. Amelia Blake sent out announcements of the marriage to local friends in Rogers, but ceremony itself was strictly a family affair. Some of Betty Blake's siblings and in-laws were busy working and unable to come home for the wedding. Meanwhile, Rogers's niece Irene, daughter of his sister Sallie McSpadden, became ill with scarlet fever, and the entire McSpadden family found themselves quarantined in their home in Chelsea. Rogers's other sisters, May Stine and Maud Lane, both had young children, but they left them in the care of their husbands and traveled the one hundred-some miles to Rogers by train with their father in order to attend the wedding.

Betty Blake worried about not having the proper clothes to wear (as did Rogers's sisters). Rogers reminded her, with true male perspective, that the wedding ceremony and what she might wear were inconsequential—what mattered was herself, their togetherness, and the future that spread before them. He also asked that her sisters not show up his sisters by dressing more elaborately, since his sisters would be arriving at the Blake house for the ceremony in their traveling outfits. Betty Blake wore a blue and white silk dress, and the ceremony was performed by a good family friend who was pastor of her local Congregational church.

However simple and private the ceremony, all of the town of Rogers embraced the new couple as they left for their honeymoon. When they arrived at the train station by wagon after the ceremony, they "found the whole town gathered on the station platform to bid us goodbye with rice and cheers."[11] The newlyweds spent the Thanksgiving holiday, the day after their wedding, in St. Louis, where they watched Jim Thorpe[12] play football in a college game and went out to the theater to see the illustrious actress Maude Adams in *What Every Woman Knows.*[13]

Betty enjoyed "this chance to see a real New York star," not yet realizing that she herself had married a man who would become one.[14] She admitted that her own view of Rogers's profession, going into their marriage, was dim. She had never seen his work in vaudeville, and when she did see it for the first time after their marriage (at Proctor's Theater in Newark, New Jersey, in December 1908), she was unimpressed. "I must confess," she wrote in her memoirs, "that I then had little interest in or curiosity about his career on the stage."[15] She and Rogers shared the view that she was an elevating as well as a stabilizing force in his life, and they believed that her rather complete alienation from his stage life was part of this quality. She embodied middle-class values and small-town ways. His daily life, in contrast, was cast with theater people, single and married, some avant-garde, some bizarre, people whose lives were framed by the road and the footlights, and for whom, most of the time, fortunes ebbed far more than they flowed. Theater people were used to sporadic hours and late nights, heavy and regular alcohol consumption, waits behind the scenes and in empty train stations, and long and constant travel to places familiar and strange in cramped railway passenger or freight cars. Their social life when they had engagements centered on the hotels, bars, and other environs of vaudeville districts in urban environments large and small.

Betty Blake, along with her family, had long held the opinion that the way Rogers made a living was a little tawdry. It was definitely unattractive as a

Program cover, Orpheum Circuit of Theatres, ca. 1909. Rogers often played the Orpheum chain, the largest big-time vaudeville circuit in the West. *(OkClaW)*

lifestyle for marriage. "From my point of view," she remembered thinking before her marriage, "show business was not a very stable occupation. All I knew about the theater and the people connected with it had been gathered from the little traveling shows that visited our town from time to time. And I could not see a life of trouping the country in vaudeville."[16] It had been just these kinds of doubts, as well as her worries over Rogers's inconsistent expressions of care and indifference toward her, his pattern of ardent contact and then lack of communication, that had made her rebuff him in the past. Once married, she assumed that the vaudeville life was an aberration that would soon come to an end, and they would settle down on a farm outside Claremore to raise a family.

But Betty Blake Rogers too found herself lured by the big city and the lifestyle that regular work in vaudeville afforded. After a bit of time in New York City just after their marriage, and a few weeks on the road becoming accustomed to the different rhythm of Rogers's employment, she found herself rather liking the feeling of a "carefree life."[17] In her first weeks in New York she learned the advantages of working a two-a-day performance schedule, which provided free time between shows to enjoy other aspects of city living. She and Rogers spent their days walking around the crowded and colorful streets of Chinatown at lunchtime, riding horses in Central Park, taking the ferry out to the Statue of Liberty, strolling past the animals in the Bronx Zoo, or going to see the latest exhibitions at the museums. Rogers suffered through the opera, which she was thrilled to attend and he was not. Old friends from Arkansas visited, and Betty Blake Rogers met new kinds of people she had never been exposed to in her comparatively sheltered life in the rural and small-town South.

Once they left to go on the western Orpheum Circuit, which Rogers signed up for on 14 December 1908, Betty Blake Rogers also discovered the extent to which her husband was a loner, even within the context of the fast and furious life of performing in one city after the next. She knew that despite his great capacity for close friendships, he had needed to be self-contained as a child, growing up the only surviving son in his family and so much younger than his sisters. He had spent long hours alone on his horse as a youngster, and as an adult entertainer he continued to spend much of his time alone once he established a career on the road. His letters to his wife written during times when they were separated are studded with references to playing solitaire. Although he was friendly, funny, and open to other vaudeville actors, he was at the same time shy. He often kept to himself outside of the theater, especially when outside New York traveling a circuit.

He was even distanced from his partner, Buck McKee, who led a very lonely life while they worked together. McKee had virtually a separate existence from Rogers except for their time in practice or on the stage. When they were on the move, McKee traveled with the horse in a boxcar; stayed separately from Rogers, sometimes bunking in the stables where Teddy was quartered; and arrived at the theaters well before Rogers to set up the ropes for the act. The two men parted ways each evening as soon as the act was over, with McKee staying behind at the theater to gather up the equipment and restable the horse. McKee often had to hunt Rogers down at hotels during the daytime and dog him in order to be paid.

But in his marriage, Rogers shifted from his solitary habits. His prophecy that he and Betty would be all for each other came true. They became a society of two. When they were separated for the first time in their marriage for a few weeks in April—May 1909 (while Betty Blake Rogers visited her family and Rogers continued to perform in nearby states), Rogers experienced the kind of loneliness and longing that had characterized Buck McKee's existence on the road apart from his New York actress wife for a long while. As Rogers wrote to Betty on 29 April 1909, "We dont know how much we are to each other till we are seperated."[18] Or, as Buck McKee told an interviewer in Grand Rapids, Michigan, in May 1909, he did most of the talking to journalists for the publicity for the act because "Bill's too shy." Besides, "since he's married he's impossible. Doesn't care a gingersnap whether they say he's the best lassoist or the worst, in creation." His eyes were all for his wife, whom McKee described as "better than all right. She's Bill's pal, I'm beginning to learn when 'three's a crowd.'"[19]

While pursuing his vaudeville career, Rogers continued to negotiate, through his father and tenants who were living on the land, to improve the property on the old homeplace in Rogers County. He directed his father to buy up or lease sections of the land in order to consolidate areas of grassland or grazing pasture, farmland, and water resources into a good-sized, workable farm. He also gave his wife one of the rental houses he owned in Claremore. He did this to enable her to have her own discretionary income from the rent and to have something she could look forward to doing what she thought best with once they were back living in the area.

But after less than a year of married life, the idea of settling down on a farm had grown rather distant in Betty Blake Rogers's mind. By her own account, the first months of marriage were very happy times for her and Rogers. They were only unhappy when they were apart. In December 1908 he signed a major contract with the Orpheum Circuit, the dominant vaudeville

chain operating west of Chicago, with theaters that rivaled B. F. Keith's palatial operations.[20] The result was that the newlyweds traveled together while
Rogers fulfilled his solid bookings. After seeing much of the country and
learning to swim on her back in the ocean at Atlantic City, the issue of stability did not seem quite as centrally important to Betty Blake Rogers as it once
had. "I was growing reconciled to show business," she observed, "and our
promised return to Claremore kept being postponed."[21] With the western
Orpheum Circuit successfully completed, July 1909 saw Will and Betty Blake
Rogers headed not to Oklahoma, but back to life in New York.

1. Newspaper clipping, *Minneapolis Journal*, ca. 14–20 February 1909, scrapbook
A-2, OkClaW.
2. In a period when Will Rogers was competing in roping contests, supervising his
father's ranch in Indian Territory, and working as a cowboy on large cattle spreads in
Texas, Owen Wister made summer trips to Wyoming cattle country. Wister's
Virginian, a story about cattle handling and ranch life in Wyoming in the 1870s and
1880s, brought western themes from popular dime novels into American literature and
offered an idealized West to Anglo-Saxon easterners uneasy about industrialization
and immigration. In it, Wister established paradigms for the genre and strongly influenced mainstream America's conception of the West. The popularity of the novel
shaped ideas of the loner, law-bringing, cowboy as the quintessential Anglo-Saxon
American hero—one who appeals to women, has a loyal and sometimes comic sidekick and an intelligent horse, and sometimes uses violence against other men to exert
moral force in a chaotic or lawless world.
3. See Will Rogers to Sallie McSpadden and Folks, 1 October 1908, below.
4. See *PWR,* 2:330–31, 334 (Will Rogers to Betty Blake, 5 December 1906, with
enclosure, Rogers to Nina, ca. week of 26 November 1906) and Will Rogers to Betty
Blake, 23 September 1908, below.
5. Ibid.
6. See Will Rogers to Betty Blake, 23 November 1908, below.
7. See Will Rogers to Betty Blake, 27 October 1908, below.
8. Will Rogers to James K. (Sandy) Blake, 20 November 1908, OkClaW. See also
Biographical Appendix entry, BLAKE SIBLINGS).
9. See Will Rogers to Betty Blake, 12 and 19 November 1908, below.
10. C. L. (Cap) Lane to Betty Blake, 18 November 1908, OkClaW.
11. Rogers, *Will Rogers,* 103.
12. The versatile athlete James (Jim) Thorpe (1888–1953) was born near Prague,
Okla., of Potawatomi and Kickapoo, Irish, and French heritage. He was a football star
at Carlisle Indian School in 1907–9 and 1911–12. He won the pentathlon and
decathlon events at the Olympics in 1912. He played major league baseball for the
New York Giants and other teams from 1913 to 1919 (Hickok, *Who's Who of Sports
Champions,* 778; see also Fall, *Jim Thorpe;* Schoor and Gilfond, *Jim Thorpe Story;*
Wheeler, *Jim Thorpe*).
13. American actress Maude Adams (1872–1953) was best known for her roles in
plays by James M. Barrie, including *Quality Street* (1901), *What Every Woman Knows*
(1908), *The Legend of Leonora* (1914), and *A Kiss for Cinderella* (1916). When Will and
Betty Blake Rogers saw her the day after their wedding, she was famous from an

extremely popular run in the lead of Barrie's *Peter Pan* (1905) (Davies, *Maude Adams*; Froham, *Maude Adams Book*).

14. Rogers, *Will Rogers,* 103.

15. Ibid., 104.

16. Ibid., 97.

17. Ibid., 106.

18. Will Rogers to Betty Blake Rogers, 29 April 1909, OkClaW.

19. Clipping, "Lassoed a Bride," Grand Rapids, Mich., ca. May 1909, vaudeville scrapbook, CPpR.

20. The origin of the powerful Orpheum Circuit was dated to 30 June 1887, when the first Orpheum Theatre in San Francisco opened. Behind the theater's construction was the impresario Gustav Walter, a German immigrant who had arrived in San Francisco in 1874. The city already was an active site of popular theater for its growing population, with minstrel shows, melodramas, music halls, and burlesque theaters.

Walter was a pioneer in San Francisco variety theater. He opened the Fountain, a concert saloon on Kearney Street, and managed the Vienna Gardens. His next venture was the Wigwam Variety Hall, which presented a mixed bill of opera and vaudeville acts. In 1886 Walter started building his most impressive endeavor, the Orpheum, on O'Farrell Street between Stockton and Powell Streets. Seating 3,500, the spacious theater was embellished with expensive accoutrements, including boxes with gilt scrollwork and an elaborately designed stage curtain. The Orpheum was the first theater in the West built on a scale that matched B. F. Keith's lavish houses.

The Orpheum (also called the Orpheum Opera House) became San Francisco's most popular theater from the time it opened. Walter presented programs that included opera, drama, European imports, and vaudeville acts ranging from canines to comedians. His eclectic programming appealed to a broad audience of the working class, women, and the wealthy. Orpheum admission prices were low: 10 cents for balcony seats, 25 cents for orchestra seats, and 50 cents for box seats. Admission for children was 10 cents. Around 1897 Walter began vaudeville-only bills and opened a booking office in New York to engage the best talents.

Driven by his success in San Francisco, Walter established his second theater in Los Angeles. He leased Child's Opera House on Main Street and renamed it the Orpheum Theatre, opening on 31 December 1894. With two theaters under his control, Walter had the beginnings of a circuit. Next he established a theater in Sacramento, Calif., but then faced financial difficulties. He had overextended his holdings and could not pay a $50,000 liquor bill, which stemmed from serving patrons alcoholic beverages in theater lobbies. He was consequently forced to sell his interests around 1897 to Morris Meyerfeld, Jr., and Dan Mitchell.

When Meyerfeld named Martin Beck as the Orpheum's manager, he chose a shrewd and aggressive businessman who would eventually create the biggest circuit west of Chicago. Born in Liptó Szent Miklos in Eastern Europe, Beck (1867–1940) first worked in Chicago as a waiter and music-hall show producer. In search of a new opportunity, he moved to San Francisco, where he met Gustav Walter and developed an association with Meyerfeld.

With Meyerfeld's financial backing and Beck's management skills, the Orpheum organization began to build or lease big-time vaudeville theaters in cities from Los Angeles to Chicago. Besides their theaters in San Francisco and Los Angeles, the circuit in 1902 included theaters in Kansas City (1898), Omaha (1898), and New Orleans (1902). A year later they opened a new Orpheum on Spring Street in Los Angeles. By 1905 the Orpheum chain numbered seventeen theaters. In February 1908

Beck reached an agreement with the Sullivan and Considine Circuit that permitted the Orpheum to manage and book their theaters in the Pacific Northwest and Butte, Mont. By 1909 the circuit consisted of twenty-seven theaters with numerous other affiliations, including the Hippodrome theaters in England. On 19 April 1909 a new and more opulent San Francisco Orpheum opened, built on the site of the original Orpheum, which had burned down in the April 1906 earthquake. In Los Angeles the circuit in 1911 opened a lavish Orpheum on Broadway, designed by G. Albert Lansburgh and managed by Clarence Drown. Most Orpheum theaters were on the West Coast,in the Rocky Mountain states, and in the Midwest, but the circuit also had venues in Memphis, New Orleans, and Winnipeg, Canada. Most important, the theaters were located strategically, much like train stops, which permitted vaudevillians to travel a route or circuit from the Midwest to the West and back as they performed in each Orpheum city weekly.

In addition, Beck helped form the Western Vaudeville Managers Association in 1903, a merger of prominent managers in Chicago and the West, chiefly the Orpheum Circuit. In 1906 this organization allied with the Eastern Vaudeville Managers Association (headed by Keith and Albee) in a booking arrangement that essentially created a vaudeville oligopoly. (Beck agreed to book Orpheum acts through Keith's United Booking Offices [UBO].) A territorial agreement was reached, with the Orpheum controlling vaudeville west of Chicago and Keith-Albee keeping control east of Chicago.

The Orpheum also had a network of offices around the world. The general offices of the Orpheum Circuit were initially in San Francisco, headed by its president, Morris Meyerfeld, Jr. In Chicago Beck, as general manager, oversaw the Orpheum's executive offices, which included booking, production, and administrative functions. By 1909 the executive offices, with Beck in charge, were in New York's New Longacre Building on Times Square. In addition, the Orpheum had representatives in London, Paris, and Melbourne; a central foreign office in Berlin; and even a representative in Asia.

In New York, Beck ruled over a well-run business modeled on current organizational practices. During the early 1900s streamlined organizational structures, often involving consolidations, were established in major industries and businesses for the purposes of administrative efficiency, cost containment, and increased productivity and profits. The two major big-time vaudeville circuits, Keith-Albee and the Orpheum, adopted these management and organizational polices from business and industry, as well as those of the successful Theatrical Syndicate, which controlled the nation's legitimate theater.

In the Orpheum's New York office various vaudeville business functions were divided into bureaus and departments: production, booking, transportation, press, and legal. Previously a closed corporation, the chain in 1919–20 became a stock-issuing corporation (the Orpheum Circuit, Inc.) registered in Delaware (absorbing the Orpheum Theatre and Realty Co., the entity that owned or leased theaters). Its properties and other assets were valued at more than $13 million. The consolidation of its various holdings established a corporation under centralized management and financial control, with Beck as president. (Meyerfeld became chairman of the board, an honorary position that led to his retirement.) The year before, the circuit had acquired the Kohl and Castle chain of theaters in the Midwest and in Chicago. The Orpheum also opened in 1919 the spacious and elegant State-Lake Theatre in Chicago, which presented four shows a day of continuous vaudeville and movies. In early 1920 the circuit claimed that it owned or leased forty-five theaters in thirty-six cities.

The consolidation allowed the circuit in the 1920s to build larger and more luxurious theaters that offered twice-a-day programs of both vaudeville and motion pictures. New showplaces were erected or acquired in Kansas City (1921), Minneapolis (1921), St. Paul (1923), Oakland (1925), St. Louis (1925), Los Angeles (1926), Sioux City (1927), Seattle (1927), and San Francisco (1927). Beck was voted out of office by the stockholders in 1923, and Marcus Heiman became the Orpheum president. (Beck became a Broadway theater owner and built the Martin Beck Theatre in 1924.)

By the late 1920s, with the arrival of sound movies, vaudeville's heyday was over. As early as 1915 silent films were drawing a larger audience than vaudeville, and there were many more movie theaters than vaudeville houses in major cities. By the mid-1910s the Orpheum Circuit was adding feature films to its vaudeville programs, a trend that continued through the 1920s. During this decade some Orpheum theaters became exclusively movie houses. In December 1929, for example, the Los Angeles Orpheum staged its last vaudeville show and changed to film programming.

The development of talkies created chaos in the vaudeville industry. In an effort to further consolidate and to protect their theater holdings, the Orpheum merged with the Keith-Albee chain in 1927. In October 1928 the newly merged company, Keith-Albee-Orpheum, combined with the Radio Corporation of America and the Film Booking Office to form Radio-Keith-Orpheum (RKO). The Orpheum theaters became RKO movie houses. Thus the Orpheum's legacy was a large national network of movie theaters that once were vaudeville houses (Berson, *San Francisco Stage*, 91–97; Connors, "American Vaudeville Managers," 34–37; *EV*, 30–31, 280–81, 290, 381–83; *DAB* 11, supp. 2:33–34; Gagey, *San Francisco Stage*, 179, 207–8, 210; Goodwin, *Fitzgeralds and the Kennedys*, 429–42; Kibler, *Rank Ladies*, 15–20; *NYT*, 17 November 1940; *Orpheum Circuit* 1925; "Orpheum Circuit Agrees with Sullivan-Considine," *Variety*, 30 November 1907; "Orpheum Circuit Closes Deal with Sullivan-Considine," *Variety*, 8 February 1908; *Orpheum Circuit of Theatres*; Russell Harley, "Short History of the Orpheum Theatres, San Francisco, 1876–1977, typescript, CSf-PALM; Singer, "Vaudeville West," 120–22, 142–52, 174–77, 180–82).

21. Rogers, *Will Rogers*, 109.

Article from the *Detroit Free Press*
11 September 1908
Detroit, Mich.

BILL ROGERS, COW-PUNCHER, HAS
A HEART-ARMOR PIERCING MANNER
WESTERNER WITH CHEROKEE BLOOD, SLIM LEGS IN CARELESS
CHAPARRALS, AND A FETCHING-DRAWL, SEEMS TO FIT
THAT FEMININELY ADORED TYPE OF WISTER VIRGINIAN.
By Bertha V. O'Brien.

Tall and straight and lithe as an Indian, humor twinkling in his keen blue eyes and latent strength portrayed in his every movement, the Virginian[1] stood back in the wings of the Temple theater yesterday and talked about cow-punchers and the rest of the world.

He wasn't Dustin Farnam[2] but so immensely like the posters that hang in half the girls' rooms in the country that you'd scarcely know the difference. There was the half slouching length of limb encased in leather, the blue flannel shirt open at the throat, the soft, worse-for-wear hat and the devil-may-care, good-humored smile that sets the boys out there apart from the rest of the world. Only "Bill" Rogers doing breath-taking cow-boy stunts at the Temple this week isn't a Virginian.

"I reckon that Virginian they tell about was all right," he said in that slow persuasive drawl, that's warranted to pierce bullet-proof heart armor. "But say, I want to tell you that one night a lot of us were sittin' out there 'round the camp fire readin' that there book, because we fellows out in the territory had been hearing a powerful lot about it and readin' about the play and all that, and so we sat 'round and listened and took it all in until it come to that place where the fellow that's supposed to be the hero goes to work and hangs his old pal for cattle stealin'.

THREW BOOK IN FIRE.

"Well, we couldn't swallow that, so we just threw the book into the fire and says 'gol durn that Virginian—he wasn't no cow-puncher.' I don't know what they did 30 years ago but I know that the boys don't string up their old pals, do they Buck?"[3]

Buck McKee, erstwhile sheriff in Oklahoma, now helping Bill in his vaudeville stunt, assented with a lazy nod. "When they gave me the job of sheriff out there I jest let the good fellows get away from me even if the law was after them. The only ones I took in was the mean devils that wasn't worth living anyhow," said Buck, drowsily.

"Nationality?" echoed Bill, shifting his weight of bone and sinew from one spurred foot to the other. "Well I reckon I'm about as real an American as you can find. My father and mother were part Cherokee and I've got enough other mixtures to make me kind of a scramble or hash. Dad's a great old fellow.

"Fired" from College.

"They've got a town out in Indian Territory named after him; he's the president of a bank and about a hundred other things. Dad didn't reckon on my getting into vaudeville. Ain't it funny? He wanted me to go to college and grow up—well you know how—to be a fine gentleman and all that, but say all the schools I was fired from! I've been all over the world—Australia, Africa, Europe—broke horses for the British durin' the Boer war, been shot—see the scars, and every gol darned thing you can think of, but the nearest I ever came to being killed was one time in Frisco."[4]

Bill dug down into his leather pouch and drew out a package of pink gum. "Have some?" He offered genially, before he took his share.

It's a Good World.

"It was an awful fool way I came near to being killed and I guess the joke's on me. You see another guy and me were coming into Frisco one night after we'd been traveling some and we were clean tired out so that we could lay down and sleep any old place. We hiked to a hotel, got a room and us for the feathers. I guess I went to sleep before I struck 'em, but anyhow I didn't know a thing until I opened my eyes and blinked at a pretty nurse who was tellin' me I'd ought to be mighty glad I hadn't joined the happy hunters. The doctors had given up trying to pump the illuminatin' gas out o' my system and a bunch of students thought they'd experiment so they went to work and brought us to. I'm strong for students ever since and kind o' sore on doctors.[5] I'm not hankerin' after passing in [my] checks yet. This world's a pretty good place for me. . . .

PD. Printed in *Detroit Free Press*, 11 September 1908. Scrapbook A-2, OkClaW.

1. Rogers, of course, was an Indian (as well as a cowboy), born of part-Cherokee, part—Scotch-Irish parents in Indian Territory, and a citizen of the Cherokee Nation.

The similarities, in terms of sex appeal, between Rogers's lean cowboy stage persona and Wister's western literary hero with the southern accent were not lost on Bertha O'Brien.

2. Silent-film star Dustin Farnham (1874–1929) premiered in the lead role as the Virginian when Wister's popular novel was first adapted for the stage in 1903. In 1914 he starred in the film version of the story (Katchmer, *Eighty Silent Film Stars*, 265–88; Payne, *Owen Wister*, 211–27).

3. Rogers is referring to a subplot in *The Virginian* in which the Virginian participates in hunting down and punishing a gang of cattle rustlers and horse thieves. The captured men turn out to include a cowboy named Steve, formerly one of the Virginian's best friends, who has gone bad out of greed. Steve is judged by all concerned to be a better man than his companions in crime who go unpunished. He conducts himself like a gentleman when he is taken prisoner and is held overnight for execution without a trial. He maintains his honor by not naming names of other, uncaptured friends who were involved in the thefts, and he approaches death bravely when he is hanged come morning by the Virginian and the other members of the posse. The Virginian later privately breaks down and sobs over the fate of his friend, and he suffers nightmares over the unfortunate turn that the basically good man took toward lawlessness. Despite the emotion that Wister had his hero display in the aftermath of meting out justice, Rogers evidently felt that when it came to a matter of honor—to a tussle of right and wrong in which legality is weighed against friendship, and good character against bad—that the laws of the heart and cowboy camaraderie should overcome the laws of property (see Wister, *The Virginian*, chaps. 30–32 [374–421]).

4. For a detailed account of Rogers's family heritage and the period of his life that he describes here, see *PWR*, volume one.

5. For a report of this incident when Rogers was overcome by gas, see *PWR*, 1:208–10; and Excerpt from Unpublished Autobiography, ca. late 1910, below.

Article from the *Rochester Herald*
ca. 15 September 1908
Rochester, N.Y.

WILL ROGERS TALKS POLITICS.

"My father is a Democratic state Senator in Oklahoma,"[1] said "Wild Bill" Rogers, the quaint and picturesque cowboy, performing with his Indian pony at the Cook Opera House this week, "but I reckon I don't know what my politics are. I'm something like Taft[2] on religion. His father was a Unitarian, but I reckon big William chucked it, and like myself, he doesn't know what he is. There is one thing mighty sartin, howsomever, and that is that "Bill" Bryan[3] is agoin' to make Taft travel a might fast clip. Ten days ago I left 'Frisco to fill my engagement at Mr. Moore's theater here, and I reckon I didn't hear a single word of praise for Mr. Taft on the entire trip, while Bryan sentiment was everywhere. Every city and village we passed had Bryan banners flying in the breeze. O' course you might expect that in the west, but when I passed through the same states four years ago, by golly, it was all Roosevelt. You know Roosevelt was a sort of a cowboy once, or ruther he claimed he was, and that helped him consid'able, but between you and me he never was a real, sure-enough cowboy, 'cause he had plenty o' money all the time, and a sure-enough cowboy never has any money. Roosevelt is like that there cowboy, the Virginian, I saw in the play, that allowed his pal to by hung for stealing cattle. A sure-enough cowboy would never allow his pal to be hung for anything. He would give him a horse and gun and tell him to beat it for Mexico. I don't know whether I'm agoin' to vote this year, but if they don't stop me I reckon I'll vote for Bryan. The last thing my old dad said to me when I left Oklahoma City was 'Bill, you vote for Bryan in November, and remember if I learns as how you voted for Taft when you all get home I'll beat your head off with a neckyoke,' and by hominy, I reckon he'd do it, too."[4]

PD. Printed in *Rochester Herald*, ca. 15 September 1908. Scrapbook A-2, OkClaW.

1. Clement Vann Rogers was a longtime Downing Party politician within the Cherokee Nation. He was elected to the Cherokee Senate in 1903 and served in the last Senate before Oklahoma statehood. He was affiliated with the Democratic Party after statehood, and was a supporter of William Jennings Bryan. Although he remained politically active, he did not serve as a senator under the state system. He was a banker and leading businessman in the town of Claremore, Okla. Will Rogers's son, Will Rogers, Jr., carried on the family tradition set by his paternal grandfather when he became a Democratic representative from California in the 1940s. For an overview of Clement Vann Rogers's life, see *PWR*, 1:536–43; see also Biographical Appendix entry, ROGERS, William Vann.

2. William Howard Taft (1857–1930), who was born and raised in the Mount Auburn section of Cincinnati, Ohio, was a lawyer, judge, law professor, and secretary of war (under the Theodore Roosevelt administration) before he was elected president of the United States on 3 November 1908. In his 1908 campaign against Democratic candidate William Jennings Bryan, Taft's religious beliefs were repeatedly raised as an issue. He refused to discuss his own spiritual beliefs in the face of charges of atheism. After his election he revealed that he was a Unitarian and that he did not believe in the divinity of Christ or in orthodoxy of creed. He did, however, favor the conservative social influence of sincere religious practice, just as he favored conservatism in politics (D. Anderson, *William Howard Taft*; J. Anderson, *William Howard Taft*; DeGregorio, *Complete Book of U.S. Presidents*, 393–406).

3. William Jennings Bryan (1860–1925) of Nebraska was the Democratic Party nominee for the presidency in 1896, 1900, and 1908. He was nominated at the Democratic National Convention in Denver in July 1908. He received an overwhelming vote of the delegates on the first ballot, followed by a wild demonstration of cheering support that lasted over an hour and a half. The Democratic platform called for restricted government bureaucracy and corporate influence. It favored tariff reduction, antitrust laws, the strengthening of federal protections, nationalization of the railroads, conservation of natural resources and wilderness areas, the independence of the Philippines, and the rights of workers, including the creation of a system of workman's

compensation insurance. Bryan lost to Taft, who was seen both as Roosevelt's political heir and as a break from his reformist spirit; Bryan, who headed the Progressive wing of the Democratic Party, was perceived as overly liberal and antibusiness (Ashby, *William Jennings Bryan*; Bryan, *Memoirs of William Jennings Bryan*; Bryan, *Speeches of William Jennings Bryan*; DeGregorio, *Complete Book of U.S. Presidents,* 398–99; Glad, *Trumpet Soundeth*).

4. Rogers and his father had their differences when Rogers was young, but by this period they were close, and Clement Vann Rogers regularly handled business affairs at home in the Claremore area for his son. The cowboy image Rogers maintained in the entertainment world was counterbalanced by real-life concerns about livestock dealings and ranch land back home in Oklahoma. Rogers wrote to his father the day this interview was published and gave him his opinion on a livestock investment. He sent home $100 and reported that he was in Rochester for the week and not sure where he would be headed next or whether he would be working in the next week (Will Rogers to Clement Vann Rogers, 14 September 1908, OkClaW). He was headed to Pittsburgh.

Rogers appeared on the bill in Rochester, N.Y., with Felix Adler, Clayton Kennedy and Hattie Rooney, Peter Donald and Meta Carson, the Otto Brothers, Anne Blancke and Co., and Winona Winter (whom the author of a Keith performance report described as "the GREAT BIG HIT OF THE bill"). Rogers came last on the program, and made "the same big hit as before. He has added nothing to the act, or detracted nothing from it" (manager's report by J. H. Finn, Cook Opera House, Rochester, N.Y., ca. 14 September 1908, KAC-IaU). The program ended with a kinetograph on William Jennings Bryan.

Manager's Report, Grand Opera House
21 September 1908
Pittsburgh, Pa.

GRAND OPERA HOUSE.[1]

PITTSBURG, PA. Sept. 21st, 08.

FRANK PARKER & CO. 17 min. Interior. Heavy Weight Juggler. This is a good act for the three a day section.

LEONARD & DRAKE—3 shows. Singing, talking and imitations. Olio. 9 min. Only fair.

BIMM, BOMM, BRRR—17 min., closing 5 min. olio in one. Garden. Novelty Musical Trio. I think this act alright on any bill up to 8:30. Would not care to play them much later.

BURTON & BROOKS—19 min. Interior. Closing in one 7 minutes. These gentleman tried a now [new] talking act on Monday afternoon which was very bad. I had them go back to their old act and they are doing very well.

SIX LITTLE GIRLS & TEDDY BEAR—14 min. Garden, closing in one 3 min. This act never commences and if I had it for $250 less I would feel that I had been cheated. There is absolutely nothing to the act and I cannot see how it ever got by the first week.

LAVEEN-CROSS & CO.[2]—Roman Sports and Pastimes. 16 minutes, special. There is absolutely no necessity for the big production these people carry and were they to simply do their act at about $200 it would be much better. The work of Laveen & Cross is exceptionally good, being almost as good as the Bellclaire Bros.[3]

WINONA WINTER[4]—16 min., olio. Going very big. I know of no one _that_ ~~who~~ plays for us who receives more applause than Miss Winter.

THOS E. SHEA[5] & CO. in "The Bells", 32 Min., special. The production of Mr. Shea is very good. The act, of course, is dramatic and holds the attention of the audience throughout. Mr. Shea receives good advance applause and finishes with 3 and 4 curtains. I am sure that he has drawn us [*illegible crossout*] some money.

JOHNSON & HARDY—17 minutes. street. Singing comedians. Better than anything of the kind we have ever played. A big hit at every performance.

WILL ROGERS—12 minutes, full stage, wood. Lariat throwing. I think the novelty of Mr. Roger's act has about worn off. While he does practically the [same] work he has done on his previous visits here, our patrons do not seem to have the same interest and I am sure we do not want to play him again.

REESE BROS.[6]—11 min. Garden, close in one. Colored acrobats, singing, talking and juggling batons. 3 shows. A good act for the 3 a day section. A little rough and would not recommend it after two or eight o'clock.

John P. Harris.

TD. KAC-IaU.

1. The Grand Opera House in Pittsburgh was managed in this period by Harry Davis and John Harris. It had a seating capacity of 2,646 people, with a 48- by 80-foot stage (*GHNTD; JCGHTG*).
2. LaVeen and Cross were comic acrobats who did pantomime playlets in vaudeville. They were still working together in 1925, when the Jackson, Fla., *Journal* reported that "burlesque becomes a high art in the hands of these actors" (12 October 1925; clipping file, NN-L-BRTC; Laurie, *Vaudeville,* 137).
3. The Bellclair Brothers' acrobatic act included Ben Bellclair (1886–1949), who spent many years in vaudeville. The Bellclair Brothers were often mentioned with LaVeen and Cross as high-class acrobats. The last fourteen years of Ben Bellclair's life, he was a member of the staff of the Industrial Council of the Cloak, Suit and Shirt Manufacturers, Inc., of New York. He lived on Long Island with his wife and daughter, and was survived at his death by three brothers (*VO,* 4:22 June 1949).
4. See Biographical Appendix entry, WINTER, Winona.
5. Thomas E. Shea (1861–1940) was head of one of the most successful stock companies in the United States for many years. The company performed both in the United States and in England. Shea was best known for playing Dr. Jekyll-

Mr. Hyde leading roles. He was born in East Cambridge, Mass., and performed in amateur productions there while working at a local sugar refinery. He married Nellie Burkett of Belfast, Me., in 1892, and she became the leading lady of Shea's stock company, which he had formed in the 1880s. In addition to touring with their major productions, the company did condensed or tabloid versions of Shea's plays on the Keith Circuit in vaudeville. Shea gave silent-screen actor Dustin Farnham his start in his stock company in Winterport, Me. (*NYT*, 24 April 1940; *VO*, 3:1 May 1940).

 6. The two Reese Brothers, who began in circus entertainment, had been vaudeville acrobats since at least the turn of the century. They also appeared as comic actors with Bert Williams and Aida Overton (Walker) in *The Policy Players, Clipper,* and *Sons of Ham* (1900)—all Bert Williams and George Walker productions—with Williams and Walker's Policy Players Co. of New York City (Sampson, *Blacks in Blackface,* 278, 311, 448; Sampson, *Ghost Walks,* 210).

To Betty Blake
23 September 1908
Pittsburgh, Pa.

Wednesday

Dear Dear Betty

 Your little note just come and it has made me feel terrible

 honest Betty I feel afful

 I know you thought from the way I wrote in the last letter that I loved the woman No you were all wrong I wrote that way cause I did not want to appear like I was *knocking* her after all that had happened. Still you are right when you say that I have not treated you square. No I have not Betty it seems that I havent treated any one square. I have *lived a lie* and now I am reaping the harvest of it please make a little allowance for me dear I am not myself now and seem to have no mind of my own

 I am *scared* and dont know what to do.

 Betty: this is all of what comes of doing wrong I done the greatest wrong that any one could do and I have wished and prayed a thousand times since that I had not done it.

 No I am no man I am the weakest child you ever saw if you knew me better I am easily led and can be pulled into almost anything. I have no mind of my own I just drift and drift. God knows where too.

 Now listen dont you think of deserting me in all this. I need you and want you and I am hoping that this will all soon be at an end and I will be my own old self again.

 I'll admit I havent treated you right honest if you know how that hurts me Betty you wouldent say it, but its the truth.

Well I will stop   its show time. Im *bad* dearie   *all bad* but I am trying to do better and live better.

Write to me girl.

Your Billy.

Armory Theatre[1]
Binghamton, N.Y.
next week.

ALS, rc. OkClaW. On Hotel Antler, Fifth Avenue, Pittsburgh, letterhead.

1. Rogers played the Armory Theater in Binghamton, N.Y., along with Ben Berger
and Brother (bicylists); Bijou Russell (a song-and-dance team); the Musical Goolmans
(a "refined novelty" act); Edgar Allen and Co. (who did the skit *A Fortune Hunter's
Misfortune*); and Lillian Mills and Elula Morris. E. M. Hart was manager of the
Armory, and the bill with Rogers played to full houses (*NYDM*, 8 October 1908;
Variety, 3 October 1908).

To Sallie McSpadden and Folks
1 October 1908
Binghamton, N.Y.

Thursday, 1908

My Dear Folks—

Well I guess you all think I had deserted you but I been pretty busy and
only got a chance to write to papa. I got Mauds letter yesterday. Well I am just
kicking along   same old way and going pretty well   things are none too good
in this business this year   still I will be all right if I can keep working   It is
raining up here for the first time in months   this country was all about to
burn up with forest fires. the fair is on here now.

I am sho sorry I missed the two big fairs down there   I will get those
things yet some day.

So May has a boy[1] and is getting on fine   well I am sho glad. So Johny[2]
has gone off with a show   Well I'll be the ruination of my Nephews yet. they
will gradually *gather in* after they get a little *wiser* and find out where and what
is best   you know that prowling and *show off* feeling is just like a case of billiousness   ~~the~~ if its in your system the ~~better~~ ▲ quicker ▲ you get it off the better. At any rate if the *son* and *Nephews* of our dear father acomplish nothing
besides a roaming disposition. We can always rest assured that the opposite sex
of the family will follow in the beloved footsteps ▲ of ▲ their *dear* mothers and
grandmother. that being acomplished *is all that can be asked*

Well now to dispose of seriousness and come back to every day life again   I got the much sought after *Bank Statement.* You have often heard of a fellow looking for *trouble* and then finding it. Well there was the most striking instance of it you could find.

[I]t looks like a plot to a Jewish play. or. a Chinese Laundry bill. I am going to publish it as a *Rebus* in the paper. I think they made a mistake and sent me the clearing house sheet. or some of Godbeys livery stable³ statements I *either* am the *poorest* mortal in Rogers County Cowwescowwee district, party of the first part heretofore mentioned.   sign here *his mark* (EASY) ▲(that my mark allright.▲

or

I have a mortgage on the aforesaid bank and a balance so big that a horse couldent jump over it.

I dont know what it is but think I will wind up by *owing myself money* and to cap it all it seems that my old ▲dearest▲ friend Morgan⁴ (Wonderful Man) is going to stand by and see me enter bankruptcy and not even offer a helping hand   He is looking out for my interest *so well* that he wont pay me money cause he is afraid I will drink it up and ruin my young life. Now in return for his generosity and sincere affection I am going to reward him abundantly by issueing him a life time lease on the old Homestead and also paying him a small *bounty* of some 500 shekels a year for the privalege of having him and it shall also be in the agreement that I shall defray all expenses of an exploring party to penetrate the *deepest depths* of those weedish jungles once a year to ascertain if my victim still survived and if not by what means did he pass away. was it by *overflow, house falling on him,* or ▲was it▲ seeing so many people passing along all those much traveled roads. or a mosquito bite.

Thats the only way I can ever hope to get even with him is by making him stay there forever.

You know papa wrote me I should sell the farm and I told him yes for 20 thousand. Well I never heard from him since   that was a month ago.⁵ I'll bet he is beseiged night and day with men laying the 20 thousand at his feet and he dont know which one to take and rather than make them mad he wont accept any of them.

I am writing him now that I meant *20 cents* instead of 20 thousand. and does he think 20 cents will be too much.

Well I will have to stop and go fool the unsuspecting public for a brief space of 12 minutes   as long as they dont catch me at it its all right

Well I will stop again   Write to me Next Week.

Grand Opera House

Syracuse[6]

New York.

Lots and Lots of Love to all

Your old Bro. Bill

ALS, rc. OkClaW. On Arlington Hotel, Binghamton, N.Y., letterhead.

1. Rogers's sister May Rogers Yocum Stine (1873–1909) gave birth to four children who lived beyond childhood: her son by her first marriage to Matthew Yocum, Johnny Yocum, and two sons and a daughter with her second husband, Frank Stine. There were other babies born who did not live past infancy or early childhood. There is no record of a surviving male child born in 1908, unless genealogists have been mistaken and her youngest surviving child, Owen Gore Stine, was born around October 1908 instead of in January or February 1909, as usually assumed (see *PWR*, 1:556; Collins, *Roping Will Rogers Family Tree*, 28).

2. A reference to May Stine's son, Johnny Yocum, who was born in 1893 and as a teenager participated in roping contests just as Rogers had in his youth.

3. C. F. Godbey was the cashier and treasurer of the First National Bank in Claremore. Rogers's father was a chief officer in the bank and owned a nearby livery stable.

4. Morgan, not to be confused with Rogers's friend Tom P. Morgan (see *PWR*, 2:498–501 [Biographical Appendix entry for Tom P. Morgan]), was a local man with whom Rogers had business dealings and whom he did not like much. Morgan was apparently living on Rogers farmland and raising hogs in 1908, and seems not to have made some payments, perhaps of rent on the land. Rogers wrote to his father, "You take all that you have a Mortgage on of old Morgans hogs. Wagon and all cause I am tired fooling with that old *skunk*" (14 September 1908, OkClaW). He wrote to his father again about Morgan on 24 October 1908, urging him to "pay all the money I have there and all you collect and get from Morgan and the houses" (OkClaW).

5. Rogers wrote to his father on 21 September 1908, saying, "Now in regard to selling the farm I dont like to do it but if you can do it for $20,000. Twenty thousand dollars You said there was 350 acres at $50 an acre at least that would be $17,500 Well I wont take that but if you can get twenty all right and I dont care much about it at that" (OkClaW).

6. E. A. Gridgman of the *New York Daily Mirror* reported that Rogers was joined at the Grand Theater in Syracuse by Quinlan and Mack, Lewers and Mitchell, Charles Kenna, Frosini, Saona, and the Gartelle Brothers, making up "a good bill, which drew big business" (*NYDM*, 17 October 1908).

To Betty Blake
ca. 10 October 1908
Syracuse, N.Y.

My Betty—

Well dear just a line as I am getting out of here tonight after the show at 11:40 and get to Montreal at 10 in the morning   this is one of the towns you have to play Sunday in but not in Canada   only 6 days

Well *hon* I just think of you all the time and am just most crazy to see you and it wont be so long till I do either.

I cant hear yet just where I go after Montreal but will wire as soon as I find out.

Now you write all the time. Say are you in the store   you did not say, tell me.?

Aint it funny   this is the town I sent you the little *Hdkf.* from that time. I kinder have a warm place in my heart for it when it does what I *hope* it ~~does~~ _ *will* _[1]

Well. By By my Darling Sweetheart. I hope you may never regret sticking by a *bum* like I am.[2]

Your own Boy

Billy.

ALS, rc. OkClaW. On The Vanderbilt hotel, Syracuse, N.Y., letterhead. Postmarked 11 October 1908.

1. Rogers had sent Betty Blake a lace handkerchief as a Christmas gift, telling her that he had purchased it during his time in Argentina from an elderly Indian woman who told him he should give it to the woman he would marry. He carried it with him all through his travels in South Africa, Australia, and New Zealand, and then in 1906 sent it to Betty Blake, telling her, "I kinda prize it. And you might do the same" (see *PWR,* 2:136; Rogers, *Will Rogers,* 98).

2. Betty Blake forgave Rogers his confessed trespasses, and they made plans for the future. His eagerness to see her and hear from her became a theme of his correspondence. On 8 October 1908 he had cabled her, "Everything turned out great   will see you in few weeks" (OkClaW). He was on his way from Syracuse to Montreal, Canada, to appear at the Princess Theater.

The Princess Theatre, managed by the Canadian Theatre Co. and under the direction of Jess Burns, offered *Casino Girls* with Idalene Cotton and Nick Long, along with "Vaudeville including Will Roger[s] 'The Broncho Buster' and 'Champion Lasso Thrower,'" a comedy sketch by the Fitz Gibbon McCoy Trio, and Wixon and Eaton, "Roman Travesty Artists" (playbill, scrapbook A-2, OkClaW).

To Betty Blake
19 October 1908
Auburn, N.Y.

Monday.

My Own Betty.

Say *Hon* what is the matter   I did so expect to get a letter when I got here this morning but none came and last week only one in reply to the first wire I sent from Syracuse   did you get offended at anything in my letters   I cant imagine it at all.

I am just now sending you by mail three separate *parcels* two of them containing Books. *The Devil "Togeather"* and ["]*A little brother of the Rich.*"[1] Hope you will like them if you havent read them before as they are the three books of the year. And in another parcel 6 pairs of gloves and 6 pairs *of Female Hosiery.* Now the reason *one of them,* of my getting these is that I bought them last week in Canada and are supposed to be cheap up there

I hope you wont be offended at me sending you the Stockings. They are *bum* and I dont think you will like them but you can ▲ try ▲ and give em away.

I hope they fit. I mean the gloves as I thought I remembered your size as 6 1/4.

Now let me hear from you kinder often wont you dear   will wire you next weeks address.[2]

Your same old Billy.

ALS, rc. OkClaW.

1. Robert Herrick's *Together* was indeed one of the biggest books of 1908. Herrick (1868–1938) was an English professor at the University of Chicago from 1893 to 1923. He wrote a series of novels dealing with determinism and free will, especially explorations of the characters of corrupt professionals and businessmen, and the ways in which ethical values of individual liberty and moral responsibility clash with materialism and power (Hart, *Oxford Companion,* 369–70, 851; Rogal, *Chronological Outline,* 180; Traub, ed., *American Literary Yearbook,* 1:120).

Joseph Medill Patterson (1879–1946), author of *A Little Brother of the Rich* (1908), also wrote muckraking novels critiquing the inhumane aspects of modern industrialism and capitalism. A member of the Socialist Party (U.S.) national executive committee in 1908–12, Patterson oversaw the compilation of the *Socialist Campaign Book,* produced by the National Headquarters of the Socialist Party in Chicago in 1908, one of the years that labor leader Eugene V. Debs made a run for the presidency on the Socialist ticket. While Herrick wrote of reform of corrupt practices within the railroad corporations, and the price of this corruption for the individuals involved in business, Patterson and Debs favored the rights of labor to organize industrial unions to circumvent the power of railroad monopolies and were concerned with the collective cost borne by working people. Patterson's other books included *Rebellion* (1911) and an account of pacifism, *The Notebook of a Neutral* (1916).

2. Rogers wired Blake from Auburn again on 23 October 1908 to tell her that he would be playing the Poli's Theater in Wilkes-Barre, Pa., the next week (OkClaW). He wrote to his father the next day, telling him he was planning to come home for Christmas and saying that he was eager to have financial problems settled so that he could have some money available through a short-term note (24 October 1908, OkClaW).

In Auburn, Rogers appeared at the Grand Theatre, operated by the Auburn Amusements Co. The bill included Society Entertainers Tony Williams and Rose Ethel (in the playlet *A Night at the Club*); the Four Musical Kleis's (Introducing Master John Kleis); Madden and Fitzpatrick Co. (doing the play *The Turn of the Tide*); comediennes Watson and Little (In their Vocal Comedietta, *A Matrimonial Bargain*); Rogers (Presenting His Original Novelty, "A Study in Rope"); Willie Weston

("Imitating People You Know"); and Hayward, Pistel, Hayward & Co. (In their Comedy Success, *The King of Blackwellis*) (Grand Theatre playbill, scrapbook A-2, OkClaW).

Rogers was an "added feature" at the Poli in Wilkes-Barre. He appeared with the "Reading, Singing, Scenic Novelty" *A Night with the Poets*; the Avon Comedy team; Johnson and Hardy; Sadie Jansel (formerly of the Fascinating Flora Co.); George H. Wood; and the Damm Brothers. An electrograph was shown at the close of the show (Poli, Wilkes-Barre, Pa., playbill and clippings, scrapbook A-2, OkClaW).

To Betty Blake
27 October 1908
Wilkes-Barre, Pa.

<u>Tuesday.</u>

My Gal Betty.

Well my own sweetheart your dear letter come yesterday and I just love it and you more all the time. you always kinder cheer me up with your letters and I will sho be glad to see you and I am crazy for the time to come.

I am so sorry you say you wont get you a *pony* now cause I do so want you to have one. but you keep on the lookout for one and if you see one why that offer always holds good and you must *buy it*

Yes dear those books do show a lot of heart aches and misfortune and it makes me sad to read them but it is just all what you make it as you say and God and Love is all there is after all

"G" hon you are a smart girl and I have read so little and really dont know a thing and I will just ~~be able~~ love to have you tell me oh so many many things that I dont know cause I want someone that I can look up to and not a *bum* like myself. I just know you will be dissapointed in me cause you think I am wise cause I have traveled but I dont know a thing only the bad side that I should not know.

Well this is the jumpiest season   I still dont know yet where I go next week and may have to lay off but I will wire you later on.

Did you get the last book I sent you and the letter in it

Here is a little clipping from todays paper here   my act is going pretty good   This is a new Theatre and the first time I ever played here.

I hope I get a letter from my girl tomorrow   I am getting crazier about them all the time

I am going over tonight and see the first part of a show as I am on late. Robert Edison[1] in, "Call of the North."[2]

I always hate to tell you about all these cause there is my girl away out there and has to [be] content with an *Uncle Tom* show

Nevermind Kid this aint *dog days* but still every pup has them so yours is coming.

Well I will stop as there *aint much news in town* and I must eat a little even if I am in love I do occassionally eat.

Write me a long letter all about *"Togeather"* and tell me your view.[3]
Your own old Bill.

ALS, rc. OkClaW. On Redington Hotel, Wilkes-Barre, Pa., letterhead.

1. Robert Edeson (1868–1931) played regularly in New York productions throughout the 1890s, appearing at the Garrick theater, the Lyceum, the Herald Square theater, and several others. He became a star of Richard Harding Davis's *Soldiers of Fortune* at the Savoy in March 1902 and continued a string of star engagements through 1907, appearing in both New York and London. His career began to decline in 1908, and he did not regain his former star stature (*OCAT*, 225; *WhMuDr*, 107; *WhoStg*, 144–45).
2. *The Call of the North* was a play in four acts by George Broadhurst based on Stewart Edward White's story *Conjurer's House*. It was produced by Henry B. Harris at the Hudson Theatre in New York in August 1908, with Robert Edeson heading the cast and doing the staging (Mantle and Sherwood, *Best Plays of 1899–1909*, 565). It toured from New York to Albany, Chicago, Kansas City, and Wilkes-Barre, among other cities, in 1908–9. It was made into a film in 1921 (program, NN-L-BRTC; *NYDM*, 5 September 1908; *Theatre Magazine* [October 1908]: xxiv).
3. Rogers cabled Betty Blake four days later to tell her that he was "laying off next week" and would next be at the Hotel Preston, his regular place to stay in New York City (31 October 1908, OkClaW).

To Betty Blake
ca. 11 November 1908
Chelsea, Okla.

Rogers traveled from New York across country by rail through Rogers, Ark., where he visited with Betty Blake before proceeding to Oklahoma and the town of Chelsea, where his sisters Sallie McSpadden and Maud Lane lived. There are two letters to his fiancée postmarked 11 November 1908—this one, written en route after his stop in Rogers, and the following letter, written the afternoon of his arrival in Chelsea.

My Intended Wife.

(Dont that sound great it will sound greater when that middle word is *disected.*).

Well Hon I got in all O.K. but my train was 40 Min late out of Rogers and I come near going back up there and annoying you for a little longer

Well I get out of here at 11:15. Aint that a fine wait wish I could get you by long distance Phone I would just spend all my money telling you how much I love you, cause I sho do *feel good* and I dont feel so lonesome either cause I am just living on expectations and for the future and *you*   Well Sweetheart I sho do sympathize with you about now cause I can picture you having your *trouble* and a lot of it at that

Well I wish there was some way old Bill could help you through it but guess you will have to go it alone in this *nerve breaking* business cause I would be of no use.

I do so hope and pray you make it all right. its *you alone* that I want but at the same time I should hate to cause any of your folks any worry or uneasiness cause I know how they all love you and want to see you happy. I will tell the folks at home and know all will be fine cause they all like and love you

Here is that clipping I forgot to give you   Now you take *heed.* And here is *your* 50. not mine, *yours.* Now dont you *utter* a *murmur* cause what I have is *"yourn"* and you might need this little bit for something   but what you havent got you wait till you get east and get. You must remember all the fine clothes in the world on you could not make any more of a hit with me. dont worry about your *suit* not coming   you can get one in St. Louis   thats only one day longer to wait and just what you have looks might good to Willie. You always did hear my views on this clothes thing for a wedding and I always did express them long before we knew when ours would be a bit *hurry up*   I hate the sound of that preparing thing   I want *you you*   not clothes   I will let you get all you want when we get east   I dident see Harry Osborne   his store was closed before I got here.

Guess I wont cause a disturbance at 2 a.m. tonight when I arouse the McSpadden or Lane domicile and have them slaughtering the fatted *rooster* for breakfast.

Just think I wont get your letter tomorrow   not till *Thursday.*

Hope all the folks are well   you see I havent heard from there in over two weeks

I must run down and see the Gulagers one night while here and have a *chat* with dear old Mary[1]   She will be the most pleased person cause she always did *boost* you great.   really more than —— as I was saying before.

Well my own Sweetheart, its getting along late   will send you a line tomorrow and all other days and you must too. Goodnight Darling   just think in 16 more days. Bill loves you oh just lots, lots, more all the time.

Your own Billy.

ALS, rc. OkClaW. On St. Louis and San Francisco Railroad Eating Houses letterhead. Fred Harvey, Manager.[2] Postmarked 11 November 1908.

1. Mary Gulager (b. 1880) was Rogers's cousin and a good friend. She was also friends with Betty Blake, whom she had met when Blake lived for a short time in Indian Territory when all three were teenagers. She was the daughter of Rogers's maternal aunt, Martha Schrimsher Gulager (*PWR*, 1:200n.2).

2. Frederick Henry Harvey (1835–1901) began work as a mail clerk on the Hannibal and St. Joseph Railroad in 1862. As a railroad employee, Harvey saw a business niche for a chain of clean, high-quality, restaurants connected by rail. He took his plan to the Atchison, Topeka, and Santa Fe Railway. The first restaurant opened in Topeka, Kans., and was an instant success. Within ten years there was a Harvey House every hundred miles on the Santa Fe rail line. The railway included the motto "Fred Harvey Meals all the Way" in its advertising (Poling-Kempes, *Harvey Girls*, 38). By 1900 the Fred Harvey Co. and the Santa Fe Railway developed a chain of luxurious hotels to complement the restaurant business.

Fred Harvey's other innovation, and perhaps the one best known, was the concept of the Harvey Girls. Harvey had become dissatisfied with the staffs of waiters hired from the local populations for his restaurants. They did not bring the necessary spunk, freshness, respectability, and standardization to his chain. He conceived the idea of bringing in young women from the East and Midwest to staff the restaurants. These women had to be of good character, and had to sign contracts for twelve, nine, or six months. They were paid $17.50 a month, plus tips, and room and board—a very good rate of pay. They lived in a Harvey dormitory and had to be in by ten at night. Their uniform consisted of black shoes and stockings, ankle-length, long-sleeved black dress, and white apron and collar, and they wore their hair tied back. On the job the waitresses had to employ the "Harvey Way," an assemblage of rules of mannerism, etiquette, and work style. This concept of a standardized staff presentation went on to become the norm in American restaurants.

Will Rogers was a great enthusiast of Harvey Houses and the Harvey Girls. He wrote: "In the early days, the traveler fed on the buffalo. For doing so, the buffalo got his picture on the nickel. Well, Fred Harvey should have his picture on one side of the dime, and one of his waitresses with her arms full of delicious ham and eggs on the other side, 'cause they have kept the West supplied with food and wives" (quoted in Poling-Kempes, *Harvey Girls*, 102).

Rogers made as great an impression on Harvey Girls as they had made on him. Opal Sells Hill remembered Rogers as being a frequent passenger on the Santa Fe line in the 1920s: "All the girls knew who he was and used to go and stand on the porch of the Harvey House to watch him perform in the street. Everybody watched him. Later, I became the Harvey Girl he always requested to serve him. We became great friends. He'd call me by name when he came into the Amarillo dining room and then he'd say, 'Bring me some of that corn bread and red beans or some of those delicious ham and eggs!' Everybody knew what he wanted; and he'd get it, even at dinner time. He was a great favorite at the Harvey House" (Poling-Kempes, *Harvey Girls*, 142; also 31, 33–38, 102–3, 148; see also Cox, "Fred Harvey, the Righteous Restaurateur," 133–34, 138; Morris, *Harvey Girls*, 21, 25, 30–31).

To Betty Blake
11 November 1908
Chelsea, Okla.

Wednesday

4 P.M.

My Own very own Betty

Well Sweetheart   I got in at 4 aclock, this morning. train two hours late I walked up to Sister Sallies and sneaked in and they did not know I was on the place   I went up and went to bed and early this morning Sallie come in the room to get something and found me in bed.

We phoned Papa and he came up from Claremore and is here   the whole two famalies all stay all night over at Mauds and then tomarrow we will all drive out 8. miles to my other Sister May's Stine. she lives out in the country you never met her did you   She is dandy just like the other two   I am the only *bum* in the troop. Well I told them all about it at dinner[1]   in a kind of a kidding way I started it and then told them I just know they will be pleased as they like you and think that you will take good *care of me.* Well, I will get your letter tomorrow and will be so glad to hear from you. Oh! I got your letter sent on from New York.

The folks are outside ~~wait~~ waiting in the buggy for me and I want this to go on this train.

I will write you tomorrow after your letter   still I go to the country all day but will write late tomorrow night.

With all my love.

Billy.

ALS, rc. OkClaW.

1. Both Rogers and Betty Blake waited awhile after making marriage plans to tell their respective family members. Rogers chose to tell his sisters, Sallie McSpadden, Maud Lane, and May Stine, the big news in person. His sisters welcomed Betty Blake into the family, and in later life Betty Blake Rogers and Sallie McSpadden grew especially close. On 14 November 1908 Sallie McSpadden wrote the following kind letter to Betty Blake (OkClaW):

My Dear Bettie:—
Willie has joyfully told us the all important news of your and his approaching marriage and I am only sending you this little letter this morning to tell you how glad I am.
After having spent a week with him, during a Washington engagement, I realize how very lonely his life is and with his accustomed good judgement, I feel that he is doing just the right thing at the right time and place and congratulate him on the wise choice he has made. I assure you you will find a warm welcome in our home, not only from Tom and I, but from the entire 'troop,' as Willie so aptly puts it. A man who has been such an ideal brother as has this dear brother of mine could not be other than the dearest husband in the world and you

need feel no hesitancy in giving your self into his keeping. I not only *hope,* but believe that you will be 'the one woman and man' in the world to each other and after all—thats all there is to life. My love and good wishes shall follow you both wherever you be and at all times. Tom wishes you both to remember that there will always be a plate and room in the kindergarten that is maintained and managed by

Sister Sallie

Maud Lane wrote similarly to Betty, on 18 November 1908 (OkClaW). "My own dear girl you dont know how glad I am to have you for a sister," she wrote. "Cap and I have loved you from the very first and now that you are to be one of us we are so glad, I am sure you are the only woman for my dear boy, you see I think I love him just a little more than the other girls for I cared for him when he was a dear baby and to me he has ever been the dearest brother in the world and I want him to be just as happy as can be, but in this wish my dear I dont forget you and all the good things that should be yours. I do hope in this marr[i]age you will find love, peace and happiness, to me marr[i]age is truly a divine institute and if husband and wife truly love each other there is not greater joy on this earth than marr[i]age. I am praying my dear that such will be the union of you and my darling boy."

Not to be outdone, C. L. (Cap) Lane wrote his own letter to his prospective sister-in-law. In it he revealed that Will Rogers was not the only wit in the family. Lane cautioned Betty that marriage was like opening a prize package—you had to close your eyes and open the package, and not until then would you really know if congratulations were in store. He then went on to warn her, tongue in cheek, about the soon-to-be bridegroom's strange behavior since the news of the engagement had come out. "Far be it from my intention to knock on your Little Willie, but dear Betty I must be candid with you, and while what I am about to tell you, to a certain degree reflects on my own family, I cannot remain silent, when I see a girl, trusting her future happiness into the hand of one who at times is mentally incapable. Them are harsh words, but I will tell you of a few, only, of his acts." He went on to ponder whether there could be a "predisposition to insanity" in the family "and that being hereditary[,] would account for Willie's antics." Will Rogers had always seemed rational on his prior trips home to see his family, but on his last visit "his act has been that of a crazy man, he sits around in a deep study for a few minutes, then jumps up singing and dancing, at other times he seems [to] be in an ecstatic condition of mind paying no attention to any one, and seems to me like some one walking in his sleep, you know how it is." He went on to describe a change in diet—Rogers, who loved beans with onions piled on top, suddenly refused to eat the onions. Then he took "things like letters, photos etc that formerly he was very careful and jealous of" and "now thinks very little of as he has torn and burned up two & one half bushels" full, and "without apparent regret, in fact seems to delight in it." He had also taken "a distaste to Jewelry, has rid himself of cuff buttons, stick pins, rings and things, sending them away, the Lord only Knows where." (As Betty Blake well knew, Rogers had sent most of these items to his bride-to-be to have them reworked into pieces she could wear. As part of his purging of his past relationships and dalliances, he also returned gifts of jewelry to his old girlfriend, as he had promised Betty he would do [see Will Rogers to Betty Blake, 20 November 1908, below].) Cap Lane ended his list of evidence of devotion to Blake, couched in mock horror, by reassuring Betty that he had only her happiness in mind in telling her these things, and if she needed "verification of the facts, ask any married man." Betty Blake sent her love back to Cap Lane, and told Maud Lane to tell him that she had "read and re-read his letter. Tell him I'm pretty good at bronco-bustin'" (Betty Blake to Maud Lane, ca. 23 November 1908, OkClaW).

Betty told the news of the impending wedding to Mary Quisenberry, in Rogers, Ark., by mail. Quisenberry wrote back, "Of course you could not have surprised me more than I was when I got your letter this morning. I was simply paralyzed for a minute, but I am so glad for you Bettie and know you are going [to be] one of the happiest girls in the world. The few times that I saw Will (I may call him that since he is to be my new brother) I liked him very much and I know he is *awful nice* or Bettie would not like him." She ended by saying that she and her husband joined "in love and best wishes for the bride-to-be and congratulations for the groom" (Mary Quisenberry to Betty Blake, ca. 29 October 1908, OkClaW).

To Betty Blake
12 November 1908
Chelsea, Okla.

Thursday, 4:30 P.M.

My Own Darling Betty,

Well Dearie I got your dear sweet little note and it did make me feel oh so happy and "G" but I do love you and oh how I will try to make you happy.

I have just this minute come in from my sister Mays where Maud, Sallie, Papa and I all drove out and spent the day, oh, Betty I am so happy and so glad that it is so soon now, aint you. Cause I just could not wait long for you the way I want and love you now. My folks are so well pleased and just think it fine and love you and think you are grand. They have always been kinder afraid I would grab on to some old show girl or some bum and now that they know it is you they are tickled to death. I dont know how [now] about just when I will get over there. I do so want to come Sunday and am very apt to do it. I will wire you Saturday if I do and if not I will come about Tuesday or Wednesday and we will plan just *what—when* and *how*. I will go down to Claremore tomorrow and spend the day and I want to go up to the farm some one day. I am going south by Tahlequah from your home this time will spend a day and night there and go south on that No. 5   that I will come in on the day before. I am just crazy to come Sunday and will I think.[1] Now listen Sweetheart dont worry and feel bad cause you have not got just as you would like but what do you care. Dont you think old Bill will understand and I want you all the more and *not clothes*. You can get just what you want in St. Louis and New York. Say that day we had planned on is Thanksgiving *a fine day* and I think it would be good just like we had planned dont you.[2]

Well Dearest, Sister is waiting to take me home up to Sister Sallies. I will be so glad to get your letter tomorrow.

Well Goodnight *my own very own* two weeks from Today.

Your own Billy.

Rogers sent this telegram confirming his intention to visit Betty Blake in Rogers, Ark., shortly after their wedding. (*OkClaW*)

ALS, rc. OkClaW. On C. L. Lane, Corner Drug Store, Chelsea, Indian Territory, letterhead.[3] Postmarked 12 November 1908.

1. Apparently Betty Blake was crazy for him to come on Sunday, too; he cabled her the next day that he had "got your letter and tickled to death sure   I will be there Sunday on no 6   lots of love   Billy." Flustered while sending the first transmission, he wired her again minutes later to say, "I mean no 5 instead of 6" (WR to Betty Blake, 13 November 1908, received 8:53 A.M. and 9:05 A.M., OkClaW).

2. Betty Blake and Rogers were indeed married on 25 November 1908, as they had planned.

3. Rogers's brother-in-law, C. L. (Cap) Lane, was a Chelsea businessman and druggist who owned a large drugstore in the town (see *PWR*, 1:498–99).

To Betty Blake
19 November 1908
Claremore, Okla.

Thursday, A.M.

My Almost *Wif*

Well *hon* your little letter come today and it was just like you and I loved it even if it was short.

I got in last night or rather just this a.m. at 4 aclock. I stayed over in Muscogee a few hours longer than I expected and then come home last night by the way of Vinita.

I did not get to see Sandy in Gibson and I wish I had but I had some Business with the Trent boys in Muskogee and had to go there.[1] I will write to Sandy today.[2]

Say hon, your ring just come and I am sending it on to you today by registered mail. It is not as large as I wanted but it is a pure white, perfect stone. You see I told them by all means that what I did get I wanted to be perfect and not some big yellow thing. You can exchange it if you like when we get back there. I want to have one of those pins made into a ring and if I can have it done in Claremore today will send it to you also.

Say what do you think? Sister Sallies children or one of them have got the Scarlet Fever and of course could not be able to come. They are hardly in bed but the house is all quarintined and no one can get in or out. I will write you tomorrow and tell you something more definite but perhaps Maud and Papa can come.[3] I am running down to Claremore this eve for a few hours.

Well old Mary[4] was just tickled to death and so is all the people I have seen. Oh I sho am proud of my *wif,* and cant understand how this did not happen long ago   it was all your fault that it did not.

Yes Sweetheart we will get that first train and say guess what we will see in St. Louis Thanksgiving afternoon, a great Football game. ~~Charli~~ *Carlisle Indians* against *Washington University.*[5] I have always wanted to see ~~them~~ those Indians play. They are one of the greatest teams in America. *Wont* you like it.

Well I must stop. "G" I dont think of a thing but you all the time and oh Girlie how I do love you and how I will try and make you happy. You are just the grandest girl in all the world. Oh I love love Love you with all my heart and am so so happy.

Your Billy

ALS, rc. OkClaW.

1. References to Betty Blake's brother, James K. (Sandy) Blake, and to Rogers's friends and distant cousins, brothers Richard Owen (Dick), Thomas Brown (Tom), and Spi Trent. Rogers's father, Clement Vann Rogers, had helped pay for Spi Trent to go to a business college, and Trent worked as a bookkeeper in a family business in Okmulgee, Okla. The boyhood closeness between Rogers and Spi Trent did not last, and Rogers was later dismayed by Trent's unabashed willingness to trade on their former relationship in pursuit of financial gain. Rogers and Betty Blake both became very close to Spi Trent's brother Tom Trent in the next few years, when all three spent time living in New York (see *PWR*, 1:198n.1, 562–64 [Biographical Appendix entries for Richard Owen Trent, M.D., and Spi Trent]; see also Will Rogers to May McSpadden,

27 July 1909, note 2, Betty Blake Rogers to Clement Vann Rogers, 30 July 1909, and Will Rogers to Betty Blake Rogers, 10 August 1909 and note 1, below).

2. Rogers wrote to James K. (Sandy) Blake on 20 November 1908 (OkClaW). He told him he had passed through town but had not had a chance to stop and see him:

> Well old boy I guess that Dear Sister of yours has made known to you *our* desires and should you approve of it I just want to tell you that I will do all in my power to try and make her happy and will try to live up to the high ideal you have set in caring for her as you and your dear folks have so well done in the past.
>
> I sho do admire you Sandy for the unselfish way you have cared for your folks [his mother and sisters]. And she certainly does appreciate it and loves you as well she should.
>
> Now I will just try and take up the part of caring for her and looking out for her where you have done so well. Now if I do what you have done you wont ask for more cause there would be no more to ask for.
>
> Perhaps you are not aware that I have loved that girl for many years since Oolagah in fact. And I have been all over the world and she is the only *real* girl I ever saw.
>
> Now Sandy our home wherever it may be on the road or at home is always your home and you can come once a year and stay a year if you will. And we not only ask you but *want* you.
>
> I wish you could come over. I know I would feel some better if I had you there but if not we hope to see you back east on a trip to see us real soon. We will show you a time.
>
> Well I better quit before I get sentimental (and that dont take long either when I get strung out about Betty).
>
> I will try and prove myself a *real* brother to you.
>
> Will Rogers.

3. Maud Rogers Lane had written to Betty Blake the day before to tell her about the illness in the family and how her and Sallie McSpadden's Thanksgiving plans had thus been disrupted. She said she wished that Betty Blake and Will Rogers would come back to Oklahoma after the wedding so that the Rogers family members could see them, "but now that Sallie is shut-in, it is better as you have arranged. Irene has Scarlet Fever took sick Saturday night, she is doing quite nicely and we are hoping none of the other children will take it. I cant go over there but talk to them every day. We had planned to spend Thanksgiving with sister May but I guess we will have to give that up now" (18 November 1908, OkClaW). Maud Lane was apparently hedging around the fact that she had not been formally invited to come to the wedding in Arkansas. On 21 November 1908 she wrote to Betty Blake again, saying she was "so glad you decided to ask me down. I have been most dead to go all the time but dident dare, but now you can depend on me I will surely go." The McSpaddens were still quarantined when she wrote and would be unable to go, as would the Lane children, who were "all in school, but Lasca[,] so Mr. Lane will have to stay home to keep her." Maud Lane ended her letter by observing that she and Clement Vann Rogers would be the only Rogers family members who could come to Arkansas—indeed, they could go even farther, to New York, where Betty and Will were going to live. "Papa and I are the only ones who have no cares and can go any place at any time," she wrote, "even as far East as New York" (OkClaW).

4. Mary Gulager.

5. The Carlisle Indian School was the first federally sponsored off-reservation vocational boarding school for American Indians. Established by then army lieutenant Richard H. Pratt in Carlisle, Pa., the school opened its doors in 1879. Its motto, "Kill the Indian and save the man," graphically described its mission to "Americanize" and "civilize" the Indians. Constructed on the model of manual-labor institutions, the school instructed its students in basic academic skills but placed heaviest emphasis on

household skills for girls and farming and manual trades for boys. Daily life was imbued with military discipline, and students, wearing uniforms, drilled and marched to classes.

The Carlisle School also instructed its students in sports, and by the 1890s it had organized a football team proficient enough to play college ball. The Carlisle Indians played the best college teams and developed a national reputation. On 26 November 1908 the Indians played St. Louis University (not Washington University as Rogers thought beforehand), and defeated them 17–0 in a game played in St. Louis. The Carlisle team won ten games, lost two, and tied one during the 1908 season (*Chicago Daily Tribune*, 27 November 1908; *LAT*, 27 November 1908; *NYT*, 27 and 29 November 1908; Steckbeck, *Fabulous Redmen*, 11–15, 74–77; Weeks, *Farewell, My Nation*, 223–26).

The newlywed Rogerses took the train from Rogers, Ark., to St. Louis and saw the Carlisle Indians play on Thanksgiving Day. That same evening they went to the theater and saw Maude Adams in *What Every Woman Should Know* (Collins, *Will Rogers: Courtship and Correspondence*, 184).

To Betty Blake
20 November 1908
Claremore, Okla.

Friday, 2 P.M.

My Almost *Wif,*

Well Sweetheart, it is only a few more days and you and I will be .1. and I will be oh! so happy and I just think of it all the time and just want my own Girl   oh how I do want you Sweetheart.

Now Betty I dont know just who will be down with me besides Papa and perhaps Maud and Cap. Sallie dont know yet and hardly thinks she can come. Her children are just doing fine, still they cant let them out and my Sister May will be in town tomorrow and dont hardly think she can come on account of the baby and really I dont know but will let you know. It will perhaps be Papa and Maud and Cap and *perhaps me* if I can possibly get off.

Say Hon about those announcements   "G" I dont know I have so *darn* many friends or *supposedly friends* all over the Universe and I would not know where to stop or dont remember half of them and all my vast army of connections and if I should overlook a cousin or a dozen then the devil would be to pay and I have thought so little of who to send them too that I dont see any use of it now. I know I should only send them to my dearest friends but I have been away so much and all that   I dont know who they are and do you think that it would be all right to let it go   honest dear, I dont know who I should tell you   I dont remember even half of my near relatives.

Now hon I sent you a package by registered Mail today containing a ~~bun~~ little bunch of pins and diamonds. is there a jeweler there that can do that for me. The cluster pin I want you to make a ring   the Horseshoe you can do with as you think best   a bar pin of some kind for your collar and the locket for your chain around the neck   have that Masonic charm taken off   it is only stuck on and if you have one of your little pictures a good one put it in there   I only had that little post card one in there of me ▲ and ▲ on one side for ~~you~~ ▲ yours ▲   Now I wanted you to have that done there and you will have them on the trip east   I hope you can get that one made into a ring cause it will be swell. I wish you could have some kind of a ring made out of that horseshoe pin cause it would be fine   The little pin of mine I just sent you to look at *not* for you. it is mine   it and my big ring is all I have. all the other I give to you. Wear that locket, he can take off that Masonic pin part   it has been commented on more than all my other stuff put togeather

I sent the cuff buttons and two rings back to ——[1]   and wrote and told her I did not care for them just as I had told you I would and I feel good over it now that all that dreadful thing is over.

Yes the plans you spoke of are all O.K. Anything you plan is good. Yes we will get that first train out. I wrote Sandy yesterday. Wish he could come over I wouldent mind him. is that Lee Adamson there   just poison him for a few days with my regards will you. Thank the Lord Bill Marshall cant be there.[2] Have you a suit case *hon*   by putting in there just what you want you will not have to get into your trunk till N.Y. I will get you a dandy little traveling bag and you can discard the big grip or suitcase. did you mean to come direct from the train up there. By, By, My[l]ove. I will write you tomorrow, with all oh, just all my love.

Your Billy.

ALS, rc. OkClaW.

1. In this letter, as in Rogers's letter of 11 November 1908, the apparently unspeakable names of the ex-girlfriend or ex-boyfriend are consigned to oblivion and represented by long dashes.

2. References to Betty Blake's brothers-in-law, her sister Anna's husband Lee Adamson and her sister Cora's husband Will Marshall. Betty Blake had been visiting Cora and Will Marshall in Oologah when she first met Rogers. Both Adamson and Marshall worked for the railroads and had difficulty getting time away from their jobs (see *PWR*, 1:187nn.3,4).

To Betty Blake
21 November 1908
Claremore, Okla.

Saturday. Eve.

Claremore.

My Own Betty

Well, hon I am down here on a little visit for a few hours and go back on the eve train.

Well *hon* I am sho a loving you these days and will always   oh I just know it and oh we will be so happy and just happy all the time.

Well Sweetheart it is only a day or so and we will be all for each other

I will be up at Chelsea now till Tuesday Night when we will leave   I think it will be Maud, Cap, Papa and —— I dont know if Sister May can come and of course Sister Sallie cant come   still the children are not sick at all.

Did you get that bunch of stuff and could that fellow, jeweler fix them for you. if not can have it done in N.Y.

Well hon I must *get* this off on this train and you can get it tomorrow and how I do wish I *was* down there tomorrow (Sunday) and the long old quiet drive in the hills cause it will be some time before we get to go again and how I did love those old drives and I think you did too.

I do hope your mother will not go to a lot of trouble because that is the very thing I wanted to avoid.[1]

By. by.   My Very Own

Your Billy.

ALS, rc. OkClaW. On First National Bank, Claremore, Okla., letterhead. Postmarked 22 November 1908.

1. Most of the details of the wedding planning fell to Betty Blake's mother Amelia Blake, who sent out announcements and organized the wedding, which took place in her home. Betty Blake wrote to Maud Lane about the same time that Rogers wrote this letter to her, warning her in part that the whole thing would be a simple affair. She told Lane she was glad she could come "on Wednesday" (the day of the wedding) and that she hoped "all the rest can come. My mother is expecting you all. We are making no *special* preparations. I will be married in my suit, and it will all be rather a 'shirt waist' affair" (Betty Blake to Maud Lane, ca. 23 November 1908, OkClaW).

To Betty Blake
23 November 1908
Claremore, Okla.

Monday. Eve.

My very very Own.

Well *my Betty* it is only two more days and "G" this has been a long old Week   about the longest I ever saw

Well I come down last night from Chelsea and up to the farm today at Oologah   went up on the train and drove out from there and back in time to get the local back to Claremore and will go up on this afternoon train to Chelsea. Say but I did think of you a lot while up at old Oologah and I sent you a wire from there[1]   did you get it and think of how I used to see you at that old Depot   those were fine old days

Say but it looks lonesome up there. The old farm is looking pretty bad but I dont want to sell it and will keep it and think it will still be all to the good for us yet. I have turned the management of it over to Buck Sunday[2]   that Injun boy   you remember him in the store. He is a good business boy and will see to it all for me and it will relieve papa of it all   cause he is getting so he cant do business any more.

Well we will go up to Monette[3] on that tomorrow afternoon train and will get a good nights rest and feel refreshed for a *strenerous* day

Are you scared, *hon*   I am not. Maud and May are coming and perhaps Cap.[4]

Say how do we go   from the train to your house and be married right away ~~and~~ is that the way I understand it to be.[5] if it is as soon as we get there I will not change my clothes   just have on a dark traveling suit that I will be married in. remember no *dressing up*. My sisters will just have on what they wear down there, so dont let those sisters of yours be all dressed up[6]

Just think Sweetheart in two days from now how we will be   and I just know we will be happy and I will just do all I can to please you and try to make you love me more and not let you ever feel sorry that you left home for me. Oh Betty I am so happy and I do love you with all my heart and just want you more all the time

I hope I get a dandy letter from you when I get to Chelsea this eve   do you know it seems that you have *kinder* neglected me since I came away but I know you thought of me lots and that is just as good.

Well Goodbye Sweetheart My Own, my own. only a day ▲ after you get this ▲ and I will [be] yours forever and you all mine.

Your   Billy.

ALS, rc. OkClaW. On First National Bank, Claremore, Okla., letterhead. Postmarked 24 November 1908.

1. Rogers cabled Blake from Oologah, to say: "Back to the scenes of our childhood wish you was at this old Depot now   love Billy" (23 November 1908, OkClaW). Rogers and Blake first met at the Oologah train station in the fall of 1899. Although Rogers was still decidedly boyish, he and Blake were not children—both were twenty years old. She was visiting her sister Cora and Cora's husband Will Marshall, who worked as the depot agent in Oologah, and was standing at the counter one day when Rogers came into town from his father's ranch to see if a banjo he had ordered had arrived by rail. He was struck by her immediately, but was too shy to speak much to her at the time (see *PWR*, 1:155, 185).

2. The Sunday family, who were Cherokee, were prominent in business in Oologah and in Cherokee Nation politics. They owned a livery stable and general merchandise store in Oologah (*PWR*, 1:558–59).

3. Monett, Mo., a town thirty-five miles east of Joplin, Mo., and some fifty miles from Betty Blake's hometown of Rogers, Ark., was a changeover stop on the train ride from Chelsea, Okla., to Rogers, Ark. After their wedding, the Rogerses took the train from Rogers to Monett and then changed over to a "stateroom in the through train to St. Louis." The fact that Rogers had made these arrangements reminded his new wife "that he was an experienced traveler and a man of the world" (Rogers, *Will Rogers*, 103).

4. Sallie McSpadden sent a note of regret that she could not attend, along with a gift, wishing Betty Blake "a long happy and prosperous life, with just clouds enough to make a beautiful sunset" (Tom and Sallie McSpadden to Betty Blake, 24 November 1908, OkClaW).

5. Betty Blake actually had a little scare involving the arrival of the train with her beloved and his family members in Rogers. "My mother's house was but a few blocks from the railroad station. If we left home when the train whistled, we could be at the depot by the time it arrived," she recalled. "That morning I remember hearing the whistle and looking through the window of my room upstairs to watch my brother drive away to meet Will and his family." Her brother returned with an empty wagon. "I was on the verge of tears before he finally explained that the train was in two sections that day and that the wedding party was on the second section" (Rogers, *Will Rogers*, 102).

6. There had been quite a bit of concern among the women about the proper thing to wear. Betty Blake Rogers recalled that it was "a small wedding, with just the two families present . . . I wore a blue and white silk dress and I remember well my going-away suit of dark blue broadcloth, ordered 'special' from Marshall Field's in Chicago, with hat and veil to match" (Rogers, *Will Rogers*, 102–3).

Wedding Announcement
25 November 1908
Rogers, Ark.

Mrs. Amelia J. Blake
announces the marriage of her daughter
Betty
to
Mr. William P. A. Rogers[1]
Wednesday, November the twenty-fifth
nineteen hundred and eight
Rogers, Arkansas

PD. OkClaW.

1. Rogers's formal name was William Penn Adair Rogers. He was named for his father's friend, the Cherokee Nation politician William Penn Adair (1830–80) (see *PWR*, 1:482–85 [Biographical Appendix entry for William Penn Adair]).

Marriage License of Will Rogers and Betty Blake
25 November 1908
Bentonville, Ark.

MARRIAGE LICENSE

STATE OF ARKANSAS   COUNTY OF BENTON

To any Person Authorized by Law to Solemnize Marriage—Greeting:

You are hereby commanded to solemnize the Rites and publish the Bans of Matrimony between Mr. <u>William P. Rogers,</u> of <u>Claremore,</u> in the County of <u>Rogers,</u> and State of <u>Oklahoma</u> aged <u>29</u> years, and <u>Miss. Bettie Blake,</u> of <u>Rogers,</u> in the County of <u>Benton</u> and State of Arkansas, aged <u>28</u> years, according to law, and do you officially sign and return this License to the parties herein named. Witness my hand and Official Seal this <u>16th.</u> day of <u>Nov.</u> A.D. <u>1908.</u>

<u>W. E. Hill</u> Clerk.
_____ D. C.

CERTIFICATE OF MARRIAGE

State of Arkansas

}

County of <u>Benton</u>

I, <u>John G. Bailey</u> do hereby certify that on the <u>25</u> day of <u>November</u> 190<u>8</u>, I did duly and according to law, as commanded in the foregoing License, solemnize the Rites and publish the Bans of Matrimony between the parties therein named.

Witness my hand this <u>25</u> day of <u>Nov</u> A.D. 190<u>8</u>

My Credentials are recorded in County Clerk's Office <u>Bentonville</u> County, Ark., Book <u>B</u> Page <u>629</u>

CERTIFICATE OF RECORD

State of Arkansas,

}

County of Benton.

I, <u>W. E. Hill</u> Clerk of the County Court of said County, certify that the above License for and Certificate of the Marriage of the parties herein named, were, on the <u>26</u> day of <u>Nov</u> 190<u>8</u>, filed in my office and the same are now duly recorded on page <u>396</u> Book <u>"G"</u> of Marriage Records.[1]

W E Hill Clerk.

_____ D. C.

PD, with typed and autograph insertions. OkClaW.

1. Rogers's hometown newspaper, the *Claremore Progress*, reported that "a very pretty home wedding took place Thanksgiving day at Rogers, Ark." (the wedding was actually the day before Thanksgiving) "when *William*, son of Hon. C. V. Rogers, of our city, was married to Miss Bettie Blake, at the home of the bride's mother in Rogers. The ceremony took place at one o'clock in the presence of the immediate families of the contracting parties. After an elegant repast had been served the happy couple left for New York. Will enjoys a large circle of friends here who wish him and his bride many years of happiness (*CP*, 28 November 1908). Betty Blake's hometown newspaper also announced the wedding, observing that it "has created much interest owing to the prominence of the bride in local circles" (*Rogers Democrat*, 19 November 1908).

Western Vaudeville Association Contract
14 December 1908
Chicago, Ill.

Will and Betty Blake Rogers headed east from St. Louis after their brief honeymoon in that city. Rogers's first professional appearance after his marriage was at Proctor's Theatre in Newark, N.J. He played there the week ending on 12 December 1908, and that was the first time his new wife saw him perform his stage act. He played the next week (13–19 December) at the Colonial Theatre in New York with Ruth Allen, the Stewart Sisters,[1] the Exposition Four,[2] and others.[3] During that time he signed a contract to go out on tour on the Orpheum Circuit. Rogers and his act, including Buck McKee and Teddy, would play in cities in the South, working their way up to the Midwest. Betty Blake Rogers would accompany her husband on this tour.

WESTERN VAUDEVILLE ASSOCIATION
AND UNITED BOOKING OFFICES
OF AMERICA, N.Y.

IT IS IMPERATIVE that artists send photographs and billing matter, ten days in advance, to the Theatre they are booked in, NOT TO THE AGENCY. A failure to comply with the above is sufficient cause for cancellation.

N.B.—If you have pictorial paper notify each Theatre where it can be procured.

MAJESTIC THEATRE BUILDING

CHICAGO ILL.

S. H.

CONTRACT   No.

This Agreement, made and entered into on the <u>14</u> day of <u>DEC.</u> <u>1908</u> by and between <u>THE ORPHEUM CIRCUIT CO.</u> party of the first part, and <u>WILL ROGERS</u> party of the second part:

Witnesseth: That for and in consideration of the mutual covenants and agreements of the parties hereto, as hereinafter set forth, **It is hereby Mutually Agreed** between them as follows:

The party of the first part hereby agrees to employ and does hereby engage and employ, the said party of the second part, to perform, and the party of the second part hereby agrees to perform for the said party of the first part <u>HIS</u>

specialty consisting of <u>LASSO ACT</u> to the satisfaction of the party of the first part at the <u>ORPHEUM</u> Theatre in the City of[4]

	MEMPHIS[5]	MAT.	MON.JAN. 4/09
"	N. ORLEANS	"	MON.JAN. 11/09
"	KANSAS C.	"	SUN.JAN. 24/09
"	OMAHA	"	SUN.JAN. 31/09
"	ST.PAUL	"	SUN.FEB. 7/09
"	MINNEAP.	"	SUN.FEB. 14/09

or at such other theatre or place of amusement in said city of _____ or at such other city as the party of the first part may designate, for <u>SIX</u> weeks, commencing <u>MAT.MON.JAN. 4/09</u> 1___ at Rehearsal 9 o'clock A.M; said party of the second part to give <u>TWO</u> shows daily, at such hours as the said party of the first part shall designate, subject to the rules of the said Theatre, in all respects. In the event that the said party of the second part shall faithfully carry out and strictly observe all of the conditions hereof, said party of the first part hereby agrees to pay to said party of the second part the sum of <u>300.00 THREE HUNDRED</u> Dollars for each week of said engagement

Said party of the second part shall put said party of the first part in possession of all photos, lithos, stage and property plots of the said artist (party of the second part), relating to the act or acts, at least ten days before the beginning of said engagement.

Said party of the second part hereby agrees not to play or perform at any club or other place in the said city _____ prior to, during or within two weeks after said engagement: and it is expressly understood, should the party of the second part violate this clause of this contract, they agree to forfeit all salary due or to become due under this contract as liquidated damages to party of first part.

It is hereby mutually agreed that incompetency or drunkenness of the artist or artists said party of the second part), or his or their failure to appear at said Theatre at the hour when said engagement is to begin, or at any time when the said acts should be performed, shall be sufficient cause to annul or discontinue said engagement without notice.

It is further agreed that the said party of the first part may deduct from the above stipulated compensation an amount equal to the ratio which the number of acts, to be performed under this contract by the party of the second part, bears to the compensation to be paid to the party of the second part hereinabove mentioned, for each act which the artist (said party of the second part) fail to perform under said engagement.

Said party of the first part may cancel the said engagement at any time after their first performance or prior to the third performance of said party of the second part, upon paying to said party of the second part a sum equal to one seventh of the weekly compensation hereinabove mentioned.

Either party to this contract may cancel same by giving two weeks notice.

This contract is entered into through the instrumentality of the Western Vaudeville Assn. and in consideration of the services rendered to the parties hereto in procuring this contract, the said parties hereto agree to and do hereby save the said Western Vaudeville Assn. harmless from any and all claims of every character whatsoever which the parties hereto or either of them may sustain because of the failure on the part of either party hereto to faithfully carry out the terms of this contract.

It is further agreed that this agreement, having been made through the Western Vaudeville Mgrs' Assn., Chicago, Ills., and United Booking Offices of America, N.Y. a commission of <u>10</u> per cent. shall be deducted from the salary payable to the artist under this contract.

In Testimony Whereof the parties hereto have hereunto set their hands the day and year first above written.

CASEY[6] — AGT.   <u>THE ORPHEUM CIRCUIT CO.</u>

<u>Will Rogers</u>

PDS, with typed insertions. JLC-OkClaW.

1. The Stewart Sisters were a dance act, originally from Lancashire, England. They were in vaudeville in Europe and America for many years. They began as a "Dancing Doll," "Six English Blossoms," or "English Dancing Dolls" act, and the number of sisters in their act decreased from six to four to three over time. They came from Great Britain to appear at the St. Louis World's Fair and then appeared at the French Grand Opera in New Orleans (1904–5). In the next few years they played summers in England, circuit work in the United States, and appearances in Germany, living together in a flat in New York City as their primary home. "We manage our own business affairs, one girl acting as secretary, one superintending the wardrobes (though we all work on those), another attending to the baggage, hotels, etc. In this way each of us gets some time for reading, music, and other forms of recreation. . . . we are very practical English girls" (*Toledo Courier Journal,* 2 September 1907). From 1907 to 1909 there were four sisters appearing together, all between the ages of eighteen and twenty-five. From 1910 through 1915 there were three sisters appearing as the Stewart Sisters with Escorts, in an eleven-minute, full-stage, singing and dancing act with three women and three men. Where the earlier sister act had featured "37 different character dances" (ibid.), the escorted version of the act emphasized musical comedy and showy costume changes. The sisters were working with the escorts as a sextet, doing "English Pantomime and Dancing Novelty" at Loew's Theatre in New York in October 1914, and Rogers appeared with them again in January of that year (*Vancouver World,* 3 October 1914; see also Reviews from the Palace Theatre, ca. 5 January 1914, below). By 1916 the three sisters remaining in the act—Emmie, Pearl,

and Jean Stewart—were appearing alone without escorts. They were described as a distinguished act. They did a series of dances of their own arrangement, including "A Country Gallop," "Tulip Time in Holland," and "An Acrobatic Frolic." Emmie Stewart was reportedly the choreographer of the group. The *Detroit Journal* of 5 January 1915 described their work as "Dainty dances, very clean" (*Variety*, 19 November 1910; Locke env. 2169, NN-L-RLC).

2. The Exposition Four were a group of musicians who started out as amateurs in Pittsburgh's Hill district, where they had all grown up together. Composed of three brothers (Russell, Woodruff, and Newton Alexander) and their friend (James Brady), the Exposition Four were known for their versatility and professionalism. The Alexander brothers were the sons of J. W. Alexander, a Pittsburgh photographer and businessman who was at one time a partner of Samuel Scribner. The four young men went to public schools and gained experience playing dances and social affairs in their neighborhood and around the city. They were discovered by Gus Hill, and they played Hill shows for six years. They made their vaudeville debut at the Grand Theatre in their hometown and were appearing together on the circuit in 1905. They played the Farm in Toledo in August 1907, and "with instrumental music, songs, and comedy, made a great hit and encored many times." In their act they did a series of song and dance numbers with many quick changes of costume and makeup. They received consistently favorable reviews, and were described as "one of the best musical acts in vaudeville" (unmarked clippings, scrapbook, ser. 3, 456:67–69, NN-L-RLC). Rogers played again with them in 1915 (see Victoria Theater Playbill and Reviews, 26 April 1915, below).

3. For documentation of these appearances, see vaudeville announcements, *NYDM*, 12 December and 26 December 1908; *NYT*, 14–19 December 1908; vaudeville program, Colonial Theatre, scrapbook A-2, OkClaW. See also Rogers, *Will Rogers*, 104.

4. The text of Rogers's schedule from "ORPHEUM MEMPHIS" to "SUN.FEB.14/09" was typed over the printed contract text from "at the _____" to "part may designate." Additional text of contract reads sideways in left margin, *"Read Carefully the Club Clause under this Contract. It will be rigidly enforced."* Text in right margin reads, "[Fi]rst Part does not pay for Exe." Text in bottom margin reads, "Party of the First Part does not pay fare."

5. Rogers's act played in Chicago and St. Louis before going to Memphis. The 19 December 1908 *Variety* announced that he was to open at the Majestic Theater in Chicago on Monday "as start of a western tour booked by Pat Casey." He was playing in St. Louis commencing with the matinee on Monday, 28 December 1908, and headed from there to Memphis (playbill, scrapbook A-2, OkClaW).

6. Rogers's agent, Pat Casey, emerged from the "war" between Klaw and Erlanger and the UBO as the "adjuster for acts holding Klaw and Erlanger contracts." Once the "end of the K. & E. contracts has arrived, Mr. Casey intends to become a booking agent . . . prompted by the United people to make this move, receiving their assurance of warm patronage." The Pat Casey Agency opened in New York City on 1 April 1908, and business immediately boomed. Casey operated the agency in a variety of different buildings until 1916. His ads stated that he was "Fully Versed in the proper handling of acts to the Artists' Best Interests." After closing the agency, he joined first the Vaudeville Managers Association and later the Keith-Albee vaudeville circuit as an executive. In 1926 he shifted from vaudeville to films, becoming a member of the Association of Motion Picture Producers and a labor arbitrator for the movie industry (*Variety*, 21 March 1908, 14 December 1908; see also *NYT*, 8 February 1962; see also Biographical Appendix entry, CASEY, Pat).

RESULTS *The Pat Casey Agency* INC. **RESULTS**

PAT CASEY

Experience
And
Efficiency
Enable
Our
Experts
To
Develop
And
Promote
Talent

Trade advertisement for Pat Casey, Rogers's vaudeville agent in 1908. *(National Vaudeville Artists, Eighth Annual Benefit, 11 May 1924)*

Buck McKee to Maud Florence McKee
29 December 1908
St. Louis, Mo.

Tuesday,

St. Louis, <u>Dec 29, 1908</u>[1]

Precious Little Sweet heart:—

Enclosed find money order for $4.<u>00</u>. You can get it cashed at your substation up there by having Mrs. AE, or some body to identify you. Sign "Mrs. Maude McKee"—

Now that is all I could get hold of this morning, but I will send more later & also your Mother's $25.<u>00</u>.

Go down to that Iron factory at 20<u>th</u> St. between 7<u>th</u> & 8<u>th</u> Aves. I think it is about 6 doors west from the 7<u>th</u> Ave cor. & on the down town side of the St. It dont look like a shop from the front   It looks like an office. The lettering is on the glass window or door. You can find it. Get the four plates for the bottom of Teddies shoes—have them laced together with wire & ship them by express, without wrapping, to Will Rogers, Lasso Expert, Orpheum Vaudeville Theatre, ~~Orpheum Circuit~~, Memphis, Tenesee. You can go to any express office with them, or else give them to Mr. Pitchfork & have him attend to it. He would only be too glad to get a chance to accomodate you that much I know. It would be a boon pleasure to him. The amount due on them is $2.<u>25</u>. See that they are tagged & addressed carefully & plainly.

You can have the ballance of the $4.<u>00</u> & I will send more soon.

There is no particular hurry about sending them any certain day, just so they reach Memphis by the time we get there. If you send them from N.Y.C. by Friday or Sat. it will do.

It is raining here this morning.

Tell the foreman I went away & forgot them in my hurry, I had so many things to see after. Tell your Mother I will not forget the $25.<u>00</u>.

Be careful this bad weather & dont get your feet wet & get sick. Use that catarrh remedy regularly—that is what I bought you the atomizer for, so make good use of it.

Must get this off in the mail now. So bye=bye for the present.

Love & Kisses as ever.

Buck.

ALS, rc. BMc-C. On Havlin's Hotel (European), Havlin's Theatre Building, St. Louis, Mo., letterhead. Jeff Caspers, Proprietor.

1. A newspaper account reported that Rogers and McKee played at the Grand Opera House in St. Louis. The Opera House had a seating capacity of 2,100 and charged prices from 25 cents to a dollar. The Havlin's Theatre building, where McKee stayed, had a theater located on the ground floor. It advertised that it was illuminated with gas and electricity. The playbill in Rogers's vaudeville scrapbook, however, places him and McKee at the American Theatre in St. Louis the week of 28—31 December 1908. The bill was made up of the Okuras (Imperial Japanese Jugglers and Pedal Balancers); Tom Barry and Madge Hughes (in a first appearance in Their Dramatic Novelty, *A Story of the Street,* A Little Character Study of the East Side, with a Sentimental Touch); Europe's Most Brilliant Concertinist, Francini Olloms; Virginia Harned (in a comedy she wrote, *The Idol of the Hour*); Ececentric Dancing Comedians Jack Hallen and Sully Hayes; Morrisey and Rich (Refined Entertainers); and the Noted Vocalists, the Basque Grand Opera Quartette (Mme. Suzanne Harris, Soprano; Mr. Charles Morall, tenor; M. D'Arras, Baritone; M. Rerrard, Basso); and Will Rogers (King of the Lariat, "assisted by Buck McKee, ex-sheriff of Pawnee Co., Okla.") (American Theatre playbill, vaudeville scrapbook, CPpR).

Review from Will Rogers's Scrapbook
ca. 30 December 1908
[St. Louis, Mo.]

As Rogers traveled with his act, his well-trained bay horse Teddy became a favorite with the other performers and audiences alike. Wandering tamely behind Buck McKee through the streets of the cities where they performed, and doing his tricks with bright-eyed alacrity on stage, Teddy achieved his own kind of star status.

INTELLIGENT PONY.
"TEDDY" LIKES SUGAR, LOVES HIS MASTER AND
IS WISE IN MANY WAYS.

Lovers of horseflesh should not fail to get a glimpse at and, if possible, form the acquaintance of "Teddy," the cayuse employed by Will Rogers, the lasso thrower at the Grand theater, in his rope throwing feats. "Teddy" is an intelligent animal, eats sugar from the mouth of his master, and is fond of carrots, apples and sweetmeats of all kinds. He is devoted to Cowboy McKee, who rides "Teddy" a greater portion of the act. He will follow McKee about the streets like a dog, stand patiently at the curb and wait until he comes out of a store, and if the master remains too long will whinny his disapproval. "Teddy" bows his acknowledgement of applause, knows his way to the stable where he is fed, wears rubber shoes and resins his feet in order to keep from slipping. He has had years of experience on the broad prairies, where he was classed as one of the best cow ponies in the country.

PD. Unidentified clipping, ca. 1908. Scrapbook A-2, OkClaW.

Buck McKee to Maud Florence McKee
31 December 1908
St. Louis, Mo.

Thursday night,

ST. LOUIS, <u>Dec. 31, 190<u>8</u></u>

My Precious Little Wife;—

I got no word from you today & I am very much worried   I am afraid your Mother is worse, or you are sick yourself, or something.

I feel greatly depressed this evening some how. I am afraid you are in distress. I do hope I will get a letter in the first delivery in the morning with good news that your little Mama is better, & that you are well & all right, & more cheerful than you were when last you wrote. My heart aches for you tonight. I am—O! so lonesome. I wish I could jump on the train & go to you tonight. I pray God will be good to you, & protect you from all harm and grief, & restore your Dear Mother to health.

This has been the lonesomest week I have ~~never~~ ▲ever▲ put in in vaudeville. I have actually suffered ever since I left you last Friday morning.

Maudie Darling, I sent you a special delivery letter this after noon with a money order in it for $10.<u>00</u>, it was all I had & Bill had to borrow that for me from the stage manager, (who by the way is a westerner himself & has been in Oklahoma City.) & an all round good fellow.)[1] Bill will draw some from the front of the house tomorrow I guess & then I will send you some more. Use what ever is necessary to take good care of your mother & I will keep you supplied with plenty after this week. Will send your mother's $25.<u>00</u> later.

Take good care of her & of yourself. Address me next, Orpheum Theatre, Memphis Tenesee.[2] We play St. Paul & Minneapolis the last of Jan. & first of Feb. I hope I can have you join me then. We have a straight R.R. route from there on. & I will be a little "a head of the hounds" financially by that time I hope.

You try to work your end of the string the best you can meanwhile. Get to work on your act if you can at once & get ready.

I will correspond with Pat Casey about booking as soon as you have anything tangable to approach him with. *Do your best.* Cheer up. Keep busy. Be good. God bless you.

Love & Kisses & best wishes for a Happy new year,

Your loving husband,

Buck

ALS, rc. BMc-C. On Moser Hotel and Silver Moon Restaurant Co., 809–815 Pine Street, letterhead. Eighteenth Street Cars to and from Union Station pass the door, E. T. Weldon, Pres., E. E. Whitson, Sec'y & Treas.

1. The manager of the Grand Opera House in St. Louis was John G. Sheehy (*JCGHTG*, 241).

2. McKee wrote across the top of the letter, "Next week—Orpheum Theatre, *Memphis, Tennesee.*" Will and Betty Blake Rogers visited the Rogers family in Chelsea and Claremore in January 1909 while en route to engagements in St. Louis, Memphis, New Orleans, and Kansas City (*CR*, 1 January and 22 January 1909). A former teacher of Rogers's, W. S. Dugger, saw Rogers's performance in January and wrote the following letter to Clement Vann Rogers on 10 January 1909:

1079 Monroe Ave., Memphis. Tenn.,
Jan. 10, 1900 [1909].
Hon. C.V. Rogers:
Claremore, Okla.,
Dear Mr. Rogers:—Your son, William, has taken our city by storm. His company is the best that has appeared at the Orpheum at Memphis this season. On the main floor standing room could not be obtained at Saturday's matinee. With others I was compelled to secure a seat in the rear of one of the balconies. Willie's acting was superb. I did not know he was in our city until I saw him walk out on the stage. Immediately I recognized him. I took six o'clock dinner with him today. Several girls, one in particular in auto, wanted to meet him. I did not know he was married until I had told the girls I would introduce him. I was delightfully surprised when I met his elegant wife. They seem devoted to one another, and perfectly happy. This did me a great deal of good as I am always interested in my former school boys. I met you in Claremore, but suppose you have forgotten. Have always been especially fond of Willie.

Now about the company with which Willie is traveling. It is the very highest class known to the theatrical world. I met the ladies and know many of their relatives, so Willie is in good hands.

The Orpheum at Memphis is one of the highest class theatres in the South and one of our most popular playhouses. To this theatre all of our best people go.

Have written you these few lines because I feel a mutual joy in Willie's success. You have my very best wishes for your future success and happiness. May I ask you to remember me to Mr. Chas. McClellan and family? Believe me, I am your friend,

W.S. Dugger

(reprinted in the *Claremore Messenger*, 15 January 1909, OkClaW).

Rogers and McKee played the Orpheum in Memphis at Main and Beal Streets, where Max [Pabish?] was the resident manager. Appearing on the bill were acrobat Charles Matthews (The Champion Jumper of the World), assisted by Miss Doris Reece (in an Exhibition of Record Leaps); dancers William Alexis and Della Schall (The Happy Pair, in a Combination of Twists, Skirts, Turns and Steps); comic actor Henry Horton (Late Star of Eben Holden), assisted by Louise Hardenburgh and Co. (presenting the Pastoral Comedy in Two Acts, *Uncle Lem's Dilemma*, by Edward Locke); the Swor Brothers (Those Two Artists in Ebony Make-up, Impersonating Southern Negro Characters); Mr. and Mrs. Harry Clarke (Banjoists Extraordinary); and Winona Winter (The Little Cheer-up Girl, late star feature of *The Dairy Maids* and *The Little Cherub*). Rogers, the "Oklahoma Cowboy," closed the bill "In World Wonderful and Astonishing Roping Feats" (Orpheum theater, Memphis, playbill, scrapbook A-2, OkClaw). Buck McKee wrote his wife, "We leave for New Orleans at 11-40 tonight. . . . Then to K.C. after that" (Buck McKee to Maud Florence McKee, 10 January 1909, box 1979, folder 12, BMc-C).

The same group played the New Orleans Orpheum at St. Charles and Poydras Streets the week of 11–17 January 1909 (Orpheum theater, New Orleans, playbill, scrapbook A-2, OkClaW). McKee wrote to his wife, "We have the same show with us as last week, but we scatter from here some go east & some go west" (Buck McKee to Maud Florence McKee, 13 January 1909, box 1979, folder 13, BMc-C). Indeed, just as McKee reported, a revised cast (still including the Swor Brothers, but missing the other performers from the Memphis and New Orleans engagements) appeared with him and Rogers at the Kansas City, Mo., Orpheum at 9th and May Streets, 25–31 January 1909. The bill there featured The Four Orans (Miss Lizzie and Messrs. Julius, George and Robert Oran, in their new novelty *On the Sea Shore*); Miss Sue Smith (The American Girl, in Some Songs); Miss Adeline Dunlap and Mr. Frank McCormack (and their company's *The Night of the Wedding* by Richard Duffy); Oscar Lewis and Sam Green (in the New Comedy Creation, *Engaging a Cook*); The Misses Hengler (May and Flora, the Daintiest and Classiest of all Musical Comedy Stars); the Swor Brothers impersonation act; and Rogers (Who Has Astonished America and Europe with His Roping Feats, assisted by Another Cowboy and Trained Cow Pony) (Orpheum theater, Kansas City, Mo., clippings and playbills, scrapbook A-2, OkClaW; *NYDM*, 6 February 1909).

Will and Betty Blake Rogers and Buck McKee went from Kansas City to Omaha, Nebr., where the bill was made up of Morris and Morris (Grotesques, in *Fun on a Broom Handle,* A Clean Sweep in Comedy); Clivette (the Man in Black) and "The Veiled Prophetess" (The Only Living Exponents of Psycho-Astralism); Miss Julia Kingsley and Co. (In the Sparkling Comedy, *Supper for Two*); the First American Tour of Mr. Charles Matthews and Doris Reece; Staley and Birbeck's Novelty Transformation, *The Musical Blacksmiths*; the Swor Brothers; and Rogers (Orpheum theater, Omaha, clippings, playbill, and program, scrapbook A-2, OkClaw).

Maud Florence McKee to Buck McKee
6 February 1909
New York, N.Y.

. . . I was right here in this room from [*word illegible*] untill Monday Jan. 29, 30, 31ˢᵗ   So there.   "Now about *my not expecting you to* be ▲ a ▲ *hermit* "but be careful" I mean simply this "I do not expect you to sit alone in your lonely room but go to the *other shows* and *club affairs with* the *boys but be careful of women* "thats all"   Flirting sometimes leads to serious trouble. You [*word illegible*] Yes, I repeat, Bill Rogers, has *not* done right by *you,* whose fault was it that you owed him $61.90? *his own*!, how *dare* he *cancel work* when he has another in the act, *he lays off too* D *much* to dare cancel any work, and why should his wife cost him so much she is an *ordinary woman* who has been *brought up in very moderate circumstance and show's it*   don't forget that. I did not know you wished to hear about Mama in every letter as I could have very easily told you, the truth is she say[s] you are starving me to death here, so now maybe that will hold you for a while at least.

Playbill for the St. Paul, Minn., Orpheum, advertising Rogers as The Oklahoma Cowboy, 7 February 1909. (OkClaW)

Now Sweetheart Baby, You know I Love You and I am frank and open hearted with you but your Love, Sweetheart causes jealousy and anxiety which there is absolutely no ground for   You can rest in peace and contentment Buck Darling because I will Love you and be true to you a life time if you are good to me   Sweetheart, the writing on the last page of this letter looks like you had been *drinking*   Please don't, Buck Darling, for my sake, don't   I want you to live long my Sweet Baby. You surely were not yourself when you wrote this, it looks like Bobbies writing. I do hope all your "william questions" are answered satisfactorily for once. don't be always "imagining" I am *hiding* [*things*] from you, "what have I to hide? *Please tell me I have made a great big spoiled Baby of you* and *you can't be happy away from me* and I am D— glad of it, So there—   Now write me *every* day Buck Dear. Thanks for $2.00[1]

> All My Love—Kisses
>
> Your Loving Wife
>
> Maudie

ALS, rc. Box 1972, folder 18, BMc-C. The first page of the original letter is missing from the repository. Postmarked 6 February 1909. Envelope addressed to Mr. Buck McKee, Orpheum Theatre, St. Paul, Minn., c/o Will Rogers; on Howard, Guile, and Co., Savoy Hotel, Victoria Street, Montreal, letterhead.

1.   These were very hard emotional times for Maude Florence McKee and Buck McKee. She was laid off from her chorus-girl vaudeville job in New York at the end of January, she and Buck McKee were missing one another, her mother was very ill, and money was tight. It was tighter when Buck McKee did not receive payments from Rogers when he expected them, and thus was not able to send home to New York what his wife and mother-in-law were depending upon to get by.

While she was afraid he would fall prey to evil elements on the road, be seduced by flirtation or friendship into becoming unfaithful to her, or succumb to the beckoning comforts of liquor, he experienced anxiety about her unemployment and welfare in New York. She was looking for work, and he was worried that her expectations were not running high enough. "All you seem to have an ambition for is to find a job just like Joe Harts Crickets, or Polly Pickles Pets. I reckon if nobody happens to get up another act just like either one of them you will do like Thompson's Mule did when he swam across the river & laid down & starved to death for want of water at the old familiar water trough which had gone dry," he wrote to her in his reply to the above letter, on 11 February 1909. He later told her he had dreamed "someday to see you in an act of your own, when you could be your own boss, & hold your head up & be respected, & recognized as a lady & a vaudeville Star." He wished he could be in New York to do something with the agents and the booking offices to help her realize her potential, and he suggested she think about taking a role in western melodrama (Buck McKee to Maud Florence McKee, 11 February 1909, box 1979, folder 19, BMc-C). Both took out their anxieties and worst fears on each other, and both also always came back to the fact of how much they loved each other. After castigating Maud for not trying hard enough in looking for work, and not aiming high enough while she did so, Buck McKee underlined that *"I love you & I cant be happy nor contented away from you. I wish I had you here with me now. There will be no more of this kind of separation* after *this trip if I have to quit my job & work on the street to be with you*" (ibid.). He wrote his wife long love letters from the road. He wrote her a beautiful and romantic description of the Louisiana countryside as his train traveled to the New Orleans engagement in early 1909, then observed, "I love everything that is natural. I hate acting" (13 January 1909, box 1979, folder 13, BMc-C).

Buck McKee suffered from not being able to provide more than he was able to make in the Rogers act, and he told his wife that he hoped someday to be able to quit vaudeville and do something better. In the meantime, she needed to find work in show business herself in order for the three of them to get by.

The contrast between their poverty and separation and the Rogerses' new-found happiness and togetherness was particularly hard for Maud Florence McKee to swallow. "Bill Rogers does not do right by you," she wrote her husband on 1 February 1909 (box 1979, folder 16, BMc-C). She suspected that Betty Blake Rogers was using up money earned from the act that had previously been distributed in part to McKee. McKee slipped into a deeper and deeper depression as the act continued along the western Orpheum Circuit. He felt exhausted by the travel and performance schedule, and worried that Teddy was exhausted, too. He reported being lonesome and "depressed . . . the time seems so long and tedious . . . I feel as if I would go crazy sometimes." And without money, there was little he could afford to do to provide a lift from the drudgery and unhappiness of his loneliness on the road: "I feel the curse of poverty tonight," he wrote Maud from Spokane. In the same letter, he wrote cryptically about his despair over the issue of honesty and loyalty between husbands and wives, voicing his disdain over the rampant and open infidelity in vaudeville and stating that he and Maud were "at least one couple who are on the level with each other. That is why I am so sensitive on that point . . . *I really believe in you, & sad to say you are about the only one I ever did really believe in*" (Buck McKee to Maud Florence McKee, 12 March 1909, box 1979, folder 22, BMc-C; see also Buck Mckee to Maud Florence Mckee, 29 December and 31 December 1908; 10 January, 13 January, 11 February, 24 February, and 12 March 1909; and Maud Florence McKee to Buck McKee, 25 December 1908, 19 January, 27 January, 1 February, 6 February, 13 February 1909, BMc-C).

Article from the Butte *Anaconda Standard*
27 February 1909
Butte, Mont.

ROBBERS USE AXE TO DESPOIL ACTORS
HAUL MADE FROM TRUNK IN "THE PARK" APARTMENTS.
MAN AND WIFE ARE VICTIMS

MYSTERY SURROUNDS CRIME IN VIEW OF BELIEF
THERE WAS NO ONE IN BUTTE EXCEPT OWNERS WHO KNEW OF THE CACHE—ROGERS IS AN ACTOR.

No little mystery is attached to the robbery of the room of William Rogers and wife in "The Park," on Park street, near the Montana street corner, while they were at the Orpheum theater Thursday night. Mr. Rogers is on the

Orpheum circuit and will open a week's engagement with his partner in a lariat-throwing act at the matinee this afternoon.[1] The thief who committed the
crime was discerning, disturbing nothing in the apartment except a money
box in a wardrobe trunk. The box was taken away intact, with its contents,
consisting of about $200 and jewelry of as much value. Not a clew was left,
and the police are the more puzzled in view of the fact that Mr. and Mrs.
Rogers had only just arrived from Minneapolis and, as far as known, there was
no one in the city who knew the whereabouts or disposal of their valuables.

However, they were very careless in leaving not only their trunk unlocked,
but also the room. The sheet iron drawer in which the money and jewelry was
kept was fastened. To pry it from its moorings an axe was used by the thief and
this he left behind him. The police have taken charge of it, believing it may furnish some clew to the perpetrator. However, they have discovered nothing that
would shed light on the case up to last night.

CAME TO BUTTE ALONE.

Mr. and Mrs. Rogers came to Butte alone. No other actors were with
them, and they had met none of the fraternity in the city up to the time they
left their room. The theory, however, is that someone must have obtained
knowledge of the deposit box of the trunk and its contents in some mysterious way, carefully prepared to steal the valuables and going to the room with
full knowledge that the occupants had left. He probably carried the big, full-
sized axe concealed under a coat or long [hol]ster. To reach the Rogers' room
he had to climb two flights of stairs to the third floor. Yet no one, as far as can
be ascertained, saw any suspicious characters about the block. However, this
is not surprising in view of the numbers that are passing freely in and out at
all times.

Nothing but the lock box in the trunk was disturbed, despite that there was
costly wearing apparel to be had simply by lifting it from its resting place. Nor
were the rooms on either side of that occupied by the Rogers' entered.

WHAT IS MISSING.

The money missing consisted of two $50 bills, some smaller currency and
considerable silver. The jewelry taken included a gentleman's gold watch,
lady's chatelain watch, a locket in the shape of [*words illegible*], a stickpin consisting of a gold piece, pair of opera glasses, and a number of fancy handker-
chiefs, besides other trinkets of less value.

Captain of Police Buckner and Detectives Williams, White and [Morrisey]
are at work on the case. They held a number of interviews with the drayman

who delivered the trunk from the station. He took the trunk no further than the hallway on the third floor, whence the owners moved it into the room about 4 o'clock in the afternoon of the robbery. Mr. and Mrs. Rogers are certain there could have been no clinking of the coin when the trunk was moved about, as it was packed with paper. They, as well as the police, are in a quandary in the matter. The money was the total of their savings [. . .].[2]

PD. Printed in the Butte, Mont., *Anaconda Standard*, 27 February 1909. Scrapbook A-2, OkClaW.

1. Rogers and McKee played the St. Paul, Minn., Orpheum at Fifth and St. Peter Streets the week of 7 February 1909. The bill was made up of Spanish equilibrist Joe Garza; dancers Charles DeHaven and Jack Sidney (the Dancing Waiter and the Guest, formerly a feature with *Edward's School Boys and Girls*); the Eight Melani's (A Tuneful and Picturesque Ensemble Act) in a first appearance in St. Paul; Porter J. White (and His Company, Appearing in *The Visitor*, by Oliver White, Author of *Superstition*, etc.); blackface performers Frank White and Lew Simmons (in their Black-Face Character Study, *On the Band Wagon*); and, also in her first American appearance, Parisian beauty Joly Violetta (the Celebrated Beauty, Assisted by the Brazilian Dancer Mons Arnaud); and Rogers (Orpheum theater, St. Paul, Minn., playbill and clippings, scrapbook A-2, OkClaW; see illustration p. 95).

Rogers continued with the regular two-a-day schedule, with performances at 2:15 every afternoon and at 8:15 every evening (*Variety*, 13 February 1909). He appeared at the Minneapolis Orpheum at Seventh Street near Hennepin Avenue the week beginning 14 February 1909. There his fellow performers were Gus and Arthur Keeley (Comedy Physical Culture); Arcadia (Operatic Prima Donna and Violin Virtuoso); Mr. and Mrs. George A. Beane (in *A Woman's Way*, an old story made new in telling); Rogers, Teddy, and McKee, in an unusual middle spot; the Basque Grand Opera Quartet (Mme. Suzanne Harris, soprano, Mr. Charles Morati, tenor, M. D'Arras, baritone, M. Ferrand Basso, in a Repretoire of Songs from the popular Operas in French, Italian and English); the headliners, the Russell Brothers (James and John Russell) with Flora Bonfanti Russell as the ballet dancer in *Our Servant Girls*; and the Three Moshers (a comedy cycling act, formerly Mosher, Houghton, and Mosher, featuring Tom, Daisy, and James Mosher with Albert Hayes). The program closed with the kinodrome motion pictures, *No Petticoats for Him* and *The Auto Heroine*. W. L. Landon was the stage director at the theater (Orpheum theater, Minneapolis, program, 14 February 1909, OkClaW; Orpheum theater, Minneapolis, playbill and clippings, 14–20 February 1909, scrapbook A-2, OkClaW; *NYDM*, 27 February 1904; *Variety*, 20 February 1909).

The Russell Brothers, known as "The Irish Chambermaids of Vaudeville," were a female-impersonation act, in which James (d. 1914) and John Russell appeared as Irish serving girls (*EV*, 456). Flora Bonfanti Russell (b. 1890) was the daughter of James Russell. She was described as the "little soubrette with the Russell Brothers in 'The Great Jewel Mystery'" in 1906. She was the protégée of well-known dance teacher Marie Bonfanti, with whom she had begun studying at the age of nine. "She has just turned sixteen and is already one of the best dancers in the profession," announced the *New York Mirror* on 24 November 1906. In 1907 she starred in *The Hired Girl's Millions* as "the ingenue lead" and supporting actress to her father and uncle: "a very pretty young woman, possessing a charming personality and fine stage appearance as well as being blessed with a good singing voice" (clipping, Locke env. 1980, NN-L-RLC). She did Parisian toe dancing in that production. Her character was an employee in a department store who was orphaned but became an unwitting heiress to a fortune. In supporting roles, the Russell Brothers played the McCann sisters (as part of their specialization in cross-dressing and female impersonation). The 23 August 1907 *Rochester Post* called *The Hired Girl* a "mixture of melodrama, farce and musical comedy." The Russell family act in 1909, called *Our Servant Girls,* was similar to their past act, and Flora Russell continued to do French ballet in the midst of the spoofs. The Russell Brothers split up when James Russell retired from the act in 1913. After his brother's death, John went to England and appeared in vaudeville there. Flora Russell did parts in musical comedy, and in 1913 toured with *Mutt and Jeff* (*Detroit News,* 2 November 1914; *New York Telegraph,* 13 January 1907; *Toledo Blade,* 1 February 1913; *Vanity Fair,* 1 February 1907; clippings, Locke env. 1980, NN-L-RLC).

The bill in Butte, Mont., included Mark Caron and Dick Farnum (comedy acrobats); Surazall and Razall (musical comedians in *The Music Publisher* by J. R. Lazar, with Ada Razall as Miss Birdie Newcomer, a Flip Chorus Girl, and Sam Surazall as Sam, the Music Publisher, and as Paderewski); Joly Violetta, assisted by M. Arnaud in parodies and Brazilian dances; banjo players Mr. and Mrs. Harry Clarke (In a Repertoire of Popular and Classic Music); Mr. S. Miller Kent and his Players, in the comedy playlet *Marriage in a Motor Car* by Edgar Allen Wolff (featuring Mr. Kent as Harold Mattews, Miss Donah Benrimo as Olive Van Ortan, Miss Dorothy Keene as Merian, the Maid, and Alphonse as Himself); Harry L. Webb (The Man who Talks and Sings); and Rogers (Orpheum theater, Butte, Mont., playbill and clippings, scrapbook A-2, OkClaW; *NYDM,* 6 March 1909).

The Rogerses went from Butte to Spokane and Seattle, Wash., and then Portland, Ore. Many of the same performers went with them, including the S. Miller Kent stock company with the motor car playlet, the Clarke husband-and-wife banjo-playing team, and dancers Joly Violetta and Monsieur Arnaud (*Variety,* 6 March, 13 March, 20 March, and 27 March 1909; Orpheum, Spokane, Wash., clippings, 7–13 March 1909; Orpheum, Seattle, Wash., clippings, 15–21 March 1909; and Orpheum, Portland, Ore., clippings, 22–28 March 1909). In Portland the bill was presented in the following order: Caron and Farnum; Surazall and Razall; Joly Violette and Arnaud; the S. Miller Kent players; Mr. and Mrs. Harry Clarke; the Grand Opera Diva Mlle. Zelie de Lussan (Prima Donna of the Metropolitan Grand Opera House, in Operatic Selections and Ballads, with Signo Angelo Fronani at the Piano), and Rogers (Orpheum theater, Portland, Ore., playbill, scrapbook A-2, OkClaW).

At the end of March they were in San Francisco, and they went from there to Salt Lake City, where the bill for the week of 5 April 1909 included the Amoros Sisters (Josephine and Charlotte, Parisian Novelty Gymnasts, in a combination of aerial skill and Arabian tumbling); the Clarkes; Surazall and Razall; a presentation of *At the Sound of the Gong,* a dramatic episode of *The Prize Ring,* by Messrs. McDonald and W. J. Ferry, staged by May Tully with Tom Wilson, Arthur Sullivan, Elsa Berrold, Bill Russell, Bob Johnson, and Jack Straw in acting roles; Novelty Gymnasts Tony Wilson and Mlle. Heloise (Originators of the Tramplin or Bounding Mat); Imro Fox (Unique Comic Conjuror and Deceptionist, in *The Box of Cagliostro*); and Rogers (Orpheum theater, Salt Lake City, playbill, scrapbook A-2, OkClaW). In Denver, the line-up for the week of 12 April 1909 was the Amoros Sisters; American Virtuosos, the Milch Sisters (Violin—Piano—Vocal); Mr. Claude Gillingwater (in the comedy sketch, *A Strenuous Rehearsal*); the Clarkes with their banjos; Wilson and Heloise; Imro Fox; and Rogers (Orpheum theater, Denver, playbill, scrapbook A-2, OkClaW).

Having to go from Denver to Louisville, Ky., gave Will and Betty Blake Rogers a chance for another stopover trip to the Claremore region, where they visited Rogers's friends and family on 20 April 1909 (*CP*, 17 April 1909; *Talala Gazette*, 29 April 1909). Betty Blake Rogers then went on to visit her own family, while Will Rogers left to keep engagements in Louisville and Cincinnati.

2. Will and Betty Blake Rogers began a savings plan as soon as they were married. Maud and Cap Lane had suggested it to them as their own method of putting aside funds for the future when they were first wed. The Rogerses got a strongbox and each day slipped a dollar bill or silver dollar into it. They carried the box on the road with them, along with the jewelry that he had invested in or given to her, and some of her own treasures that they had received as wedding gifts or he had mailed to her in the past. The act was laid off for one week while the Rogerses made the "long jump from St. Paul to Butte, Montana," and they arrived a few days before other people on their bill (Rogers, *Will Rogers*, 107). They went out ice skating, and when they came back to the hotel, the box had been broken into by someone with an ax. Betty Rogers "was brokenhearted" (ibid., 108). Rogers tried to cheer her up by telling her how brave Maud Lane had been when her brand-new house, just being finished by workmen, burned down. She had managed to laugh soon after at the antics of the anguished painters who tried in vain to stop the fire from spreading before themselves escaping the flames. Betty was not much cheered by the comparison, but he maintained his attitude of bemusement toward the theft a few days later as he went off to the theater; the *Butte Inter Mountain* reported that "in spite of the fact that Will Rogers had been robbed of $700 worth of money and jewelry in a local rooming house the first night he was in town, he pulled off his act very merrily" (clipping, Butte, Mont., ca. 1 March 1909, scrapbook A-2, OkClaW). The *Butte Miner* attributed the crime to prowlers, and said that the Rogerses had inadvertently left the door of the room unlocked (27 February 1909).

To Betty Blake Rogers
25 April 1909
Louisville, Ky.

Sunday, 10.30 a.m.

My Own Own Dear Wife,

Well hon, here I am and say but it is lonesome and I sho do miss you all the time and more than ever now since I got here and it is as lonesome as the D_____

Well old hon, after you left I got off the train and Dr Bushyhead[1] was out on the Platform waiting for me and I was with him up to 11_____ oclock when my train left. we just sit around down at the Drug store and talked. then on the train Joe Chambers[2] was on going up to Chelsea to the dance that night. Got to St. Louis it was about noon   train a little late. Went down on the stage at the American Theatre[3] and saw all the boys and at 2 oclock out to the Ball Game   saw the Worlds Champion Chicago team[4] play St. Louis and beat them too   then back and sent you a lot of Music   addressed it to Dick[5] so you would be sure and get it. sent the Real Slivers Rag. learn it good so you

can play it when you come   couldent get the words to Loving Rag. then had
Supper. also sent clem[6] that one piece Slivers Rag, too. then back on the stage
behind and saw part of the show at the American and left at 10.10 P.M. on the
Southern Railway   sent you a wire from Depot   did you get it. got here at 7
a.m. and there is no Hotels in this town but this big one so I finally just come
here and got a nice little single room for $1.25 a day. *not* with bath of course
and I can only have it till Tuesday as they have a big Convention of some kind[7]
but I will find me one by that time and I dont mind moving as I have nothing
but comb and brush and collar. it is a ~~beautiful~~ nice hotel   nothing like the
Baltimore though

Buck had got in yesterday all O.K.

It is nice and warm here. I am billed second up next to the Headliner. The
Country Kids that Kid act from Newark   you remember that was with me
are the Headliners. I close the show. open this afternoon   that act is the only
one that I know personally[8]

Well I'll bet you are just getting ready to have one glorious feed for dinner
today and I sho would like to be there too and after dinner we would go for a
good old drive but I'll bet it wouldent be as good as the one we took at home
would it   I enjoyed that more than any drive I ever had. and we were looking
at *our own* things then.

I know you had a good time with Sandy.[9] hope he got to go home with you
and you all will be having a big reunion today. Give my love to Mama and
Dick and all of them and tell them how I wish I was there and that I will be
before long.

Old Honey Bug I got that Dandy picture of you just right here in front of
me and it sho does make me wish for you. I feel *"awful"* lonesome today   its
been such a long old day and it is not noon yet   maby it will be better after I
get to work. I got me a lot of Sunday papers and I will read till Show time
Now if they have any dances and card parties you just go to all of them cause
I want you to have a good time and you must get you some new clothes
too   I will send you the money   I want you to look nice   Get Tom Morgan
to Show you the Variety. last weeks of the Denver shows. and see what it says
about your old *Hussy*.

Well my Sweetheart Wife I must close cause you might want this long a letter all the time. With all the Love of your old Husband   I sho do miss you
and love you a lot.

Your only,

                                                                                    Billy.

ALS, rc. OkClaW. On Seelbach Hotel Co., 4th and Walnut Streets, Louisville, Ky., letterhead.

1. The Bushyheads were a prominent Cherokee family and relatives of the Rogerses. Dr. Jesse Bushyhead, M.D., was Rogers's cousin, the son of former Cherokee principal chief Dennis Wolf Bushyhead and his wife, Rogers's maternal aunt, Elizabeth Alabama Schrimsher Adair Bushyhead. Dr. Bushyhead was a Claremore, Okla., physician, and Rogers had known him all his life (see *PWR*, 1:485–86 [Biographical Appendix entry for Jesse Crary Bushyhead, M.D.]).

2. There were two men named Joe Chambers who lived in the Claremore area. Joseph Walker Chambers (1883–1956) was born in the Cooweescoowee District of the Cherokee Nation (Rogers County, Okla.) and worked as a druggist at the Owl Drugstore in Claremore (*HRC*, 139). The other Joseph Chambers, born 31 March 1886, was a member of an old Cherokee family. This Joe Chambers was among the young men who were invited to Pocahontas Club meetings and parties in 1903. He became a lawyer and was active in historic preservation in Claremore (DuPriest et al., *Cherokee Recollections*, 13, 92; *OCF*, 1:152).

3. The American Theatre in St. Louis advertised that it played "legitimate attractions." The theater had a seating capacity of 1,726 (*JCGHTG*, 103).

4. The Chicago Cubs won their third straight National League pennant in 1908 with the help of a famous base-running mistake by Fred Merkle of the New York Giants. Merkle was the runner at first base as the Giant's winning run was scored against the Cubs. Instead of advancing to second, he watched the runner cross home plate and began trotting off the field as it began to fill with exuberant fans. As a result, authorities declared the game a tie, putting the Cubs and the Giants in a dead heat for first place with one game to go. The Cubs were victorious. They went on to win the 1908 World Series against the American League Detroit Tigers in a five-game (4–1) series (Cohen and Neft, *World Series*, 23).

5. Betty Blake Rogers's sister, Theda Blake, who lived in Rogers, Ark. A few days later Rogers wrote to ask, "Do you think you can get Dick to come back with you for a while[?] I hope you can[. I]t would do her a lot of good" (Will Rogers to Betty Blake Rogers, 28 April 1909, OkClaW).

6. Clement Mayes McSpadden, Rogers's nephew (*PWR*, 1:508). Rogers's sister Sallie McSpadden reported in a 27 April 1909 letter to her brother that "Clem received and learned 'Silvers' you sent him. I think its very catchy. He had the two step, but we all like the slow-drag best" (OkClaW). She told Rogers that Clem's eye was better and that he was working in Claremore, taking the train to and from Chelsea each workday.

7. As Rogers explained in his next letter, the Boilermakers were coming to town for a convention and had engaged all the rooms (see Will Rogers to Betty Blake Rogers, 26 April 1909, below).

8. In Louisville, Rogers played at B. F. Keith's Mary Anderson Theater, which offered vaudeville and moving pictures and had a seating capacity of 1,450 (*JCGHTG*, 76). The week's bill for the end of April was headlined by Gus Edwards' Kountry Kids (In a One-Act Truly Rural Musical Comedy, *Miss Rose's Birthday*, written by Edwards). Happy Jack Gardner (Burnt Cork Monologist and Singing Comedian) and Grace Cumings and Co. (In the Merry Sketch, *A Mail Order Wife*) preceded Rogers, who came in the middle of the program. Rogers's act was followed by singer Anna Woodward (Late Soloist Holcomb's Pittsburg Band); Rice and Elmer (in *A Rube's Visit to Chinatown*); the Hughes Musical Trio (Instrumental Experts in a Classy

Offering); and Marie Yuill and Robby Boyd (The Gay and Giddy Duo). The closing kinodrome feature was *C.Q.D. or Saved by Wireless* (Mary Anderson Theater, Louisville, playbill, vaudeville scrapbook, CPpR; Mary Anderson Theater, Louisville, clippings and playbill, scrapbook A-2, OkClaW).

9. Betty Blake Rogers's brother, Sandy Blake.

To Betty Blake Rogers
26 April 1909
Louisville, Ky.

My Dear Wife.

Well Hon it is just after the Matinee Monday and I come right home to write to you and I enjoy it too   I am not doing it cause I think I should   I love to write to you and tell you all I do.

Well last night after I wrote you the last letter did you get both letters[1]   I read a while and played Sol a while and then went to bed but it sho was lonesome and I did not go to sleep very soon and woke up early and had a hard time (can you imagine that) staying in bed till 11 oclock   it seemed like three or four. then went to the little old Restaurant and had breakfast 25 cents. and then to the Theatre and practiced a while. not very long it is real hot down here and read the papers and then walked around town with one of the (Boy) Kids in the act and back and worked   we dont have many at Matinees but good at night.

Here are the three clippings from the three papers[2]   very fine aint they they seem to like the act great here

We are talking of having a ball game   the Performers against the Stage hands.

I have to leave this hotel tomorrow as there is a convention of Boiler Makers coming in here for convention and had engaged all the rooms.

We leave here Saturday night after the Show and open in Cincinnatti Sunday. Columbia, Theatre.[3] ~~then~~ I will about get a letter from you tomorrow and I will be glad too. as soon as I finish this letter it is not sundown yet   I am going to walk down to the River, Ohio, and see all the boats.

Oh say did you have all those Professional copies of Music in your Trunk that was sent to me in Salt Lake. What did We do with them   I just happened to think I hope you have them. And you must play a lot and drive and ride every chance you get and also dance and play cards and just have lots of fun.

I wont write you such a long letter but I will write you *every few days*

Love to all. and most all of it for you.

Your old boy.

Bill.

ALS, rc. OkClaW. On Seelbach Hotel Co., 4th and Walnut Streets, Louisville, Ky., letterhead.

    1. Rogers wrote to his wife in the morning and again in the evening, when he got home from the night show. He had "stopped at one of those little Dairy lunch places where you have saw the chairs all sitting around the Wall with one big arm where you sit your plat   Well I had Milk and Pie and come on home and now is the lonesome time   I have some papers   will play Sol and read but I am pretty tired. . . . Well both shows just went fine   my act could not of went better   the talk is a big hit down here among these Southerners. I wont get up till late and then I am going to practice   I went over every night and stood back on the stage and saw the whole show   it aint so good." He sent Betty a set of amusing postcards featuring children (Will Rogers to Betty Blake Rogers, 25 April 1909, OkClaW).

    2. Rogers enclosed three reviews of the Mary Anderson Theater program clipped from local Louisville papers, including items from the *Courier Journal* and the *Herald*. He highlighted a paragraph of praise for his act in the *Herald* column, "The Theater," which said he topped "anything in the cowboy line which has so far left the grazing lands of the West for the richer pasture of vaudeville. There is a freshness about his humor—it is the humor of the soil—an apparent lack of self-consciousness—and a degree of skill displayed, which must be rare, even, 'Down in Oklahomy,' as Rogers would say. He is assisted by a 'right peart' pony and another Western youth, who allows himself to be lassoed and otherwise treated with Western indignity just to make a vaudeville holiday. This act is about the most sensational of its kind ever seen in Louisville, and certainly the most amusing" (clipping, enclosure in Will Rogers to Betty Blake Rogers, 26 April 1909, OkClaW).

    3. Rogers played the Columbia Theatre, managed by M. C. Anderson, in Cincinnati, the week commencing with the Sunday matinee, 2 May 1909 (see Will Rogers to Betty Blake Rogers, 2 May 1909, below).

To Betty Blake Rogers
27 April 1909
Louisville, Ky.

My Own Darling Wife

    Well Sweetheart your first letter come last night earlier than I had expected and I sho did love it and you too.

    I am sorry you got so scared in Ft Gibson but I cant blame you for that is one tough town   you should of made Sandy have you put up stairs

    Well I am down here at a kind of an Actor Hotel and have a very good room at $1.00 a day   and it is very good   several of the boys are here   it is a *Stag* Hotel.

    Well yesterday after I wrote you I went down on the river and it is away up and a lot of those little tough Kids they call River Rats were playing there and I sat and watched them for a long time   they were the toughest customers I ever (saw) *not seen*   then had dinner and went to the room and read and then to the show and straight home   had Milk and Pie and did not even have a glass of beer all day[1]   then read and played Sol and went to bed and got up at 11. but it sho is lonesome in an old room and in an old bed   I look around all the time thinking you are there.

Oh I tell you hon, I sho do miss you and will be glad when you come back but I want you to have a good visit and you can come to Indianapolis[2]   I guess I can stand it that long.

I am going to send Shea[3] that $150 tomorrow as he is going to go to Europe Saturday   No I did not hear a thing of Obrien   it dont matter I guess they done all the[y] could and it did not cost as much to get here as I at first thought it would anyway

Now hon you get you some clothes while you are home   order them and tell me and I will send you the money to get just what you want.

I sent you the clippings yesterday   did you get them

Now you have a good time hon but you must write often cause I love to get your letters.[4]

I am just home after matinee.

With all the love and a million kisses to my own dear Wifey.

                                                                                                Billy.

ALS, rc. OkClaW. On Nic Bosler's European Hotel, Louisville, Ky., letterhead.

1. Here, during his first separation from Betty Blake Rogers since their marriage, Rogers was getting an idea of the kind of loneliness that Buck McKee had been experiencing for the entire tour. Like Maud Florence McKee, Betty Blake Rogers seemed to need reassurance from her husband that he was not drinking as a form of solace on the road.

2. Rogers appeared in Cincinnati the first week of May 1909. Then his route was changed from Indianapolis to Forest Park Highlands in St. Louis for the week of 9–15 May. He made a quick trip home to Oklahoma after playing in Cincinnati and before heading to St. Louis (Will Rogers to Betty Blake Rogers, 3 May 1909, OkClaW; *Rogers County Democrat*, 8 May 1909; *Variety*, 15 May 1909).

3. Mort or Joe Shea, both New York vaudeville booking agents. Rogers told his wife, "I wired Shea that $150.00. I got it from the Manager last night. I wrote him the right kind of a letter too" (28 April 1909, OkClaW). On Mort Shea, see *PWR*, 2:518–19 (Biographical Appendix entry for Maurice A. Shea).

4. Rogers wrote to several family members in his lonely state, and the result was a flurry of answers in his week in Louisville. Sallie McSpadden wrote a reply letter to her brother the same day he was writing here to his wife. She was glad to have heard from him and sympathized with how much he missed Betty, saying she was sure Betty "will be ready to join you next week." (Rogers underlined this section of the letter and sent it to Betty Blake Rogers, writing below the marked passage about the next week, "How about it Kid[?]") (Sallie Rogers McSpadden to Will Rogers, 27 April 1909, OkClaW). Sallie McSpadden gave her brother all the news on the family. May Stine had been to visit and had gone "home Sunday afternoon in a fine good humor." Her son Clem, husband Tom, and father Clement Vann Rogers were busy working and traveling to

look after business. She was trying to keep in touch by mail with Johnny Yocum, sister May's eldest son, who had gone out on his own as a teenager. She was not sure how the local elections had turned out yet, but she said, "I so hope the booze men lost." She told Rogers that the man living on his farm was working very hard and doing an admirable job with the property, and she filled him in on the latest in the sensational Bullette murder case, in which a woman named Ruth Yarbough was accused of murdering John Bullette, a prominent citizen from Delaware, Okla., and committed suicide after being placed under arrest (see also *Rogers County News,* 7 July 1909). Clement Vann Rogers wrote his son on the next day, 28 April 1909, telling him whom he had been visiting and conveying information about the status of deeds on the land for the "old Home Place" (OkClaW; see also Will Rogers to Clement Vann Rogers, 29 April 1909, OkClaW).

Rogers wrote to Betty Blake Rogers again on 28 April 1909, when he was not yet the recipient of these letters. "I did not get a letter all day yesterday or today but know I will get one tonight," he told her. "I havent heard from papa or a soul since I got here only the one letter from you and I have read it through a dozen times. I dident know I was so stuck on you hon, but I sho am. and I think of you all the time and will be offul glad to see you I tell you." He told Betty how tired he had been feeling. He had been practicing hard at his roping in midday, after the matinee performance. He signed himself, "All my love to my Own Sweetheart Wife. Lots and Lots Love and Kisses. Billy" (28 April 1909, OkClaW).

To Betty Blake Rogers
30 April 1909
Louisville, Ky.

Friday Eve. 5. P.M.

My Dear Sweetheart Wife,

Well last night I got your short letter and looked for another but none came but I will get it tonight

I got a letter from Papa and will enclose it. tells about his trip. you must write him every day or so for he does love to hear from you. I did not think Spi would be mean about those deeds   I wrote him a long letter last night and thanked him   also wrote to Papa about some more land I wanted to buy up around the old place   I want all I can get reasonable cause it will never get any cheaper

Well old pal it has finally after about a month got as far as Friday on the week   I was in bed just after the show last night and up at 10:30 and practiced hard till show time   They are having big Ball Games here but I am on so late I cant get out to see them. suppose it will be the same way in all the towns.

Where are all those drives and horseback rides you had planned   get you a horse and fly at 'em.

I am going to get up at 7 aclock and go out to the big race track where they are training all the fast horses for the Kentucky Derby which will be run here

Monday. The old Millionare who owns this Theatre, Cincinnatti and Indianapolis has a fine bunch out there and his Trainer who has been in to see the show asked me to come out and see them exercise them. The Track is quite a noted one in America and is called Churchill Downs.[1]

Wish you was here to go along.

There was a big wind storm here all yesterday and last night   done a lot of damage all over.

I got me a lot of papers and will go up and read for a while then eat and go to the show and will get a letter from my own wifey and it will make me think of her more than ever and wish she was here.

Now you write long letters and tell me all you do. All my love and kisses to my dandy sweet Wife.

                                                                                               Billy.

ALS, rc. OkClaW. On Nic Bosler's European Hotel, Louisville, Ky., letterhead.

1. The Kentucky Derby of 1909 was won by Jerome (Rome) Bristow Respess's horse Wintergreen. The winner led a field of ten horses and finished a length and a half ahead of his nearest rival. Wintergreen won the stake of $5,000.

Brewing company owner and banker Rome Respess (1863–1939), son of a southern planter, was a breeder and owner of fine Kentucky thoroughbred racehorses. His best horse, Dick Welles, was both a winning performer and one of the outstanding sires of his time. Respess owned Highland Stock Farm near Florence, Ky., and an interest in racetracks in Kentucky, Ohio, Arkansas, and Lousiana (*EAB*, 15:46; *NYT*, 4 May 1909 and 26 July 1939).

Rogers wrote to his wife on 1 May 1909 to report on what happened at the racetracks. "I went out to the Track and it is great," he wrote. "Met and had breakfast with *Rome Respass* the Millionaire horse owner who owns the horse that will win the Derby Monday   he is just like some old ranchman and was dandy to me   had a fine breakfast right in the Stables. He then showed all his horses and I met the Secretary of the Fair Grounds and jockey Club. and he took me all over the club house and gave me a dandy picture   (Which I mailed to you today)   it is a print from a drawing of one of this fellows Repass's horses that will run. its a great picture   hope it dont get broke in the Mail. oh I met ever so many big horse men   they are all grand bunch of fellows saw all the horses run and exercise" (OkClaW).

To Betty Blake Rogers
2 May 1909
Cincinnati, Ohio

                                                                       Sunday 5:30 P.M.

My Own Sweetheart Wife.

Well here I am in the Germany of America   got in at 8 oclock this morning   left last night at 7 P.M. and the best part of all of it was that your dear sweet letter was here and I went right to the Theatre at once cause I expected it and I was sure glad cause I was afful lonesome   I did not know a soul and the show did not start for hours and if I had not of gotten it I dont know how bad I would of felt[1]

I am at this hotel   pay 1.50 a day for a nice little front room without bath but there is one next door

It is a pretty swell place. I eat at a nice little restaurant across the street have had about 6 dishes of Strawberries at different times all day   just finished a couple just now

Well the old act went great this afternoon   they were great laughers   I am billed about third or fourth here as there is a big show.[2]

Buck today as he reached down off of the Pony to pick up the rope out on the stage   the strap that he was holding on too with his other hand broke and he fell all over the stage on his right *ear.* of course it did not hurt him cause he was right at the floor any way but it was sho funny. The stage is very slick and old Teddy like to fell twice.

That Woman mystifier Anna Eva Fay[3] is the Headliner and she does all that stuff having the audience write on a tablet questions and later on she tells them the answer. so she closes the show. she goes on No. 6. then has to have time to frame up the answers so she always goes on last again   she does like two acts. I have a dandy place No. 7. I am glad I am not closing cause it is a late, long, show.

Hon the little Pictures are dandy and just as cute as they can be of my Gal and I have looked at them a thousand times

There is another big Kid act on the bill just like the one last week with 10 Kids in it in a schoolroom scene.

This being Sunday I dont know if it ▲ this letter ▲ will go out at once or not.

I wonder what you are doing today. I'll bet you are having such a good time you dont think much of the time of me   I wish Sunday would hurry up and pass cause its lots more lonesome than the other days.

Well hon I will mail this. With all my love I am always your

Billy.

ALS, rc. OkClaW. On Hotel Havlin, Cincinnati, letterhead. European Plan, John H. Havlin, Prop.[4]

1. Rogers played at the Columbia Theatre in Cincinnati with The Hughes Musical Trio (Versatile Instrumental Virtuosos); Frank Odell and Rose Kinley (A Skillful Acrobatic Comedy and Novel Dancing Speciality); Howard Truesdell & Co. (In His Latest Comedy, *Two Men and a Bottle*); Violet King (England's Great Violinist and Clever Entertainer at the Piano); Harry W. Fields and His Napanees (In the Condensed Musical Comedy, *Fun in a School Room,* presented by Mr. J. A. Sternad)

(this was the act Rogers described as "another big Kid act," in comparison to Gus Edwards's children's act, with which he had just finished appearing); and Eva Fay (The Woman of Mystery) who appeared (as Rogers pointed out to Betty) twice in the course of the bill, in the sixth and closing slots. Rogers followed Fay's first act, occupying (as he says) the seventh position on the bill, and was followed by Miss Ray Cox, a comedienne, who did a skit called *See the Baseball Game.* It was a bit of a treat for Rogers to be able to leave the theater a little early. He often closed programs because of his use of a horse on stage, but the nature of Fay's act dictated a different arrangement in Cincinnati (Columbia Theatre, Cincinnati, playbill, week of 2 May 1909, scrapbook A-2, OkClaW).

2. The next day Rogers wrote that "I done a bad act last night and should of been roasted for it but I did great today and it goes good with the audience here" (Will Rogers to Betty Blake Rogers, 3 May 1909, OkClaW).

3. Mind reader Eva Fay (d. 1931) had just experienced a very difficult several months when Rogers shared the bill with her in May 1909. Fay was born in Delhi, India, of English–East Indian parents, and it was there she met and married her husband, John T. Fay, a fellow mind reader. He was a member of a family of several mind readers, including his mother, a famous spiritualist and psychic vaudeville performer named Anna Eva Fay, who was a hit in the 1880s and 1890s, and continued to perform on stage until the early 1920s. John T. Fay appeared in his mother's act until the turn of the century, when he began peforming with his wife. Eva and John T. Fay worked Hammerstein's Roof Garden in New York together in 1906 as The Fays. They did the western vaudeville circuit in 1908 for the Casey Agency, and drew good crowds. They had finished a performance in Oakland one night shortly before Christmas 1908, and had checked their bags at the train station, preparing to travel to Denver for their next showing, when John T. Fay excused himself from the dinner table they were sharing in a restaurant, went to the men's room, and shot himself. Eva Fay, whose home was in Melrose Highlands, Mass., brought her husband's body to Boston for burial, which took place 27 December 1908. She soon went back to work on her own. In her act she appeared blindfolded and identified objects held up by members of the audience. In the second part of the act she would answer questions, usually of a highly personal nature, posed by members of the audience about themselves. She was assisted by a staff who infiltrated the audience and sold Fay's booklets about spiritualism and psychic abilities. When she worked the Hippodrome in October 1909, a reviewer said, "She is variously described by the local critics today as genii, Buddhist, Mahomet, incarnated oracle, Delphi, and her weird fascination has aroused the utmost interest" (*New York Telegraph,* 4 April 1909). She worked at Hammerstein's in 1910 with Bert Williams and was still appearing in her act during that decade (*EV,* 168–69; Oakland, Calif., *Morning Telegraph,* ca. 21 December 1908; *New York American,* 12 September 1931; *New York Times,* 14 September 1931; *Toledo Blade,* 22 March 1913 and 21 January 1916; *Vanity Fair,* 24 August 1906; *Variety,* 30 April 1910; scrapbook ser. 3, 422:45–70, NN-L-RLC; clipping file, NN-L-BRTC).

4. The Hotel Havlin catered to theatergoers and performers. When Rogers was still in Louisville, he received a letter from the hotel proprietor John H. Havlin, wooing him to stay at the hotel when he came into town for his next engagement. The letter described the hotel as brand-new and fireproof, with rates starting at "$1.50 and upwards" without baths. Located "directly opposite the Lyric Theatre and next door to the Grand Opera House, in the very heart of the city," the Hotel Havlin was "regarded by all as the headquarters for all visiting members of the theatrical profession." Rogers did stay at the hotel. While still in Louisville he wrote in the mar-

gin of the typed letter he had received from Havlin that he would "cut out the upwards" in the cost of the $1.50 rooms, and he sent the letter to Betty Blake Rogers to let her know where he would be staying (John H. Havlin to Will Rogers, 29 April 1909, OkClaW; *JCGHTG*, 235, 241).

To Betty Blake Rogers
4 May 1909
Cincinnati, Ohio

Tuesday, 2 P.M.

My Own Dear Wife,

Well this is earlier in the day than I usually write as I generally wait till after the matinee   But I got up at 10 oclock and went to the Theatre ~~and~~ to get a nice long letter from you before breakfast—but I am sorry to say I was dissapointed as I only got your *note* and it was about the chilliest little thing I had ever gotten from you in a long time. I am afful sorry hon you felt bad but am glad you know it was not about me and that you are so perfectly at home and feel that you had never left.

But dont worry dear I am not silly enough to think you mean all those things you just felt a little upset when you wrote and you dont mean things like you say them I know and its mean of me to tell you of them but you had promised to write a long letter Sunday and I guess thats why I noticed it so much

I am ~~sorry~~ sorry now that I sent you the letter from Sister Sallie cause I know you did not like the little part in there where she says Betty she thinks will be ready to join you in Cincannatti because your whole attitude seems to be to give people the impression that you are not in love with me and you do hate to have them think that you are   But I dont think you really mean it its only that you are afraid someone will tease or kid you about it. Well after breakfast this morning I went back to the theatre a[nd] worked for three solid hours and I am just about all in but will go over and do my show pretty soon

Here is the paper[1] telling of the big race and my friends horse won it   the one I had breakfast with and that is this horses picture that I sent to you, Wintergreen   I was in his stall and met the jockey and all   The race was run yesterday   I could of won a bit of money on it for I knew this horse would win but I knew you would not like me to bet and i did not bet a cent   That Owner Respass in the picture is a fine old fellow and I am glad he won.

This is actually a more lonesome week than last week (I did not think it possible)   I dont know a soul and there is no one but me stops here

Hon here is $20.00   I will put in this letter   it is all I have and I know you need some   I will send you some more in a few days   I just happen to have this and will send it now.

Say where is that letter you was going to send me that you got from some one.

Now dearie you write me a nice long letter and if you feel like saying a little sarcastic thing just leave it out and see how much nicer it will sound. My letters may not have been as long as you would of liked but you must remember I have not a thing in the way of news to interest you   all days are the same to me. and at that I have written more and also *more letters* than you   you spoke of writing twice one day but I notice you dident do it. The day you said you staid home from a club to write me you wrote *4* ▲ little ▲ Pages—Just think it over and see

Well must get to the show shop   I do hope you feel good by now and wont feel bad any more and write and _____ lots to the old boy who takes things as he knows you mean them and not as you do and say. Yours always the same

Billy.

ALS, rc. OkClaW. On Hotel Havlin letterhead.

1. The enclosure clipping regarding the horse race is no longer extant.

To Betty Blake Rogers
4 May 1909
Cincinnati, Ohio

Tuesday Night
11:30 P.M.

My Dear Sweetheart Wife,

I wrote you once today but I have just come in to the hotel after the show I was in a saloon and had about 4 glasses of beer and am home ready to go to bed—but I dont know   I feel so lonesome some way tonight (I do all nights for that matter) but more than usual tonight and so I will write you just a little note

Oh here is a little Kodak picture those two little Milch Sisters in Denver took   they sent them to Buck   they took a lot of him and the Pony   they took this out in the alley by the stage one day as I was going   I was reading a paper   I leave here Saturday Night at 1 oclock and get to St Louis at 10:30 Sunday morning and open at Matinee   I think I will get a place to stop out near there if there is a hotel in or near the grounds and they tell me there is

When ▲ will ▲ you be up. dont make it too long cause I am sure lonesome for my little girl

Well hon I will stop and go up and see if I can go to sleep and get up early and hope I get a nice long letter from my own wife "G" but that seems great just to know you are all mine and I do love you oh, but I love you. Goodnight

My only only Love.

A million kisses. Your boy,

Billy

ALS, rc. OkClaW. On Hotel Havlin letterhead.

To Betty Blake Rogers
5 May 1909
Cincinnati, Ohio

Wednesday 2 P.M.

My Own Dear Wife

Well hon I went over to the Theatre today and I *almost* got a letter.

I dont know what you mean in your letter where you refer to my good time in Louisville and hope I have as good time here   you wrote as if I had been having a gay time and all I can recall is going to the track to see the horses and I dont know that it was a particular good time. I enjoyed it yes   But I dont know where the good time come in Louisville nor have I discovered it here either.

Are you sore about something I did or havent done or what is the matter I dont understand the peculiar little chilliness of your last three letters   My Lord I am not doing anything and have tried my very best to write you often and tell you all I do. and to not do a thing that would displease you.

You know when you went home you could stay just as long as you wanted to or come back just when you wanted too and you know I how glad I will be to have you back. without you saying "if you want me back that week."

I want you to come just as soon as you can—and have had your visit out I know you are having a good time and are enjoying yourself cause you dont even have time to write.

I am just home from a long practice and oh but it is hot   I will now go over and do my matinee. dont do a thing but eat-sleep-read-and play a little Sol—till I get sleepy at night.

Now Betty dont feel sore or hurt about anything—I havent done anything "G" I dident think you would mind me going out to that track and I just happened to meet those men. My I am not having any good times   I never was as lonesome in my life

If I do anything you dont like tell me about it   dont take it out in not writing and in saying sarcastic things

Must get over and do my stunt. Now Sweetheart please dont be this way with me   I am trying to do the best I know how to please you and you know I want to do anything that will allow you to enjoy yourself. Now come up to St. Louis any time of the week you want too.[1] your old boy who loves you more than all the world.

Billy.

ALS, rc. OkClaW. On Hotel Havlin letterhead.

1. Later in the day Rogers received the desired letter from his wife. He cabled her: "YOUR GOOD LETTER JUST COME PLEASE LEAVE ABOUT SUNDAY LOVE BILLY" (Will Rogers to Betty Blake Rogers, 5 May 1909, OkClaW). After he got off work that night, he wrote to Betty again ("This is the 2nd letter and a Telegram today"), to say that "just after I come off from my act your *dandy good regular* letter come and I feel so good and love you so much and oh how I wish you was here   I would just love you to death" (5 May 1909, OkClaW). He regretted his criticisms in the above letter, which he had mailed that morning, and talked of arrangements for Betty Blake Rogers to come into town. He wrote to her again on Friday to say, "I said some mean things in some of my letters and I did not mean a one of them. You are so good to me and I am the one who is wrong and you must forgive me cause I dont mean a bit of it and I will show you when you come '*home*'" (7 May 1909, OkClaW).

To Betty Blake Rogers
6 May 1909
Cincinnati, Ohio

Thursday   2 P.M.

My Dear Wife,

Well hon I did not get a letter today cause it come last night and I did not much look for one.

Here is $25.00   now I dont know if this is enough   you would not tell me what to send but if it is not we can send it to Dick as soon as you come

Guess you got the $20.00 in the other letter   Oh but it is hot here today and we are having a Womans Matinee. No Men admitted   this Anna Eva Fay is going to tell them a few secrets   I guess it is one grand *Bunco*   I got a letter this morning from the Press agent at Indianapolis and he said I was to be there the week after St. Louis.[1] the week that I was to be in Milwaukee but I have not been notified of it from the office so I dont know which one will go to   it dont make any difference anyway   I dont know yet just what will do after Chicago   have got a couple of agents hustling for me some parks and may get them and then I may not   so it might be possible we would be open after Chicago   still you cant tell yet.

They all say that Grand Rapids week is great   right out on a lake— fishing— rowing— and lots of fun   I want to get us a place to stop out near
or in the park in St. Louis next week   wouldent you like it better than in town
I have been over to the Theatre and been ▲ practicing ▲ working and oh how
I did sweat   it sho is getting hot on these old stages now when all those lights
are up.

Well only three or four days and I will be with my own little wife and I will
sho be glad cause it is certainly lonesome.

You decide yourself what trains to come on and I will sho be glad to see
you cause I sho do love you a heap, your own

Billy.

ALS, rc. OkClaW. On Hotel Havlin letterhead.

1. Rogers played at the Forest Park Highlands in St. Louis the week of 9–15 May
1909. Appearing with him on the program were Borani and Nevara in a novelty act;
the comedienne Grace Armond; the musical duo Berry and Berry; and the Clipper
Comedy Quartette of comedians and singers. Rogers, who came last on the bill, was
the headliner. His act was listed as Will Rogers and Co. (Comedy Lariat Act) (Forest
Park Highlands, clippings and playbill, scrapbook A-2, OkClaW; *Variety*, 15 May
1909). Rogers went to Indianapolis from St. Louis, and to Grand Rapids before
appearing in Chicago.

Reviews from Indianapolis Newspapers
ca. 19 May 1909
Indianapolis, Ind.

ROGERS'S LASSO HURLING WAYS.

Will Rogers is an amusing stage character. He is a genuine Oklahoma cowboy, born in Indian Territory, and loves his lariat and his horse—"critter," as
he calls [him]. His lasso hurling makes him a favorite of this week's bill at the
Grand.[1] Mr. Rogers, if the dignity of the prefix "Mr." does not grate upon his
sense of humility, was one of a bunch of boosters from Oklahoma a few years
ago who came to Indianapolis. His monologue, accompanying his manipulation of ropes, is characteristic of the West.

"I'm goin' to try a fool trick," he says, as he makes his rope behave like a
trained creature. "I'll try to throw this one around the critter's neck and this
other one around the other thing," referring to the assistant on the mount. The
lassoing of the horse and the rider, both at the same time and around the neck
of each, is the climax of the cowboy's display of skill.

Rogers talks the same off the stage as he does before the footlights. He
gives the impression of being a big, good-natured boy, happy in the extreme.

He has been on the stage for four years, during which time he has been seen in Europe and America.

Teddy, the horse used by Will Rogers, the Oklahoma cowboy, in his lariat-throwing exhibition at the Grand this week, is fond of motion pictures and insists upon [fe]tching them from the back of the sheet [after] every performance. Teddy, in the words of the Oklahoman, is "jest a common ranch horse," but "he's a lively critter and can throw up a little dust when he gits started." In addition to his treat of loaf sugar Teddy is permitted to stand behind the sheet, with his bridle hanging from the bit to the floor, in Western fashion. He is given the whole stage and follows the pictorial characters. Teddy is especially interested in the "chase" pictures and apparently takes delight in the rapid action in such films. He wears rubber shoes and does not disturb anybody while he looks on and crosses and recrosses the stage with every aspect of gleeful appreciation.

Buck McKee, Mr. Rogers's assistant, is a Western rider, and, next to Rogers, Teddy's best friend. Buck takes Teddy out for daily exercise. The horse and the cowboy, without bridle, saddle or whip, are conspicuous figures on downtown streets this week. McKee, a curly-haired ranchman, has won many bets on Teddy's training. The horse will gallop on the street and stop at a signal or a word from the rider. Leicester Square, one of the most congested places of traffic in London, saw Teddy and McKee. The horse and rider also gave exhibitions on Broadway, New York.

PD. Printed in Indianapolis *News* and Indianapolis *Star*, ca. 19 May 1909. Clippings, scrapbook A-2, OkClaW.

1. Rogers, with Teddy and Buck McKee (sidekicks referred to, in a blurb of the program in *Variety* of 22 May 1909, as "a horse, a pal and many feet of rope") played the Grand Theater in Indianapolis with Sam Chip and Mary Marble (in *In Old Edam*, a musical fairy tale); the Bison City quartet; Mack and Marcus (silent cartoonists from San Francisco and Philadelphia); Roberts, Hayes and Roberts (a dance act); aerialists Frobel and Ruge; the Hughes Musical trio; and instrumental viruoso Florence Wilson.
Rogers went from Indianapolis to the Ramona Theatre at Reed's Lake in Grand Rapids, Mich. There Gus Edwards' Kountry Kids rejoined him on the playbill (In a One-act Trury Rurl Musical Comedy Entitled *Miss Rose's Birthday* written by Edwards), as did Mack and Marcus the cartoonists. (Mack was from the San Francisco *Chronicle* and Marcus from the Philadelphia *Enquirer*. They were making a "Special Appearance in Vaudeville, In the Entertaining Pictorial Act *Evolution*.") The program was rounded out by Jewell's Manikins, a mechanical exhibition on stage of *Toyland Vaudeville* (With the New Snow Ballet and Other Specially Devised Features). Betty Blake Rogers went with Rogers to Grand Rapids. She drew the eye of a member

of the local press, who wrote an account of Rogers, his wife, and his act that was a little hazy on the details. "If 'all the world loves a lover,' Will Rogers, the sinewy young fellow whose lariat throwing is one of the features on Ramona's bill this week, must be the center of interest among his associates," the local article stated, "for he brings with him a slender, dark-eyed, shy little Oklahoma [Arkansas] maiden to whom he was wedded only last week [six months ago]. They are spending the first week of their honeymoon at Ramona resort, where they idle away the morning hours in rowing, fishing, and gathering the wild flowers which smother the place at this time of year" ("Lassoed a Bride," unidentified clipping, Grand Rapids, Mich., ca. May 1909, vaudeville scrapbook, CPpR). Whether they had been married one week or six months, the Grand Rapids engagement provided a backdrop for the kind of honeymoon vacation that Rogers had promised Betty in his letters before she rejoined him on the road.

Notice from the *Chelsea Reporter*
10 June 1909
Chelsea, I.T.

Friday noon your Uncle Clem Rogers started for the biggest city in the United States, Chicago, to see his son William, who is giving exhibitions in the theatres there with his intelligent horse.[1] Mr. Rogers was accompanied by his niece, Miss Mary Gulager, of Tahlequah, and granddaughter, Miss Estelle Lane of Chelsea.[2]

PD. Printed in CR, 10 June 1909, OkClaW. Reprinted from *Rogers County News*.

1. Rogers played the Majestic Theatre in Chicago the week beginning Monday, 31 May 1909. He appeared there with a very large bill of performers that included the Johnson Students (Comedy Dancing and Juggling Specialists); Gladys Lillian Parry (Violiniste); Munson and Munson (With a Comedy Musical Number); Miss Minnie Kaufmann (The Extraordinary Lady Cyclist); Harry Fidler and R. Byron Shelton (The Boys Who Sing, Play, Mimic and Impersonate Those Two Colored Boys); Chinko (The Youthful Juggling Genius, from the London Musical Halls, in a Return Tour in America); the mimic Fanny Rice (Merrily, Cheerily, Verily Yours, Presenting Her Original Creation, The Miniature Mimic Stage); singer Mabel McCane (The Musical Comedy Favorite, In Her Own Selected Songs); cartoonists Mack and Marcus doing the same act they presented in Grand Rapids; Marie Dainton (First Time Here, The Celebrated English Mimic, Impersonator of the Stars of the Legitimate Stage and Music Hall Favorites); Harrison Armstrong (presenting His One Act Play, *Circumstantial Evidence*); and R. C. Herz (Late Co-Star with Benee in *The Soul Kiss*, In Monologue). Rogers wound up the program in the last slot with his roping act, billed as The Oklahoma Cowboy Who Has Astonished America and Europe with His Lasso (Majestic Theatre, playbill, vaudeville scrapbook, CPpR). *Variety* reviewed the Majestic show. Armstrong's troupe, listed in the eleventh spot on the bill, was described as the headliner, and "its success was emphatic." Marie Dainton's impersonations were deemed "not well imitated," while Mack and Marcus's did "a novel act called 'Evolution'" and Fiddler and Shelton were "different from any other colored act seen in years. One particular point is their refinement. They scored a deserved hit."

Rogers, coming at the end of the long list of people to be reviewed, was said to have "interested as he always does. The show this week is high class vaudeville" (*Variety*, 5 June 1909).

    2. Estelle Lane was the eldest daughter of Rogers's sister Maud and her husband Cap Lane.

Betty Blake Rogers to Clement Vann Rogers
13 July 1909

Atlantic City, N.J.

July 13th

My dear Mr Rogers—

We leave tomorrow afternoon for New York.[1] We have had such a good time here that we sorter hate to leave. We have been going in the water every day and its great,   Im not afraid now and I go out and swim with Billy— He has taught me how to float and swim on my back—   Oh, we have have had some great times and are both as black as niggers—[2]   Im so tanned you would hardly know me—   There are hundreds in the water every day—   Its the greatest thing here—

Billy ~~this~~ ▲ thinks ▲ he will work next week, he has several weeks booked for summer but they all come later—   I will let you know at once if we leave New York next week—   The weather has been so delightful here, cool and a good breeze all the time, we have not felt the heat once—but will in New York I bet—   We were going to take a boat trip today, dressed and went down to pier to start but the sea was so rough the boat did not go out, I was sorry, we had counted on it so and some way I wanted to get *sea sick* just so I could tell about it some time—

Billy gave me, for my very own—one of the little rent houses he has in Claremore—   He said I could have the nicest one—so I want you to take care of it for me—you pick out the best one for me and every month I want you to put the rent in the bank in my name—   Im just tickled to death to have this all for my own and Im going to do wonders with it in *my name* and don't you let Billy touch it—   you tell me which one is the best and all about it—   I'm greatly interested in my new possession and just tickled to death to have it for myself—asn't it good of Billy to give it to me? When Im home sometime I'll fix it up and make a real pretty place out of it.

    Lots of love from Bill and your daughter

Betty

ALS, rc. OkClaW. On The Albany Hotel, Broadway and 41st Street, New York, letterhead. Sent in The Dunlap, Atlantic City, N.J., envelope.

1. Will and Betty Blake Rogers followed up their honeymoon behavior at the lake in Grand Rapids with a seaside vacation in Atlantic City. He appeared at Young's Pier and Theatre in Atlantic City at the end of June 1909. The bill included Harris' Big Vaudeville Co. (Every Afternoon and Evening); Leech (And His Three Rosebuds); impersonator Edna Luby (As Vesta Victoria and Rose Stahl); Rogers (The Lariat Thrower); musicians Pearl and Yosco (The Dago and the Musician); The Great Westin (Eminent Character Impersonator); Honey Johnson (Black Face Comedian); and Dilla and Templeton (in *The Goblin's Den*). The bill closed with a kinetograph called *New Views*. Rogers's scrapbook from the period has the playbill pasted on a page surrounded with pictures of himself and Betty in bathing suits grinning and frolicking in the waves (Young's Pier and Theatre clippings and Atlantic City photographs, vaudeville scrapbook, CPpR; *Variety*, 26 June 1909).

2. Both Betty Blake Rogers and Will Rogers were known to casually use the pejorative slang term for African Americans, as was common in the social environments in which they had grown up. Rogers was raised within a well-to-do Confederate slave-owning family whose ongoing relationship to poorer African Americans was paternalistic. The Rogers family were used to having African American employees working on their ranch and in their household, and Rogers's sisters employed black domestic servants. Later in his career, when Rogers used the word *nigger* during a radio broadcast, he was befuddled at the outraged calls that came into the station in protest of his use of a term that was offensive to many, and which many listeners equated with advocacy of a position of white supremacy. In addition to being used to hearing the term within his family, Rogers was surrounded with like use of slang terms to describe blacks, Jews, and members of white ethnic groups within the vaudeville world. In his own defense, he explained that he regarded the term as one of familiarity or intimacy rather than of racism, and in response to the angry radio listeners, he told how as a motherless child he had been largely raised among the African American families of the ranch-hands and women domestic servants who worked at the Rogers ranch, and insisted that he had many friends among people of color, inside the entertainment industry and out. He indeed maintained ties with the families of Rabb and Houston Rogers, who had helped to raise him, and even when he had gained celebrity status, went out of his way to visit them and to quietly help their family members in times of need.

2. WILL ROGERS AND CO.
July 1909–February 1911

Will Rogers and Betty Blake Rogers with an unidentified friend on the boardwalk in Atlantic City, N.J., 1909. *(OkClaW)*

THE PERIOD BETWEEN MIDSUMMER 1909 AND EARLY SPRING 1911 WAS A TIME of consolidation and reconfiguration for Will and Betty Blake Rogers. An unexpected death in the Rogers family drew them both closer into the family circle. Rogers's professional life also took a turn, as he decided to pursue a different direction in his act.

The death in the family was that of Rogers's youngest sister, May Stine, who died of illness at Sallie McSpadden's home in Chelsea in late July 1909. May Stine had given birth to a child the year before she died and had attended her brother's wedding in Arkansas. She had had a difficult life, with much hard work and tragedy, and of all the Rogers children who lived to adulthood, she was the least well-to-do. At the same time, she maintained a sunny disposition. When, on the last day of her life, she was told that her death was approaching, she accepted the news calmly and with solid religious faith. Family members gathered in her room to pray, and she said goodbye to everyone, including the servants in the McSpadden household, who had always been kind to her and her children. She left behind three young children whose care over the next several years continued to be a concern for her sisters and brother. May Stine had been ill before, and Sallie McSpadden misjudged the severity of her final illness, not realizing her sister's condition until it was too late to summon Will and Betty Blake Rogers from far-away New York in time to either see May or attend her funeral, which took place the day after her death. Will agonized over the shocking news, while Betty was drawn ever more firmly into the family.

To Sallie McSpadden, who wrote a letter conveying the details regarding May's death,[1] Betty Blake Rogers became more like a sister. To Clement Vann Rogers, she had already become another daughter. Even before May Stine's death made her a correspondent on intimate matters, she had been writing to her father-in-law on a regular basis. These letters give much of the information available about her and Will's life in New York. She was faithful in letting Clement Vann Rogers know what was happening in his son's career. "I'm sending you a picture Billy & I had made at Niag[a]ra Falls— & I will also send you some good newspaper articles about Billy— Lots of love Betty" she wrote in a typical letter on 9 November 1909.[2] She often signed her letters

"Your daughter." In addition to conveying news about Rogers's work and whereabouts, she confided in Clement Vann Rogers about financial matters and expressed her own desire for a measure of economic independence—even if she used the funds she saved on her own to purchase presents for her husband. Her letters contain a balance of news about New York and concern with matters in Oklahoma. Although the plan for the Rogerses to settle eventually on a ranch in Oklahoma remained intact, and Rogers continued to acquire and rent out property back home, New York had become a second home for the newlyweds. "We go to New York next week and it will seem good to me," Betty wrote to Clement Vann Rogers on 2 November 1909. "New York is next to home." Betty also reported that things were good between her and Will: "We have been married just one year and a mighty happy year it has been," she wrote as Thanksgiving 1909 approached. A year later, on the second anniversary of their marriage, the couple were still happy and living in New York.[3]

Will Rogers, meanwhile, was building a foundation for his future success and winning a name for himself appearing in towns large and small. Doing "small time" vaudeville on the road, he later explained, was essential to the development of quality stage work. Traveling to different houses gave performers a chance to learn their trade, perfect their acts, and learn how to adapt their material to a wide variety of audiences. Some performers "make the mistake of playing just on Broadway," he observed. If they did so, they grew stale as they failed to renew their techniques and material. More important, they became only known in a small entertainment circle in New York and did not build a wide base for their popularity. Because he participated on the circuit and won star status in local reviews, Will Rogers became known to audiences in different regions of the United States. He credited the success of fellow vaudevillian Al Jolson in radio, film, and the musical stage to the fact that Jolson, despite his successes, was willing to "play everywhere he could," and because of this, "he would draw anywhere."[4]

In the spring of 1910 Rogers decided that he had finished some of his developmental training with his old act and wanted to move into something new and more daring. He began to change his act. First, he supplemented it with other performances, reaching back to connections from his Wild West show and roping contest days to do so. At the same time that he continued to play in twice-a-day vaudeville with Teddy and Buck McKee, he began making special appearances in arena shows.

The first major appearance of the year was with his old friends, the Mulhalls, in a show they mounted with arena director Jim Gabriel in

St. Louis. The appearance was part of a deal Rogers made with Zack Mulhall over the question of ownership of Rogers's old roping pony, Comanche. The two men had not been on speaking terms since the summer of 1905, when Mulhall had wanted Rogers to continue with his Wild West show and Rogers had decided instead to stay in New York to try his hand in vaudeville. In something of a practical joke (one that Rogers evidently did not find too amusing), Mulhall ended up with custody of Comanche in the summer of 1905, either by kidnapping the horse, as some tell it, or by purchasing him away from someone to whom Rogers had decided to sell. After nearly five years of ill feeling, in March 1910 the two men entered into an agreement that Rogers should get Comanche back. In the next month, and apparently as part of the same deal, Rogers appeared with his old friends Charley and Lucille Mulhall, J. Ellison Carroll, and Tom Mix in a show in St. Louis on 7 April 1910. In a flashback to their younger days, Rogers and Lucille Mulhall wowed the crowd.

Whether the idea of bringing a heightened Wild West aspect into his vaudeville act came to him as cause or effect of his reassociation with the Mulhalls, the appearance in St. Louis triggered a change in direction for Rogers's vaudeville performances. After performing in St. Louis with the Mulhall show, he made special appearances with the Buffalo Bill's Wild West and Pawnee Bill's Far East combined show in Madison Square Garden, New York. He also reconnected to his roping contest days by appearing as a fancy roper at an event in Tulsa featuring champion roper J. Ellison Carroll. After dabbling in this way in other people's promotions, he came up with a show of his own. For one week in June 1910 he mounted his own Will Rogers' Wild West show. The show was produced at the Big Hip stadium in Philadelphia, and Rogers worked it in between regular vaudeville engagements. The Will Rogers' Wild West show combined cowboys, cowgirls, roping, and equestrian feats (both fancy high-schooling style and western rough riding) with vaudeville and circus-style acrobatic, trapeze, animal, and musical acts in an open-air venue.

While Rogers was engaged in reaching back to the associations of his youth and experimenting with the Wild West format, Lucille Mulhall left the big-arena venue for a time to develop her own Wild West act for the stage. There was evidently a mood for change in the air, and both Rogers and Mulhall were simultaneously exploring ways to combine the Wild West and vaudeville forms. Rogers tried changing horses and altering the format and personnel of his act. In effect he developed two acts: one with a horse and McKee, and another that was a group equestrian act. By mid-July 1910 Teddy, who had been with the act since its inception, was gone from Rogers's regular routine. Will and Betty Blake Rogers spent the late summer vacationing in Oklahoma,

Lucille and Zack Mulhall, ca. 1909. *(Mulhall Family Collection, Martha Fisch, Guthrie, Okla.)*

and Teddy was put out to pasture at the Rogerses' Oologah ranch. Rogers acquired new horses, and in the autumn of 1910 he began to try once more, as he had briefly in Europe in 1907, to assemble his own successful Wild West act for the stage. He was connected through friendships to the complicated network of Wild West performers and horse trainers who had experience in the circus, roping contest, and Wild West show worlds. He had also gained a great deal of firsthand business knowledge about mounting acts from his years observing the ways of booking agents and theater managers on the vaudeville circuits. Calling on old friends and others who had a good reputation as riders, he put together a group act featuring women equestrians who would do a miniature Wild West show on the vaudeville stage. He hoped that times were more auspicious for support of a group of performers than had been the case during his short-lived attempt at a similar act a few years before. Betty Blake Rogers's letters reflect the hard work Will Rogers put into getting the new act together and the enthusiasm they both felt for what they called the Big Act. As she put it, "he was eager to try out something a little more spectacular" than what he had been doing in his old act. In spite of the previous financial failure of a bigger act, "he was determined to try again."[5]

Mary Turner, a promoter for the Tompkins Wild West show, described Rogers's initial Big Act concept as "a big stage act with contrasting girl riders."[6] In the fall of 1910 Rogers signed up the well-known cowgirl Goldie St. Clair, a Buffalo Bill show performer who had recently won the woman's bucking-horse championship in Cheyenne, Wyoming. He also recruited fancy rope artist Florence LaDue, who was married to his friend, trick rider Guy Weadick, with whom she had starred in the Miller Brothers' 101 Ranch Wild West Show. Rope dancing was provided by Hazel Moran and traditional trick riding by Tillie Baldwin, while Arlene Palmer did Cossack-style riding like that seen in the Buffalo Bill, Pawnee Bill, and Miller Brothers' 101 Ranch shows. All the performers whom Rogers headlined were considered at the top of their profession, and in the years ahead each broke new ground for women in rodeo competition, helping to establish the place of women's contests in the sport.[7] Unlike men, who came into roping contests and rodeo from experience as hired hands or professional cowboys, women more often came into the competitions out of ranch work they had done growing up on family spreads. In hiring women for the act, Rogers showed a willingness to accept the female athletes he knew as capable both in their riding skills and in their ability to project star quality to audiences. In some ways, his Will Rogers and Co., with its cast of women awing the audience while Rogers spun his rope, prefigured the career Rogers would have with the *Ziegfeld Follies,* in which his cowboy act was framed by the presence of many beautiful women. In Will Rogers and Co., however, the emphasis was not only on the women's appearance, but also on the astounding things they could do, and instead of simply providing a beautiful backdrop, they appeared front and center on the stage.

The production of the act was very much a matter of friendship. Rogers's good friends Mabel Hackney Tompkins and her husband, seasoned Wild West arena director Charles Tompkins, helped put the act together and train the horses. Mabel Hackney Tompkins had won many awards as a professional rider who specialized in international show jumping as well as riding in Wild West shows. She provided the eastern high-school horse flavor to the act. Like Goldie St. Clair, she had performed with the Buffalo Bill show. Rogers came to New Hope, Pa., where the Tompkinses wintered stock, to talk over his ideas for the Big Act and to look over their ponies and equipment. The horses for the act were kept for a time in New Hope, and the act premiered in nearby New Jersey.[8]

Once it reached rehearsal and trial runs, the act was clearly in need of revision. In his first conceptualization of the Big Act, Rogers served as narrator of the women riders' spectacular feats. As one rider after another burst into the audience's view on horseback, Rogers stood to the side of the stage and kept up a constant patter of jokes and explanations. The act closed dramatically with Goldie St. Clair riding a bucking horse onto the stage. St. Clair was known in Wild West circles for her feisty personality as well as her gorgeous long hair. Betty Blake Rogers recalled that when St. Clair emerged on stage she made a strong visual impact because she "was young and pretty, with long blonde hair that hung down her back."[9]

Rogers had been worried all along that the Big Act might be just too big. He admitted after the first week's run that his fears had been justified. The act, as first conceived, was indeed too large to be workable or profitable. Theater managers also had been lukewarm because they wanted Rogers himself to have more of a starring role. Rogers let go some riders, making sure to find other work for them, and pared down the act to just four riders and horses. Charles Tompkins joined the group as a bronco rider, and Rogers combined the fancy-riding aspects of the group act with his old lariat act with Buck McKee, creating a new group act in a different configuration from the original all-girl concept. The bronco riding remained, but at the heart of the act was Rogers with his commentary and rope.

Will Rogers and Co. was both a link to Rogers's past and, as it turned out, part of his evolution toward the monologue mode of entertainment for which he became internationally famous. After this he left the Wild West format behind. Betty Rogers remembered Harry Jordan, a theater manager in Philadelphia, turning to her backstage during a performance of the group act and saying, "why does Will carry all those horses and people around with him? I would rather have Will Rogers alone than that whole bunch put together."[10] Rogers had underestimated his own star quality. His image on stage was also changing. He was more and more being recognized for what he said as well as what he did. He was now seen as a witty comic and commentator on the events of the day, not just as a cowboy who could thrill audiences with amazing twirls of a rope. By the end of March 1911 Rogers was ready to leave both the old act and the Big Act behind, and go solo. He simplified his act to a man alone with a lariat on the stage.

1. See Sallie Rogers McSpadden to Betty Blake Rogers, 29 July 1909, below.

2. Betty Blake Rogers to Clement Vann Rogers, 9 November 1909, OkClaW.

3. Betty Blake Rogers to Clement Vann Rogers, 2 November and 27 November 1909, OkClaW.

4. *TDW*, 21 May 1933; see also Rogers, "Broadway Ain't What She Used to Be," 21–22, quoted in Fisher, *Al Jolson*, 10.

5. Rogers, *Will Rogers*, 98.

6. Mary A. Turner to Homer Croy, 10 September 1952, HCP-MoU.

7. Goldie St. Clair (Irene Wooden, b. 1885) was a pathbreaker for women in rodeo. She won a world bucking-horse championship at the Jamestown Exposition and World's Fair in 1907 and was famous for her breakneck rides on bucking broncos. Along with Lucille Mulhall and Bertha Blancett, she was a high-profile veteran of Wild West shows and roping contests. St. Clair, Mulhall, and Blancett, along with trick ropers Florence LaDue and Tillie Baldwin, were all considered top athletes of their time. They each spent many years competing, and for LaDue, Baldwin, and St. Clair, the stint with Will Rogers and Co. was one job among many over a long career.

All the leading women involved in Rogers's act would gain wider fame in 1912, when Guy Weadick mounted the renowned Calgary Stampede. Weadick gave cowgirls real superstar status for the first time, by including a full range of women's contests in the Stampede. For LaDue, the venue gave opportunities to shine in fancy roping and trick riding. LaDue (Florence Bensel, 1883–1951) had met Weadick during the 1905 Cummins Wild West Congress of North American Indians and had toured with him in vaudeville, including the Rogers act. She then did a western stage show called *Wyoming Days*. She and Lucille Mulhall competed in Calgary in 1912 for the title of world champion. In a close contest, the top award went to LaDue, who won the title again in 1913 in another closely fought rivalry with Mulhall. In the pre–World War I years LaDue continued to win headlines in contests, including the New York Stampede of 1912, in which Tillie Baldwin and Bertha Blancett also competed.

Baldwin (Anna Matilda Winger, 1880–1950), the first woman bulldogger, had an unusual background. Born in Norway, she did not learn to ride until she immigrated to New York as a young woman, when friends taught her to ride at a local stable. She became a star with the Miller Brothers' 101 Ranch Wild West show in 1912. She excelled in several rodeo events, including relay races, trick riding, and bronc riding, as well as bulldogging. In 1912 she began wearing innovative bloomer attire in competitions rather than the more common divided skirts, which limited the ability of women to do elaborate gymnastics in trick riding. She won the all-around cowgirl title at the Pendleton Roundup in the same year. Baldwin was victorious as the only woman in an otherwise all-male field in the Roman race in the Winnipeg Stampede of 1913. In the race, the rider stands on two horses running side by side, with one foot on each horse's back and the reins for each mount in one hand. The race was run each day of the event, with the decision being based on the cumulative score. Baldwin and LaDue both gave exhibitions of riding and trick roping at the 1919 Calgary Stampede. Baldwin began her own Wild West show in 1921, and toured the United States with the show. She married William C. Slate in 1925, taught riding at a riding academy near her home in Connecticut, and continued to make occasional appearances in Wild West shows. LaDue stopped participating in competitive rodeo in 1916, but continued doing exhibitions and making vaudeville and Wild West appearances with Weadick. She and Weadick went to England with the Miller Brothers' 101 Ranch show in 1914, where they played with the Anglo-American Exposition in London. World War I ended most Wild West and Stampede performances, but both rodeo and the Miller Brothers' show experienced a resurgence in the 1920s, which was the heyday for women competing in events later reserved for men. The Weadicks retired in 1950, the year of Baldwin's death, and Florence LaDue died a year later (GWP-GA; *Billboard,* 12 December 1908, 4 February 1911, 13 January 1912; *Daring Beautiful Western Girls*; Frederiksson, *American Rodeo,* 150; LeCompte, *Cowgirls of the Rodeo,* 27, 46–55, 61, 76, 172–73; Russell, *Wild West,* 81, 82–83. See also Biographical Appendix entry, LaDue, Florence).

8. See *PWR,* 2:523–26 (Biographical Appendix entry for Charles and Mabel Hackney Tompkins).

9. Rogers, *Will Rogers,* 109. St. Clair was twenty-four years old when she worked with Rogers's act. On Will Rogers and Co. and the performers involved in the act, see also *Billboard,* 12 December 1908; Herb McSpadden to Paula M. Love, 26 February 1972, OkClaW; Buffalo Bill's Wild West vertical file, WBaraC; Russell, *Wild West,* 93.

10. Rogers, *Will Rogers,* 110.

Betty Blake Rogers to Clement Vann Rogers
19 July 1909
New York, N.Y.

New York, <u>July 19, 19</u>09
Monday

My dear Mr Rogers—

You[r] letter written July 13th came day or so ago—   We came in here last
Wednesday night—   We are at this "Preston" Hotel, small but very nice—
Billy thought it would be cooler than at the Albany[1]—   It is very pleasant, we
have a big room, big windows—   We are only 4 blocks from river and get
such a dandy good breeze all the time—   We have not felt the heat [at] all
since we came here—

I have just come in from a long walk—   Im sorter lonesome today—
Billy left about ten o'clock to go down to Long Island to see his lots down
there—   He has never seen them you know and I was sorter anxious to have
him go and look them over—   He has 3 lots near Hampstead and ~~one~~ 2—
(almost 3)—acres of land at Deerpark—   Hampstead is quite a place you
know and I think he should sorter know what he has there—   He will get
back about 4 or 5 o'clock this p.m.—   Hampstead is only 20 miles from New
York but Deerpark is farther & sorter hard to get to   so I don't expect Billy
back until later this afternoon[2]—

This hotel is directly opposite the Madison Square Garden, and is the
same hotel Billy stopped at when he was here with Mulhall the first time—
It was the old Putnam Hotel then, but has been improved since and the name
changed to Preston—   We were over to Madison Square Garden last night
and went up on the roof and also ~~on~~ up on tower—   We had a fine view of
the city from there—

I hardly think Billy and I will get home this summer, but we will come in
fall or winter some time—   We are coming home late in the winter and fix
our home up and next summer ~~you~~ will find us there keeping house and living like *white folks*—   We are just crazy for it and plan all the time just how
we are going to fix things—   Won't it be dandy—   We will all have the best
time and we can see you and be with you every day.[3]

Billy has 4 weeks work—   Newport, Brighton Beach[,] Rockaway. We are
laying off next week and may go up in the mountains & spend the week—
Address your letters here—   "Preston Hotel, 26th St. and 4 Ave["]—

Lots of love

Betty

ALS, rc. OkClaW. On Hotel Preston, Fourth Avenue and Twentieth Street, Opposite Madison Square Garden, letterhead. Samuel Glantz, Prop.

1. When they first arrived in New York, Will and Betty Blake Rogers lived at the Albany Hotel at Broadway and 41st Street.

2. Betty Blake Rogers recalled in her memoirs that in Will Rogers's "vaudeville days—along with the furs and diamonds, Will was making weekly installment payments on Long Island real estate. A well-known vaudeville team, turned salesmen, had convinced ballad singers, acrobats, dance teams and others, that a fortune awaited them at the far end of the island, on a weekly-payment basis, as soon as the transatlantic liners began docking at Montauk Point, and that was to be very soon. Long after, when we were married, we found Will's city lots in the middle of an old man's cornfield. But never were we able to locate definitely his supposed acreage near Deer Park" (Rogers, *Will Rogers,* 100–101). This early bad experience in real estate investment did little to dissuade Will Rogers from a lifelong fascination with the acquisition of land. As he established a career in New York, the Rogerses lived on Long Island, and over his lifetime he owned real estate in Oklahoma, on Long Island, and in California. Even after his success as a film star and the establishment of his family ranch in the Pacific Palisades above Santa Monica, he loved to travel the western countryside looking at other properties.

3. Rogers picked up summer work in resort areas. He was soon offered a contract with Percy G. Williams's Greater New York Circuit that changed his and Betty's plans to return to live in Oklahoma. "Will had promised," Betty Blake Rogers remembered, "to give up the theater at the end of the tour and we had made glowing plans for our home in Claremore. But at the end of the tour an offer came to play the Percy Williams houses in the East at $300 a week. This was more than Will had ever been paid, and even I agreed that the offer should be accepted" (Rogers, *Will Rogers,* 108). The Percy G. Williams Circuit, contracted in connection with the UBO, included the Orpheum Theatre in Brooklyn; the Alhambra, Bronx, Gotham, and Colonial theaters in New York; and the Greenpoint Theatre in Greenpoint. On the same day, 10 August 1909, Rogers arranged for other engagements through the rest of 1909 and into the first few months of 1910. He signed with F. F. Proctor's Amusement Enterprises for additional work in the New York area, with B. F. Keith Theatre Co. for work in Boston, with the B. F. Keith Hippodrome Co. for work in Cleveland, and with the B. F. Keith Amusement Enterprises for work in Philadelphia. All the contracts, including the Percy G. Williams contract, were for $250 a week, 10 percent of which went off the top to ("deducted and immediately paid over to") the UBO (vaudeville contracts, 10 August 1909, OkClaW). On Rogers's signing with the Keith Circuit in 1906, and the business politics between Keith, Proctor, Williams, and other vaudeville promoters, see Introduction to "Caught in the Vaudeville Wars," *PWR* 2:303–9.

To Clement Vann Rogers
27 July 1909
New York, N.Y.

In July Will and Betty Blake Rogers received the tragic news that Will's sister May Stine had died. The youngest of the three surviving daughters in the Rogers family,[1] May Stine had had a difficult life, marked by violence, illness, and tragedy.

My Dear Own Papa,

you cant imagine what a shock it was when we got Sallie's telegram   We did not even know she was sick.

Well this is certainly a sad blow to all of us and I do wish I could of gotten there for the funeral   But as I could not get there I guess there is little use of us coming as I have to go to work again next week. But we will be there before long.

Poor May she had had a lot of trouble in her life[2] but it seemed to of been all over and she was getting along so happily and well the last few years and it seems too bad that it come so soon but God knows best and all things are done for the best. But it will be hard on all of us to give her up   We were always such a happy family and so enjoyed all being togeather. and all loved each other so much. Poor Sallie and Maud   I know they are just heart-broken.

Well we have all of us children been wonderfully fortunate in having such a kind and loving Father as you have been to all of us. not only financially but by every word and action. and though our dear sister has gone she is happy and you should be happy to know that through all of her life you and Sallie and Maud have done every little thing possible to help her and make her life more pleasant and that should be a great consolation to you all

I dont know what arrangements you all will make about the children but I want to pay for the schooling at least for at least one of the boys.[3]

Well I will hear in a day or so telling me how it all happened   I know that everything was done for her that possibly could of been done and I do hope she did not suffer[4]

Well I will stop and write again as soon as I hear   With all our love and Sympathy. your loving

Son and Daughter.[5]

ALS, rc. OkClaW.

1. Two other daughters were born to Mary America Schrimsher Rogers and Clement Vann Rogers. They were Elizabeth (b. 1861) and Zoe (b. 1876), both of whom died in infancy. Will Rogers had also had two brothers, Robert (1866–83), who died of illness as a teenager, and Homer (b. 1878), who died in infancy.

2. At her death, May Stine was survived by her second husband, Frank Stine; her son Johnny Yocum, of her first marriage; and two young sons and a daughter by her second marriage. The children of her second marriage were Jacob (Jake), born in 1900; Mattie (Lanie) born in 1903; and the baby, Owen, born ca. 1908 or 1909. Three other children, Willie, Zella, and Vera, had preceded May Stine in death, having died in infancy or early childhood. For a time after May Stine's death Owen Stine

was taken in by Maud and Cap Lane, and Lanie Stine lived with the McSpaddens, while nine-year-old Jake Stine stayed with his father. By November 1909 Jake was living in Texas with his paternal grandmother, who wrote to Will and Betty Blake Rogers about his progress, and Frank Stine had taken Owen back into his care, apparently to the distress of Maud Lane. Betty Blake Rogers wrote to Clement Vann Rogers on 6 November 1909 to say that she had heard from Maud and was "sorry Mr Stine took the baby—surely he will not try to keep it" (OkClaW). Stine later took custody of Lanie as well. While Rogers's sisters helped raise the children, Rogers assumed some financial responsibility for their welfare.

3. May Stine's children each inherited some property from Clement Vann Rogers at his death, and Will Rogers did take responsibility for their schooling. Lanie Stine studied at the Ursuline Academy in Paola, Kans., and Rogers paid for her room and board. When Frank Stine had difficulty supporting the children, Rogers purchased the Oklahoma property that had been left to them by their grandfather and paid out the purchase money to them in the form of periodic stipends or support payments made through their father. Later, during Rogers's Hollywood years, Betty Blake Rogers's brother, Sandy Blake, who acted as business manager for the Rogerses, continued to come to the aid of Owen Stine. Blake shielded Will Rogers from knowledge of some of the numerous legal scrapes and personal indiscretions in which the young man became involved in Texas (*PWR*, 1:557).

4. The exact cause of May Stine's death and the nature of the illness that made her bedridden are not known for certain; apparently, close acquaintances were not aware of her illness and even Rogers's sisters were shocked at its severity. According to Sallie McSpadden's eyewitness account of Stine's death, Stine seems to have had a weakened heart and to have died from heart failure while under medical treatment. She died in the early morning hours of 25 July 1909, in the care of Sallie McSpadden and the McSpadden family in Chelsea. She was thirty-six years old. Will Rogers later, rather cryptically listed "confinement" as the cause of his sister's death on an insurance application form, and the *Claremore Progress* of 30 July 1909 reported her death as a result of "lingering illness" (see *PWR*, 1:554–58 [Biographical Appendix entry for May Rogers Yocum Stine]).

5. Betty Blake Rogers wrote to Clement Vann Rogers on 28 July 1909, telling him, "It hurt Billy so much because we could not come home. But we could not have gotten there in any way until Tuesday. . . . I will write you tomorrow, and so will Billy— He feels so badly now he can't write— Lots of love from Billy and your daughter Betty" (OkClaW). (Betty Rogers's letter was dated "Wednesday, July 27," but Wednesday was the 28th.)

To May McSpadden
27 July 1909
New York, N.Y.

27 July 1909

My Dear May[1]—

Just got your address from your Mama today   we had wrote for it long before but she had just forgotten to send it.

Well you know by now of our poor Little Sister May's sudden death   it certainly was a sudden shock to us as we did not even know she was sick till

Sunday Morning about 10 oclock   we got your Mamas wire and we would of gone but we could not of gotten there till Tuesday and they wired not to come that would be to late. I did hate it so not to be there and we thought a lot of you up there alone and wished we knew your address.

Well this will be pretty hard on all of us to be without her, of course you and I cant realize it fully till we go home and not find her there and those poor little motherless children and your Mama and Aunt Maud it will just most kill them and Poor Papa. they had all bee[n] so near May and had done so much for her and she had always been so jolly and we had all had such good times togeather.

Its hard on all you children cause you all did think so much of your Aunt May and she did of you and so enjoyed having you all out there   I will get a letter in the Morning telling me all about it.

Now May write and tell us all you are doing up there and when you intend to go home   we want you to come and see us before you go. I dont know yet just where we will be but I expect in or around New York. I think I work in Newport, R.I., next week but am not sure yet   I am not working now   we have been back from Atlantic City about two weeks.

Are you there with your Cousin Maud or are you alone   Tom Trent is here[2]   he will be down   he just come in and will spend the evening here in the room with us   he sends his love to you   he will be here when you come down   he is studying voice

Betty is not feeling well   not sick only just a little pain   she said she would write to you tomorrow. Now write us at once and tell us how you are.

With all our love

Uncle Willie

Hotel Preston
    4th Ave 26 Str
    New York

ALS, rc. OkClaW.

1. May McSpadden (1891–1978), daughter of Tom and Sallie McSpadden, was one of Will Rogers's favorite nieces. She had always been very close to her uncle, and had corresponded with him when she was a child and he traveled to Argentina and South Africa. May received her primary education at the Chelsea Academy in her hometown. She graduated from the Cherokee Female Seminary in Tahlequah in May 1907, and went on to receive a teaching credential from Northeastern State Normal School, Tahlequah. She was a student at Lake Chautauqua, N.Y., the summer that May Stine died. May McSpadden became a highly respected teacher in public and Indian schools in Foyil and Ardmore, Okla. She married Walton Charles Poole of Chelsea in May 1919 (*PWR*, 1:294–95 and 528–29 [Biographical Appendix entry for May McSpadden Poole]).

2. In her letter to Clement Vann Rogers of 27 July 1909, Betty Blake Rogers wrote that "we are expecting Tom Trent here today to spend the day with us— He was with us last night— and you don't know how good it is to be with some one from home. Billy and I have felt so badly, have felt that we were so far away from home and to meet up with Tom here and at this time has been good for us" (OkClaW). Tom Trent continued to be a good friend to the Rogerses when they were in New York. In December 1910 he was still living in New York and visiting with them when they also lived in the city. He had studied singing and was "trying to get a position on the stage in some singing and dancing act" (Betty Rogers to Clement Vann Rogers, 12 December 1910, OkClaW).

Sallie Rogers McSpadden to Betty Blake Rogers
29 July 1909
Chelsea, Okla.

Thursday.

My Dear, Dear Bettie:—

Each day your letters have come and each one leave[s] its own message of your and my precious brother's sorrow in the death of our little sister.

I could not write sooner for it seemed that I was some how to blame for not having written you sooner, and yet, I am sure she was sicker than this when we had Lenskor with her in Oologah. None of—nurse, Dr. and all— thought her in danger—though we all knew she was seriously sick—till after 4 o'clock Saturday evening— I wrote my card, Willie, to you, after 4 and at 4:30 the nurse called the Dr. who came immediately and in that short time her life was passing beyond the skill of mortal man though even then neither nurse or Dr. despaired, but administered the proper medicines and she seemed to be doing very well, only much weaker.

When Dr. came a little past eight and told us she could scarcely live tell midnight, I felt that it was too hard to bear— Her heart, which it seems had never been very strong simply gave way, and no drug—not nitro-glycerine— nor even the "Saline solution" which they tell me is used only as a last resort stimulated her at all—or for only an hour or so.

Maud tells me she has written you, very clearly, all the details of her sickness[1] but oh, my dear ones, if there is any comfort in a mother dying and leaving her little ones, surely we have that comfort in the sweet testimony she left us. Her mind was remarkably clear to the end and when she told us all to be very quiet and asked Tom to lead us in a short prayer, it seemed that my heart would break. Poor Tom could scarcely control himself at all, but did the best he could for the little sister that he had petted. Very much as he always did Ella and Rue. She spoke of you saying "We are all here but Willie and do you think there is any other Dr. can do me any good?" Oh, my brother when I told her

that the Dr. said she had only a little while to live, her even voice did not qua-
ver though mine was broken with sobs and she replied, "Well—we must all
meet death—   Call the Dr. and the nurse." We did so, she thanked them both
for what they had done for her and said she was satisfied. She called for every
child, by name, and even called for John and Alice—(the cook and the boy,
you know)   Alice kissed her just as the children did, and she said "Alice
you've been so good to me and my children." She told Lanie she was going to
Heaven   That she had prayed all night. Oh, Willie, since she had to go, it was
beautiful to have her go in that way—   After kissing every child goodbye, she
asked Clem to raise her up. He did so and Cap slipped his arm around her
and with her beautiful eyes looking, I truly believe, into Heaven, the soul of
our poor storm tossed little sister was wafted without even a tremor, to the
gates of Paradise, there to hold sweet communion with our loved mother and
her own three little ones, who have preceded her. She was dressed in a simple
white dress, and her face looked so calm and peaceful—   not a trace of sorrow or suffering but as I looked at the little toil-hardened hands folded so
peacefully I could not help thinking "Rejoice for the Lord brings back his
own. ["]

I'm sure Maud has told you of the kindness of the Claremore and Oologah
people. Truly one must be in deep sorrow to sound the depth of love and sympathy of one's friends. Lanie and Owen are both doing quite well. Maud and
I went out with Frank yesterday and cleaned and put the house in order and
packed up a few little mementos for the children, which when they are grown
will be priceless to them from having been their mothers. Among other things
were the lovely drawn work pieces that you had given May. For the next
month, at least, Frank will continue to live there and keep on with his work at
the lease. Jake will stay with him till school opens—   now, dear, don't think
we are all perfectly heartless in allowing poor little Jake to be out there, but if
you were here I could explain more reasons than one for this. It will make it
more bearable for Frank to have Jake with him night and morning. Being a
boy he can go with his papa to his work each day and they have a splendid
horse and buggy and will come to us every Sat. night and Jake will come during the week also. I hope you, too, see that it is better.

Dear Bettie: Never for one moment did I ever feel that in loving you my
precious brother loved me less, for I knew his great big noble heart was capable of loving both wife and sisters, but, ah, how glad I am that when this great
sorrow came upon him, he had your love and your sympathy and the sweet
comfort of the presence of his wife. He could not have borne it alone, and so
even in this dark hour we may see little rifts of sunshine, if we only seek them.

May God in His infinite care and tenderness, be very near you both and bring you safely to the ones who love you so dearly, at home, is the wish of your devoted

Sister Sallie

ALS, rc. OkClaW.

1. Maud Lane's letter is not extant.

Article from the *Claremore Progress*
30 July 1909
Oologah, Okla.

After five weeks of sickness Mrs. Frank Stine died at Chelsea last Saturday and the remains were brought here on Monday and buried in Oak Hill cemetery. No one here knew of her sickness and when the word came to prepare a grave for her everybody was surprised and shocked. The family had made their home here for several years, up to about 18 months ago. She had been raised here and on the old Rogers farm out on the Verdigris river. To know her was only to become her friend, young and old were all glad to meet Mae Stine. She being a daughter of Col. C. V. Rogers, of Claremore, gave her an extensive and honorable relationship in several parts of the county. Her friends were numerous as attested by the large number of people attending her burial from Chelsea, Claremore and this place. She was placed beside two of her infants who had preceded her over the river. The bereaved family have the deep sympathy of this community. A daughter, a wife, a sister and a mother rests from the turmoil and strife of this life.[1]

TD. Oologah news reprinted in *CP*, 30 July 1909.

1. Elsewhere in the paper the *Claremore Progress* reported correctly that May Stine had "died Sunday morning"; similarly, the Claremore *Rogers County News* reported on 28 July 1909 that she had been taken ill "two weeks ago" and that her death "occurred Sunday morning, July 25th." May Stine's funeral was held in the Southern Methodist Episcopal Church at Oologah on Monday, 26 July 1909, "and the interment was made near that place" (see also *Claremore Messenger*, 30 July 1909).

Betty Blake Rogers to Clement Vann Rogers
30 July 1909
New York, N.Y.

New York
July 30th

My dear dear Mr Rogers—

Your good letter came this morning and we were so glad to hear again from you. You write such good letters, and tell us everything in such a dear sweet way that it makes us feel good— You are a good father and we love you, we love your good letters because they are just like you— Of all the dear letters we have gotten from home Billy and I like yours the best and they do us lots of good too. It is just next to being with you.

This has been a sad week for poor dear Billy, we have both felt badly, and have felt so far away from home and our loved ones— But you all have been so good to write us every day, and tell us just everything, and everything you tell us about our sisters illness is sweet and makes us feel better about it all. Your letters have been such a comfort to Billy— He loves you, and admires you so much. he reads your letters over and over—

I have just come up from breakfast, Billy left me there and went up town to see his agent— I came right on up to the room. It is very warm today, the first real warm day we have had. Our room is larger, with plenty of windows, a good breeze so we don't feel the heat so much—

Tom Trent was down last night, he comes over to see us every day— He is a nice boy, good and very particular about his friends and the people he goes with— Tom seems mighty nice and I like him splendid— Billy and I enjoy him so much, and he seems crazy to be with us all the time.

We got a nice letter from May McSpadden— She leaves there next week and is coming here to see us— We will be so glad to have her and can take her to so many places that she will enjoy— I am writing to her today—

Billy gave me that $20.00 that was refunded on my ticket, and I want you to put it in the bank in my name, and you know he gave me one of the little rent house[s] there in Claremore and I want the rent money put in in my name too— Im going to start a bank account, all of my own and Im going to try to save something here to add to it too. I want it all kept seperate from Billys and some of these days I will surprise him with a *big* bank account.

We won't get home for awhile, not until winter I guess. Billy does not know yet just how his work is going to be for next season, he will know soon tho and then we can make our plans and will know just what we are going to do.

My mother and sisters are all well— My sister Dick, that you met in Chicago is improving all the time and will soon be as strong as ever, her little trip with us did her lots of good, she has been improving all the time since— If it gets to[o] warm for you in Claremore, and you don't go west you had better take a little trip over to Rogers [Ark.]— At the Electric Springs there is a good hotel and a good man has it this summer— It is cool down there all the time, quiet and the water is fine— I just believe you would enjoy a week or so at this spring, it is beautiful there in the summer and the folks from home say the hotel down there is good.

I must quit now I have some work I want to do before Billy comes and he will be coming soon— With lots of love to our dear good father, and all the folks— Your daughter

Betty

ALS, rc. OkClaW.

Rogers's Performance Calendar
9 August 1909–26 July 1910

Despite the grief he experienced over his sister's death, Rogers had a heavy schedule before him that he needed to fulfill. The following calendar was written in list form in Rogers's hand and pasted in his vaudeville scrapbook.

AUG.	9.	Phila
"	16	Newport.
"	30.	Alahambra.
SEP.	6.	WATERBURY
"	13	EASTON
"	27.	UNION HILL.
OCT.	4.	UTICA.
"	11.	BUFFALO.
"	18.	TORONTO
"	25.	OTTAWA
NOV.	1.	HARRISBURG
"	8.	NEWARK
"	15.	NEW ROCHELLE
"	22	ALBANY

"	29	BOSTON
DEC.	6.	STAR. BROOK.
"	13.	GAIETY
"	20.	HAMMERSTEIN
"	27	[*Illegible*]
JAN.	3.	NORFOLK.
"	10.	BRONX.
"	17.	[*Greenpoint?*]
"	24.	ATLANTA C. [*Atlantic City*]
"	31.	DETROIT.
FEB.	7.	Rochester.
"	14.	JOHNSTOWN.
"	21.	CLEVELAND.
"	28.	PHILA.
MAR.	14.	SPRINGFIELD.
"	21	NEW HAVEN.
"	28	MERIDAN.
APR.	11.	FIFTH AVE.
"	18.	ALAHAMBRA
"	23	COLONIAL Buffalo Bill
MAY.	2.	BUFFALO B
"	9	BUFFALO "
"	16	YONKERS
"	30	WILLIAM PENN.
JUNE	6.	MURRAY HILL
"	13.	PHILA, BALL, [R].
"	20.	BOSTON
JULY	18	ATLANTA
"	26.	CHATANOOGA

This was the last time used [*word illegible*] Teddy

AMS. Scrapbook A-3, OkClaW.

Manager's Report, Keith's Philadelphia Theatre
9 August 1909
Philadelphia, Pa.

PHILADELPHIA SHOW

AUG. 9-09.

VAN BROTHERS. 20 min. open in two, close in one. One man works straight, the other comedy. This is a very good act and could hold a strong spot on any bill. The man playing a peculiar instrument like the zither, certainly caught the house and he was compelled to give four encores. Both are expert musician[s] and the crowd liked them from the start. The comedy is good, but the musical work is really excellent. They play cornet, trombone and saxophone. Close in one with a saxophone duet.

AL. WHITE'S FOUR DANCING BUGS.[1] 13 min., opens in two, close in one. This is an excellent dancing act. The initial lunatic idea is novel, and the work throughout is expert and outside of the beaten track. There are three changes of costume, and some of their dancing is of the kind that we very seldom see. It certainly got the crowd immensely. Should be booked.

WILL ROGERS. 10 min. F[ull].S[tage]. There is no need to say anything about Will Rogers and his act, except to say that it is just as interesting and as expert as ever. Good applause and a strong finish.

DOHERTY SISTERS.[2] 14 MIN. Two mighty pretty girls who have improved immensely since their last appearance here. Their songs and dances are full of life although they have acquired the cafe chantant flavor from abroad. Make good in this spot.

FRED HALLEN & MOLLIE FULLER.[3] "A Lesson at 11 P.M." 21 min. F.S. A good lively sketch that has a very obvious plot, but there is plenty of laughter throughout. Trades on domestic infelicity and a lesson taught by a third party. The audience liked it. A good applause finish.

MARIE DAINTON.[4] 16 min. in one. A very swee[t] and winning personality. Her imitations of English celebrities are much stronger than the American, but everything was appreciated and enjoyed. Miss Dainton has great talent and will develop into one of the biggest hits yet. Will undoubtedly score strong with out [our] evening audiences. We have billed her big, and think she will draw well for the balance of the week.

WILLY PANTZER TROUPE. 17 min. F.S. Same act as presented here before, with some improvements. Really very strong acrobatic work of the higher line. The little chap was particularly a hit. Good applause throughout and a strong close. This act needs no comment except to say that it is better than ever.

AL. JOLSON.[5] 15 min. in one. There is certainly lots of life and ginger in Jolson's act. He sings new and clever songs with big dash, and his line of talk is immense. The crowd would not let him go this afternoon, and whether he told stories, sang, imitated or whistled, he was a big hit; in fact, this man will simply carry the evening audiences off their feet. He is beyond question the best blackface entertainer that has come on the Circuit in recent years.

KITA BANZAI TROUPE. 16 min. F.S. Well known on the Circuit; just as artistic and entertaining as ever, the two little chaps particularly making good with the audience which applauded liberally.

KINETOGRAPH. "A Chinese Wedding." A mighty interesting travel film. "Haunted by Policemen." All that could be desired in a comedy film.

GENERAL REMARKS. This is one crackerjack bill from start to finish. There is not a dull act in it, nor a dull line. With any sort of favorable weather it would pack the house; but as this is the hottest day of the year, the temperature being 100 on the street, we cannot expect to[o] much.[6]

C. E. BARNS

TD. KAC-IaU.

1. Al White (1878–1957) was a former minstrel player who became a veteran vaudeville performer, theater operator, and dance teacher. Born in England, he was sponsored in the United States by comedian Billy Carrol. He began his U.S. career at Atlantic City, N.J., where he remained a popular performer. He was one of the original members of Dumont's Minstrels. In 1906 he formed one-half of the team of Evans and White as a minstrel act on the Keith Circuit. He often played on the same bills with Gus Edwards, the Four Cohans, Eddie Cantor, and George Jessel. He became a resident of Philadelphia and operated a vaudeville-film house there as well as a dancing school and studio. (*VO,* 2:16 January 1957).

2. The Doherty Sisters (Anna and Lillian Doherty), an American song-and-dance act, were regulars on European and South African tours. A clipping of 1 July 1905 described them as "American girls of petite and pleasing appearance."

> They made their debut a few years ago and jumped into immediate favor with the patrons of vaudeville. A well-known European agent who saw them in New York engaged them for the Empire circuit in South Africa and they appeared at Johannesburg, Cape Town and other places with great success. They then returned to England and, with the prestige gained in South Africa, had no difficulty in filling long and profitable engagements in London at some of the leading halls. Managers made them big offers, which they accepted when they had finished their time in England. The principal cities of Europe were visited, and their magnetism and nimble feet carried them through triumphantly. Even in St. Petersburg they were so well received that their engagement was extended twice and they were offered a return date. They came back to their native land a few weeks ago and immediately began playing a series of engagements booked for them during their European tour. They have been most successful in the West and will make their New York reappearance at Hammerstein's Paradise Gardens on July 17, when they will display the elaborate wardrobe secured by them in Paris.

The Doherty Sisters played in *The Ginger Girls* after they completed their tour of Europe in 1907. They worked under Western Vaudeville Association management in

1908, with bookings in Chicago and London. Anna Doherty, the "plump member of the Doherty Sisters team, made her debut as a single entertainer at the Union Square and scored a decisive success" in August 1907. The sisters continued to work both singly and in their joint act. Anna Doherty was married to the Irish comedian William A. Inman (son of one of the Inman Sisters). On 1 March 1909, the *New York Telegraph* reported that she was suing Inman for divorce after the mysterious disappearance in September 1908 of their two-year-old son Billie, who had been in his father's care on the U.S. vaudeville circuit while his mother was appearing in Europe. Other accounts said the two reconciled and had another child, a boy, in June 1909. Anna Doherty was frequently compared to Eva Tanguay in reviews; indeed, she mimicked Tanguay and copied the contents of her act, and some critics faulted her for her lack of original material. In 1916–17 Anna played leading roles in stock-company productions at the Knickerbocker Theatre (clippings, series 3, vol. 368, pp. 133–48, NN-L-RLC).

3. Molly Fuller (1865–1933) was already a veteran comic performer when Rogers appeared on the bill with her in Philadelphia. She had appeared in *Peck's Bad Boy* (1884), *The Twentieth Century Girl* (1895), *The Gold Bug* (1896), and *Aunt Hannah* (1900), and had teamed with various other actors to do sketches in vaudeville. She suffered from ill health in her later years, becoming blind in 1917. She died at her home in Hollywood on 5 January 1933 (*VO*, 2:10 January 1933).

4. Marie Dainton (1872–1938), a mimic who was new to the U.S. vaudeville circuits, came fresh from a successful run in London music halls. She was making her debut in Philadelphia. Despite her popularity in Britain, her act did not go over particularly well in the United States, where many people in the vaudeville audiences were not familiar with the English celebrities she mimicked, and critics found her to be unskilled at her craft. Dainton was born in Russia and began doing imitations on the stage at York in March 1894. She soon became a success in London. She did musical comedy work, and had previously appeared before American audiences in *The Belle of Bohemia* at the Casino Theater in New York in 1900. The biggest hit of her career was *The Chinese Honeymoon,* which enjoyed a thousand-night-long run and in which she starred. Dainton died in London after a short illness in February 1938 (*NYT*, 2 February 1938; *VO*, 2:9 February 1938; Dainton file, NN-L-RLC; Keith's Philadelphia Theatre playbill and reviews, vaudeville scrapbook, CPpR).

5. Al Jolson (ca. 1886–1950), who first gained fame as a blackface minstrel and musical comedy singer and performer, also became a star in radio and film, with a career that spanned several decades. The Keith's Philadelphia Theatre playbill described him as the "Blackface Comedian Who Wins Them All" (vaudeville scrapbook, CPpR). Along with Fanny Brice and Eddie Cantor, he was among those who brought Jewish humor to the stage.

The son of a cantor, Al Jolson was born Asa Yoelson in Strednicke, Russia. He immigrated to the United States in the early 1890s and lived in Washington, D.C. The family Americanized their name to Joelson, and some years into his performing career, Jolson further simplified the spelling. Like Will Rogers, Jolson suffered the loss of his mother in his youth, and he was an independent-minded boy. He made his way into show business with a brief stint in the circus. Influenced by the performances of Fay Templeton and Eddie Leonard, Jolson began performing in whiteface circa 1899. One of his first appearances was on the legitimate stage in a Washington, D.C., production of Israel Zangwill's *Children of the Ghetto.* He sooned joined his brother Harry (born Hirsch) Jolson (1882–1953) in New York City to do vaudeville and burlesque. Over the years they appeared together as a brother duo, individually in single acts, and as a team or trio with other, more senior vaudevillians. Al Jolson teamed with Fred E.

Moore in 1901 as Joelson and Moore. The two moved between vaudeville and the Victoria Burlesquers company. In the spring of 1902 they joined Al Reeves's Famous Big Co., and in the fall of the same year they went on tour with Lawrence Weber's Dainty Duchess Co., appearing throughout the East and Midwest. Al Jolson also continued to work on and off with his brother Harry. They developed a burlesque act called *The Hebrew and the Cadet,* in which Al played the straight man to his brother's comic characterization of a Hasidic Jew. In 1904 the brothers joined Joe Palmer to form the trio of Joelson, Palmer, and Joelson. It was during this time that they changed their performing names to Jolson, and it was also during this time that Al Jolson began to appear in blackface. Harry Jolson left the trio in November 1905, and Al Jolson continued in the duo of Jolson and Palmer until he developed his own single act. He began playing as a single in San Francisco in 1906, working on perfecting his blackface technique as a singer of coon songs. While working on the West Coast he met Henrietta Keller (1888–1967); they married in September 1907 and divorced in 1919. In November 1906 he joined the Walter Sanford Players, a stock company in residence at the Globe Theatre in San Francisco. The big break in his career came in August 1908, when he joined the famous Lew Dockstader's Minstrels. By 1909 he was the main draw for the show as it toured the United States, and he appeared on vaudeville within the aura of this minstrel fame. Having made the switch from supporting actor to star as a minstrel singer, he continued to do his vaudeville act and also entered musical comedy. Over the next decade he headlined a series of popular productions at the New York Winter Garden Theatre, including *La Belle Paris* (1911), *Dancin' Around* (1914), and *Sinbad* (1918). During these musical comedies he would rivet audiences with vaudeville-like sets of songs, many of which he made into standards. His records began selling in the millions in 1912. His film career began with the semi-autobiographical film *The Jazz Singer* (Warner Brothers, 1927), a classic in the transition from silent pictures to sound, and continued with *The Singing Fool* (1928), which made Jolson into a film star; *Mammy* (1930); *The Singing Kid* (1936); *Rhapsody in Blue* (1945); and others. He also was well known as a radio performer. He made his debut on commercial radio in the National Broadcasting Co.'s *Dodge Victory Hour.* Broadcasting from New Orleans, he was featured in a special program, with Will Rogers, Paul Whiteman, and Fred Stone joining in from Beverly Hills, New York, and Chicago, respectively. During the program Jolson sang two sets of songs and told stories. His radio career continued with *Presenting Al Jolson* (1932) and *Kraft Music Hall* (1934). Jolson had a reputation as a superb entertainer but an egotistical and difficult person in private life. He was married to his second wife, Alma Osborne, from 1922 to 1926. His third wife was fellow entertainer Ruby Keeler, whom he married in 1928 and divorced in 1939. Jolson was a popular entertainer of U.S. troops overseas during World War II, and his career, which had ebbed for a time, surged again in the postwar years. His biographical film *Jolson Sings Again,* made for Columbia Pictures, became the top grossing film of 1949. He died of a heart attack in San Francisco in October 1950. The 1952 Warner Brothers film *The Story of Will Rogers,* starring Will Rogers, Jr., and directed by Michael Curtiz from a story by Betty Blake Rogers, featured a clip of Jolson singing his hit *Swanee* (*EV,* 272–75; Fisher, *Al Jolson*; Freedland, *Jolson*; Goldman, *Jolson*).

    6. George M. Young reported in *Variety* that the weather was so miserably hot when Rogers appeared in Philadelphia that the house was extremely small, even given the strength of the bill. Young hated Marie Dainton's performance, stating that "Dainton made her first appearance here and did not add anything to the credit of English mimics." He implied that her act had been something of a punishment for the

stalwarts who had turned out despite the heat. The rest of the bill received higher praise, as Young deemed it "well balanced" and reaching "a good average." "Al Jolson won over the big hit. He is a newcomer here and won himself into favor at once, holding his audience all the way through." Young thought Fred Hallen and Mollie Fuller did a good job with poor material and that the Doherty Sisters "did nicely." "Will Rogers," he judged, "was back with his rope, mustang and droll talk, and 'smeared on' a plum good novelty in the wild west line." Al White's Four Dancing Bugs included two boys and two small girls. Young felt this new act was clever and would become a "dandy routine." The Kita-Banzai Troupe "put a strong finish to the show with the clever tumbling" (*Variety,* 14 August 1909, clipping, vaudeville scrapbook, CPpR).

To Betty Blake Rogers
10 August 1909
Philadelphia, Pa.

12:30 P.M.

My Own Darling Wifey

Well Dear here it is another old lonesome night   have been sitting down stairs for a long time talking to a gang (not drinking much) just *blathering*

Well I got in all O.K. today on the same train   had a shave and a bite to eat and then to work and tonight we had the best audience of the whole week and the old act went great. Donnelly has not come back from Atlanta yet

Well I guess May and Tom[1] have seen all of N.Y. by now   Dont you go prowling around too much   you just stay close home and let them do all the going   you dont kneed to go. Well old baby Doll it looks lonesome tonight and I wish I was there but I will be tomorrow but tonight I feel offul tired and sleepy and think I can go right to sleep and dream of my own Dear little wife I wont write you much   will see you so soon

Goodnight my old Dear   I sho do love you   a million kisses and all my love

your Billy.

ALS, rc. OkClaW. On Leisse's Hotel, European Plan, 818, 820, and 822 Walnut St., Philadelphia, letterhead.

1. Tom Trent and May McSpadden. May McSpadden came to visit the Rogerses in New York City before heading home to Oklahoma after her studies in New York state. Tom Trent took her out sightseeing. "Billy has been in Philadelphia," Betty told her father-in-law, "and its been mighty nice for us to have Tom to run around with." She sent home a "little souvenir of the statue of Liberty" for Clement Vann Rogers in care of May (Betty Blake Rogers to Clement Vann Rogers, 14 August 1909, OkClaW).

To Betty Blake Rogers
11 August 1909
Philadelphia, Pa.

Night about 11:30 P.M.

My Own Darling Wife,

I should of wrote to you this afternoon and you would of gotten it the first thing in the morning but I did not think of it not getting there but now I see that this will not get there till tomorrow eve.

Well Dear I opened up O.K.   done a pretty good act both shows and went good   got a nice hand tonight on my entrance. Tonight was Baseball Night had the two teams there Philadelphia and Detroit and I used several ball gags in my act and they done fine   I have a good place on the bill early but a good place and I am sho glad   Say Hon but it sho is lonesome here tonight   I am in my room writing this and I sho do wish for you   I dont see how I could let you stay in N.Y. next year   its too lonesome   I'll bet you are lonesome too aint you dear   I hope you dont get afraid. I will be there tomorrow night about 1 oclock. and it is lucky that I am on early cause 10 oclock is the last train out   if I was on late I could not come   aint you glad I sho am   I am here for the night at the old hang out. have met a lot of people I knew and have been sitting down talking to them   Donnelly is in Atlantic City   will be up tomorrow. Wish he was here tonight   I would make him sleep with me   it is so lonesome.

Here is a Programme   see how the way I am on the programme[1]   Dear this has been the hottest day of the year here   oh but I am about roasted now and at work oh but it was fierce   oh! got a wire today from Casey to play the Alahambra, 125th St., N.Y. August 30. pretty good eh.

Well Dear I must stop or melt.

With all my love to you my own Dear Wife   I do love you so and miss you so much. goodnight Dear[2]

your Billy.

xxxxxxxxxx

ALS, rc. OkClaW. On Leisse's Hotel, Philadelphia, letterhead.

1. Rogers was listed third on the Keith's program and described as "The Lasso King–With His Broncho" (playbill, vaudeville scrapbook, CPpR).
2. Rogers wrote to Betty again on Saturday, at around 12:30 A.M., telling her he wanted to write "cause how I dont like this lone thing, and I will be glad when tomorrow night comes." Donnelly had still not arrived in Philadelphia, and it had been another very hot day. "Well old Baby Doll," Rogers told his wife, "I wish you was over here right now cause I sho do miss you and want you bad." He signed off so as to get

a letter written to Joe Shea (14 August 1909, OkClaW). Writing on the same day, Betty Blake Rogers told Clement Vann Rogers that she would be going to Newport, R.I., with Will for the next week, where he would play Freebody's Park Theatre (14 August 1909, OkClaW).

Betty Blake Rogers to Clement Vann Rogers
18 August 1909
Newport, R.I.

Newport   Aug 18th—

My dear Mr Rogers—

By this time May is home and perhaps you have seen her. We miss May this week— it was so good to have her with us.

It has been raining ever since we struck this place, and has been cold too— I wish you all had some of the rain—

Billy and I took a long walk this morning— It was the cliff walk[1]— which runs back of the beautiful summer homes here and right on the waters edge—   the coast is rocks & cliffs here and is beautiful—   This morning we passed Cornelius Vanderbuilt's home, Mrs. O. H. P. Bellmont, Golets, and dozens of other mansions we did not know whose they were[2]—   These "swells" have all been down to the show this week and all seemed to like Billys act—   They applauded uproariously—   We are going to take an automobile trip around the city   there are many interesting things to see—   Newport is over 200 years old—   the church is here that Geo Washington attended and the pew that he sat in is still preserved[3]—

We go back to New York from here—   you write to us at Preston Hotel 4th and 26th st. We got the letter you sent to New York—   It was sent here—

Lots of love to you all

Betty

ALS, rc. OkClaW.

1. The day before she wrote this letter, Betty Blake Rogers sent Clement Vann Rogers a postcard depicting a "View along the Cliff Walk, Newport, R.I." and reported on the rain (17 August 1909, OkClaW).

The Cliff Walk is a three-and-a-half-mile-long path on Newport's eastern shore. It originally provided landing points for fishermen along the rocky coast, but became one of Newport's most famous natural attractions for visitors. Tourists came not only to enjoy the dramatic views of the sea, but also to gawk at the architectural wonders that had sprung up, for it was mainly along the Cliff Walk that robber barons built their ornate and ostentatious mansions.

2. She is referring here to three well-known Newport mansions, all designed in somewhat fantastical form by architect Richard Morris Hunt. The Breakers, perhaps the most famous of the robber baron homes, was imperial in scale and Italian

Renaissance in style. It was built for Cornelius Vanderbilt in 1892–95. Belcourt Castle was designed by Hunt for Oliver Hazard Perry Belmont and his wife, the former Mrs. William K. Vanderbilt. Ochre Court, a late Gothic/French Renaissance/Beaux Arts mansion, was planned by Hunt in 1888 for Ogden Goelet, a wealthy New York real estate developer. Ochre Court was among the first monumental homes built, and Goelet in effect sparked the Newport building trend. Like The Breakers and Belcourt, Ochre Court was monumental in scale, but was built on a small, suburban-sized lot (Downing and Scully, *Architectural Heritage of Newport, Rhode Island,* 171–73; see also Baker, *Richard Morris Hunt,* 314, 334–72).

3. The city of Newport, located on the southern tip of Rhode Island at the opening of Narragansett Bay, was settled in 1639 by religious dissenters from the Massachusetts Bay Colony. It evolved from a major seaport city and commercial center into a leading summer resort, popular especially among southerners, who came to escape the heat of their home states, and among New Yorkers, who worked in the city during the week and joined their families in Newport on the weekends. At the time of the Rogerses' visit the colonial heritage of Newport remained much in evidence in the commercial, domestic, and religious architecture of the original section of the city. Touro Synagogue, built in 1763, is the oldest synagogue in the nation, and Trinity Episcopal Church, on Queen Anne Square, has been in continuous use since it was opened in 1726. George Washington attended Trinity Church, and the pew he used has been preserved there (Newport Historical Society, Newport, R.I.).

Buck McKee to Maud Florence McKee
18 August 1909
Newport, R.I.

Wednesday morning
Newport, R.I., 8, 18 1909

My Precious Little Wife:—

Yours just received. I know that was why I didn't hear from you yesterday—because I forgot to tell you the name of the Theatre.[1] But this is a sweet little letter & cheers me up. It is nice here this morning only a little chilly yet, but the rain seems to be over. Yes I wished I had brought my overcoat, but I guess I wont need it any more now this week. This *is* sure a blue, bleak place when it is bad weather all night. I will address this letter to *"your house."* I sent the others to [Gerts] thinking you would be there nights & would not have to get up & get dressed & spend four hours fixing your hair & selecting an immaculately clean waist to go out & get you mail.

Say you had better get you Mother to go out to see Coyne *"the first bright day you have."* It is time he was making a report of some kind on that case. I expect to make it my business to see him my self as soon as I get back there. Also you go in & see Joe Shea occasionly.

Well now kid there is no occasion for me "holding one hand on my pocket-book"—for it is empty & absolutely harmless—so that leaves both hands free to use on the other thing if necessary for it's protection. You say I *"must not get into fights"*—Well now supposing I was to be attacked & asaulted by a bunch of these high-plumed old hens wouldn't you want me to put up a fight? Or would you want me to meekly submit to their evil designs & then come home to you all pecked to death like an old subdued rooster? What*???*

No, Darling, I havn't caught any cold yet although I had a good chance to yesterday. I was wet all day. But I am not subject to catching cold—(thank the Lord,) The only thing that bothers me—is billiousness when I drink coffee & beer. I am not using either this week.

Yes, Sweetheart, I was awfully disappointed to at the way the day passed Sunday. I hardly had a word with you atal. *Dam those railroad guys any way.* I should have had all the afternoon & evening with you if I could have used that midnight train for this jump. I *begrudge every hour* I am detained away from *you*, & I *hate* the hindering cause[.] Never mind Darling it wont always be like this. We will be very happy yet—when we can be together all the time. *I love you, Kid,. God bless your precious little heart* You are *an Angel to me. I worship you.*

Darling I will not mail this yet. I see a letter from Joe Shea here for Bill & I will wait until he comes down or opens it & see what is doing for next week. So long for the present.

Later—

Just saw Bill & he says the letter from Shea says that he is trying to fix New Roshelle for next week. That is what he has been saying for the last three weeks. I doubt very much if we get it. I guess it is a question of the salary. They dont want to pay the price.

We will most likely *lay* off next week. We have Alhambra the week following.[2]

Will see about getting the money for the Simpson business tomorrow.

Bill paid the $8.^{00} ballance on the old Castleberg account—so that is all settled at last Thank God.

Hope you are feeling better by this time. Take care of your self. Dont go out & get wet.

Love and kisses.

Buck

ALS, rc. BMc-C. First section of letter on letterhead from George P. Lawton, Livery, Sale and Boarding Stables, and Carriage Repository. Horses and Carriages of All Kinds Bought and Sold on Commission. Park Stables, Corner Touro and Spring Streets. Second section of letter (following "Later") on letterhead (and return address) from Central House, Open the Entire Year,

H. F. Finnegan, Proprietor, 14 Bath Road. Letter addressed to Mrs. Maud McKee, c/o Killingsworth's, 67 West 106th St., New York City, N.Y.

1. Will Rogers, Teddy, and Buck McKee played at Sheedy's Theatre in Freebody Park, Newport. The bill included The Three Navarros (European Equilibrists); Gertie DeMilt and Her Boys (Singing and Dancing Stars); Lydell and Brown (in *Varieties*); George B. Alexander (The Happy Hobo); Billy K. Wells (The Hebrew Orator); Clarence Wilbur and his Ten Funny Folks (in *The New Scholar*); and Kelly and Catlin (The Natural Comedians). Rogers finished the bill. He was incorrectly described as "The Texas Cowboy" as well as the more familiar "Lariat King" (Sheedy's Theatre, Newport, R.I., playbill and clipping, vaudeville scrapbook, CPpR). Rogers, "with the aid of a pony and his driver," received a good review in the *Newport News*, which reported on his "remarkable feats, throwing with one and two hands, catching the horse and the rider at the same time," and doing "a number of fancy movements, jumping through the loop, and tying knots in a rope by throwing it and gradually reducing the size of the loop" (clipping, vaudeville scrapbook, CPpR).

2. They played the Alhambra Theatre, at Seventh Avenue and 126th Street, the week of 30 August–4 September 1909. Joining them on the bill were The Daleys (Expert Skaters); Sue Smith (The American Girl); William H. Macart and Ethlynne Bradford (In a Tabloid Comedy Drama Special, *A Legitimate Hold-Up*); Harry B. Lester (The Jovial Jester); Eva Taylor and Co. in a comic sketch; Imro Fox (Comic Conjurer and Deceptionist); singer Louise Dresser; and George Felix and Lydia Barry, with the Barry Sisters, Emily and Clara. As was often the case, Rogers had the last live spot on the show, before the closing vitagraph (Alhambra Theatre, New York, playbill, vaudeville scrapbook, CPpR).

Variety described the Alhambra bill as a happy one, with three comedy sketches combined with "good specialty material" making up a nice "light show" (*Variety*, 4 September 1909; see also *NYDM*, 11 September 1909). Rogers and McKee traveled from the Alhambra to Waterbury, Conn., where they appeared at Poli's Theater.

The *Waterbury Republican* gave the act good advance press, stating that Rogers "has been a headliner on the prominent vaudeville bills of the country. The act is radically different from anything we have had here, and should prove quite a sensation." At Poli's Buck, Will, and Teddy joined the Zardi Troupe (Acrobats Extraordinary); Lewis and Young (Singers and Dancers); Bonita (Late Star of *Wine, Women and Song*), assisted by Lew Hearn (In an Original Travesty on *Three Weeks*); Lyons and Yasco (The Harpists); Hal Davis (presenting *The Vital Question*, By Lester Lonegan, an intense one-act drama of the hour); and Eddie De Noyer and the Dainty Danie Sisters (Musical Comedy Stars in *Oh, You Tramp!*). The Rogers act closed the show, which was brought to the audience by Mrs. Hastings' Corset Shops ("Corsets to make Thin People Look Plump"), which, as a line printed in the midst of the playbill announced, were "to be found in every large town in New England" (Poli's Waterbury Theatre playbill and clipping, vaudeville scrapbook, CPpR). The ad showed Poli's concern with attracting female audiences (see Oberdeck, "Contested Cultures").

To Clement Vann Rogers
19 September 1909
New York, N.Y.

Sunday.

My Dear Papa,

Well I got here today and found your letter here telling me about the farm and I am so glad you went up there cause I think that fellow is pretty good man and if I get 4. or. 5. hundred dollars it will be more than I ever got all put togeather[1]   yes I want to get all that land around there if you can buy it for me   I think now is the time   it wont be any cheaper   I want all that north pasture as I dont own the creek at all yet.

I am laying off this week as I was not booked but after a week or so will be at it pretty steady all winter and will soon clear up my note there   you see I have not worked only a little all summer as there was no theatres open much I dont much look for Betty for at least two more weeks as her sister is still very bad. I want you to come back with her and travel a couple of weeks with us will be up at Buffalo and Niag[a]ra Falls and Toronto Canada[2] about then and you can see some great country

Well I will close   I just come home from church at one of the big churches here.

Lots of love to all

your loving son
Willie

ALS, rc. On Hotel Preston letterhead.

1. Everyone seemed cautiously optimistic about the tenant management of the old Rogers farm and thus about the status of the Rogerses' bank accounts and debts. In a letter Betty Blake Rogers wrote to her father-in-law from Harrisburg, Pa., several weeks later, she said, "I think Billys farmer did fine this year. I hope the corn turns out good." She noted that the money from the crop would "look mighty fine put in the books to my audit and I would take it away from Billy too but I want him to apply that to his note there at the bank and get that cut down some" (Betty Blake Rogers to Clement Vann Rogers, 6 November 1909, OkClaW).
2. Rogers played in Toronto and Ottawa the last two weeks in October. Betty Blake Rogers, who apparently made a trip home to Rogers, Ark., in September to be with an ill sister, accompanied Rogers to Canada in October, but Clement Vann Rogers did not.
Before going to Canada, Rogers, McKee, and Teddy appeared at the Hudson Theatre in Union Hill, N.J. They were on the bill with Luce and Luce (Refined Musical Act); comedian Austin Walsh (Sunny Smile Smearing Spokesman); Morton and Russell (Protean and Change Artists); Mr. and Mrs. Gene Hughes (Presenting *Sup[p]ressing the Press* by Fred J. Beaman, with Gene Hughes as Robert Olmstead, who

believes himself a criminal, Line Crews Hughes as Agnes Olmsted, who thinks she has committed a crime, and Charles McCarren as Will Overton, Mrs. Olmsted's brother, in a one-scene play set in Mrs. Olmsted's drawing room on Fifth Avenue). An intermission followed the first drama, and the second half of the show opened with Will H. Ward and Co. (In a Dramatic Play, entitled *When the Devil Comes to Town*, written by Will H. Ward, with William W. Ward as a German tailor, Mrs. W. W. Ward as his wife, Mae Scullen as his daughter, Willis Reed as a modern evil, and Del Netra as a newsboy, in a three-act play set in a tailor shop and a mansion). The last two acts were Hallen and Hayes (Eccentric Dancing and Talking Act) and Rogers (Hudson Theatre, Union Hill, N.J., playbill and clippings, vaudeville scrapbook, CPpR).

The beginning of October saw the Rogers act at the Shubert Theatre in Utica, N.Y. According to *Variety*, the playbill there was made up by Ida Fuller (a fire dancer); Land and O'Donnell (acrobats); Moore and Young; Walsh, Lynch, and Co. (appearing in *Huckin's Run*, the "big hit" of the bill); the Girls from Melody Lane; and Charles and Fannie Van (*Variety*, 9 October 1909).

The second week in October Rogers appeared at Shea's Theatre in Buffalo, N.Y., with Max Yorke's Dogs; Suzanne Rocamora (Dainty Singer of Dainty Songs); the Exposition Four (Alexander Bros. and Brady, Musical Experts); Howard Truesdell and Co. (In the Novel Farce, *A Corner in Hair*); Nellie Nichol (Songstress Comedienne); (World Famous Eccentrics) Spissel Brothers and Co.; and Frank Fogarty (The Dublin Minstel). Rogers closed the program (Shea's Theatre, Buffalo, playbill, vaudeville scrapbook, CPpR; *NYDM*, 23 October 1909).

Betty Blake Rogers to Clement Vann Rogers
2 November 1909
Harrisburg, Pa.

Tuesday

My dear Mr Rogers—

your good letter came to Ottawa just as we were leaving. We got in here Monday morning, have a nice hotel near the theatre and right across from the capitol— The capitol buildings and grounds are beautiful[1]— This is a mighty pretty place and only 18 miles from the big Indian school Carlisle University— The street cars run out to this school and tomorrow Billy and I are going out. We saw the Carlisle Indians defeat Washington University in St Louis last thanksgiving when we stopped off there on our way east.

Its mighty good to get back in the states again— Toronto is a big town and Ottawa a beautiful city but I don't like Canada and Im glad to get *back* *"home"*.[2] We go to New York next week and it will seem good to me— New York is next to home[3]—

Billy is doing a nice show this week and has had some good reports in the newspapers. The theatre here is very pretty and does a splendid big business.[4]

Im glad Chas Carter is cured of the rheumatism—   He is certainly a fine
man and I know you all had a good jolly time in Chelsea—   I hope Billy and
I see him in Washington sometime—

Im going to buy Billy a watch, the chain and a masonic charm   It will cost
$50 and I am going to pay for it out of my own money—   I want to give it to
him the 25th of November. That is our wedding anniversary. We will have been
married one year—   I don't want Billy to know anything about this so when
you write don't you mention it—   I will write a check for the money when I
make the purchase—   I just wanted to tell you so you would know, but don't
you mention it in your letters because I want to surprise Billy[5]—

I will write to you again soon. Lots and lots of love to you from Billy and

Your daughter
Betty

What kind of trouble did Christian get into—   you said in your last letter that
the officers had brought him home from California

Im sending $15 for my bank account. Put it there to my credit—   Billy gave
it to me.

Hotel Preston
4th Ave. & 26th St.
New York

ALS, rc. OkClaW. On Hotel Columbus, 3rd and Walnut Streets, Federal Square, Harrisburg,
Pa., letterhead. Maurice E. Russ, Proprietor.

    1. Betty Blake Rogers found Harrisburg to be "such a pretty town." She wrote to
Clement Vann Rogers that "we went through the capitol—   oh, its beautiful—   the
finest one in the United States, and it certainly is a beauty—   The most beautiful decorations and we were told the dome is supposed to surpass (in beauty) the dome of St
Peters cathedral in Rome—   the grounds are pretty too—   Billy and I have spent
most all our time over there" (6 November 1909, OkClaW).
    2. Rogers received his usual good reviews in Toronto and Ottawa. The *Toronto
World* described him as "a wizard with the lariat," and the Toronto *Mail and Empire*
praised him for his "amusing and original line of patter" as well as his skill with the rope.
In Ottawa the *Evening Journal* found his act to be the "most unique item," with Rogers's
skill all the more impressive because of the small stage space in which he had to work.
The Ottawa *Evening Citizen* included Buck McKee in its praise, saying that "Will
Rogers and his partner, in expert lariat throwing, gave a wonderful exhibition. In talk
and manner Rogers seems the part and he does almost incredible things with ropes.
Their own horse is also used in some of the lasso work and the entire act is one which
holds the undivided attention of the audience" (clippings, vaudeville scrapbook, CPpR).
    3. Will and Betty Blake Rogers returned to New York on the afternoon of 7
November 1909, traveling by train the day after he closed at the Orpheum Theater in
Harrisburg and the day before he opened at Proctor's Newark Theatre in New Jersey.

4. Rogers was booked in Harrisburg as "The Real Western Cowboy," as usual in the last slot on the bill. He was joined at the Orpheum by MacRae and Levering (Expert and Eccentric Bicycle Artists); J. T. Doyle (Songs and Talks); Joe Kane (Late Co-Star with Max Rogers, of Rogers Bros., being presented by Pat Rooney) with Some Girls; Minnie St. Claire (The Girl from Missouri); John P. Wade and Co. (A Breath of Fresh Air, In the Southern Classic Playlet, *Marse Shelby's Chicken Dinner*); Kenney, McGahan and Platt (Potpourri of Comedy, Music, and Song) (Harrisburg Orpheum playbill, vaudeville scrapbook, CPpR).

The cast received enthusiastic reviews from the Harrisburg press. In the style of election reporting, the headline of one review read, "Whole Vaudeville Ticket Elected: Western Candidates Lead Party by Large Plurality." The article stated that the show at the Orpheum represented a victory for vaudeville. "Will Rogers," the writer observed, "knew how to get what was coming from the public. . . . He is the only candidate that electioneered on horseback, and the beautiful animal he rode and his evident love for it did much to advance him in popular favor. One of his feats was with a lariat that stretched from the rear of the stage to the main entrance of the theatre. Mounting his horse with the lariat coiled, he whirled it about his head with the loop gradually enlarging till it filled almost the width of the stage and circled far out over the audience. The upper district cast a solid vote for Rogers." The Harrisburg *Telegraph* reviewer also was thrilled by the performance, writing that "around at the Orpheum are two cowboys direct from the wooly West, who give us the most novel act ever seen here. One of the boys is adept with the lasso and the other an expert horseman, and in a pretty stage setting, representing a woods scene, they offer an act that is the most realistic production of real Western life of anything we have ever had. The cowboy of the stage with a lasso in each hand and then a Western horse, with his rider, gallops across and the cowboy catches the rider about the neck with the lasso while he has the horse lassoed about the four feet. The horse is a fine specimen of Western horses and he goes through antics with his rider on his back that prove the latter to be an expert horseman. All the while they are offering this decided novelty they have a patter that savors of Western sayings and Orpheum audience are enjoying their offering immensely." The Harrisburg *Patriot* simply said that "Will Rogers, cowboy and hunter from the great West, is this week giving Harrisburg the sensation of its life" (clippings, vaudeville scrapbook, CPpR; see also *NYDM,* 13 November 1909).

5. Betty Blake Rogers was evidently excited about this surprise for Rogers, for she wrote about it again in her 6 November and 9 November 1909 letters to Clement Vann Rogers. She ended up writing a personal check to the friendly manager of the Preston Hotel, who gave her cash in return to use to purchase Rogers's jewelry. "I signed the check Betty B. Rogers and felt awfully big too," she wrote her father-in-law, hiding the watch away for the anniversary on the twenty-fifth. She told Clement Vann Rogers to address her "next week at #560 West 113th St., New York, N.Y." (9 November 1909, OkClaW).

While Betty Blake Rogers was planning their anniversary celebration, Rogers played Proctor's Theatre Newark the week of 8–13 November 1909. The bill opened with Wentworth, Vesta and Teddy (Comedy acrobats introducing the champion of acrobatic dogs); Jas. P. Conlin and Lillian Steele (Fun at the Piano); and two motion pictures, *Fun with the Manikin* and *The Bogey Woman.* The bill continued with "America's Representative Character Comedienne," Gracie Emmett and Co. (In One Round of Continuous Laughter, *Mrs. Murphy's Second Husband,* with Gracie Emmett as Mrs. Honora Murphy, Nellie Collins as Bedilia Jenkins, Ben J. Mills as David Jenkins, and George F. Weber as Frederick J. Mawson); singer John McClosky; and

Flo Irwin and Co. (In George Ade's Farce, *Miss Peckman's Carouse,* By Arrangement with Kurt Eisfeldt, a play set in a western city of 25,000 inhabitants, during a Temperance revival, with Flo Irwin as Susan P. Peckham, a reformer; Tom Springer as Horace Peckham, a lawyer; Sidney Broughton [the company's manager] as Thomas Barrett, a man-about-town; Frankie Raymonde as Mrs. Barrett, a jealous wife; and R. V. Mallory as Henry, a law student). The bill continued with Howard and North (in *Those Were Happy Days*); and a new Gus Edwards act, Gus Edwards's Holland Heinies with Jane Priest and A Company of Ten (First Time on Any Stage, in a Dainty Dancing Comic Opera in One Act Entitled *The Goose Girl of Morken*), featuring musical numbers especially written for the act by Edwards: "My Holland Daisy," "Goosie," "Nobody Knows It But You and I" and the "Holland Heinies March." The players were Lorraine Lester, Josephine Dougherty, Loretta Moore, Adele Mason, Anita Moralles, LaVivian Brodrick, Louise Owen, Victor Foster, and Janet Priest in the lead, as the Goose Girl. The Gus Edwards play was followed by three more acts: Gertrude Mansfield (Song Reading); The Great Lester (The Accomplished Ventriloquist); and Rogers (The Cowboy and His Horse). Photographs of a vacationing Betty Blake Rogers were pasted all around the clipped playbill from Proctor's that Rogers saved in his scrapbook (Proctor's Newark Theatre playbill, and photographs of Betty Blake Rogers, vaudeville scrapbook, CPpR; see also *Variety,* 13 November 1909).

Rogers next played Loew's New Rochelle Theatre. He appeared in the fifth slot on the bill, after the Erretto Brothers, Juliet Wood, Keaner Brisco, and the Who Trio, and before Oscar Lorraine and the final act, Billie Burke (Loew's New Rochelle playbill, vaudeville scrapbook, CPpR).

Article from *Variety*
22 November 1909
New York, N.Y.

While vaudeville life was difficult for the performers on the road, it was also a harshly competitive business among the various booking offices and agents who elbowed each other for talent, and between the powerful controllers of the largest circuits and big theaters versus the small-time theater owners and operators. Shortly before his first wedding anniversary in 1909, Will Rogers found himself in the middle of a dispute stemming from one of these rivalries.

BREAK BETWEEN THE UNITED AND THE JOE WOOD OFFICES?

ACT BOOKED THROUGH THE LATTER "PULLED OUT," THE
WOOD HOUSE BEING DECLARED "OPPOSITION" BY
PROCTOR. KERNAN LEAVES A DEFI.

There have been various happenings in connection with the bookings by the United and Joe Wood which portended a discordant note. The agencies have been supposed to be in friendly affiliation.[1]

The most serious event occurred on Thursday of last week, when Will Rogers, the lariat thrower, was notified by the Proctor end of the United office that unless he canceled his engagement at Loew's Theatre, Elizabeth, N.J., forthwith, he (Rogers) would not play Proctor's, Albany, this week, as booked.[2] There is also a "Proctor's" at Elizabeth, playing the same style show as Loew's. The latter house belongs to the Loew Enterprises, which controls thirteen popular priced theatres in and about New York City, all booked through the Joe Wood agency.

Jos. Schenck, the general manager for Loew Enterprises, said on Monday to a Variety representative when questioned regarding his stand under the prevailing condition: "I have placed the matter before the United and am waiting for a reply. If our houses are declared 'opposition' by the United, I want to know it, not because we care, but I do not want to misinform acts. We can secure all the acts we want and don't intend to do an injustice to any who may care to play our circuit under the impression they can work the United time afterwards.

"We had some trouble in Elizabeth before with the Banda Roma, which Proctor took away from us. Mr. Rogers offered to play his engagement out, but I advised him to leave, he having opened at the Thursday matinee.

"Loew Enterprises will not submit to underhand methods, nor will it submit to the 'stealing of acts' from interests supposed to be friendly. If there is no satisfactory answer returned to us, we will notify Mr. Wood we will not stand for it, and if Mr. Wood cares to continue in his present relation, he will do so without our houses."

PD. Printed in *Variety*, 22 November 1909. Clipping, vaudeville scrapbook, CPpR.

1. In 1909 Joe Wood booked vaudeville acts as the head of the Metropolitan Vaudeville Exchange. He had some fifty "small-time theaters" in the New York—New Jersey area on his books, including the Imperial Theatre on 116th Street and Lenox Avenue, which was considered "an incubator for future headliners" (Laurie, *Vaudeville*, 240—41). At the same time, the UBO had thirty-two small-time houses on its books. In 1909 Joe Wood's business was taken over by Pat Casey (Rogers's agent), who booked the small-time theaters for the year ahead. His brother Dan Casey was made treasurer of the organization, while Joe Wood, stripped of most of his control of the business, acted as an agent. The business was then taken over again, this time by People's Vaudeville, headed by Joe Schenck, who booked the houses for Loew's.

Joe Wood was a legendary figure at the time for having built up what was called the "small-time" business in the first place. He began as a producer of novelty acts. He wrote the librettos and scores for his own productions and staged them himself. When he began booking the acts in addition to producing and writing them, he entered into a new career. He opened an office in the Sheridan Building and carried on his bookings in a semi-secret fashion to protect himself from bigger booking agencies that were interested in maintaining or expanding their monopolies. He became enormously successful, controlling bookings for some two thousand vaudeville acts and becoming known in the business for his uncanny skill in recognizing acts that would become future headliners and would move from the small-time onto the big-time circuit. It was his success that did him in, bringing about what one contemporary described as his "dethroning." After his rather audacious move into the same building that housed the UBO, his prosperity became impossible for the bigwigs in the industry to ignore, and his enterprise was taken over. After losing his agency, Wood started again with just a few acts. By 1910 he was busy rebuilding his business (Grau, *Business Man in the Amusement World*, 95–96).

2. When Rogers signed the contract with F. F. Proctor's Amusement Enterprises in New York on 10 August 1909, he agreed to appear at Proctor's Newark Theatre on 8 November 1909 and at Proctor's Albany Theatre on 22 November 1909 at a rate of $250 per week, with a portion of that sum going to the UBO. He was booked with B. F. Keith Theatre Co. of Boston, E. F. Albee and S. K. Hodgdon, managers, for a two-a-day Boston appearance the week of 29 November. Five percent of that booking went to his agent, Pat Casey, and the same percentage to the UBO (vaudeville contracts, 10 August 1909, OkClaW).

Betty Blake Rogers to Clement Vann Rogers
27 November 1909
Albany, N.Y.

Saturday

My dear Mr Rogers—

I came up here[1] Thursday to eat Thanksgiving dinner & celebrate our wedding anniversary. Billy and I had a big turkey dinner in our room & we so enjoyed it— We have been married just one year and a mighty happy year it has been. I go back to New York Sunday & Billy goes to Boston[2]— He will come to New York the following Sunday— I will write you next week from New York.[3] Lots of love

Betty

Address
#560 West 113th st.,
 New York
 N.Y.

ALS, rc. OkClaW. On Kenmore Oaks Hotel Co., J. A. Oaks, Pres. and Treas., Albany, N.Y., letterhead.

1. Rogers played at Proctor's Albany Theatre Thanksgiving week, beginning 22 November 1909. Appearing on the same bill were The Hickman Brothers and Co. (Paul and Harry Hickman, with Retta Merrill, presenting *A Detective Detected*); Hilda Hawthorne and Johnny; John P. Wade and Co. (again doing their standard skit, *Marse Shelby's Chicken Dinner*); Peter Donald and Meta Carson (The Scotch Comedian and His Bonnie Lassie, Presenting *Alex McLean's Dream*, with Peter Donald as McLean, on his way from the Scotch Ball, and singing his own songs "I'm Gettin' Se Daft about Mary" and "My Heart Aye Wams tae the Tartan"; Meta Carson as both Mrs. McLean and an old sweetheart of McLean's; and Dinna Kent as a Policeman). The play was

followed by Pianologue Artist Augusta Glose (Songs! Incidents! Wit! Delight! Music! Distinctly Classy!); Swan and O'Day (Blackface Comedians and Dancers); and Fred Walton (the renowned pantomimist) and Co. (In a new comedy entitled *Ballo-in-Maschera,* with Rene Doret as the Lady in Black, Raymond Lymora as the Cavalier, George Selby as the Attendant, and Fred Walton as Pierrot, with Mr. Baker at the piano). Rogers closed, billed as The Cowboy and His Horse (Proctor's Theatre, Albany, playbill, vaudeville scrapbook, CPpR; see also *NYDM,* 4 December 1909).

2. The next stop for Rogers and McKee was Keith's Theatre in Boston. Things did not go very well with the overall bill. The line-up started off without "any enthusiasm" from the audience for The Three Donals, who were acrobats. They were followed by Browning and Lavan in the sketch *The Recruiting Officer,* which flopped badly in the afternoon performance on opening day but did better in the evening. Benjamin Chapin and his company did *At the White House,* a reworking of an old act that failed to arouse much interest from the audience. Then came Doherty and Harlowe, who did better than their predecessors, but were in a "hard spot" and "hardly strong enough to lift the lump in this bill." After Doherty and Harlowe had lightened things a bit, Rogers did his act. Coming on at 3:10 P.M. in a show that began at 1:43, he worked for ten minutes with a full stage. "Rogers held the interest in very good shape this afternoon," wrote the Keith reviewer, "and his talk livened up matters a bit and got quite a few laughs." Rogers, who came uncharacteristically in the middle of the bill, was followed by four more acts: French burlesque singer Albert Chevalier; Beatrice Ingram (in the sketch *The Duchess*); Lillian Shaw (with new and good "stuff"); and The Tasmanian Van Dieman Troupe (six women acrobats, who provided "a splendid picturesque closing act"). The kinetograph for the afternoon was *Quaker City Auto Races,* which the reviewer found "exciting" (Manager's Report, Keith's Theatre, Boston, 29 November 1909, KAC-IaU; see also *NYDM,* 4 December 1909).

3. Will Rogers wrote to Clement Vann Rogers from New York on 10 December 1909 to say that he and Betty had not heard from him for "several days— and we have not written either cause Betty has been sick for a week in bed but is getting O.K. now and will be out by tomorrow I think I am working over in Brooklyn this week and also next week then I play in New York the week of Christmas." He told his father that the people he and Betty were boarding with on West 113th Street were from Muskogee, and asked if Buck Sunday, who was managing the Rogers farm back in Oklahoma, had sold the corn yet (OkClaW).

Rogers played Hammerstein's Victoria, at 42nd Street and Broadway, Christmas week, 20—25 December 1909. The playbill was Hearn and Rutter (Singers and Dancers); Wallace Galvin (And His Hands); Farrell-Taylor Trio (Presenting Their Comedy Musical Skit, entitled *The Minstrel Man*); Stepp, Mehlinger and King (Vaudeville's Cleverest Entertainers); Valeska Suratt and Co. (Presenting the Parisian Playlet, *The Belle of the Boulevards*); Barrows-Lancaster and Co. (In the Dramatic Farce, *Tactics,* revised by Margaret Mayo); Avery and Hart (Colored Comedians); and Will Rogers (The World's Greatest Lariat Thrower) (Hammerstein's Victoria, New York, playbill, vaudeville scrapbook, CPpR; *NYT,* 19–26 December 1909).

Will Rogers's Real Estate Statement
ca. 1909
Claremore, Okla.

Despite his wanderlust, Will Rogers maintained a long-lasting claim to Oklahoma as home. Like his father, who held rental properties and owned a business in Claremore as well as the old ranchlands outside Oologah, Rogers invested in local real estate. His small savings income came from the modest rents his father collected for him from tenants on family land. These funds were deposited in the First National Bank of Claremore, which Clement Vann Rogers helped to found and direct. During most of his vaudeville years, Rogers assumed that show business would be a temporary livelihood and that as he grew older, he would return to ranching. Early in their marriage, he and Betty Blake Rogers talked about returning to Claremore, establishing a ranch there, and living near his family members and old friends, and not far from her relations and acquaintances in Arkansas. In 1911 Rogers purchased acreage outside Claremore where he intended to build a future ranch home.[1] After his father died, Rogers accumulated additional family acreage near his Oologah birthplace.[2] Rogers's entertainment career continued to flourish, however, and he never returned to Oklahoma to live. The Rogerses established permanent residence elsewhere—first in New York, where they lived while he worked in vaudeville and in the Ziegfeld Follies, and then in southern California, where he worked in films. Even after moving to California, he never abandoned the idea of retiring or developing a regular second ranch home on his Oklahoma property. Upon his untimely death, and at Betty Blake Rogers's wish, his land on the outskirts of Claremore became holdings of the Will Rogers Memorial. The family home and ranchland where Will and Betty lived in Pacific Palisades, California, meanwhile, became the site of the Will Rogers State Park.

AD, rc. OkClaW.

1. Rogers had earlier purchased real estate outside New York. On 1 July 1908 he bought land in Suffolk and Nassau Counties, Long Island, N.Y. (list of papers belonging to William P. Rogers in tin box to be delivered to John T. McSpadden and held by him, OkClaW). He and Betty Blake Rogers established a home on Long Island and lived there during his *Follies* years.
2. See introduction to part two, above.

STATEMENT OF WILLIE ROGERS
ROGERS CO. TAX [for] YEAR 1909

	Lot	Block	Value	Tax	
Claremore City	1	66	800	34	00
West 53 ft	2	66	400	17	00
	7	66	150	6	38
	8	66	1200	51	00
				$108	38

	Acres	Sec	Twp	Range		
Sw ne Se. and North 20 acres Lot 4	30	24	23	15	3	96
Se 10 acres Lot 10, S 9.60 Lot 9	1,9.6	18	23	16	5	15
Sw 10.07 acres lot 108 Se 10 acres lot 5	20.07	18	23	16	5	28
Se 10 acres lot 11 Sw 10.06 acres lot 11	20.06	18	23	16	5	28
Lot 4 and North half Ne Sw	69 93	18	23	16	18	48
Lot 3 and Se 9 20 acres Lot 5	49.24	18	23	16	13	01
W et. 20 acres lot 5 and lot 9	59.81	18	23	16	15	79
S [illeg] Sw & Lot 8	31 34	18	23	16	8	27
Lots 10-12 and 14	73 37	18	23	16	19	36
Please return this statement with remittance				Total	202	96

To Frederick Hawley
ca. 7 February 1910
Rochester, N.Y.

HELLO GANG[1]—

Say, where do you Rabbit Tracking Punks come in to be playing again at a regular theater so quick? Is that house going to the pups, or what? You all ought to be threshing corn or digging wheat.

I wouldn't ever write to you or speak to you, only I want *something*. Where were you rums when I was at the Bronx and Greenpoint?[2] You showed up just about like I got forty weeks booked. Nothing, no.

Say, I want that big pair of spurs, the ones with the jinglebobs on them, the ones you don't wear. I want to try out a bum imitation of Fred Stone in his rope dance and want big gads for it. (I may only use them one show 'cause some one will shoot me.) But I got some stuff framed up and might get away with it. If it's any good I will order a pair and return yours or buy them. If not, I will return them. I will practice on it till I play Phila. in three weeks and pull it there, as they have played there.[3] Now express them up here C.O.D., P.D.Q., or there will be a new Greaser wanted in the Madam's act. (Get that. Her Act?)

I took your lousy suggestion and got a black drop and I guess it does help, although I haven't had my salary raised more than twice since I had it. I tell everybody that it was your idea (as I don't want the blame myself). I hope I run on to you grave fliggers some time, but I am halfway decent since I left you.

I am this week here at a *regular* theater.[4] The stage is so big I am working in one.

Well, Idiot Caviar say. I want to buy the little 41 gun of yours. What will you take for it? I am going to either turn booking agent or train robber one.

Well, I must stop. I can't spend all my time writing to you cornfield canaries. Good night.

WILL ROGERS

Temple, Rochester, N.Y.

Next week Johnstown, then Cleveland Phila. three weeks Poli, then open from Hell to Harlem.

I do want to buy the gun sure enough.

PD. Printed in *American Musician*, 7 February 1910. Clipping, vaudeville scrapbook, CPpR.

1. Rogers's letter was reprinted in the "Rubs" column with the following introduction: "Frederick Hawley and Will Rogers, who are well known in the vaudeville world, are having quite a time these days corresponding. Fred Hawley has been advising Will Rogers lately how his act should be presented. The result of which is the following letter, which is so typical of Rogers that I take delight in publishing same." Rogers addressed the letter to "The Bandit, E. Frederick Hawley, Long Acre Building, New York City."

2. Rogers had begun the year in Norfolk, Va., at the Colonial Theatre, where, as *Variety* reported, he closed "with a whirl" (*Variety*, 8 January 1910). The Colonial was managed by W. T. Kirby for the UBO. Rogers was joined on the Norfolk bill by Charlie Nevins and Lydia Arnold (in *Little Miss Manicure*); operatic artists J. K. Murray and Clara Lane (In their New Singing and Comedy Sketch, *A Quiet Honeymoon* by Donney and Willard); Conlin, Steele and Carr (Funmakers); conjurer Imro Fox (The Original Comic Conjurer and Deceptionist Producing His Latest Problem, *Asrah*, A Lady Defying the Laws of Gravitation); Hal Davis and Inez McCauley (Presenting *The Unexpected*); Six American Dancers (an act with three men and three women). Rogers, who came last, was a hit; one local reviewer called him a "wonder" who had the crowds flocking to the theater. The show was brought to the Colonial by MacDonald's Dairy Lunches: "All over Norfolk for Men only." Cartoonist J. E. Williamson drew sketches of all the acts on the bill, including one of Rogers, McKee, and Teddy, with Rogers handling lariats simultaneously in both hands, one encircling McKee's head and the other Teddy's (Colonial Theatre, Norfolk, playbill and Norfolk clippings, vaudeville scrapbook, CPpR).

Rogers returned to New York from Virginia to play at Percy G. Williams's Bronx Theatre, which was part of the Orpheum chain. He appeared there with Jeters and Rogers (Comedy Skaters); A. O. Duncan (America's Best Ventriloquist); the Leonard's and Anderson Co. (in *When Caesar C's Her,* A Satire on Bernard Shaw's *Caesar and Cleopatra*); the Long Acre Quartette (Vaudeville's Popular Singers); Joseph Hart's *Futurity Winner;* singer Carrie De Mar (Whom Joseph Hart Presents in a Series of New and original Songs, including "Nobody's Satisfied," and Her Success of Two Continents, "Lonesome Flossie"); and Willard Simms and Co. (in *Flanders' Furnished Flat*). Rogers came at the end of the bill, as The Champion Lasso Expert. A local reviewer joked that Percy Williams had been lax in planning the facilities at the Bronx Theatre—he should have included stalls, since there were three horses on the bill (Teddy and two other horses that appeared in Hart's racetrack playlet, *The Futurity Winner*). Williams quipped that "if they are going to make a stable out of his theatre then he will have to serve oats at intermission" (Bronx Theatre playbill and unidentified clipping, vaudeville scrapbook, CPpR; see also *NYDM*, 22 January 1910).

The Greenpoint in New York was the next stop for Rogers in mid-January 1910 (*Variety*, 15 January 1910).

3. Rogers was booked for Philadelphia for the week of 28 February (see Manager's Report, Keith's Philadelphia Theatre, 28 February 1910, below).

4. Rogers played Young's Pier Theatre, Rochester, N.Y., where W. E. Shackelford was manager, at the end of January 1910 and was in Detroit at the Temple Theatre the first week of February. He was at the Temple Theatre in Rochester the following week (week of 7 February 1910), from which place he wrote the letter to Hawley.

Rogers played Young's Pier Theatre (High-Class Vaudeville under Direction of Ben Harris) the week of 24 January in the third spot on the program. He came after Otis Harlan's act and J. K. Murray and Clara Lane (in the Delightful Musical Comedy

Sketch Entitled in *A Quiet Honeymoon,* by Downey and Willard). He was followed by Gillahan and Murray; Miss Sydney Shields and Co. (in the Interesting Comedy Sketch, *Broadway USA,* by Allen Gregory Miller, set in the Law Office of Bruce and Co., England, with Hudson Allan as Robert Greenwood, An American; Maurice Barrett as Bruce, an English Barrister; and Miss Shields as Mildred Hampton, an English girl); Miss Billie Seaton (Breezy Singer of Breezy Songs); and Musical Gracey (Presenting Original Novelties, Including His Latest Invention, the *Musical Mission Lamps*). A clipping of a review of the performance reported that Rogers "has a lot of new talk that keeps his audiences laughing all during his act. When he impersonates George Cohan, doing a dance while whirling the lasso, he makes a big hit, and ends his act throwing a forty-foot lasson while on horseback" (Young's Pier Theatre, Rochester, N.Y., playbill and unidentified Atlantic City clipping, vaudeville scrapbook, CPpR).

At Detroit's Temple Theatre, Rogers was back in his accustomed last slot on the playbill, preceded by The Three Nevaros (Original Equilibrists in a Pantomimic Novelty); Cadets de Gascogyne (High-Class Vocalists); Jack Horton and Mlle. La Triska (The Clown and the Human Doll); Eleanor Gordon and Co. (Including Joseph Sullivan in *Tips on Taps*); Lou Anger (The German Soldier); Edwin Stevens (Creator of the title role in *The Devil,* Assisted by Miss Tina Marshall in *An Evening with Dickens*); and Charlie Case (Funniest of All Monologists, With More Stories of His Father). A clipping Rogers saved reported that Edwin Stevens was "an actor in the best sense. He sits at a table in full view of his audience and, with a few make-up touches, a wig and an attitude incarnates himself into a flesh and blood Dickens creation. . . . Next in honor on the program comes Will Rogers, real cowboy from out of the west, who delights the eye and makes the blood flow a bit faster with his splendid lassoing, the picture being much helped by the beautiful pony which, with its rider, is so often caught in the unerring lasso" (Detroit Temple Theatre playbill and clipping, vaudeville scrapbook, CPpR).

Rogers played at the Rochester Temple Theatre the week of 7 February 1910. He appeared in the fourth slot, after Rosaire and Doreto (The Captain and the Sailor); The Reiff Brothers and Miss Murray (Smart Singing and Dancing Offering); and Horton and La Triska (The Clown and the Human Doll). He was followed by the Cadets De Gascogyne (Stellar Singing Act); Edwin Stevens and Tina Marshall (in *An Evening with Dickens*); Harry B. Lester (Monologist and Singer); and Annette Kellermann (The Celebrated Water Witch, The Diving Venus). The show closed with the showing of a templescope, custom film footage described as "a series of magnificent clearness" in promotional material. A local reviewer writing in the *Post Express* praised Teddy's wonderful intelligence and questioned the authenticity of Rogers's southern drawl (Rochester Temple Theatre, playbill and clipping, vaudeville scrapbook, CPpR).

Article from Will Rogers's Scrapbook
ca. 21 February 1910
Cleveland, Ohio

WILL ROGERS TELLS CLEVELAND LADS HOW TO ROPE THE FEROCIOUS LONG-EAR

EXPERT APPEARING AT HIPPODROME[1] OFFERS PRACTICAL POINTERS ON PITCHING AND SWINGING THE LOOP
(By Victor Slayton)

Here are some hints on the gentle art of roping steers, intended for the pleasure of Cleveland lads. Of course, this is not the time of year to play cowboy. The season doesn't really open until the summer's first wild west show has come and gone. But information, like livestock, has to be caught while it's going. Goodness knows where Will Rogers will be when the grass begins to sprout. So we might as well ask him while we can and file his answers away for seasonable reference.

Rogers has been appearing this week at the Hippodrome, where he is on the program as a "cowboy lariat thrower." That language, it may be explained, is such as no self-respecting cow puncher would use, except in jest. A cow hand may be peeler or a war hawk or any one of a number of things, but he'd have to be feeling merry indeed to call himself a cowboy. As for lariat, that would be an awful word to spring in the cow country. A rope's a rope, the same as a pigging string is a pigging string, and you might as well call it a lasso as a lariat, if you wish the real cattle person to deem you an untutored upstart.

As we were saying, Will Rogers does some wonderful roping at the Hippodrome, with the able assistance of Teddy, the most rope-broke horse in captivity, and Buck McKee, a raven-haired and well-developed son of the west, after whom the bad man in the "Round-Up" was named.[2] These practical pointers on roping are authoritative, being related by Rogers to your Uncle Dudley, who tried his own unpracticed hand at roping the wild ones some years ago—but cautiously picked out the young ones.

Your rope can be almost anything that's heavy enough. About 30 feet of half-inch manila used to be the happy thought in New Mexico. For play purposes, 3-8 or even 1-4-inch rope will be found plenty large, and 20 feet long enough. For that matter, the same length of heavy sash cord would be pretty sure to hold anything the boys can catch anywhere around here except out Clark avenue way. Moreover, woven sash rope is pleasanter to the touch, manila rope having whiskers. Which is one reason why cow punchers wear gloves.

At one end of your rope tie your hondo (phonetic spelling.) That means a hard and fast loop two or three inches in diameter. Your father can show you, if he goes fishing. If he's a yachtsman, make him show you an eye splice. This little rope ring is sometimes bound with rawhide, or fitted with a metal thimble, (also called a hondo), to give it weight, but this is unnecessary. Run the other end of your rope through the ring and you're ready to rope something.

The simplest throw is the pitch, used in roping on foot, as in catching horses in a corral, where swinging a loop around the head would cause the herd to take fright and mill. In pitching a rope the loop is carefully laid out on the ground behind the roper and trailed along as he advances on his prey. As in every sort of throw, the loop should be caught in the right hand about 18 inches from the hondo and the single part of the rope with it, so that two thicknesses of rope are in the hand and the hondo hangs down from the right or thumb side of the hand. The part of the rope not needed for the loop is coiled and held loosely in the left hand.

In preparing to pitch the loop see that it lies fairly on the ground, untwisted and open. Then, as the pony you mean to catch dashes by, cast the loop with a quick jerk that will cause it to open just in time for the horse to stick his head in it. Unlike most throws, this pitching thing is really easier to do than to tell about.

In roping from horseback the pitch of course is impossible. The puncher falls in behind his prey, riding fast enough to keep within throwing distance, takes down his rope from the thong in which it has hung coiled at the right of his saddle horn, jerks out a loop and swings it around his head. The swing is usually from right to left—clockwise, the manual training teacher might call it—only, of course, it swings in a horizontal plane. When the loop becomes large enough and the moment is propitious, the rope is hurled with considerable force at the beef critter's horns or head or feet, as the case may be, making due allowance for the animal's speed.

There's a peculiar twist of the wrist required to keep the loop open during the swing, but it's easily acquired. It's absolutely necessary to keep the loop open and untwisted, however, for no catch can be made with a fouled loop. The loop can be large or small according to taste; it's considered modest to swing a small one. But it should be several feet long to go with.

These are the principal throws and with them various feats of fore-footing and "busting" can be accomplished. Then there's the Hooley Ann (another phonetic spelling), which is a tricky pitch, the loop being laid out in front of the roper and jerked back with a swing behind the head and a back-handed cast. Then there are no end of fancy movements, known in various parts of the cow country by various names, such as the Johnny Booker [Blocker] and the three-days-in-Mexico.

It's too bad that space doesn't permit telling the boys about the big roping and tying contests they still have in the west; about McGonigle and Carroll, the champions; about Rogers' early appearances at the St. Louis fairs; how he went with the Mullhall show to New York five years ago and, instead of going back to Oklahoma with the outfit, stayed and went into vaudeville. It would be a pleasure to tell how he and a side partner went to South America to show the native riders and ropers up and were themselves shown up by the gauchos, but maybe that wouldn't be kind.

PD. Clipping, ca. 21 February 1910, vaudeville scrapbook, CPpR.

1. Keith's Hippodrome was the largest and most popular vaudeville theater in Cleveland with a capacity of about 3,500. The theater, which was designed by the firm Knox and Elliott, was dedicated on 30 December 1907. It opened with fanfare in early 1908. A *Variety* reported described the theater: "a palace for any city; for Cleveland it's a wonder, with a seating capacity of 4,100; a width of 130 feet, and a depth of 220 feet" (*Variety*, 4 January 1908). The theater was on the ground floor of two office buildings. Two entrances led to the auditorium, one on Euclid Avenue, the other on Prospect Street. A key midwestern theater in the Keith-Albee chain, the Hippodrome presented acts arranged by the UBO. With a huge stage, it was built to accommodate all types of entertainment, from opera to the circus. Like its New York counterpart, it had a 455,000-gallon water tank in front of the stage for spectacular water acts. The theater had a tracked ramp leading to the stage that provided easy access for horses and other large animals. The Hippodrome advertised 1,500 seats at 25 cents for the daily matinee. Around 1930 the theater was redesigned by Thomas Lamb, and eventually it became a movie theater. Its last performance was a double feature on 2 May 1980 with fewer than sixty people in the audience. The theater and its two buildings were demolished by early 1981, and its artifacts were sold before its razing (Fowler, "Hippodromes," 20; *GHNTD*, 541; *JCGHTG*, 70; scrapbook A-3, OkClaW).

2. *The Round Up* was a western drama in four acts by Edna Day. It was produced by Klaw and Erlanger in New York at the New Amsterdam Theatre in 1907 and traveled to other venues in 1908 (Mantle and Sherwood, eds., *Best Plays of 1899–1909*, 542).

Manager's Report, Keith's Hippodrome
21 February 1910
Cleveland, Ohio
KEITH'S HIPPODROME

Feb 21 at 1910
Cleveland, Ohio.

GALETTI'S BABOONS.[1] Did not appear.

5 MUSICAL MAC LARENS. Time 11. Open F.S. palace, close in 1. 4 young women, 1 man. They play a number of instruments well. They wear kilties and close with a well executed Highland fling and jig. Generally pleasing.

MAKARENKO TROUPE.[2] Time 15. F.S. Garden. 3 women, 5 men. Gorgeously costumed. They open with what I imagine is the Russian edition of Grand Opera. It sounds well and gets much applause. They finish with some great wild dancing which took very well all over the house. First class in every particular.

MIGNONETTE KOKIN.[3] Did not appear.

MADDEN & FITZ PATRICK CO. 2 men. C.D.F.[4] Time 28. "The Turn of The Tide." A good comedy sketch ending with a pathetic touch. It gives apt opportunity for a vocal solo and piano playing, both of which are interpolated neatly.

SPISSELL BROS & CO.[5] Time 11. F.S. Spec. 3 men, 1 woman. Pantomime and acrobatic comedy. High class material for the line. Laughs frequent.

VALERIE BERGERE & CO.[6] Time 25. "The Sultan's Favorite." Special F.S. 3 women, 2 men. Bergere is a great favorite here and hence was greeted with advance applause and encouragement throughout. The sketch is very light and farcical and in my opinion does not give Miss Bergere a chance to display her well known ability to advantage. The theme is novel and the setting highly attractive.

LEW HAWKINS.[7] In 1. Time 16. Black face monologist with some songs. Generally poor with one or two bright moments.

WILL ROGERS. F[ull].S[tage]. woods. Time 10. Male assistant horseback rider. Rogers is an expert lariat manipulator. He has an odd line of comedy conversation that fits in well with his work. He was a hit.

HIPPOGRAPH.

Ned Hastings.[8]

TD. KAC-IaU.

1. Galetti's Baboons was one of several primate acts current on the circuits. The baboons rode cycles and did acrobatic tricks. Other primate acts included Wormwood's Monkeys, Alleina's Monkeys, and Jean Clairemont's Circus Monkeys. Animal trainer Frederick Galetti headed Galetti's Baboons, and his wife, Mignonette Kokin, was regularly booked along with the Galetti act for the same bills. The collaboration was not without incident. Once one of her husband's baboons injured Kokin, and she had to be hospitalized for two weeks (*EV*, 14; *Indianapolis Star*, 27 February 1908).

2. The Makarenko Troupe—Daniel, Julia, and Zara—adapted Russian folk songs and dances for the stage, including "whirlwind Cossack dances" and "weird Siberian folk songs." They were new to Cleveland audiences (Keith's Hippodrome, Cleveland, playbill, vaudeville scrapbook, CPpR; Locke env. 1249, NN-L-RLC).

3. Toe dancer and singer Mignonette Kokin did impersonations of English, French, Russian, and Scottish characters in song and dance, using several costume and character changes in her act. She worked both the Proctor and Keith Circuits and was

a favorite in San Francisco, as well as in English and Australian music halls. One of her trademark gimmicks was using a camera to show the audience film of her quick changes with her maid and dresser in her dressing room between the separate parts of her performance. "Miss Kokin does all neatly and costumes them with a novel touch by moving pictures showing the detail of her costume changes," reported a reviewer. "Characteristic dances done in her neat style close each imitation. It is a pleasing act" (*Cincinnati Inquirer,* 2 March 1908; see also *Broadway Magazine,* 1 December 1900; Los Angeles *Examiner,* 31 December 1912; *Pittsburgh Post,* 26 November 1907; San Francisco *Call and Post,* 28 October 1915; *Toledo Blade,* 10 September 1907; *Variety,* 14 December 1907; Locke env. 1060, NN-L-RLC).

4. "C.D.F." or "Centre Door Fancy," refers to a type of set needed for the act, namely box-shaped scenery that was called "fancy" because of its elaborately decorated arch (Page, *Writing for Vaudeville,* 46).

5. The three Spissell Brothers, headed by John and Frank, were comedy acrobats who worked their highly physical Three Stooges—style slapstick routines into comic-dramatic skits. They performed with Jennie Mack as the Spissell Brothers and Mack from 1907 to 1912, with bookings both in Europe and the United States. Frank Spissell appeared in the act in full clown costume, while the other brothers wore street clothes and amusing hairdos, and Jennie Mack was the straight person, specializing in different dialects and accents. Publicity shots for the team included such gags as the photograph used by the UBO in 1908, showing a pier full of vaudevillians waving goodbye to the three Spissells, with Frank fully costumed and made up as a clown, as they rowed a tiny rowboat out to sea. The caption announced the act's departure for a vaudeville tour in Europe.

Most of the Spissell acts were a take-off on their successful romp *The Continental Waiter,* which they performed at the Cleveland Hippodrome. It was an eleven-minute, full-stage performance that started out in semi-serious fashion with a handsomely dressed young German man (one of the Spissells) and woman (Jennie Mack) sitting down to an elegant meal. The waiter comes out to serve them but becomes entangled with a hatrack, whereupon a "drunk takes his place at an adjoining table and becomes involved in more funny acrobatic nonsense with the waiter. The service of a meal to the German and girl works up to a general roughhouse, the waiter being the mainstay of the comedy." Between the drunk, the waiter, and the elegant European, a "break-neck speed of knockabout and startling falls" begins, and soon pandemonium strikes the restaurant, complete with tumbling runs and pratfalls that destroy the props. The act was a big hit. The Spissell Brothers and Mack *Cafe de Paris* number, also performed in 1910, was very similar. The *Pittsburgh Leader* of 7 August 1910 reported that the "Spissell Brothers and Mack are comedians first and acrobats afterwards. Their comedy is not entirely silent nor is it altogether of the knockout variety. The quartet of them, one member of which is a dainty, dashing gazelle, make the 'Cafe de Paris' a lively little skit." They used humorous makeup and did some spoken word and some mimicry. Mack was described as "a pretty and sprightly comedienne who, while the three acrobatic comedians are indulging in eccentricities, is making the ludicrous accompaniment noises which accentuates the comedy. Her hands and feet are kept busy ringing a bell here, blowing whistle there, inflating a fog horn bellows, simulating a screech owl, fabricating a steamboat warning, turning a huge police rattler to imitate the effect of a man falling downstairs, shaking a box filled with broken glass to make the sound of a sudden crash and in diverse and sundry other ways contriving to produce a din and hubbub that add materially to the ridiculousness of the situations."

The Spissell brothers also performed without Mack as Spissell, Spissell, and Spissell, and in 1911 they began appearing as Frank Spissell and Co. Frank Spissell died in Plainfield, N.J., in August 1912, a few days after becoming ill during a performance at the Majestic theater in Chicago (*Variety*, 14 December 1907, 27 June and 15 August 1908, 2 October 1909, 2 August 1912; Locke env. 2131, NN-L-RLC).

6. Valerie Bergere (1872–1938) was a French actress who made her American debut in a San Francisco stock company in 1892. She appeared in *On the Bowery* (1894), *Madam Butterfly* (1901), *The Great Ruby* (1901), *Billie's First Love* (1903), *The Red Mouse* (1903), and *His Japanese Wife* (1904). She worked as a vaudeville and musical comedy actress for over forty years and also appeared in films. Her last stage appearance was in *Moon over Mulberry Street* in 1935, and her last film was *Miss America* for RKO in 1937 (*VO*, 2:21 September 1938). The Hippodrome playbill described her as "vaudeville's favorite actress" (vaudeville scrapbook, CPpR).

7. Blackface comic star Lew Hawkins (1865–1931) was a veteran of vaudeville. He was called an "oldtime minstrel favorite" in a Keith press release of 6 January 1913 and was typically billed as the "Chesterfield of Minstrelsy." Hawkins began as a clog and jig dancer in San Francisco in 1872, going on stage when he was still a boy. He teamed with J. W. Kelly, who was known as the "rolling mill man." They first performed in Chicago. In 1884 he teamed with Ben Collins to form one of the standard blackface acts of vaudeville. The team ended with Collins's death in 1893. In his single act Hawkins specialized in song parodies. The *Rochester Post Express* of 1 April 1913 reported that he made "rhyming songs and stories out of the names of automobiles, popular magazines, a deck of cards, etc." The *Peoria Journal* of 24 April 1912 praised Hawkins because his humor was clean: "he has learned that smutty or risque fun is not what true Americans are demanding. Accordingly his patter is clean and wholesome and ridiculously funny." Hawkins suffered severe bouts of ill health in 1912 and 1914, but recovered and returned to the stage. He was still performing in 1916. Hawkins was quoted in an interview as saying that "minstrelsy has disappeared because of the high cost of living. . . . That's why the day of the minstrel entertainment is no more." He pointed to high salaries that prevented agents from getting group acts together as the main cause of minstrelsy's decline. He retired in Benton Harbor, Mich., where he died 18 January 1931 (*Variety*, 26 February 1910; *VO*, 2:21 January 1931; Locke env. 649, NN-L-RLC).

8. Ned Hastings (1888–1969) was manager of the Keith Circuit Midwest theaters from 1906 to 1928. He was a Harvard University track star and graduated in the class of 1905. After college he worked as a *Cleveland Press* reporter and press agent for the Prospect Theatre in Cleveland. When the theater burned down in 1908, he moved on to work in theaters in Indianapolis and in Louisville, Ky. He was based at Keith's theater in Cincinnati from 1916 to 1928. After the demise of vaudeville, he became the public relations director of the Cincinnati Zoo and held that post until his retirement in June 1961 (*Variety*, 16 January 1969).

Manager's Report, Keith's Philadelphia Theatre
28 February 1910
Philadelphia, Pa.

PHILADELPHIA SHOW.

FEB. 28–1910

MARCEL & BORIS. 9 Min. F.S. This is a very versatile act. The man works with two boys, both of whom are skilled hand-balancers, tumblers and jugglers, and one of them is an exceptional musician with the mandolin and violin, the latter mainly trick work which got a good hand. Some of the feats were absolutely unique, never having been seen here before and winning strong applause. Starts off the show very well.

JOHN BIRCH. 12 min. in one. This is well known on the circus. Gave his characteristic melodrama number with the aid of various hats, closing with a shower of hats from the flies. Fair applause.

CHAS. B. LAWLOR[1] & DAUGHTERS. 20 min. F.S., close in one. Good advance hand. Have a lot of very original songs which they offer with four changes of costume. The two girls sing quite well and make a pretty stage picture. Good applause for each selection and fairly good close.

EVA FAY. First Part. 19 min. F.S. Performed this part of her act after the regulation manner, being tied in a chair and covered with a velvet cabinet. Received fair applause. Mrs. Fay is a pretty woman and has a pleasing personality which goes a great ways to popularize her act.

WILL ROGERS. 12 min. F.S. Well known on the circuit. Advance applause showing that he is quite a favorite here. Did his regulation stunts and introduced his usual comedy. Always a thoroughly good act for us.[2]

CARSON & WILLARD. 14 min. in one. Same act as presented here before, with some variations. The parodies were strongly applauded and the "Salome" finish got a very strong hand.

"HOLLAND HEINIES." 20 min. F.S., close in one. Miss Priest is the feature in this act. Songs are fair and somewhat reminiscent of Edwards' "School Days" songs and situations. Fair applause after each selection. Stage setting good and all told the act will pull up stronger with more appreciative houses than we had today which was the limit for listlessness and preoccupation owing partly to the dismal weather and partly to the strike situation.

EVA FAY. 19 Min. F.S. Second Part. Miss Fay is blindfolded and covered with a veil and answers questions after the well known method. Has a fine strong voice and refined personality. Received many laughs for her jokes and evidently had the audience mystified and interested throughout. Closed well.

STUART BARNES.[3] 20 min. in one. Advance applause. Good line of monologue and some new and fetching songs. Considerable laughter and applause
throughout and a good finish. Barnes is a favorite here and always holds this
spot with credit.

FOUR LUKENS. 3 Min. F.S. Typical high-bar casting act, very skilful and at
times thrilling. Received advance applause and a good hand after each one of
their feats. Makes an excellent [c]loser for any show.

KINETOGRAPH. "In India." Interesting travel film, colored. "Two Chums
Looking For Wives." Usual comedy. Kinetograph series quite up to the standard.

GENERAL REMARKS. This is a good all-round bill and should play well for
the balance of the week without shifting. Very hard audience today, everybody
seeming to be overawed by the strike which threatens to assume even more
serious proportions and keeps everybody guessing.

C. E. BARNS.

TD. KAC-IaU.

1. Charles B. Lawlor (1852–1925) was best known as the songwriter of the popular song *The Sidewalks of New York*. Born in Dublin, Lawlor immigrated to the United
States in his twenties and became a U.S. citizen in 1884. He began his career as a
church concert soloist and opera singer. In 1887 he moved to New York and began
writing songs for his own vaudeville act and for other performers. He often collaborated with James Blake (no relation to Betty Blake Rogers's family). His other well-known
songs included *Irish Liberty* and *Pretty Peggy* (*AmSCAP*, 423–24; *NYT*, 1 June 1925).
2. Rogers went from Philadelphia to Springfield, Mass., where he played last in the
lineup at Poli's theater, with Suzanne Rocamora (Presenting a Repertoire of Songs);
Ward, Clare, and Ward (in *The Twin Flats* by Searl Allen); Paul Quinn and Joe Mitchel
(Presenting Their Own One-Act Comedy, *The Lemon City Land Agent*); and the Seven
Laskys's Imperial Musicians (Vaudeville's Greatest Musical Act, Messrs. Weingetz,
Armstrong, Harvey, Wilson, Storey, Hadded and Cohen). The local *Springfield Daily
News* said Rogers looked "as though he stepped out of the ochre covers of 'Deadwood
Dick's Last Shot,'" while another reviewer found Teddy to be "one of the most lov-
able chaps that ever walked the boards at Poli's" (Poli's Springfield playbill and clip-
pings, vaudeville scrapbook, CPpR; see also *Variety*, 19 March 1910).
Rogers continued on his Poli's tour with an engagement in New Haven, Conn.,
the week of 21 March 1910. There he appeared with ice sculptor Luigi Marabini
(Chisels Figures of Fancy Out of Huge Blocks of Ice); The Three Dolce Sisters
(Refined Singers and Dancers); Joe Kane and Oscar Ragland (In a New Comedy
Creation, *Coming East*); George Auger (The Giant Actor) and Co. (Present that most
Extravagantly Costumed, Original and Humourous Playlet, *Jack the Giant Killer*;
George Auger is the Tallest actor on earth, and his Lilliputians are the Smallest Cast);
The Original Madcaps (the Most Agile and Skillful Ensemble Act in Vaudeville); and
Dolly Connolly (Artistic Syncopist of Song) with Percy Wenrich (Composer of
"Rainbow" and "Put On Your Old Gray Bonnet") (Poli's New Haven playbill, vaude-
ville scrapbook, CPpR; *Variety*, 26 March 1910).

3. Stuart Barnes was a big-time act, earning $400 a week in 1909. He had made a hit playing in Europe in 1908. A reviewer of his act at the Colonial Theatre in 1911 said that "Barnes, with his immaculate evening dress, white gloves and silk hat, had his usual quota of new material and landed his usual big hit. Two things are sure about Barnes—he knows how to wear a dress suit and how to land the point of a joke, either in song or monologue" (*Variety,* 28 October 1911). Barnes (whose wife sued him in 1909 when she discovered he had been married before and never legally divorced) centered much of his humor and commentary on marriage and relationships with women. A *Variety* review of 26 March 1915 noted that "his monologue deals mostly with domestic problems, a very hard subject to extract comedy out of without offending. The laughter and applause that greet Mr. Barnes shows he successfully does so." Another *Variety* review of 2 January 1909 observed that the "panning that Stuart gives the wives was doubly effective in Harlem, where the old man gets to the theatre only when he brings home two tickets and takes the real head of the house with him." Barnes followed his monologue with a song, often choosing something by Irving Berlin. The *New York Mirror* review of his 23 January 1909 appearance at Hammerstein's Victoria stated that a "few of his political jokes seemed in rather poor taste and did not meet with any hearty applause. . . . Mr. Barnes is steadily rising as a monologist and happily keeps his talk and songs new and up to date" (*Variety,* 16 October and 31 December 1907, 7 March and 22 July 1908, 5 March and 25 June 1910, 16 November 1916; Barnes clipping file, NN-L-BRTC).

From Zack Mulhall
22 March 1910
St. Louis, Mo.

St. Louis   Mo   March 22, 1910

Will Rogers Polis Theatre
New Haven Conn[1]

Wrote you to-day, accept your proposition, You can have Commanche[2]

Jack [Zack] Mulhall

TG, rc. Vaudeville scrapbook, CPpR.

1. Rogers played Poli's Theatre in Meriden, Conn., the week of 28 March–2 April 1910. He appeared with Valveno and LaMore, Marron and Heins, Marie Yuill and Bobby Boyd, Jeannette Lowrie, John Harvey and Helen Case, Holly and the Boys, and Brown and Harrison (*Variety,* 2 April 1910).
2. In March 1910 Mulhall and Rogers, who had not been on speaking terms since 1905, apparently came to an agreement in regard to the horse, with Rogers offering to appear in a Mulhall show in exchange for the return of Comanche. The transaction never took place, despite Mulhall's agreement to give Comanche back. The arrangement about the horse seem to have gotten caught up in legal entanglements connected to Mulhall's larger financial problems (see Will Rogers to Clement Vann Rogers, ca. 25 October 1910, below). Rogers did see the horse again (in the fall of 1910, in Knoxville, Tenn.), but Comanche ended up not with Rogers's family in Oologah, as Rogers had hoped, but pastured by Mulhall down in Florida, "where he grew sleek, fat

and happy." Comanche died "in his Florida meadow" ca. 1912, "full of honors and triumphs and remembered by hundreds of cowboys around the rodeos as the king of cow ponies" (Rogers, *Will Rogers,* 87–88; see also McSpadden, "Horses and Horse Collars").

Article from *Billboard*
16 April 1910
St. Louis, Mo.

In April 1910 Rogers reunited with his old friends the Mulhalls to appear in a Wild West show directed by Jim Gabriel in St. Louis. Later in the month he followed up his St. Louis appearance with the Mulhall show by performing with Buffalo Bill's Wild West and Pawnee Bill's Far East Combined Shows at Madison Square Garden, New York. He made a special appearance in St. Louis and worked the Buffalo Bill show at the same time that he was in New York doing vaudeville. Some months later he brought his own brand of Wild West performance to the vaudeville stage.

MULHALL WILD WEST SHOW

April 7, in the St. Louis Coliseum, before an audience of 8,000 people, James Gabriel, arena director[,] started the first performance of the Mulhall Wild West Show, and with a company of one hundred performers gave an exhibition that pleased.

There are eighteen numbers to the program and each act shows the full skill of the participant. The features of the performance were the acts by Lucille Mulhall, J. [E]llison Carroll, Charles Mulhall, Tom Mix and Helen Gabriel, although every act presented was greeted with hearty applause. The performance ran smoothly with the exception of the narrow escape from serious injury of Charles Mulhall. After riding the plunging broncho twice around the arena, he essayed to leap from its back to the saddle of another horse, when his foot became entangled in the stirrup and the bucker plunged away, dragging him full length through the arena, kicking and bucking viciously. Mulhall was dashed against the concrete coping time and time again, and the animal's heels missed his head by a hair's breadth, while the alarmed cowboys tried to capture the runaway. Mulhall was finally released and, dazed, but unhurt, he bowed gracefully to the audience and retired.

Colonel Mulhall has a meritorious company. His daughter, Lucille, is famous the country over as a daring horsewoman and steer roper. Little Mildred Mulhall bids fair to equal her sister. Charley Mulhall is the best

Lucille Mulhall performing on her horse, Governor. (*Mulhall Family Collection, Martha Fisch, Guthrie, Okla.*)

broncho buster in the world. Colonel Zack himself is a bright star. Then there are Jim Dennison, J. Ellison Carroll and many other famous riders and ropers.

Colonel Mulhall has all the things other wild west shows have, and goes them many better. He gives races and chases and stagecoach attacks and water hole fights and bride chases, where the cowboys contest for a girl on horseback, the first man lifting her off her saddle getting her as his wife. In addition to this there is a trapeze act by cowboys and cowgirls that is thrilling in the extreme.

Miss Helen Gabriel, although but 16 years of age, was exceptionally clever in her rough riding and feats of horsemanship, and especially in the act, A Chase for a Bride, where she is cast from one horse to another. She was wildly applauded for her work.

Lucille Mulhall showed the greatest skill and daring in her saddle and lariat feats, one of which was the roping and throwing of a bull. She and Willie Rogers performed remarkable and seemingly almost impossible feats. One of her specialties was the throwing of a lasso over her back with an almost uncanny accuracy of aim. Her act with her trained horse, "Governor," was one of the best of the kind that St. Louis has seen. He is not only a high school horse, but a college graduate, to judge from his grace and the thoroughness of his training.

The main act is the bull fight. Three picadors and one saucy lady in Carmenesque costume entered the ring preceded by the bandrillos on horseback, and followed by a fife and drum corps. The band struck up the "Habanero" from Carmen, and the lady lighted and smoked a cigarette to prove she was Spanish and danced while the knock-kneed picadors flirted with the "bull." The latter was just a long-horned, razor-backed Texas son of a sirocco. He took long-horned stabs at the red and yellow flags the picadors waved at him, and then ran around the arena while the women smoked and danced. A banderillo threw himself upon the steer and bore him to the earth, got a half Nelson and toe hold on him, and let cowboys leap upon and tie him. In all, it is a very fine show.

The show will remain all week and will next visit Kansas City, then on to Chicago before taking the road for an extended season. James Gabriel has trained his people well and although the Coliseum could not be had but for two rehearsals, yet, he had the performance go with much dash and spirit. The week will prove profitable, as the sale is good, and having made a big start, we can add another truly big show to our list of summer features.[1]

Will J. Farley.

Printed in *Billboard*, 16 April 1910.

1. Rogers saved an unidentified clipping of the Coliseum show in his vaudeville scrapbook. The review praised Lucille Mulhall and Rogers for their rope-and-horse tricks in language almost identical to that of the *Billboard* review (clipping, "Crowd Thrilled When Mulhall Falls Off Horse," CPpR). The Coliseum show was advertised in the *St. Louis Republic*, 3 and 10 April 1910.

Rogers went from St. Louis to New York to appear at Keith and Proctor's theater on Fifth Avenue with Irene Franklin (assisted by Burt Green); W. C. Fields (Greatest of Tramp Jugglers); Hoey and Lee (The Jolly Jesters); Dolan and Lenharr; The Ruby Raymond Trio; and The Robert Demont Trio. Rogers was placed next to last on the bill, between the two trios (*NYT*, 10 and 12 April 1910).

The week of 16 April 1910 Rogers played the Orpheum's Alhambra Theatre on Seventh Avenue and 126th Street in New York, appearing last on the bill with The Dixie Serenaders (Colored Entertainers); Seymour Brown and Nat D. Ayer (in an Original Comedy Sketch, *Undiscovered Genius*, Introducing Their Latest Song Compositions, featuring their hit from the "Follies of 1909," "Moving Day in Jungletown"); The Frey Twins (Statue Wrestlers; First Time Here); Pat Rooney and Marion Bent (The Popular Favorites, In Their Latest Skit, *At the Stand*); Lionel Barrymore, Doris Rankin, and McKee Rankin (In the Realistically Dramatic Playlett, entitled *The White Slaver*); Geo. Austin Moore (Dialect Singing Comedian); the Top O' th' World Dancers (And the Original Famous "Collie Ballet" in *Kris Kringle's Dream*); and, in a return engagement, Jack Wilson and Co. (in *An Upheaval in Darktown*) (Alhambra Theatre, New York, playbill, 18 April 1910, vaudeville scrapbook, CPpR; *NYT*, 17 April 1910; *Variety*, 16 April 1910).

Article from *Variety*
30 April 1910
New York, N.Y.

Two Bills

Buffalo Bill's Wild West and Pawnee Bill's Far East Combined Shows opened Tuesday evening at Madison Square Garden, New York, for a three-week engagement. In his annual greeting to the big Garden audience Col. William F. Cody declared that this will mark his last appearance in New York with the organization. In a voice plainly affected by emotion "the old scout" bade farewell to two generations of amusement seekers. His speech was simple and to the point and the show started immediately. Major Gordon W. Lillie (Pawnee Bill) did not appear in the arena.[1]

From 8:15 until exactly 11 o'clock there was not an instant's pause in one of the best entertainments Col. Cody has ever headed. A few changes are noted, although none of them is of importance, and all the familiar spectacles are on exhibit. When the audience filed out of the Garden there was a general comment that the Wild West had never been better or more interesting.

The Far Eastern exhibit has been extended somewhat in size and time consumed, and the latter half condensed to bring the whole show within the time limit. It was noticeable toward the close Tuesday evening that the displays were being run off as quickly as possible. Especial credit is due to the arenic director who put the show in shape. In spite of the lightning speed there was not a slip or hitch in the proceedings.

The displays are seventeen in number, an innovation being No. 11, called a Grand Military Tournament, in which all the horsemen combine in their native dress and equipment for a short but elaborate drill. Another novelty for the show is Rhoda Royal's double high school display in two improvised rings.[2] One is a "liberty" routine worked by six beautiful blacks. Nothing startling is developed, and Tuesday night some of the evolutions were rather rough, possibly because the horses had not yet become accustomed to the presence of Rossi's Musical Elephants, which were in the arena at the same time, awaiting their turn. The elephant act is newly equipped with trappings and costumes and the animals never worked better. The second turn of the equestrian display involved two well trained ponies in a series of novel tricks, together with several tiny ponies. In the Far East gathering much attention is attracted by a big troupe of twenty Arabs having a capital round of whirlwind acrobatics. The "levitation" trick used as a "solo" last year is among the absentees, happily, being replaced by a first rate sextet of Russian dancers (two men and four women). If the troupe of Hindu dancers who cavort about the east side of the field is not the same that was employed in Gertrude Hoffmann's[3] act, they are remarkably alike.

The cowboy, cowgirl, Indian and foreign riders were up to the best the show has ever carried and the stock is in extraordinary good condition. The ginger of the horses contributed a good deal to the snap of the performance. A splendid lot of Indians, a little above the usual quota, give picturesque exhibitions of riding and native life on the plains.

It is worth recording as an incident that the feature of the rope throwing display was the appearance in the central portion of the arena of Will Rogers. The Oklahoma cowboy was in his element at the finish of the episode when he raced around the ring spinning his wide "crinoline" loop, the other workers having withdrawn to one side to give the feat prominence. Rogers is playing the Colonial this week and worked the Garden shows in addition.[4]

George Connor ("Buckshot")[5] the versatile cowboy-secretary, had the standard-bearers post in the cowboy division. The Grand Review is well dressed and the riders superbly mounted. The Pony Express rider followed. Then came the rope throwing. Ray Thompson's equestrian exhibit is slightly changed by the addition of the six blacks owned by Rhoda Royal and later worked in the "liberty" style. "Ray Bailey" and "Irma G," or their successors go through the same remarkable series of feats while the Royal sextet show simpler high school work, under the guidance of men and women riders.[6]

"The Deadwood Stage Coach" is again on view, the battle between cowboys and Indians and later with U. S. Cavalry being worked better than formerly to show the shifting of the victory. Devlin's Zouaves do their familiar drill.

"Football on Horseback" has developed into a real game involving skill, shiftiness and real headwork by the riders. The game is now three years old and the players have worked out combination plays and trick formations for ground-gaining quite as complicated and interesting to watch as a well executed college football maneuver. From a novelty riding freak, horseback football has evolved into a keen contest of brains and riding skill quite the equal of polo. Tuesday night the cowboys scored twice within ten minutes of play, and the teams galloped off with the audience still at tiptoe of interest. The display could have been twice as long without wearying.

Improvements are noted in the staging of "The Battle of Summit Springs." Buffalo Bill is first shown entering from the Madison Avenue gate and riding into the cavalry camp to summon the soldiers. The troopers ride off through the Fourth Avenue set scenery. A change of picture is made and the Indians march down the mountain and pitch camp. The rest of the episode then proceeds as in former years, ending with the battle and the duel between Buffalo Bill and Tall Bull. The cavalry drill was there with its thrill and the bucking bronchos and "cowboy fun" made its old-time appeal. The cowgirl rider in this division is missing this year. The wild riding of the Cossacks and the final salute bring the entertainment to a finale.

Just as the audience was rising to depart the curtains at the Fourth Avenue end were drawn and a pretty tableau, showing an Indian posed on horseback and dressed in full war panoply of paint and feathers, on a tall set rock with a miniature Indian camp just below, was disclosed under the combined calciums of the lighting battery. Across the base of the tableau appeared in illuminated letters the single word "Farewell."

Rush.

Printed in Variety, 30 April 1910. Clipping, vaudeville scrapbook, CPpR.

1. The emotional farewell speech and announcement of the last performance in a particular setting became standard fare in Cody's tours near the end of his career. In their coverage of the Madison Square Garden show, which opened on 26 April 1910 for the week, the *New York Times* reported that Buffalo Bill's show had become "a

classic ethnological exhibit of the manners and customs of a certain period in American history and of a race which is fast vanishing from the earth," and noted that with Cody's aging, it would "either pass into less famous hands or disappear altogether." There is no doubt that the show that Rogers joined was delivering high quality for the genre. The *Times* concluded its enthusiastic review of the New York version of the show by stating that when the performances were over at the end of the week, it would be "the end of one of the best of the Buffalo Bill Shows" (*NYT*, 26 April 1910). Ever a master of publicity, Cody had the Combined Shows give an exclusive, full-dress-rehearsal performance to newspapermen on the night of 10 April 1910. Lillie had acted as an interpreter for the Buffalo Bill shows in the 1890s. The Pawnee Bill and Buffalo Bill shows merged in 1908, with Lillie acting as business manager and Cody as showman. They mounted their first big collaborative show in Madison Square Garden in April 1909, with the western aspects far dominating the Far East side of the show. The Buffalo Bill shows closed for the last time in 1913 (*Billboard,* 12 December 1908; Russell, *Wild West,* 83; *Variety,* 1 May 1909). See *PWR,* 1:487–88, 502–3 (Biographical Appendix entries for William F. Cody [Buffalo Bill] and Gordon William Lillie [Pawnee Bill]). See also programs, Pawnee Bill's Historical Wild West, WBaraC.

2. The *New York Times* reported that "Rhoda Royal and Ray Thompson have each trained five horses to do various evolutions, and the ten horses, with riders, were next introduced [after the Mexican lasso-throwing portion of the program]. Miss Royal—at least one must imagine it was she—concluded this exhibition by urging her horse almost to destroy the laws of equilibrium by balancing as far back as possible on his hind legs, while she clung to the saddle, her hands dangling loose" (*NYT*, 26 April 1910). This trick was actually the trademark of Ray (Minnie) Thompson, and it was probably she, and not Rhoda Royal, who performed it.

3. Gertrude Hoffman (1886–1966) was a dancer who achieved her greatest prominence in the 1920s. She headed her own troupe, "which played concert halls around the country." At the height of her fame she was said to have "some of the aura of a Martha Graham." She was best known for her Dance of the Seven Veils, considered in its day to be something of a sexual shocker, done on the theme of Salome. Hoffman was managed by her husband, Max Hoffman (1875-1963), who was also musical director for the Shuberts and for several editions of the *Ziegfeld Follies.* She toured in vaudeville beginning in 1908 and had "an act that specialized in Russian dances." Her son, Max Hoffman, Jr., was also a vaudeville dancer (*VO*, 6:2 November 1966).

4. Rogers appeared during the last week of April 1910 both at Madison Square Garden with the Wild West show and in vaudeville at the Colonial Theatre at Broadway and 62nd Street. He performed last on a bill at the Colonial that also featured Wills and Hassan (Acrobats); Oscar Lorraine (The Character Violinist, First Time Here); Maurice Freeman (The Well-Known, Talented Actor, First Time Here), supported by Nadine Winston and Co. (in *Tony and the Stork*); Dan Burke Assisted by Mollie Moller and His Wonder Girls (The Misses Craig, Densmore, Benner, Russo, Carleton and Boyne, in *At Lake Winnipesaukee*); Julius Tannen (The Natural Monologist, First Time This Season); Lew Dockstader (The King of Minstrelsy, First Time Here); and Gus Edwards's Schoolboys and Girls (In a Young Comic Opera in One Act, entitled *Graduation Day,* With the Original "Sassy Little" Lillian Gonne and the Dancing Gordon Bros. and Frank Alvin). Rogers was advertised on the bill as appearing "First Time This Season, Champion Lariat Expert" (Colonial Theatre, New York, playbill, 25 April 1910, vaudeville scrapbook, CPpR; see also *NYT*, 24 April 1910). A review by "Wynn" printed in *Variety* observed that "Will Rogers closed

the show with his lariat throwing. His talk sounds good after all the dialect comedians have finished" (undated clipping, vaudeville scrapbook, CPpR).

Rogers remained for a stint in New York state in May. He traveled up to Buffalo for the first two weeks, then played the Warburton Theatre in Yonkers, where Joseph E. Schanberger was manager, the week of 21 May 1910. At the Warburton he appeared with Fennel and Tyson (in *The Soph and the Fresh*); The Marshells (Singing and Dancing); Albert Rees (The Man with the Freak Voice); Harriet Burt and Co. (in *Silver Idaho*); Hawley Olcott and Co. (Presenting their Novelty Comedy *Monday Afternoon*); and Elizabeth Brice (Late of Jolly Batchelor Co.) and Charles King (Late of Yankee Prince Co.). Rogers (The Oklahoma Cowboy) came last on the bill (Warburton Theatre, Yonkers, N.Y., playbill, vaudeville scrapbook, CPpR; *Variety*, 21 May 1910).

At the beginning of June, Rogers played at the Murray Hill Theatre in New Jersey, one of Arthur Buckner and Joseph E. Shea's theaters and part of the Columbia Amusement Co. He appeared there the week of 6 June 1910 with Siebert and Strauss; Mr. and Mrs. Harry Thorne; Clara Nelson; John J. McGowan and Cale; Billy (Single) Clifford; Sa-Haras (In an Unusual Exhibition of Second Sight and Thought Transference); and Caicedo. Rogers had the fourth slot, after Nelson (Murray Hill Theatre, N.J., playbill, vaudeville scrapbook, CPpR). Rogers then went to Philadelphia in mid-June.

5. George Vincent Connor (Buckshot) (1851–1944) was a veteran of the circus. He began working as a candy butcher with the Van Amburgh wagon show in 1881 and became a trick roper, rider, and equestrian director. He was associated with several major circuses and Wild West shows, including Barnum and Bailey, Sells Brothers, Sells-Floto, Ringling Brothers, Hagenbeck-Wallace (in which he appeared along with Ray Thompson in 1918), the Buffalo Bill shows and the Miller Brothers' 101 Ranch show. He was working with the Ringling Brothers and other circuses in the 1940s. He died at home in Chillicothe, Ohio, in November 1944 (*Billboard*, 28 March 1914, 8 July 1918, 16 December 1944; route book, John Robinson Ten Big Shows, 1917 season, and route book, Bud E. Anderson's Jungle Oddities and Three-Ring Circus, 1940, WBaraC).

6. Expert trick rider Minnie Thompson, of Dallas, Tex., was the wife of horse trainer Ray Thompson, who worked for the Barnum and Bailey Circus and for Buffalo Bill's Wild West and Pawnee Bill's Far East Combined Shows in 1909–10. He had previously directed the high-school horses for Buffalo Bill in 1907–8. Minnie Thompson performed on horses Ray Thompson had schooled, and with time their identities merged in her stage name. Minnie Thompson was often referred to as Miss Ray Thompson, Mrs. Ray Thompson, or simply as Ray Thompson when she performed. Barnum and Bailey route books pictured them as "Ray Thompson and Wife with Their High-School Horses," with "Mr. Ray Thompson" in a portrait on one side and "Mrs. Ray Thompson" on the other. Many publicity shots from the 1909–10 era feature her hanging upside-down in the saddle along the back of a rearing Irma G, with captions identifying her simply as Ray Thompson. Minnie Thompson was a veteran of the Buffalo Bill shows, having performed with them before in April 1909 at Madison Square Garden, New York, and in London. She was also a regular with the Barnum and Bailey Circus. She performed with the New Hippodrome Circus as well as the Buffalo Bill show in 1909 and was still with the New Hippodrome Circus in 1912. She was famous for working her horses without bridles. Ray Thompson worked for the Hugo Brothers Three Ring Circus in 1912 and continued to train high-school horses for many different circuses in Europe and the United States well into the 1940s. The

Thompsons' horses, Joe Bailey, Virgil T, and Irma G, were well known on the circuit. The Thompsons traveled with their daughter, born in December 1906. Minnie Thompson had first met Ray Thompson when she was a belle in Dallas and she saw Sultan, a Ray Thompson horse, in a parade. She asked her wealthy father to purchase Sultan for her. When approached regarding the sale, Ray Thompson replied that the only way the young woman could get the horse was to marry the owner. She did so, and began performing on Ray Thompson horses with the Barnum and Bailey Circus soon after. The confusion over the name Ray Thompson (which was also used by an unrelated stage actress of the period) became greater when the Thompsons had a son, Ray Thompson, Jr., and later there was yet another Mrs. Ray Thompson, also a rider. Minnie and Ray Thompson apparently divorced, for Ray Thompson was reportedly married to another equestrian, Kathryn Thompson, a rider with the Barnes Show in Indiana, in 1917. He and that Mrs. Ray Thompson were separated in 1920 and divorced in 1923 (*Atlanta Constitution,* 7 October 1906; *Billboard,* 27 August 1910, 24 April 1920, 16 June 1923, 1 September 1945, 27 April 1946; *Milwaukee Journal,* 21 June 1909; *New York Daily Tribune,* 2 May 1910; *New York Telegraph,* 2 May 1910; *Variety,* 4 December 1909; Buffalo Bill's Wild West and Pawnee Bill's Far East Combined Shows clipping, featuring "Miss Minnie Thompson and Her Reinless Wonder 'Virgil T,'" 1911, "Trained Western Range Horses," Buffalo Bill's Wild West Combined with Pawnee Bill's Great Far East program, 1909, and Ray Thompson High School Horses, with Mr. and Mrs. Ray Thompson, flyer, small collections file, WBaraC; Locke env. 2345, NN-L-RLC).

Article from the *Philadelphia Inquirer*
14 June 1910
Philadelphia, Pa.

RODGERS' WILD WEST HIT AT "BIG HIP"

COWBOY LIFE AND PASTIMES FEATURE OF EXCELLENT BILL CONTAINING THRILLS, COMEDY AND BURLESQUE

Murky skies and threatening rain early in the day did not deter more than five thousand persons from attending the performance at the Big Hip, at Broad and Huntingdon streets, last night. Those that went were well rewarded, for the bill of offerings was one of the best that this open air amusement place has presented.

In exhibitions of cowboy pastimes, showing his dexterity with the lariat, in roping horses, tying up "bad men"; forming crinolines, yards and yards in circumference, in the middle of which he performed all kinds of gyrations, Will Rodgers who has been seen here in high class vaudeville, repeated all his former successes, and then some more.

On the open field Rodgers has a better opportunity to display his skill than on a theatre stage, and last night the performer took advantage of the chance and a thrilling and interesting exhibition was the result. In addition to his own performance, Rodgers has gathered about him other men from the plains, who, with himself, in scenes portraying the methods and manners of cowboy life, form a Wild West show of considerable merit. To complete the atmosphere of the circus, there was, as part of the evening's entertainment, Colonel Boon's Animal Alliance and Jungle Carnival in marvelous exhibitions.

There was plenty of comedy in the screaming rough and tumble specialty of LaMaze, Bennett and LaMaze, in an act that is well described by its name, "Bumps, Jumps and Thumps." Breakaway Barlows showed some sensational and daring perch and ladder work. In clever tumbling, balancing and other difficult acrobatic stunts the Garnellas made a pronounced hit, as did Caprice R. Lewis, whose marvelous performance on a swinging trapeze was a thrilling exhibition, deserving of the applause it received. There were many other acts on the big bill that contained funds of thrills, comedy and burlesque. One of the features of this amusement place is the Banda Bianca, a musical organization whose selections were well received.[1]

PD. Printed in *Philadelphia Inquirer*, 14 June 1910. Clipping, vaudeville scrapbook, CPpR.

1. In addition to this review, the *Philadelphia Inquirer* carried advertisements for the show and an advance notice. The largest advertisement declared entertainment at the "The Big Hip (Phillie's Ball Park)" at Broad and Huntingdon" the "Apex of Arenic Achievement, Advanced and Augmented . . . This week–Nightly at 8 O'Clock . . . WILL ROGERS' WILD WEST Introducing prairie pastimes, frontier types, dexterous gunplay, lariat throwing, lasso maneuvers, antics peculiar to the American cowboy and exhibitions of border life that will be signalized by a magnitude and diversified perfection that will eclipse anything ever attempted in fancy, rough and daring equestrianism." The featured acts advertised were Colonel Boone's Troupe of Trained Lions; The Breakaway Barlows (ladder and perch experts); The Comedy Four singers; the aerialist Caprice R. Lewis; acrobatic acts The Six Garnellas and La Maze, Bennett and La Maze; and "ten other acts of equal prestige." All this could be had in grandstand seating at prices of 10 or 25 cents. An article in the same issue announced that a "program of unusual merit has been prepared for this week at the 'Big Hip.' Will Rogers' Wild West outfit, with all the primitive and picturesque modes and methods peculiar to cowboy life and Indian intrigue, heads the bill, and by way of a special feature Colonel Boone's troupe of performing lions has been added. Independent of the tuneful instrumental numbers executed by the Banda Bianca, vocal selections will be introduced by the Comedy Four." The article went on to list the acts and concluded that the upcoming event would be a "program of unusual strength" (advertisement and article, *Philadelphia Inquirer*, 12 June 1910; see also advertisement, *Philadelphia Inquirer*, 18 June 1910). Rogers saved a *Philadelphia Evening Item* review, "Wild West at the 'Big Hip'," which declared that the work of Rogers's "aggregation of Wild West artists" had "aroused the utmost enthusiasm during the time they occupied the arena. Every distinct type of horsemanship known to equestrian art was revealed, together with lasso technique, sharp-shooting and other pastimes characteristic of the turbulent West was shown. It was all very thrilling and worth seeing time and time again" (undated

clipping, vaudeville scrapbook, CPpR; see also *Variety,* 18 June 1910). Rogers went from this successful experiment in Philadelphia to Boston, where he appeared as a guest artist in an open-air show at the Airdome.

Article from the *Boston Globe*
21 June 1910
Boston, Mass.

AIRDOME ON BALL GROUNDS.

CAPITAL PROGRAM, INCLUDING SOME WELCOME COMEDY ACTS, PROVIDED FOR THIS WEEK.

With absolutely perfect weather, the second week of the now widely-known Airdome opened at the American league ball grounds on Huntington av last evening with a program as fresh as the cooling breezes which blew over the spacious lot. The open-air feature of this enterprise is appealing to an ever-increasing number of Bostonians and residents of its suburbs.

Although the acts were well varied last evening, there were plenty of the laugh-producing nature befitting a summer night's amusement. The clown element was well represented and the buffoonery of these men tickled the audience immensely.

One of the noteworthy acts was that of Will Rogers, the cowboy and master of the lariat. His throwing and handling of the pliable ropes was a delight to behold, and when he easily "roped" his partner and the horse the latter was mounted on as well, the applause was tremendous. As trapeze artists the Flying Martins proved themselves to be of the front rank. . . .[1]

PD. Printed in *Boston Globe,* 21 June 1910. Clipping, vaudeville scrapbook, CPpR.

1. Although the *Boston Globe* article continued with another three paragraphs about the various acts in the show, Rogers's scrapbook clipping ended at this point.

Variety also reviewed the show. "Adverse weather," so hot that "the city wilted at night," had plagued the opening of the "Airdome in the American League baseball grounds on Huntington Ave." The Airdome had opened for the first time on 14 June 1910 and was sharing its space for afternoon American League baseball games with other sorts of entertainment, including night-time vaudeville acts, Sunday-evening concerts, and moving pictures (*Variety,* 25 June 1910; see also *Boston Globe,* 19 June 1910). An unidentified clipping in Rogers's scrapbook reported that the audience the night Rogers appeared was "large and well pleased" and that Rogers had made a particular hit, with "one of the best western acts that has been seen in Boston for some time." Rogers was billed, in the midst of the city's scorching weather, as "A Breeze from the Prairies" (clipping, vaudeville scrapbook, CPpR; see also advertisements, *Boston Globe,* 16, 19 and 22 June 1910).

Review from the *Atlanta Constitution*
21 July 1910
Atlanta, Ga.

AT THE CASINO.

The largest attendance of the week at the Ponce de Leon Casino was recorded on Wednesday. The great seating capacity of the theater, next to the largest lower floor seating in Atlanta, was practically tested at the popular bargain matinee, and at night a great gathering enjoyed the splendid performance that has been presented to open the season this summer.[1]

A great deal has been said for the show and the manner in which it is being produced. It is conceded by the theatergoers to be one of the cleverest bills of vaudeville that has been seen in Atlanta, full of interesting numbers, with pleasing variety and containing acts that are actual drawing cards.

Will Rogers, the lasso expert, has become a great favorite and a rattling good entertainer. He can do almost anything with a rope, and aside from the unique originality of the act it is instructive. Ben Welch,[2] the star comedian, has scored a real hit with his crisp monologue and parodies, and the Primrose Quartette is really one of the cleverest acts that has been seen here this season.[3]

Daily bargain matinees are offered, and the night performances will be given as usual.[4]

PD. Printed in *Atlanta Constitution*, 21 July 1910.

1. The Casino Theatre, under Wells management for Forsyth-Keith Vaudeville, was making a transition to offering "real" vaudeville entertainment to rival that offered by the Orpheum and the Forsyth. Bookings formerly set up for the Forsyth were transferred out to the park. Prices were 10 cents for children and 25 cents for adults for matinees, and 50 cents for night performances. The Casino had reserved seating on the lower floor for 900 patrons. The acts during the week when Rogers helped the Casino break into the summer business were all recruited from Keith theaters (*Atlanta Constitution*, 17 and 19 July 1910).

2. Ben Welch (d. 1926), was well known in New York as an upbeat comic who did Jewish and Italian characterizations. In his performance at the Casino Theatre, he had the audience roaring at the beginning of his act, but ended on a note of pathos. The latter tone was more the trademark style of his brother, Joe Welch (1869–1918), who was also a high-profile New York comic, but whose gags were based on his characters' chronic dim view of life. The Welches' parents emigrated from Germany to the United States in the 1860s, and Ben and Joe Welch grew up on New York's Lower East Side. Both did impersonations of Jewish peddlers as well as Germans and Italians. Joe Welch specialized in a characterization of an unfortunate Jewish merchant. He began his work in variety in the late 1880s and moved into Broadway, vaudeville, and film. His trademark opening line was "Und I vished dot I vas dead!" (Distler, "Rise and Fall of the

Racial Comics," 163; see also 161–64). He brought his character from variety to the legitimate stage in 1901 with *The Peddler,* in an unsuccesful attempt to rival David Warfield's hit play, *The Auctioneer.* He continued playing Jewish charcters on stage between 1906 and 1916. He also made films from 1912 to 1918, including a film version of *The Peddler* in 1917. Ben Welch remained active in vaudeville into the 1920s. He "did a lively, fast-talking Jewish pushcart type, in exact contrast to Joe. For a time he teamed with Jules Jordan, of Jordan and Harvey, in which the pair characterized the breezy, jolly type of Jew" (Gilbert, *American Vaudeville,* 292). Ben Welch went into burlesque and was extremely successful. In the last years of his life he went blind (he lost his sight in the middle of an act, while on stage), but he continued to work, using a straight man, Frank Murphy, as his partner to guide him on stage and thus conceal his disability from his audiences. Welch's professionalism helped set the standard for the Ponce de Leon bill (*EV,* 542–43; Laurie, *Vaudeville,* 175–76).

3. The *Atlanta Constitution* advertised "Keith Vaudeville" at the Casino, the theater at Ponce de Leon Park, "Out in the Cool Woods, Free from City Heat" (17 July 1910). Another paper reported that "those who journeyed out to Ponce de Leon Monday night for the initial performance at the Casino expecting to see a mild edition of the vaudeville which has been on view at the Forsyth were agreeably surprised. The bill was fully up to the high standard which was set by that popular playhouse and if, as many supposed in advance, the summer acts cost less than those of the regular season, the fact was not apparent." Special praise was reserved for "Will Rogers, the lariat expert. There have been lariat artists in Atlanta before, but none in the same class with Rogers. What he can't do with a rope is not worth telling. He does everything with a lariat except cook a meal, shave himself or commit suicide." Another clipping described Rogers as "a big, jolly fellow" and "real cowboy" who "now commands a salary in one week equal to the pay he received for a year's work on the ranch. He is a star card in the principal vaudeville houses, and with his horse, is a character that wins friends in every city" (unidentified clippings, vaudeville scrapbook, CPpR). Rogers shared the bill with Matthiessen's Ponce De Leon Orchestra; The King Brothers (Exponents of Physical Culture); the hefty men of The Primrose Quartette (1,000 Pounds of Harmony); Alsace and Lorraine (a male and female team of Wondrous Electrical Musicians); The La Petit Emilie Bicycle Troupe (Featuring the 3 Vecchi Sisters formerly of the Kaufman Troupe [and one man]); and Ben Welch. Welch, who was presented as the New York headliner, pleased the crowd and received a good round of applause, but he was unexpectedly upstaged as a comic by Rogers, who surprised everyone by entertaining as much with his comedy as with his "pandora box" of a lariat (Ponce De Leon Park, Atlanta, playbill and clippings, vaudeville scrapbook, CPpR; *Atlanta Constitution,* 19 July 1910). The news spread around town about Rogers and his colleagues, and the audiences grew larger with each performance, making the opening week of the summer entertainment at the Casino a huge success (*Atlanta Constitution,* 23 July 1910).

4. Rogers and Teddy went from Atlanta to Chattanooga, Tenn., where they were described in reviews as "Will Rogers & Co.," an act combining "horse, cowboy, and lariat." Rogers received rave reviews, with the Chattanooga *Daily Times* touting him as the "most skillful artist ever seen in this city," and one depicting the "days when the cowboy and the vacquero alike vied with each other to make life on the mesa and Rio Grande more interesting" (clippings, vaudeville scrapbook, CPpR). It was Teddy's last performance with Rogers. From Tennessee Will and Betty Blake Rogers visited Rogers, Ark., and the Chelsea-Claremore area, and Teddy was sent home to Oklahoma to be put out to pasture (*CR,* 18 August 1910).

Article from the *Rogers County News*
8 September 1910
Claremore, Okla.

Rogers's faithful pony Teddy was retired and put out to graze in Oologah in August 1910. Soon afterward the plan for Teddy's happy retirement went badly awry when he and another horse that had been sharing his pasture disappeared through a break in the fence. Rogers's nephew, Herb McSpadden, was dispatched to search for the pony. Rogers urged his family to advertise for return of the horse, no questions asked. Notices like the one below appeared in the local papers, and McSpadden rode about the countryside examining horse herds and asking after Teddy. The horse was finally found, but not until the McSpaddens received a lead almost a year and a half after Teddy disappeared. As Betty Rogers put it, "Teddy, who had been the idol of boys on the streets, who had played in the leading vaudeville theaters of America, the music halls of Europe and before the King of England," was located "hitched to a plow." The famous bay pony was being used to work the fields for an elderly Cherokee share-cropper. Herb McSpadden explained to the farmer the special circumstances, pur-chased Teddy from him, and returned the horse to the Rogers land in Oologah, where he was pampered and "lived to be very old."[1]

Willie Rogers is mourning the loss of his valuable show horse, which either strayed or was stolen from a pasture in Chelsea last Saturday. This animal had been shipped a few days ago from the east to Chelsea to pasture out. It was in company with another horse which is also missing. The animal that Mr. Rogers values so much is the one he has staged in every quarter of the states and in Europe, within the last five years. It has a brand A. C. on left hip, and a cut on the left front leg, recently made by coming in contact with barb wire. Mr. Rogers offers a reward of $[1]25 for the return of the horses.

PD. Printed in *Rogers County News*, 8 September 1910.

1. Rogers, *Will Rogers,* 111. Herb McSpadden later became the foreman of the Rogers Oologah ranch. He recalled that Teddy was lost on 18 August 1910 and recovered in February 1912. Clement Vann Rogers was distraught at the loss, and Sallie and Tom McSpadden put out circulars around Chelsea, Oologah, and Claremore, trying to locate the pony. They got no response. Herb McSpadden locat-ed information on the other horse (which he owned) that had been lost along with Teddy, and learned that it had died. Finally, in February 1912, the McSpaddens found that "Teddy had been taken up as a stray in Mayes County and sold on the street in Pryor at a Sheriff's sale for $25.00." Herb McSpadden went out to Pryor to investigate, and with the help of the sheriff was able to trace the horse from the sale to a "sharecropper's place [at] the north edge of Rose Prairie east of Grand River." He explained to Teddy's new owner what had happened, paid him $50 to repurchase the horse, and brought Teddy home to Oologah. Teddy lived until the fall of 1917 (Herb McSpadden to Paula Love, 26 February 1972, OkClaW; see also McSpadden, "Horses and Horse Collars").

Article from the *Tulsa Post*
22 September 1910
Tulsa, Okla.

ROPING CONTEST GOOD AND DRAWS BIG TULSA CROWD

The roping contest at the Fair grounds yesterday, conducted by J. Ellison Carroll,[1] and a band of fifty Oklahoma and Kansas riders, afforded great pleasure to the large crowd of Tulsans, who journeyed out to witness the contest, which is ranked among the best of sports.

The roping of steers was in itself a great attraction, as from fifteen steers turned loose from the corral only three were missed.

After a fifty feet start the rider would chase, lasso and tie the steer, some making the time less than one-half minute.

Frank Johnson, of Broken Arrow, winner of last year's trophy, won again this year, in 29 1-4 seconds.

C. H. Johnson of Cedarvale, Kansas, was second in 29 3-4 seconds.

Lou Gentry of Council Hill, was third in 31 1-4 seconds and Millard Holcomb, fourth, in 31 1-2 seconds; all others making commendable time.

The roping of steers from an auto by Mr. Carroll was novel, and done in very good time.

From the whole herd and during the entire performance only three steers were injured, two of these were only slightly hurt, the other having its leg hurt, was knifed and taken to the butcher, within the minute.

The feature of the program was the work of Billie Rogers of Claremore.

Mr. Rogers is the greatest fancy rope artist in the world and is at present on the Orpheum circuit, doing vaudeville.

PD. Printed in *Tulsa Post*, 22 September 1910. Scrapbook A-3, OkClaW.

1. Rogers's friend J. Ellison Carroll (1862–1942) was an award-winning roper most famous in roping circuits for having defeated Clay McGonigle (another friend of Rogers's) for the championship in what was reputed to be the biggest steer-roping contest ever mounted in the West, held in San Antonio in 1904. The victory won Carroll the title of world's champion steer roper. In the estimation of many people involved in the roping contest circuit, Carroll, McGonagile, and Joe Gardner were considered the best ropers of all time. Carroll was of the old school of ropers and ranchmen, a veteran of both roping contests and cattle drives, and similar in nature and expertise to the men with whom Rogers had grown up. He was part of the circle of friends with whom Rogers had associated as a young man, including Tom Mix, the Mulhall family, and the cowboys involved with the Miller Brothers' 101 Ranch. Born in San Patricio County, Tex., Carroll worked as a cowboy in the Texas Panhandle in the 1880s and herded his own cattle there in the 1890s. When steer-roping contests were outlawed in

Texas in 1905, he moved north to Oklahoma, where he ranched with his brother, R. M. Carroll, and continued to compete. He later returned as a cattle rancher to Texas, establishing the 07 Ranch near Big Lake. He was a sheriff and county commissioner in Reagan County, Tex., in the 1930s. He is a member of the National Cowboy Hall of Fame (Porter, *Who's Who in Rodeo*, 44–45).

Performance Schedule from Will Rogers's Scrapbook
ca. 24 October 1910–4 April 1911
Eastern Circuit, U.S.A.

In the fall of 1910 Rogers combined his routine vaudeville appearances, using a new horse, with the development of a new group Wild West act. The Big Act, as he and family members called it, featured Rogers doing a running monologue from the side of the stage while a set of equestrians, trick riders, and ropers performed feats of skill on horseback. The riders—initially all women and all well known in Wild West circuits—demonstrated eastern and western styles of riding and represented various international cultures in their costumes. The Big Act premiered in December 1910 but did not last long in its original form. Rogers modified it almost immediately in response to financial pressure and criticism from theater managers. Managers, upon whose opinions contracts depended, were reluctant to book the act because they found it unwieldy, and they wanted Rogers to take more of a starring role in the show. Rogers himself, after a week's trial run, decided that the show was too big. By January 1911 he had reduced the size and configuration of the Big Act and made his own lariat work part of the performance, in effect combining a smaller version of the group act with his old act done just with a horse and Buck McKee. Even this version of the group show proved too expensive to prosper during a downturn in the vaudeville market, and Rogers abandoned the new enterprise by spring of 1911.

Last Weeks with old Act With Horse.[1]

Casino—Brooklyn.

Empire— "

Miners—New York.

Orange—Bayonne.

N. Brunswick Patterson.

Rehersed big act with girls[2]

Bayonne. "*closed*"

3rd Ave. Kee[?].

Prospect in Bronx.

Pittsfield.

Lawrence

Columbia. NY

Albany—Schenenectady

Star Brooklyn.

Prospect Cleveland.

Detroit.

Rochester

Washington.

5th Ave.

Providence.

Keiths. Phila.

AD. Scrapbook MF & ZF, CPpR.

1. After retiring (and losing) Teddy in August 1910, Rogers began acquiring other ponies to train for the stage. At first he felt that none of them worked as well as his old pony, but with more time spent in training, the new acquisitions soon fit well into both the single and group acts. After spending a happy vacation at home in Oklahoma in the late summer of 1910, Rogers began putting together what he and Betty Blake Rogers referred to as the Big Act, which was first billed as Will Rogers and His Broncos and then, in its modified form, as Will Rogers and Co. In between ongoing vaudeville engagements, Rogers returned to Oklahoma in October 1910 and "bought the little gray pony of Vivian Ross and O. K. Osment's bay pony and will train them for stage work" (*CM,* 14 October 1910; see also *Rogers County News,* 13 October 1910). He also bought a dun filly from his friend Tom Isbell of Vinita. Betty Blake Rogers used the filly for pleasure riding before Rogers chose her as his prime replacement for Teddy in the old act. Rogers's nephew, Herb McSpadden, who helped him acquire the Oklahoma horses, recalled that "the big act required several horses; Eastern girl on a high school horse; Western girl on a cow pony; Mexican girl; Cossack girl. Maybe So. America & Australia. [H]ad the cowgirl ride a bucking horse in the act" (Herb McSpadden to Paula Love, 26 February 1972, OkClaW).

2. Not only did Rogers get new horses, he also recruited new talent, initially all women, to join him on stage. He hired Buffalo Bill show performers Goldie St. Clair and Mabel Hackney Tompkins, Miller Brothers' 101 Ranch Wild West Show veteran Florence LaDue, roper Hazel Moran, trick rider Tillie Baldwin, and Cossack-style rider Arlene Palmer. Charles Tompkins and Buck McKee were both part of the later, revised version of the act that performed in 1911 (Mary A. Turner to Homer Croy, 10 September 1952, HCP-MoU). See also *PWR,* 2:523–26 (Biographical Appendix entry for Charles and Mabel Hackney Tompkins), and Biographical Appendix entry, LaDue, Florence.

To Clement Vann Rogers
ca. 25 October 1910
New York, N.Y.

New York.

Tuesday Night.

Well I got here all O.K. and got started in to work but I sure do miss my old Pony   have tried two already and neither of them are any good but when Herb gets here with the others I can use any of them and after a few days they will be all right   I think I will use the little yellow one for my act as its smaller and easier to ship.[1] I just gave one hundred dollars for her   Betty said you all heard I gave two hundred.

I saw old Comanche in Knoxville, Tenn. They are all tied up there by the courts   I will get him back again but he is about all in now   but he looks pretty good

I wired Betty to come on   its lonesome up here and then I want to get us a flat and keep house all winter and you are coming back here and see us when I get this other act to going. Which ought to be just before Christmas.[2] I sure did hate to leave and I tell you I had the best time there this summer I ever had and I never did hate to leave home as bad as this time.

I am going to write to you every few days and tell you just how we are and say Papa dont you think I ought to put an ~~ad~~ notice in the papers and offer $125.00 for those two ponies   some one has them and that is about as cheap as they would give them up and if Teddy is all right when we get him if we ever do why I can ship him on here   Now I will pay most anything to get him but dont make it less than $125. Then people will hunt for them. make it that and no questions asked where they were found or anything   get Sallie to have it done   a notice in the Paper   also cards   lots of them printed and mailed ($125.00 Reward *and no questions asked* where they were found at for—and so on with description.)   do this   I *dont want* that *old* pony to be out all winter.

Love to all the folks and lots for you   I hope you stay most of the time at Chelsea

Willie

My address is this Hotel.

ALS, rc. Pettyjohn collection, WHC-OkU. On Hotel St. Francis, 124–25 West 47th Street, New York, letterhead.

1. Things ended up working out fine with the dun filly Rogers bought from Isbell. On 10 November 1910 Rogers wrote to his father, "I used the little yellow Pony in my act last night and she just worked fine. I gave only $100 for her but I would not take $500 for her I will try the others too" (OkClaW). Betty Blake Rogers also reported that her husband was pleased with the new horse.

2. Betty Blake Rogers wrote to Clement Vann Rogers from New York on 2 December 1910 that "our big act will open Monday [5 December 1910] & I hope I will soon have some good news to tell you. . . . Billy is working like a trojan getting his horses & people in shape for next Monday—   He gets up early each morning & by 8:30 has every thing ready for rehearsal—   He is awfully busy, I hardly get to see him" (OkClaW). The Big Act was given a trial run at the New York American's Christmas Fund Benefit at the Hippodrome on 18 December 1910. Billed as "Will Rogers and His Broncos," the act appeared "courtesy of Buckner and Shea." The benefit program was divided into circus, symphony orchestra, and theatrical and vaudeville sections,

and the Rogers group act came seventeenth in a lineup of twenty-two acts. Winona Winter was also on the bill (Hippodrome, New York, playbill, scrapbook A-3, OkClaW). Rogers was appearing in the Bronx at the same time that the Big Act played at the Hippodrome. For Christmas week he traveled to Pittsfield, Mass., where he appeared with the Jack Irwin Duo; Ward, Clark and Ward; Barry and Halvets; Beth Tate; and the Camille Comedy Trio (*Variety,* 24 December 1910).

Betty Blake Rogers to Clement Vann Rogers
ca. 5 November 1910
New York, N.Y.

Tuesday

Dear Mr. Rogers.

Your letter came this morning. I think it is fine that you write us so often— We are always so glad to hear from you and then we know you are feeling well and are alright.

We have just come in from the riding academy. Have been there rehearsing the new act. Our ponies look so pretty and move together nicely, the little old gray pony is sorter crazy but will be all right Im sure when they work her more— We have everything but the high sc[h]ool horse and Billy has two or three in view— It won't be much trouble to get one.[1]

I had a nice letter from Estelle,[2] she told me you all would be together Thanksgiving and that you would have a big time— Im sorry Billy and I cannot be with you— We will have to have our little celebration alone— Its our wedding anniversary too you know— Nov. 25th We have been married two years.

Billy sends his love to you and with lots from your daughter

Betty

ALS, rc. Pettyjohn collection, WHC-OkU. On Hotel St. Francis, New York, letterhead.

1. Rogers used Mabel Hackney Tompkins's "high school horse Vardius to represent the English style–side saddle, tailored habit, and top hat" (Mary A. Turner to Homer Croy, 10 September 1952, HCP-MoU).
2. Rogers's niece Estelle Lane (Neal), the eldest daughter of Maud Rogers Lane and Cap Lane.

Betty Blake Rogers to Clement Vann Rogers
ca. 12 November 1910
New York, N.Y.

Saturday

My dear Mr. Rogers—

I have just come up from breakfast and Billy has gone to see about his horses. He bought such a beautiful pony yesterday black and white spotted— He only gave one hundred and fifteen dollars for it and that was very very cheap. The man who owned him was holding out for $200.00. The pony was sold at a big sale. The horses we brought back with us are all fine. Billy uses my pony (the little yellow one he got in Vinita) in his act and he likes her so much. She does the work as well as Teddy did. The weather here is very nice now. Its cold, but we have had the sun the past few days.

I ~~was~~ spent the day yesterday with Mrs. Winter and her daughter Winona— you remember the girl you met in Chicago that played in the "Golden Girl"[1]— They will be in New York for some time and Im so glad for I love them dearly and so glad to be with them here. Billy will work right in and around New York now for several weeks. He is busy all the time getting everything in shape for the act. He has four horses now and has gone today to see about getting a high-school horse. Billy has been very conservative and I think we are going to get this act on much cheaper than we first thought.

What did you think of the election?[2] We were so pleased over it all— Excitement in New York was very great—

My love to you and Billy sends his love

Your daughter
Betty

ALS, rc. Pettyjohn collection, WHC, OkU. On Hotel St. Francis, New York, letterhead.

1. See Biographical Appendix entry, WINTER, Winona.
2. The 8 November 1910 elections resulted in sweeping victories for the Democratic Party on both the state and national levels. In Congress the Democrats gained control of the House of Representatives for the first time in almost twenty years. The New York Democrats won the governorship and both houses of the state legislature. By uniting behind the gubernatorial candidacy of John A. Dix, a prominent businessman and banker from upstate New York, the New York party's reform and Tammany Hall factions defeated the Republican Henry L. Stimson. Their victory was read as a rejection of the forces behind Stimson, who was inextricably associated with the political goals and ambitions of Theodore Roosevelt. (Roosevelt's reform program, known as the New Nationalism, had alienated conservative Republicans.) Low voter turnout, especially in upstate New York, indicated that many Republicans did not

vote. This resulted in the first Republican defeat statewide in the new century (*NYT*, 8 and 9 November 1910; Wesser, *Response to Progressivism*, 21–43).

Betty Blake Rogers to Clement Vann Rogers
9 December 1910
New York, N.Y.

Friday Dec 9th

Dear Mr. Rogers—

We are having pretty weather now, still have snow on the ground, but the sun is bright and warm and its just fine to be out—

The big department stores here are beautiful, the Christmas goods and display is so pretty— I wish each day the children could be here, they would so enjoy seeing the beautiful toys— I hope you can be with us Christmas— it isnt long you know. The time goes so quickly I can hardly realize Christmas so near—

The big act is going pretty good, its so big Billy is afraid now he will have to cut it down some to get it on the regular stages[1]— He is working with it all the time & we both think that it will make money— We got your good long letter and was so glad to get it— Im sorry for Lanie and Owen and only hope that later Frank will let them go back to the girls— Im afraid he won't be able to care for them as they have been used to and as they should be cared for— Pauline is home today and Billy and I can imagine the happiness in the McSpadden *family,* I should love to see Pauline and do so hope she comes home ▲much▲ benefited by her long course of treatment[2]—

My love to you all

Betty

ALS, rc. OkClaW. On Hotel St. Francis, New York, letterhead.

1. On 12 December 1910 Betty Rogers wrote to Clement Vann Rogers that "Billy will bring the new act into New York about Tuesday, he is out now getting his stuff brought over and to get everything shaped up, the act is working fine but Billy thinks he will have to take out some of the horses— Its too big and hard to handle on the stage, he intended doing this any way when he took the act out on the road— Some of the managers want him to take out two of the horses and in their place add his own act, they would give him big money for this— Until we get the act in New York tho we won't know just what to do about that" (OkClaW).

2. References to Frank and May Rogers Stine's children Lanie and Owen Stine, who had been living in Chelsea with their aunts, and to Tom and Sallie McSpadden's nine-year-old daughter, Pauline (Paula) McSpadden, who as a toddler had suffered from infantile paralysis and remained in fragile health. She had been sent to live in a sanitarium in St. Louis in an effort to build her strength (OkClaW; see also *PWR,*

1:505–6). Betty Blake Rogers wrote to Clement Vann Rogers on 12 December 1910 that "Billy worries so about Lanie and Owen, he feels badly about the way Frank has done and wants to know what kind of report Frank gives to the Judge and just what will be done about it— I know you worry about the children too— But I suppose we will just have to wait and see. I think later he will want Maude and Sallie to take the children back, Im sure he will get tired of caring for them" (OkClaW).

Excerpt from Unpublished Autobiography
ca. Late 1910
New York, N.Y.

Rogers wrote this autobiographical account for Variety founder Sime Silverman,[1] but it was never published.

Sime asked me how I got in[to] show business and why I stayed. I got into it cause I couldn't make a living at anything else and how I stayed is a wonder to a lot of audience[s]. How I horned into it is a pretty longwinded tale and in unloading it on you you would think I was telling the story of my life. I was born at Claremore in the Cherokee Nation, Indian Territory, now Oklahoma, on the same ranch I still have there. The county was named for my father, who was the oldest resident of the county and a member of the constitutional convention of Oklahoma. My mother was a quarter-breed Cherokee. My father was a one-eight[h] and I'm ~~more~~ sure proud of my Cherokee blood cause they are some tribe. Mixed blood hold the same rights and land as a full blood.

My father tried to make something out of me and sent me to half a dozen different schools. I hardly ever would stick the year out. The last one was a military school at Booneville, Missouri. I broke out of there and headed for Texas and New Mexico, as I was leary of going home to my dad. I worked on ranches and finally I and another boy went to California with a shipment of cattle and up to Frisco and that night something happened. He says he didn't blow the gas out. Maybe there was a leak. I was asleep when he come in. Anyhow they dug us out of there the next morning and hauled us to a hospital and believe me bub I didn't know a fighting thing till late that night. That was just bull luck. The main doctors gave me up but a lot of young medical students and just by practicing on me they happened to light on some nut remedy (that no regular doctor would ever think of) and I came alive. Well I landed back home pretty badly buggered up. This stuff had located in my system. I went to Hot Springs to boil it out and when I would get in a hot room they would all think the gas was escaping some place.

I had heard that the Argentine Republic was a great ranch country so I sold a bunch of my cattle and took a boy named Dick Paris with me and we hit the trail for South America. We come to New York to take a boat but found it easier to go by way of England. We landed up in a little hotel down by the Battery. We started to cross the street and he jerked us up on the sidewalk and said, Get on the sidewalk and [*illegible*] get run over by anything bigger than a man. We was here a week and never got further uptown than the City Hall. If we had ever got as far up as 42nd Street we would have thought we was in Albany.

We sailed on the Philadelphia. Well I didn't even last to see Sandy Hook. Oh doctor, I sho was sick. And you talk about boats doing things. Say bub, this baby cut some capers. A bucking horse, why this baby did everything but rare up and fall back. If it could go on the stage and do all those tricks it would make these kickers go back to Brooklyn. It did a flip flap Browny Rudolph in a [*illegible*] all in a swing. I couldn't have any luck eating and I lay on my broad back that whole trip. When I come on deck the last day they thought a new passeneger had got on board. Well after not having luck enough to die we finally [*illegible*]

We went up to London and wanted to see everything and noticed that Picadilly Circus was billed bigger than anything else on all the buses. But when we got there we soon learned it wasn't much of a show. But I'll give the Picadillies credit. They got a great location if they ever want to put on show.

We happened to ooze our way into an opera house and saw an awful [*illegible*] little guy. I didn't know he amounted to much. I saved my program and afterward learned it was Dan Len[o] and he was a top [*illegible*] on all the showbills and was as big a man in England as Joe Keaton in Muskegon. We stood a good chance of getting beheaded there down by the headquarter ranch where his royal loftiness hangs out. They have planted around what they call the King's own lifeguards. They sit back on a big truckhorse in a little covered coupe and wear a high lambswool muff on their nob for a hat and enough swords and capes and harness to put out a number two show. My partner thought the first one we eased into was a statue. Then we saw he still wore all this and lived. Dick asked him to gouge this old bobtail fly [*illegible*] in the ribs and see if he couldn't get him to [*illegible*] Then a London Robert directed us to drift on down the [*illegible*] But we was safe from that geezer on the horse cause you would have to give him three days notice to shed some of that wardrobe so he could handle his artillery. Can you imagine a flock of those located in front of the White House when Roosevelt was there? But different nations have different ideas of humor.

We mooched on up around the Bank of England and Dick discovered we were being watched. The made us feel sorter important. You see our dress was not what you would call decidedly English. I guess they figured we looked tough enough to assassinate the king or crack the bank. But we didn't even know the king and couldn't even count English money we had seen so little of it.

The old village was pretty busy just getting ready to crown King Edward so we went out to the Tower of London to get a peek at this [*illegible*] and it was what you would call considerable headgear. If [*illegible*] could get their lunch hooks on about a peck of those [*illegible*] they would have the other two thirds of the actors in hock for life.

Then we caught a boat for Buenos Aires and that dealt me another [*illegible*] of misery for 23 days. Just seems like I was right on the verge of dying and then not do it. And the other guy no matter that old tub did a [*illegible*] spin he could sit right on the rail over the back and chew old star navy and spit on the ocean and every time they ring a bell to change the watch he thought it was a dinner bell and stampeded for the lunch box. And to rub it in every time he would come in to where I lay he would be eating. He come back to dinner from there and I laid around a lot.

On those ranches, those good native gauchos or poolers down ther get 15 dollars a month in rag money. That's 42 cents on the dollar of regular money. Well I didn't prosper or do much good down there. Besides those guys could throw a rope further than I could throw a rock. They couldn't do any tricks but they could sho [*illegible*] that old rawhide out there and hang beef on the end of it every shot. When I went to check up to leave the country I found I didn't have enough dough to make the first payment on a soda cracker. Well I worked my way out of there on a cowship. Had every old kind of animal on there, horses, hardtails, mules, cows and a way up high where the crows went [*illegible*] to be was woolly [*illegible*] sheep.

Well if there's anything I hate worse than going on early at Hammerstein's it's sheep. Add to this conglomeration [*illegible*] of all nationalities. Not a one could spit a word of English and we were to act as waiters for this 3000 head. A German ship crew, an Irish veterinarian who spent most of his time working on me. But last and not least of this zoo was an Englishman that [*illegible*] the whole layout. He was a regular legit. I soon found I couldn't rassle with a bale of hay and a dose of seasickness at the same time and they couldn't fire me so I was appointed the nightwatchman on the decks with the cows. Well after I did get so I could eat things without a return ticket on it, why we didn't have anything to eat. I reckon that Englishman figured we could graze on that day old alfalfa. I finally figured out a way to land some extra nourishment. Some of those cows had calves. Well I got a rope and tied em off and later on would go and milk these old milk cows. They were harder to get to than the back end of that sixth floor. After bearfighting those old snaky heifers around there and getting more bumps than all the Jimmy Rice imitations put together I would get my little cupful and take it up to the cook, who was tickled to get fresh milk in the middle of that ocean to use in his cooking. He would load me up a bunch of [*illegible*] everything that this Englishman couldn't eat for dinner. I would leave a call with him and go back on watch.

25 days and we lobbed into Durham and it was just before the close of the Boer War and I got a job trying to help break horses up at the British [*illegible*] station. You know these American or Australian horses killed and crippled more soldiers than the Boers. Lots of them were just Western broncos that had never been broke. And then they expect some of these yeomanry that had never rode anything worse than a 'Ansom Cab and couldn't ride in a boxcar without the door ceiled up to crawl up in the middle of these old scruffy broncs in a little Pan Cake saddle. Why, it was nothing less than suicide. When a whole company would get new horses and they would holler Company Mount, in ten seconds you couldn't see nothing but loose horses and Tommies coming up digging the dirt out of their eyes and wondering if the Boers was after them. Those fellows had as much chance staying on top of some of those horses as a man would have of sneezing against a cyclone. But you have to slip it to em for nerve cause soon as they got their bearings they wanted to take another fall out of the bloomin bleeder.

But sometimes nerve can be taken for damn foollishness. There was one regiment of high collars from London that had more money than ability that was known as DeWitt's Remounts. After having tea and their nails manicured they would start out with all of these fancy uniforms and good horses. DeWitt would catch em and take their horses and part of their wardrobe and guns and turn em loose and let em go get mounted and then get em again. They were about as handy around a war as a she bear in a drugstore.

When the war stopped I joined Texas Jack's Wild West show at Johannesburg. I showed him my little tricks with a rope and he put me in that night. That was my first shot at the show business and I was sho scared, leary eyed. I thought a fellow ought to do roping in a show just had to be a curly wolf and do all sorts of curious things with a rope or set up and fan a Bronc with one hand and roll a cigarette with the other like you've all heard of but nobody has ever seen. And don't let any four carder kick that load in you cause there is some high Weavers in some of those contests.

When I got in the ring that night I couldn't slip up on the bank and throw a rope in the creek. I couldn't a doubled that rope up and hit the ground with it. I tangled myself up in that rope so I guess they thought I was doing a Houdini. Finally when Jack saw I wasn't going to be able to choke myself he come in and drove me out. Then it come time to show how real wild cowboys conquer untamed mustangs, buck jumpers. I told Jack I better not take out a stack in this bronc affair cause he was liable to get the top of his tent punctured with a weak roof cause I haven't got a single medal on my person for remaining on the hurricane deck of any outlaw Cayouse. I told him to bring out some nice little crowhopper and if the saddle horn was on solid I'd try cause I sho did need that job. And that's a big old wall-eyed mickle-done Australian Bronk. He certainly did look the part. But I found out afterwards they considered him a joke and he couldn't throw a wet saddleblanket. Well I screwed that old [*illegible*] down on him and got a death grip on that old apple and away we went, him just hitting a high lope around this little ring and me hanging on three [*illegible*] like a monk. But I wasn't going to turn loose of that horn cause I didn't know what minute he might bog his head and I couldn't set on a fence and [*illegible*]. All he did was run into a long tent pole at the edge of the ring and break it and the gaslight that lit the [*illegible*] pole it bent the rope and throwed the whole works in the dark. This turned on a half-breed panic. When the lights finally came on he was standing there [*illegible*] and hanging on to that horn like an actor to his top-money contract. It must have been a big hit, cause everybody laughed.

But we had a boy there that was a bronc [*illegible*]. Poor boy. Any time that old rancher took a setting on one of those bugs and heads that skate was in for a fine cleaning. He rode [*illegible*] with hands in the air [*illegible*] free and scratching. Us other punks didn't have any license to even scratch his side. I stayed a year and we showed everywhere down there. Of course I thought to be a regular Wild Wester I had to have a name so I christened myself The Cherokee Kid and had [*illegible*] heads made.

Then I got Australia in my suit so Jack gave me a letter to Wirth Brothers.

Well I throwed in with that troupe and stuck almost a year. Played all over South Africa. Well I took a shot at everything. Did a clown in the leaps and did a coon song in black face in the concert. All about playing so many different parts in the drama. Well then I got Australia into my suit and so I let a chuck for there. He gave me a letter to Wirth Brothers, who are the big circus of Australia.

Well I paid for the privilege of spending another 20 days of agony on another ocean, the Indian. And say it sho was on the warpath when I breezed over it. Well all that peeved me was that I had to go American instead of European. That old cowboy who did make some coin off me. Well I didn't think it was possible to be so sick and still live. That little passover was 21 days bounding "agony."

It was my extreme good fortune to be on a boat that did not touch Australia but went right on to New Zealand five days further and then reloaded. And you had the pleasure of a small matter of five days to get back to where you had almost been ten days previous. What wonderful transportation arrangement especially for a Jasper that gives up going to Hoboken on a ferry boat.

Well again fate was cruel to me and I survived the trip and joined the Wirth show in Sidney. And my roping act also a trick riding act that certainly had a nice little [illegible]. And we toured. It was just like a vaudeville show, only one act at a time, one show a day, no Sundays. We toured through Australia and then as Clef would say, I was overstuffed with pleasure when I heard they was to sail for New Zealand. Well the only consolation I had was they said even the captain got sick. Say that little New Zealand is just what I would call a regular country. The best system of government in the world, great scenery and the natural resources of the country are great. Of course I thought I had to have a Wild West name so I christened myself the Cherokee kid, a name that I would tell I got back in America and realized what a fine joke they were.

A man come to try to get us to go to a show that showed all the coast towns in India straight settlement China. Said he would pay me good salary all the time. Had me all excited till he said it was easy as we only showed about a third of the time as we were on the boat traveling the rest of the time. Well I don't know what kept me from hitting him right then and there. Old "coolies" out there ain't never going to see unless Mr. McAdoo stretches out one of his tunnels further than he ever has yet beli[e]ve me.

The show had finished New Zealand and was going back to Australia. Well I couldn't see any luck having another boat ride going further away from home again. So I left them—like so many have left the Barnum show—*Flat* and I headed for America. Well now comes the crossing trick of all this seasick stuff and I hope to chew up my best rope if it ain't just as recorded. Made a day trip by train and had to take a boat for just one night to get to Auckland where I was to get the boat coming from Australia to Frisco. Well our train pulled up side of this little skiff that night and we all stacked out of there into the boat which was tied to the dock.

Well I figured the way to do it is got right to bed. Well there was no state room. The men had one big room full of bunks. I didn't take time to take off my clothes. I hit the alfalfa. But I prepared myself. I got one of those cute little tin lunch buckets that you hangon the side of your bunk. Well I layed there and rolled around and commenced to feel uneasy in certain parts and finally I couldn't wait longer and man I was sick. Well this had been going on for some distance when some old wool said to another one, I wonder what's the matter. Ain't this thing going to go? Well, that shows you what a big mess of imagination will do for you. But then too there's a curious sort of smell on all boats that if I got a whiff of it in the inside of the Mojave desert I sho would take ill. They would make more of those men turn their shooting coal into that scoundrel and make it get under faster instead of having the horde of em painting and varnishing all the time wouldn't be so many people seasick.

Well I got back to Frisco after being gone almost three years during which time I had made a complete circuit of the world and made in such a way that I had travelled over 50,000 miles [*illegible*]. I had started in first class, yes and put on the old double barrel behavior for dinner too. You ought to get use floating down the main aisle of the dining saloon with this Hart Schaffner Marx hand me down wedding suit. I got my white tie dirty putting it on and I had to wear galoshes and I do hate em. I must have been a hit when I come in cause everybody laughed. Then I traveled second class, then third class, then when I was companion to those she cows was what might be called no class at all. It took me three years to get enough money to get back home, and say George Cohan's trademark sho looked good when I sited it astride Golden Gate.[2]

I landed back here just before the World's Fair in St. Louis and worked there with Colonel Mulhall that year. Well I had the stage fever and another boy and I got a job for a week at the old Standard in St. Louis with a [*illegible*] barley. I showed the act to old Col. Hopkins and he liked it and wrote to Murdoch in Chicago and he finally gave me a week at the old Chicago Opera House.

AMS. Private collection of Will Rogers, Jr., from typed transcription by Ben Yagoda. On Hotel St. Francis, New York, letterhead.

1. See Biographical Appendix entry, SILVERMAN, Sime. Rogers wrote this autobiographical statement for Silverman ca. 1910–11, while he was living at the Hotel St. Francis, but it was never put into print. Donald Day printed a revised version of it in his *Autobiography of Will Rogers,* and Ben Yagoda referred to it in his biography, *Will Rogers* (see 353n.74). The autobiographical account is significant as much for its style—with Rogers developing the kind of humorour writing he would use later in his journalism—as for its content.

2. For extensive documentation of this period of Rogers's life, from his birth in Indian Territory through his schooling and travels leading up to his appearance at the St. Louis World's Fair in 1904, see *PWR,* volume one.

To Clement Vann Rogers
5 January 1911
New York, N.Y.

Lawrence, Mass.

My Dear Dear Papa.

Your letter just come and we were so glad to get it cause you always tell all the news.

I am so glad you are getting all of your business straightened out cause then you will know just how you stand and wont Worry about your different affairs   I am mailing to you today the abstract that Johnstone made and you can get the farm all straightened out too. Who is the Lawyer that is doing it. Now we are expecting you back here right away and in case we go to Europe which we may do you are to go along for a few weeks any way.

We are thinking of going over pretty soon and have a trip mapped out for you Sallie and Maud   it wont cost much and We will all go over togeather and then you all can come back when you like   it wont cost you all over $250, or $300 a piece   now Sallie and Maud can afford that and we will just all go over and have one big time   I will write them later all about it as I will know more when I get to New york next Week. A little ocean trip would be the finest thing in the world for you.

Well the big act I put on did not do so well and I saw it at once and only played it one week then I took part of it out and put it in my act and I think I can get quite a bit more money for my act   I have a girl from Pawnee Oklahoma and her husband and she rides a bucking horse in my act and I still use Buck and three ponies besides the Bucker 4 horses and 4 people   She is a great rider and I have a great Bucking horse. I have 6 horses in all but I only use 4 of them in this act   I bought a pretty spotted horse   looks like Toms old Spot and he is good and I have two Buckers and the three ponies   they all work good   The little bay Blue Starr one is just a second Teddy. the other act was two big and they would not pay me enough money to afford to keep it but I got all the people other jobs and they are all doing Well. I think I will get some money with this act. this is a bad year back here and its hard to get work but this act is certainly going great with the audience.

Now Maude you and Sallie this is no joke   We will all just go to Europe I will find out all about the cost next Week   you could make it in 6 Weeks Papa could stay with me while you all and Betty and Bettys sister Dick may go if we do and you all could take in all of it   I am figureing on an engagement in Paris and if I get it it starts Feb 15. so hurry up   We would go by

London as I want to put on a trial show for the Managers so I could come back there from Paris. Now ~~you~~ we all could go over togeather and then you could take side trip to Scotland and Ireland then all over to Paris and you could come home by way of Venice, Rome, Naples and Perhaps the Holy Land all in three or four Weeks over there. Papa could stay with me Betty could go with you all then you could sail home from Naples   he could meet you there and Betty come back to where I was   Now can you beat that for somewhere around $350.00 or what if it costs more thats the trip of a lifetime for all of us.

Now I will write you all next Week   Now Papa we are sending you by express a present for your Birthday   wish we were there to help you celebrate and eat a big dinner   Say ask my Godbey[1] to send me please a statement at the bank and see how I stand

Well I must close

Write to the same address in N.Y. St. Francis Hotel, as we will be there next Week as I dont think we work[2]

Lots of Love to all of you and go to getting your Money ready cause this will [be] some trip   What will Cap and Tom say.[3]

With all our Love
Billy and Betty.

ALS, rc. OkClaW.

1. C. F. Godbey, cashier and treasurer of the First National Bank of Claremore, Okla., where Rogers kept his accounts.
2. Rogers played with the modified group act in Lawrence, Kans., the week of 2–8 January 1911. In the rest of the month he went from Kansas to Columbia, N.Y., on to Albany and Schenectady, and back to Brooklyn. February brought him to Cleveland, Detroit, Rochester, N.Y., and Barrington, R.I., and then back to New York to the Fifth Avenue Theatre in early March. His Will Rogers and Co. played Providence and Philadelphia in March 1911 (*NYT,* 5 and 7 March 1911).
3. Betty Blake Rogers wrote to Sallie McSpadden on 7 January 1911 that "we are leaving here Sunday at noon, will go to Boston then down to New York on boat. We may go to Europe soon. . . . We want you and Maude and Mr. Rogers to go with us" (OkClaW). Clement Vann Rogers had already written to McSpadden to tell her about the invitation to Europe (9 January 1911, OkClaW).

Review from *Variety*
14 January 1911
New York, N.Y.

Will Rogers and Co. (3).

Wild West.

18 Mins.: Full Stage.

Columbia.

Will Rogers explains the reason for his new act to the audience in few words. He says "I've been getting away with this junk for so long that I thought you would get wise to me sooner or later so I went out and dug up a little new stuff with which to bunk you for a few more years." Rogers is doing an act quite different from his former offering, even though the rope is still the main feature. It is Rogers though who is liked. His personality, careless manner and broad grin are worth more than the most intricate tricks that could be figured out. Some of the lariat throwing has been dropped to allow Rogers to give an imitation of Fred Stone in his lariat dance. Rogers is a surprise when he starts dancing, and gets away with it big. To make it more difficult, he shows how George Cohan would do the dance were he to start throwing the rope. This brought a storm of applause. With the dancing goes talk in which Rogers "kids" his imitations. There are many laughs folded in the few remarks. As a finish Rogers introduces a young girl about whom he tells wonderous tales as regards broncho riding. A broncho is lead out and with the aid of two men the young woman is placed in the saddle, holding her position easily while the horse jumps and dives all over the stage. It makes a bully good finish to an all around entertaining specialty that is an improvement over Roger's former act, which was good enough.

Dash.[1]

PD. *Variety* clipping, 14 January 1911. Scrapbook MF & ZF, CPpR.

1. Dash was the pseudonym for Charlie Freeman, who was Sime Silverman's brother-in-law and the younger brother of Silverman's wife, Hattie Freeman. An accomplished athlete, he played professional football for Syracuse. He was known as a gambler, betting on horses and other sport events. Although he knew little about show business, Sime hired him after two issues of *Variety* had been published. He proved to be an excellent critic and writer. Freeman married Amelia (Carrie) Claire, member of the juvenile vaudeville act, Felix and Claire. Later in his career he was a booking agent for the Palace (Gilbert, *American Vaudeville*, 375–76; Laurie, *Vaudeville*, 485; Spitzer, *Palace*, 184; Stoddart, *Lord Broadway*, x, 32, 53, 95–96, 99, 133, 374).

Article from the *Chelsea Reporter*
19 January 1911
Claremore, Okla.

C. V. ROGERS ENTERTAINED.

A very notable day in the life of Hon. C. V. Rogers of Claremore was that of Wednesday, January 11, 1911, as that was his 72nd birthday and his daughter, Mrs. Tom McSpadden, entertained for him at her hospitable home. Mrs. McSpadden was ably assisted throughout the entire day by her sister, Mrs. C. L. Lane. The weather man's assistance had been engaged for some time previous, so the day was bright and warm. The dinner party was composed of all "out of town" guests and were all ladies immediately related to the family. When all were seated it was no small degree of pride that our hostess felt in entertaining so distinguished a company, for be it known that 45 years ago these same guests were the reigning belles of the Cherokee nation. Not one present was less than 65 years of age and all are bright intelligent and entertaining women today.

The dining room wore a very festive appearance and the long table was laid for 16 guests. Both dinner and supper were served and the excellent menu was prepared entirely by Mr. Rogers' two daughters, who had catered extensively to their father's taste in the service of his dinner.

A telegram of love and congratulation from his son, Will Rogers, and wife, of New York was read at the dinner table and seemed to bring the only absent members of the family very, very near indeed.

Among the notable guests present was Mrs. Margaret Timberlake of Vinita, a sister of Mr. Rogers, and who is three years his senior. Mrs. Timberlake was a member of the first class of graduates of the old Cherokee Female seminary.

Mrs. M. L. Gulager, a sister-in-law, and Mrs. E. M. Alberty felt that the occasion was of sufficient importance to warrant them making the rather tiresome trip from Tahlequah. Miss Mary Gulager accompanied her mother and was a decided acquisition to the company.

The Claremore guests were Mesdames Juliet Schrimsher, a sister-in-law, Mary E. Lipe, a cousin, and Lou Lane. Mrs. Emma Drake of Chelsea, a classmate of Mrs. Lipe, was also present.

Each guest contributed, not only her presence, but also her charming personality and enthusiasm of years. Each wore, other than a placid smile, a becoming "memory cap," that all combined made this a very special occasion.

Quite a number of friends from town called during the afternoon to offer their congratulations to Mr. Rogers on having passed his 72nd mile stone and still retaining the erect carriage, health and vigor of early middle life.

Each guest was served with a cup of canuchy, the Cherokee national drink.[1]

It may not be amiss to give here, very briefly, a sketch of life of a man who has been such a prominent figure in the affairs of his country.

He received his education at the Baptist mission of Going Snake district and at the male seminary in Tahlequah. The civil war broke out during his early married life and he enlisted in the Confederate army, serving under Gen. Stan[d] Watie and later being put in command of his regiment.

In the early 70's he filled a two years' term as district judge and was then elected to the Cherokee senate and for eight years represented Cooweescoowee district in that capacity.

President Cleveland then appointed him one of three "appraisers of intruder property," and his last public service was that of assisting to make the constitution of Oklahoma, which convention assembled at Guthrie in 1906.

Very few men living today are so conversant with the history of the Cherokee people or have served them longer or better and we speak the sentiments of all his friends when we wish for Mr. Rogers unstinted peace and prosperity through the remainder of his life.

PD. Printed in *CR*, 19 January 1911. OkClaW.

1. Canuchy is made from crushed hickory nuts that have been condensed into and stored in a ball. The ball is boiled in water, and the nutmeat dissolves into broth. This is strained of shells and consumed as a drink or soup, often with sugar added. It is sometimes served with hominy grits or rice.

Keith Circuit Contract
17 February 1911
Philadelphia, Pa.

B. F. KEITH'S AMUSEMENT ENTERPRISES.

Agreement made this <u>17th</u> day of <u>February</u> 191<u>1</u>, by and between B. F. KEITH, of Brookline, Mass., hereinafter called the first party, and <u>WILL ROGERS & COMPANY</u> hereinafter called the "artist."

1. The artist promises to render and produce upon the terms and conditions hereinafter contained, a certain <u>BRONCHO BUSTERS</u> act or specialty with <u>four</u> persons therein for <u>ONE</u> weeks, commencing <u>MARCH</u> 27th 1911, at KEITH'S THEATRE, in Philadelphia, Pa., or in such other theatres or cities as the first party may require, in consideration of which and of the full and complete performance of the promises of the artist hereinafter set forth, each of which is of the essence of this agreement, the first party agrees to pay the sum of ——SIX HUNDRED——($600.00) Dollars upon the conclusion of the final performance by the artist at the end of each week during the term of this agreement.

2. It is understood that this is a vaudeville engagement and that the artist shall pay all transportation. If the artist is to render said act in more than one place hereunder, the average cost of such transportation between the places where such act is to be given, rendered or produced hereunder, shall be not over Twenty-five Dollars per person.

3. S. K. Hodgdon of 1493 Broadway, New York City, is acting for the first party in employing the artist.

4. The artist promises to abide and be bound by the rules and regulations in force at the theatre where the artist may be required to render or produce said act hereunder, to report for rehearsals at 10 A.M., on Mondays of each week, to furnish complete orchestrations of music, to render and produce said act at each performance to the personal satisfaction of the first party or the management of said theatre at least 2 times each day and not over 14 times in each week, and an additional performance on holidays or special occasions, when required; to eliminate any part of said act when requested by said first party or such management, and at least two weeks before the beginning of each engagement hereunder to deliver to the first party the necessary billing, scene and property plots, complete set of photographs sufficient for a large frame, program and press matter, time of act, and the route, if any, upon which the artist may be scheduled for two weeks immediately prior to the beginning of said engagement, and a failure to perform any of these conditions shall entitle the first party to forthwith cancel this agreement. . . .[1]

14. The artist acknowledges that this agreement and the engagements set forth herein were procured for him solely by and through the United Booking Offices of America, the exclusive booking agent of said artist, and therefore authorizes the first party to deduct 5% from the aforesaid salary at the end of each week, and pay the same over to the United Booking Offices of America.

IN WITNESS WHEREOF this agreement has been duly signed and sealed the day and year first above written.

APPROVED
By   60136
FEB 21 1911

<u>B. F. Keith, By S. K. Hodgdon</u> (L.S.)
(Artist sign here giving address.)
<u>Will Rogers & Co</u>(L.S.)
<u>1493 Broadway</u> ▾ <u>NY</u> ▾

PDS, OkClaW.

1. The abridged clauses covered standard agreements regarding sickness, cancellation of the agreement, judgment of professionalism of an act, salary, faithful performance, copyright, and other issues.

3. THE OKLAHOMA COWBOY AND THE WALL STREET GIRL
May 1911–September 1912

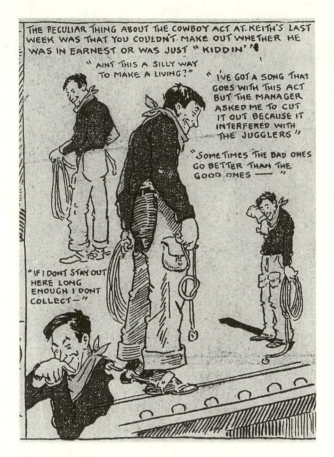

Newspaper cartoon clipping from the *Columbus Sunday Dispatch*, 8 October 1911, from Will Rogers's scrapbook. *(OkClaW))*

THE TWO-YEAR SPAN FROM THE SPRING OF 1911 TO THAT OF 1913 WAS A pivotal period in Rogers's life and career. In the spring of 1911 his show-business career was at a standstill. His attempt to organize a group Wild West act for the vaudeville stage had ended as a financial failure. The expenses associated with the show were enormous, especially the costs of costumes, travel, and salaries. With little publicity, his cowboy and cowgirl troupe never obtained major engagements. This was the first of Rogers's several show-business failures. Another was his money-losing film production company in 1922. Lacking management skills, he had a difficult time running a business.

Ever since his first vaudeville engagements, Rogers had worked with a horse and assistant. Although a popular vaudevillian in 1911, he was not a household name coast to coast. Nor was his popularity equal to vaudeville stars such as Eva Tanguay, Nora Bayes, Lillian Russell, May Irwin, Vest Tilley, Harry Houdini, Elsie Janis, and many other headliners, all of whom made over $1,000 a week.

To enliven his act, Rogers needed to "reinvent" himself, something he had to do several times in his career. His last vaudeville appearances in 1910 lacked novelty. Although the manager of Keith's Philadelphia Theatre called Rogers a "good act" in 1910, he was hardly excited by his performance. The act was getting old. "Did his regulation stunts and introduced his usual comedy," he wrote.[1] Although vaudevillians seldom suffered from overexposure, since they played to a different audience each week, Rogers had made two or three visits to cities on the Keith Circuit. Fortunately, Rogers possessed an insatiable drive to try something new—in this case a single act.

Single acts in vaudeville were extremely common, especially among stand-up comedians and monologuists. By deciding to go single, Rogers was taking a chance. Lariat tricks would not be enough to make his act different. To be a success, he would have to add spice to his act through comic patter, imitations, and other devices.

Several people influenced Rogers's decision to perform a single act. When Harry Jordan, the respected manager of Keith's Theatre in Philadelphia, suggested backstage to Betty Blake Rogers that her husband should perform alone, Rogers took the advice. Betty recalled that after hearing Jordan's opin-

Max Hart, the theatrical agent who played a prominent role in shaping Rogers's persona as The Oklahoma Cowboy. *(NN-L-BRTC)*

ion, "Will went back to the original act with which he started in vaudeville—just himself and his rope."[2] Another influence was Fred Stone, now a Broadway song-and-dance celebrity. Rogers taught Stone roping tricks that Stone used in his lariat dance in *The Old Town* (1910). In his autobiography, Stone recalled how he received a telegram from Rogers, asking, "Would you mind if I give an imitation of you doing the rope dance?" "I wired back that I didn't mind at all and I would teach him what he needed to know about dancing."[3] Max Hart, Rogers's new talent agent, also played a key role in promoting him as a single act.[4] Hart (1874–1950) became his agent sometime during the spring of 1911, when he saw Rogers perform. A flamboyant personality with a flair for selling his clients to booking agents and theater managers, Hart was popular with big-time vaudevillians. His clients included Fanny Brice, George Jessel, Buster Keaton, W. C. Fields, Fred Stone, and Eddie Cantor. In his reminiscences, Cantor recalled that Hart was "the top theatrical agent in the world. He not only handled the biggest money-makers in the business, he had so many next-to-closing acts that he was once able to threaten the Keith circuit—they'd meet his demands for increased pay for his clients or he'd bring vaudeville to a halt by yanking out his next-to-closing acts."[5]

A master at publicity, Hart purchased large advertisements for his clients in *Variety* and other trade papers. During Rogers's second week at Chicago's Majestic Theatre in June 1911, Hart placed a sizeable newspaper advertisement listing the rave reviews Rogers had received there. The advertisement highlighted Rogers's new single act without a horse as well as Hart's personal direction.[6]

Rogers was fortunate to have found Hart at this point in his career. It was probably Hart who recommended Rogers for his part in the Broadway musical comedy, *The Wall Street Girl*. As Rogers's agent, Hart must have played a role in changing his vaudeville billing to The Oklahoma Cowboy. Over the last eight years Rogers had had a series of monikers: The Cherokee Kid, Lariat Bill, The Lariat King, The Man with the Horse, The Plainsman, and several others. "The Cherokee Kid" and "The Oklahoma Cowboy" connoted different meanings: Rogers was now rarely identified on the stage and in the press as a Cherokee born in the Indian Territory. His current billing related to the new state of Oklahoma and a poignant western symbolic figure, the cowboy. As The Oklahoma Cowboy, Rogers represented both the new America that was being created out west and the archetypal western hero, a figure that was widespread in popular culture at this time. Basically, Rogers's new billing Americanized him, even though Rogers was neither an Oklahoma resident nor a practicing cowboy, but an entertainer who lived in New York. Audience identification with Rogers as The Oklahoma Cowboy would last his entire career. Rogers's public persona would later reappear as the cowboy philosopher in his writings, as the common man from Claremore in his films, and as the crackerbarrel topical humorist in his radio broadcasts.

Rogers was well aware that his roots in the American heartland made him unique on the stage and understood that he should exploit this image as much as he could. As a vaudeville single, Rogers used more homespun humor in his act. In his early vaudeville days, Rogers had made offhand remarks while doing his rope tricks. Now he relied increasingly on comic patter in his routine. He poked fun at other performers on the playbill and joked about his rope tricks, whether he did them perfectly or missed them. Although he was yet to get his humor from the newspapers, he began to tell a few political jokes. He had a standard gag about Theodore Roosevelt's return to politics ("I wonder what become of him. . . . Well, sometimes they come back, but not often").

During this period Rogers started to create his own style of humor. His comedy revolved around an understated delivery, a southwestern drawl, the homely metaphor, and the lighthearted quip. As a vaudeville single Rogers stood out from the regular comic fare on the variety stage. Personifying a lariat expert and cowboy humorist from the plains, Rogers's stage character was the opposite of the ethnic urban comedians whose humor derived from European sources and the immigrant ghetto: the Irish, such as Pat Rooney and J. W. Kelly; the German, or "Dutch," such as Gus Williams and Joseph Emmet; and the Jewish comics, such as Joe Welch and Barney Bernard.[7] The racial comedians relied on stereotyped characterizations of newly arrived immigrants. In their routines they used hyperbole, punch lines, self-deprecation, and double entendres. In Rogers's repertoire there was no slapstick, facial makeup, or risque gags, no bladder or baggy pants.

Rogers's single act, with its emphasis on understatement and humility, also contrasted with other forms of vaudeville humor. He was unlike the rambunctious eccentric comedians, such as Joe Cook, Herb Williams, and the teams of Rice and Prevost or The Elinore Sisters, who combined ethnic comedy with slapstick. These so-called nut acts stressed exaggerated clowning, knockabout antics, acrobatic stunts, fake bone crunching, and the throwing of props and furniture. While Rogers appealed across the board, risque and sexually brazen acts toyed with Keith Circuit guidelines for family humor. They often inspired a mixed response, from riotous laughter in the "low-brow," largely masculine, galleries to a tight-lipped appraisal from more "high-brow" patrons in the orchestra section, including middle-class women. Also popular were comic monologuists, such as Fred Niblo, George Fuller Golden, Louise

Henry, and James J. Thorton, who personified class and regional stereotypes, such as the clever Yankee and the country bumpkin. Rogers's routine also differed from the tramp comics, such as W. C. Fields and Nat Wills; the blackface comics, such as Frank Tinney and George (Honey Boy) Evans; "coon" singers like May Irwin, Marie Dressler, Fay Templeton, and Sophie Tucker; or the grotesque comics, who presented stock low-comedy characters with odd bodies or voices, or mismatched clothes.

Rogers's humor related more to the crackerbarrel literary tradition of American humor. This lower-class, white male tradition dates back to the eighteenth century and Benjamin Franklin's characters, Poor Richard and Silence Dogood, two witty, common-sense sages. Seba Smith's Major Jack Downing and Charles Farrar Browne's Artemus Ward were two rustic humorous characters created by popular nineteenth-century writers. Rogers's comedic style and speech patterns descended from southwestern American sources: the literary tall-tale humorists of the nineteenth-century frontier, the campfire yarns of backwoodsmen and cowboys, and the farfetched stories about the country yokel.

The success of Rogers's heartland humor parallels changes in the composition of the vaudeville audience. The racial comics were popular in the 1880s and 1890s, when variety theater was primarily located in cities and in immigrant areas. As promoters transformed vaudeville into a more refined, middle-class entertainment between 1900 and 1910, the popularity of ethnic comedians declined. The expansion of vaudeville across the country was another factor. Urban ethnic comedians were popular in New York and Chicago, but when national circuits established big-time theaters in rural states, such as Iowa and Kansas, those comedians had less appeal. By 1910 a broader spectrum of theatergoers preferred subtle humor to exaggerated comedy, wisecracks to slapstick. Rogers's act of lariat tricks and homely humor better matched vaudeville's growth into the hinterland and its emphasis on clean humor and morality.

Rogers added new material to his single act, including several impersonations. He not only imitated Fred Stone's lariat dance from *The Old Town,* but also mimicked the patriotic and spirited style of George M. Cohan's song "You're a Grand Old Flag." He added to his repertoire a parody of the comedian Eddie Foy, who was known for his farcical dancing and singing. Sometimes Rogers did a little comic singing himself. His rendition of the Ozark tune "Houn' Dawg" in a nasal twang drew considerable laughter from the audience. Rogers continued to make humorous comments about other performers on the bill. He began chewing gum on stage and stuck the wad on the proscenium arch—a Rogers trademark that he would use regularly in the *Ziegfeld Follies.*

Rogers's career took a new turn when he obtained a role in *The Wall Street Girl,* a musical comedy that opened in New York on 15 April 1912. This was Rogers's first appearance on Broadway; *The Girl Rangers* had never made it to the Great White Way. At this time many vaudeville headliners were moving to roles in Broadway musicals and revues: George M. Cohan, Al Jolson, Nora Bayes, Eddie Cantor, and Bert Williams, to name a few. For these performers, musical comedy meant not only more money and fame but also an opportunity to experiment and expand their routines beyond the constricted twenty-minute vaudeville format. As a result, the American musical theater was energized by vaudeville talent.

The origin of the American musical can be traced back to 1866 when *The Black Crook,* a potpourri of song, dance, melodrama, comedy, spectacular scenery, and gorgeous costumes, opened at Niblo's Garden in New York. The sold-out extravaganza ran for sixteen months and demonstrated the audience potential for musical comedy entertainment. For several decades thereafter the musical was dominated by urban and ethnic themes. For example, the musical plays of Edward (Ned) Harrigan and Tony Hart, such as *The Mulligan Guards' Ball* (1879), featured Irish American characters and other ethnic types that reflected the urban immigrant experience. Similar ethnic characterizations were found in the popular variety shows of Joe Weber and Lew Fields at their American Music Hall (1896). In their Mike and Meyer routine Weber and Fields used "Dutch" (German-Yiddish) dialect to burlesque recent immigrants. Their shows combined the humor of travesty and parody with musical extravaganza to create a form that foreshadowed the revue. Considered the most popular American musical in the nineteenth century was Charles Hoyt's *Trip to Chinatown* (1891), a farce that ran for 657 performances. The distinctive early black musical theater, exemplified by *Clorindy* (1898) and *In Dahomey* (1903), and featuring Bert Williams and George Walker, was also a vital genre, with books and music far ahead of its time.[9]

Rogers performed in *The Wall Street Girl* when the American musical was in a transitional stage between shows derived from Viennese operetta and innovative forms of the 1920s that used American themes and idioms, such as George Gershwin's *Lady, Be Good!* (1924) and Jerome Kern's *Show Boat* (1927). The Broadway musical from 1907 to 1914 was dominated by operettas with sentimental waltzes, cheerful melodies, and romantic plots. The immensely popular and influential *Merry Widow* by the Hungarian composer Franz Lehar (1870–1948) opened at the New Amsterdam Theatre on

21 October 1907. Numerous Americanized operettas followed, such as Victor Herbert's *Naughty Marietta* (1910) and *Sweethearts* (1913), Otto Harbach and Rudolph Friml's *Firefly* (1912), and Sigmund Romberg's *Student Prince* (1924). During the 1911–12 season over forty new musicals were performed, most having hackneyed plots, undistinguished librettos, and overly sentimental music. Songs in a musical were rarely integrated into the plot or related to character development.[10]

By contrast, there were productions that suggested the American musical was changing and becoming less dependent on European influences. Considered a forerunner of the modern musical comedy was L. Frank Baum's *Wizard of Oz* (1903), with music by Paul Tietjens and A. B. Sloan, and starring Fred Stone and Dave Montgomery. George M. Cohan began to create unique musicals with well-written books and bouncy songs based on American themes, such as *Little Johnny Jones* (1904) and *George Washington, Jr.* (1906). The revolution in the American musical, however, did not really get under way until 1915–19, and it flourished in the 1920s.[11]

In 1912 New York's Times Square (the area between Forty-second and Forty-fifth Streets where Broadway and Seventh Avenue intersected) was the focal point of the American theater. That year Rogers appeared in *The Wall Street Girl* at the George M. Cohan Theatre, located at Broadway and Forty-third Street in the center of Times Square.

The move to Times Square actually began before the twentieth century, when theaters such as Hammerstein's Victoria began to be built farther uptown, a trend that corresponded with the city's changing demography. Important to the growth and accessibility of Times Square was the completion on 27 October 1904 of the first phase of the IRT subway line, which ran from downtown City Hall, north on Fourth Avenue to Forty-second Street, and then on uptown. Due to its location on the subway route, the Times Square station became the city's busiest stop.

From 1900 to 1915 many new theaters were built in the area from Thirty-eighth Street to Fifty-ninth Street and between Sixth and Eighth Avenues. Among them was the lavish New Amsterdam Theatre (1903), where Rogers would perform in the *Ziegfeld Follies*, starting in 1916. Two other notable theaters were the Lyceum (1903) and the huge Hippodrome (1905), built for spectaculars. By 1905 seven major legitimate theaters were located on West Forty-second Street. At the end of that year the *New York Dramatic Mirror* (itself located at 121 West Forty-second Street) called Times Square New York's new Rialto. The offices of producers, theatrical agents, trade papers, and music publishers were all situated there. It was the headquarters of the two organizations that controlled the American legitimate theater: the Shubert brothers and the Theatrical Syndicate. Also new hotels (the Metropole and Astor), restaurants (Shanley's, Rector's, Churchill's, and Murray's), and theatrical clubs were located in the district. By the time Rogers appeared in *The Wall Street Girl,* the Times Square area was not only New York's entertainment hub but also the center of America's commercial culture in the performance arts.[12]

The Wall Street Girl was called a musical play and featured a score written in part by the Viennese-trained composer Karl Hoschna (1877–1911). Due to Hoschna's untimely death, several other composers were hired to create the music. The book by Margaret Mayo and Edgar Selwyn had a western theme, with the story primarily set in a Nevada mining town where the daughter of a Wall Street stockbroker invests in a profitable mine, prevents her father's financial ruin, and marries her partner. Rogers's Oklahoma Cowboy persona was a natural fit to the western story line. His roping repertoire in act 2, really a replay of his vaudeville routine, occurred in a mining town scene. Although *The Wall Street Girl* was not a box-office hit and lasted only seven weeks on Broadway, Rogers himself received rave reviews. Critics mentioned him as one of the musical's best performers.

Important changes in Rogers's personal life also occurred during this period. In 1911 he and his wife decided that New York should be their home. Their decision was influenced by the city's role as the center of the vaudeville industry. The booking headquarters of the Keith and Orpheum Circuits were located in New York, as well as the offices of other chains. Vaudeville agents and theater managers were likewise located in the Times Square area. After living in a midtown hotel and rooms at West 94th Street, the Rogerses found permanent quarters in an apartment at 551 West 113th Street in Morningside Heights, a growing area of middle-class apartment buildings.

Shortly after the Rogerses' move, two significant events happened. Their first child, William Vann Rogers (better known as Will, Jr.), was born on 20 October 1911. Eight days later Clement Vann Rogers died. Rogers canceled his engagement at Hammerstein's Victoria to attend his father's funeral in Chelsea, Oklahoma. Although the father-son relationship was often somewhat strained, the elder Rogers's strong character and entrepreneurial drive were dominant influences on his son. Clement Vann Rogers was initially disappointed that Will did not become a rancher and cattleman. In his final years, however, he became reconciled to his son's show-business career. He enjoyed seeing his son perform and would brag to others about his accomplishments in vaudeville. He was also proud that his grandson was given his middle name, Vann.

Dying intestate, Clement Vann Rogers left an estate that was divided equally among his three living children and the children of the late May Stine. Much of the real estate the family members inherited was on the Old Home Ranch near Oologah—a small part of the many thousands of acres that the Rogers family had once controlled in the Cherokee Nation. In September 1912 Will Rogers bought the acreage of his sisters Maud Lane and Sallie McSpadden, and he also purchased that of May Stine's children in 1913, all in addition to the Claremore property he purchased in 1911.[13]

1. Manager's Report, Keith's Philadelphia Theatre, 28 February 1910, above.

2. Rogers, *Will Rogers,* 110.

3. Stone, *Rolling Stone,* 169; see also Yagoda, *Will Rogers,* 125–26.

4. See Biographical Appendix entry, HART, Max.

5. Cantor, *Take My Life,* 96.

6. See Clipping from Will Rogers's Scrapbook, ca. 19 June 1911, below.

7. On the history of ethnic humor in vaudeville, see Distler, "Rise and Fall of the Racial Comics."

8. Gilbert, *American Vaudeville,* 251–92.

9. Mast, *Can't Help Singin',* 1–24; Toll, *On with the Show!* 172–206.

10. Bordman, *American Musical Theatre,* 230–77; *OCAT,* 423, 475–76.

11. Mates, *America's Musical Stage,* 181; Mordden, *Broadway Babies,* 22–33; *OCAT,* 559.

12. Frick, *New York's First Theatrical Center,* 151–68; Henderson, *City and the Theater;* Knapp, "Historical Study of the Legitimate Playhouses on West Forty-second Street between Seventh and Eight Avenues"; Stern et al., *New York 1900,* 46, 203–22; Taylor, ed., *Inventing Times Square;* van Hoogstraten, *Lost Broadway Theatres.*

13. See also Will Rogers's Real Estate Statement, ca. 1909, above.

———

Review from *Variety*
6 May 1911
New York, N.Y.

Once again, the Victoria Theatre in New York played an important role in Rogers's career. His second vaudeville engagement with a horse and an assistant had occurred at the Victoria Theatre in June 1905. This time he made his first appearance as a single act at Hammerstein's Victoria Theatre. He would never again perform with a horse on stage as a regular part of his routine. In his new act he wore a bright cowboy outfit with chaps and spurs on his boots. Expanding his repertoire, he imitated Fred Stone's lariat dance as performed by Stone on the Broadway stage. His twelve-minute act included a "Yiddisher" dance within the circle of his lariat.[1] Seated on a wooden box, he told stories mixed with quips. Rogers appeared on the Victoria bill with an all-star cast. The following review, which compares a vaudeville bill to a baseball game, exemplifies the clever writing for which Variety *was known.*

HAMMERSTEIN'S

It's one long grand bill at the corner[2] this week. The umpire called the game at 7:55 and the Gordon Bros.[3] stepped to the plate. The boys did their best in front of the few fans, but after a couple of long fouls flied out to right. Di Pace Bros. followed with a couple of high class selections on the mandolin and guitar. They took three long sweeps and retired to the bench without having touched the sphere.

Will Rogers doing a single was up third. Although the pitching was full of curves and fast ones Will managed to connect and placed a pretty single between second and short. Rogers as a single is in right and should keep going in the same direction. He should be hitting in the .300 class at the end of the season. Hoey and Lee playing on their own grounds had some trouble, but managed to bunt Rogers down to second.

John C. Rice and Sally Cohen found things a trifle hard at the opening with "The Primroses" sketch, and were up with two strikes and three balls, when they found one to their liking and nailed it up against the fence for two bases, scoring Rogers.[4] The finish aroused the audience to noisy enthusiasm. The piece is full of bright, snappy material, and the finish just can't go wrong.

The Six Kirksmith Sisters, newcomers to the big league, were up next.[5] They started quietly although their past performances must have been known on "The Corner" for the girls received a reception. They improved as they went along and followed the Rice and Cohen swat, with a b[s]ingle to left center, that never stopped rolling until they had completed the circuit, pushing Rice and Cohen over the pan ahead of them. These six girls will have no trouble whatever finding any sort of pitching and should have a long career in the big league. McIntyre and Heath closed the first part coming up with the bases clear. "The Man from Montana" proved as funny as ever and the black face comedians, although they stood up to the plate a trifle longer than necessary, hit long fouls to all parts of the enclosure before they straightened one out that went fair.[6]

The game was then called for ten minutes after which, with whetted appetites, the fans filed back to the stands. The Arlington Four were the first to face the pitcher after the intermission.[7] Following a stormy session during which the fans gradually became seated, they managed to hit to short right for a clean single. Felix and Claire were placed too far down in the batting order. "The Kids" had too many old time sluggers to follow and their efforts, although sincere, were only good for a sacrifice which advanced the Arlington Four to second. Amelia Claire gets better with each showing, but young Felix, who is beginning to grow some, must show something that will take him out of the child wonder class. Montgomery and Moore hit clean for two bases, although they were all but caught in an endeavor to stretch the two-sacker into a triple.[8] The Arlingtons scored on the hit. Frank Morrell was pretty well up against it down next to closing.[9] The fans were beginning to tire of the long game, and moved towards the entrance, but many remained to see Frank out and he finally squeezed one through first and second that put Montgomery and Moore on third. Sam Mann and Co. next to closing hit a long fly to deep center, going out themselves, but scoring Montgomery and Moore and advancing Morrell to second.[10] The Heuman Trio with a few ardent fans still left retired the side, leaving Morrell on third.

The game was played with a brand new Ball, Ernest (New Acts).[11]

Dash.

PD. Printed in *Variety*, 6 May 1911. Clipping, scrapbook A-3, OkClaW.

1. "Will Rogers," *NYC*, clipping, scrapbook A-3, OkClaW. The reviewer commented: "No other man in his line can get away with the talk as Rogers does, his stories and his quips getting plenty of laughs last week. . . . Rogers doesn't need any assistants—he can go it alone very nicely."

2. Hammerstein's Victoria Theatre was known as The Corner because it was on the northwest corner of Seventh Avenue and Forty-second Street.

3. The Gordon Bothers were called a "goofy" act, and their routine was compared to "Jeffy [the] boxing kangaroo" and "Big Jim, the skating and dancing bear" (Laurie, *Vaudeville*, 164).

4. John C. Rice (1858–1915) and Sally Cohen were a popular husband-and-wife comedy sketch team. Earlier, Rice's partner in the legitimate theater was May Irwin. She appeared in the historic 1896 Edison Vitascope film, *The May Irwin Kiss* (an episode from Irwin's 1895 Broadway play, *The Widow Jones*). Born in a small town in New York state, Rice was named John C. Hillburg. His parents were Swedish immigrants. Rice began as a contortionist and then became a comic actor. On stage he gained notice in *Aunt Bridget's Baby* (1891) with George W. Monroe and later starred in Herbert Hall Winslow's *Knotty Affair* (1891). Rice and his vaudeville partner, Sally Cohen, married around 1890. As a young actress, Sally Cohen appeared in Bob Miles's Juvenile Pinafore. She and Rice were among the first performers from the Broadway dramatic stage to appear in vaudeville. They were well-known variety regulars for over fifteen years and in 1909 were earning $600 a week. In 1915 Rice was in Philadelphia preparing for a Sigmund Lubin film with Marie Dressler when he died at the Hotel Majestic from complications due to Bright's disease and neuraemia. Two months earlier Rice and Cohen had performed together in vaudeville at New York's Colonial Theatre. The couple had one daughter, Gladys (*FilmEnc*, 680; Laurie, *Vaudeville*, 52; Musser, *Before the Nickelodeon*, 65, 80, 83; *NYT*, 6 June 1915, 17; *VO*, 1:11 June 1915).

5. The Six Kirksmith Sisters was a musical act (Laurie, *Vaudeville*, 68).

6. James McIntyre (1857–1937) and Thomas Heath (1853–1938), the headliners on the bill, performed the sketch *The Man from Montana*. McIntyre and Heath, who performed from 1874 to 1924, were among the most prominent blackface minstrel artists of their time. Born in Kenosha, Wis., McIntrye began his show-business career at age ten as a clog dancer and in the circus, and as a member of Kate Pullman's company. Born in Philadelphia, Heath ran away from home at age twelve and lived in the Carolinas. Heath had three partners before McIntyre: James Mott in a dance-and-patter act; Frank Mullen in a small-time vaudeville act; and George Howard in a performance of clogs and jigs. According to one anecdote, Howard was unable to perform one night in 1874, and McIntyre replaced him at the Tivoli Theatre in San Antonio, Tex. Soon McIntyre and Heath toured with tent shows and circuses, traveling to small towns where they did a clog dance on a barn door stretched between two wooden horses. In New York they were a big success at Tony Pastor's Music Hall and at Koster and Bial's Music Hall. In 1881 they toured with the Barnum and Bailey Circus, and in 1893 they were with Weber and Fields's company.

McIntyre and Heath pioneered the use of narrative situations for their gags, and the characters they played had a streetwise intelligence that was new for blackface routines. The act was based on minstrel shows of the pre–Civil War era, particularly the Christy Minstrels, led by blackface performer E. P. Christy, as well as the work of Stephen Foster. Of all the minstrel acts, theirs was the closest in style to the *Amos and Andy* radio show. Some accounts suggest they created the buck-and-wing dance.

Both performers created stereotyped characters that degraded African Americans. Heath played a pompous "dandy" character named Henry (pronounced "Hennery") with shiny clothes and a pillowed belly. McIntrye acted the comic part of Alexander, a naive, sorrowful character with a whiny voice, the victim of Henry's schemes. Like other blackface minstrel performers, they used caricatures that exploited African Americans through exaggerated dialect and stereotyped portrayals. Words in their routines such as *coon* and *nigger* reflect the racism of the time. An example of their repartee is as follows: "If it takes two yards of cloth to make a shirt, how many shirts can you get out of one yard? Answer: It all depends on how dark de night is and how many shirts is on de line" ("The Georgia Minstrels," clipping, NN-L-BRTC).

McIntyre and Heath had one of the longest associations as a team in the history of the American stage. During their time together they performed in every entertainment medium: vaudeville, minstrel shows, musical comedy, burlesque, motion pictures, circuses, and radio. Although there were constant rumors of a feud between the two, they remained friends after their stage career, both living on Long Island. When McIntyre died from uremic poisoning in 1937, Heath, now eighty-four and bedridden as a result of a paralytic stroke, was not informed of his death. A year later Heath died of a heart attack at his Setauket, Long Island, estate (clipping file, NN-L-BRTC; *EV*, 341–42; Gilbert, *American Vaudeville*, 83–85; Grau, *Forty Years Observation of Music and the Drama* 192–93; Laurie, *Vaudeville*, 139–40; Mantle and Sherwood, eds., *Best Plays of 1899–1909*, 493; *NYT*, 20 August 1938, 15; *OCAT*, 450–51).

7. The Arlington Four were a quartet of young men who performed song, dance, and blackface comedy. They dressed as messengers and performed buck-and-wing dancing. They also did imitations, including an imitation of Bert Williams. Their names were Lee, Lane, Manny, and Roberts. Roberts, who was an African American, was one of the first black performers to join white vaudevillians in a variety act. In May 1912 they headed the bill at the Orpheum in Peoria, Ill. (clipping file, NN-L-BRTC; Laurie, *Vaudeville*, 76).

8. Florence E. Moore was a female clown, known as "The Girl of Many Faces," and Billie (Kin) Montgomery was a piano comedian. They were the first to introduce wooden brogan shoes for use on the stage (clipping file, NN-L-BRTC).

9. Frank Morrell (ca. 1877–1925), whose birth name was Frank Cairns, was a singer. He began in vaudeville as a member of That Quartet, a popular act for many years. When the quartet broke up, Morrell did a single act. He retired from the stage due to a long illness arising from gangrene and lived in San Diego. An attempted comeback in 1923 was thwarted because of ill health. In San Diego he worked as a deputy sheriff. Both his legs were amputated because of blood poisoning, which led to his death in 1925 (*VO*, 1:18 November 1925).

10. Sam Mann was a comic actor who did ethnic humor in burlesque and vaudeville shows, and also appeared in the Yiddish theater. He specialized in German, Irish, and Jewish dialect parts. Of Russian-German descent, he immigrated to the United States with his parents as a child. He was the brother of Louis Mann (b. 1864), also an actor who did ethnic comedy work. Sam Mann did short comedic plays or farces on the vaudeville circuit. The *Milwaukee News* in 1911 reported on his appearance at the Majestic theater, saying that "Sam Mann is a German comedian who doesn't overplay his hand. For that reason he is about twice as effective as he would be if he was conceited and resorted to broader burlesque. Give Sam a goatee, a red nose, a comedy fiddle and several beers of assorted sizes, with a few actor folk who know their business, and he will bring down the house as positively as the sun rises and sets" (partially dated clipping, Locke env. 1298, NN-L-RLC). Indeed, two of Mann's claims to fame were his ability to gulp down a pitcher of beer as part of the humor in his act and nevertheless maintain his lucidity, and his smashing of perfectly good violins on stage.

Mann's specialty in the 1911–14 seasons was a playlet about a German orchestra leader called *The New Leader,* which he performed at Keith theaters and on the Orpheum Circuit. This was the playlet his dramatic company performed at the Victoria Theatre. A mixture of farce and burlesque, it was in part a play on The Cherry Sisters act. Two women dressed to impersonate The Cherry Sisters auditioned for an imaginary vaudeville act, while Mann played the straight part from the orchestra pit, feigning great dismay over what was happening on stage and interacting with the audience. The *Chicago News* of 27 May 1913 said of the act at the Palace that "Sam Mann is there with his hair on end, his dialect in a twist and his comedy ablaze with fun as the troubled leader of an orchestra at a vaudeville rehearsal. It is about as uproarious bit of farce as could be crowded into fifteen minutes and Sam is immense in a serious, agitated manner. So are supporting comediennes and comics."

In the 1915 season he did a new show, *Lots and Lots of It,* in which he played a real estate agent with "shades of humor and pathos that made the Potash and Perlmutter stories famous" (unidentified clipping, 5 January 1915, Locke env. 1298, NN-L-RLC). In between his vaudeville circuit engagements, Mann appeared on the stage. He played Jewish roles with the Hans Nix Co., the part of an Irishman in *Singing Girl of Killarney,* and a German character in *Morning, Noon, and Night.* He supported Louise Dresser in *Broadway to Paris* at the New York Winter Garden in June 1913. He played a role in Yiddish theater as Morris Perlmutter in various productions of *Potash and Perlmutter.* He was still working as an actor into the 1930s (clipping file, NN-L-BRTC; Locke env. 1298, NN-L-RLC; *NYT,* 30 April 1911; *Pittsburgh Post,* 8 December 1910; see also Manager's Report, Keith's Philadelphia Theatre, 10 May 1915, below).

11. Ernest Ball, a new act, was a piano player (Laurie, *Vaudeville,* 328). Also on the bill were Bertie Lawrence, The Marvelous Dunns, The Bowen Brothers, Morris and Eddie, and motion picture views (*NYT,* 30 April 1911, 2 May 1911).

Notice from *Variety*
27 May 1911
New York, N.Y.

Will Rogers sold a couple of ponies last week. He needs them no longer in vaudeville, where Rogers is now appearing as a "single turn," assisted by a few lariats and some talk. Johnny Collins and Geo. McKay[1] are the boys who think they picked up a bargain in the bronchos. They are now negotiating for the saddles, not having previously thought of it.

PD. Printed in *Variety,* 27 May 1911.

1. The entertainer George W. (Red) McKay (1880–1945) had a long career in vaudeville and motion pictures. Born in Minsk, Russia, with the family name of Reuben, he grew up in a Jewish orphanage in Cleveland, Ohio. At age fourteen McKay, as he was now known, became a singing and dancing waiter in a Chicago restaurant. As a vaudevillian he teamed with Johnny Cantwell (the *Variety* article might have mistakenly referred to Cantwell as Collins). McKay appeared in vaudeville with his wife, Ottie Ardine, who earlier had been a featured act on the Keith and Orpheum Circuits. In addition to playing in Gus Edwards's musical *The Merry-Go-Round* (1908), he also appeared in the musical comedy *Honey Girl* (1920) and *Broadway Brevities,* the latter produced by his brother, Ben Reuben. McKay and his wife appeared in the film short *Back from Abroad* in 1929. Under contract to Columbia Pictures, McKay played parts in several films, including *Men in Her Diary* (1945), his last film. He also had a minor role as Mr. Van Heusen in Bing Crosby's *Going My Way* (1944). McKay died in Hollywood on 3 December 1945 (*EV,* 368; Laurie, *Vaudeville,* 298; *VO,* 3:5 December 1945; *WhoHol* 2:1113; *WhScrn,* 1:469).

Article from the Dallas *Morning News*
31 May 1911
Dallas, Tex.

After performing at Hammerstein's Victoria, Rogers appeared on the bill at Brooklyn's Orpheum Theatre the week of 8 May.[1] Next he traveled home to visit his father and sisters, arriving about 24 May.[2] From there he went to Dallas, where he performed at the Lake Cliff Casino, a summer theater in the city.[3]

AMUSEMENTS.

LAKE CLIFF CASINO.

Cleverness of an unusual kind is displayed by Will Rogers at the Casino this week. Rogers is a genuine cowboy—or was, until he commenced amusing the public from behind the footlights. He handles the cowboy "rope" in a manner that mystifies. He makes one jerk and four knots appear as if by magic in the long strand which he holds coiled in his hand. With capable right arm a-swing, he whirls a gigantic loop about his body, as he nimbly dances in and out of the circling loop, albeit great Mexican rowel spurs are attached to his booted heels. For an encore last night he gave a distinctly genuine cowboy yell, that made Western folk believe they were back at home on their broad prairies. Other acts this week include Alice Raymond and company[4] in a spectacular musical number; Van Hoven, the mad magician; Thomas and Hall;[5] Yakka Egawa, Japanese woman slack-wire artist; Ashley and Lee[6] and the Casinograph. Matinees are given daily at 3 P.M., with evening performances at 8:30. The bill will be changed tomorrow, beginning with the matinee performance.

PD. Printed in *Dallas Morning News*, 31 May 1911.[7]

1. At Brooklyn's Orpheum Rogers was on the playbill with Irene Franklin (1876–1941), the popular impersonator, singer, and comedian. She was accompanied by her pianist, composer, and husband, Burton Green. Also on the playbill were the following acts: The Thomas J. Ryan-Richfield Company in *Mac Haggerty, Osteopath*; Valerie Bergere and Company in her latest set *Judgment*; The Avon Comedy Four; Mack and Orth; Paul La Croix; The Aurora Troupe; and The Grazers (*EV*, 191–93; *NYT*, 5 May and 7 May 1911).

2. The *Rogers County Leader* of 26 May announced that "Hon. Clem Rogers received a telegram Monday from his son Will, asking him to meet him on Wednesday, as he would stop off to visit with his sisters and their families. Will is en route to Dallas, where he is to appear next week."

3. The casino was located in Lake Cliff Park, which was advertised as "America's most Beautiful Summer Garden." Free band concerts were given on Sunday afternoons and evenings (*Dallas Morning News*, 28 May 1911).

4. Alice Raymond and her company presented *A Night in Egypt* (*Dallas Morning News*, 30 May 1911).

5. Hilda Thomas and Lou Hall presented a skit called *The Substitute*. Lou Hall (ca. 1861–1921), born Louis F. Balzer, and Thomas were a singing and piano vaudeville act for many years. As late as 1921, Hall was doing a comedy sketch called *She's a Traveling Salesman*. On 18 June 1921 he died in Chicago from blood poisoning as a result of an operation (*Dallas Morning News*, 30 May 1911; *VO*, 1:24 June 1921).

6. Ashley and Lee did a routine about life on New York's Lower East Side: "One of the team does a bit of character work as the proprietor of a delicatessen store, where customers are few, in a very humorous way, and the other is a blase 'rounder' to the manner born. Their song parody on names and places is original, and they have been encored again and again throughout the week" (*Dallas Morning News*, 30 May 1911).

7. On 1 June 1911 the *Rogers County News* reported that "the *Dallas Morning News* comments favorably on the work of Will Rogers. . . . They are billed at one of the summer theatres for one week for a different play each evening."

Clipping from Will Rogers's Scrapbook
ca. 19 June 1911
Chicago, Ill.

Max Hart, Rogers's new vaudeville agent, played a key role in Rogers's career at this time.[1] Hart influenced Rogers to perform a comedy monologue with rope tricks. He obtained a booking for Rogers at Chicago's Majestic Theatre[2] as The Droll Oklahoma Cowboy. "The Oklahoma Cowboy" moniker was used regularly during this stage of Rogers's career. It would be associated with Rogers for many years and helped communicate his stage persona to the public. Rogers was such a success that he was held over for a second week.[3]

HELD OVER FOR ANOTHER WEEK AT MAJESTIC, CHICAGO

WILL ROGERS

THE DROLL OKLAHOMA COWBOY
IN HIS NEW SINGLE OFFERING, ALL ALONE, NO HORSE

This is the second time in the history of this playhouse that an act originally booked for one week was held over because of its success.

WHAT THE CHICAGO PAPERS SAY

A COWBOY THAT LASSOES AN AUDIENCE.

BY RICHARD HENRY LITTLE.

Will Rogers, the Oklahoma cowboy, was one of the most pronounced hits on the program. The accomplished Mr. Rogers not only delights the audience with his amazing dexterity with the lasso, but even more with his running fire of small talk. The great beauty of Mr. Rogers' conversation is that he never is quite through.

He makes a remark and apparently marks a period by doing some trick with the lasso and the part of the audience that sympathized with his statement applauds madly. Then Mr. Rogers drops another remark that is diametrically opposed to his first statement and starts another section of the audience to great applause. But as this tumult drops down he makes still another comment along the line of the original thought that is a trifle more pertinent than either of the first two and differs widely from both.

The remarks of Mr. Rogers, when published properly, look something like an extract from the Congressional Record, because of the "applause," and "great laughter," and "long continued demonstration" that must be scattered through the published text of his discourse.

"Tribune."

The bright stars of the bill (it's a cold afternoon when the Majestic doesn't have at least two) are Will Rogers, the Oklahoma cowboy, who does remarkable things with a lariat, and eight young women who announce themselves as the "original Berlin madcaps." Rogers has a shame-faced humor of his own which never misses fire, and his imitation of Fred Stone's lariat dance is a startlingly well-done replica of the original.—"Record-Herald."

Will Rogers, a wonderful lariat thrower, is another big hit with the crowd. He has a grace and facility all his own, and with them a real instinct for comedy, that makes good with a vengeance. He does Fred Stone's lariat dance as well as Stone himself, and that's going some.—"American."

That Broadway cowboy, Will Rogers, who can do more different things with a lariat than a newspaper poet can with a rhyming dictionary, is the principal cause of applause at the Majestic this week. He is the most thoroughly practiced greenhorn in vaudeville. He may have been a real roper and rider before he took to the varieties; at any rate the audiences accept him as the real thing. But it matters not whence he came; he's as much an artist with a round-up and corral wheeze as he is with the rope. In his act he gives an imitation of Fred Stone's lariat dance, which Stone did as an imitation of Rogers. The imitation is bad for Stone, for Rogers does both the rope work and foot work better than the man who confesses he is a comedian.—"Journal."

Wild Bill Rogers is an artist. Why an artist? Because, in place of trying to nourish the sympathies of his audience for the act, he contrives to make them sorry for his stage fright. This is practical heart interest, and his lariat tricks and apparently unstudied conversation score the more heavily for that feeling of pity for his embarrassment. There is no necessity, for he walks away with the bill, even when Eddie Foy is finally off the stage. Mr. Rogers makes his ropes tie themselves into knots and untie again. He offers an imitation of Fred Stone in his famous lariat dance in "The Old Town," which would do credit to the greatest Scarecrow of the generation.[4] He pretends to give an imitation of the same form of poetry of motion as George Cohan would attempt it, and suggests that the versatile manager would find himself thoroughly hanged in the midst thereof.[5] But the feature of the act is not his cleverness with the lariat; it is the surprising manner in which he plays upon the sympathies of an audience willing enough to be sorry for a stage fright that doesn't exist. And in so doing he throws the antics of Hamlette Eddie Foy into the Stygian shade.—"Inter-Ocean."

The unquestionable hit of the evening was none other than Will Rogers and his lasso. Rogers never missed an opportunity to get his point over. Throughout the turn he had his audience just where he wanted them.—VARIETY.

DIRECTION, Max Hart

PD. Clipping, ca. 19 June 1911, scrapbook A-3, OkClaW.

1. See Biographical Appendix entry, HART, Max.
2. The Majestic Theatre opened on 1 January 1906 with a vaudeville show. The theater was located on the ground floor of the eighteen-story Majestic Theatre building, designed by E. R. Krause and situated in the center of Chicago's Loop at 22 West Monroe. A major force behind the theater's construction were the partners George Castle and Charles E. Kohl, well-known vaudeville theater owners in Chicago. The Majestic offered a bill of twelve to fifteen acts that ran continuously from 1:30 P.M. until 10:30 P.M. With four levels of seating and boxes, the theater had a capacity of 1,965 people. The Majestic was considered to be a first-class theatre and over the years offered drama, musical comedy, vaudeville, and burlesque. It was purchased by the Orpheum Circuit in the 1920s. In 1945 it was bought by the Shubert brothers and renamed the Shubert in memory of Sam Shubert (*EV*, 290; Frick and Gray, eds.,

Fred Stone, Broadway musical comedy star, dressed as a cowboy. Stone was Rogers's closest friend, and they shared a love of frontier life and the stage. *(Photo by Moffett, NNMuS)*

Directory of Historic American Theatres, 60; Grau, *Business Man in the Amusement World,* 323–24; *JCGHTG,* 86; *Orpheum Circuit* 1925).

3. During Rogers's first week (12–18 June) he appeared with the famous comedian Eddie Foy (1854–1928). Also on the bill were The Madcaps, Yates Motoring, Mlle. Bianci, and other acts. During his second week (19–25 June) Rogers performed on the same bill with the singer and actress Louise Dresser (1878–1965). Other acts were Edward-Davis and Co. (In a Brilliant New Play); Harry Fox and Millership Sisters (Unequaled Comedy Trio); The Four Hustings (In a Riot of Laughter); Taylor, Kranz and White (The Great Rathskeller Artists); Three Escardos; Corinne Francis; and The Narrow Brothers (clippings and playbill, vaudeville scrapbook, CPpR).

4. Stone taught Rogers his rope dance routine that he used in *The Old Town.* Rogers danced to the tune of "I Am a Cowboy with Gun and Lariat." *The Old Town* opened at Broadway's Globe Theatre on 10 January 1910. The musical play, produced by Charles Dillingham, ran for 171 performances. Stone played a leading role and performed a lariat dance (Mantle and Sherwood, eds., *Best Plays of 1909–1919,* 409; Rogers, *Will Rogers,* 113; see also Biographical Appendix entry, STONE, Val Andrew [Fred]).

5. According to Betty Blake Rogers, her husband was dancing to the tune of Cohan's signature song "You're a Grand Old Flag," which Cohan had introduced in the 1906 musical *George Washington, Jr.* (*OCAT,* 154; Rogers, *Will Rogers,* 113).

From Fred Stone
29 June 1911
Tromso, Norway

Fred Stone sent Rogers a postcard from Norway. An outdoorsman, Stone was on his way to Greenland to hunt polar bear. As he waited for his chartered steamboat to be repaired, Stone visited an encampment of what were then known as Laplanders (Sami) to see their roping skills.[1] The postcard he sent Rogers depicts a Laplander in native costume with a lasso. Stone and Rogers shared a passion for the art of roping, and Rogers's imitation of Stone's lariat dance in The Old Town *(1910) was now a permanent routine in his act.[2]*

Thursday June 29. 1911

Tromso, Norway.[3]

Dear Will.

This is a funny way to rope but they do the trick.[4] I will bring you one of their ropes. We sail for Greenland tomorrow for Polar bear.[5] Good luck to you & Wife

Your friend

Fred Stone

APCS, rc. OkClaW. Printed on the back in bold type were the words "Verdenspostforeningen. Brevkort fra Norge. (Novège)." Addressed to Mr. Will. Rogers, c/o St. Francis Hotel, 47th Street, New York, N.Y., USA.

1. Stone wrote in his autobiography that the Laplanders "cheerfully posed for pictures and gave me an exhibition of their roping, which is altogether different from ours. In return I showed them how the American cowboy spins the rope and did fancy catches for them which they had never seen before" (Stone, *Rolling Stone*, 173).

2. On the act, see Biographical Appendix entry STONE, Val Andrew (Fred).

3. Tromso is a seaport city located on a small island between South Kvaloy and the Norwegian mainland in northern Norway. It was founded in 1870 and became an important regional center for fishing, fur trading, and shipbuilding (*WNGD*, 1230).

4. The postcard shows many loops of rope curled around the Laplander's right hand, while his left hand appears ready to throw the rope.

5. Stone went to Greenland with three people: Edward Farmer, an experienced fisherman and hunter; Robert Burnes, a trapshooter and moose hunter; and Arthur Houghton, who managed *The Old Town* company. They hired a German guide named DeGisbert who chartered a sixty-five-year-old steamship, the *Fonix*. The ship encountered rough seas, and Stone became seasick. During the voyage the engine stopped running, the hold filled with water, and the ship had to be steered through ice fields in a dense fog. Some 150 miles from Greenland the hunters spotted a polar bear on an ice floe. Taking his camera and rifle on a whaleboat, Stone went out to the ice floe and killed the bear. Later, he roped two cubs that were brought on board; DeGisbert sold one of them to the Hagenbeck animal circus. In Rogers's scrapbook was an article on Stone's trip describing how he had taken movies of the polar bears. Stone declared that his next trip would be to Ellesmere Land in northern Canada to take more movies and to lasso the musk ox. "If I can get Will Rogers, the Indian cowboy, who does such wonderful roping, I'll take him along to work with me" (scrapbook A-3, OkClaW; see also Stone, *Rolling Stone*, 172–81).

Clipping from Will Rogers's Scrapbook
4 August 1911
Claremore, Okla.

In late July Rogers returned to Claremore to visit his father.[1] While there he purchased land that later became the site of the Will Rogers Memorial, built in 1938.[2]

W. P. ROGERS BUYS TOP OF "PREP" HILL.

W. P. Rogers has purchased of Mrs. J. M. Boling[3] the twenty acre tract of land lying along the top of the Preparatory hill;[4] the consideration being $8,000, or $400 per acre. This is one of the most desirable unimproved pieces of property near the city and some time is destined to be covered with many elegant homes. It is an ideal location for building purposes.

PD. Printed in *CWP*, 4 August 1911, clipping, scrapbook A-3, OkClaW.

1. Betty Blake Rogers was visiting her parents at Rogers, Ark. Will Rogers left Claremore on 3 August (*CWP*, 4 August 1911; see also *HRC*, 33).

2. Betty Blake Rogers deeded the land to the state of Oklahoma. The Memorial contains the library and museum dedicated to preserving the legacy of Will Rogers. It

holds Rogers's letters, documents, films, artifacts, and personal memorabilia. Will and Betty Blake Rogers are buried on the grounds. Today, it is a popular tourist attraction.

  3. James M. Boling was a Claremore physician and the director of the town's First National Bank. Clement Vann Rogers was also on its board of directors. Boling was a member of the Indian Territory Medical Association. At its meeting in Muskogee on 8 December 1891, he presented a paper, "Ovarian Hyperaemia and Hemorrhage," as part of the Obstetrics and Gynecology section program. Mrs. Boling had purchased the land in early May 1909. The *Claremore Progress* of 8 May 1909 reported as follows: "Mrs. J. M. Boling this week purchased of Miss Ella Talbert twenty acres of land on the Talbert Hill, just west of the city and east of Third street. Mr. Bayless having his bridge about completed, the street once open will make it just a nice distance from the main business part of town. Dr. and Mrs. Boling intend to build a home there some time not too far distant. There could be no more ideal location, none more beautiful in all Oklahoma, lying as it does, high with a rolling east slope, giving a fine view of our city, looking right down Main street and surrounding country, with just enough trees, a spring of water and a draw through one corner to give it a rustic appearance, water to supply a fish pond, then add to all this stone right on the ground for building purposes, just joining the electric light and gas and water mains" (quoted from *HRC*, 31). W. E. Sunday, a friend of Rogers and the real estate agent who arranged the sale, recalled that Mrs. Boling initially wanted $8,500 for the 20-acre plot that was valued at $1,000. Sunday felt he could get it for less. Rogers wanted the land desperately and told Sunday, "Darn your lazy soul, don't you let that get away from me!" Sunday telephoned Mrs. Boling and pretended that Rogers did not really want the land and was about to leave by train for New York. Worried that she would lose the sale, Boling made an offer of $7,500. Sunday felt the price was still too high and told Rogers to offer $6,500. "For God's sake, offer it," Rogers said. Boling agreed, and the sale was made. The warranty deed transferring the land to Rogers was dated 23 October 1911. Later, when Rogers and Sunday visited the property, Sunday asked why Rogers had wanted the property so much. Rogers replied: "Oh, some of these days, I'll come back here and build a home where I can sit and look down on all you Claremore folks" (Sunday et al., *Gah Dah Gwa Stee*, 134–35; see also *PWR*, 1:558–59; Clinton, "The Indian Territory Medical Association," 27, 32; DuPriest et al., *Cherokee Recollections*, 155).

  4. The name of the hill was derived from the preparatory school located across the street (Collins, *Will Rogers*, 210).

Performance Schedule from Will Rogers's Scrapbook
7 August 1911–March 1912
Eastern Circuit, U.S.A.

Rogers's single act was well received in Chicago, and the recognition enabled his agent Max Hart to obtain engagements through the UBO. Returning to New York, Rogers began his tour of the Keith-Albee Circuit with a performance at the Victoria Theatre's Paradise Roof Garden.[1]

Single Act.

Aug 7.   Hammersteins[2]
           Boston.[3]
           Montreal.
           Buffalo.
           Toronto.[4]
           Syracuse.[5]
           Erie.
           Cleveland.
           Columbus.
           Alahambra N.Y.[6]
           Union Hill.
           Hammersteins
           Hammersteins-5th Ave. X[7]
           Newark.[8]
           Greenpoint.[9]
           Orpheum.[10]
           ~~Greenpoint~~▲Bushwick▲[11]
           Trenton.[12]
           Baltimore[13]
           Atlanta.[14]
           Phila.[15]
           Scranton[16]
           Colonial. N.Y.[17]
           Orange—Bayonne.[18]
           Bijou. Phila.[19]
           Hammersteins[20]
           Providence[21]
           Bridgeport[22]
           New Haven[23]
           Worcester[24]
           Spring field.
           Hartford.[25]
           Utica.[26]
           Harrisburg.[27]
           Pittsburg.[28]
           Detroit
           Rochester
           5th Ave.[29]

AMS. Vaudeville scrapbook, CPpR.[30]

1. The playbill and other pertinent theater history are noted here, unless there is a document in the August 1911–March 1912 time period that refers directly to the theater and Rogers's performance.

2. From 7 to 13 August 1911 Rogers played with an all-star cast at Hammerstein's Roof Garden theater atop the Victoria Theatre. Headlining the bill was the famous dancer Ruth St. Denis (1879–1968), who performed the East Indian dances, "The Cobra" and "The Nautch." St. Denis played her first vaudeville engagement in 1906, and thereafter she frequently appeared in major variety theaters. After her marriage to the dancer Ted Shawn (1891–1972), they performed together on the vaudeville stage, and their Denishawn Co. played the Palace in 1916. Innovative dancers who created a unique style, they specialized in exotic ethnic and folk dances that differed from traditional ballet and evoked styles from Asia, Europe, Algeria, and Mexico, as well as Native American themes. The inclusion of modern dance in a vaudeville program magnified the problem of presenting high and popular culture on the same program. Shawn recalled that "those who spent hard-earned quarters to watch a seal twirl a trumpet were not *always* receptive to the dance of Denishawn." He also called the theater managers, agents, and bookers "the most sadistic, ghoulish, and horrible people encountered in a long professional life" (Loney, "Denishawn in Vaudeville and Beyond," 180). By contrast, the ballroom style of Vernon and Irene Castle was more easily accommodated in a variety program. Large salaries were what drew artists from the legitimate stage to vaudeville. Vaudeville provided St. Denis and Shawn with a good income, and they sent dance companies on vaudeville tours.

Another feature on the program was Gus Edwards's School Boys and Girls, a popular children's act produced by Gus Edwards (1879–1945), a well-known vaudevillian, producer, and song writer whose productions had often appeared on the same programs with Rogers. Other performers included Yvette (Singing Violinist); The Five Piroscoffis (Foreign Pantomime Jugglers); Luciana Lucca (Singer); Berg Brothers; Sherman, Krantzman and Hyman; Kramer and Spillane; Gordon Brothers (Singers and Dancers); F. A. Clement; Bedini and Arthur; and motion pictures. Rogers opened the second half of the program (*DE*, 415–17; *EV*, 155–58; "Hammerstein's," clipping, scrapbook A-3, OkClaW; *NYT*, 6 August 1911).

3. Rogers performed at Boston's Keith Theatre 14–19 August 1911.

4. Rogers appeared at Mike Shea's Theatre in Toronto 4–9 September 1911. Shea (1859–1934) operated other theaters in Buffalo and upstate New York. Accommodating an audience of 1,400 people, the theater was part of the Keith-Albee Circuit and engaged artists through the UBO (*EV*, 463; *GHNTD*, 555).

5. Rogers performed at Syracuse's Grand Opera House 11–15 September 1911. Rogers had previously played there the week of 18 December 1905 (see *PWR*, 2:245, 246n.1). At this time the theater was still operated by the Shubert brothers, and its bookings were handled by the UBO (*GHNTD*, 543; *JCOTG*, 177). Also on the program were a flying ballet; Charlotte Parry in *The Comstock Mystery*; and The Alfalfa Junction (Syracuse Grand Opera House clipping, scrapbook A-3, OkClaW). Betty Blake Rogers visited her husband in Syracuse, leaving New York on 13 September and staying until 17 September. Together she and Will Rogers visited the New York State Fair and saw Zack Mulhall (Betty Blake Rogers to Clement Vann Rogers, 18 September 1911, OkClaW).

6. Rogers performed at New York's Alhambra Theatre 9–14 October. The Alhambra was operated by Percy G. Williams and later by Keith-Albee when Williams

sold his properties in 1912. Opening on 15 May 1905, the Alhambra seated 572 on the first level, 277 on the second level, and 320 on the third level. It was located in Harlem at Seventh Avenue and 126th Street. A big-time vaudeville theater, it offered two shows a day, a matinee at 2:15 P.M. for 25 cents and an evening performance at 8:15 P.M. On the bill with Rogers was Mabel Hite, a well-known singing comedienne, in *20 Minutes of Foolishness*. With her husband Mike Donlin, a professional baseball player, she performed baseball acts, including one called *Stealing Home* (Frick and Ward, eds., *Directory of Historic American Theatres*, 175–76; Laurie, *Vaudeville*, 59, 118, 124–25). Other performers at the Alhambra included Jones and Deely; 6 Musical Spillers; The Bathing Girls; Stuart Barnes; Bounding Gordons; The Daleys; and Bert Leslie and Co. in the new comedy *Hogan the Painter* (*NYT*, 8 October 1911; Robinson, "A Stroll through Harlem," 10–11).

7. The *X* was written because Rogers's two engagements at Hammerstein's Victoria and Proctor's Fifth Avenue Theatre were canceled due to his father's death on 28 October. Rogers traveled to Claremore for the funeral on 31 October (see Obituary for Clement Vann Rogers, ca. 29 October 1911, below).

8. Rogers performed in Newark 6–11 November 1911.

9. Rogers appeared at Percy G. Williams's Greenpoint Theatre in Brooklyn 13–18 November 1911. Greenpoint, a district in northern Brooklyn, had a population of approximately 100,000. Recognizing its audience potential in 1907, Williams bought the Greenpoint Theatre property on Calyer Street. Formerly a church, the Greenpoint Theatre was the first vaudeville house in the district. With the Greenpoint, Williams's Metropolitan Circuit had six theaters in the greater New York area ("Another House for Williams," *Variety*, 4 May 1907; DiMeglio, *Vaudeville U.S.A.*, 131; *ENYC*, 152; *EV*, 559–60; Laurie, *Vaudeville*, 357; Snyder, *Voice of the City*, 93; "Williams Goes with Keith," *Variety*, 16 February 1907; *WNGD*, 466). The dancer Princess Rajah was the playbill's headline feature (see Clipping from Will Rogers's Scrapbook, ca. 5 March 1912, note 3, below). Others on the program included Marguerite Haney and Company; Wilfred Clarke and Co.; Richardson's posing dogs; Bixley and Lerner; Lyons and Yosco; and The Kemps (*NYT*, 12 November 1911).

10. Rogers performed at Percy G. Williams's Brooklyn Orpheum Theatre 20–25 November 1911. Heading the program were the vaudeville stars Nora Bayes and Jack Norworth, billed as "The Happiest Married Couple of the Stage." Bayes, a singer and comedienne, sang Norworth's tunes, such as "Shine on, Harvest Moon." Bayes was also a top Broadway performer. Others on the program included the blackface act Tim MacMahon and Chappelle; The Pullman Porter Maids; Conroy and LeMaire (a blackface team in the skit *The Pinochle Fiends*); Leon Rogee; O'Brien, Havel, and Klyde; Belle Hathaway's monkeys (a baboon catching plates); and Wentworth, Vesta, and Teddy (*EV*, 27–30, 307–8; *JCOGT*, 85; Laurie, *Vaudeville*, 83, 140–41, 163; *NYC*, 19 November 1911).

11. Percy G. Williams's Bushwick Theatre, which opened in 1911, was considered among Brooklyn's most prominent and elegant vaudeville theaters. It was located at Broadway and Howard Avenue in Bushwick, then a fashionable district in northeast Brooklyn, which the borough had annexed in 1855. Designed by the well-known architect William McElfatrick, the theater was constructed in a modernized Renaissance style with a flamboyant terracotta and limestone façade embellished with large cherubs, sculpted pediments, and six large, columned rectangular windows. Inside were elaborately decorated boxes that featured musical instrument themes in plaster relief. A noted feature was a room located under the stage for animal acts. The Bushwick seated 2,500 and was a popular theater in Williams's circuit. When Williams

sold the theater to Keith-Albee in 1912, it continued as a vaudeville house, and eventually movies were added to its program. With the decline of vaudeville, it became the RKO Bushwick movie theater in the 1930s. By 1970 the building had been converted into the Pilgrim Baptist Cathedral, but after a few years it was permanently abandoned (*ENY,* 149; Frick and Gray, eds., *Directory of Historic American Theaters,* 168; *GHNTD,* 538; Robinson, "Brooklyn's Magnificent Ruin," 22–23).

Rogers was billed as "The Lariat Comedian" at the Bushwick. Other performers included Princess Rajah (Just Returned from Europe in a Series of Classical Dances); McMahon and Chappelle and Their Pullman Porter Maids (In a Melange of Fun); Laddie Cliff (Late Star of Folies Bergere, England's Clever Boy Comedian and Dancer); Amoros Sisters (Those Two French Girls); Sutcliffe Troupe (Novelty European Entertainers); Hibbert and Warren (Blackface Comedians); York and Adams (Hebrew Comedians); and The Savoy Trio (*NYT,* 26 November 1911; Bushwick Theatre, Brooklyn, playbill, scrapbook A-3, OkClaW). On 30 November Rogers and twenty-one other vaudeville acts under contract to Percy Williams went to Blackwell's Island to present a show for prisoners on the island. Other performers included Lillian Russell, Nora Bayes and Jack Norworth, and Al Jolson (*NYT,* 29 November 1911).

12. Rogers was at Trenton, N.J., 4–9 December 1911. He performed either at Keith's Trent Theatre or at the Taylor Opera House (*GHNTD,* 538).

13. In Baltimore, Rogers performed at the Maryland Theatre 11–16 December 1911. The Maryland Theatre had a seating capacity of 1,972. At this time the theater belonged to the Keith-Albee Circuit, and booking was handled by the UBO (*GHNTD,* 532; *JCOTG,* 143). Joining Rogers on the Maryland playbill were William Rock (1875–1922) and Maude Fulton (1881–1950), a sensational singing and dancing act. Rock was noted for his characterizations. He teamed with Fulton until 1916, when she turned to a film career. Rock's new partner was the chorus girl Frances White, and they made a popular pair, appearing at the Palace Theatre and in the *Ziegfeld Follies* (*Baltimore Sun* clipping, scrapbook A-3, OkClaW; *EV,* 424–26; *WhoHolly,* 620).

14. In Atlanta, Rogers performed at Keith's Forsyth Theatre 18–23 December 1911. The theater was located on the ground floor of a granite-and-brick, eight-story office building, which was part of a larger business and real estate development project in the North Forsyth section of Atlanta. The office building was located on the northwest corner of North Forsyth and Luckie Streets, near the Piedmont Hotel, a new million-dollar post office, and court house. The building also contained ground-floor shops, a rathskeller in the basement, and a roof garden used for outdoor performances. The theater was considered modern for its time and was especially noted for the elimination of large beams and columns in its construction. Its French Renaissance interior was marked by a domed ceiling and elaborate wall decorations. The large stage could handle everything from vaudeville to extravaganza. The Forsyth had a seating capacity of 1,454, with private boxes, orchestra, balcony, and gallery (Brown, "The Forsyth Theater and Office Building," 63–66). The Forsyth was advertised as "Atlanta's Busiest Theatre," and its bookings were arranged through the UBO (Forsyth Theatre, Atlanta, playbill, scrapbook A-3, OkClaW). On the program with Rogers were The Florentine Singers, described as the best vocalists of the season. Reviews praised Rogers's roping skill as well as his imitations of Fred Stone, Eddie Foy, and George M. Cohan (*Atlanta Constitution, Atlanta Journal,* and *Atlanta Georgian and News* clippings, scrapbook A-3, OkClaW; *GHNTD,* 527).

15. Rogers appeared at Keith's Philadelphia Theatre during Christmas week, 25–30 December. Rogers performed here early in his career and several times there-

after (see *PWR*, 2:163–65). The manager's report, written by C. E. Barns, noted that Rogers's act was seventeen minutes long and used the full stage. "Went quite as strong 'alone' today as he has done on previous occasions with a more pretentious act," Barns wrote. "He has introduced a lot of amusing cowboy talk which gets the laugh all over the house, and his tricks with the rope are better than ever." Others on the bill were The Stanleys; Those French Girls (Trapeze Act); Three White Kuhns (Musical Trio); DeWitt, Burns and Torrance; Leonard and Russell (Songs, Comedy, and Dancing); Lolo (Mind Reader, Archery, and Sharpshooting); Raymond and Caverly; and The Diving Norins (Diving Act). The Keith report summarized the program as follows: "A capacity holiday crowd enjoyed this show from start to finish if one is to judge by the constant applause, and in some places, acts were actually stopped the applause was so big. With plenty of comedy and fun, for the children, this ought to be a strong business week for us" (Manager's Report, Keith's Philadelphia Theatre, 25 December 1911, KAC-IaU).

16. From 1 to 6 January 1912 Rogers performed at Sylvester Z. Poli's theater in Scranton, Pa., a UBO-affiliated theater. The Scranton theater, which opened on Labor Day 1907, was located on Wyoming Avenue. It had a seating capacity of 2,500. In 1911–12 Poli leased Scranton's Academy of Music, an opera house, across the street. In 1925 he sold his theater in Scranton to M. E. Comerford. The theater was renamed the Penn in 1930 and was permanently closed in 1960 (*GHNTD*, 548; King, "Sylvester Z. Poli Story," 13, 18). Appearing on the same bill was Jesse L. Lasky's production *California,* described as a musical spectacle and operetta with a cast of sixteen. To accent the western theme, the theater personnel wore western outfits ("Good Show at Poli's," clipping, scrapbook A-3, OkClaW). Lasky (1880–1958), a vaudevillian turned producer, organized several popular big-act and flash-act musical comedies for vaudeville with traveling scenery, an all-star cast, special costumes, and music. Lasky's Feature Play Co. produced *The Squaw Man* (1914), the first full-length motion picture filmed in Hollywood. Lasky later was head of production at Paramount (*EV*, 299–300; *FilmEnc*, 792; Laurie, *Vaudeville*, 67, 232).

17. Rogers performed at Percy G. Williams's Colonial Theatre 8–13 January 1912. The theater, which opened as the Colonial Music Hall on 8 February 1905, was built by Fred Thompson and Elmer Dundy, who had constructed the New York Hippodrome and Coney Island's Lunar Park. Located at 1887 Broadway at Sixty-second Street, the Colonial was built in the Hell's Kitchen area of Manhattan and thus represented the expansion of New York's theater farther uptown to attract residents of new apartments. Outside it featured a Federal-style façade, while the interior, which seated 1,265 in the orchestra, balcony, and gallery, resembled an English music hall with balconies near the stage. In April 1905 the theater was sold to Percy G. Williams, who presented first-class vaudeville. The Colonial constantly drew packed houses, and in the gallery noisy spectators threw pennies at the acts they booed. When Williams sold his interest to B. F. Keith in 1912, the theater was renamed Keith's Colonial and continued as a big-time vaudeville theater. In 1917 E. F. Albee refurbished the interior. In 1923 the theater became a venue for all-black musical comedies with the premiere of *Runnin' Wild,* which introduced the Charleston dance. In 1925 Walter Hampden leased the theater, and he featured Shakespeare and other classic plays until 1931, when the Colonial (then named Hampden's Theatre) became an RKO neighborhood movie house (the RKO Colonial). Between 1956 and 1971 it was used as a television studio by NBC and later ABC. Rebekah Harkness bought the theater, and in 1974 it became the home of the Harkness Ballet. When the ballet proved unprofitable, the Harkness Theatre offered other dramatic and musical productions.

Harkness eventually sold the theater at a large loss, and it was demolished in the summer of 1977, to be replaced by condominiums (van Hoogstraten, *Lost Broadway Theatres*, 91–93).

Rogers had appeared here the week of 30 December 1907, when he was part of a playbill that featured Jesse Lasky's *California*. Also on the 12 January 1912 program were the famous actors Sydney Drew and Lionel Barrymore in the automobile comedy *Stalled*. Other performers included Yorke and Adams (Hebrew Comedians); Shirley and Kessler (Singing and Dancing); Willie Weston (Songs); The Six Musical Cuttys (Musical Novelty); Collins and Hart (Burlesque Strong Men); and The Seven Picchiano Troupe (Acrobats) (*NYT*, 7 January and 9 January 1912). The critic Robert Speare commented that Rogers "the Cowboy Comedian" was "developing into a real actor." His jokes when he missed a rope trick were so funny, Speare wrote, that "it soon was apparent that every one was wishing him to miss, in order that he would spring one of those original yarns" ("Colonial's Bill Is Full of Hits," clipping, scrapbook A-3, OkClaW).

18. From 15 to 20 January 1912, Rogers probably performed at the Orange Theatre in Bayonne, N.J. Brooklyn's Orpheum appears on a typed itinerary list in scrapbook A-3 (OkClaW), but he had already performed there in November 1911. Except for Hammerstein's Victoria, big-time theaters rarely booked the same performer again so soon.

19. From 22 to 27 January 1912 Rogers probably performed at Keith's Bijou Theatre in Philadelphia (New York's Alhambra Theatre appears on the typed itinerary list in scrapbook A-3 [OkClaW], but Rogers had performed there in October 1911). Located at Eighth and Race Streets on the former site of an old church, the Bijou was Keith's oldest Philadelphia vaudeville theater and had opened on 4 November 1889. Seating some 1,400 patrons, it was advertised as "The Drawing Room Theatre of Philadelphia—High Class Refined Entertainment" (Glazer, *Philadelphia Theaters*, 68). The Bijou was designed by the architect J. B. McElfatrick in what one critic described as "Morrish–Pullman Car." Its façade featured a large arch ornamented with stained-glass windows that were bordered by sculpted angels with musical instruments. Floral designs, busts, Corinthian columns, and medallion windows also embellished the exterior. The name "B. F. Keith's Bijou Theatre" was embedded in the top of the arch. The Bijou was the first Philadelphia theater to show motion pictures. On Christmas day 1895 a film was shown on a projector called the eidoloscope, invented by the Latham family, and the following year the Bijou exhibited Lumière's cinematograph. When Keith opened his new Philadelphia theater on Chestnut Street in 1902, the Bijou became the home of stock companies until 1905. That year it resumed its vaudeville performances, which went on until 1912, when the theater began offering burlesque shows. In 1924 it was renamed the Garden, a Yiddish theater. Burlesque was resumed in 1927 and lasted until the 1940s, but during this time the theater was often closed by the police due to its lewd performances. By the 1960s the famous Bijou, now called the New Garden, was playing B movies. The historic theater was demolished in 1967, and the Metropolitan Hospital was constructed on the property (Glazer, *Philadelphia Theaters*, 68–69).

20. Rogers returned to perform at Hammerstein's Victoria, New York, 29 January–3 February 1912. He opened the second half of the bill. The *Variety* reviewer called him "the most unique monologist vaudeville ever owned" ("Hammerstein's," clipping, scrapbook A-3, OkClaW). On the playbill he was described as "Introducing Western Sports and Pastimes." The headliner on the all-star program was the magician Harry Houdini, who had just returned from a world tour. Listed fifth were

Flournoy E. Miller (1887–1971) and Aubrey Lyles (advertised as "Colored Comedians and Dancers"), a well-known black vaudeville team. Graduates of Fisk University, the pair wrote plays and popular songs, and co-produced the popular black musical, *Shuffle Along* (1921). In 1903 they had had their own repertory company and starred in the road shows of *In Dahomey* and *Sons of Ham* (*AmSCAP*, 510; *OCAT*, 624; Sampson, *Blacks in Blackface*, 246–47, 373–74, 458–59; and Sampson, *Ghost Walks*, 242, 280, 293, 326, 331, 401–2, 445). Also featured were Havel and Bend (In a Comedy Juggling Act); Chalk Saunders (Comedy Cartoonist); Martine Brothers (Comedy Trampolinists); Clark and Bergman (In a Baseball Flirtation, Introducing Songs and Dances); Six Musical Cuttys (The World's Greatest Musical Family); Joseph Hart's *Dinkelspiel's Christmas* by George V. Hobart; Marshall Montgomery (The Whistling Ventriloquist); Daisy Harcourt (The Clever English Character Comedienne); Avery and Hart (Colored Comedians); Bert Melrose (Featuring the Melrose Trick); and New Victoriascope Views (Hammerstein's Victoria Theatre, New York, playbill, week beginning matinee 29 January 1912, scrapbook A-3, OkClaW; see also *NYT*, 28 and 30 January 1912).

21. Rogers appeared at Keith's Providence Theatre 5–10 February 1912. He had previously played there in late November 1905 (for the theater's history, see *PWR*, 2:233n.3). Rogers was advertised as the "Ranch Raconteur," an example of the growing popularity of his yarn spinning. He was listed third but was moved to the sixth spot because of the success of his fourteen-minute act. The theater manager, Charles Lovenberg, reported: "Mr. Rogers did very well; for that reason moved down to this spot, altho[ugh] I would have preferred to have a new act in this position" (Keith Report Book, Providence Show, week of 5 February 1912, KAC-IaU). Lovenberg was disappointed with the show as a whole, noting that many acts "fell pretty flat," especially those that had worked well in larger cities. Other performers were as follows: Rem-Brandt (Ben Olch, Cartoonist, Presenting a Novel Picture Painting Act Using Compressed Air and Liquid Colors); O'Meers Sisters and Co. (Three Girls on the Wire); Carl McCullough (The Dynamic Comedian Presenting *Footlight Impressions*); *High Life in Jail* (A Travesty on Prison Life with W. H. [Bill] Mack); Fay, 2 Coleys and Fay (Frank Fay, Gertrude Fay, Clarence Coley, and Hattie Coley in *From Uncle Tom to Vaudeville*); Charles Cartmell and Laura Harris (In Some New Songs and Dances); Weston, Fields, and Caroll (Snappy Singers of Snappy Songs); Clarence Wilbur and His Funny Folks (In *The New Scholar*). Two motion pictures opened the program, *Quick a Plumber* and *Mr. and Mrs. Suspicious*. Closing the program was the film *The Ventriloquist's Trunk* (Manager's Report Book; Providence newspaper clippings; and Keith's Providence Theatre playbill, week of 5 February 1912, KAC-IaU).

22. Rogers performed at Sylvester Z. Poli's Bridgeport Theatre in Connecticut 12–17 February 1912. He had performed there previously in late April 1908. The theater was built in 1875 as the Hawes Opera House and was later called the Park City Theatre. Poli bought the theater in 1901 at a public auction and renamed it Poli's Plaza Theatre. It burned down in 1925 and was demolished in 1930. In 1912 Poli built a new theater in the town, and another in 1922, Poli's Palace Theatre (King, "Sylvester Z. Poli Story," 12, 14–16, 18). Also on the bill were the actress and comedian May Tully and her company in *The Battle Cry of Freedom*, and Howard and Howard in *The Porter and the Salesman* ("May Tully & Co. and Others Are Pleasing at Poli's," *Bridgeport Daily Standard* clipping, scrapbook A-3, OkClaW).

23. Rogers performed at Poli's Theatre in New Haven, Conn., 19–24 February 1912. In March 1908 Rogers had had to leave his engagement because his father was ill.

24. Rogers appeared at Poli's Theatre in Worcester, Mass., between 26 February and 2 March. He had performed there earlier in February 1908 (see *PWR*, 2:397–98 and 398n.1). Poli built the theater in 1905 by acquiring property that had recently been destroyed by fire. Inside were horseshoe balconies decorated with cherubs. As a Poli brochure explains, Poli was especially proud of his theaters in Worcester and New Haven: "In several of the theaters, notably those in New Haven and Worcester, there are some exceedingly fine designs in the way of grand foyers and marble staircases that are most striking in their artistic conception and arrangement and contribute to the ensemble of beauty that makes the Poli theaters objects of universal admiration" (*S. Z. Poli's Theatrical Enterprises*). The existence of Poli's theater angered Keith, who had the rival Park Theatre in Worcester, and it led to a feud until Poli allied with Keith in 1906. In 1912 Poli renamed his theater the Plaza Theatre; it was demolished in 1941. In 1912 he built Poli's Grand Theatre, a larger venue, which was demolished in 1925 to make way for Poli's new Palace Theatre (King, "Sylvester Z. Poli Story," 13, 14, 18).

25. Rogers appeared at Poli's Theatre in Hartford, Conn., 11–16 March (see Hartford newspaper clippings, scrapbook A-3, OkClaW). Rogers had performed there in late February 1908 (on the theater's history see *PWR*, 2:404–5n.3).

26. Although documentation does not exist, Rogers could have performed from 18 to 23 March 1912 at the Orpheum Theatre in Utica, N.Y. (*GHNTD*, 543).

27. Although documentation does not exist, Rogers could have performed at the Orpheum in Harrisburg, Pa., from 25 to 30 March 1912. The Harrisburg Orpheum used Keith-Albee's UBO for its bookings (*GHNTD*, 546).

28. Rogers saved clippings from his performance at the Grand Opera House in Pittsburgh, Pa., where he might have played between 1 and 6 April 1912. Rogers had first played there in late December 1905 (on the theater's history see *PWR*, 2:246n.2).

29. Rogers's name was not mentioned in Keith and Proctor's Fifth Avenue Theatre advertisements in the *New York Times* from 21 March to 15 April. Rogers opened in *The Wall Street Girl* on Broadway on 15 April 1912. Of the two remaining dates (Rochester and Detroit), Rogers could have performed at only one of the theaters, if any. The Keith Circuit theatres were Detroit's Temple Theatre and Rochester's Cook Opera House. Rogers had performed earlier at these theaters (on the Temple Theatre see *PWR*, 2:206n.1; on the Cook Opera House see *PWR*, 2:209n.4).

30. All the locales and theaters except Rochester and the Fifth Avenue are in order as in the original document. Those two items appear in a separate list written opposite Utica and Harrisburg in the original document. On the left side of the scrapbook, Rogers had handwritten an earlier schedule listing his performances under the heading "Last Weeks with old Act With Horse." A typed schedule listing theaters and dates from 14 August 1911 to 11 February 1912 can also be found in scrapbook A-3, OkClaW.

To Clement Vann Rogers
ca. 21 August 1911
Montreal, Quebec, Canada

Montreal, Canada.

Monday.

Dear Papa.

I just come in here this morning from Boston   will be here all Week till Saturday Night[1]   Next Week I go to Buffalo. here is $141.40 give it to

Godbey to send to the Insurance people for my old Insurance that I have had for long time. and in few weeks I will send that to pay the insurance that I took out from Ball.

I look for Betty this week to come to New York   if she does I will go by there Sunday and spend the day and into Buffalo Sunday night. Is Mrs. Boling still living up at the place   tell her to be sure and get me a good old Man to put on the place to take care of those trees and flowers for me.[2]

I want to keep that place up good.

Tell Buck to write to me. I will write you every week.

Love
Willie

Write to Sheas Theatre.[3]

Buffalo   New york.

I will get it there next week when I get there.

ALS, rc. OkClaW. On Welland Hotel, McGill College Avenue, Montreal, letterhead. G. Fuller proprietor.

1. Rogers performed at the Montreal Orpheum 21–27 August 1911. He was billed again as The Oklahoma Cowboy and did imitations of Fred Stone and George M. Cohan. Other performers on the bill were the comedy team Johnny Neff and Carrie Starr in *The World's Greatest Musician*; The Eight Palace Girls (Singers and Dancers from the Palace Theatre, London); Al Fields and Jack Lewis (In *The Misery of Handsome Cab*); George Yeomans and the Dorians (In *Terrible Night*); and The Three Dooleys (Bicycle Act). The Orpheum, with a seating capacity of 1,800, was a big-time showplace for vaudeville in Montreal (clippings from *Montreal Daily Star* and *Montreal Daily Herald*, scrapbook A-3, OkClaW; *GHNTD*, 555; Laurie, *Vaudeville*, 186, 230).
2. Mrs. Boling had sold land to Rogers (see Clipping from Will Rogers's Scrapbook, 4 August 1911, above).
3. Rogers performed at Mike Shea's House of Vaudeville in Buffalo from 28 August to 2 September. He was advertised as The Droll Oklahoma Cowboy. Also on the bill were The Eight Palace Girls; Conroy and LeMaire; Welch, Mealy, and Montrose (The Base Ball Fans); Elsie Faye (The Act Dainty); The Musical Spillers (Original Rag Time Players); Millard Brothers (Comedy Bar Artists); Una Clayton and Players (In Her Own Unique Comedy, *A Child Shall Lead Them*); and the kinetograph (All New Pictures) (Shea's House of Vaudeville, Buffalo, playbill, week of 28 August, scrapbook A-3, OkClaW).

Betty Blake Rogers to Clement Vann Rogers
21 August 1911
Rogers, Ark.

In this letter, Betty Blake Rogers conveys the news that she and Will plan to settle in New York. Several factors influenced their decision, including the imminent birth of their first baby. Since New York was the center of the American theater world, settling there would allow Rogers access to the offices of the leading vaudeville circuits, managers, and agents. The New York area would remain the Rogerses' home until 1919, when they moved to California.

My dear father Rogers.

I have been so busy the past few days getting ready to go back to New York. I leave here tonight at 9:30 pm and get in New York City Wednesday evening about six o'clock. My sister[1] is going with me and we are at once going to get apartments and start house keeping[2]

Billy will come in to New York next Sunday and spend the day with us.[3] We hope to be settled by then and have a good home cooked dinner for him.

Im feeling just fine and am sure I will stand the trip allright

I have about all my baby clothes made. I am expecting the youngster about the fifteenth of October.[4] Billy wants a boy of course, but I do not care which it is. If it is a boy I am going to name it after Billy. I would name it for you but there are so many Clems in the family Im afraid they would get mixed up.

I will write you just as soon as I get to New York. You write to me to the St. Francis Hotel, West 47 st., New York City.[5]

We will stay there until we find suitable apartments.

Lots of love to you from your daughter

Betty

ALS, rc. OkClaW.

1. Theda Blake (1875–1966), one of the seven Blake sisters (see Biographical Appendix entry, BLAKE SIBLINGS).

2. At first the Rogerses lived at the St. Francis Hotel on West 47th Street. They then resided in an apartment at 203 West 94th Street and moved on 7 October 1911 to an apartment at 555 West 113th Street.

3. Rogers was unable to visit his wife in New York because of train connections (Betty Blake Rogers to Clement Vann Rogers, 25 August 1911, OkClaW).

4. William Vann Rogers was born on 20 October 1911 (see Notice of Birth of Will Rogers, Jr., ca. 20 October 1911, below, and Biographical Appendix entry, ROGERS, William Vann).

5. The St. Francis Hotel was located at 124–26 West Forty-seventh Street in the Times Square theater area. The hotel manager was D. E. Dalton (letterhead, Betty Blake Rogers to Clement Vann Rogers, 28 August 1911, OkClaW). The St. Francis Hotel was one of several hotels on West Forty-seventh Street in the midtown area that attracted people in the theater. Several apartment hotels catered to the newly married, such as the nearby Hotel Somerset at 150 West Forty-seventh Street, built around 1900 and designed by Clarence Luce (Stern et al., *New York 1900*, 274–75).

From Clement Vann Rogers
29 August 1911
Claremore, Okla.

Claremore, Okla. <u>Aug 29th</u> 191<u>1</u>

Dear Willie & Bettie

St. Francis Hotel, New York City

Today is Tuesday the 29th. I got one letter from Willie with $141.40 to pay on his insurance at Little Rock & one from Bettie the day she left for New York City to stay a while. Times are a little bit dull here   Boling & his wife left the Hill place yesterday & they said they got a good man to take care of the Property of yours on the Hill. He is a young man so they say. They reported him to Wm. Sunday[1]   I went up to Chelsea last Saturday & come back Monday. They were all well. They live on watermelons & peaches.

Sallie & Morris will come down tomorrow to do some Trading & take Dinner with me at the Hotel Mason.[2] I got a notice from Clerk Frye of my Paving Tax on Block 113, Lots 12 13 14 & 15 ~~first~~ & this is the Lots the Rock Barn is on & the Paving Tax that is put against me on these 4 lots is $182.74 & have to be paid by Sept 1st[3]   This is a heavy Tax on this Property but it have to be paid. That is over 3 months Rent on the Barn & Lot. Johnie Yocum is up about Lenapah.[4] I dont think he is going to School. They sent Mrs. D. W. Lipe to hospital at Kansas City   she lost her mind[5]   Hay Crops are sure fine since the Rain   Their will be lots of Hay Their will be quite a lot of corn & World of watermelons every whare in this country. The weather here is quite cool & nice now & have been since the Rain last week. I cant say whare Mr. & Mrs. Bolling will go & live. They will move their things from the Hillside today

I keep in very good Health all the while

Write when you can[6]

from your Pa

C. V. Rogers

ALS, rc. OkClaW. On First National Bank, Claremore, Okla., letterhead. John Dirickson, president, C. V. Rogers, vice-president, C. F. Godbey, cashier, and R. A. Patton, assistant cashier. Capital and surplus $60,000.

1. William Esther Sunday (1877–1959), a close of friend of Clement Vann Rogers (see *PWR*, 1:558–59).

2. Sallie McSpadden, and probably Maurice Rogers McSpadden (1905–1968), Sallie and Tom McSpadden's youngest child.

3. Clement Vann Rogers owned a Claremore livery stable built of stone. The property was valued at $4,185 on 23 December 1908. Rogers received a statement of

paving taxes totaling $182.74, a figure that included $70.63 in interest (dated 18 August 1911 and signed by W. H. Fry, city clerk). Rogers waited one day before the deadline for payment and received a receipt for paid taxes signed by W. H. Fry on 31 August. On 29 June 1910 Rogers signed a contract with the New State Paving and Construction Co. to pave the uncovered portion of the alley in block 113 where his barn was located. The brick pavement over a five-inch construction base cost Rogers $509.19. In return for his agreeing to the paving, the town permitted the rock barn to stand as is for twenty-five years or during the life of the building. William Henry Fry (b. 1868), city clerk of Claremore, signed the 20 July 1910 agreement. A leading Claremore political and business figure, Fry served also as the first mayor of Claremore and as justice of the peace. He was in the mercantile business and later in the hardware and mortuary business. He married Charlotte V. Gibbs (d. 1957) in 1889, and they had six children (Collings, *Old Home Ranch*, 63; contract, 29 June 1910; document, 20 July 1910; receipts, 19 July 1910 and 31 August 1911; statement of paving taxes, 18 August 1911, Clem V. Rogers file, OkClaW; *HRC*, 201–2).

4. Rogers's nephew, John Vann (Johnny) Yocum (1893–1952), was the son of Rogers's sister, May Rogers Yocum Stine, and Matthew Yocum. Lenapah is located in northern Nowata County, Okla. Its post office was established in April 1890. The town's name stems from the word Lenápe, the original name for the Delaware Indians (Shirk, *Oklahoma Place Names*, 124).

5. DeWitt Clinton Lipe's second marriage in March 1871 was to Mary Elizabeth Archer (see *PWR*, 1:503–5).

6. Will Rogers wrote back to his father from rooms at the Elks Club in Erie, Pa. He reported that Betty, who was in an advanced stage of pregnancy, had just spent a week with him in Syracuse, N.Y., and that she had given him Clement Vann Rogers's letter. She had headed back to New York City "feeling fine," and Rogers heard "from her every day." Rogers praised his father for his newsy correspondence and advised him to send all his letters to Betty at their apartment in New York. She would take care of forwarding them to Rogers on the road. Rogers told his father that "We have a nice place in New York. 5 rooms and bath and we are figuring on you and Maud and Sallie all to come back here this winter and see us or if you don't want to get out in the winter you can come early in the spring." Rogers also reported that he had "just fixed Jake Stine [his young nephew] up a nice box and sent him today to Texas a winter suit and underwear, stockings, waists and a sweater." He also advised his father to "look after my place up on the Hill" (Preparatory Hill in Claremore) and to keep the maintenance up on "the old home place in town . . . take those fences down and cut all those old dead trees out of the yard and clean it up . . . and keep it as we may want to use it." Rogers was headed from Pennsylvania to Ohio (Will Rogers to Clement Vann Rogers, 20 September 1911, OkClaW).

Excerpt from Manager's Report, Keith's Hippodrome
26 September 1911
Cleveland, Ohio

B. F. KEITH'S HIPPODROME

Sept. 26, 1911.

Cleveland, O.

WILL ROGERS:—Presenting a line of entirely new stuff, and giving us a little of Montgomery & Stone, Eddie Foy and Geo. Cohan. Very liberal applause. Opens and closes in one. 14 m.

This act goes to Columbus.[1]

H. A. Daniels.

TD. KAC-IaU.

1. Advertised as "One of Vaudeville's Big Novelties," Rogers received rave reviews at the Hippodrome. He was also the subject of a feature article written by William Sage in the *Cleveland Leader* of 27 September 1911. The article covered Rogers's early experiences and his performance at Berlin's Wintergarten in which he roped a German fireman who stood in the wings. Accompanying the article was an illustration showing a fireman with an axe being roped ("New Views of the Spotlight People," scrapbook A-3, OkClaW). Also mentioned in the manager's report and in scrapbook clippings were the following performers: Robert DuMont Trio (Comedy Acrobatic Act); Majestic Trio (Vocalist and Musicians with Banjo and Mandolin); Hayward and Hayward (in the Sketch Entitled *Holding Out*); Frank Stafford and Co. (Featuring Stafford's Wife and a Dog in *A Hunter's Game*); Haines and Vidocq; Gus Edwards's School Boys and Girls; and *The Hold-Up* (A Miniature Melodrama with Percival Lennon in the Role of Lonesome Joe). Reviews noted that *The Hold-Up* featured a mock train that ran across the stage. It was advertised as "the climax of realism," featuring a 150-ton engine and loaded freight cars, dashing across the stage at a real speed of a-mile-a-minute" (scrapbook A-3, OkClaW).

Manager's Report, Keith's Theatre
2 October 1911
Columbus, Ohio

REPORT OF COLUMBUS SHOW, WEEK OF OCTOBER 2
—W. W. PROSSER[1]

THE JUGGLING BURKES:—Two young men in a club juggling act of excellent value. Their work is quick and showman-like throughout and their various stunts were well received, applause being frequent and a very strong finish was scored. Terrace in two. 9 min. (This act is open)

WATSON AND LITTLE:—Man and woman in a classy little singing and talking number, "A Matrimonial Bargain." Both have pleasing voices and both are good lookers. The woman makes a particularly striking appearance. They have a good line of talk, all of which seemed to catch on very well, none of the points being missed, and most of them getting over in good shape. They sing nicely, and all in all the act was thoroughly satisfactory from start to finish, and pleasing throughout. The finish was strong. Olio in one, 17 minutes. (This act is open)

THE OLD SOLDIER FIDDLERS:—They were given an ovation at the rise of the curtain and had not the slightest trouble in arousing unqualified enthusiasm. A sure-fire hit all the way through with bows galore. Special in three and street in one, 28 minutes.[2] (This act goes to Dayton.)

FELIX AND CAIRE:—This well known pair was seen in this town for the first time today. Their opening number was but fairly well received but subsequent to that they had everything their own way. Their songs and dances as well as their impersonations were unmistakable hits. The finish was very strong. Center door, fancy in two and olio in one, 21 minutes. (This act goes to Cincinnati).

WILL ROGERS:—"The Oklahoma Cowboy." This fellow was a riot. His inimitable bits of talk in conjunction with his dexterity with ropes and lariat made the biggest kind of a hit. He went like a cyclone throughout and could hardly get away. Garden ~~and~~ in five and conservatory in one, 19 minutes. (This act goes to New York)[3]

CHARLES LEONARD FLETCHER AND COMPANY:—In "His Nerve," a legitimate playlet of the Raffles type, which was admirable presented. The story is a dramatic offering, of sufficient strength to maintain undivided interest throughout. The story is well worked out, and the success of the star and his associates was pronounced. There were several bows. Library set in four, 22 minutes. (This act goes to Syracuse)

NELLIE NICHOLS:—This clever comedienne came out and established herself thoroughly with the audience with her repertoire of songs. She all but stopped the show. She was a big hit from start to finish. Olio in one, 14 minutes.[4]

THE RIALS:—Man and woman in a comedy novelty offering of the flying ring order, including juggling and tumbling. The woman works straight and the man impersonates a dude. This act went well and finished strong. Palace in four, 9 minutes

MOTION PICTURES:—O.K.

TD. KAC-IaU.

1. The B. F. Keith's Theatre in Columbus, Ohio, seated 1,650 people and accommodated a seven-piece orchestra. As a theater in the Keith-Albee Circuit, its booking was handled by the UBO (*GHNTD*, 544; *JCGHTD*, 71–72).

2. The Old Soldier Fiddlers were considered "sure-fire applause getters." One member was John A. Pattee, who was sixty-seven years old in 1911. The act used fiddles claimed to be from the Civil War period (John A. Pattee clipping file, NN-L-BRTC; Laurie, *Vaudeville*, 67).

3. Reviewers who saw the show at Keith's Theatre commented on Rogers's dry spontaneous humor and called him an "amusing monologuist" with "delicious little" jokes. Questioned about who wrote his material, Rogers replied: "Why theer ain't a line I didn't put in myself: feel sorry for the man who couldn't write better stuff than that, but it's my line of talk, and it's all the line of talk I know; just Oklahoma talk and ranch talk." A large cartoon depicting Rogers in various poses with rope in hand appeared in the *Columbus Sunday Dispatch* of 8 October 1911. Each pose featured one of Rogers's jokes. Quotes from Rogers's self-deprecating humor accompanied each page: "Ain't this a silly way to make a living?"; "If I don't stay out here long enough I don't collect"; "I've got a song that goes with this act but the manager asked me to cut it out because it interfered with the jugglers"; and "sometimes the bad ones go better than the good ones." Rogers next played New York's Alhambra Theatre, 9–14 October 1911 (clippings, scrapbook A-3, OkClaW; see also illustration, 210).

4. The daughter of Greek parents, Nellie V. Nichols (1885–1971) became a successful vaudeville and screen actress. As a young woman, she was a clerk in her father's clothing store in New York's Bowery district. She first gained experience with a stock company in Los Angeles, and in 1905 she was with the Fishers Stock Co. in San Francisco. In 1907 she joined Henry W. Savage's touring company in *The Sultan of Sulu*. On the vaudeville stage Nichols was noted for her singing and dancing imitations of ethnic characters. One popular number was "Will Someone Name My Nationality?" about a girl who cannot understand her heritage because her mother is Irish and her father is Jewish. Nichols also parodied popular songs, such as "Alexander's Rag-time Band." Nichols was a big-time vaudeville regular and was frequently booked for thirty-five straight weeks. Keith Circuit report books testified to her popularity, including audiences so entertained they demanded she stay on stage well past the time allotted for her number. In April 1912 she was the headliner on the playbill at New York's Fifth Avenue Theatre. Other times she was with touring companies performing in such plays as *Buster Brown* (1908) and *The Newlyweds and Their Baby Company* (1908). Nichols performed as late as 1919 in vaudeville. In April of that year she headed the bill at Keith's Theatre in Toledo. Her screen debut was in 1930 in *Playing Around*. Other films included *Women Go On Forever* (1931) and *Manhattan Merry-Go-Round* (1937) (Kibler, *Rank Ladies*, 40; Nellie Nichols clippings, Locke env. 1615, NN-L-RLC; report books, KAC-IaU; *WhScrn*, 2:344).

Betty Blake Rogers to Clement Vann Rogers
7 October 1911
New York, N.Y.

As this letter reveals, Betty Blake Rogers found a new apartment in a building at 551 West 113th Street in Morningside Heights, a growing uptown residential district. At this time a large number of side-street apartment buildings, catering to the lower middle class, were being built between 110th and 114th Streets and between Broadway and Riverside Drive. Nearby were such landmarks as Columbia University, Barnard College, St. Luke's Hospital, and the Cathedral of St. John the Divine. The Morningside Heights apartment would be home for the Rogerses for several years.[1]

#551 West 113th St.

New York City

Saturday Oct 7th

My dear father Rogers.

We are moving today to another house. We think it is much better than this one and think we will like it much better.

Billy will be here Sunday   He works here in the city for several weeks and Im so glad.[2] It will be fine to have him home for awhile. We are going to have a nice big dinner for him tomorrow.

It is raining today and the weather is quite disagreeable. I expect it will be getting much colder.

I will write you a good letter right soon. Now when you write address our letters to #551 West 113 St. Tell Maude and Sallie that we have changed our address and that when we get straightened up I will write to them.

Lots of love to you from your daughter

Betty

ALS, rc. OkClaW.

1. The Rogerses moved on 7 October 1911 from 203 West 94th Street. Morningside Heights was among the last areas of the city to be developed due to the lack of public transportation. The extension of the IRT subway into the area in 1898 generated rapid commercial and residential development. Despite the area's impressive landmarks, the construction of numerous apartment buildings similar in style created a feeling of urban uniformity (Stern et al., *New York 1900*, 417–19).

2. Rogers performed in New York beginning with his engagement at the Alhambra Theatre, 9–14 October 1911. Located in Harlem at Seventh Avenue and 126th Street, the Alhambra was very close to the Rogerses' new apartment. Rogers would have vaudeville engagements in the New York and New Jersey area until 10 December.

Notice of Birth of Will Rogers, Jr.
ca. 20 October 1911
New York, N.Y.

Will and Betty Blake Rogers's first child, William Vann Rogers, was born on Friday, 20 October 1911.[1] The birth of Will, Jr., or Bill, as he became known, was reported in several New York papers. At the time of his son's birth Rogers was appearing at the Hudson Theatre in Union Hill, New Jersey. Rogers saved the program, and on the page listing the performers he wrote next to his name: "Little Bill was born this week."[2]

SON COPS POP'S ACT.

Will Rogers became the father of a boy last Friday.

The rope fellow states his boy has already stolen part of his act (the finish—when the yell happens).

PD. Unidentified clipping, ca. 20 October 1911, scrapbook A-3, OkClaW.[3]

1. William Vann Rogers was born in a nursing home at 4:30 A.M. At birth he weighed 7 pounds, 8 ounces, and his height was 20 inches. His first name derived from his father; his middle name, Vann, was the middle name of his grandfather, Clement Vann Rogers, and the surname of his great-grandmother, Sallie Vann, Will Rogers's paternal grandmother. Apparently, Will Rogers asked the doctor to use the name Will Rogers, Jr., on the birth certificate. According to C. L. Lane, Clement Vann Rogers "was considerably worked up over his grandson" and proud that the baby's middle name was Vann (C. L. Lane to Betty Blake Rogers, 26 October 1911, OkClaW). Clement Vann Rogers died eight days after his grandson was born (Baby's History Book, OkClaW; Collins, *Will Rogers,* 213). Betty Blake Rogers's mother, Amelia Blake, traveled from Rogers, Ark., to New York to help with the birth, arriving on 28 September 1911 (Betty Blake Rogers to Clement Vann Rogers, 2 October 1911, OkClaW).

In the baby book, a gift from Estelle and Ethel Lane (Will Rogers's nieces) for Christmas 1911, there is a list of gifts received from friends and relatives. Among fellow vaudevillians, Mabel Hite gave a Japanese kimono, and Myra Keaton, Buster's mother, a powder puff. Clement Vann Rogers mailed the new baby beaded moccasins and black wool stockings. Will Rogers deposited $250 in the Franklin Savings Bank on Forty-second Street and Eighth Avenue for his son. Maud Lane gave a jacket, and Sallie McSpadden, a shawl. In a letter to her new nephew, Sallie wrote: "My Dear Little Boy:—Each stitch taken in this little shawl confirms, for you, an unlimited amount of love, and that you may grow to manhood a joy to your parents, a blessing to your friends and an honor to your country is the wish of your Aunt Sallie" (Sallie McSpadden to William Vann Rogers, 21 October 1911, OkClaW). Tom Morgan, the Rogerses' good friend from Rogers, Ark., wrote a humorous congratulatory letter: "Whether or not he is a bouncing boy I do not know, but you can drop him on the floor and see" (Tom Morgan to Betty Blake Rogers and Will Rogers, 22 October 1911, OkClaW; see also Baby's History Book, OkClaW; Clement Vann Rogers to Will and Betty Blake Rogers, 23 October 1911, OkClaW; Biographical Appendix entry, ROGERS, William Vann).

Photographs of Will Rogers, Jr., born on 20 October 1911, from Will Rogers's scrapbook. *[OkClaW]*

2. At the Hudson Theatre Rogers was listed as the fifth act on the bill. Other acts were as follows: William Lucifer and Lucian Kibler (the Whirlwind Acrobat and the Loose-limbed Comique); Mae and Bert Mack (The Ginger Girl and the Dancing Kid); Emily Green and Co. (Presenting the Playlet *A Minnesota Romance* by Charles Horwitz); Will "Mush" Rawls Supported by Ella Von Kaufman (In a Minstrel Comedy *The Willing Worker*); Della Fox (the Comic Opera Star); King, Bennett, and Fields (Those Frisco Boys); Gordon Brothers (Champion Bag Punchers); "Bob" (the Boxing Kangaroo); and the Photoplane (Novelty Pictures) (Hudson Theatre, Union Hill, N.J. program, OkClaW).

3. Rogers's scrapbook A-3 contains numerous photographs of Rogers and his wife holding the infant. Also pasted in the scrapbook was Rogers's ticket (lower grandstand ticket stub, section 9, row AA, seat 21) to the third game of the World Series at the New York Polo Grounds between the National League's New York Giants and the American League's Philadelphia Athletics on 17 October 1911. The Athletics won 3 to 2 in 11 innings. The Athletics' Frank Baker hit a home run to tie the game at 1 to 1 in the ninth inning (thus earning his nickname Home Run). The Athletics scored twice in the eleventh inning with Harry Davis singling in the deciding run (the Giants countered with one run in the bottom half of the inning). It was a pitchers' battle between the Giants' Christy Mathewson and the Athletics' Jack Coombs, both of whom pitched all eleven innings. Mathewson also pitched a complete game in game one of the series. The Athletics won the series, four games to two. The original Polo Grounds had burned down on 14 April 1911 but was rebuilt and opened on 28 June. A concrete-and-steel structure, the new Polo Grounds had more seating (it could seat 34,000 people) (*BE*, 2590; Ritter, *Lost Ballparks*, 160–61).

Maud Lane and Sallie McSpadden to Betty Blake Rogers
21 October 1911
Chelsea, Okla.

Chelsea Okla

815 AM

Mrs Will Rogers,

551 West 113 st

Delighted a̶s̶t̶ₜatₐ[1] W Vs safe arrival   hope he gets you up by six each morning and cries to go to the theatre with his dad each evening, and his his auntie and grand mother take him for a noon day airing six days in the week, call for express package,

Maud & Sallie

TG, rc. OkClaW. Western Union Telegraph Co. Night letter. Received at 2753 Broadway, New York.

1. The original telegram was typed "ast" instead of "at." Someone wrote a large *t* over the *s* and hand-deleted the typed *t*.

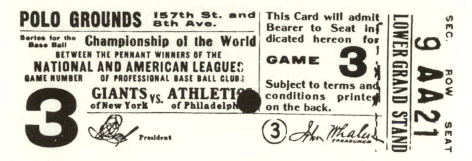

1911 World Series ticket, from Will Rogers's scrapbook. (*OkClaW*)

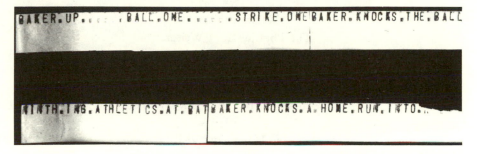

1911 World Series tickertape, announcing historic home runs by Frank (Home Run) Baker, from Will Rogers's scrapbook. (*OkClaW*)

Hammerstein's Victoria Theatre Playbill
23 October 1911
New York, N.Y.

Rogers returned to Hammerstein's Victoria Theatre to perform his single act. He was part of a bill that included several well-known vaudevillians.

HAMMERSTEIN'S
WEEK BEGINNING MONDAY MATINEE, OCTOBER 23, 1911.
Matinee Every Day.

1   Overture
Medley Two-Step—"I Want a Girl" . . . . .Harry Von Tilzer[1]
Conductor of Orchestra, Mr. Geo. May.

2   Williams and Kramer
Colored Singers and Dancers.

3   Smith Brothers
                    In an Aerial Novelty.

4   Lieut. R. Eldridge and Sallie Randall
                A Novelty from the Phillipines.[2]

5   Rose Young and Friedman
                        Entertainers.

6   Will Rogers
                World's Champion Lasso Thrower.

7   William Dillon
                The Popular Song Writer.[3]

8   Thos. J. Ryan-Richfield Company[4]
        Presenting Their Latest One-Act Comedy by Will M. Cressy[5]
                (A Sequel to "Mag Haggerty's Father)
                        —Entitled—
                    "Mag Haggerty's Visit"
                            Cast.
Mike Haggerty . . . . .Thos. J. Ryan
Mrs. Ma-shay-on, nee "Mag Haggerty" . . . . .Sallie Calhoun
Schone, Mrs. Ma-shay-on's footman . . . . .Rhineas Fanning
                Time—The evening before St. Patrick's Day.
                    Place—Mike Haggerty's Home.

9   Chas.—Cartmell and Harris—Laura
                In Some Songs and Dances.[6]

10   Charlie Case
                "The Man That Talks about His Father."[7]

11   Charlotte Parry
        In Her Latest Protean Playlet, "Into the Light."[8]

12   Victor Moore
                Emma Littlefield and Company[9]
                In the Original of Bare Stage Acts, entitled
                "Change Your Act, or Back to the Woods."

NOTE—The action takes place after the Monday Matinee in a Metropolitan Vaudeville Theatre where no audience is present.

13   Hoey and Lee
                                   Hebrew Comedians.

14   Scott Brothers
                                   Comedy Acrobats.

15   New Victoriascope Views

PD. Scrapbook A-3, OkClaW.

1. Harry von Tilzer (1872–1946), born Harry Gunn, wrote many songs for vaude-villians. Born in Detroit, von Tilzer grew up in Indianapolis, and at age fourteen he joined a circus. Next he was a singer with a vaudeville touring company. His song-writing career commenced around 1892 when he began writing tunes for Tony Pastor. Also a song publisher, von Tilzer published the early work of George Gershwin and Irving Berlin. He produced musicals and was a charter member of the American Society of Composers, Authors and Publishers (ASCAP). In 1911 he wrote "I Want a Girl Just Like the Girl That Married Dear Old Dad," the year's hit tune, which was played as the overture at Hammerstein's (the lyrics were by William Dillon, who per-formed in the seventh spot on the bill. Among von Tilzer's other popular tunes were "A Bird in a Gilded Cage" (1900), "Wait Till the Sun Shines, Nellie" (1905), and "When My Baby Smiles at Me" (1920) (*AmSCAP*, 757; *EAM*, 186–87).

2. Lieut. R. Eldridge did sand paintings, and Sally Randall sang. Eldridge and Randall were among the best "art" acts in vaudeville. Other vaudevillians did rag pic-tures, paintings of animals and landscapes, and clay modeling (Laurie, *Vaudeville*, 212).

3. William A. (Will) Dillon (1877–1966) was a popular song-and-dance man and noted songwriter. Born in Cortland, N.Y., Dillon performed in minstrel and medicine shows. He toured with Harry Lauder's troupe in vaudeville in the United States and performed with the troupe in London. For the Scottish star he wrote "At the End of the Road." Dillon retired from acting in 1912 after two automobile accidents. He sub-sequently went into the construction and finance business in Ithaca, N.Y., and also was a theater owner. Dillon wrote the lyrics to many popular songs. He was a founder of ASCAP in 1914 (*AmSCAP*, 176; Laurie, *Vaudeville*, 198; *VO*, 6:16 February 1966).

4. The husband-and-wife comedy team of Thomas J. Ryan (ca. 1855–1928) and Mary Richfield (d. 1921) were well known for their Irish sketches. Ryan and Richfield introduced the idea of sequels in their sketches that centered on the character of Mag Haggerty. The first, *Mag Haggerty's Father* (1901–2), concerned an Irish bricklayer whose daughter, married to a gentleman, tries unsuccessfully to teach her father the manners of high society in an Atlantic City, N.J., resort hotel. Others between 1904 and 1909 included *Mag Haggerty's Daughter*; *Mag Haggerty's Reception*; *Mag Haggerty in Society*; and *Mag Haggerty, M.D.* Ryan maintained that these stories were based on an Irish friend, Tim Haggerty. Critics admired Ryan's real-life portrayal of Irish char-acters. Noted for his brogue on stage, Ryan amused audiences with his tag line "Is it?" His wife, Mary Richfield, also received critics' accolades for her portrayal of the colleen

Mag. Their characterizations generally avoided ethnic stage stereotypes, and this made them popular with the Irish working class. Irish organizations, such as the Brooklyn Gaelic Society, appeared regularly at their performances, and the pair were made honorary members of the society (Laurie, *Vaudeville*, 49; Staples, *Male-Female Comedy Teams in American Vaudeville*, 87–89).

5. William M. (Will) Cressy (1863–1930) was a prolific and talented playwright who wrote many skits and playlets for the vaudeville stage. Born in Bradford, N.H., Cressy was first a stage actor; he began playing in vaudeville in 1900. Soon he was writing numerous one-act plays both for himself and for other performers. On stage he often appeared with his wife Blanche Dayne, the two playing likeable rural types in scenes with realistic sets. By 1908 he claimed to have written 101 playlets. Among them were the Mag Haggerty sketches made famous by Ryan and Richfield. Cressy was the first president of the Vaudeville Comedy Club, organized in 1906, and he was prominent in other show-business organizations. In 1914 Cressy wrote the book *Continuous Vaudeville*, a humorous book containing anecdotes about actors, managers, and others associated with the theater. Cressy lived in New Hampshire, where he operated a hay and grain business (*EV*, 116, 526; Gilbert, *American Vaudeville*, 359–62; Laurie, *Vaudeville*, 49; *WhMuDr*, 80–81; *WhoStg*, 107).

6. Charles Cartmell (ca. 1882–1938) and Laura Harris (ca. 1881–1937) were a husband-and-wife, song-and-dance team that toured the United States and Europe. Harris's father, Thomas Harris, once performed as a dancer before Abraham Lincoln, and later performed with his daughter and Cartmell in their act. Cartmell was born in Columbus, Ohio. He and his wife lived in Freeport, Long Island, an actors' colony, and were members of the local Lights Club (Laura Harris and Charles Cartmell clipping files, NN-L-BRTC; *VO*, 2:16 November 1938).

7. Charlie Case (1858–1916) was a popular African American monologue comedian. His obituary claimed that his mother was an albino and his father an Irishman, and that he was a blackface comedian. Case began his show-business career performing in beer halls. His routine dealt with family life when he was a child and dwelled particularly on his wayward father. Case wrote his own routines and was known for a quiet and intimate style of delivery. Because of his nervousness on stage, he twiddled a rag or a string in his fingers. Case was known for his generosity and played at many benefits. He died accidentally while cleaning a shotgun (*EV*, 49; Gilbert, *American Vaudeville*, 9, 176–77, 283; *NYDM*, 9 December 1916, 11; *VO*, 1:1 December 1916).

8. The vaudevillian Charlotte Parry (ca. 1873–1959) performed in the United States, Great Britain, and Australia. She was known for her quick-change act. Her most famous routine was *The Comstock Mystery*, in which she played seven characters. In the playlet *Into the Light*, she played an Italian woman accused of murder and all the witnesses in the trial. Parry retired when she married Joshua Lowe (Jolo), the *Variety* representative in London. She lived there until her husband was killed in an automobile accident, shortly after World War II. She died at the home of her daughter in North Carolina at age eighty-six (Laurie, *Vaudeville*, 97; *VO*, 5:11 November 1959).

9. Victor Frederick Moore (1876–1962) was born in Hammonton, N.J., and appeared on stage in Boston in 1894–95. As a young actor, he performed with various repertory and stock companies, and began working in vaudeville in 1901. In 1902 he paid $125 for the rights to *Change Your Act, or Back to the Woods*, the sketch he performed at the Victoria Theatre. Moore met the actress Emma Littlefield (1883–1934) in 1903. They married that year and performed the act together for twenty-five years (their salary started at $60 and rose to $2,500 a week). Set backstage at a theater, the sketch deals with a struggling vaudeville team being canceled for a performance and

ridiculed by a stagehand. Born in New York City, Littlefield made her stage debut in 1901 in Fall River, Mass. She began her vaudeville career in 1903 with a female partner. She and Moore appeared in *Forty-five Minutes from Broadway* (1906) and George M. Cohan's musical *The Talk of New York* (1907). Between vaudeville engagements, Moore often appeared on the New York stage. After Littlefield's death in 1934, Moore continued to have a successful career on Broadway in the 1930s and 1940s. In 1932 he played Vice President Alexander Throttlebottom in George Gershwin's Pulitzer prize–winning musical *Of Thee I Sing*. The Throttlebottom name entered the popular lexicon as a term for an ineffectual politician. As early as 1915 Moore performed in movies, and over the years he gained considerable fame playing many comic roles, especially a chubby, kind-hearted little man. His best screen roles were as Barkley Cooper in *Make Way for Tomorrow* (1937) and as Sen. Oliver P. Loganberry in *Louisiana Purchase* (1941). He appeared in such films as *Swing Time* (1936) with Fred Astaire, *Star-Spangled Rhythm* (1942) with Betty Hutton, and *True to Life* (1943) with Mary Martin and Dick Powell. He had a memorable role in *It Happened on Fifth Avenue* (1947) and also appeared in *The Seven Year Itch* (1955) with Marilyn Monroe. In addition, Moore performed on radio and in early television. At age seventy-six he was voted best actor in the New York Critics annual poll for his role as Gramps in the 1953 Broadway revival of Paul Osborn's *On Borrowed Time*. He died of a heart attack in 1962 at an actors' home in Long Island (*EV*, 354–55; *FilmEnc*, 968; Gilbert, *American Vaudeville*, 83; *NYT*, 24 July 1962, 27; *OCAT*, 487; *VO*, 5:25 July 1962; *WhMuDr*, 228; *WhoStg*, 285, 320–21).

Clipping from Will Rogers's Scrapbook
ca. 24 October 1911
New York, N.Y.

One reviewer noticed that Rogers told a gag about Theodore Roosevelt at Hammerstein's Victoria Theatre. It was a forerunner of his political jokes, which dominated his routine in the Ziegfeld Follies *and brought him international fame.*

HE NEEDS NO COMPANY.

It was at Hammerstein's where Will Rogers first appeared doing a "single." From that day the managers have never again desired that he should surround himself with a company of men and horses. Rogers and his rope supply enough fun for both the managers and the public. Will never stops roping, also he never stops talking, even when he is singing and dancing. He has some witty talk, too.

"You remember," he asked, "when Teddy Roosevelt came back from a long tour of the West? Or can't you remember that? You must remember Roosevelt, don't you?" Well, Teddy was a pretty good fellow, when he had it. I wonder what has become of him?"

After the laugh had subsided he continued:

"You know, they do say that sometimes they come back," and then after this laugh has subsided: "But not often."

PD. Unidentified clipping, ca. 23 October 1911, scrapbook A-3, OkClaW.

From Clement Vann Rogers
25 October 1911
Claremore, Okla.

The following letter was Clement Vann Rogers's last correspondence with his son.[1] It deals largely with his successful attempt to buy back much of the ranch land he had lost during the allotment process.[2]

Claremore, Okla., <u>Oct. 25th</u> 1911

Dear Willie & Bettie & William

Today is Wednesday & I got your letter wrote on last Sunday & got it this morning   Dr Bushyhead   Godby & Buck Sunday read it.[3] All glad to hear from you   We are sure having some nice weather now. Buck Sunday have got all the Papers in fine shape on the old Home Place with our 10 acres on the Place allotted to Rosa Patterson on the old Home Place[4]   we cant fine [find] her no place nor fine [find] anyone that knows her or place she lives. I dont remember her nor when she lived   The Gus Lowery Papers are all fixed up all right & Buck have got the Deeds to all the land on the said Farm but this 10 acres Rosa Patterson Allotted[5]   we will still try & find her

Willie I think you are making a mistake in wanting some of that land back of the Field cleared out. The Timber on that land is worth a lot of money just as it stands. I will go up and look at the crop & see how the Renter is doing on Said Place   I will go up next week & I will try & sell the corn their

My Health continues good & I still go up to Chelsea every Saturday & come back on Monday & I still eat at the Mason Hotel. Tom & Sallie is going to Tahlequah next week. A few days ago they sold a lot of their fine jersey cows & calves at big Prices $50.00 & $185.00. My Horse is still a little lame   He is in fine fix. Herb McSpadden will be Home soon[6]   Buck said he would send you a few papers today. I sent William Vann Rogers a pair of beeded Moccasins & 2 pr of stockings

Now Willie dont Fret about the old Home Place as it is in good Shape & if we can fine Rosa Patterson we then can have the Tittles all perfect & you will have one of the best Farms in this state. I still hold to my Rock Barn & what few Houses I have here in Claremore   My Rents amount to about $114.00 per month.

I will take your letters up to the Girls next Saturday.

Love to All

Your Pa, C. V. Rogers

ALS, rc. OkClaW. On First National Bank, Claremore, letterhead.

1. Clement Vann Rogers wrote his son and daughter-in-law four letters between 17 and 25 October. They were very warm in tone; he was looking forward to the birth of his grandchild. On 19 October 1911 he wrote that he was in fine health for a man his age (seventy-two). Nine days later he died during the night, on Saturday, 28 October, at his daughter Sallie McSpadden's home in Chelsea (Clement Vann Rogers to Will Rogers and Betty Blake Rogers, 17 October 1911, 19 October 1911, and 23 October 1911, OkClaW).

2. Clement Vann Rogers was originally allotted 69.93 acres and Will Rogers 78.84 acres. Before his death, Clement Vann Rogers bought back 214.70 acres from individuals who owned allotments on his former ranch (List of Taxable Lands Owned by C. V. Rogers, Rogers County, Claremore, Oklahoma, Clem V. Rogers file, OkClaW). Rogers died without a will, and therefore his real estate holdings were divided equally (one-quarter interest) among his three surviving children and the late May Stine Yocum's four living children from her two marriages. In 1912 Rogers bought the land owned by his two sisters and May's children (agreement between Sallie C. McSpadden and John T. McSpadden and William P. Rogers, 21 September 1912, Clem V. Rogers file, OkClaW). Over the years Will Rogers purchased or leased more land on the old home ranch, and eventually he had over sixteen hundred acres. In 1936, one year after his death, the ranch land was sold by Betty Blake Rogers for $15,920, and most of it is now covered by a large reservoir (Collings, *Old Home Ranch*, 136–39).

3. Dr. Jesse Crary Bushyhead (1870–1942) was Will Rogers's first cousin and a prominent Claremore physician (see *PWR*, 1:485–86 [Biographical Appendix entry for Jesse crary Bushyhead, M.D.]). C. F. Godbey was cashier at the First National Bank. Buck Sunday (1877–1959), a childhood friend of Clement Vann Rogers, was a rancher and also active in the real estate business. At this time he handled Clement Vann Rogers's property interests as well as the real estate owned by Will Rogers (*PWR*, 1:558–59 [Biographical Appendix entry for William Esther Sunday]).

4. On 16 March 1905 Rosa Patterson was allotted 11.34 acres (appraised value $56.70) of lot 8 from Rogers's ranch (section 19, town 23, range 16) (Department of Interior Commission to the Five Civilized Tribes, Certificate of Allotment No. 40212, Clem V. Rogers file, OkClaW). In an undated document, Clement Vann Rogers listed the land he bought from individuals who had secured allotments from his ranch. The first entry stated that he had purchased the entire acreage back from Rosa Patterson at $4 an acre (total $45.36) (undated document, The Convention to Form a Constitution for the State of Oklahoma letterhead, Clem V. Rogers file, OkClaW).

5. Augustus (Gus) Lowery (also spelled Lowry) was allotted 21.27 acres from lot 14 (section 19, town 23, range 16). Clement Vann Rogers also bought this acreage back. In addition to his purchases from Patterson and Lowery, he also bought property from the following individuals: Spi (Martin) Trent (69.98 acres), Jane Hicks (10 acres), Jesse Ross (65.71 acres), and Mariah Ross (36.56 acres) (List of Taxable Lands Owned by C. V. Rogers, Rogers County, Claremore, Okla., and undated document, The Convention to Form a Constitution for the State of Oklahoma letterhead, Clem V. Rogers file, OkClaW). See also *PWR*, 1:562–64 (Biographical Appendix entry for Spi [Martin] Trent).

6. Rogers's nephew Herb McSpadden had graduated from the Cherokee Male Seminary at Tahlequah in 1910 and began running his family's ranch in 1914 (see *PWR*, 1:509–10 [Biographical Appendix entry for Herbert Thomas McSpadden]).

To Clement Vann Rogers
28 October 1911
New York, N.Y.

Rogers penned his last letter to his father on 28 October. Clement Vann Rogers died that night.

Saturday

Dear papa.

just a note   we got your letter and the dandy little Moccassins and stockings and Betty and baby and I were tickled to death with them   you all have sent him some awful pretty things   Sallie and Maud sent some beautiful things and Spis wife too.[1] We are doing fine   Betty will write you   she sat up today.

Love Willie

ALS, rc. OkClaW.

1. Spi Trent's first wife was Allie Belle Williams, with whom he had three children. She sent a little jacket and silk boots (see Baby's History Book, OkClaW).

Obituary for Clement Vann Rogers
ca. 29 October 1911
Claremore, Okla.

On Saturday night 28 October, Clement Vann Rogers died at his daughter Maud Lane's home in Chelsea. As the patriarch of the Rogers family, a significant figure in Cherokee Nation politics, and a successful rancher and businessman, Rogers was widely known in the area, and his funeral was attended by many people. He was mourned by hundreds of friends in Oklahoma. On learning the news of his father's death, Rogers immediately left New York for Claremore, canceling his engagements at Hammerstein's Victoria Theatre and Keith and Proctor's Fifth Avenue Theatre.[1]

C. V. ROGERS

C. V. Rogers, familiarly known as Uncle Clem, one of Claremore's oldest and most respected citizens, died Saturday night at the home of his daughter, Mrs. J. T. McSpadden, in the town of Chelsea, and will be buried at that place Tuesday afternoon at 3 o'clock. Mr. Rogers had been in failing health for several years and his death was not unexpected by those intimately acquainted with him. He died sometime during Saturday night and was found Sunday morning by his daughter when she went to his room to call him for breakfast.[2]

Mr. Rogers was one of the most prominent citizens of the Cherokee people and was noted far and wide as a most philanthropic and public spirited citizen; he was a friend of the school children, and every person in distress could find a ready helper in Uncle Clem Rogers. He amassed a fortune in his time but a large portion of it had been devoted to charity before he died.

He was vice president of the First National Bank of this city from the time of its organization until his death.

Mayor E. A. Church has issued a proclamation requesting every business house in this city to close its doors from 3 to 4 P.M. Tuesday afternoon as a mark of respect for our distinguished citizen.

Clement Vann Rogers was born Jan. 11, 1839 in Going Snake district of the Cherokee Nation, near the present site of the town of Westville in Adair county. His parents were Robert and Sallie Rogers nee Vann. He attended the male Seminary at Tahlequah for several years, although he was not a graduate of that institution.

In 1857 he moved to Rabb's Creek west of the town of Oolagah and established a trading post with the Osages; this was the first trading post ever established in the Cooweescoowee district which at this time embraced nearly all the Cherokee Nation west of the Grand River. In 1858 he was married to Miss Mary A. Schrimsher, a sister of the late Judge John G. Schrimsher. To this union six [eight] children were born, three of whom survive the deceased, they are Mrs. J. T. McSpadden, and Mrs. C. L. Lane of Chelsea, and Wm. P. Rogers of this city.[3]

At the commencement of the Civil war Mr. Rogers espoused the Cause of the Southern Confederacy and served with distinction as a soldier and a statesman throughout the four years. He enlisted in Company G of the First Regiment of Mounted Cherokee Volunteers under Captain James L. Butler; Col Stand Watie being Colonel of the regiment, he was elected First Lieutenant in this company and in 1863 was elected Captain of Company C of the same regiment.

He was a member of the Senate of the Confederate Council from 1862 to 1865.

After the War he settled on the Verdigris river about 3 miles east of the town of Oolagah, where he later built a palatial home and improved what was known far and wide as the best farm in the Cherokee Nation. About this time he also embarked in the cattle business and became wealthy. He was elected as judge of Cooweescoowee district in 1877, serving his country in this capacity two years.

In August, 1879, he was elected as Senator of the Cherokee Council, was re-elected in 1881, 1883 and again in 1889.[4] In 1898 and 1899 he served on the commission to provide for the relinquishment of the title to their lands by the Cherokee people paving the way to individual allotment.

Grover Cleveland in June, 1893, appointed Mr. Rogers a member of the commission to appraise the improvements of intruders in the Cherokee Nation.[5]

His first wife died on May 28, 1890, and on June 8, 1893, he was married to Miss Mary A. Bibles, daughter of the Hon. John Bibles; she died January 17, 1900.[6]

In 1907 he was elected a delegate to the Oklahoma Constitutional Convention, where he served with distinction, he being the oldest member of that body.[7]

The present county of Rogers was named in his honor as a fitting tribute to a long and useful life spent in its boundaries. After the Constitutional Convention Mr. Rogers' health failed rapidly and he gave up active interest in politics and business. He continued to make his home in this city until the day of his death, always spending Sunday with his daughters at Chelsea. He was on one of these visits when death called him.

PD. Printed in *CDP,* ca. 29 October 1911. Scrapbook A-3, OkClaW.

1. Rogers was held over for an extra week at Hammerstein's Victoria and was also booked to perform at the Fifth Avenue Theatre. At Hammerstein's he would have been on the playbill with Irene Franklin, and at the Fifth Avenue Theatre with Ruth St. Denis and her company (clippings, scrapbook A-3, OkClaW; *NYT,* 29 October 1911). Betty Blake Rogers recalled that her son, nicknamed Bill, was just one week old when Uncle Clem, as many affectionately called him, died. She wrote: "I had just received a package from Uncle Clem—three pairs of little black wool stockings with pink-and-blue toes and heels, and a pair of tiny beaded Indian moccasins—when the message arrived. . . . Will was terribly hard hit by the news and left immediately for Oklahoma" (Rogers, *Will Rogers,* 120). Betty remained in New York to care for the baby.
2. Clement Vann Rogers, who lived in Claremore, regularly went to see his daughters' families in Chelsea on the weekends. He would take the train to Chelsea on Saturday, spend the night at Maud Lane's house, and then go to Sallie McSpadden's home for Sunday. Maud's daughter, Estelle, discovered her grandfather lying dead in bed on Sunday morning. His death was diagnosed as heart failure. The funeral on 31 October 1911 was held at Chelsea's Southern Methodist Church and was conducted by Rev. J. L. Gage. Rogers was buried in the cemetery at Chelsea. The bodies of his first wife, Mary America Schrimsher Rogers, his son Robert, who died as a teenager, and two infant children, Zoe and Homer, were moved from the Rogers ranch and buried next to his grave (clippings, scrapbook A-3, OkClaW; *CR,* 2 November 1911;

Keith, "Clem Rogers and His Influence on Oklahoma History," 95; Yagoda, *Will Rogers*, 123).

3. Clement Vann Rogers and his first wife had eight children counting Elizabeth, Zoe, and Homer, who died in infancy. Three of the eight were still living at the time of his death (see Will Rogers's Family Tree, *PWR*, 1:474). His second marriage, to Mary Bibles, was childless.

4. Rogers served as a senator in the Cherokee Nation for five terms beginning in 1879, 1881, 1883, 1899, and 1903 (see *PWR*, 1:540–41).

5. Principal Chief C. J. Harris appointed Rogers; the other two members were appointed by President Grover Cleveland.

6. Rogers and Mary Bibles were married on 15 January 1893. She died at the age of thirty-four and was buried in Claremore (*PWR*, 1:548–50 [Biographical Appendix entry for Mary Bibles Rogers]).

7. Rogers was elected in 1906 to the Constitutional Convention.

Clipping from Will Rogers's Scrapbook
ca. 5 March 1912
Springfield, Mass.

THE THEATERS
JUST FOR A JOKE.
HOW WILL ROGERS HAPPENED TO SING THE "HOUN DAWG" SONG.[1]

Will Rogers, the Cowboy comedian at Poli's,[2] has been singing the "houn dawg" song about three weeks. He first broke it in at New Haven. It occurred to him that there might be some fun in it for him, so he pulled the clipping out of his pocket, as he has been doing this week, and gave it to the orchestra leader. Rogers says it wasn't much of a song but it served his purpose of getting some fun out of it. On the bill with him that week were Princess Rajah,[3] Yvette, violiniste, J. C. Nugent[4] in a dramatic sketch and a team of acrobats.

The audience gave him so much applause that Rogers said he would give them a treat and let them hear a quartet sing the song. Much to the surprise of the actors he dragged on the stage with him Rajah, Yvette, Nugent and one of the acrobats. It mattered little to Rogers whether any of them could sing, and as a matter of fact none of them could. However, on they came, some of them with their makeup. Rajah grabbed up a long muff and after Rogers had had his fun she sprung a little joke of her own. She drew from the muff the snake which she uses in her Cleopatra dance and there was a hasty exit of the quartet. Rogers, in commenting on this joke, said: "I didn't suppose she had the doggoned snake in that muff," but he appreciated Rajah's ready wit in turning the tables on him, even if the others failed to appreciate the subtlety of the joke.

As to the "houn dawg" song, Rogers says it is a familiar drone in the Ozark mountains, on the Arkansas and Missouri border line. Mrs. Rogers came from that region and the song is no novelty to her. Her mother, in fact, when first the song began to attract notoriety recognized it instantly as one that had been familiar to her from her childhood days. There are several other similar songs peculiar to that section.

Rogers has received from the Witmarks an orchestration of the song which he has been trying out.[5] After he settles upon the version that is best to his liking he will utilize it in his act. The Witmarks claim to have obtained the music from an obscure firm of publishers in St. Louis who, in turn, claim that they paid a fabulous sum for the song. Rogers thinks he is about the first professional to sing the song on the stage and that was because of his familiarity with the region where it originated.

Rogers says further, that down in that section a wealthy land owner has developed a summer resort and for a diversion every fall for his guests he has inaugurated what is called an "old fiddlers' contest." This is open to all the fiddlers of that region and one of the most important conditions is that no one shall be allowed to enter the contest who can read music. The proprietor of the resort pays the expenses of the mountaineers for a week, transportation included, and puts up money prizes. It provides a gala outing for the mountaineers, also proves a diverting entertainment for the guests.[6]

PD. Unidentified clipping, ca. 5 March 1912, scrapbook A-3, OkClaW.

1. The "Houn' Dawg" song was a popular craze at this time. Supposedly originating in the hills of the Ozarks, the song was sung by Missouri Democrats at their party convention. It eventually became the Democrats' unofficial theme in the 1912 presidential race. Its opening lines went as follows:

> Every time I come to town
> The boys keep a-kickin' my dawg aroun';
> Makes no difference if he is a houn'
> They gotta quit kickin' my dawg aroun'.

(Springfield newspaper clipping, scrapbook A-3, OkClaW; see also Yagoda, *Will Rogers,* 126).
2. Rogers performed at Poli's Theatre in Springfield, Mass., 4–9 March 1912. Rogers had previously performed there in February 1908 (on the theater's history see *PWR,* 2:404n.2).
3. Princess Rajah was discovered by William Hammerstein either at a Coney Island sideshow or at Huber's Museum on Fourteenth Street where she was a snake charmer. She performed a "Cleopatra Dance" with a snake, in which she gazed upon the statue of her dead lover, Antony, moving "every muscle in her body, the whole being a weird spectacle." She danced holding a chair in her teeth as she whirled about the stage. The Princess became popular and was part of the Salome dance craze. A

reviewer once described her performance: "She dresses in gauze and beads, mostly beads, to accentuate the play of her muscles, and twists and turns in all manner of ways, but the suggestion is only of sorrow and of death" ("Princess Rajah's Great Hit," Princess Rajah clipping file, NN-L-BRTC; see also *EV*, 449–51; Gilbert, *American Vaudeville*, 244, 246–47; Kibler, *Rank Ladies*, 50; Laurie, *Vaudeville*, 49, 392, 396).

4. John Charles Nugent (1878–1947) was a stage and film actor, as well as a prolific playwright and theater commentator for *Variety*. Born in Niles, Ohio, Nugent started as a child in show business and got his initial training with repertory and stock companies. He began in vaudeville with his wife Grace Fertig Nugent and later added their two children, Ruth and Elliott, to the act, which often appeared in the headliner position. Nugent wrote his own vaudeville sketches, and with his son Elliott (1899–1980) he wrote many Broadway plays, including his most famous comedy *Kempy* in 1922. He went to Hollywood to act, write, and direct films for Metro in 1929. He was known for advocating American style and content for the U.S. theater, rather than imitating European work. An advocate of actors' rights, he helped instigate the first White Rats strike with a fiery speech given to the membership (Laurie, *Vaudeville*, 49, 148, 180, 312; *OCAT*, 398, 513; *VO*, 3:23 April 1947).

5. M. Witmark and Sons was a leading song publisher and among the first to exploit the rising popular music trade. The firm was started in 1885 by three Witmark brothers, Isidore, Julius, and Jay. They initially began business at their family home at 402 West Fortieth Street. In 1886 they published their first hit, "President Cleveland's Wedding March." In 1888 they moved their office to the Demorest building at 32 East Fourteenth Street in Union Square, and then to 841 Broadway. They published a series of hits, including "Throw Him Down, McCloskey," "I Long to See the Girl I Left Behind," and "The Wedding of the Lily and the Rose." Julius Witmark was a performer at Tony Pastor's theater and encouraged performers to sing his brothers' songs. Isidore Witmark was a composer and wrote the music to the 1902 Broadway musical comedy *The Chaperons*, which ran for only forty-nine performances. The Witmark firm represented such composers as Victor Herbert and George M. Cohan. In 1893 the company moved uptown to 49–51 West Twenty-eighth Street, better known as Tin Pan Alley, where other song publishers and pluggers had offices (*AmSCAP*, 844; Bordman, *American Musical Theatre*, 182; Frick, *New York's First Theatrical Center*, 120–21; Mantle and Sherwood, eds., *Best Plays of 1899–1909*, 412)

6. In addition to his imitation of Fred Stone's lariat dance from *The Old Town*, Rogers showed how George M. Cohan and a "Yiddisher cowboy" would do the dance. He also continued to burlesque Eddie Foy. "He also has lots of fun with his comments on preceding acts," wrote one reviewer ("Will Rogers Gives the 'Houn' Song' at Poli's," *Springfield Daily News* clipping, scrapbook A-3, OkClaW).

Review from the *New York Times* 16 April 1912 New York, N.Y.

A turning point in Rogers's career was his appearance on Broadway in The Wall Street Girl, *a musical comedy that opened on 15 April 1912.[1] Rogers appeared in the second act, performing his roping routine. This was his introduction to the Broadway stage—a precursor of his years with the* Ziegfeld Follies, *beginning in 1916.[2] The following* New York Times *critique typifies the mixed reviews the show received.*

"WALL STREET GIRL" IS RATHER TAME.

BLANCHE RING STRUGGLES VALIANTLY WITH NOT VERY TUNEFUL ROLE AT COHAN THEATRE.[3]

TWO HIGH SPOTS STRUCK

THE STAR'S SINGING OF "DEEDLE-DUM-DEE", AND WILL ROGERS LARIAT THROWING AND QUAINT REMARKS.

The Wall Street Girl, a musical play in three acts; book by Margaret Mayo[4] and Edgar Selwyn,[5] lyrics by Hapgood-Burt,[6] music by Karl Hoschna.[7] George M. Cohan Theatre.

James Greene	.Harry Gilfoil[8]
John Chester	.Charles Winninger[9]
Dexter Barton	.William P. Carleton[10]
Bertie Longman	.Clarence Oliver[11]
Rev. Dr. Leonard	.Paul Porter[12]
Jordan	.Cyril Ring[13]
Pinch	.Charles Silber
Walker	.Jack Wellekens
Simons	.Ralph Shipman
Harris	.William Bourn
West	.Robert Thumston
Mrs. Williams	.Maude Knowlton[14]
Pearl Williams	.Florence Shirley[15]
Lawrence O'Conner	.Wellington Cross[16]
Sunshine Reilley	.Lois Josephine[17]
Glen Underwood	.Helene French[18]
Rosie Dale	.Ivy Paget
Grace Sinclair	.Catharine Hurst
Eddie the Torrant	.Helen Turner
Mazie Blackburn	.Kathryn Salnpolis
Trixie Allen	.Cleo Le Moyne
Jemima Greene	.Blanche Ring

There were two high spots in "The Wall Street Girl" produced, with Blanche Ring as the star, at George M. Cohan's Theatre last evening. One of them was the "Deedle-Dum-Dee" song, sung by Blanche Ring herself, and the other was that extraordinary lariat performer, Will Rogers, who did his

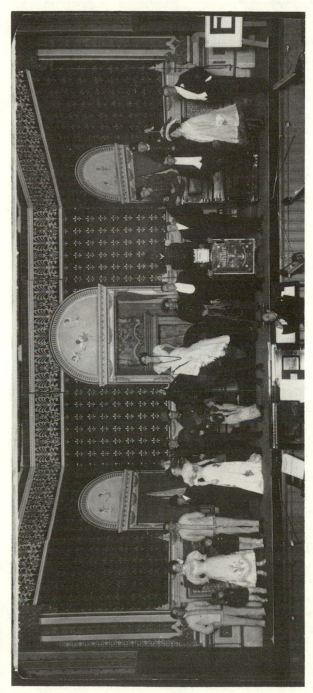

Cast of *The Wall Street Girl*. Rogers is standing to the right of the horse. *[OkClaW]*

regular vaudeville act, but who undoubtedly scored the success of the evening, doing things with ropes and conversing in his quaint way with the audience.

Somewhere during the action William P. Carleton, as a Wild Westerner in New York, remarked that he hadn't seen a good show in years and Miss Ring replied, "That's not strange. There aren't many."

It is unfortunate not to be able to say that "The Wall Street Girl" is an exception to this rule. A curious fact in regard to Miss Ring's career is that whenever she has not been a star she has run away with any performance in which she has been connected. But once with her name emblazoned in electric light she seems to be at a disadvantage.

Last night, for instance, she struggled valiantly with not very humorous or tuneful material, and it was scarcely her fault that she did not make more of this than she did.

There is very little plot. What there is, is connected with a mannish daughter of a Wall Street millionaire, who falls in love with a Westerner, and who eventually marries him.

This plot gives an opportunity for a second act laid in Reno, which, however, has absolutely nothing to do with divorce. It does provide a chance for the girls to appear as cowboys, however, and allows an opportunity for an Indian rag-time dance. It also gave Will Rogers his opportunity to introduce his specialty, ending with his imitation of Eddie Foy, illustrated. "It's a pretty knot, is it not? Is it not." And somewhere in his act Harry Gilfoil perpetrated an epigram, in reply to the minister's.

"Do right and fear no man!"

"It should be" replied Gilfoil, "Don't write and fear no woman!" It was also in this act that Miss Ring sang "Whistle It" and asked the house to join her with only moderate success, however, when one remembers "Umpty-ti-Addy" and others of that like. However, give the song time.

Miss Ring, as has been said before, struggled with all her health, spirits and abundant charm and temperament, but she seldom had a chance to exert herself to any great effect. When she did she made the most of it. She was asked for a curtain speech, and, with Mr. and Mrs. Jerry and Miss Josephine Cohan[19] facing her in the box, she thanked the audience in behalf of herself, her brother, Cyril, a member of the cast; her sister, Frances, playing in "Get Rich Quick Wallingford," and her sister, Julia playing in vaudeville.[20] It's almost like the Drew family![21]

Harry Gilfoil had scarcely a look-in, and it cannot be said that he got many laughs. William P. Carleton played the Western lover according to Hoyle, Charles Silber was an amusing Pinch, and Lois Josephine did some neat dancing.

PD. Printed in NYT, 16 April 1912, OkClaW.

1. There are several stories about how Rogers joined the show. Blanche Ring claims that she saw Rogers perform in Texas and that she wanted him to do his act in her upcoming musical. She got her manager and the show's producer, Frederic McKay, to see Rogers on the stage, and McKay also liked him. They made Rogers an offer, and he accepted it. Ring liked to boast that she had discovered Rogers. She said, "I put him in the business," and said that Rogers called her his "first boss." Rogers joined the show when it opened in New York; his name does not appear in playbills from the show's preview in Rochester, N.Y., in late March 1912 (Interview with Blanche Ring, September 1958, 8, 10, Oral History Popular Arts Collection, September 1958, NNC; *Rochester Post Express* review of *The Wall Street Girl*, Wellington Cross clipping file, NN-L-BRTC; on Ring, see also Biographical Appendix entry, RING, Blanche).

By contrast, McKay said that Rogers sought the job and that one day in New York he wandered into McKay's New York office. "Like to use you," said McKay. "But I've never seen your act and don't know what you can do." Rogers arranged to do his act on Sunday at the Columbia Theatre, and McKay signed him for $125 a week. According to McKay, George M. Cohan commented about Rogers during the dress rehearsal, saying, "That fellow's good" ("How Rogers Landed on Broadway," unidentified, partially dated clipping from Provincetown, Mass., HTC-MH).

Originally the rights to *The Wall Street Girl* were held by the stage star and producer Lew Fields. Needing money for a new venture, Fields sold his interests to McKay (Fields and Fields, *From the Bowery to Broadway*, 291). Most critics agreed that despite a weak plot, it had enough action to please audiences and that Ring held the show together with her catchy songs. Rogers was singled out by many critics and received rave reviews for his expert roping act (see Advertisement from Will Rogers's Scrapbook, ca. 16 April 1912, below). In its first New York run, the show lasted seven weeks with fifty-six performances.

2. *The Wall Street Girl* was described as a three-act musical play. Its story line, based on the theme of the wealthy eastern woman who goes west, appealed to urban audiences and could be interpreted as part of the Wild West fad in American popular culture at this time. The plot focuses on Jemima Greene (Blanche Ring), the daughter of a Wall Street stockbroker (act 1 takes place in the private office of Greene and Longman, Wall Street brokers). She buys a half-interest in a Nevada mining operation, goes to Reno, and falls in love with her partner Dexter Barton, played by W. P. Carlton. She eventually marries him in New York and saves her father from bankruptcy with money from the successful mine (act 3, the final act, takes place in her father's home on Fifth Avenue). The story gave Ring many opportunities to sing the show's tunes, which included "Whistle It"; "Deedle-Dee-Dum"; "I Should Have Been Born a Boy"; "Indian Rag"; and "I Want a Regular Man." The last of these, written by Benjamin Hapgood Burt, became a Blanche Ring standard (Bordman, *American Musical Theatre*, 276).

Rogers fit in well with the musical's western theme. In act 2, which takes place in a town outside Reno, the scenery displayed a background of saloons, restaurants, and hotels around a boxing arena (Reno was then a popular locale for prize fights). Wex Jones, critic of the *New York Evening Journal*, wrote that the stage was full of "whirling characters," such as girls with boxing gloves, men in fighting togs and chaps, cowgirls, miners, Indians, ministers, brokers, and "moving picture men" ("Blanche Ring in 'The Wall Street Girl', a Jolly Jumble of Mirth," clipping, scrapbook A-3, OkClaW).

Within this context Rogers appeared performing his lariat stunts. Called "Lariat Bill, expert with the rope" in the playbill, he was actually a specialty act and had nothing to do with the plot during the play's initial Broadway run (*Wall Street Girl* playbill, week beginning Monday evening 15 April 1912, scrapbook A-3, OkClaW). However, during its second New York run in November 1912 at the Grand Opera House, Rogers was given an expanded speaking role (see Synopsis of Scenes from *Wall Street Girl* Program, 19 September 1912, below). He played "Lawrence O'Connor, who has the moving picture rights" (Wellington Cross, who was not in the second New York run, originally performed this part). He was also given separate billing as "Will Rogers (Specially Engaged)," which reflected his success in the production (*Wall Street Girl* playbill, week beginning Monday evening 18 November 1912, Grand Opera House, NNMus; see also *Seattle Daily Times* clipping, [June 1912], scrapbook A-3, OkClaW, which reports that in *The Wall Street Girl* next season Rogers "will have a speaking part and be featured in the billing").

Betty Blake Rogers attended opening night and later described the event: "We rode to the opening on the subway and I remember how nervous I was and how anxious for Will's success" (Rogers, *Will Rogers*, 120–21). According to her, the play's opening night was interrupted with news that the British ocean liner *Titanic*, on its inaugural voyage to New York, had hit an iceberg and sunk (over 1,500 of the 2,200 passengers aboard drowned). She wrote: "Then Will came on stage and interrupting the action of the play, announced that the ocean liner *Titanic*, on its maiden voyage had struck an iceberg and gone down at sea with a shocking loss of life" (Rogers, *Will Rogers*, 121). However, news of the *Titanic* disaster began to circulate in the early morning of 15 April, many hours before the show opened. The headline of the *New York Times* of 15 April announced that the *Titanic* had hit an iceberg and was sinking at midnight, with the last wireless heard at 12:27 A.M. (the first urgent wireless from the *Titanic* was on 14 April at 10:25 P.M.). The reviews in the New York papers on 16 April did not report that the sinking of the *Titanic* had disrupted opening night on 15 April. The *New York World* review on 16 April mentioned the extent of the tragedy, not the sinking itself. It reported that "men who went out at the end of the first act brought back news of the extent of the Titanic disaster. The tidings spread throughout the theatre, and there was a noticeable change in the attitude of the audience, the spirit of gayety lessening greatly" (see "'Wall Street Girl' Is Quoted High on List," clipping, scrapbook A-3, OkClaW). Years later, after attending the premiere of the film *Cavalcade* (1933), which contained a *Titanic* scene, Rogers told a reporter that he recalled the sinking affecting the performance, but he did not mention that he had told the news of the disaster to the audience ("Will Rogers Impressed With 'Titanic' Scene in Film," unidentified clipping, Will Rogers Personality File, PP). The *New York Times* on 16 April reported that the *Titanic* had sunk at 2:20 A.M. and that probably 1,250 passengers had perished. Thus, the *Titanic* was in the process of sinking during the show's opening night, 15 April. Since there were no newspaper reports that Rogers had interrupted the show on opening night, this event probably did not happen. It is more likely that the dramatic news on opening night was the final sinking and the number of casualties. It was these reports that were circulating in the audience that night (see Bryan and Frances Sterling, "*The Wall Street Girl*," *Will Rogers Roundup*, newsletter of the Will Rogers Cooperative Society, June and August 1992, CPpR). On Sunday 21 April Rogers participated in a special *Titanic* relief benefit at the Cohan theater with Blanche Ring, George M. Cohan, Fanny Brice, Cross and Josephine, Frank Tinney, Nat Goodwin, and many others (*NYT*, 21 April 1912).

VIEWS OF THE INTERIOR OF GEORGE M. COHAN'S NEW THEATRE
NEW YORK CITY.

Broadway musical comedy star George M. Cohan (inset) and the interior of Cohan's
New Theatre in New York, where *The Wall Street Girl* played. *(HTC-MH)*

3. George M. Cohan's Theatre was located at 1482 Broadway, at the southeast corner of Broadway and Forty-third Street, in the rear of the twelve-story FitzGerald Building. The theater was named after the famous musical comedy performer and designed by the architect George Keister in the early Italian style. The lobby and auditorium (seating 1,100) were embellished with murals depicting Cohan and his family and paintings of scenes from Cohan's Broadway hits. Purple silk bordered with silver also adorned the walls. Centered on a wall directly above the stage was a large painting of Cohan standing on a pier gazing at a boat on the ocean with the words "Give My Regards to Broadway" emblazoned at the top. The theater opened on 13 February 1911 with the comedy *Get-Rich-Quick Wallingford,* written and produced by Cohan. This was followed by the musical farce, *The Little Millionaire,* starring Cohan. Musicals and Sunday-night film shows dominated the theater's offerings in the 1920s. Its final theater production was the operetta *The DuBarry* in 1932. In the following six years it was a movie theater, but financial losses forced the owners in 1938 to sell the building at auction for $100,000; the purchaser was the New York Life Insurance Co. Shortly thereafter, the building was demolished, and stores were constructed at the location in early 1939 (Henderson, *City and the Theatre,* 239; Mantle and Sherwood, eds., *Best Plays of 1909–1919,* 424, 452; van Hoogstraten, *Lost Broadway Theatres,* 129–133).

4. Margaret Mayo (1882–1951) was born Lillian Clatten on a farm near Brownsville, Ill. She was educated as a girl in Oregon and Wisconsin and attended Stanford University for one year. In 1896 she appeared on stage at the Garrick Theatre in New York in the production *Thoroughbred,* directed by Charles Frohman. She enjoyed a short acting career and in 1903 began to write plays. *The Wall Street Girl* was a collaboration with her husband Edgar Selwyn, whom she married in 1901 and later divorced. Mayo's plays included *Polly of the Circus* (1907), *Baby Mine* (1910), *Twin Beds* (1914), and *Rock-a-Bye Baby* (1918). Among those, the three-act comedy *Baby Mine* was her biggest success, running 287 performances at the Daly Theatre. She also wrote screen scenarios for the Goldwyn Motion Picture Co. In 1951 Mayo died in Ossining, N.Y., from complications due to a spine fracture (Berg, *Goldwyn,* 67; Mantle and Sherwood, eds., *Best Plays of 1909–1919,* 402, 422, 470, 499, 528, 577, 630; *NYT,* 26 February 1951; *OCAT,* 470; *VO,* 4:28 February 1951; *WhMuDr,* 220; *WhoStg,* 307–8).

5. A well-known stage actor, playwright, film director, and producer, Edgar Selwyn (1875–1944) was born Edgar Simon in Cincinnati, Ohio, the son of a Polish Jewish merchant. At the age of seventeen he went to Chicago looking for work. Finding himself poverty stricken, he attempted suicide by jumping off a bridge into the Chicago River. The river, however, was frozen solid, and Selwyn was unhurt. While walking off the ice, however, he was robbed at gunpoint. The thief, recognizing Selwyn's dire straits, pawned his gun and split the proceeds with him. Selwyn dramatized the incident in his play *The Rolling Stones.* His first appearance on stage was in 1896 in *Secret Service* at New York's Garrick Theatre. After that, he acted in stock-company productions, obtained supporting roles, and then began to get larger parts in Broadway plays. As a producer, his biggest theatrical hit was Bayard Veiller's *Within the Law* (1912), which ran for 541 performances at New York's Eltinge Theatre.

With his brother Archibald (Arch, ca. 1877–1959), also an actor, Selwyn operated Selwyn and Co., which became the American Play Co., a prominent production firm, which created many Broadway hits. Selwyn at one time operated the Selwyn, Times Square, and Apollo theaters on Forty-second Street. In 1912 he began to produce movies with his brother for their All-Star Feature Films Co. In 1916 they joined with Samuel Goldwyn (then Goldfish) to establish the Goldwyn Pictures Corporation (the syllable *-wyn* in the name representing the Selwyns). At first the Selwyn brothers rejected Goldwyn's offer, but then Goldwyn went to Margaret Mayo, Edgar Selwyn's wife, and pleaded with her. Excited by Goldwyn's enthusiasm for the film business, she convinced her husband and brother-in-law to join with Goldwyn. They produced numerous silent features, which made both Selwyn and Goldwyn pioneers in film history. (Rogers would make his first silent films for Goldwyn Pictures, beginning in 1918 with *Laughing Bill Hyde.*) In 1925 Selwyn was Goldwyn's best man at his wedding to the actress and screen writer Frances Marion. In 1920 Selwyn went independent, and two years later Goldwyn was edged out of the company. In 1924 Goldwyn Pictures merged with Metro Picture and Louis B. Mayer Productions to form Metro-Goldwyn-Mayer (MGM). In 1929 Selwyn became a writer and director for MGM, directing such hits as *The Sin of Madelon Claudet* (1931), with Helen Hayes starring in an Oscar-winning role. During the last twelve years of his life Selwyn was an executive with MGM, where he produced routine films. In 1944 Selwyn died in Los Angeles as a result of a cerebral hemorrhage (Berg, *Goldwyn*, 66–68, 83, 138–39; *FilmEnc*, 538, 934, 1228; Mantle and Sherwood, eds., *Best Plays of 1909–1919*, 451-53, 475–76; *NYT*, 14 February 1944; *OCAT*, 24, 607; *WhoStg*, 391–92; *VO*, 3:16 February 1944).

6. Benjamin Hapgood Burt (ca. 1876–1950), American lyricist and composer, was born in Rutland, Vt. During his early years he was an actor and performed with the Weber and Fields Co. (1900–1901). Between 1904 and 1906 he wrote more than sixty special numbers for major stage productions. His main collaborator was Karl Hoschna. Among Burt's songs were "Well, I Swan," "The Pig Got Up and Slowly Walked Away," "My Gal Irene," "Here Comes the Groom," and "I'd Rather Two-Step Than Waltz." Burt died in Amityville, N.Y., on 17 September 1950 (*AmSCAP*, 94; *WhMuDr*, 57).

7. Karl Hoschna (1877–1911), composer and arranger, was born in Kuschwarda, Bohemia. He was educated in Austria at the Vienna Conservatory of Music, where he specialized in the oboe. After graduating with honors, he became an oboeist in the Austrian army band. He arrived in the United States in 1896 and joined the Victor Herbert orchestra. A copyist for the Witmark Music Publishing Co., he wrote arrangements and selected songs for publication. He began collaborating with the lyricist Otto Hauerbach (later Harbach, 1873–1963), and in 1905 their musical *The Daughter of the Desert* was performed on Broadway. Hoschna and Hauerbach had a string of successful Broadway musical comedies that included *The Three Twins* (1908), *Madame Sherry* (1910), *The Girl of My Dreams* (1911), and *The Fascinating Widow* (1911). Among Hoschna's popular songs were "Bright Eyes," "Cuddle Up a Little Closer," "Girl of My Dreams," and "The Mood You're In." Hoschna died on 23 December 1911 after he had composed some of the music for *The Wall Street Girl* (*AmSCAP*, 345; Ewen, *American Popular Composers*, 94–95; *NYDM*, 3 January 1912).

8. Harry Gilfoil (1865–1918), whose birth name was Frank B. Graff, was born in Washington, D.C. At age seventeen he began his stage career. Gilfoil performed in numerous comic plays by the writer Charles Hale Hoyt (1860–1900), such as *A Stranger in New York* (1897). His greatest success in a Hoyt play was his role in the popular farce *A Trip to Chinatown* (1890). He had a lead part in Klaw and Erlanger's *Liberty Belles* (1901), a Broadway musical comedy. One of his comedic specialties in vaudeville was whistling and mimicry. Gilfoil lived in Brooklyn for many years. Afflicted with heart and kidney disease, he died on 17 August 1918 at his home in Bayshore, Long Island (Chapman and Sherwood, eds., *Best Plays of 1894–1899*, 208; Harry Gilfoil clipping file, NN-L-BRTC; Mantle and Sherwood, eds., *Best Plays of 1899–1909*, 396; *NYT*, 11 August 1918, 17; *OCAT*, 359–60, 679).

9. The popular actor Charles Winninger (1884–1969) was born in Athens, Wis. Winninger had a show-business career that spanned fifty years during which he performed in vaudeville, Broadway musicals, film, radio, and television. He came from a theatrical family; his mother and father, Franz and Rosalie Winninger, were musicians. They formed the Winninger Family Concert Co., which performed in variety, tent, and medicine shows, as well as concerts and stage shows. As a young boy, Winninger toured with his family. In 1900 he and his brothers formed the Winninger Brothers Repertory Co. With the troupe he performed character roles, comedy bits, and specialty numbers. He toured with them until 1906. In 1910 he made his Broadway debut in *The Yankee Girl*. Winninger married its star, Blanche Ring, in 1912; they divorced many years later. In 1915 he started his film career with the Elko Comedy Co., followed by features for Universal in the 1920s. Winninger played in numerous musical revues; his most memorable stage role was as Cap'n Andy in the Jerome Kern musical *Show Boat* (1927). In 1930 he returned to Hollywood, performing in films for Universal and the Fox Film Co. Winninger also performed on radio from 1932 to 1934 as the skipper Captain Henry in *Show Boat*, a popular variety hour. Under contract to MGM, he appeared as Judy Garland's father in the film *Little Nellie Kelly* (1940) and *Ziegfeld Girl* (1941). Other films included *State Fair* (1945) and *Give My Regards to Broadway* (1948). Winninger also ventured into television, playing Dad Farrell on *The Charlie Farrell Show*, a situation comedy. Winninger died in Palm Springs, Calif., on 27 January 1969 (*BEWHAT*, 923; Brooks and Marsh, *Complete Directory to Prime Time Network TV Shows*, 113; Dunning, *Tune In Yesterday*, 551–53; *EV*, 419; *FilmEnc*, 1469; *LAT*, 28 January 1969; *OCAT*, 720; *WhoHol*, 2:1838; *WhScrn*, 1:773).

10. The stage and screen actor William Probert Carleton (1873–1947) had a long career in plays and on the screen. On stage he performed in the musical comedies *The Cadet Girl* (1900) and *Broadway and Buttermilk* (1916). Between 1921 and 1938 he appeared in numerous films. Among them were *A Wife's Awakening* (1921), *Bobbed Hair* (1922), *Homeward Bound* (1923), *Half-a-Dollar Bill* (1924), *Girl without a Room* (1933), *The Perfect Clue* (1935), *The Bohemian Girl* (1936), and *La Zandunga* (1938) (*WhScrn* 2:69).

11. Clarence Oliver's specialty was playing youthful parts, because of his breezy and direct manner. Although his parents wanted him to become a Methodist minister, his first intention was to be a professional baseball player or a racehorse jockey. He became a jockey, but was tossed by a horse and suffered severe injuries. During his acting career he appeared in numerous plays, including *She's In Again, Laff That Off,* and *Broadway Jones*. He and his wife also performed in vaudeville as a team on the Keith Circuit in an act called Liver and Opp. On screen he played roles with Madge Kennedy and Mae Marsh, among others ("Played in Vaudeville," *Boston Herald*, 28 November 1926, Clarence Oliver clipping file, NN-L-BRTC).

12. Paul Porter (1886–1957) was an actor and theater manager. On stage he appeared in numerous productions, including *Another Man's Shoes* in 1918. His greatest success came during the 1920s as the Sewer Rat in *Seventh Heaven*, Bully Boy in *Little Old New York*, and Jimmy in *Burlesque*. He appeared on Broadway with Peggy Wood in the 1937 *Miss Quis*. Porter made his home in New York (Mantle and Sherwood, eds., *Best Plays of 1909–1919*, 637; *NYT*, 19 October 1957; Paul Porter clipping file, NN-L-BRTC).

13. The actor Cyril Ring (1893–1967), the brother of Blanche Ring, had a long Broadway career and appeared in many shows, including *Back Seat Drivers* (1928). Under contract to Warner Brothers, he went to Hollywood in 1924, where he had an

extensive career that ended in 1947. On screen he played in Abbott and Costello's *One Night in the Tropics* (1940), the Marx Brothers' *Cocoanuts* (1929), and Laurel and Hardy's *Great Guns* (1941). He also played in the 1947 film *Body and Soul,* with John Garfield. Upon his retirement from the screen he was the manager of the Beverly Hills Club, a popular restaurant for show-business people. He died in Hollywood on 17 July 1967 (Cyril Ring clipping file, NN-L-BRTC; *WhoHol,* 2:1429; *WhScrn,* 1:617; *Variety,* 19 July 1967).

14. Born in California, the actress Maude Knowlton first appeared on the New York stage in 1898 as Miss Brewster in *Trelawney of the Wells.* The following year she had a role in *Brown's in Town.* In 1906 she played Mrs. Barrington in *What the Butler Saw.* That same year she performed with Rose Stahl in *The Chorus Lady,* a popular four-act comedy, which ran for 315 performances at New York's Savoy Theatre. The fabulous gowns for this role were designed by White Studios (Mantle and Sherwood, eds., *Best Plays of 1899–1909,* 513, 518; Maude Knowlton clipping file, NN-L-BRTC; *WhoStg,* 271–72).

15. The actress Florence Shirley (1893–1967) was best known for her film career, which extended from 1939 to 1952. She played supporting roles with the actress Norma Shearer in *We Were Dancing* and *Her Cardboard Lover.* She also appeared in the Greta Garbo classic, *Ninotchka* (1939). Also in 1939 she performed in the film adaptation of Mary McCarthy's novel, *The Women.* As late as 1952, she played in *Deadline, U.S.A* and *Stars and Stripes Forever* (*FilmEnc,* 1240; *WhoHol,* 2:1552; *WhScrn,* 1:660).

16. Wellington (Duke) Cross (1887–1975) was a stage actor and vaudeville performer. His career in vaudeville started in Chicago, where he teamed with Lois Josephine in a man-and-woman act. Other vaudeville appearances were in an act called Cross and Dunn, a four-person song-and-dance revue. He also appeared in the one-act satire *Wives.* He received excellent reviews for his performance as Billy Early in the Broadway hit musical comedy *No, No, Nanette* (1925). Backstage during a performance he met cosmetics executive Elizabeth Arden, and went to work for her as vice president of her firm from 1928 until his retirement in 1958. Cross's home was in Manhattan, where he died on 12 October 1975 (Mantle and Sherwood, eds., *Best Plays of 1909–1919,* 558; Wellington Cross clipping file, NN-L-BRTC).

17. Lois Josephine, Wellington Cross's partner, was a Broadway singer and dancer. The two met in Chicago when he needed a partner immediately for a vaudeville act. They rehearsed for a few hours and then began work at $50 a week, six shows a day, with ten performances on Saturday and twelve on Sunday. They graduated to the big time and played the Orpheum Circuit. In 1913 they appeared at the Winter Garden for the Shuberts. Josephine continued her career on Broadway and appeared in the three-act musical play *Oh, I Say!* (1913) and with Cross in the musical revue *Town Topics* (1915). Will Rogers also performed in the latter show. On 23 September 1915, the opening night of *Town Topics,* Cross and Josephine sent a telegram to Rogers with the message: "IM AFRAID YOULL BE A HIT" (OkClaW). Josephine also played on the same bill with Rogers in shows at Florenz Ziegfeld's *Midnight Frolic,* a nightclub located on the top floor of the New Amsterdam theater (Lois Josephine clipping file, NN-L-BRTC; Mantle and Sherwood, eds., *Best Plays of 1909–1919,* 513, 558; *NYDM,* 18 February 1914, 24; Wellington Cross clipping file, NN-L-BRTC).

18. Helene French was a stage and screen actress who was born in 1863 in Ohio and died in 1917 in Los Angeles (*WhScrn,* 1:258.)

19. Jere J. (Jeremiah John, called Jerry) Cohan (1848–1917) and Helen Frances (Nellie) Costigan Cohan (1854–1928) were the mother and father of George M. Cohan and his sister Josephine. The son of Irish immigrants, Jerry Cohan (born

Cohane or Kohane) was born in Boston. He served as a surgeon's orderly in the Civil War and afterward worked as a saddle and harness maker. In the 1870s he began his show-business career in minstrel companies and vaudeville, appearing as The Ethiopian Comedian, a single act that featured singing, clog dancing, Irish fiddling, and harp playing. In 1874 he married Helen Frances Costigan, born in Providence, R.I., and also of Irish heritage. She had never been on stage before when she joined her husband in vaudeville. Billed as Mr. and Mrs. Jerry Cohan, they performed clog dances and comic sketches. They also had parts in *The Molly Maguires,* an Irish variety show. In 1883 B. F. Keith hired them to do their act in his museum in Boston. They became Keith regulars and appeared also at his Bijou Theatre. At the Bijou the Cohan children, George and Josephine, joined their parents' act and toured with them in the melodrama *Daniel Boon on the Trail.* The family next performed in two troupes organized by Jerry Cohan, the Irish Hibernia and the Bijou Comedy Co. In 1889 the family created a vaudeville act called The Cohan Mirth Makers, which included a brass band. The parents performed a one-act comedy sketch, their daughter a dance act, and their son a buck-and-wing dance in his own skit called *The Lively Bootblack.* Their performance concluded with the entire family acting in Jerry Cohan's original comedy *Googles Doll House.* As The Mirth Makers, the Cohans did 601 performances. By 1892 they were known as The Four Cohans and eventually became the highest paid family act in vaudeville. In their family act, Josephine Cohan performed her dance specialty, George Cohan did buck-and-wing dancing and performed comic parts, and the parents acted in sketches. The Four Cohans starred in New York stage musical comedies written by George M. Cohan. The parents continued to perform in their son's musicals, including *The Yankee Prince* (1908), *The Little Millionaire* (1911), and *Broadway Jones* (1912). In 1917 Jerry Cohan died from hardening of the arteries at his home in Monroe, N.Y. Helen Cohan passed away in 1928 (Cohan, *Twenty Years on Broadway,* 1–57; *EV,* 105–7; Gilbert, *American Vaudeville,* 185; Mantle and Sherwood, eds., *Best Plays of 1899–1909,* 388–89, 432; McCabe, *George M. Cohan,* 1–82; Morehouse, *George M. Cohan,* 15–75; Odell, *Annals of the New York Stage,* 15:704; Stein, ed., *American Vaudeville As Seen by Its Contemporaries,* 298; *VO,* 1:3 August 1917 and 29 August 1928; *WhoStg,* 92).

20. Frances Ring (1882–1951), sister of Blanche Ring, was a successful actress. She started her career in the play *Lost in Siberia* (1898) and in the revivals *Down in Dixie* and *Secret Service.* Between 1903 and 1912 she appeared in many plays, often in lead roles. One of her biggest successes was as Fanny Jasper in *Get-Rich-Quick Wallingford,* a four-act comedy written and produced by George M. Cohan. A box-office hit, it opened at New York's Gaiety Theatre on 19 September 1910 and ran for 424 performances. She appeared in several films in Hollywood, where she died on 15 January 1951 (Chapman and Sherwood, eds., *Best Plays of 1894–1899,* 115, 178–79, 247; Mantle and Sherwood, eds., *Best Plays of 1909–1919,* 424; *OCAT,* 288–89; *WhoStg,* 365–66; *WhoThe,* 516; *WhScrn,* 2:395).

21. The Drews were a famous English theatrical family. John Drew (1827–62) and his wife Louisa Lane (1820–97) were popular English stage performers. Their son John Drew (1853–1927) and daughter Georgiana Drew (1856–93) also acted on the stage. Georgiana married the actor Maurice Barrymore (1849–1905). Their children, Ethel Barrymore (1879–1959), Lionel Barrymore (1878–1954), and John Barrymore (1882–1942), had extremely successful acting careers on stage and in films (*OCAT,* 58–60, 211–12).

Blanche Ring, star of *The Wall Street Girl* and other Broadway musical comedies. *(NNMuS)*

Advertisement from Will Rogers's Scrapbook
ca. 16 April 1912
New York, N.Y.

A shrewd promoter, Max Hart took advantage of every opportunity to publicize Rogers's act. He bought advertisement space in newspapers to highlight his client's good press reviews in The Wall Street Girl.

WILL ROGERS THE DROLL OKLAHOMA COWBOY ON BROADWAY WITH BLANCHE RING IN "THE WALL STREET GIRL"

"AMERICAN."
By Alan Dale.[1]

The "entertainment" at George M. Cohan's Theatre should be called "Miss Blanche Ring." And then, in smaller type, the name of Will Rogers, the lasso expert. Miss Ring and Mr. Rogers were the headliners. The other turn that redeemed "The Wall Street Girl" was, as I said before, Mr. Will Rogers, "expert with the rope." Mr. Rogers is droll person, and some of his "gags" were funny. He opined that while he felt certain of himself in a fifty-cent show, he was not so sure in a two-dollar entertainment. Mr. Rogers need have no qualms. Two-dollar entertainments are elusive affairs, and they need an occasional recruit. The rope manipulation was exceedingly clever, and it looked as though Mr. Rogers would have to work overtime. His quiet work and his subdued speech were splendid reliefs from the ear-splitting racket of the other performers.

NEW YORK "HERALD."

And there is a fine specialty act introduced from vaudeville—Mr. Will Rogers, who throws the lariat, dances with it and in it, meanwhile giving imitations of footlight favorites and keeping up a running monologue that drew hearty laughs from the audience.

NEW YORK "TRIBUNE."

And there was Will Rogers, the lariat thrower, who produced the only real humor of the evening.

"Morning Telegraph."
By Rennold Wolf.[2]

After Miss Ring's, the biggest individual success of the evening was registered by Will Rogers.

"World."
By Charles Darnton.[3]

Meanwhile Will Rogers came out and threw his hat into the ring he made with a rope. By the same token he came out of vaudeville. A man brought up on the plains seldom looks for a broader field. But Rogers is more than a cowboy—he's an artist. While pretending to throw a bluff last night he threw a rope over "The Wall Street Girl" and dragged off the first honors of the performance. Everything he did was done apologetically. But no apologies were necessary. Aside from his skill, Rogers displayed a sense of humor as fresh as a breeze from the Western prairie. He talked of himself and of "Teddy"—but never seriously. Without betraying the slightest effort he "roped" the house [. . .].[4]

"Evening Telegram."

Will Rogers with a well managed lariat and an equally well managed monologue was as popular with the audience as Miss Ring herself.

"Evening Sun."
By Acton Davies.[5]

There was a poet with his lariat who had come out of the West and inserted himself right in the middle of the play[6] who was worth his weight in gold to the management. His specialty, to which Miss Ring wisely gave plenty of rope was really one of the cleverest exhibitions of lariat throwing which this town has seen. Having lost the programme we cannot do the artist full justice this morning and give him the ineffable joy of seeing his name in the papers. But any one who can do so many marvelous things with a little piece of hemp really need not care much what the world in general says about him. If anything really jars him all he has to do is to go out and lasso it.

BROOKLYN "DAILY EAGLE."

WILL ROGERS AND HIS LARIAT, RECRUITED FROM VAUDEVILLE, THE ONLY REAL HIT.

The Reno act was the setting for the only hit of the evening. Will Rogers, well-known and liked by the patrons of vaudeville houses, gave his lariat performance and caught Broadway by storm. Not only is Rogers wonderfully clever with the rope, but he is a comedian who should be given a real part in the play.

VARIETY.

Will Rogers scored a genuine hit in the second act with his lariat specialty. Will says, "I knew it was alright at fifty cents, but I was a little afraid of it at $2."

"GLOBE."
By Louis Sherwin.[7]

"The Wall Street Girl" is Pleasant Diversion of a Tenuous Kind—Will Rogers Makes an Engaging Impression in a Very Brief Time.

But the one who makes the success of the evening, next to Miss Ring, is Will Rogers, with his lassoing act, fresh from vaudeville. It is not so much due to his rope throwing, which is passably clever. The thing that gives him his instantaneous popularity is his amazing geniality. He does his little tricks so pleasantly and with such good humor that in three minutes you find yourself liking the man regardless of what he does. He is not on the stage more than ten minutes altogether, but by the end of that time everybody is sorry that he has to leave it.

"EVENING JOURNAL."
By Wex Jones.

And it's in this scene that Will Rogers gets an excuse for appearing. He is the young man who takes a rope and makes it do a turkey trot in the air. In fact, he can make a simple piece of rope act something scandalous, and this, together with his unique drawling monologue, really makes him the biggest feature of the whole show.

Direction of Max Hart

PD. Unidentified clipping, ca. 16 April 1912, scrapbook A-3, OkClaW.

1. Drama critic Alan Dale (1861–1928), whose real name was Alfred J. Cohen, was born in Birmingham, England. He moved to New York, where he worked as an apprentice to writer Leander Richardson. Dale started out as a drama critic in the 1880s, when several New York morning newspapers added evening editions that printed theater reviews. In 1887 he became the drama critic for the *New York Evening World* and next joined the *New York Evening Journal,* working there until 1895. That year he moved to William Randolph Hearst's *New York American,* where he gained fame as a critic with a breezy style who would not hesitate to pan a play, even one by a famous playwright. He was a favorite of Hearst for a time because his reviews increased sales of the *American.* Bearing a waxed mustache and pince-nez, Dale was a dapper figure on the Broadway scene. Actors and actresses feared his reviews, and producers sometimes banned him from premieres. He was, nonetheless, one of Broadway's most influential critics, whose reviews could make or break a production. Dale admired the work of the composer Jerome Kern, boosted his songs and musicals in his reviews, and in so doing played a role in his rising reputation. Dale also wrote sketches and plays, including the satire *The Madonna of the Future* (1918). He also wrote several books on the theater. In failing health, Dale died while traveling by train from Plymouth to Birmingham, England (Bordman, *Jerome Kern,* 37–38, 63, 78, 81–82, 88, 90, 145, 153, 178, 188, 228, 273, 286, 288; Grau, *Business Man in the Amusement World,* 236; Mantle and Sherwood, eds., *Best Plays of 1909–1919,* 620–21; *OCAT,* 180; *VO,* 1:23 May and 30 May 1928; *WhMuDr,* 82).

2. Born in Ithaca, N.Y., Rennold Wolf (1874–1922) was a dramatist and journalist. After graduating from Cornell University, he became a lawyer and moved to New York in 1901. Around 1906 he joined the *New York Morning Telegraph,* a theatrical daily, as a dramatic critic. With Gene Buck, he wrote the book for the *Ziegfeld Follies* of 1915, 1918, and 1919. He collaborated with drama critic and writer Channing Pollock (1880–1946) on several musical plays between 1911 and 1917. In addition, Wolf wrote film scenarios and theater criticism for several magazines (Mantle and Sherwood, eds., *Best Plays of 1909–1919,* 457, 476, 511, 526, 537, 553, 616, 626, 631; Grau, *Business Man in the Amusement World,* 235; Leavitt, *Fifty Years in Theatrical Management,* 607–8; *OCAT,* 552–53; *WhMuDr,* 328; *WhThe,* 4:2607; see also Wolf's article on the vaudevillian Nora Bayes from the *Green Book Magazine* (1914), reprinted in Slide, ed., *Selected Vaudeville Criticism,* 6–14).

3. The drama critic Charles Darnton (ca. 1870–1950) was born in Adrian, Mich., and began his journalism career at the town's newspaper. For a time he was reporter and drama critic on the *Detroit Evening News.* Darnton's move to the *New York Evening World* in 1902 as drama critic was a turning point in his career. Here he built his reputation for excellent theater criticism that panned mediocre plays and praised the hits. Soon he became known as "the dean of New York drama critics." Legend has it that he was the first critic to have his name and a quotation from a favorable review on a New York theater marquee. He was on the staff of the *Evening World* for twenty-one

years. When the newspaper merged with the *New York Telegram,* Darnton went to Hollywood, where in 1931 he began a screenwriting career with the Fox studio. He died in Hollywood (*NYT,* 21 May 1950; *VO,* 4:24 May 1950).

4. An excerpt from the *New York Times* review of 16 April 1912 (printed above) has been deleted here.

5. Acton Davies (1870–1916) was born in Quebec, Canada. He came to New York in 1887 and was employed by the New York Gas Co. He began contributing to New York newspapers and eventually became a reporter in 1890. In 1893 he succeeded Charles Dillingham as drama critic for the *Evening Sun,* a position he retained until 1914. On the newspaper he became known for his unique and lively style. His critiques were merciless and well respected by theater people, although a few times he was physically assaulted by actors and managers whose work he had panned. He also covered the Spanish-American War for the *Evening Sun* and was its correspondent in Puerto Rico. After leaving the *Evening Sun,* Davies joined the *New York Tribune* for a short time. A proponent of the legitimate stage, he wrote an article in the first issue of *Variety* that criticized vaudeville, calling it "a place where a great many bad actors go before they die." "I have got a grudge against it," he wrote. "Vaudeville has robbed me of too many happy hours in the variety theatres to ever expect a boom from me" ("What I Don't Know about Vaudeville," *Variety,* 16 December 1905, reprinted in Stein, ed., *American Vaudeville As Seen by Its Contemporaries,* 83; see also Stoddart, *Lord Broadway,* 86; and Davies's 1913 review of the British music-hall singer Marie Lloyd, reprinted in Slide, ed., *Selected Vaudeville Criticism,* 129–30). Davies also wrote short stories, film scenarios, and a novel, *The Grand Finale.* Late in life he was publicity representative for the Shuberts. Davies died in Chicago in 1916, from rheumatism of the heart (*NYT,* 13 June 1916; *VO,* 1:9 June and 16 June 1916; *WhMuDr,* 85).

6. The following words were deleted from the original at this point: "just when 'The Wall Street Girl', was beginning to die hardest" (Davies, "Blanche Ring Keeps Her Audience in Jolly Good Humor," *Evening Sun* clipping, scrapbook A-3, OkClaW). It was obviously removed to avoid saying anything critical about the show. Davies, however, generally praised the show and gave a rave review to Blanche Ring.

7. Louis Sherwin was born in 1880 in Germany; his full name was Hugo Louis Sherwin Golitz. He was the son of Amy Sherwin, a well-known soprano, and Hugo Golitz, an impresario. He began his newspaper career in the West with the *Los Angeles Times* and the *Rocky Mountain (Denver) News.* He became drama critic for the *Denver Republican,* and in 1910 joined the staff of the *New York Evening Globe,* where he gained his reputation as a first-rate drama critic (*WhMuDr,* 280).

Article from the *Oregon Daily Journal*
1 July 1912
Portland, Ore.

The Wall Street Girl finished its run on 1 June 1912 after fifty-six performances. Rogers rejoined the show in late September for its tour of the East, Midwest, and South. In early June he and his wife traveled to Oklahoma to visit relatives and friends, and to look after business interests. Then in mid-June Rogers resumed his vaudeville career on the Orpheum Circuit in the Pacific Northwest, with engagements at Spokane, Seattle, and Portland.[1] During his Portland performance another reviewer noted that he was using more jokes about "famous men" in his routine.[2]

To Travel 2500 Miles to Spend Day with Son

Just to pass a few hours with his 8-months-old son, Will Rogers, cowboy, is to travel more than 2500 miles, although he bade goodbye to the child less than a fortnight ago. Rogers' engagement at the Orpheum will end next Sunday night.[3] Early Monday morning the performer will board a train for Kansas City and thence speed to Claremore, Okla., where his wife and child await him. Four days' travel by train will bring him to his goal in Oklahoma. Then, after a visit lasting only a few hours, the lariat-thrower will have to depart for Chicago, in time for a matinee performance next Monday.[4]

"That's crossin' plains with a vengeance," said Rogers, "but I have to do it to see that boy of mine."

PD. Printed in *Oregon Daily Journal*, 1 July 1912, scrapbook A-3, OkClaW.

1. Rogers performed at Spokane and Seattle during the last two weeks of June, at the Orpheum theaters. The Seattle Orpheum, built in 1911, was a richly decorated theater with a staircase of imported marble. Outside, an onyx tablet engraved with the Orpheum name was placed above the entrance. Both theaters belonged to the Northwest Orpheum Circuit, which was managed by John Considine, and the Orpheum company booked the performers (Elliott, *Variety-Vaudeville in Seattle*, 55–56, 67; *Orpheum Circuit* 1925). At Spokane and Seattle, Rogers performed with the same vaudevillians who were on the Portland program (see *Spokane Daily Press* and *Seattle Post-Intelligencer* clippings, scrapbook A-3, OkClaW).
2. In Portland, Rogers continued to perform his imitations of Stone and Cohan, as well as to make amusing comments about Theodore Roosevelt and other "famous men," as the reviewer from the *Morning Oregonian* put it. Rogers joked about Roosevelt, who was making a comeback as the presidential candidate of the Progressive Party in the election of 1912 against William Howard Taft, the Republican candidate, and Woodrow Wilson, the Democratic candidate. The reviewer quoted Rogers as follows: "'I wonder what's become of him these days?'" he said. (Cheers from the Taftites.) 'Sometimes they come back, though'—(counter cheers from the rough riders)—and when he completed the sentence by adding 'but not often' the applause from 'The big Billers' was deafening" (*Morning Oregonian*, clipping, scrapbook A-3, OkClaW).
3. During the week of 1 July 1912, Rogers performed at Portland's Orpheum, a large theater that seated 2,000 people. Vaudeville was so popular in Portland that the Orpheum Circuit used six different theaters up to 1925. In 1916 the circuit took over the Helig Theatre, which became the main showcase for Orpheum attractions. Also on the bill were actress and comedian May Tully (In a Skit Called *The Battle Cry of Freedom*, a Satire on the Divorce Question); the brothers Jack and Phil Kaufman (Comic Blackface Vocalists); Chinko (Juggler); The Four Lyric Latins (singers); Bert Terrell (Dutch Character Vocalist); and Minnie Kaufman (Cyclist) (*GHNTD*, 541; "Men and Music Orpheum Leaders," *Oregon Daily Journal*, 3 July 1912; *Orpheum Circuit* 1925; playbill, *Oregon Daily Journal*, 4 July 1912).
4. Rogers returned to Chicago's Majestic Theatre during the week of 15 July. The reviewer from *Billboard* wrote that Rogers's monologue in his twenty-minute act was "topical and refreshing in its brightness" (clipping, scrapbook A-3, OkClaW). Also

featured on the bill were the singer and comedian Winona Winter, a friend of Will and Betty Blake Rogers; the famous John Tiller's London dance company, in the sketch *Fun in a Harem*; and Tiller's twelve Sunshine Girls in songs and dances. Other performers were Nip and Tuck (Comedy Tumblers); Maud Ronair and Joe Ward (Presenting *Ocean Breezes*, written by Keller Mack and Frank Orth); Ruby Norton and Sammy Lee (Singing and Dancing Skit); and the Kinodrome (Majestic Theatre program, week of Monday, 15 July 1912, scrapbook A-3, OkClaW). On Sunday afternoon 21 July Rogers participated at a memorial performance for Hugh E. Keough at Chicago's Colonial Theatre. The secretary of the Keough Memorial Committee wrote: "You have been placed at 2:28 o'clock which will give you ample time to return to the Majestic as we will have a taxi waiting at the theatre for you" (letter from Hugh E. Keough Memorial, 18 July 1912, OkClaW; see also Keough Memorial playbill, Colonial Theatre, 21 July 1912, scrapbook A-3, OkClaW). From 22 to 27 July Rogers might have performed at the Majestic Theatre in Milwaukee (see *Milwaukee Daily News* clipping, scrapbook A-3, OkClaW).

During the week of 29 July he was appearing at Detroit's Temple Theatre with Winona Winter. Also on the program were Franklyn Ardell (Assisted by Ann Walter in *The Suffragette*); Del Franco's Monkey Circus (From the London Hippodrome); Keno, Walsh, and Melrose (Full-Around Funsters); Gray Trio (Pianosongolists); Coogan and Parks (Songs—Dances—Patter); Marlo-Aldo Trio (a Gymnastic Novelty); and Mooreoscope Pathe Weekly (the Moving Picture Newspaper). The playbill advertised "an even temperature of 68 degrees maintained on the hottest days" (Temple Theatre playbill, week starting Monday, 29 July, scrapbook A-3, OkClaW). On the significance of air-conditioning technology, and the use of air-conditioning in marketing to draw theater audiences, see Cooper, *Air-Conditioning in America*.

Following Detroit, Rogers probably appeared at the Ramona Theatre in Grand Rapids, Mich., 5–10 August. At the Ramona he was on the bill with Jack Wilson's *1912 Review*; The Five Melody Maids and a Man; Ronair and Ward (Musical Sketch); Belle Story (Singer and Comedian); the Gordon brothers and their boxing kangaroo; and Pathe's Weekly (*Grand Rapids News* clipping, scrapbook A-3, OkClaW).

Article from the *Chelsea Reporter*
29 August 1912
Chelsea, Okla.

Clem McSpadden, Rogers's nephew, died in Los Angeles on 20 August 1912 from typhoid fever, which he caught while working as a railroad surveyor in New Mexico. He was buried in Chelsea, Oklahoma. Rogers was visiting his relatives at the time, and undoubtedly attended the funeral.[1]

Special Correspondent.

IN MEMORIAM.

Last Thursday our little city was shocked by the telegram bearing the sad news that Clement McSpadden had passed away at Los Angeles, Calif., of typhoid.

Clem, as he was familiarly called, was born near Chelsea, Dec. 20, 1886, and departed this life Aug. 20, 1912, being twenty-five years of age. He grew to manhood in Chelsea and was held in high esteem by everyone.

The deceased was in the employ of the Santa Fe railroad surveying, at Choves, N.M., when he took sick and was sent to Los Angeles, a distance of eleven hundred miles. This was their closest hospital and his wife was at this place also.

His parents, Mr. and Mrs. J. T. McSpadden, left here Aug. 18 in response to a message telling them of their son's serious illness, but death came before they reached him. They immediately made arrangements to bring the body home for burial, arriving here Sunday morning. Funeral services were held at the M. E. Church, South, Sunday afternoon, Aug. 25, conducted by Rev. J. J. H. Reedy, former pastor of the Episcopal church at this place.[2] The remains were laid to rest in the Chelsea cemetery. The funeral was one of the largest ever attended here.

He has left a wife, father, mother, brother and sisters to mourn his early departure. Their sympathizing friends are numbered by their acquaintances.

PD. Printed in *CR,* 29 August 1912.

1. See *PWR,* 1:508 (Biographical Appendix entry for Clement Mayes McSpadden).
2. Clem McSpadden's father and mother, John Thomas McSpadden and Sallie McSpadden, were members of the Methodist Episcopal Church South and were both involved in local church affairs (*HRC,* 301). The Rev. James J. Hamilton Reedy, the son of a Presbyterian minister, was born in 1852 at Curwensville, Pa. He grew up in Freeport, Ill., and moved with his family in 1868 to Council Bluffs, Iowa, and in 1876 to Nebraska. Reedy received his training for the Episcopal ministry at the Theological Seminary at Topeka, Kans. In 1889 he was ordained deacon at Trinity Church in Council Bluffs. After living in Denver, Colo., from 1900 to 1906, Reedy went to Oklahoma, where in 1908 he taught Cheyenne Indians at the Whirlwind School, near Watonga. In 1908 he was inducted into the priesthood at St. Paul's Church in Oklahoma City. From 1909 to 1911 he was pastor of Episcopal churches in Vinita, Chelsea, Claremore, and Afton, Okla. In 1911 he was appointed curate of Trinity Church in Tulsa and served in that capacity until 1935, when he was made curate emeritus (Botkin, "Indian Missions of the Episcopal Church in Oklahoma," 45; Meserve, "Trinity Episcopal Church, Tulsa," 270n.12, 273).

Synopsis of Scenes from *Wall Street Girl* Program
19 September 1912
Poughkeepsie, N.Y.

On 19 September 1912 the road tour of The Wall Street Girl *began in Poughkeepsie, New York, at the Collingwood Opera House. Rogers was given a speaking part and an opportunity to sing two songs. Rogers traveled with the show from mid-September 1912 to May 1913, performing in cities on the East Coast, in the Midwest, and in the South.*[1]

SYNOPSIS OF SCENES.

ACT I—Private Office of Greene & Longman, Wall Street Brokers.
ACT II—Outside of Ring. Town near Reno, Nev.
ACT III—Room in Mr. Greene's home on Fifth Avenue.

Time . . . Present.

MUSICAL PROGRAM
ORCHESTRA UNDER DIRECTION OF J. ALBERT BROWNE

ACT I.

1. Opening Chorus (Hoschna and Burt) . . . . .Clerks and Bookkeepers
2. "Under the Love Tree" . . . . .Miss Sullivan and Mr. Thompson[2]
3. "I Should Have Been Born a Boy" (Brown & Ayer)[3] . . . .Miss Ring and Ensemble
4. "I Want a Regular Man" (Hoschna and Burt) . .Miss Ring and Principals
5. "On the Quiet" (Hoschna and Burt) . . . .Mr. Porter and Mr. Thompson
6. Finale (Hoschna and Burt) . . . . .Company

ACT II.

1. Opening Chorus (Burt and White) . . . . .Ensemble.
2. "If You Only Will" (Burt) . . . . .Miss Malone[4] and Mr. Rogers
3. "Come On Let's Razoo on Our Little Kazoo" (Spink) . . .Miss Ring and Chorus
4. "The Indian Rag" (Brown and Ayer) . . . . . .Mr. Carleton and Ensemble
5. "Oh You Naughty Wicked Kid" (MacCarthy)[5] .Miss Sullivan and Ponies
6. "Every Day" (Jones and Daniels) . . . . .Miss Ring and Mr. Carleton
7. Finale (Brown and Ayer) . . . . .Company

ACT III.

1. Opening—"You're Some Girl" (Brown and Ayer) . . . . .Miss Malone and Mr. Rogers.
2. "Spoony Land" (Madden and Fitzpatrick)[6] . . . . .Miss Sullivan and Mr. Thompson
3. "I Can Drink" (Burt) . . . . .Mr. Porter
4. (a. "Deedle-dum-dee" (Burt and Hein)[7] . . . . . . .Miss Ring and Chorus
   (b. Request Numbers . . . . .Miss Ring
5. Finale (Hoschna and Burt) .Entire Company

PD. Scrapbook A-3, OkClaW.

1. By the time the show reached New York City's Grand Opera House in mid-November, Rogers's two songs, "If You Only Will" and "You're Some Girl," were no longer performed, and he was not given any new songs to sing (Grand Opera House, New York, *The Wall Street Girl* playbill, 18 November 1912, NN-Mus; see Chronology at the front of this volume for the theaters where Rogers performed on tour in *The Wall Street Girl*).

2. Alice Sullivan and Elmer Thompson.

3. A. Seymour Brown (1885–1917), lyricist, author, and actor, was born in Philadelphia. He acted in vaudeville from 1911 to 1914. As a composer, he wrote songs for Broadway stage scores, including *The Newlyweds and Their Baby* (1909), *The Matinee Idol* (1910), and *Adrienee* (1923). Among his most popular songs were "Rebecca of Sunnybrook Farm" and "Chin Chin." Brown collaborated with Nathaniel Davis (Nat) Ayer (1887–1952) on many songs, including the 1911 hit, "Oh, You Beautiful Doll" (Brown wrote the lyrics). Born in Boston, Ayer went to London as a young man with the singing troupe American Ragtime Quartet. He stayed in London, where in 1916 he wrote music for revues. His most popular show tune was "If You Were the Only Girl." A prolific composer, Ayer wrote the show score for *Somewhere in England* (1919). He died in Bath, Somersetshire, England (*AmSCAP*, 81–82; *EAM*, 106; Short, *Fifty Years of Vaudeville*, 113, 161, 174).

4. Geraldine Malone.

5. Joseph McCarthy (1885–1943) was a well-known songwriter of his time. Born in Somerville, Mass., he first sang in Boston cafes and worked as a music publisher in the city. His first song hit was "That Dreamy Italian Waltz" in 1910. In 1912 he wrote "You Made Me Love You," a tune Al Jolson introduced in *The Honeymoon Express* (1913) and made famous. Another McCarthy hit was his lyrics to "I'm Always Chasing Rainbows" (1918), with music by Harry Carroll (1892–1962). Between 1912 and 1928 McCarthy wrote the scores for many musicals, such as *Kid Boots* (1923) and *Rio Rita* (1927). He also wrote the music for several editions of the *Ziegfeld Follies*. With the composer Harry Tierney (1890–1965), he wrote "Irene," the hit title song in the 1919 musical comedy that was made into a film in 1940. McCarthy also wrote many songs for the movies, but they were never as popular as his Tin Pan Alley tunes (*AmSCAP*, 489; Craig, *Sweet and Lowdown*, 337; *OCAT*, 447).

6. The lyricist Edward Madden (1878–1952) wrote songs for many Broadway shows, including *Rogers Brothers in Panama* (1907), *The Mimic World* (1908), *The Girl and the Wizard* (1909), *He Came from Milwaukee* (1910), *La Belle Paree* (1911), and

Little Boy Blue (1911). Two popular compositions were "By the Light of the Silvery Moon" (music by Gus Edwards) and "Moonlight Bay" (music by Percy Wenrich). Madden also wrote special songs for singers such as Fanny Brice, who sang his "Fol de Rol dol Doi" in *The Whirl of Society* (1912) (*AmSCAP,* 464; Goldman, *Fanny Brice,* 58, 69; Grossman, *Funny Woman,* 66).

The composer Michael J. Fitzpatrick (1863–1950) broke into show business as an actor with Harrigan and Hart productions. He also performed a song-and-dance act with his brother William. At one time he had his own band. Fitzpatrick composed songs for minstrel shows and then for Broadway musicals. He wrote the music for such songs as "Daddy's Mill" and "Ham and Eggs" (*AmSCAP,* 227).

7. The composer and conductor Silvio Hein (1879–1928) wrote many Broadway stage scores. Born in New York, Hein may have studied music in Vienna and Trieste. He composed songs for approximately twenty-four musicals. His popular songs included "Heart of My Heart," "Arab Love Song," and "I Adore the American Girl." He was a founder and charter member of ASCAP and its first director until 1928 (*AmSCAP,* 323; *EAM,* 105; *OCAT,* 333).

4. ON THE ROAD TO THE PALACE
March 1913–October 1914

Broadway's famous Palace Theatre where Rogers appeared in vaudeville for the first time, in January 1914. *(Wurts Collection, NNMuS)*

AFTER ROGERS FINISHED HIS ROAD TOUR WITH *THE WALL STREET GIRL*, HE IMMEDI-ately returned to the vaudeville stage. He began a period of exhausting travel as he played dates weekly in the Midwest, South, and West. It was a valuable peri-od in his career, in which he continued to perfect his act of rope tricks and humorous patter. He increasingly emphasized gags in his routine. He continued to joke about missing with his rope and to tease other performers on the play-bill. But he began making more quips about current topics, as well as dropping in one-liners about personalities such as Theodore Roosevelt and Henry Ford. Critics began to notice that Rogers's act had improved and that it now had a better balance between lasso stunts and funny remarks.

From 17 March to 10 June 1913 Rogers performed in theaters affiliated with the Western Vaudeville Managers' Association (WVMA), an organization composed of more than ten circuits.[1] With offices in Chicago, the association booked theaters primarily in the Midwest, South, and West: the Orpheum, Gus Sun, Butterfield, Allardt, Theilen, Finn and Heiman, and Interstate chains. It furnished attractions for more than three hundred theaters. The organization's publication promoted the WVMA as follows: "From its head-quarters in Chicago, its interests reach out over the entire country from the Atlantic in the East to the Pacific in the West, from Canada on the North and Southward to the Gulf of Mexico and the Mexican line. In no section of this country of ours is this office without its representatives and its theatres."[2]

The WVMA had strict regulations, quite similar to those of the Keith-Albee Circuit. The acts it sent out on the road had to be respectable and fam-ily-oriented. The association's rules specifically prohibited foul language and misbehavior of any type: "Everything of a vulgar, suggestive, profane or sacri-legious nature is forbidden in this theatre. The use of the words, HELL, DAMN, and GOD, except in serious or reverent sense, must be eliminated, as also expressions such as 'For Gawd's Sake'. The resident manager has authority to cancel acts which refuse to comply with this rule after having been requested to do so."[3] Performers often felt constrained by the pervading moral codes in big-time vaudeville. In his routine Rogers joked about the censorship. "The man dont even alow a fellow to cuss a little when he misses out loud," said Rogers.[4]

After an engagement at the Majestic Theatre in Chicago, Rogers played at theaters in smaller cities in Wisconsin, Illinois, and Indiana. A split-week policy existed at these houses. Rogers performed at one theater Sunday through Wednesday and then moved to another theater for performances Thursday through Saturday. Rogers traveled the Interstate Circuit in Texas, with engagements in Fort Worth, Dallas, San Antonio, and Houston. While performing in Houston at the Majestic Theatre, Rogers received the news about the birth of his daughter Mary. The only daughter of Will and Betty Blake Rogers, Mary would become an actress, and she had a very close relationship with her father.[5]

During 1913 and 1914 Rogers toured the Orpheum Circuit. On 10 June 1913 he began a trip that took him to cities in Canada, the midwestern states, and California during a six-month period. At his first stop on the tour in Winnipeg, Manitoba, Rogers appeared on the same program with Eddie Cantor and George Jessel, then young entertainers with Gus Edwards's Kid Kabaret, which featured both comic and singing performers.[6] In his autobiography, Cantor recalled an incident when Kid Kabaret was last on the playbill and "fourth from closing was a cowboy who did the best roping act you've ever seen. . . . This cowboy was the first guy I'd ever met from west of the Bronx and I worshiped him—Will Rogers. We called him Bill."[7] Cantor had a long association with Rogers; the two later performed together in the *Ziegfeld Follies.*

George Jessel recalled Cantor telling him that Rogers was a potential star: "Only two years ago he was doing a roping act with a trained horse, and now [1913] all he does is talk, chew gum, and do tricks with a rope, and he's getting $1,000 a week."[8] Jessel recalled that Rogers was captain of the baseball team during the Orpheum tour. Usually the vaudevillians would play against teams composed of performers who were playing at another vaudeville theater. In Seattle they played against a team from the Empress Theatre, a Sullivan and Considine house. The local paper reported that "Will Rogers, the Oklahoma cowboy, captains the Orpheum nine and the Empress players are headed by Joe Birnes, storyteller, who also may pitch. The Orpheum team is comprised of members of Gus Richards' [Edwards's] Kid Kabaret principally."[9] On one occasion they beat a baseball team of stagehands, and as the winner Rogers was presented with a silver cup on stage. "Rogers made a speech of thanks with the same tender hesitancy that later made him one of the most beloved figures in America," wrote Jessel.[10]

Rogers's engagement in Winnipeg, Canada, led to the publication of his first article in the program of the Winnipeg Stampede. Rogers performed in

Winnipeg in June, two months before the Stampede, which took place 9–16 August 1913. The Winnipeg Stampede was a frontier-day celebration that featured among other events a rodeo with the best ropers in the country.[11]

In late July 1913 Rogers visited his relatives in Claremore and Chelsea, Oklahoma, for two weeks. Then he boarded a train for San Francisco and on the way sent postcards to his wife and son who remained at home in New York. In San Francisco and Los Angeles, Rogers performed at the Orpheum theaters. In his routine Rogers continued his imitations of Fred Stone and Eddie Foy. But he also turned to ethnic stereotyping, emphasizing an imitation that he called a "Yiddisher cowboy" and one-liners about the Irish and Germans. He also began incorporating into his act a few props. On stage was a stepladder from which he did some roping tricks. He rode a unicycle as he twirled his lasso.[12] Most critics applauded Rogers's new jokes and antics.

After California, Rogers began traveling east, stopping each week at Orpheum theaters in such cities as Salt Lake City, Denver, Sioux City, Omaha, Kansas City, Des Moines, Minneapolis, and Chicago. The tour concluded with a Christmas engagement in New Orleans.

The highlight of Rogers's vaudeville career during this period was a January 1914 performance at the famous Palace Theatre in New York. The Palace opened in March 1913 and became the most renowned vaudeville theater in the country. For a performer, playing the Palace represented the pinnacle of achievement in the variety field. Rogers had improved his act since he last appeared in New York, and he received rave reviews for his performance at the Palace. After eight years of constant, rigorous travel from one theater to another, Rogers was at the apex of his career in vaudeville.[13]

In late January Rogers achieved another significant feat by performing at three New York theaters during just one week: Hammerstein's Victoria Theatre, Keith's Union Square Theatre, and the Alhambra Theatre. Headlines claimed that Rogers had broken a record by appearing at three theaters the same night, a feat that was accomplished by clever scheduling.[14] At the Victoria Theatre he appeared on the same all-star program with his friends The Three Keatons and Bert Williams, and at the Union Square Theatre with his friends Pat Rooney and Marion Bent.[15]

In the spring he toured the Keith-Albee Circuit with many engagements in the Midwest. Then in late May he and Betty Blake Rogers traveled to England, where Rogers made a well-received, month-long appearance in the revue *The Merry-Go-Round.* Returning to the United States in mid-July, Rogers was off again on another Orpheum tour, beginning with engagements in California cities. At train stops along the way he sent postcards to his fam-

Marion Bent (*center*) with husband Pat Rooney II (*right*) and son Pat Rooney III (*left*). The Rooneys were good friends of Rogers and appeared several times on the same vaudeville playbill. The Rooneys autographed this photograph to their manager, William Morris. (*Photo by Adeda, gift of Ruth Morris White and William Morris, Jr., NNMus*)

ily, who were staying at the Blake family home in Rogers, Arkansas. In California he performed at Orpheum theaters in San Francisco, Oakland, and Los Angeles. He also played at new Orpheum theaters in Sacramento, Stockton, and San Jose. The legendary actress Bertha Kalich from the Yiddish and Broadway theater was the headliner at each stop; Rogers received second billing. He appeared for the first time in San Diego at the Spreckels Theatre and one day went to Tijuana, Mexico, to see a bullfight. The return trip east included engagements in Salt Lake City, Denver, Lincoln, Omaha, Kansas City, and Sioux City. The tour was the culmination of Rogers's busiest and most successful vaudeville period.

1. See Will Rogers's Vaudeville Calendar, 17 March–10 June 1913, below.
2. *Vaudeville Managers' Protective Organization, 1912 Yearbook,* 21.
3. *Vaudeville Year Book, 1913,* 19.
4. Vaudeville Act Performance Notes, ca. 30 October 1914, below.
5. See Biographical Appendix entry, BROOKS, Mary Amelia Rogers.
6. See Review from *Seattle Post-Intelligencer,* ca. 15 July 1913, below.
7. Cantor, *Take My Life,* 104; see also Cantor, *My Life Is in Your Hands,* 133–38; Wertheim, *Will Rogers at the Ziegfeld Follies,* 175–91; Biographical Appendix entry, CANTOR, Eddie.
8. Jessel, *World I Lived In,* 18.
9. "Footlight Rivals to Play," clipping, scrapbook A-3, OkClaW.
10. Jessel, *So Help Me,* 26.
11. See Article by Will Rogers from *The Stampede,* 9–16 August 1913, below; Biographical Appendix entry, WEADICK, Guy.
12. See Vaudeville Act Performance Notes, ca. 30 October 1914, below.
13. See Reviews from Palace Theatre, ca. 5 January 1914, below.
14. See Review and Listings from Three Theater Engagements, ca. 25 January 1914, below.
15. See *PWR,* 2: 510–13, 520–23, 526–32 (Biographical Appendix entries for Pat Rooney and Marion Bent; The Three Keatons; Bert Williams and George Walker).

———

Will Rogers's Vaudeville Calendar
17 March–10 June 1913
United States and Canada

Mar	17,	Majestic, Chicago[1]
Mar	24,	Milwaukee
March	31,	Orpheum Theatre, Madison Wis[2]
April	3,	Majestic " LaCrosse, "[3]
"	6,	Lincoln " Chicago[4]
"	10,	Majestic " Springfield, Ill[5]
"	13,	Orpheum " So. Bend, Ind.
"	17,	Walker Opera House-Champaign, Ill.[6]
"	20,	[~~Empress Theatre, Decatur, Ill.~~]▲Alton, Ill▲[7]
"	24,	New Grand Evansville, Ind[8]
"	28,	Open
May	5,	Fort Worth, Texas[9]
"	12,	Dallas "[10]
"	19,	Houston "
"	26,	San Antonio "[11]
June	10,	Winnipeg Starting Orpheum Circuit[12]

TD. Scrapbook A-3, OkClaW.[13]

1. In this document the theaters and the vaudevillians with whom Rogers performed are annotated only if they are not mentioned elsewhere in this or earlier sections.

2. The Orpheum Theatre in Madison, Wis., was opened in November 1911 and had a capacity of over 1,000. It was the third theater built by the Orpheum chain in Wisconsin. Later it was called the Garrick Theatre and catered to students at the University of Wisconsin. At that date it offered a stock company, silent films, and traveling dramatic and musical performances. It was renamed the New Madison, and then was demolished in 1957. On 31 March 1927 the circuit opened the deluxe New Orpheum Theatre, seating nearly 2,500. It offered a program of five acts of big-time vaudeville and films that was changed every Sunday and Thursday. Eventually it adopted an all-film policy ("Movie Theatre History in Wisconsin," 7; *Souvenir and Opening Program of the Orpheum Circuit's New Orpheum Theatre*).

3. In LaCrosse, Wis., Rogers appeared on the same bill with the Cherry Sisters (see Review from *South Bend Tribune*, 15 April 1913, below).

4. The Lincoln Theatre on Lincoln Avenue in Chicago belonged to the Finn and Heiman Circuit, which was affiliated with the WVMA (*Vaudeville Year Book, 1913*, 49).

5. Just at the time Rogers appeared at the Majestic in Springfield, Ill., the theater had switched to offering vaudeville. Before that it had offered legitimate theater. The Majestic was located on the ground floor of a three-story building and had a seating

capacity of 1,706. In the 1920s it offered high-class vaudeville two times a day, with three shows on Saturdays and Sunday. Springfield's growth could support another theater, and the New Orpheum Theatre, seating nearly 3,000, opened on 30 April 1927. It was built at a cost of more than $1 million and presented five acts of vaudeville and feature films (*GHNTD*, 529; *Souvenir and Opening Program of the Orpheum Circuit's New Orpheum Theatre*).

6. The Walker Opera House in Champaign, Ill., belonged to the Finn and Heiman Circuit, which was affiliated with the WVMA. Its manager was Sam Harris. The Orpheum opened its own vaudeville theater in Champaign, Ill., in 1914, which also served the Urbana area. At the Walker Opera House, Rogers was on the same program with Cameron and O'Connor, who performed a comedy act called Hired and Fired; The Three Lorettos, a musical act; and the comedian Al Carlton. In the 1920s the Orpheum Circuit built a larger theater for vaudeville and photoplays (*Champaign Daily News* clipping, scrapbook A-3, OkClaW; *Orpheum Circuit 1925*; *Souvenir and Opening Program of the Orpheum Circuit's New Orpheum Theatre*; *Vaudeville Year Book, 1913*, 49).

7. Rogers probably performed at the Hippodrome in Alton, Ill. It was operated by the WVMA, which booked Orpheum-affiliated theaters. It had a capacity of about 1,000 spectators (*GHNTD*, 528; *Souvenir and Opening Program of the Orpheum Circuit's New Orpheum Theatre*).

8. Located on Sycamore Street in Evansville, Ind., and managed by a Mr. McGowen, the New Grand Theatre began presenting vaudeville in 1908. At this time it was a theater on the Finn and Heiman Circuit. It became an official part of the Orpheum Circuit in 1920. It was situated on the ground floor of a five-story building and seated 1,200 people. At the time it was the main theater in Evansville, which had a growing population and was a center for furniture manufacturing (Evansville newspaper clippings, scrapbook A-3, OkClaW; *GHNTD*, 529; *Souvenir and Opening Program of the Orpheum Circuit's New Orpheum Theatre*; *Vaudeville Year Book, 1913*, 49).

9. Rogers performed in Fort Worth, Tex., at the Majestic Theatre 5–10 May 1913. This was the first of four stops in Texas arranged by the Interstate Amusement Co. Managed by Charles Mussett, the Majestic had a capacity of 1,400 people. The Interstate Amusement Co. was a circuit allied with the WVMA. In 1913 the Interstate had sixteen theaters in Arkansas, Illinois, Kansas, Kentucky, Missouri, Oklahoma, and Texas. The headliner on the Fort Worth program was Amelia Bingham doing *Big Moments from Great Plays*. Others were Gannon and Tracey (a two-girl act); Keno and Green (singers and dancers); Vera Berliner (violinist); and The Levolas (wire walkers) (*Fort Worth Star* clipping, scrapbook A-3, OkClaW; *GHNTD*, 550; *Vaudeville Year Book, 1913*, 47).

10. Rogers appeared at the Majestic Theatre in Dallas, Tex., 12–17 May 1913. The Majestic belonged to the Interstate Amusement Co. Circuit. While in Dallas, Rogers participated in an afternoon Wild West show at Fair Park, which was attended by more than five thousand spectators. The show was arranged by the Shriners. Rogers was praised for his dexterity with the rope: "Principal features on yesterday's program were trick roping by Will Rogers of Claremore, Ok., who fastens three men on horseback abreast, roping a man on horseback with a rope in each hand, and other clever tricks" (*Dallas Morning News* clipping, scrapbook A-3, OkClaW). According to *Variety*, Rogers also rode bucking broncos (clipping, scrapbook A-3, OkClaW; *Vaudeville Year Book, 1913*, 47).

11. Rogers appeared at San Antonio's Plaza Theatre 26 April–1 May 1913. The theater was part of the Interstate Amusement Co. Circuit and was managed by Lloyd

Spencer. It had a capacity of 1,004 customers. Playing before a Texas crowd very familiar with lariat tricks, Rogers demonstrated a level of skill that drew high marks from reviewers; wrote one critic, "Residents of Texas are more or less familiar with feats of the lariat by reason of the fact that this section is still important as a 'cow county', but those who yesterday witnessed the initial performances of the Plaza Theater bill for the current week had their eyes opened by Will Rogers' unique act. Rogers is a plainsman and went through long years of arduous schooling in acquiring his wonderful cunning in manipulation of the noosed rope. That he learned the lesson well is evidenced by the sure way in which he puts the lariat through all sorts of difficult evolution" ("At the Plaza," clipping, scrapbook A-3, OkClaW; see also *GHNTD,* 550; *Vaudeville Year Book, 1913,* 47).

12. In Winnipeg, Canada, Rogers performed at the Orpheum Theatre 10–15 June 1913. The Winnipeg Orpheum opened in 1911 and was the first of the circuit's theaters in Canada. It had a seating capacity of 1,900. The theater was housed in its own building, built in a classical style. By the mid-1920s it featured both vaudeville and photoplays. Winnipeg marked the start of an Orpheum Circuit tour that would take Rogers to other cities in Canada, including Calgary and Edmonton. He also performed in Seattle and Spokane, Wash., and Portland, Ore., before returning to Claremore, Okla., in late July. Touring with Rogers in Canada and the Pacific Northwest were Gus Edwards's Kid Kabaret with Eddie Cantor and George Jessel (Frolicsome Boys and Girls, Kompany of Klever Kid Komics); Jane Connelly (Comedian); Rose Valerio Sextette (Speed Fiens); Helen Trix (Pianosongwhistleress); La Valera and Stokes (Dash of Spanish); and Brent Hayes (On the Banjo) (*Orpheum Circuit 1925; Souvenir and Opening Program of the Orpheum Circuit's New Orpheum Theatre;* Orpheum clippings, scrapbook A-3, OkClaW; see also Review from *Seattle Post-Intelligencer,* ca. 15 July 1913, below).

13. The entries for 17 and 24 March were handwritten in the lower right corner. The 10 June and Alton, Ill., entries were handwritten also. Handwritten to the left of the 13 April entry was the notation "1913."

Review from the *Milwaukee Journal*
24 March 1913
Milwaukee, Wis.

ROGERS' OWN BRAND

LARIAT ARTIST IN VARIETY BUT ACT IS THE SAME.
COWBOY SHATTERS TRADITIONS OF VAUDEVILLE, WHICH
ARE BELIEVED TO DEMAND CONSTANT CHANGE.

Will Rogers, besides making a lariat do almost everything but talk, is more or less a shatterer of traditions. Those who make it a habit to see him every time he comes to town were convinced of that Monday afternoon in the Majestic.[1] Vaudeville, in which Mr. Rogers is at present finding congenial employment, means variety—always something different. As a matter of fact, Noah Webster[2] goes so far as to assert that "variety show" is preferable to "vaudeville show."

But Rogers is not different. Like Tennyson's brook, he goes on forever.[3] Seeing him for the third time reveals nothing that one has not seen at time No. 1 or time No. 2, except that the Fred Stone imitation from The Old Town is omitted, and that Mr. Rogers has apparently cut down the time of his act.[4]

Among the visits referred to above was Mr. Rogers' appearance here in Blanche Ring's musical comedy, The Wall Street Girl, but the Rogers brand is the Rogers brand in musical comedy and in vaudeville—or, in deference to Mr. Webster, variety. Now, his apparently ingenuous manner is not ingenuous at all, and his running fire of comment, which he reels off, as it were, on the spur of the moment, is simply a manifestation of a good memory. His jokes are always the same, even to his relieving himself of the end-let of Yucatan as "excess baggage," when he trips over the lariat at always exactly the same place.[5]

Yet everbody laughs his fill with enjoyment.

PD. Printed in *Milwaukee Journal,* 24 March 1913. Scrapbook A-3, OkClaW.

1. Milwaukee's Majestic Theatre was part of the Orpheum Circuit. Occupying the ground floor of an office building on Grand Avenue, it opened on 24 August 1908. At that time Milwaukee had a population of about 300,000. Seating about 2,000 patrons, the Majestic was the Orpheum's main theater in Milwaukee for eight years. It initially had a policy of two shows a day, but by 1923 the theater offered a mixture of continuous vaudeville and films. In 1928 the Majestic offered only movies, and it closed permanently in 1932. In response to Milwaukee's population growth, the Palace Orpheum was built in 1916. In 1928 the Orpheum Circuit opened a more luxurious theater, the New Majestic at Grand Avenue and East Water Street, with a seating capacity of 3,000 (*GHNTD,* 552; Headley, "Theatres of Milwaukee," 3; "Movie Theatre History in Wisconsin," 5; *Orpheum Circuit* 1925; *Souvenir and Opening Program of the Orpheum Circuit's New Orpheum Theatre*).
2. Noah Webster (1758–1843), American editor, lexicographer, and educator, published *An American Dictionary of the English Language* in 1828 (*WNBD,* 1045; Snyder, *Defining Noah Webster*).
3. A reference to a line in Alfred Lord Tennyson's poem "The Brook," where the brook replies, "For men may come and men may go, But I go on for ever" (Stange, ed., *Poetical Works of Tennyson,* 218).
4. According to the *Billboard* review, Rogers's act was twelve minutes long (clipping, scrapbook A-3, OkClaW).
5. This particular program ushered in the new vaudeville season at the Majestic after its stock-company performances. Also on the nine-act playbill were Belle Storey (vocalist); *Waiting at the Church* (a playlet written by Edgar Selwyn and William Collier and presented by Edward Abeles and his associates); and a boxing kangaroo (Milwaukee newspaper clippings, scrapbook A-3, OkClaW).

Review from the *South Bend Tribune*
15 April 1913
South Bend, Ind.

It is more interesting to talk with Will Rogers half an hour than to read the best cowboy story in the world. Rogers is the genuine article. All that you have read of the boyishness of the cowboy, his contagious humor, his high spirits and his irrepressible grin is warmed over stuff compared with the first hand impressions you get from Rogers.

He told a long list of corking stories yesterday afternoon and it was the hardest sort of hard luck that tore him away to go over to the Orpheum[1] to do that wonderful roping of his, with his original brand of fun adding to the delight of the performance. . . .

Rogers has a great act, which he sticks to pretty regularly, but he varies it with little touches of humor occasionally, for instance, if the players stand in the wings while he is performing, he likes to coil his rope around them and draw them out on the stage for the amusement of the audience. In Chicago, Saturday night, three girls in a sister act, who had slipped on kimonas and came upstairs to watch him, were all caught in a single throw and yanked before the audience. It will be strange if he does not catch some one unawares at the Orpheum before his engagement is over.

Rogers likes to "kid" the other acts on the bill and most of his patter is made up of things in reference to the acts that preceded him. This of course, changes at every engagement and indicates his original humor and dry wit.

A few weeks ago in LaCrosse, Wis., he was on the same bill with the original Cherry sisters, who hold the world's record in presenting the poorest act and getting away with it.[2] Rogers had a lot of fun guying the act, but when he made the statement that the Cherry sisters were evidently named before lemons were discovered the older member of the team became outraged and had him arrested.[3] He had quite a time squaring the affair and since has been a bit cautious in reference to his personal remarks.

PD. Printed in *South Bend Tribune,* 15 April 1913. Scrapbook A-3, OkClaW.

1. South Bend's Orpheum Theatre opened in 1910 and featured vaudeville programs for twelve years. It occupied the ground floor of a two-story building and seated 1,045 patrons. This theater eventually became too small for the city's rising population. On 2 November 1922 the Orpheum Circuit opened the Palace, a larger, more lavish theater seating 2,600 that offered a program of vaudeville acts, a feature photoplay, screen news, and a comedy film. At that time the original Orpheum became a motion-picture house. In 1924 the Orpheum Circuit took over the Oliver Theatre where touring stock companies performed and feature photoplays were shown. On 16 February 1927 anoth-

er Orpheum theater opened, the Granada, showing only first-run films. Thus, by 1927 the Orpheum Circuit had four theaters in the city (*GHNTD*, 529; *Orpheum Circuit* 1925; *Souvenir and Opening Program of the Orpheum Circuit's New Orpheum Theatre*).

2. The singing Cherry Sisters were Addie (1859–1942) and Effie Cherry (1878–1944). At first their act included three other sisters: Jessie (d. 1903), Ellen or Ella (1863–1934), and Elizabeth or Lizzie (d. 1936). Raised in Marion, Iowa, on a farm, the young girls would go to Greene's Opera House in Cedar Rapids to see a show. The five sisters first went on stage in the local area, performing a one-act sketch called *The Gypsy's Warning*, in order to earn money to attend the 1893 World Columbian Exposition in Chicago. There they met a theatrical agent who booked their act. As The Charming Cherry Sisters—Something Glad, Something Sad, they performed *The Gypsy's Warning* as well as songs, such as "Don't You Remember Sweet Alice Ben Bolt?" They sang terribly, dressed in ungainly outfits, and looked like local farm girls who should not be on stage. Their performance began to make a name for them as vaudeville's worst act. Wherever they played, the audience would hiss and throw items at them. Managers hired them as a joke act, and patrons were encouraged to throw vegetables at them.

The Cherry Sisters were brought to New York by Oscar Hammerstein. At their debut at Hammerstein's Olympia Theatre Roof Garden on 28 November 1896, a net was strung in front of the performers to protect them from the vegetables and fish that audiences were invited to throw. At the height of their career they were earning $1,000 weekly as regulars on the Keith and Orpheum Circuits. A critic once wrote about the act: "They were just a quartette of incompetents, and were so indifferent as to their reception by the public, that they were in demand for many years, at a salary far higher than would have been accorded them if they had possessed real ability" (Grau, *Business Man in the Amusement World*, 245).

When Jessie died in 1903, the sisters temporarily retired and returned to Iowa, where Effie Cherry operated a bakery in Cedar Rapids. She and Addie decided to return to the stage, while Ellen and Elizabeth remained on the farm. Known as the "vegetable twins," they performed as a duo. They closed their act with a rendition of "Ta-ra-ra-boom-de-ay." In the mid-1920s they returned to Iowa again. By the early 1930s they had spent most of their earnings from vaudeville, sold their farm at a rock-bottom price, and were living in a Cedar Rapids rooming house. Addie died in 1942 and Effie in 1944 (Avery Hales, "Cherry Sisters" [reprint from *Coronet*, December 1944, 92–96], in Slide, ed., *Selected Vaudeville Criticism*, 46–50; *EV*, 93–94; Slide, *Vaudevillians*, 25; *VO*, 2:20 March 1934, 3:28 October 1942 and 4 August 1944).

3. Although Rogers was on tour with The Cherry Sisters, there is no evidence that this event happened. The week before, at the Majestic Theatre in Springfield, Ill., Rogers and The Cherry Sisters were on the same program. In his scrapbook, Rogers wrote "GREAT" on top of the review headlined "Cherry Sisters and Will Rogers Divide between Them the Honors of the Show." The review mentioned that Rogers joked about other acts on the bill, and probably he made fun of the Cherry Sisters (clipping, scrapbook 1914, CpPR).

Telegram from L. H. Adamson
18 May 1913
Rogers, Ark.

While in Houston, Rogers received the following telegram announcing the birth of his daughter, Mary Amelia Rogers. Writing to his daughter on her nineteenth birthday,

Rogers recalled her birth: "You was born on Sunday afternoon in Rogers, Ark. at lit-tle 'Mamoos' House. Dad was playing a little Vaudeville Theatre in Houston. Texas. The Majestic. I got the wire and went on the stage for my Matinee and told em about you."[1]

ROGERS ARK MAY 18TH 1913

WILL ROGERS

MAJESTIC THEATRE HOUSTON TEXAS—[2]

LITTLE BETTY ARRIVED TWO PM WEIGHT EIGHT POUNDS
MOTHER AND BABY DOING FINE

L H ADAMSON[3]

TG, rc. OkClaW. On Western Union Telegraph Co. letterhead.

1. Will Rogers to My Daughter, ca. 18 May 1932, OkClaW. Mary Amelia Rogers (1913–90) was born in Rogers, Ark., where Betty Blake Rogers had gone to stay with her mother, Amelia Blake, while her husband was on his vaudeville tour. The baby was named Mary for Will Rogers's mother and Amelia for Betty Blake Rogers's mother. She had a career as a stage and film actress, using the name Mary Howard. Rogers's only daughter, she was very close to her father and was deeply shocked by his unexpected death. Rogers's warmth and love for his daughter were expressed when he wrote her on the occasion of her twentieth birthday; "Well dear even if you are all grown up and a fine girl, you are still daddys baby girl. . . . It seems funny writing to a grown lady, why dear this is the first love letter I have written to a young lady in yars and yars, but it is a love letter, and I am in love with you, and hope you are happy and fine, and you will hurry home and see me. Love and Kisses from old Dad" (Will Rogers to Dear Old Lady Rogers, ca. 18 May 1933, OkClaW; see also Arkansas Department of Health, Delayed Certificate of Birth, filed 27 October 1987, copy, OkClaW; Biographical Appendix entry, BROOKS, Mary Amelia Rogers).

2. Rogers performed at Houston's Majestic Theater 18–24 May 1913. The theater belonged to the Interstate Amusement Co. Circuit and was managed by W. S. Sachtleben. Built in 1910 and located on Texas Avenue, this was the second Majestic in the city. The first, also a vaudeville house, was at 1309 Congress Street. Both were built for Karl Hoblitzelle, owner of the Interstate chain. On the program with Rogers were Vera Berliner (violinist); Keno and Green (Presenting *Hands across the Street*); The Levolas; and The Gannon and Tracy Girls ("Texas, Houston," 12; *Vaudeville Year Book, 1913,* 47; *Houston Daily Post* clipping, scrapbook A-3, OkClaW).

3. Lee H. Adamson married Anna Blake, Betty Blake Rogers's sister, on 12 April 1899 in Silver Springs, Ark. At the time of his marriage Adamson lived in Rogers, Ark., and was employed as a foreman for a construction company. He later helped build the Rogers ranch in Pacific Palisades, Calif. Adamson worked as a foreman on the project and as the engineer who laid out the roads. The Adamsons had one son, Richard (BBC-RHM; Collins, *Roping Will Rogers Family Tree,* 135; Sandmeier, "To the Docents [of] Will Rogers State Historical Park"; Notes, Letters, and Sketches to Lee Adamson, Incoming Correspondence from Will Rogers Regarding Development of Ranch, scrapbook 559-1-5788, CPpR; see also Biographical Appendix entry, BLAKE SIBLINGS).

Telegram to Betty Blake Rogers
18 May 1913
Rogers, Ark.

HOUSTON TEX MAY 18, 13

MRS WILL ROGERS,

ROGERS ARK.

HURRAH FOR YOU BOTH MESSAGES CAME JUST AS I WAS GOING ON DID SOME
ACT SEND NIGHT LETTER TO RICE HOTEL WITH ALL DADDYS LOVE.[1]

BILLY   750 P.M.

TG. OkClaW. On Western Union Telegraph Co. letterhead. In right margin stamped and hand-written, "Phoned to Mrs Rogers, Time 8 pm, By AYH."

1. Rogers had received a telegram dated 18 May 1913 from the families of his sisters Sallie and Maud, signed "McSpaddens and Lanes." It was also sent to the Majestic Theatre. On the same day they sent a congratulatory telegram to Betty Blake Rogers, urging that Mary be called Maud (OkClaW).

Review from the *Seattle Post-Intelligencer*
ca. 15 July 1913
Seattle, Wash.

Rogers began an Orpheum Circuit tour on 10 June 1913, making stops in cities in Canada and in the states of Washington and Oregon. During the tour he appeared on the same program with Eddie Cantor and George Jessel, who were touring with Gus Edwards's Kid Kabaret.[1]

COWBOY ROGERS ORPHEUM[2] WINNER

GUS EDWARDS' "KID KABARET" A FLOCK OF

HAPPY AND PRECOCIOUS COMEDIANS.

HELEN TRIX SHINES. . . .[3]

The new bill at the Orpheum was "all bumpy" with hits last night and the much-heralded "Kid Kabaret" of Gus Edwards, good as it proved to be, ran a dead heat for popularity with Will Rogers, the Oklahoma cowboy, and Helen Trix, the "pianosongwhistleress," which is hard to pronounce but remarkably easy to witness. Will Rogers' magical roping and tricks with the lariat, accompanied by a droll and wholly original line of quiet humor, certainly was the individual triumph of the first night's performance and the surprised audience expressed approval with persistent and spontaneous applause.

Fifteen or more of the most remarkable precocious elves on the stage make up the big act offered by Gus Edwards and his own capital minstrelsy and blackface comedy set a pace that the youngsters come near equaling.[4] It is a beautiful scene, too, and little Betty Washington with her violin is a musical and dancing feature of the "feature." The demure and whimsical Jane Connelly with her "company" of two good comedians present a playlet that is genuinely funny in a discreet and natural way.[5] Melvin Stokes, a young dramatic tenor, of great intensity and remarkable musical gifts, with La Valera, a Spanish dancer, add much life, color and brilliant melody to the program.[6] The Rose Valerio sextet, "speed fiends on a taut wire," conclude the acting numbers with a bewildering series of rapid evolutions, acrobatics and dancing upon slack and taut wires.[7]

It is a program of marked excellence, rapidity, novel and clean numbers, and it is quite fair to say that the astonishing humor, dexterity and naturalness of Will Rogers, the rope-juggling buckaroo from Oklahoma, rather overshadows the others with his absolutely unique "turn." Besides being a marvel in the way of rope manipulation and cowboy dancing, this act is funny during every second of its performance and gets the audience in an indescribable manner. It seems to be the real thing, from the lingo of the cowpuncher himself to the greasy chaps, dusty sombrero and raucous cattle yell with which he responds to the applause.

PD. Printed in *Seattle Post-Intelligencer*, ca. 15 July 1913. Scrapbook A-3, OkClaW.

1. Gus Edwards (1879–1945) was born Augustus Edwards Simon. His parents, Morris and Johanna Simon, immigrated to the United States from Hohensollern Province, Germany, when Edwards was eight years old. Edwards grew up in Brooklyn, where he went to school at night and worked in his uncle's tobacco-processing plant by day. Only one year after arriving in New York, Edwards was employed by vaudevillian singer Lottie Gilson to sit in the audience and to repeat the song from his seat. The idea of their act caught on and became a vaudeville standard called the "singing stooge," and was described in a popular song of the period called "A Song in the Gallery."

At the age of seventeen Edwards formed his own act called the Newsboy Quintet, which performed at Hyde and Behman's Music Hall. The following year the act toured with The Four Cohans, and in 1898 it toured with the boxer turned vaudevillian John L. Sullivan. Edwards then began to write his own songs. In 1899 he formed a partnership with Will D. Cobb, and together they wrote "I Couldn't Stand to See My Baby Lose," "The Singer and the Song," and "You Are the Only Girl I'll Ever Care About," among other songs. On Broadway they wrote songs for *The Wizard of Oz,* starring Montgomery and Stone. Edwards and Cobb also wrote songs for the *Ziegfeld Follies.* The pair published two important Tin Pan Alley songs: "Goodby, Little Girl, Goodby" (1904) and "If a Girl Like You Loved a Boy Like Me" (1905). In 1905 Edwards began publishing his own music, and his "Sunbonnet Sue" (1906) sold a million copies. In 1908 he began to produce stage musicals, beginning with *The Merry-Go-Round* at New York's Circle Theatre. That same year Edwards composed "School Days," the song that was to be his trademark. It sold 3 million copies of sheet music.

Its lyrics caught on with the public: "School days, school days, dear old golden rule days. Readin' and writin' and 'rithmetic, taught to the tune of a hickory stick" (Cantor, *As I Remember Them*, 11). On stage in the act called *School Days* the catchy tune was sung by Edwards as the teacher and forty children singing and dancing. The act was performed for twenty years on vaudeville stages with variations.

From that time on Edwards specialized in children's acts. The motto he displayed on his office wall was "Give the Kid a Chance." Actors and others who got their start with Edwards included Eddie Cantor, George Jessel, Elsie Janis, Walter Winchell (journalist), Mervyn LeRoy (film director), and Groucho Marx. In his eulogy for Edwards, Jessel stated: "I sat on his knee and he taught me to sing" (*VO*, 3:14 November 1945). Some children were as young as five and six. They did not attend school, but were taught to read and write by a tutor employed by Edwards. One of the popular jokes about Edwards was that "Gus is hanging around the maternity wards now, looking for fresh talent" (Cantor, *As I Remember Them*, 12). In Edwards's Kid Kabaret the children pretended they were nightclub singers and dancers. Cantor remembered, "We were a group of boys and girls who dressed up in our parents' clothes and gave our own cabaret" (Cantor, *As I Remember Them*, 14). Jessel, who was fifteen, wore on stage a high hat, white vest, and spats, carried a cane, and performed comedy bits with Cantor. Cantor believed that the Kid Kabaret act was a valuable training school for young actors.

In 1928 Edwards began to write for Hollywood. He wrote *The Hollywood Revue of 1929* and also had a role in the MGM film. In 1932–33 he appeared in Paramount's *Screen Songs*. In 1930 he returned to vaudeville with a new children's act. Edwards retired in 1938 due to ill health. Bedridden for the last six years of his life, he died bankrupt due to high medical bills in Los Angeles. The story of his life was produced in 1938 by Paramount and starred Bing Crosby (*AmSCAP*, 102; Cantor, *My Life Is in Your Hands*, 129–33; Ewen, *American Songwriters*, 145–47; Jessel, *So Help Me*, 11–27; Jessel, *World I Lived In*, 14–17, 19; *OCAT*, 226; *OF*, 1:176; S. J. Woolf, "Gus Edwards Academy," *NYT Magazine*, 23 March 1941; *VO*, 3:14 November 1945; see also Biographical Appendix entry, CANTOR, Eddie).

2. The Orpheum in Seattle was initially a theater operated by the Sullivan and Considine Circuit from 1904 to 1908. In 1908 Considine entered into an agreement with Martin Beck's Orpheum Circuit creating the Seattle Orpheum Co., with Beck owning 40 percent of the stock. The agreement permitted Beck to manage Sullivan and Considine theaters in the Northwest and to book the theaters' acts. At this time Seattle's Orpheum offered shows twice daily, and reserved seat prices ranged from 10 to 75 cents. Its seating capacity was 1,986. From 1911 to 1915 the circuit's acts performed in a new Orpheum at Third and Madison Streets. The chain built another Orpheum in 1917 and a third in 1927 (Elliott, *History of Variety-Vaudeville in Seattle*, 50, 52, 54–56, 67; *GHNTD*, 551; *Orpheum Circuit of Theatres*; *Souvenir and Opening Program of the Orpheum Circuit's New Orpheum Theatre*).

3. Helen Trix (1892–1951) was born in a small town in Pennsylvania, studied piano in Europe, and returned to the United States as a singer with a British accent. During the time Jessel toured with her on the Orpheum Circuit, he recalled that she "was the first gentlewoman I had ever known, and I have to admit it was she who started me on my lifetime habit of reading and educating myself because of my lack of a formal education" (Jessel, *World I Lived In*, 16–17). Trix was also a composer and producer for the London musical *"A" to "Z"* in which she and her sister were featured performers. She also appeared in the London production of *The League of Nations* (1920). One reviewer wrote of Trix that she "is a 'raggy' girl who also does a boy

impersonation that has many people guessing" (*AmSCAP*, 373; Jessel, *So Help Me*, 24–25; Jessel, *World I Lived In*, 16–18; *NYT*, 20 November 1951; "Orpheum," *Spokane Press*, clipping, scrapbook A-3, OkClaW; *VO*, 4:21 November 1951).

4. According to the playbill, there were twenty in the company. In addition to Jessel and Cantor, the troupe included Eddie Buzzel, George Price, Leila Lee, and Gregory Kelly. Buzzel was either fourteen or fifteen, and Lee was about six (Cantor, *My Life Is in Your Hands*, 129).

5. Jane Connelly (d. 1925) was married to Erwin Connelly, with whom she often performed in vaudeville and in film. She and her husband were known for the sketches *A Cup of Tea* and *Foolish Wives* (*VO*, 1:4 November 1925).

6. Melvin Stokes was a dramatic tenor, and La Valera was a Spanish dancer ("It's Novelty Week on Orpheum Bill," *Seattle Sun*, clipping, scrapbook A-3, OkClaW).

7. The Rose Valerio Sextette was a high-wire act called "a speedy set of wire walkers and dancers" ("Orpheum," *Spokane Press*, clipping, scrapbook A-3, OkClaW). Also on the playbill was Brent Hayes, a banjo player.

To Betty Blake Rogers
ca. 8 August 1913
Albuquerque, N.Mex.

At the end of July Rogers left Portland, Oregon, to visit his sisters and other relatives in Chelsea and Claremore, Oklahoma. He spent time at his father's ranch in Oologah.[1] *He also saw his family, who were then in Rogers, Arkansas. On 6 August Rogers left for San Francisco to resume his vaudeville tour on the Orpheum Circuit. At train stops he mailed postcards to his wife and son.*[2]

Going over from Rogers that day left my coat on train with my ticket to California in it and dident miss it till next day. But as I went through Tulsa they had it there. Hope I wont forget to remove myself from the train when get to Frisco.

APC, rc. OkClaW.[3]

1. Rogers's trip home was reported in the local papers (see *CM*, 1 August 1913; *CR*, 7 August 1913; *CWP*, 1 August 1913, 8 August 1913).

2. Rogers sent his wife a card postmarked 7 August 1913 from Amarillo and Albuquerque. Like the other cards, it was addressed to her mother's house in Rogers, Ark., at 307 East Walnut Street. The postcard had a picture of cattle and alfalfa in the Pecos Valley, N.Mex. Above one of the steers Rogers wrote, "Billy Rogers Jr Farm in 30 years *Hence.*" The next day he sent another card to her postmarked from Winslow, Ariz., that depicted a Santa Fe train in Crozier Canyon, Ariz., where there were several productive mines. He wrote: "Winslow. Ariz. Here for breakfast. This is the town Clem and Alice worked in." Rogers was referring to his nephew Clement Mayes McSpadden (1886–1912) and Clem's wife Alice May Beretta. Clem McSpadden, a civil engineer, had worked as a surveyor for the Santa Fe Railroad Co. near Chaves, N.Mex. On 9 August Rogers mailed a card postmarked San Francisco and Barstow that on the front had a painting of the Petrified Forest in Arizona by Thomas Moran. Rogers wrote above the illustration: "Clem surveyed this petrified forest just before he

took sick." In 1912 McSpadden died of typhoid fever in California. One postcard that Rogers sent pictured a Pueblo boy from Isleta, N.Mex., a village thirteen miles west of Albuquerque. The card was addressed to "Little Billy Rogers," postmarked 8 August 1913 from Winslow, Ariz., and sent to the Walnut Street address in Rogers, Ark. The next day Rogers mailed a card to his son postmarked San Francisco and Barstow that depicted a Walapai Native American squaw and papoose (see *PWR*, 1:508 [Biographical Appendix entry for Clement Mayes McSpadden]; also Article from Chelsea *Reporter*, 29 August 1912, above; postcards, OkClaW).

   3. The postcard pictured Native Americans painting pottery. Printed above Rogers's message was this description: "San Ildefonso Indians Painting Pottery. The Pueblo of San Ildefonso is easily reached by Rail from Santa Fe, New Mexico. A quaint old town of 150 people on the east bank of the Rio Grande. This tribe is skilled in the art of Pottery making of a cheap grade. Red and Black and Black and Brown predominating. They can also be seen at work in the Patio of the Palace of the Governors at Santa Fe." Located in northern New Mexico on the Rio Grande River, San Ildefonso is associated with the Eastern Pueblos, a group that also includes Taos, Santa Clara, Nambe, and San Juan. They have their own distinct culture, social organization, and ceremonies. The San Ildefonso Native Americans are known for their skill in the art of pottery making and design, a southwestern Native American tradition that dates back some fifteen hundred years. Their pottery is distinguished by elaborate, carefully sculpted curves and angles. They are also recognized for their distinct black-on-black pottery. Their most famous artist is María Martínez, known for her intricate black-burnished pottery. The language of the San Ildefonso is Tiwa, a Tanoan tongue (Marquis, *Guide to America's Indians*, 7, 17, 18, 88; Sturtevant, *Handbook of North American Indians* 10: 685–92, 696, 728, 754).

   The postcard was one of a series of seven that Rogers sent his wife depicting Native American life in the Southwest. Among them was one showing San Ildefonso Indians making and sanding pottery. Rogers wrote: "The Depot platform is just full of *these* Women with this pottery." Others show an Isleta family dressed in costume; an Isleta woman weaving a belt; visitors attending a religious festival in Taos, N.Mex.; Hopi three-storied houses in Oraibi, Ariz.; and a Hopi Snake Dance. On the postcard depicting the Hopi three-storied houses that required ladders to reach the upper floors, Rogers commented: "All of them seem to prefer upper Berths. They are all the go out here. I had one last night." On another card he commented further about the Hopi houses: "Talk about your flat buildings." Above an image of an Isleta woman weaving a belt, he wrote, "Me Heep Big Injun." Clearly, he did not identify personally with southwestern Native American culture.

Article by Will Rogers from *The Stampede*
9–16 August 1913
Winnipeg, Manitoba, Canada

As far as can be ascertained, "Various Style of Roping" is Rogers's first published article, since his letters from abroad were printed in the Claremore and Chelsea, Oklahoma, newspapers (1903–4). Rogers wrote it as part of the program for the Winnipeg Stampede, a week-long event that featured spectacular riding, roping, and other Wild West show competitions. The Stampede was organized by the cowboy promoter Guy Weadick, a friend of Rogers.[1]

VARIOUS STYLES OF ROPING
By Will Rogers

There are several different kinds of roping which may be divided into the following styles: Steer roping, Horse roping, Calf roping and Fancy roping.

Steer roping is done from horse back. The roper catches the steer, throws him and ties him. Men who follow this particular line of work have horses trained especially for that purpose. The roper makes a study of how to make every second count. The man of the horse ranch may be a great horse roper, still he could not catch a steer in time, and quick time. A man may be a good corral roper on foot, yet could not sit up on a horse and catch with any degree of accuracy whatever. Another man may be first class in roping horses from horse back, but put him on the ground and he could not catch a thing.

Calf roping is an art in itself. A man may be the best calf roper in the world and be unable to go out and catch and tie a steer in anything like quick time. Of course there are exceptions in all these instances, but I am only speaking now as a general rule.

Fancy and trick roping, such as spinning and making fancy catches, is another different line of roping. This line of work originated in Old Mexico, and is called the New Mode of roping. There are several explanations given as to how fancy roping was first originated. It is my contention that making the circle of the rope originated first when someone was taking the tangle out of his rope, swung it around and it fell into a circle, which when practiced he discovered he could keep open. The first man to bring this kind of rope work into the United States was Vicente Orepso, the Mexican who will be remembered for several years with the Buffalo Bill Show. I think he first joined the show in 1893 or '94 and was with them until three or four years ago.[2] He was the first roper that any of the present day fancy ropers ever saw, and up to this day I have never seen a man exhibit the same accuracy and style that he did. He did not have as extensive a routine of tricks as the different ropers of to-day, but he seldom missed and his catches were long and clean. He was a great straight roper, and that is saying a whole lot, as many of the fancy ropers of to-day are poor straight ropers. He was a wonder at catching loose bucking horses that had got their man, or had become loose in the arena and were free to run where they pleased. In catching these runaway horses he always threw a small loop and got them right around the throat latch, not the middle of them or hind leg, or around the saddle horn.

Fancy roping is advancing all the time, and you, who are fortunate enough to attend "The Stampede," will see the greatest bunch of fancy ropers in the world. Every one of them excel in some particular little trick or stunt that he can do better than the other one, but as to who is the best on the general average on all the tricks remains to be seen when the judges' decision is awarded at the end of the contest.

Among the better exponents of this style of roping is Fred Burns, who has originated many tricks and especially fancy catches.[3] His catches are long and clean. Another is Chester Byers, a boy, I am proud to say, I taught some of his first tricks, and who for the last few years has been teaching me some new ones.[4] He is one of the quickest to learn a trick, and he has a lot of original ones of his own. I consider he is easier and slower in action than any of them. He is good in all lines of fancy roping and spinning, still I think Burns excels them all in fancy catches. Bee Ho Gray is another leader in fancy roping. He has originated as many hard tricks as anybody, lots of which he is the only one doing to-day. He is great with either hand, and is the best one handling one rope over the other that I ever saw. Sammie Garrett is also another good one.[5] Montana Jack Ray, great. Tommie Keirnan, look out for him as he can handle the rope mighty easy—can do anything that he ever saw anybody else do, but probably not with such ease.[6] Hank Durnell, while not with the same ease as Byers, does it all. Tex McLeod, Hutton, Homer Wilson,[7] and a bunch of others equally as good. Do not overlook Fred Stone, the actor of Montgomery and Stone. He has had the best boys in the business teach him, and at the present time bids fair to excel lots of them in a little while. The Mexicans are the best on catches. They do lots of hard tricks which are not understood by a great many of the ropers who are the best to do fancy catches while on horse back, still they do not do any tricks like jumping through the loop.

Tex McLeod, the present champion, I have never seen work, but I know from hearsay that he is good. If he wins against his opponents this year my hat is off to him, or any of them, even the losers, as they are all good and have worked hard to learn what they know. If you do not believe it, pick up a rope and try and do a trick with it yourself, so give them all credit.

Florence LaDue, the present lady champion, is very fast and graceful with her spinning.[8] She has a large routine of catches. I have not seen her work lately, but she was always good on all around fancy roping. Hazel Moran is a very good graceful spinner. When I last saw her work she did not do many catches, but everything she does she does well. There are several other lady fancy ropers, among them Jane Bernaudy, Grace Shultz, Bertha Blancett,[9] who are all good.

The end of the week will tell who is the best of the bunch, as all those who consider themselves as good as the best will be here to participate in all lines of cowboy and cowgirl sports and contest for the largest cash prizes ever given.

PD. Printed in *The Stampede*, 9–16 August 1913, URL-CLU. Souvenir program of Canada's Second Annual World's Greatest Frontier Days' Celebration.

1. The first stampede, in 1912, was also organized by Guy Weadick (1885–1953) in Calgary, Canada, and was called the Calgary Stampede. Nothing on this scale had ever been held. Weadick envisioned the show as a monument to an Old West, populated by cowboys, cowgirls, Native Americans, prospectors, and pioneers, that was fast disappearing. The 1912 Calgary Stampede received a mixed reaction. Audiences flocked to see it—official attendance on the first day was 24,000—and the town of Calgary profited. However, the show was run haphazardly and was plagued by rain. A widely reported event was a roping contest between rivals Lucille Mulhall and Florence LaDue, a contest that LaDue ultimately won. Permission had been gained for the Department of Indian Affairs to allow representative Native American groups to attend the Calgary event. However, the ensuing spectacle of the city surrounded by tepees, and of two thousand mounted Native Americans in the parade, caused the Canadian inspector of Indian agencies to arrive at the site to supervise the proceedings. The parade also included hundreds of cowboys, buffalo and ox teams, trappers, prospectors, and cowgirls. The Calgary Stampede program listed a total of twenty-six attractions.

The next year Weadick staged the Winnipeg Stampede, called Canada's Second Annual World's Greatest Frontier Days' Celebration. Much like the Calgary event, this stampede included parades and Wild West show competitions during the week. The Winnipeg Stampede for Thursday, 14 August, consisted of fourteen different acts. Among them were Indian Ceremonial Dances; Trick and Fancy Riding by Cowboys and Cowgirls; Roping of Long Horn Steers by Cowboys; Riding of Bucking Horses by Cowboys; Riding of Bucking Horses by Cowgirls; Steer Bulldogging by Cowboys; and a Wild Horse Race.

In August 1916 Weadick organized the New York Stampede at the Sheepshead Bay Speedway in Brooklyn. Fred Stone originated the New York show, but Weadick arranged what Rogers called the "World Series of Cowboy Events." "Guy Weadick— 'guy' in name only—who manages the whole thing and produces it, has had a lot of experience in this line and has made this one the biggest ever held and the biggest prizes ever offered," wrote Rogers ("Stampede Big Event, Says Will Rogers," *NYA*, 6 August 1916). The stampede featured saddle and bareback bronco riding, cowboy trick and fancy roping, cowboy and cowgirl relay racing, steer roping, trick riding, and wild horse races. Cowboys and cowgirls came from all over to win large sums in prize money and the world championship in their event. Among the competitors were Bill Pickett, Chester Byers, Sam Garrett, Hoot Gibson, Bee Hoy Gray, Florence LaDue, Lucille Mulhall, and Clay McGonigle, all friends or acquaintances of Will Rogers. The announcing was done by Foghorn Clancy, the dean of rodeo announcers. Rogers could not participate because he was performing at Florenz Ziegfeld's *Midnight Frolic*. But he covered the event for the *New York American* and wrote articles that were published on 6 and 8 August 1916. "I want to tell you about the big Stampede down at Sheepshead Bay," Rogers wrote. "If you haven't been down to take gapeins at it, you're overlooking the best bet that ever hit this old village. . . . How the crowd did eat up the bulldogging. That's something plumb new for New York" ("Stampede Big Event, Says Will Rogers," *NYA*, 6 August 1916). Rogers praised the African American cowboy Bill Pickett, who started bulldogging by gripping the animal's lip with his teeth: "It did me good to see old negro 'Bill' Pickett, whom I first met at a contest in St. Louis in 1899. . . . Him, up there, after all these years, showin' these young men how to do it. You know, I believe in giving some credit for originality and if ever a man originated anything, he originated this game. There's not a bone in his body that ain't bent up some way. . . . He laid one down in twenty-six seconds, the fastest up to that time" ("Tossing the He-Oxen with Will Rogers," *NYA,* 8 August 1916). During the New York Stampede Rogers invited several competitors to the *Midnight Frolic,* introduced them during his act, and let some perform their roping tricks, including Guy Weadick, "Texas Shorty" Hartley, and an eleven-year-old cowboy named after Texas Jack ("Cowboys at the Frolic," *NYT,* 9 August 1916; see also the description of the evening in Clancy, *My Fifty Years in Rodeo,* 57). Theodore Roosevelt and his sons visited the Stampede on 8 August, but Rogers's article about their appearance was apparently never published (untitled typed draft, OkClaW). Although it was not a financial success, the event helped popularize the sport in New York, and Madison Square Garden eventually became the home of the World's Championship Rodeo.

Another success for Weadick was the 1919 Calgary Stampede. This event placed more attention on the competitions and offered large purses in prize money that attracted the best cowpunchers in the United States and Canada. Weadick widely publicized the event and its special shows, including an exhibition of the work of western artist Charles M. Russell (both Weadick and Rogers became close friends of Russell). The band of John Philip Sousa was hired to perform, and the Stampede was billed as being in honor of the recent Allied victory in Europe. The Calgary Stampede became an annual event in 1923; Weadick managed it until 1932, when he was fired by the Stampede board over a managerial dispute. It is still held today and attracts many competitors and spectators (Armstrong, "Guy Who Started the Stampede," 6; "Circus Gossip," *Billboard,* 23 January 1909; Clancy, *My Fifty Years in Rodeo,* 52–62; Dippie, *Charles M. Russell, Word Painter,* 135, 279, 319, 323, 374; "Guy Weadick Traveled Rocky Trail before Hitting Pay Dirt in 1912," 24; GWP-GA; Hanes, *Bill Pickett, Bulldogger,* 54, 141–45; Kennedy, *Calgary Stampede Story,* 21, 25, 28–29, 49; LeCompte, *Cowgirls of the Rodeo,* 52; Susan M. Kooyman to WRPP, 18 January 1994; Porter, *Who's Who in Rodeo,* 136–37; Weadick, "Here and There"; Westermeier, *Man, Beast, Dust,* 46; "Will Rogers—Wiley Post," *Billboard,* 24 August 1935; Yagoda, *Will Rogers,* 154; see also Biographical Appendix entries, WEADICK, Guy, and LADUE, Florence).

2. As a young boy, Will Rogers saw the celebrated Mexican roper Vincente Oropeza (1858–1923) perform with Buffalo Bill's Wild West at the 1893 World Columbian Exhibition in Chicago. From that time forward, Rogers idolized Oropeza for his roping skills. At the St. Louis annual fair in 1899, both competed in a steer-roping contest. Oropeza was a regular with William F. Cody's shows and performed in Buffalo Bill's farewell tour of Europe in 1905–6. He was with the show for about sixteen years (Russell, *Lives and Legends of Buffalo Bill,* 377, 442; see *PWR,* 1:522–23).

3. Fred Burns (1878–1955) often played a sheriff in Western films. He appeared in *Flaming Guns, Parade of the West,* and other movies (*WhoHol,* 217).

4. Chester Byers (1892–1945) was a fancy roper, known all over the world. He learned roping tricks from Rogers, and the two became good friends (see Biographical Appendix entry, BYERS, Chester).

5. Sam J. Garrett, a first-rate rodeo performer in his time, placed fifth in the cowboy trick riding and roping at the 1916 New York Stampede. He was born and lived in Mulhall, Okla. As a young boy on Zack Mulhall's ranch, he learned roping from Will Rogers. In 1905 he was with Mulhall's troupe in the Miller Brothers' 101 Ranch show. Garrett toured widely on the rodeo circuit in the United States and also performed in South America. He was a star performer in Zack Mulhall's Wild West show

in 1910. That year the Mulhall show appeared in several cities and in the Appalachian Exposition in Knoxville, Tenn. Garrett was elected to the Rodeo Section of the National Cowboy Hall of Fame in Oklahoma City (Clancy, *My Fifty Years in Rodeo*, 61; Stansbury, *Lucille Mulhall*, 101, 103, 105, 119, 123, 124, 157, 191).

6. Tommy Kirnan (1893–1937) was a well-known and talented trick roper, fancy roper, and bronc rider. Born in Bayonne, N.J., to a family of Irish heritage, Kirnan first worked for the Frank Hafley Wild West show in California. In 1911 he left the show to join circuses and the Miller Brothers' 101 Ranch Wild West show. Kirnan competed in Weadick's 1916 New York Stampede at Sheepshead Bay, where he won second place in trick riding and fourth in roping. In 1920 he won the trick-roping contest at Fort Worth, beating Chester Byers, and tied the famous rodeo champion Leonard Stroud (1893–1961) in the riding event. The next year he beat Stroud for the world championship in riding. Kirnan promoted rodeos and took shows to Scotland, Ireland, France, and other European nations. Kirnan was married to Bea Brossard, also a successful rodeo performer. The couple participated together in shows and events. They appeared in the 1924 Tex Austin Rodeo in London, England, held at Wembley Stadium. In 1937 Kirnan died at Iowa Park, Tex. He was elected to the National Cowboy Hall of Fame in 1977 (Clancy, *My Fifty Years in Rodeo*, 61–62; LeCompte, *Cowgirls of the Rodeo*, 13, 28, 83, 86; Porter, *Who's Who in Rodeo*, 70–71, 78, 104, 130, 132–33).

7. The rodeo performer Homer Wilson also managed shows for Lucille Mulhall. He was the stage manager for Lucille Mulhall and Co., a vaudeville act that appeared at the Great Northern Hippodrome in Chicago on 17 November 1913 and toured other cities. In 1914 the act played the Orpheum Circuit. In 1916 he also managed Lucille Mulhall's Round-up, a touring rodeo show, for which he handled publicity and bookings. Wilson was one of the originators of the Wild Bunch Association, the first, shortlived, professional rodeo cowboy organization, formed at Cheyenne, Wyo., in 1915 and dissolved shortly thereafter (Porter, *Who's Who in Rodeo*, 207; Stansbury, *Lucille Mulhall*, 137, 151, 159).

8. Florence LaDue, who was a member of Will Rogers's Wild West show in 1910, beat Rogers's old friend Lucille Mulhall in events at the Winnipeg Stampede (see Biographical Appendix entries, LA DUE, Florence, and WEADICK, Guy).

9. Bertha Blancett (1883–1979) was born Bertha Kaepernik, the youngest of five children. She grew up in Colorado and began to ride as a small child. As a teenager she was riding, roping, branding horses, and breaking horses at $5 a head. Her career as a competitor began in 1904 when she participated in Cheyenne Frontier Days and put on a spectacular show. A year later she was the only woman hired by the Sherwin Wild West show. When the Sherwin show closed a few months later, she joined the Pawnee Bill show, and following that the Miller Brothers' 101 Ranch show. It appears, from several notices in *Billboard*, that she was using the stage name Bertha Ross. While with the 101 Ranch show, she met Dell Blancett, a rodeo cowboy. They were married in 1909 and moved to California to do stunt riding for the Bison Picture Co. Bertha Blancett appeared in silent films with Tom Mix. While in Los Angeles, the Blancetts gave exhibitions of bucking-horse riding, steer throwing, and steer roping. They also did Wild West exhibitions during this period in South America and Mexico. Blancett continued to participate in rodeo, winning the women's bucking-horse championship in 1911, as well as other championships, including Champion Lady Rider of the World. In 1912 she won third place in the Ladies Bucking contest at the first Calgary Stampede. She was the only cowgirl to enter all four women's events. Among her numerous specialties were racing Roman style, or standing on the backs of racing hors-

es. At the 1914 Pendleton Roundup she won the cowgirls' bronc riding and relay race, as well as the Roman race. In 1915 she won a Roman racing competition in Washington state, setting a record for speed that has not been broken to this day.

In 1919 she quit rodeo after the Pendleton Roundup and worked as a guide in Yosemite Park. She returned to rodeo after several years to perform as a pick-up rider—assisting bronco riders out of the ring after competition and handling the riderless broncos—which she did until about age sixty. In 1975 she and Lucille Mulhall became two of the few women represented among many men in the National Cowboy Hall of Fame in Oklahoma City. At age ninety she traveled from California to Oklahoma to attend the ceremonies. She is also an inductee of the National Cowgirl Hall of Fame in Fort Worth, Tex. She died in her mid-nineties on 3 July 1979 ("Bertha Blancett," in Porter, *Who's Who in Rodeo*, 28–29; Bertha Kaepernik Blancett biography sheet, TxNCMHOF; *Billboard*, 20 November 1909, 2 July and 30 July 1910; Clancy, "Memory Trail"; "Foot in Each World"; Jordan, *Cowgirls*, 189–91; LeCompte, *Cowgirls of the Rodeo*, 40–41, 55, 75; Roach, *Cowgirls*, 82–93).

Review from the *San Francisco Bulletin*
11 August 1913
San Francisco, Calif.

After a long train trip Rogers reached San Francisco, where he performed at the Orpheum Theatre. Built on the site of the original Orpheum, the theater opened on 19 April 1909. The Orpheum organization viewed it as the parent and flagship theater of the chain and spent lavishly on its accoutrements.[1] As the reviewer from the Bulletin *noted, Rogers was not only the hit of an all-star playbill with his lariat dexterity but also a top-flight humorist.[2]*

If Will Rogers was nothing more than a cowboy handy with a rope, the twenty minutes he spends in dexterous juggling would justify his appearance in vaudeville, but he is also a humorist with as keen an insight to human nature as many of the world's most famous comedians. After he finishes his act at the Orpheum, one feels as if double measure had been given.

Californians still have a traditional reverence for the lariat, although it passed out of use with the departure of the herd that once roamed the foothills. In the pioneer days skillful handling of the lariat was considered a great accomplishment, and there were many stars among the early Californians; but it is doubtful if any of them reached the proficiency which Rogers has apparently attained with little effort. Beginning with a small loop, he gradually enlarges it until it swings far out over the heads of the musicians . . . and making the timid uncomfortable with its serpent-like hissing. Throughout the entire performance he keeps up a running fire of quaint humor that one cannot fail to be pleased and satisfied.

Another number of merit is given by Walter S. Dickinson, "The Ex-Justice of the Peace." He also has a humorous monologue with many human touches. It is one of the "rube" acts long familiar to patrons of vaudeville, but Dickinson does it well and earns much well-deserved applause.[3]

Whether George Ade's sketch, "Speaking to Father," has been too widely advertised, or whether it is lacking in punch, it is hard to determine.[4] It is, however, disappointing, although it has many humorous situations and is carefully staged. Of course, Milton Pollock brings out all there is in it, and he is capably supported; but the action is too rapid and the climax too unreal too [to] carry conviction. . . .[5]

Phina,[6] with three negro comedians, has an interesting act, in which she does much vigorous singing and dancing; Fred Hamill and Charley Abbate are still entertaining as on their first appearance, and Harry Divine and Belle Williams have improved their humor by cutting out the medicated dialogue and substituting more rational nonsense. The Bell family, with their xylophones and bells, repeat their musical program with the same spirit, while one of the number dances her way into the hearts of the gallery with the true Latin dash.[7]

Rameses, who someone has said answers in real life to the name of O'Brien, finishes the bill with a marvelous exhibition of Egyptian magic.[8]

PD. Printed in *San Francisco Bulletin*, 11 August 1911. Scrapbook A-3, OkClaW.

1. After the earthquake demolished the first Orpheum, the Orpheum Circuit leased the still standing Chutes Theatre on Fulton Street, where it continued its vaudeville programs. With the rebuilding of the Market Street area, the Orpheum owners wanted a downtown theater. They constructed the 1909 Orpheum on O'Farrell between Stockton and Powell Streets. Designed by the architect G. Albert Lansburgh in an ornate, neo–French Renaissance style, the Orpheum Theatre was publicized as the most expensive theater in the West. This was the first theater commission for Lansburgh, who became one of San Francisco's most renowned architects. The theater's terracotta façade was embellished with Corinthian columns and sculptures. Five entrances faced the street, and overhead was a marquee of cast and wrought iron. Seating 2,500 spectators, the auditorium was advertised as "the finest example of present-day theatre construction in America," with a modern ventilation system, improved sight lines, and excellent acoustics. Fearing another earthquake disaster, the builders made the structure as fireproof as possible, with thirty-two exits to prevent panic during an emergency. Inside, the rose-colored walls were decorated with relief work in bronze and gold leaf. The ceiling was adorned with sculptures in gold and panels that contained paintings by Cavallero. In 1929 the Orpheum became a movie theater; it was renamed the Columbia Theatre, and after a long history it burned down in 1975 (Berson, *San Francisco Stage*, 98; Gagey, *San Francisco Stage*, 179, 207–8, 210; Lansburgh, "Some Novel Features of a Strictly Fire-Proof Theater Building," 37–41; Levin, "San Francisco Story," 5; *Orpheum Circuit* 1925; *Orpheum Circuit of Theatres*; Orpheum Circuit files, CSf-PALM).

2. In San Francisco Rogers performed at the Orpheum Theatre 10–23 August. Most newspaper drama critics, such as Waldemar Young, panned the headline act, a playlet by George Ade. By contrast, Young felt Rogers and Phina (Josephine Gassman) were the best acts on the bill. Young, an agent, actor, and playwright, later wrote movie scripts for Paramount. Both the *Chronicle* and the *Bulletin* carried large cartoons of the individual performers. The *Bulletin* cartoon was headlined "Wins Success with Rope Cowboy Scores Big Hit." After San Francisco Rogers performed at the Oakland Orpheum (24–30 August) and the Los Angeles Orpheum (31 August–6 September) ("Headline Act Is Weakest on Bill," clipping, and *Bulletin* cartoon, clipping, scrapbook A-3, OkClaW; Waldemar Young Biographical File, CSf-PALM).

3. Walter S. (Rube) Dickinson (1875–1914), born in Nebraska, was noted for his country-bumpkin monologue act portraying a wisecracking farmer. After performing in small-time theaters in the Midwest, Dickinson traveled east in 1906 and found an agent in Boston, J. J. Quigley, who gave him a contract at $60 a week. Gradually he gained a reputation and earned $125 weekly when he played the Sullivan and Considine Circuit. Max Hart discovered and promoted Dickinson. In Dickinson's act the tables were turned on the image of city slickers ridiculing the rube. Sporting a white beard, Dickinson came on stage dressed in a Palm Beach suit and wearing a Panama hat. His monologue about attending a New York City society party went like this: "What interested me most was the necks of the women. Why, some of the necks I saw last night reached from the ears down almost to where the mermaids become fish! . . . My folks asked me did I think there were enough going on in New York to amuse me? And I told 'em I wasn't taking any chances, I'm taking my checkerboard with me. . . . There's one thing I didn't do while in New York, I didn't buy a gold brick—but I'm saving up" (Laurie, *Vaudeville,* 178). Dickinson was unexpectedly killed in Kansas City when a wooden canopy above the entrance to the Meuhlbach Hotel fell on him (Laurie, *Vaudeville,* 178–79; *VO,* 1:1 January 1915).

4. Born in Kentland, Ind., George Ade (1866–1944) was a playwright, journalist, and librettist. He wrote librettos for several musicals between 1902 and 1910. As a dramatist, Ade's first success was *The Country Chairman* (1903). This was followed by *The College Widow* (1904), *Just Out of College* (1905), and *Father and the Boys* (1908). Known for capturing the dialogue of contemporary youth, Ade's plays were considered entertaining and wholesome rather than serious portraits of life (*OCAT,* 11).

5. Milton Pollock had a stock company that acted in playlets on the vaudeville stage. Pollock and his company performed Ade's *Speaking to Father* on the opening playbill at New York's famed Palace Theatre on 25 March 1913 (Laurie, *Vaudeville,* 486–87).

6. Rogers had performed with Josephine Gassman, whose stage name was Phina, at the Chase Theatre in Washington, D.C., in 1905 (see *PWR,* 2:223n.5). On racial and gender stereotyping in Gassman's and similar "pickaninny" acts, see Kibler, *Rank Ladies,* 119–25.

7. The Bell family came from Mexico, and the act had ten people in it. They were one of many large family acts on the variety stage. Joe Laurie, Jr., called the Bells "one of the great musical acts" in vaudeville. They played not only mandolins and xylophones but also pipes and mixed bells. Probably their name derived from their excellent bell ringing (Laurie, *Vaudeville,* 67, 148).

8. Rameses, an Englishman, was a vaudeville magician whose stage persona was an Egyptian. He was noted for performing an act with fresh flowers, mysteriously transforming them by sleight of hand (Laurie, *Vaudeville,* 109).

Hammerstein Amusement Company Contract
13 December 1913
New York, N.Y.

After his long tour on the Orpheum Circuit, Rogers returned to New York, where he began performing on the Keith-Albee Circuit and in theaters affiliated with its agency, the United Booking Offices. Rogers secured an engagement at the Victoria. It was the theater's nineteenth anniversary, and an all-star variety bill was presented.[1] The regulations in the contract exemplify the power vaudeville managers had over performers in bookings, salary, commissions, punctuality, censorship, pre-engagement obligations, and strikes. Breach of the contract enabled the manager to cancel the agreement and to fine the performer a week's salary.

VICTORIA THEATRE AND PARADISE ROOF GARDEN,[2]
42ND STREET AND 7TH AVENUE, NEW YORK CITY.

Agreement made this <u>13th</u> day of <u>December</u> 191<u>3</u>, by and between HAM-MERSTEIN AMUSEMENT COMPANY, of New York,[3] hereinafter called the "manager," and <u>Will Rogers</u> hereinafter called the "artist."

1. The artist promises to render and produce upon the terms and conditions hereinafter contained, a certain <u>S. & D.</u> act or specialty with <u>1</u> persons therein for <u>ONE</u> weeks, at least twice each day and not over fourteen times in each week, commencing <u>January 19th</u> 191<u>4</u>, at the VICTORIA THEATRE AND PARADISE ROOF GARDEN, in the Borough of Manhattan, City and State of New York, or in such other theatres or cities as the manager may require, in consideration of which and of the full and complete performance of the promises of the artist hereinafter set forth, each of which is of the essence of this agreement, the manager agrees to pay the sum of ____ THREE HUNDRED & FIFTY ____ ($350.00) Dollars upon the conclusion of the final performance by the artist at the end of each week during the term of this agreement.

2. It is understood that this is a vaudeville engagement and that the artist shall pay all transportation. If the artist is to render said act in more than one place hereunder, the average cost of such transportation between the places where such act is to be given, rendered or produced hereunder, shall be not over Twenty-five Dollars per person.

3. A. HAMMERSTEIN, of 1564–66 Broadway, New York City is acting for the manager in employing the artist.[4]

4. The artist agrees to abide by the reasonable rules and regulations in force at the theatre: report for rehearsals at 10 A.M. on Monday of each week; furnish complete orchestrations of music; eliminate any part of act when

requested by the manager or representatives, and at least two weeks before the beginning of each engagement to deliver to the manager the necessary billing, scenery, property plots, a set of twelve photographs consisting of at least three different styles for newspaper and lobby advertising, program and press matter, time of act and the route, if any, upon which the artist may be scheduled for two weeks immediately prior to the beginning of this engagement. Failure to strictly comply with these conditions shall entitle the manager to cancel this agreement and for the failure to deliver photographs as above provided the manager may instead of canceling this agreement, deduct the sum of Ten Dollars ($10.) from the artist's salary as liquidated damages therefor to reimburse the manager for any photographs purchased or procured by him.

5. Sickness of artist will excuse performance only on delivery of duly sworn affidavits of two physicians immediately on occurrence, stating place of confinement and nature of illness to the manager, in care of s. k. HODGDON,[5] 1564–66 Broadway, New York City, meanwhile artist is not to perform for any other person.

6. If the operation of the above theatre is prevented by fire, or other casualty, public authority, strikes, or any other cause whatsoever, or the present policy thereof changed, the manager may cancel this agreement, and if prevented from giving the maximum number of performances set forth above, it shall pay only pro-rata for services actually rendered.

7. If before the commencement of, or during this engagement, the manager finds that the artist has reduced or changed the personnel or number of performers, or otherwise changed or altered the quality of the act contemplated herein, the manager may forthwith cancel this agreement, and if such change is discovered only after the artist has commenced the engagement, the manager may, at his option, permit the act to perform and deduct from the salary when payable, an amount in proportion to the decrease in value of said act, provided he gives the artist written notice of such intention to deduct before the second performance.

8. The artist agrees not to present at any time between the day hereof and the end of the term of this engagement, any act or specialty, in whole or in part, either publicly, privately or at clubs or private entertainments in the city mentioned in paragraph 1 hereof or in any place within twenty-five miles of such city unless consented to in writing by the manager or by the United Booking Offices of America in his behalf.

9. The artist agrees that if he breaches this agreement he will pay to the manager a sum equal to the salary payable to the artist hereunder, it being

agreed that the manager will sustain damages to at least that amount, in the event of such breach.

10. If claim shall be made upon the manager that the aforesaid act is an infringement of a property right, copyright, or patent right, the manager may cancel this agreement, unless the artist stipulates in writing that the manager may hold his salary hereunder and shall in addition furnish a bond with two good and sufficient sureties in an amount sufficient to indemnify the manager against any loss, damage, cost, counsel fee, or any other loss whatsoever, by reason of his permitting or allowing the presentation of said act, pursuant to this agreement.

11. The artist acknowledges that this agreement and the engagements set forth herein were procured for him solely by and through the United Booking Offices of America and therefore authorizes the manager to deduct 5% from the aforesaid salary at the end of each week, and pay the same over to the United Booking Offices of America.[6]

12. Without cause either party may cancel this agreement on two weeks written notice personally or by mail or telegram; said notice shall operate from the day the same is served or sent. Notice to the artist may be sent to his last known address, place of performance or in care of his personal representative or manager.

HAMMERSTEIN AMUSEMENT COMPANY,

By [*A. Hammerstein*]

(Artist sign here   Will Rogers (L.S.)[7]
giving address.)   1564 Broadway NY

IMPORTANT SPECIAL NOTICE:

THERE MUST BE NO NEGLECT IN DELIVERING BILLING, ROUTE, PROGRAM AND PRESS MATTER, TIME OF ACT, PHOTOS, SCENE AND PROPERTY PLOTS, AT LEAST TWO WEEKS IN ADVANCE OF THE TIME OF OPENING EACH ENGAGEMENT, AND IF NOT RECEIVED TWO WEEKS IN ADVANCE, THEN THE FIRST PARTY MAY CANCEL THIS AGREEMENT. YOU MUST FURNISH 12 PHOTOS OF AT LEAST 3 DIFFERENT STYLES—(SEE CLAUSE 4.) DON'T PUT MUSIC IN TRUNKS BUT BRING IT WITH YOU.

IF THE ARTIST DESIRES SPECIAL "PROPERTIES" OR FURNITURE OTHER THAN THOSE IN THE THEATRE HE MUST FURNISH THEM HIMSELF.

PD, with autograph additions. OkClaW.

1. In the playbill Rogers was billed second after Vernon and Irene Castle; he was advertised as "Alone—The Oklahoma Cowboy." The *New York Times* description of the playbill stated that the Castles were in a moving picture showing their latest repertoire. The *Times* advertisements also mention the performance of Wellington Cross and Lois Josephine (18 January 1914). The playbill reflected Hammerstein's policy of billing eclectic, exotic, and eccentric acts that no other variety theater could match. Other performers included Frederick V. Bowers and Co. (The Singing Riot); Charles Ahearn and Company of 12 (Brand New Cycling Scream); George B. Reno and Co. (Comedy Oddity); Charles and Fannie Van (Presenting *From Stage Carpenter to Actor*); Burns and Fulton (Diverting Novelty); Albert Wohlman and Maurice Abrahams (Popular Song Composers); John Cantwell and Reta Walker (in *Under the Gay White Lights*); Foster Ball and Ford West (Character Study, *Since the Days of '61*); Stepp, Goodrich, and King (Music, Comedy and Song); Pons and Pons (Novelty Offering); Tom Penfold (Singer); and Moran and Moran (The Tango Duo). Last on the playbill, in large type, was the well-publicized film *Damaged Goods*, based on the three-act "psychopathic drama" by Eugene Brieux. The playbill described the film as follows: "First Moving Picture of a Victim of Sin. A Story Based on the Disease Most Dreaded by the Medical Profession. The Subject Which Was Also Treated on by That Celebrate Play, DAMAGED GOODS. The Most Sensational and Powerful Sermon Ever Preached to Humanity, Vividly Laying Bare and Depicting the Innermost Secrets Which Have Aroused the Civilized World" (Hammerstein's Victoria Theatre playbill, week commencing 19 January 1914, clipping, scrapbook A-3, OkClaW; see also Biographical Appendix entry, CASTLE, Vernon and Irene).

2. There is an emblem to the left of the heading "Victoria Theatre and Paradise Roof Garden" that reads "Member Vaudeville Managers' Protective Association." Founded in 1911, the VMPA was a powerful trade organization formed by the leading vaudeville managers to oppose performers' strikes and salary demands. At one time it had 212 members who through multiple ownership represented more than one-half of the 907 vaudeville theaters nationwide. The goal was to create a new contract that protected the managers if the actor did not perform on schedule. The above contract, especially paragraph 9, exemplifies the control the managers had over the performers, and as paragraph 5 states, a vaudevillian who pleaded sickness had to have sworn affidavits from two physicians. The VMPA was organized to oppose any independent actors' union or booking agency (paragraph 6 in the above contract gave managers the right to cancel the contract should a strike occur). The VMPA was active in the successful opposition to the White Rats' strike in 1916. The association was closely linked with the National Vaudeville Artists (NVA), a company union formed by Albee and the UBO. Any vaudevillian not a member of the NVA could be blacklisted. The VMPA survived legal actions against it for restraint of trade and a Federal Trade Commission investigation in 1918 (Connors, "American Vaudeville Managers," 56–57; Snyder, *Voice of the City*, 76–80; Vaudeville Managers' Protective Association, *1912 Yearbook*, NN-L-BRTC).

3. The Hammerstein Amusement Co. of New York was a holding company that controlled the theater properties of Oscar Hammerstein and his family. Over the years Oscar Hammerstein built, bought, and sold numerous opera venues and vaudeville theaters, primarily in the New York area. His first venture was the Harlem Opera House (1889) on 125th Street, but poor management and box-office losses caused him to sell it. A grand opera enthusiast, Hammerstein built the Manhattan Opera House on Thirty-fourth Street between Broadway and Seventh Avenue in 1892. He operated the block-long Olympia Theatre, built in 1895 on Broadway between Forty-

fourth and Forty-fifth Streets, but in 1898 it was sold at auction to Marc Klaw and Abraham L. Erlanger. Hammerstein's Victoria Theatre (1899) was much more successful, and in 1915 Hammerstein sold it to S. L. Rothafel. Hammerstein built another Manhattan Opera House in 1906 and the Philadelphia Opera House in 1908, but financial problems forced him to sell these properties within a few years. Next he opened the London Opera House in 1911, but sold it in 1913 after a series of box-office failures. His last venture was the American Opera House, renamed the Lexington Theatre (1914), which presented stage and screen shows. Hammerstein sold it in 1915 to Marcus Loew (*DAB*, 4:199–200; *EV*, 226–27; *OCAT*, 318; van Hoogstraten, *Lost Broadway Theatres*, 36–51; *VO*, 1:8 August 1919).

4. Arthur Hammerstein (1872–1955), the son of Oscar Hammerstein and the brother of Willie Hammerstein, commenced his career as his father's assistant. Starting as a bricklayer, he rose to become chief designer of his father's theaters and oversaw the management of his father's theater holdings. Beginning in 1912 with the production of *The Firefly*, Arthur Hammerstein produced Broadway musicals and light operas, many by Rudolf Friml, including the hit *Rose-Marie* (1924). But he also had many flops in the late 1920s. In 1927 he built Broadway's Hammerstein's Theatre, named after his father, but was forced to sell it during the Great Depression. In 1930 he produced the film musical *The Lottery Bride*, a box-office failure. Faced with creditors demanding their money and financial losses at Hammerstein's Theatre, he declared bankruptcy in 1931. In total, he produced thirty-one shows. His famous nephew, Oscar Hammerstein II, the son of Willie Hammerstein, worked on *Rose-Marie* before writing such classic musicals as *Oklahoma!* (1943) and *South Pacific* (1949). Arthur Hammerstein died in Palm Beach, Fla., at the age of eighty-two (Green, ed., *Encyclopaedia of the Musical Theatre*, 172; Morrison, "Oscar Hammerstein I," 14; Morrison, "Oscar Hammerstein I, Part II," 21–22; *NYT*, 13 October 1955; *OCAT*, 318; van Hoogstraten, *Lost Broadway Theatres*, 236–39; *VO*, 4:19 October 1955).

5. Samuel Kahler Hodgdon (1853–1922) worked as an executive for the Keith Circuit for more than forty years and played a prominent role in the history of vaudeville. Born in Saco, Maine, Hodgdon met Keith when both were connected with a circus. When Keith opened his museum on Washington Street in Boston in 1883, he hired Hodgdon to lecture on the curios. On 6 July 1885 Keith started continuous vaudeville at his museum. To begin the program, Keith used Hodgdon's lecture "The Arctic Moon," about the Greeley Arctic Expedition. A year later Keith offered continuous programs at Boston's Bijou Theatre (1886), where Hodgdon continued his lectures, but was also assigned the responsibility of booking the acts. When Keith and his partner Albee expanded their circuit, Hodgdon was appointed booking manager, an executive position overseeing programming at the theaters. He was given the same position with the UBO when it was formed in 1906. In this role he became indispensable to the organization and its operation. Hodgdon was respected by his colleagues for his business skills and knowledge of vaudeville. When he died in 1922, many people in the variety business mourned his death. Hodgdon's funeral was held at the Palace Theatre, and the honorary pallbearers included Albee, Martin Beck, and George M. Cohan. "His funeral service at the Palace was jammed with saddened children of vaude who honestly mourned the loss of a good friend," wrote Joe Laurie, Jr. (*Vaudeville*, 483–84; see also Gilbert, *American Vaudeville*, 199–201; *NYT*, 25 April 1914; *VO*, 1:14 April 1922).

6. In 1906 Oscar Hammerstein agreed to have the UBO handle the booking of acts

for the Victoria Theatre and its Paradise Roof Garden. He was on the UB0 board of directors with Keith, Albee, Percy G. Williams, and F. F. Proctor. The theater manager deducted 5 percent from a vaudevillian's salary and sent it to the UBO's collection agency (*EV*, 515).

7. To the left of the signatures is a stamp approving the contract as of 18 December 1913.

Reviews from Palace Theatre
ca. 5 January 1914
New York, N.Y.

Rogers made his first appearance at the famed Palace Theatre in January 1914.[1] The theater had opened on 24 March 1913 to considerable publicity. Although it was a failure at first, by the end of 1913 the Palace was considered the greatest theater in vaudeville. Rogers's appearances at the Palace in 1914 and 1915 climaxed his vaudeville career.

VARIETY
PALACE

Louis Mann and Co. pleased, but a lot of the folks stirred uneasily in their seats and heaved a sigh of relief when the 42 minutes were up.[2] The piece runs several channels, jumping from the ridiculous into the pathetic so quickly one was glad when Will Rogers hove into view with his inimitable fun-making with the lariat. Rogers was forced to do most of his lasso whirling in "one" but he went over big. Roshanara closed with her classic dances.[3]

Mark.

BILLBOARD
NEW YORK PALACE
Reviewed Monday Matinee, Jan. 5.

No. 8—Will Rogers is here with his drollery and he is the same old Bill. He has incorporated a new stunt in his act, which makes an exceptionally strong finish. Three minutes in one, three minutes full, closes seven minutes in one, three calls.

NEW YORK STAR
PALACE THEATRE.
Week Ending Jan. 11.

Order of Appearance Monday Matinee.
1. Stewart Sisters and Escorts. Dancing. Excellent.[4]
2. Freeman and Dunham. Comedy skit. Went Big.[5]
3. Cole and Denahy. Dancing. A hit.
4. Jack Norworth. Songologue. Scored.[6]
5. LeRoy, Talma and Bosco. Magicians. Very interesting.[7]
Intermission.
6. Duffy and Lorenz. "In Springtime." Went very big.
7. Louis Mann and Company, "Elevating a Husband." A big and artistic triumph.
8. Will Rogers. Rope casting act. A feature.
9. Roshanara. Story dancing. Pleased immensely.

"Of course, Will Rogers, with his routine of rope tricks, had everything his own way. He's still chewin' gum an' forgettin' to use any make-up. He does the Fred Stone cowboy dance an' puts over some nifty gags about Roosevelt, finishin' with a new trick, makin' two ropes spin at once an' doin' a dance to make it harder.[8]

PD. ca. 5 January 1914, scrapbook A-3, OkClaW.

1. Broadway's Palace Theatre was planned as the greatest vaudeville showplace in the United States. Construction began in January 1912 and cost $1 million. Designed by architects Charles Kirchhoff and Thomas Rose, the Palace is located at Broadway and Forty-seventh Street. The theater is known for its spacious interior, magnificent sight lines, and fine acoustics. The domed ceiling featured two large chandeliers, and the seats were upholstered in flowered cretonne. One producer remembered the festive opening on 24 March 1913: "The opening was gala, the theatre a jewel. From the curved marble rail in the rear you could hear a whisper form the stage, and wherever you sat in the eighteen-hundred seat theatre—still one of our largest—you could see the stage clearly. . . . The two crystal chandeliers suspended from the ceiling bespoke the grandeur of royalty" (Samuels and Samuels, *Once upon a Stage,* 258). Among the performers on opening night was the comedian Ed Wynn. Despite the excitement, the opening was principally attended by show-business people, rather than the general public, and initially the new theatre was a box-office failure. By May 1913 the Palace began to gain recognition with headliners such as Sarah Bernhardt. By December 1914 *Variety* called the Palace "the greatest vaudeville theatre in America, if not the world" (*EV,* 386).

Rogers performed in vaudeville at the Palace Theatre three times: the weeks of 4 January 1914, 7 February 1915, and 18 July 1915 (a partial week). Other stars that played the Palace were Jack Benny, Bob Hope, Sophie Tucker, Al Jolson, George Jessel, Kate Smith, Eddie Cantor, and Burns and Allen. Palace shows were typically offered twice a day and consisted of nine acts. In 1915 the Marx Brothers had their first Palace Theatre booking, and it helped launch their spectacular careers. Van and Schenck also appeared there for the first time in 1915. By 1930 vaudeville was a dying entertainment form, and on 9 July 1932 the Palace presented its last variety-only show. For the next three years, the Palace offered films and vaudeville shows on the same program. In 1935 the Palace became a movie house exclusively. For a short time in 1951 the Palace regained its luster when Judy Garland performed a record-breaking nineteen weeks there. It became a legitimate Broadway theater again with the premiere of *Sweet Charity* on 29 January 1966. The event was covered by radio, television, and newspapers. The Palace eventually became a theater used for Broadway shows. In 1991 the Palace featured the Tony award–winning *Will Rogers Follies*. The historic theater has been designated an Interior Landmark of the City of New York (*EV*, 385–87; Landmarks Preservation Commission, copy, NNMuS, 1–2, 11–12, 14–18; Samuels and Samuels, *Once upon a Stage*, 258, 262; Spitzer, *Palace*, 5–6, 9, 12, 15, 36, 39, 44–45, 250, 252).

2. Louis Mann (1865–1931) made his first stage appearance at age three at the New Stadt Theatre in New York in a German-community Christmas pantomime. After leaving the University of California at age eighteen, he began his stage career in earnest by traveling through New England performing the classics on small stages and afterward joined several stock companies. He appeared in Oscar Wilde's play *Vera the Nihilist* (1883) at the Union Square Theatre in New York. He was first noticed in 1888 in his role as Mr. Utterson in *Dr. Jekyll and Mr. Hyde*. He began taking his own small companies on tour in 1890. Mann became known for his dialect roles. His most memorable success was as a German American in *Friendly Enemies* (1918). Woodrow Wilson attended the play when it opened in Washington, D.C., and spoke in praise of the play from his box. Mann co-starred with his wife Clara Lipman until about 1913, when they decided that splitting the bill would double the income. He helped form the Actors' Fidelity League during the Actors' Equity Association strike in 1919. He wrote *The Cheater* (1910) and co-wrote *Elevating a Husband* (1911) with his wife and Samuel Shipman. He had a short film career, appearing in several films in 1929 and 1930 (*DAB*, 6:244–45; *FILM*, 2:340; Harding, *Revolt of the Actors*, 144, 173–80, 199, 221; Magda Frances West, "The Manns and Their Mountains," *Green Book Magazine*, February 1913, 321–28; *VO*, 2:11 February 1931; *WhoHol*, 1046; *WhoStg*, 1:297–98; *WhScrn*, 297; *WhoThe*, 677–78).

3. Roshanara (born Olive Craddock, 1882–1926) was an Oriental dancer. She was of British origin, born in India. She learned to dance there and appeared on stage for the first time in London and then on tour with Pavlova. She came to the United States in 1913, where she organized a troupe of dancers and took them to India for training. Returning to the United States, the troupe performed with symphony orchestras. She designed the costumes for Winthrop Ames's production of *The Green Goddess*. Roshanara died at the age of thirty-four from appendicitis (*VO*, 1:21 July 1926).

4. The Stewart Sisters were a dance act, originally from Lancashire, England. They were in vaudeville in Europe and America for many years. The number of sisters in the act decreased from six to three over time. The sisters came from Great Britain to appear at the 1904 St. Louis World's Fair and then at the French Grand Opera in New Orleans (1904–5). During the next few years they played summers in England, toured

vaudeville circuits in the United States, and appeared in Germany. Their primary home was in New York City, where they shared an apartment. "We manage our own business affairs, one girl acting as secretary, one superintending the wardrobes (though we all work on those), another attending to the baggage, hotels, etc. In this way each of us gets some time for reading, music, and other forms of recreation. . . . We are very practical English girls" (*Toledo Courier Journal*, 2 September 1907). In 1907 there were four sisters appearing together, all between the ages of eighteen and twenty-five. From 1910 through 1915 there were three sisters in the act plus "escorts," performing an eleven-minute, full-stage singing and dancing act that emphasized musical comedy and showy costume changes. By 1916 the three sisters remaining on stage, Emmie, Pearl, and Jean Stewart, were appearing alone, without escorts, and were described as a distinguished act. Emmie Stewart was reportedly the choreographer of the group. The *Detroit Journal* of 5 January 1915 described their work as "dainty dances, very clean" (*Vancouver World*, 3 October 1914; *Variety*, 19 November 1910; Stewart Sisters, Locke env. 2169, NN-L-RLC).

5. William Vaughan Dunham (ca. 1881–1954) began his show-business career at the age of nineteen. His first partner until 1908 was Al Piantdosi. Then he teamed up with Jack Freeman for ten years, touring the major vaudeville circuits. They were considered one of the "great two-men singing acts" (Laurie, *Vaudeville*, 80). In addition to vaudeville, they appeared in *Passing Show of 1911, Stop! Look! Listen!* (1915), and *Hitchy-Koo* (1917). In 1917 Freeman and Dunham and Dunham's wife Grania O'Malley starred in the playlet *A Day at Belmont*. When Freeman left the act, Dunham went on the road with his wife as the team Dunham and O'Malley. Dunham retired in 1927 and opened the House of Dunham, a New York restaurant. He died in New York on 7 April 1954 (*VO*, 4:14 April 1954).

6. Jack Norworth (1879–1959), born John Knauff, was a composer, musical-comedy performer, and song-and-dance man. As a youth he spent six years at sea before going on stage as a blackface comedian for seven years. His first legitimate theater appearance was at New York's Herald Square Theatre on 30 August 1906, playing Jack Doty in *About Town*. The play was co-authored by the actress Nora Bayes, whom Norworth married in 1907. The couple were divorced in 1913, and Norworth was married several more times during his life. Norworth and Bayes's routine was a high-profile, husband-and-wife act with a running joke about Norworth as a hen-pecked husband ruled by Bayes. The team was a huge draw as much for their musical ability as for the electricity between them on the stage. Norworth continued his career on Broadway during the 1920s and in 1929 appeared in the film *Queen of the Nightclubs*. Between 1930 and 1932 he performed in a series of film shorts called *The Naggers*. He also appeared in the story of his life with Nora Bayes, called *Shine on Harvest Moon* (1942), and in *The Southerner* (1945). He appeared on Ed Sullivan's television show on the occasion of the CBS tribute to ASCAP, which he joined in 1922. Norworth wrote over three thousand songs, as well as music for the *Ziegfeld Follies* and for Weber and Fields's shows. His best known songs are "Take Me Out to the Ballgame" and "Shine On Harvest Moon." Near the end of his life, in Hollywood, Norworth was recognized for his famous baseball song each year in parades featuring the Los Angeles Dodgers. This perennial favorite is still sung by fans at major league baseball stadiums during the seventh-inning stretch (*AmSCAP*, 276; *CmpEnc*, 1519; *NYT*, 2 September 1959; *OCAT*, 511; Samuels and Samuels, *Once upon a Stage*, 83; *WhoHol*, 1245; *WhoThe*, 770; *VO*, 5:9 September 1959).

7. LeRoy, Talma, and Bosco were well-known international comedy musicians. Henri Jean Servais LeRoy was from Belgium. He started doing magic tricks in Europe

and about 1880 went to England where he gained a reputation. In 1898 he came to the United States and toured in a magic act with Frederick Powell and Imro Fox, called The Triple Alliance of Magicians. Bosco, a Russian, was a member of this troupe; Talma was his wife. At a 1905 performance at the Tivoli Theatre in Melbourne, Australia, LeRoy was described as a "little man" and Bosco, the team's comedian, as a "stout, grinning fellow, bald headed and with a beard" (Waller, *Magical Nights at the Theatre*, 128). LeRoy was noted for his illusion called "The Man of the Moment," a vanishing act in which he disappears from a box and moments later appears on a high pedestal. Another of his illusions was "The Three Graces," an astonishing vanishing act in which he and Talma disappeared. Talma executed a deft coin act, and with her partners she played tricks on audience members, from whom they produced a variety of animals. Between the illusions Bosco clowned and did humorous magic stunts, such as his "Decapitation Trick," in which he switched the heads of two ducks. The act closed with the trio producing a variety of barnyard fowl from a series of flags, the animals squawking and running about the stage as the curtain closed. Talma died in 1944, and her husband Bosco died at the age of seventy-two. LeRoy retired in the United States and was still alive in 1942 (*ABTB*, 124; Waller, *Magical Nights at the Theatre*, 128–33).

    8. The source of the last review was not identified.

Review and Listings from Three Theater Engagements
ca. 25 January 1914
New York, N.Y.

The month of January 1914 was Rogers's busiest period in vaudeville. His Palace engagement led to numerous offers. After his appearance at the Palace, Rogers performed at New York's Colonial Theatre.[1] A week later he performed at two theaters, Keith's Orpheum in Brooklyn and Hammerstein's Victoria Theatre.[2] He was held over for a second week at the Victoria. Rogers had two other engagements that week. During the week of 25 January Rogers thus performed at three New York theaters: the Victoria Theatre, Keith's Union Square Theatre, and the Alhambra Theatre. By doing a matinee and evening show at each theater for seven days, Rogers made forty-two appearances in that one week. He received considerable publicity for this unusual feat.[3] "WILL ROGERS MAKING RECORD" was the headline above a published photograph that showed Rogers roping the entire cast on stage at the Union Square Theatre. "The only act that ever played three theatres in one week," read the caption.[4]

BILLBOARD

    Will Rogers is hanging up a new record this week. Talk about the English music hall custom of playing two houses a night—that's mere child's play. Rogers is working at three theaters—Hammerstein's, the Alhambra and Union Square. That's going some, and Bill is unconcerned about the whole affair. His one best bet and favorite remark is: "Wait till Sunday night, then come around and watch me collect."

NEW YORK STAR
VICTORIA THEATRE.
Week Ending February 1.
Order of Appearance Wednesday Matinee.

1. Le Roy and Appleton. Comedy acrobats. Good.
2. Estrella Andalucia. Dancer. Good.[5]
3. Jimmy Flynn. Songs. Good.[6]
4. Marie and Billy Hart. "The Circus Girl." Went big.[7]
5. Sallie Fisher. Singing comedienne. Fine.[8]
6. Howard and Ratliff, assisted by Dorothy Hayden. Singing, dancing and talking. A laughing hit.
7. Gertie Carlisle and Her Seven Sweethearts. Pleased.[9]
8. Thirteen Girls in Blue. Novelty. Went big.
9. Will Rogers. Monologist and lariat expert. Well received.
10. Three Keatons. Knockabouts. Big favorites here.
11. Those Two French Girls. Songs, dances and acrobatics. Well liked.[10]
12. Bert Williams. Colored comedian. A hit.
13. The Four Musical Avolos. Xylophonists. Good.

UNION SQUARE THEATRE.[11]
Week Ending February 1.
Order of Appearance Wednesday Night.

1. Gormley and Caffrey. Comedy acrobats. Good.
2. Sharp and Wilkes. Singing and dancing. Well received.
3. Ted MacLean and company. "Let Well Enough Alone." Full of laughs.[12]
4. Charles and Adelaide Wilson. Musical skit. Pleased immensely.[13]
5. Stepp, Goodrich and King. Entertainers. Scored.
6. Roach and McCurdy. Rube comedians. Went big.
7. Hugh Herbert and company. "The Son of Solomon." Scored.[14]
8. Bison City Four. Singing comedians. A hit.[15]
9. Will Rogers. Lariat expert and monologist. Excellent entertainer.

A. H.

ALHAMBRA THEATRE[16]
Week Ending February 1.
Order of Appearance Monday Night

1. Mori Brothers. Risley Act. Went big.[17]
2. Mayme Remington and Mulatto Four. Singing and dancing. Scored.[18]
3. Will Rogers. Rope Act. Excellent.
4. Ashley and Canfield. Comedians. Went very big.
5. Bird Millman and company. Wire act. A hit.[19]
Intermission.
6. Kathleen Clifford. Male Impersonator. Scored.[20]
7. Louis Mann and company. "Elevating a Husband." A treat for Harlem.
8. Connolly and Wenrich. Piano and songs. A hit.
9. Prelle's Dogs. Educated canines. A feature.[21]

PD. Clippings, ca. 25 January 1914, scrapbook A-3, OkClaW.

1. The contract for Rogers's appearance at the Colonial Theatre the week of 12 January was executed on 2 January 1914, with S. K. Hodgdon representing the Keith Circuit. His salary was $350 for the week. The contract canceled Rogers's engagement at the Alhambra scheduled for that week. At the Colonial on Broadway and Sixty-second Street Rogers (advertised as The Oklahoma Cowboy) performed with the following artists: La Valera (Premiere Spanish Danseuse); Melvin Stokes (The Young Dramatic Tenor in *A Dash of Spanish*); Hickey Brothers (Acrobatic Dancers); *A Telephone Tangle* (With Dorothy Regel, Just Something That Occurs Every Day); Laddie Cliff (England's Clever Boy Comedian); *The Porch Party* (B. A. Rolfe Presents a Musical Fantasy); Morris Cronin and His Merry Men (In Mirthful Moments Magnificently Manipulated); Mary Elizabeth (Comedienne); Emma Carus (Late Star of *A Broadway Honeymoon*); and Volant (And His Flying Piano). The *Variety* reviewer noted a trait in Rogers that the performer would use often in the coming years: "Mr. Rogers has the funniest little way of hanging his head while talking to the audience" (clipping, scrapbook A-3, OkClaW). The *Billboard* reviewer mentioned that Rogers, listed number nine or next to closing on the ten-act bill, had a "hard spot" following the headliner Emma Carus (1879–1927), a well-known singer, billed as The Human Dialect Cocktail and noted for her loud voice and her ability to sing in many languages. "But the audience was with him from the start," wrote the reviewer. "Rogers opens three minutes in one, then two minutes, full stage and closes seven minutes in one. Earnestly applauded" (clipping, scrapbook A-3, OkClaW) (B. F. Keith's Greater Circuit of Theatrical Enterprises contract, 2 January 1914, and Colonial Theatre playbill, week of 12 January 1914, scrapbook A-3, OkClaW; see also *NYDM*, 14 January 1914; *NYT*, 11 January 1914; *OCAT*, 129).

2. Rogers's contract to perform at Brooklyn's Orpheum Theatre was signed 8 January 1914 and executed by S. K. Hodgdon for the Keith organization. Rogers received $350 for the week of 19 January. On the playbill with Rogers were The Myrtle Clayton Co., Madge Terry, The Trained Nurses, Farber Girls, Merrill and Otto, Ernie and Ernie, Paul La Croix, and The Flying Martins. For performers appearing with

Rogers at the Victoria the week of 19 January, see Hammerstein Amusement Company Contract, 13 December 1913, above (B. F. Keith's Greater Circuit of Theatrical Enterprises contract, 8 January 1914, OkClaW; Brooklyn Orpheum clipping, scrapbook A-3, OkClaW).

3. Logistically, it was possible for Rogers to appear at three different theaters at their matinee and evening performances. Rogers's act was twelve minutes long, and his positions on the playbills could be carefully arranged. He had the third spot at the Alhambra Theatre, the ninth position at the Victoria Theatre, and the final spot at the Union Square Theatre. Rogers went from one end of Manhattan to another. He started at the Alhambra in Harlem on 126th Street, next went to the Victoria on Forty-second Street, and last to the Union Square on Fourteenth Street. In an interview Rogers claimed that he did two more performances. One was at the Vaudeville Comedy Club (a fraternal organization, formed in 1906, that staged "Clown Nights" [*EV*, 526]), and the other was an appearance as a cowboy riding in a film for Reine Davis. Possibly Rogers's first film role, it was photographed at Rye, N.Y., and used for Davis's stage act. Rogers also performed at a benefit for the Home for Incurables (see Performance Notes, 28 January 1914, below) (*Billboard*, 14 February 1914, clipping, and "Rogers and Reine Reeling in Rye," *New York Star* clipping, scrapbook A-3, OkClaW).

4. *Billboard*, 14 February 1914, clipping, scrapbook A-3, OkClaW.

5. The playbill described Estrella Andalucia as "The Spanish Dancing Beauty" (Hammerstein's Victoria playbill, week of 25 January 1914, OkClaW).

6. Jimmy Flynn (1883–1931) was a songwriter and singer. His best known song was "My Georgia Rose." He worked as a song plugger for two music publishers, Feist and J. H. Remick. Flynn was among radio's first popular singers, appearing in a daily program on station WHN in New York. He also sang at events at Madison Square Garden. Flynn died of heart failure at Bellevue Hospital in New York (*VO*, 2:August 18 1931).

7. Marie Hart (Mrs. Mabel Markwith, 1882–1935) and Billy Hart (William Lenhart, 1864–1942) were a vaudeville team. At the Victoria they presented a novel comedy skit called *The Circus Girl*. Marie Hart retired in 1912 and died at the age of fifty-three in New Jersey. Billy Hart was also a burlesque and screen actor and died in Los Angeles (*ABTB*, 456, 465; *VO*, 2:28 August 1935; *WhScrn*, 1:316).

8. Sallie Fisher (1881–1950) performed in vaudeville, Broadway musicals, and films. She was born on a ranch in Wyoming. She grew up in Salt Lake City, Utah, where she began singing in community functions. She started her professional career at nineteen. Her first stage successes were her appearances in the Chicago productions of *A Stubborn Cinderella* and *The Goddess of Liberty*. She performed for five years as a vaudeville headliner in the playlet called *The Choir Rehearsal*. She played with George M. Cohan in *Forty-five Minutes from Broadway* (1912) and assumed the title role in *Eva* (1912–13). Other Broadway musicals included *The Prince of Tonight* (1909), *Modest Suzanne* (1912), and *Watch Your Step* (1914). In films she worked for the Essanay film company, appearing in *The Little Shepherd of Bargain Row* (1916). She died in Twenty-nine Palms, Calif., at the age of sixty-nine (*CmpEnc*, 592–93; Kinkle, *Complete Encyclopedia of Popular Music and Jazz*, entry no. 592; *VO*, 4:14 June 1950; *WhMuDr*, 121).

9. Gertie Carlisle (Mrs. Gertrude Talbert, d. 1925) was a member of the vaudeville team Midgely and Carlisle. In the act she impersonated a little girl. After the partnership was dissolved, she appeared with another partner as Kelso and Carlisle. She was married to Roy Talbert at the time of her death (*VO*, 1:24 June 1925).

10. The French Girls were the Amoros sisters (Hammerstein's Victoria playbill, week of 25 January 1914, OkClaW).

11. This was the last week for vaudeville at the Union Square—the theater where Rogers had begun his vaudeville career (see *PWR*, 2:149–50). The theater would now show exclusively motion pictures. A clipping in Rogers's scrapbook noted the symbolic significance of this event, the number of movie theaters now exceeding vaudeville showplaces: "The change in policy is significant of the trend of the times. Time was when the Union Square was heralded as the leading vaudeville theatre in America. Its annual profits undoubtedly exceeded $200,000 many years, and an engagement there was eagerly sought by the foremost players" ("Union Square Changes Policy," scrapbook A-3, OkClaW).

12. Possibly the actor Theodore N. MacLean (ca. 1878–1934), whose real name was Phinias G. McLean. He began his career with Joseph Murphy, an Irish comedian, in *The Heart of the Ozarks*. In vaudeville he teamed with William Kent. MacLean owned a stock company, wrote melodramas, and edited a theatrical trade paper. He died in New York City (*VO*, 2:3 July 1934).

13. Adelaide Wilson and Charles Cahill Wilson were a vaudeville team that performed musical skits. A singer, Adelaide Wilson was known as the "little girl with the large voice." Charles Wilson was a comedian and violinist who did straight numbers and imitations on his violin. Toward the end of their act Adelaide sang a rag number accompanied by Charles on the violin. They once did a sketch called *The Messenger, the Maid and the Violin,* which was a big hit on the Orpheum Circuit in 1912. Their skit at the Union Square was called *The Messenger Boy.* In 1914 they performed a sidewalk skit with Charles Wilson playing the violin. He later starred in the Broadway musical *Adrienne* in 1923 (biographical clipping file, NN-L-BRTC; Locke env. 2612, NN-L-RLC).

14. Hugh Herbert (1887–1952) was a stage and screen comic actor as well as a playwright. He was born in Binghamton, N.Y., and was graduated from Cornell University. Herbert was in vaudeville for twenty years. His most popular playlet was *The Son of Solomon* by Aaron Hoffman. In that piece Herbert was assisted by Thomas A. Francis and Margot Williams. Herbert wrote several farces that were produced by A. H. Woods and Sam Harris. Beginning in the late 1920s, Herbert performed in over one hundred films for such studios as Warner, Universal, and Columbia. He mostly played supporting comedy parts and was known for his zany style. Two films in the 1940s were *Hellzapoppin* (1941) and *A Song Is Born* (1948). He wrote the screenplay for the film *Lights of New York,* the first all-sound movie made by Warner. A short time after completing the movie *Havana Rose* (1951), Herbert died of a heart attack at his home in the San Fernando Valley, Calif. (*FilmEnc*, 619; *VO*, 4:19 March 1952).

15. The Bison City Quartette originally consisted of Gerard, Pike, Hughes, and Cook. Milo and Roscoe joined later. The Quartette lasted from 1895 until 1931 (Laurie, *Vaudeville*, 75).

16. The Alhambra, located in Harlem at Seventh Avenue and 126th Street, was built by Percy G. Williams in 1900 to cater to its large Jewish population. The Alhambra was sold to Keith-Albee in 1912. The Alhambra, which seated 1,400, featured vaudeville until the early 1930s; afterward it became an RKO movie house. The interior was gutted, but its brick-and-stone façade remained standing as late as 1981 (*GHNTD*, 540; Robinson, "A Stroll through Harlem").

17. The Mori Brothers came from Japan. They "juggled barrels with their feet and one brother foot-juggled another brother" ("At the Alhambra," *Morning Telegraph* clipping, scrapbook A-3, OkClaW).

18. Mayme Remington was one of several white women (including Josephine Gassman, Grace LaRue, and Louise Dresser) who performed with African American children in a "pickaninny" singing act. At one time she called her act Mayme Remington and Her Black Buster Brownie Ethiopian Prodigés (Kibler, *Rank Ladies*, 120–21; Laurie, *Vaudeville*, 56).

19. Bird Millman was considered to have one of vaudeville's most outstanding wire acts. She started with her parents in an act called The Millman Trio, which played circus and small-time theaters in the Midwest. Later she went single and eventually formed her own company. Joe Laurie, Jr., called her "the tops of 'em all!" (*Vaudeville*, 30; see also Gilbert, *American Vaudeville*, 321).

20. As a male impersonator, Kathleen Clifford (1887–1963) appeared on stage as a well-dressed man with monocle, top hat, and tails. Born in Charlottesville, Va., she performed in vaudeville at least until the early 1930s. She started as a musical-comedy performer before making a name as a male impersonator. Clifford was often referred to as the American Vesta Tilley, an allusion to the famous English male impersonator. In 1911 Clifford appeared in the opening show, a burlesque called *Hell*, at the Folies Bergere, a stylish New York supper club. She was in several films between 1917 and 1928. She lived in Hollywood and later was a florist. Clifford wrote a book called *It's April . . . Remember* about her life in Hollywood, where she died in 1963 (*EV*, 103–4, 186).

21. Charlie Prelle, a German, had a talking dog act that was very popular. He would put human masks with moveable mouths on the dogs. The dogs would move their mouths as Prelle impersonated various characters (*EV*, 130, 526; Laurie, *Vaudeville*, 115).

Performance Notes
28 January 1914
New York, N.Y.

Rogers wrote the following notes for a charity benefit appearance at the Home for Incurables in New York.[1] After reading a letter from one of its invalids and an editorial in the New York Evening Telegram, *B. F. Keith instructed Edward F. Albee, his general manager, to organize a benefit for the hospital. A show starring vaudevillians who were currently playing in Keith theaters was presented. "I have given orders that the strongest laughing show possible be given," said Albee.[2] Rogers's notes reflect a new direction in his stage talk toward topical humor. This event may be among his first charity benefits, a type of activity that he would participate in many times during his career.*

Date: <u>28 January 1914.</u>

I explained to you what fortunate creatures they were to be here where they had everything you need while out in the world; the lots of things you had to put up with. If we go to sleep we have to buy the hotel and give it back to them in the morning.

If we want to eat we have to pawn our hat and if we want to use it any more we have to redeem it.

If we want a drink we save up a year and buy it from a bootlegger and then after drinking it you go direct to the cemetery.

If you want to get married you have to marry a kid fifteen years old for if they are older than that they are a divorced woman.

If you make any money the government shoves you in the creek once a year with it in your pockets and all that don't get wet you can keep.

If you go to church the preacher will spend an hour and a half trying to keep you awake by cussing the other denominations.

If you commit burglary and go to the penitentiary when you come out you get a new suit and ten dollars. If you go to war and come back you get nothing.

If you do get a wife it's only a matter of time till she shoots you.

If she don't shoot you, she divorces you and you have to pay alimony which is just like furnishing ammunition to the enemy.

If you get in an automobile a train will hit you and if you stay on the ground an automobile will hit you.

TMS. OkClaW.

1. The Home for Incurables was incorporated on 6 April 1866 as America's first hospital for the chronically ill. Founded by Rev. Washington Rodman of Grace Episcopal Church, it was located in the area of the Bronx known as West Farms. By the early 1870s the institution had expanded and moved to a new site at Third Avenue and 183rd Street. By 1905 the hospital, which treated and cared for patients who could not receive treatment in other hospitals, had a 310-bed capacity. The Home for Incurables remained this size until 1920, when it again expanded. It is now known as St. Barnabas Hospital (*Home for Incurables Forty-ninth Annual Report*, 30, and *St. Barnabas Hospital 1991 Annual Report*, 4–7, NN).

2. Keith's quote is from "Evening Telegram Letter Brings Quick Response," *New York Evening Telegram*, scrapbook A-3, OkClaW. The article gave further details. To transport the performers to the home, automobiles were sent to the Bronx and Alhambra theaters (Rogers was performing at the latter). An orchestra and stage equipment were brought to the hospital, where the performance was presented on a small stage. Albee estimated that the performers together equaled $10,000 in weekly salaries. Besides Rogers, vaudevillians from the Alhambra included Louis Mann and Co., Connolly and Wenrich, Bird Millman and Co., Ashley and Canfield, Mayme Remington and Her Picks, and The Three Mori Brothers. Others were Bert Clark and Mabel Hamilton, Jack Wilson and Co., Maggie Cline, Minnie Dupress and Co., Keno and Green, Kirksmith Sisters, The Alpine Troupe, Andrew Kelly, Gotter and Bolden, and Prince Yamato.

Manager's Report, Keith's Chestnut Street Theatre
9 February 1914
Philadelphia, Pa.

After his week performing in three theaters, Rogers appeared at Keith's Theatre in the Bronx.[1] Then he traveled to Philadelphia, where he entertained at Keith's Chestnut Street Theatre as part of an "Old Favorites" bill. Also on the playbill were Pat Rooney and Marion Bent, who had become good friends of Rogers. One reviewer commented that they did "interlocking acts." "Rogers helps out Rooney and then Rooney retaliates on Rogers in such an amusing manner that they were the features of the show yesterday.[2]

PHILADELPHIA SHOW

H. T. JORDAN[3]   FEB. 9, 1914.

TWO TOM BOYS. 8 min. Makes a very good opener. Both girls are expert in knockabout comedy, using table and chairs and getting lots of applause for their funny falls. Could really hold a better spot on the bill.

GEORGETTE.[4] 15 min. in one. Three changes of costume, all of them very pretty. A born entertainer who held this spot very nicely. Received plenty of applause for her four numbers. Sang some new songs and some that she gave before. Closed very well.

BEAUMONTE & ARNOLD.[5] 18 min. For life, class and ginger, this act could not be excelled. From their opening in full stage with the Doctor's office up to their work in one with two changes of costume they were immense. A great line of patter and they put it over in a brilliant manner. Their dancing finish got immense applause.

MR. & MRS. VERNON CASTLE PICTURES. 13 min. Very artistic and realistic motion pictures of the latest society dances by Mr. and Mrs. Vernon Castle. Photographically they are perfect and the music is also in perfect accord with the pictures. Well received.

WILL ROGERS. 16 min. Works in one with his roping. Introduces a unicycle with which he jumps the rope, keeping the audience in laughter all the way through with his funny line of patter gotten over in his original way. Will is a great favorite here and everything that he says and does gets the usual big hand. Made an immense finish.

EDWIN STEVENS & CO.[6] "The Troubles of R. and J." 20 min. A new act with some of his old material and some that was fresh, but it all went very well as he puts everything over in a very original way. Audience gave them plenty of applause throughout, the burlesque on Romeo and Juliet getting the audience especially strong. Lots of bright material, strong close.

SALLIE FISHER. 14 min. Repeated her former hit with five numbers delightfully presented and all of them got good applause. Made a very fine appearance in some stunning gowns and made a strong close.

ROONEY & BENT. 16 min. Always great favorite here, giving variation of their popular act. Strong advance applause and were a laugh all the way through. At the finish introduced some burlesques that were very funny.

VAN & SCHENCK.[7] Advance applause. Held this hard spot very well with some good songs, although not for the most part new. Piano work particularly expert and character material O.K. Finished with a good hand.

FOUR BARDS. 11 min. Well known ground tumbling act making a very fine effect with their strong man stunts and getting plenty of applause for their brilliant work. Makes a very good closer.

KINETOGRAPH. An exceptionally good series.

GENERAL REMARKS. We advertised this as "Old Favorites' Bill" and ▲while▲ practically every act ▲shown▲ is familiar to our patrons, they are all sure-fire and seemed to please a capacity house. Possibly a little strong on singing and dancing, but as dancing seems to be the craze nowadays, probably that wont do any harm.

TD. KAC-IaU.

1. The Bronx's growing population supported a first-class vaudeville theater. The extension of the Broadway subway in 1906 facilitated the area's growth. Keith's Bronx Theatre opened in 1913 at 436 East 149th Street, near Third Avenue. It was located at the center of the vibrant "Hub," where there were other theaters, restaurants, and stores. The theater's exterior was designed in a Beaux Arts style. The theater seated 1,892 people (first level, 799; second level, 537; third level, 478; and boxes, 78). The theater was later renamed the Bronx Opera House. Over the years it presented vaudeville, drama, musical comedy, and movies. Such stars as Julia Marlowe, Ethel and Lionel Barrymore, David Warfield, the Marx Brothers, and George Burns and Gracie Allen performed there (Frick and Gray, eds., *Directory of Historic American Theatres*, 165; *GHNTD*, 540; Stern et al., *New York 1900*, 430–33).

At the Bronx Theatre, beginning on 2 February, Rogers performed with the following artists: The Grazers (In a Musical and Terpsichorean Novelty); Dora Pelletier (The Singing Comedienne); Consul and His Adopted Daughter (Appearing in a Simian Pantomimic Comedy); Lewis and Dody (The Two Sams); Irene Timmons and Co. (In an Original One-Act Playlet, *New Stuff*); Florenze Tempest (Our American Boy with Herbert Hofman); Joseph E. Howard and Mabel McCane (The Composer and the Charming Vocalist and Comedienne); Sam Mann and His Associate Players (In *The New Leader*); and The Belleclaire Brothers (Internationally-Famed Athletes) (Bronx Theatre playbill, scrapbook A-3, OkClaW; *NYT*, 1 February and 3 February 1914).

2. "Vaudeville at Keith's," *Philadelphia Evening Bulletin,* clipping, scrapbook A-3, OkClaW.

3. Harry T. Jordan was considered to be the "best-liked manager on the circuit by the actors who played for him" (Laurie, *Vaudeville,* 340). First an assistant manager at

Keith's Eighth Street Theatre, Jordan was promoted when he helped Keith acquire the building permit. Sophie Tucker remembered Jordan always greeting the performers on Monday morning. "Harry Jordan made you forget how tired you were," she wrote. "He treated you like a human being. . . . And if you were a hit, Harry Jordan would go to the front for you and get you a raise. He helped all the acts this way, and because he did, he always got the best out of them. His house had the best shows not only in Philadelphia, but on the whole Keith Circuit" (Tucker, *Some of These Days*, 148).

4. Georgette was a young singer who did character songs and musical comedy. She was described in 1913 as "a young soubrette still in her teens," who "rendered some of Eva Tanguay's and Elizabeth Murray's songs in a good voice. She has the appearance of a prodigy" (*Philadelphia North American*, 15 July 1913). She received good reviews in 1914, with critics referring to her "charming voice," her ability to carry a chorus or duet, and her cleverness on stage. The *Toledo Blade* of 15 September 1914 called her a "singing comedienne," who was "well received by first-nighters." She continued to receive similar reviews well into the 1920s, when she was teamed with another singer-actress named Victoria. The *New York Star* reported that the "charming and clever young women" were "offering their artistic musical act on the Southern time, booked by the B. F. Keith Vaudeville Exchange" (Georgette clipping file, NN-L-BRTC).

5. Bertee Beaumont and Jack Arnold did a song-and-dance act based on his compositions. Jack Arnold's real name was Jack Gluck. Beaumont was a singer whom the *Toledo Blade* of 24 April 1911 described as "a beauty of the Spanish type, who sings Italian and French songs with romantic abandon, and dances divinely." She was also a good character actress. In 1911–12 she was cast as Nina in *Nobody from Starland*, in which she sang Italian songs and demonstrated her charm and beauty. She spent two years with the company and in 1913 worked with Henry W. Savage in his musical productions at the same time as she was doing vaudeville. She appeared in Los Angeles at the Majestic in 1911. The *Seattle Post* described Beaumont as "an Italian immigrant of a sullenly amorous disposition" (12 March 1912). Beaumont was actually of German parentage and born in Memphis, Tenn. She got her start studying dancing and appeared in Richard Carle's *Spring Chicken*. She worked in Chicago for six years and in New York, interspersed with playing two-a-day in vaudeville. In 1914 she and Jack Arnold had "a classy act," wrote a reviewer. "Miss Beaumont is one of the best dancers in vaudeville and Jack Arnold has won a reputation as a writer of pleasing songs" (*Memphis Commercial Appeal*, 7 July 1914). Beaumont and Arnold performed Arnold's compositions, including "a hodgepodge of nonsense entitled the 'Doctorine'; which allows a clever song by the latter and much repartee both, the latter portion of the act being given over to dancing and singing. Miss Beaumont has a most wonderful leg motion in her high kicking and her peculiar grace, added to her stunning changes of attire" (*Columbus Dispatch*, 31 March 1914). Beaumont and Arnold performed *The Doctorine*, in which Beaumont played a woman physician, from 1913 to 1916. They also did a playlet called *The Suffragette* in 1914, mixing comedy with song-and-dance numbers. Beaumont lived in New York on West Seventy-second Street in the 1920s. The August 1921 *Theatre* magazine described Beaumont as the "queen of the comic vamps" who had "climbed up from the chorus" (*New York Telegraph*, 13 April 1918). Arnold died in 1962 (*ABTB*, 42; Bertee Beaumont clipping file, NN-L-BRTC).

6. The actor Edwin Stevens was born in 1860 in San Francisco. He played in theater in California for six years before going to New York, where his first appearance was in *Said Pasha, Star* (1889). In the 1896–97 season he appeared in *Twelfth Night*, *The School for Scandal*, and *As You Like It*. In the 1906–7 season, he traveled the

vaudeville circuit with a program called *An Evening with Dickens*. In 1910 he played in the Sherlock Holmes story *The Speckled Band* (*ABTB*, 878; *WhMuDr*, 292).

7. Gus Van (August Van Glone, 1887–1968) and Joseph T. Schenck (1891–1930) were a two-man comic singing and piano act. They were lifelong friends from their schooldays in Brooklyn. They played children's parts in their neighborhood at Brooklyn's Myrtle Avenue Picture House and at the Lenore Club in Queens, later named the Van and Schenck Club. Schenck was a piano-playing tenor able to reach higher notes than Caruso, and Van was a consummate dialect comic. One of their famous dialect acts was called *Hungry Women,* based on a song associated with Eddie Cantor, but which was in fact a staple of Gus Van's, done in a Yiddish accent. They also performed Irish dialect skits and sang Irish ballads as well as Italian numbers. Their greatest fame was between 1914 and 1919 when they were billed as "The Pennant Winning Battery of Songland." The pair played Broadway, appearing in *The Century Girl* (1916) and the *Ziegfeld Follies* of 1919, 1920, and 1921. They also appeared in cabarets and nightclubs, such as the Silver Slipper. The duo were heard in radio in December 1923 and broadcast on *The EverReady Hour* on station WEAF. They did one film for MGM called *They Learned about Women* (1930), an early sound movie that had a baseball theme. They also made several early sound-era Vitaphone shorts. Their last appearance together was in June 1930. That month Joe Schenck died of a heart attack while appearing at the Fischer Theatre in Detroit with Van. After Schenck's death, Van could not perform solo at first, but eventually he did a single, and often evoked the memory of Schenck in a song lyric. He told an interviewer in 1930 that in his mind he was always harmonizing with the departed Schenck. In 1930 he did a well-received solo act at the Palace performing dialect singing imitations. He returned there in February 1931 and September 1932. In the 1944 film *Atlantic City,* Van played himself in a featured Van and Schenck routine, with Charles Marsh playing Schenck. He appeared in the Broadway stage play *Toplitzky of Notre Dame* (1946). In appearances between 1949 and 1954, Van was a vaudeville revival headliner at the Palace Theatre with his partner Helen Kane. Van retired to Miami Beach, where he died as a result of being hit by a car. The accident occurred while he was going to the American Guild of Variety Artists (AGVA), of which he was a former president and a lifetime member (*ABTB*, 930; *EV*, 520–22; Franklin, *Encyclopedia of Comedians,* 323; *NYT*, 13 March 1968, 47; *OCAT*, 689; Samuels and Samuels, *Once upon a Stage,* 203–5; Van and Schenck clipping file, NN-L-BRTC; *VO*, 2:2 July 1930 and 6:13 March 1968).

From Frank Stine
ca. 4 May 1914
Ochelata, Okla.

Dear Will

Just a few lines to let you know that I recieved you[r] letter and check for $32.[001] I Will mail this to day Monday th[e] 4th   Maby it Will reach you this Week at Rochester N.Y.[2] the children school Will be out Friday 8th   the 2 Boys[3] Will go to Fort Worth about June the 1th For the Summer[4]   I had a letter from Sallie a few days ago—Saying She Would Pay us a visit When school Was out

This fall I Would like to go to Some good little town and = Start me a little Garage. I do not [know] Just Where I Will locate at   I Want to get to a good School for the girls   Where We can give them music lessons   they can not get the advantage out here that they can get in town.

My B[r]others Wants me to come to Fort Worth But I Would Rather go to Some Smaller Place   —   if you come home this Summer I Would like for you to come and see us   We have about 400$\underline{00}$ little chicken and Will [insure] you one good feed any way

The children are all Well and doeing fine at School this last Season   But We Want to get Where they can have Better advantage they do not [get] to go and See much out here in these hills   Well, as I have no news to Write I Will Close hoping this Will re[a]ch you in Rochester   let me here from you often

All Join me in lots of love

Frank

ALS. OkClaW, Stine Family Collection.

1. Rogers had purchased his sister's (May Rogers Yocum Stine's) interest in their father's property in Claremore and Oologah, Okla. Legally, the property belonged to May Stine's children, since she had died in 1909. Frank Stine was guardian of the children: Edward Jacob Stine, Mattie Lane Stine, and Owen Gore Stine (Tom McSpadden was the guardian of Johnny Yocum, the son of May and Matt Yocum). The children received interest from the notes on the sale. Thus Rogers's check represented payment of the interest. In an earlier letter to Rogers, Frank Stine had written that Rogers had paid in total $350 interest on each note, which had a principal of $595 each (19 March 1914, OkClaW). According to the agreement, Rogers purchased the interest of the three children for $645 each for a total sum of $1,935. In addition, Rogers paid for the education of the Stine children and helped the Stine family financially during the 1930s (see Paula M. Love note, Frank Stine to Will Rogers, 4 May 1914, OkClaW; Property Deed, filed 15 April 1913, and Guardian's Deed, filed 6 November 1914, OkClaW; *PWR*, 1:553, 553–54, 554–58 [Biographical Appendix entries for Frank Stine, Jacob Edward Stine, and May Rogers Yocum Stine]).

2. Rogers was performing at the Temple Theatre in Rochester, N.Y., the week of 4 May 1906.

3. Jacob Edward (Jake) Stein (1900–1982) and Owen Gore Stein (1909–78).

4. After May Stine's death, Frank Stine worked in the Oklahoma oil fields until he was injured in 1914. He then went to Fort Worth, Tex., his hometown. He married Leoma Allen, and they had three children. Stine operated a garage and rented a farm with his new wife and their extended family (*PWR*, 1:553).

Betty Blake Rogers to Sallie McSpadden
26 May 1914
New York, N.Y.

From mid-February to mid-May Rogers toured on the Keith Circuit, performing mainly at theaters in the Midwest.[1] By this time the Keith-Albee organization had increased its number of midwestern theaters, east of Chicago, affiliated with its booking office, UBO. This development allowed Rogers to have more consecutive performances in the region. After his Keith tour, Rogers had no engagements planned for the summer, and he decided to travel to Europe with his wife at the end of May. On 26 May Will and Betty Blake Rogers sailed on the ship Vaterland[2] *from Hoboken, New Jersey, to London, where Rogers appeared in the revue* The Merry-Go-Round, *beginning 14 June.*

11 a.m.

Tuesday

Wish you were all with us, you can not imagine *ever* the wonderful beauty of this big boat.[3]

Betty[4]

PCS. OkClaW. Addressed to Mrs. Tom McSpadden, Chelsea, Okla.[5]

1. Rogers performed at Keith's Theatre in Columbus, Ohio, 16–21 February 1914. One of two big-time vaudeville theaters in Columbus, the theater was managed by W. W. Prosser, and performers were booked through the UBO. The playbill listed the following performers, in this order: Ernie and Ernie (The Monopede and the German Girl); Wallace Galvin (And His Hands); Hayward-Stafford Co. (In *The Devil Outwitted*); Joe Morris and Charlie Allen (The Comedians with the Pipes); The Verigraph (An Optical Sensation); Clownland (A Musical Fantasy in Black and White, with Ceballos and Victor Stone and Company of Sixteen); Will Rogers (The Wizard of the Lasso); and Romeo, the Great (Most Intelligent Chimpanzee in the World). The Verigraph was described as hazy pictures on a screen viewed through lorgnettes given to the audience. At the Monday matinee Rogers lassoed Fred Stone, who was in the audience, and yanked him to the stage where he did some lasso tricks and a dance. Stone was appearing at another theater in the city in *The Lady of the Slipper* (Keith's Theatre playbill, Columbus, Ohio, week commencing Monday, 16 February 1914; "New Keith Bill," *Columbus Citizen*, clipping; and "B. F. Keith's," *Columbus Evening News*, scrapbook A-3, OkClaW).

Rogers performed at Keith's Theatre in Cincinnati 23–28 February 1914. In 1906 there were three big-time vaudeville theaters in Cincinnati: the Columbia, People's, and Casino. By 1921, with the growth of the city population to 401,247, Cincinnati had four theaters: the Columbia, Keith's, Liberty, and Palace. Managed by John J. Murdock, Keith's Theatre had a seating capacity of 2,699. On the playbill the week commencing 23 February were Harry Tighe (The Lively Comedian and His Famous Collegians); Will Rogers (The Oklahoma Cowboy. Late Star with *The Wall Street Girl*. See His Smile—Most Magnetic Personality in Vaudeville. Champion Rope and Conversation Expert. Vaudeville's Biggest Scream); Willard Simms and Co. (The

Popular Eccentric Comedian in His Unequaled Laughing Success); Charles and Henry Rigoletto (Astonishing Display of Versatility); Henry and Francus (Just Nonsense); Andy Rice (Hebrew Comedian and Parody Singer); Sidney and Townley (Songs and Dances All Their Own); Juggling Millers (Comedy Entertainers); and Cincinnati in Motion. One reviewer noted that Rogers one night played a college student in Harry Tighe's act (*EV*, 98; *GHNTD*, 541; Keith's Theatre, Cincinnati, Ohio, playbill, week of 23 February 1914, scrapbook 1914, CPpR).

From 2 to 7 March 1914 Rogers appeared at the Grand Opera House in Syracuse, N.Y. The theater had a capacity of 1,700, and its bookings were handled by the UBO. Also on the bill were the Toya troupe of Japanese jugglers. Reviewers noted that Rogers told jokes about Ford automobiles and his standard Theodore Roosevelt joke (*GHNTD*, 543; Syracuse newspaper clippings, scrapbook A-3, OkClaW; Syracuse newspaper clippings, scrapbook 1914, CPpR).

Rogers performed at Pittsburgh's Grand Opera House 9–14 March 1914. He appeared at Cleveland's Hippodrome 16–21 March 1914. The Hippodrome was a premier vaudeville showplace in the Midwest and one of Keith's largest theaters, seating 3,500. According to the *Cleveland News*, the bill featured "everything from baboons to grand opera." S. Avitabile's English grand opera staged *Cavalleria Rusticana* (*GHNTD*, 541; clipping, scrapbook 1914, CPpR).

Rogers next went to Grand Rapids, Mich., where he performed at the Columbia Theatre, doing two shows a day, from 23 to 28 March 1914. The theater was managed by F. J. O'Donnell, and its bookings were handled by the UBO. The theater seated 1,200 spectators. Rogers was the featured act and was described as "The Oklahoma Cowboy. The Wizard of the Lasso." Other vaudevillians at the Columbia were Fredrika Slemons and Co. (In the Comedy Playlet *Liz*); Edward Jolly and Wild Winifred (Grand Rapids Favorites. Musical Comedy Stars); Holland and Dockrill (Spectacular Equestrians. Champion Riding Experts); The Heuman Trio (A Cycling Sensation); Billy and Edith Adams (Presenting the Latest Songs and Dances); Sam J. Curtis and Co. (In a Marital Episode *Good-bye Boys*); and Pathe's Weekly (*GHNTD*, 534; Columbia Theatre, Grand Rapids, Mich., playbill, week of 23 March 1907, scrapbook 1914, CPpR).

Rogers next performed at Keith's Theatre in Toledo, Ohio. A UBO-affiliated theater, it seated 1,652. Spotting a monkey in the theater wings, Rogers exclaimed, "Keep that monk out of the wings—the gosh-dang thing will be doing my act before the week is over. . . . I've got to do something to uphold the human race." At Keith's Theater in Indianapolis, Ind., which seated 2,352, Rogers performed from 6 to 11 April. His wife and two children were with him at the Claypool Hotel. He commented to a reporter that when one of his children would get out of hand, he "whirls the lasso, shoots it through the air, encircles the endangered child with the noose and draws him back into the middle of the room." Rogers recalled to the reporter the time he was in Indianapolis with the Tulsa Manufacturing Association's promotional tour and put on a roping exhibition in the hotel's lobby to great applause. It "inclined me to the idea that maybe I could make my living that way" (*GHNTD*, 529, 541; Indianapolis clippings, scrapbook 1914, CPpR).

Rogers next went to Louisville, where he performed at the Keith Theatre (capacity 1,500) the week of 20 April 1914. On the bill with Rogers was Jesse L. Lasky's *The Three Types*, three women who posed as living representations of paintings. They wore scant clothing, what Rogers called "aggrivating clothes." A former vaudevillian, Lasky (1880–1958) produced one-act shows for the variety stage at this time, but he was also a film pioneer. In 1913 Lasky produced *The Squaw Man*, directed by Cecil B. DeMille, the first feature film in Hollywood. Lasky headed Paramount until 1932 (*EV*, 300; *GHNTD*, 531; *Courier Journal*, clipping, scrapbook 1914, CPpR).

For the week of 27 April to 2 May, Rogers returned to Detroit's Temple Theatre. With Rogers on the program were *The Porch Party* (A Musical Fantasy with a Company of Twelve Clever People); Melville and Higgins (In Putting on Airs); Swor and Mack (Realistic Impressions of the Southern Negro); Frosini (Accordion Virtuoso); Horton and Latriska (The Clown and the Human Doll); Mang and Snyder (Revelations of Human Physical Development and Strength); and McCormack and Wallace (In *The Theatrical Agent*) (Detroit Temple Theatre playbill, week of 27 April, scrapbook 1914, CPpR).

Rogers apparently also performed at Keith's Theatre at Atlantic City, N.J., sometime in May before he left for Europe. Atlantic City was a seaside resort that drew many vacationers; the Keith's Theatre was located out on the Garden Pier. Also on the playbill was the magician Volant assisted by Ruth Gurley, performing a flying piano trick. One reviewer wrote of Rogers, "As soon as he gets through with his act he is out and chasing himself up and down the Wooden Way [the Atlantic City boardwalk] as though his very life depended on the quantity of ozone which he can absorb during his stay." Betty Blake Rogers later wrote that she joined her husband there (Atlantic City, N.J., clipping, scrapbook 1914, CPpR; Rogers, *Will Rogers*, 121).

2. A new German ship, belonging to the Hamburg-American Line, the *Vaterland* had just made its first trip to the United States. Considered the most modern passenger vessel of the day, the ship was visited by over 16,000 people before it left for Europe. The 430 stewards and about 600 other workers threatened to strike, and demanded increased pay and better accommodations. The strike was settled just before the ship departed. It was scheduled to leave Hoboken, N.J., at 10 A.M. It sailed to Hamburg via London. Other passengers scheduled to leave on the *Vaterland* included Admiral Oscar von Truffel of the German navy and England's Lady Sybil Grey and Lady Evelyn Jones. There were approximately 1,500 passengers on board. Betty Blake Rogers recalled that on the first night they dressed formally for dinner, only to arrive at the dining room too early and to find that the attire was informal (*NYT*, 26 May 1914; "1,030 Threaten Strike on Vaterland To-day," unidentified clipping, scrapbook 1914, CPpR; Rogers, *Will Rogers*, 121–22).

3. The *Vaterland* was considered the largest line at this time, weighing 58,000 tons. Because of its weight, it broke away from the tugs towing the ship and did considerable damage in New York harbor. As the captain turned his ship to prevent it from striking Manhattan island, it hit and sank a coal barge, damaged piers, and tore two steamers from their moorings ("Largest Line Once More Breaks Adrift," unidentified clipping, scrapbook 1914, CPpR).

4. While Rogers was performing in London, Betty Blake Rogers went to Paris with Charlotte Perry, the wife of the blackface comedian Frank Tinney. Tinney was performing in London at the Hippodrome Theatre. Betty Blake Rogers also visited Berlin. She sent telegrams from the Continent to her husband at the Strand Palace Hotel in London where he was staying (Frank Tinney to Will Rogers, 11 June 1914, and Telegrams of Betty Blake Rogers to Will Rogers, 26 June and 30 June 1914, scrapbook 1914, CPpR; Rogers, *Will Rogers*, 124).

5. The postcard depicts the vessel *Vaterland* that Will and Betty Blake Rogers took to England. Rogers wrote on the top margin: "The Harbor Pilot takes these off   We are leaving the land   Im getting sick."

Review of *The Merry-Go-Round*
ca. 12 June 1914
London, England

"THE MERRY-GO-ROUND" AT THE EMPIRE.[1]

The new spectacular production seen for the first time at the Empire last night has certainly much about it that justifies that adjective to the full. Every one of the twelve scenes that constitute its two acts is as fine as taste and a lavish outlay can make it; but, unfortunately, at present there is not nearly enough of the merriment and "go" promised by the title. Scene after scene of uncommon richness and beauty is seen, but fun—the real fun that not only gets over the footlights but reaches right to the back and the top of the hall—is, speaking generally, the rarest thing in the show. After the customary dress parade in the customary dressmaker's establishment comes a whimsical scene, "The Edge of the World," in which the "hyperfuturistic impressions and strange phenomena of living and combating colours"—to quote from the programme—are decidedly staggering. Entirely delightful is the "Fete at the Palais Royal in 1796," which ends the first act. Here Miss Phyllis Bedells[2] and Mr. A. H. Majilton join in a savage sort of dance of the "apache" type. There is promise of amusement on the Racecourse Lawn which opens the second act, but the only thing that really counts is the amazingly dexterous use of the rope, or lasso, by Mr. Will Rogers, described as a "busker," who thus beguiles the time between the races.[3] "In the days of the Fan" (with a song for Miss Daphne Glenn)[4] provides some charming effects, and "Le Vrai et le faux Chic" (after designs by the French caricaturist Sem) is piquant enough. Later we have M. Ronsin's fantastic and exquisitely-blended "Garden of Flowers," where Mlle. Alexandra Balachowa and M. Michael Mordkin[5] dance to the music of Glassnov, Tchaikovsky, and others. Then the courtyard of a London hotel, with sundry droll types, American and otherwise, and finally the truly gorgeous "Mosaic Ball," in which the chief dancers appear, and Mr. Harry Clarke[6] and Miss Norah Bayes[7] give a "ragtime drama." So "The Merry-go-Round" ends even more brilliantly than it began, and, when the necessary "pulling together" has been effected, there will be cause, one thinks, to congratulate Mr. Alfred Butt on the success of his first production at the Empire.[8]

PD. Unidentified clipping, ca. 12 June 1914. Scrapbook 1914, CPpR.

   1. *The Merry-Go-Round* was described as "an inconsequential medley," written by Fred Thompson and lyrics by C. H. Bovill. It comprised a series of richly decorated

scenes that featured music, dance, song, and comedy. Located at Leicester Square, the famous Empire Theatre was situated on the site of eighteenth-century residences of the royalty and former theaters dating back to 1848. The Empire Theatre, with its luxurious interior decorated in blue, white, and gold opened on 17 April 1884 with *Chilperic,* a musical spectacle by Florimund Hervé. In 1887 the Empire Theatre of Varieties became a music hall under the management of Augustus Harris and George Edwardes. From 1898 onward it was known as the Empire Theatre. By now it had gained fame as London's most celebrated variety theater. In the 1890s the theater gained a reputation for its bohemian clientele. Inside, the theater had an opulent promenade back of the dress circle, where English dandies and aristocrats strolled with beautiful and daring young women of the Gay Nineties and ladies of the town. In 1894 social reformers pressured the city council to close the promenade's so-called scandalous environment. Entrance to the now deserted promenade was blocked with canvas screens. They were quickly torn down by an entourage led by the young Winston Churchill, who delivered a stirring speech denouncing the promenade's closing. Afterward, the rebels and their supporters in the audience paraded around Piccadilly Circus bearing the broken pieces of the screens. When Rogers was performing at the Empire, the theater was known for its hostesses, or "percentage girls," who encouraged men to buy them drinks. After 1905 the theater was used mainly for revues that featured ballet performances by the well-known ballerinas Adeline Genée, Lydia Kyasht, and Phyllis Bedells. Many great British variety stars performed there, including Yvette Guilbert, Dan Leno, Marie Lloyd, Vesta Tilley, and Harry Lauder. In the program the Empire was called "The Premier Variety Theatre, the Cosmopolitan Club and the Rendezvous of the World." *The Merry-Go-Round* was Alfred Butt's first production as managing director of the Empire, a position he held until the theater's closing. Musical productions, films, and variety were offered at the Empire in the 1920s. On 22 January 1927 the theater closed with a production of Gershwin's *Lady Be Good!* starring Adele and Fred Astaire. Metro-Goldwyn-Mayer Pictures, which bought the property, demolished the building and built a large movie theater in its place (Rogers, *Will Rogers,* 123; *Lost Theatres of London,* 30–39; Short, *Fifty Years of Vaudeville,* 118–24; *Merry-Go-Round* production files, program, 29 June 1914, VATM; "Last Days of the Empire: Dan Leno to Ben-Hur" and "Old-time Magic of the 'Empire',") clippings, Empire Theatre file, VATM).

2. Phyllis Bedells (b. ca. 1894) was an English dancer who had an extended contract at the Empire Theatre in London. The *London Bystander* of 31 December 1913 described Bedells as the "first English Prima Ballerina of the Empire Theatre." She had great success at the Empire in 1913–15, specializing in the tango and ballet. She danced the lead role in *The Dancing Master* ballet in the spring of 1914 and starred in *The Vine,* an Arcadian dance idyll, in the spring of 1915. She was still a star in 1920, when she appeared as the chief dancer in *The Golden Prime of Good Haroun-Al-Raschid* at the Alhambra Theatre. She was paired with M. Novikoff in dance performances at the Duke of York's Theatre and starred in *Johnny Jones,* also at the same theater (*Cleveland Leader,* 21 December 1913; *London Graphic,* 24 April 1915, 27 March and 26 June 1920; *London News,* 7 March and 27 June 1914; *New York Review,* 10 April 1915; Phyliss Bedells clipping file, NN-L-BRTC).

3. According to Betty Blake Rogers, her husband was engaged for *The Merry-Go-Round* by Alfred Butt after they arrived in England. Rogers had a role in scene 5 called "The Green Park," and was cast as a "busker" (British slang for a strolling entertainer). In several reviews Rogers was singled out as the "one gleam of humour in the piece" (*Town Topics* clipping, 27 June 1914, scrapbook 1914, CPpR). "An oasis in a

desert of dullness," wrote another critic (*Sporting Times* clipping, 20 June 1914, CPpR). "I did think I'd got a new joke to-night," he once said at a performance. Two reviewers suggested that Rogers should speak a little louder. Rogers told an interviewer that the success of his roping depended greatly on the audience. "It is the audience who help to keep the rope going," he said. "Sometimes when they are dumpy it seems very contrary and on other evenings when they are enthusiastic it is almost alive in its desire to please" (*Evening News* clipping, scrapbook 1914, CPpR). Reviews generally found the book of *The Merry-Go-Round* second-rate but the staging and sets sumptuous (Rogers, *Will Rogers,* 122–23; *Merry-Go-Round* production files, program, 29 June 1914, VATM).

4. Daphne Glenn was an English actress who specialized in musical comedy. In 1910 she appeared in the United States as the prima donna in *The Dollar Princess,* a Klaw and Erlanger production. The show was based on *The Merry Widow* and had a long and successful run (scrapbook, ser. 3, 512:119–21, NN-L-RLC).

5. Mikail (Mihail) Mordkin (1881–1944), born in Moscow, was a Russian ballet dancer, teacher, and choreographer who experimented with modernist forms. He graduated from the Moscow Imperial School of Ballet. For a short time in 1909 he was with the Diaghilev ballet. Shortly afterward, he teamed with Anna Pavlova for performances at the Paris Grand Opéra. In 1910 they were invited by Otto Kahn to appear at New York's Metropolitan Opera House. They created a sensation there when they performed in a special program after the opera concluded. This success was followed by a tour across the country in 1910–11. In his American appearances Mordkin specialized in a form of dramatic dance pantomime: "Pavlova and Mordkin's astounding performances merely give a suggestion, nothing more, of an art old and thoroughly established in Russia, but new to the rest of the world," said one reviewer. "It is the unfolding or enactment of a narrative—drama, opera or call it what you may—through terpischore. Not a line is spoken, not a word sung. Only the graceful movements of the ballet and the rhythmic sway of the character dancers, supplemented by music especially written for the purpose illuminate the theme, or plot" (unmarked clipping, n.d., scrapbook, ser. 2, 281:3–13, NN-L-RLC). In the *Merry-Go-Round* production he danced the "Arrow Dance" by Tchaikovsky and, with Alexandra Balachowa, "The Blind Fortune" by Schutt and "Bacchanale" by Glazunov. After living in England, Mordkin returned to Russia, where he organized his own company. In Russia he was appointed ballet master of the Bolshoi Theatre, among the highest honors in the world of dance. In the wake of the Russian Revolution he was hired to produce ballets by the Soviet of Workmen's Deputies in Moscow. He danced in southern Russia in a variety of concert halls and theaters, and also teamed with Margarita Froman in performances in Moscow in 1919–21. Known for his independent methods, he operated his own ballet school and mounted productions until he fell out of favor with Soviet officials. As a result he immigrated to the United States in late 1923. He formed a touring company and opened a ballet school in New York. In 1937 he established the Mordkin Ballet Co. for advanced students. It later became a company for professional dancers, called the Ballet Theatre, in 1939. On 15 July 1944 he died at his summer home in Millbrook, N.J. (*DE,* 312; scrapbook, ser. 2, 281:3–13, NN-L-RLC).

6. Born in New York, Harry Clarke (Harry Prince) came from a stage family. His mother performed with Edwin Booth, and his grandfather was a stage manager at Barnum's Museum. Clarke performed with Maud Grange's company, appeared in *Beauty* and *Mam'zelle,* and toured in stock companies. He managed the stock company at the Lyceum Theatre, Denver, Colo., and was a comedian for that company as

well as for San Francisco's Columbia Theatre Stock Co. He began appearing in comedy pieces in vaudeville in 1906. From 1913 to 1915 he was married to Nora Bayes (James, ed., *Notable American Women*, 1:116–17; *WhoStg*, 88–89).

7. Nora Bayes (born Dora Goldberg, ca. 1880–1928) was raised in an Orthodox Jewish family that considered the stage an immoral vocation. At age seventeen she ran away to Chicago, married Otto Gressing, and got a job singing at the Chicago Opera House and the Hopkins Theatre. In 1902 she performed at Percy G. Williams's Orpheum Theatre in Brooklyn, singing "Down Where the Wurzburger Flows," a popular drinking song by Harry von Tilzer. She went to Europe and played the London Palace in 1904. Bayes returned to the United States for an appearance in the first *Ziegfeld Follies* in 1907. She and her husband Jack Norworth achieved fame with their performance of Norworth's song "Shine On Harvest Moon." Other well-known Bayes and Norworth songs were "Turn Off Your Light"; "Mr. Moon Man" from *Little Miss Fix-It* (1911); and "When It's Apple Blossom Time in Normandy." In 1914 Bayes appeared at the New York Palace Theater as "The Greatest Single Woman Singing Comedienne in the World." In 1917 Bayes popularized "Over There," the World War I ballad, in *Two Hours of Song*. She performed the whole two-hour cabaret show herself, and also produced it. In 1919 she managed her own theater, the Nora Bayes Theatre, which was formerly Lew Fields's Forty-fourth Street Roof Garden. Throughout her career she was noted for her exuberant personality and a sometimes contentious manner. Her stage trademark was an ostrich fan, along with wildly embellished gowns and hats. Her last stage appearance was at New York's Audubon Theatre on Broadway and 168th Street. Despite large lifetime earnings, Bayes died insolvent due to her characteristic extravagant generosity. At the time of her death she had become a Christian Scientist (Busby, *British Music Hall*, 22–23; *EV*, 27–29; James, ed., *Notable American Women*, 1:116–17; Martin and Segrave, *Women in Comedy*, 64–68; *NYT*, 20 March 1928; *OCAT*, 63; Robinson et al., eds., *Notable Women in the American Theatre*, 64–66; Samuels and Samuels, *Once upon a Stage*, 80–89; van Hoogstraten, *Lost Broadway Theatres*, 152; *VO*, 1:21 March 1928; *WhThe*, 157).

8. Others in the show included Wellington Cross and Lois Josephine, who performed a Savoy Hotel scene, and Tom Smith and Phil Doyle, who did a burlesque of Queen's Theatre celebrities. The playbill also mentioned Fisher and Green, Rene Koval, James Gooden, Nell Emerald, A. H. Majilton, Harry Roxbury, and Hugh E. Wright. Performers changed as the show continued during the month of June. The show concluded with Bioscope films (*The International Polo Cup, Trooping the Colours, Royal Ascot,* and *Kine-Kartoons*) (*Merry-Go-Round* clippings, scrapbook 1914, CPpR; *Merry-Go-Round* production files, program, 29 June 1914, VATM).

To Betty Blake Rogers
3 August 1914
Kansas City, Mo.

The Rogerses returned on the Imperator, *a Hamburg-America liner, and arrived in New York on 15 July.*[1] *Will Rogers headed for Claremore, Oklahoma, for a short visit, while Betty Blake Rogers traveled to her hometown of Rogers, Arkansas, to see her family. Arriving in Claremore on 25 July, Rogers spent time socializing and checking his property interests, and made a trip to see his in-laws and family in*

Arkansas.[2] *Scheduled to perform on the western Orpheum Circuit, Rogers left by train for San Francisco on 3 August for his first engagement.*[3]

10[30] Thursday a.m.

Leaving now on Union Pacific will get Frisco Sunday morning. Got here at 8 thur a.m. Everything fine at Farm   sold the renter my share of corn and alfalfa   got in all of Farm this year over $900.

APC, rc. OkClaW. Addressed to Mrs. Will Rogers, 307 E. Walnut St., Rogers/Ark.[4]

1. Among the passengers were the banker and arts patron Otto Hermann Kahn (1867–1934), Kermit Roosevelt (Theodore Roosevelt's son) and his wife, and Alice Roosevelt Longworth (Theodore Roosevelt's daughter, married to a member of Congress, Nicholas Longworth) (*NYT*, 16 July 1914).
2. See *CM*, 31 July 1914; *CP*, 6 August 1914.
3. On his way to San Francisco, Rogers sent a postcard to his wife from Denver, Colo., with a picture of the Lakeside Promenade at the City Park. It stated that he was having breakfast in the city and was leaving for Cheyenne, Wyo. (Will Rogers to Betty Blake Rogers, 14 August 1914, OkClaW). He also sent a postcard to his daughter Mary and son Will, Jr. (Billy), with a picture of the public swimming pool at Lincoln Park in Denver (Will Rogers to Mary Rogers and Will Rogers, Jr., 14 August 1914, OkClaW). The same day he mailed a postcard to his daughter Mary, postmarked from Cheyenne and with a picture of Devil's Slide in Ogden, Utah (14 August 1914, OkClaW). Also that day he sent a postcard to Will, Jr. (Billy), with a picture of "Cowboys Racing to Dinner." He wrote: "Here's old Indians and Cowboys. Daddy" (14 August 1914, OkClaW). Postmarked from Ogden, Utah, was another card addressed to Mary Rogers with a picture of Sitting Bull (15 August 1914, OkClaW). Rogers arrived in San Francisco on 16 August in time for his engagement at the Orpheum Theatre.
4. The picture on the postcard depicts a general view of Electric Park, Kansas City, Mo.

Review from the *San Francisco Chronicle*
17 August 1914
San Francisco, Calif.

VARIED BILL FOR ORPHEUM[1] CROWDS

BALLROOM DANCING, GENUINE SINGING,
OTHER THINGS AND WILL ROGERS.
By Waldemar Young.[2]

Diversity is the flag flung at the Orpheum masthead this week of animated entertainment.[3]

Coming in as the new headliners are Mlle. Natalie and M. Ferrari,[4] presenting ballroom dances of the sort that have been the past season's foe to embonpoint. It is enough to say of them that they win a happy measure of applause for displaying, either a little differently or with an extra flourish of grace, very much the same terpsichorean line as has been exhibited by various couples in the twelvemonth. Mamselle and Monsieur are to be rated with the best of the dancers San Francisco has seen, judged by the gauge of popular approval. Theirs is a tangoesque triumph.

To them is allotted accordingly the task of upholding the terpsichorean end of a programme that gives a little of a lot of things and not too much of any. Within what classification Will Rogers, "The Oklahoma Cowboy," would fall is rather difficult to say, unless one is willing to consider him a division of vaudeville all by himself. The fact is, however, that he closes the show with lariat trickery and ad lib monology quite astonishing, for the one part, and hugely provocative of laughter for the other.

Will Rogers has been here before and the spontaneous humor of him [his] won him yesterday afternoon a rousing welcome upon his first chuckling appearance. Later, when he got the ropes to working and the talk to bubbling forth, the welcome turned into an ovation of genuine dimensions. Rogers' work all through is refreshingly different. . . .

PD. Printed in *San Francisco Chronicle*, 17 August 1914. Scrapbook 1914, CPpR.

1. On the Orpheum Theatre see Review from *San Francisco Bulletin*, 11 August 1913, above.

2. Waldemar Young (d. 1938) was the drama critic on the *San Francisco Chronicle*. Born in Salt Lake City, he was the grandson of Brigham Young. He studied at Stanford University, and his first newspaper job was with the *Salt Lake Herald*. At the *Chronicle* he was first a reporter and sports editor. Young replaced Ashton Stevens as drama critic for the *San Francisco Examiner*, but returned to the *Chronicle* as its critic. He also wrote a column called "Bits of Color around the Town." For a time, he left the *Chronicle* to become the advance agent for Gertrude Hoffman and her Ballet Russe. Young also wrote plays and farces. At one time he and William Jacobs performed on the Orpheum Circuit a comic sketch written by Young called *When Caesar Ran a Paper*, a parody on press agents. Rogers was on the same program when they performed this sketch at the Oakland Orpheum, the week of 23 August 1914 (see Review from *Los Angeles Argonaut*, ca. 7 September 1914, below). After his years as a journalist, Young turned to screenwriting about 1917. At the time of his death he was under contract to Metro-Goldwyn-Mayer. He died of pneumonia in Hollywood on 30 August 1938 (*NYT*, 31 August 1938; *VO*, 2:7 September 1938; clipping, "Hollywood, Cal., Nov. 20," *Oakland Tribune* clipping collection and Waldemar Young biographical clipping file, CSf-PALM).

3. The actress Bertha Kalich and her company was the headliner on the program. She performed the epilogue from *Mariana* by the Spanish writer José Echegaray (Waldemar Young, "Kalich Conquers as Orpheum Star," *San Francisco Chronicle*, 10 August 1914). Other performers included Mlle. Natalie and M. Ferrari (Premiere Classic and Modern Dancers); Harry R. Hayward and Frances Stafford (In *The Devil Outwitted*); Josephine Dunfee (Late Prima Donna of the Gilbert and Sullivan Opera

Co.); Britt Wood (The Juvenile Jester); Marie and Billy Hart (Present Their Own Novel Comedy Skit, *The Circus Girl*); The Trans-Atlantic Trio (In a Novel Musical Offering); and motion pictures (*NYDM*, 26 August 1914; *San Francisco Chronicle*, 16 August 1914).

4. One reviewer wrote that Mlle. Natalie and M. Ferrari were "European exponents of classic and modern dances. They are said to be a terpsichorean revelation, and were last season the sensation of the London and Paris music halls" (*San Francisco Chronicle*, 16 August 1914).

To Will Rogers, Jr.
20 August 1914
San Francisco, Calif.

Hello Son why dont you write to Daddy and tell him how you are. Daddy saw an old Seal and some Buffalo and Bears in the Park today.[1]

APC, rc. OkClaW. Addressed to Billy Rogers, 307 E. Walnut, Rogers, Ark.[2] Stamp canceled World's Panama-Pacific Exposition 1915.

1. Rogers probably saw the animals at the San Francisco Zoo. The postcard depicts seal rocks seen from the Cliff House in San Francisco. Located on the western tip of Point Lobos overlooking Seal Rock and the Pacific Ocean in San Francisco, the Cliff House has been a popular beachfront restaurant since the 1860s. There have been four buildings on the site. The first, built around 1863, was known as "the city's most modish meeting place, a favorite hangout for local political types and a trysting place for gentlemen and their paramours" (Muscatine, *Old San Francisco*, 232). A fire destroyed this building on Christmas Day 1894. Two years later Adolph Sutro rebuilt the Cliff House in the likeness of a French chateau. This building was also destroyed by fire in 1907. It was rebuilt in a more modest fashion and reopened in 1909 (Delehanty, *Walks and Tours*, 276–77; Purdy, *San Francisco As It Was*, 78–79).

2. The postcard was postmarked 20 August 1914. Rogers mailed another postcard to his son from Oakland, Calif., on 25 August 1914 that depicts the Cliff House on fire in September 1907. He also sent a card, postmarked 18 August 1914, to his daughter Mary with a picture of the Panama Pacific International Exposition seen from Presidio Heights and another on 20 August 1914 showing people swimming in an indoor pool (OkClaW).

Review from the *Los Angeles Argonaut*
ca. 7 September 1914
Los Angeles, Calif.

After San Francisco, Rogers performed at Orpheum Circuit theaters in Oakland, Sacramento, Stockton, and San Jose, California.[1] Then he went to Los Angeles, where he appeared at the Orpheum Theatre[2] 6–19 September and received the following review.

The pet of the programme this week is undoubtedly Will Rogers, the "Oklahoma cowboy." This ta[l]king individual is an expert with the lariat, and gives a brilliant exhibition of his skill in manipulating the rope. But what tickles his audience is the stage demeanor that he assumes while exhibiting it. He comes on with a good-natured, gum-chewing grin, and while partly thinking aloud and partly throwing out casual comments to his audience performs a great many dexterous tricks with the rope with the same casual, semi-detached way with which he talks. As he is roughly dressed and either not made up or made up to look sunburned and natural, his clever pose gives the turn a natural, unstudied air which greatly adds to the pleasure with which his audience receives it. And, besides, they keep their ears well cocked, because his running, half-preoccupied, gum-punctuated talk is worth listening to. It is shrewd and humorous, and entertains us quite as much as his remarkable dexterity with the rope. It is all the more enjoyable because of his shrewdly assumed air of half fumbling at it and doing nothing really clever. He talks, and chews, and grins openly at the friendly, admiring house, and all of a sudden, with a careless flirt of one hand, he has shaken the end of his magic rope into a loose but complicated knot, or he is whirling it into huge circles that mysteriously grow larger as he invisibly p[l]ays it out: or, as he weaves other double circles, one with each hand, he jumps rhythmically from one to the other, progressing across the stage in time to the music.[3]

PD. Printed in Los Angeles *Argonaut,* ca. 7 September 1914. Scrapbook 1914, CPpR.

1. Rogers performed at the Orpheum Theatre in Oakland, Calif., 23–29 August 1914. The theater opened on 30 September 1907. The Oakland Orpheum was located on the ground floor of a four-story building and had a capacity of 1,700. A manufacturing and shipping center and terminal of four transcontinental lines, Oakland in 1909 had a population of approximately 200,000 and thus could support a first-class vaudeville theater. In 1925 the Fox Theatre was purchased by the Orpheum organization and reconditioned for vaudeville. The original Orpheum was renamed the Twelfth Street Theatre. As in San Francisco, Bertha Kalich was on the bill performing *Mariana.* Rogers commented that a man "couldn't make an act good after hers" (*Oakland Tribune* clipping, scrapbook 1914, CPpR). Another act on the Oakland playbill that had performed in San Francisco was The Trans-Atlantic Trio featuring the banjoist Harry Clarke and Josephine Dunfee. Also on the program were Waldemar Young and William Jacobs in the travesty *When Caesar Ran a Paper.* (Young had reviewed Rogers's performance in San Francisco a week earlier; see Review from *San Francisco Chronicle,* 17 August 1914, above.) Others included Byrd Crowell (Soprano Soloist); James T. Duffy and Mercedes Lorenze (In the Miniature Comedy, *Springtime*); and The Mozarts (Snow Shoe Dancers in Their Novelty Dancing sketch *Snowed In* (*NYDM,* 19 and 26 August 1914; *GHNTD,* 526; *Orpheum Circuit of Theatres*; *Orpheum Circuit Book* [souvenir for the opening of Seattle's Orpheum on 28 August 1927], copy, Csf-PALM; Orpheum program, week of Sunday matinee, 23 August 1914, Oakland Orpheum file, CSf-PALM).

Rogers appeared at the Clunie-Orpheum in Sacramento, Calif., 31 August–1 September. The theater had just opened when Rogers appeared there. It had a split-week policy of offering legitimate theater the first half of the week and vaudeville the last three days of the week. It was later called the State Theatre (*NYDM*, 26 August 1914; *Orpheum Circuit* 1925; *Sacramento Bee,* clipping, scrapbook 1914, CPpR).

Rogers sent a postcard to Will, Jr., from Sacramento on 31 August that depicted the grounds and rear of the State Capitol building. He wrote that "this is right under Daddy's window" (OkClaW).

Rogers performed at the opening nights of the Orpheum Theatre in Stockton, Calif., 2 and 3 September 1914. Others on the bill were Billy Hart (In *The Circus Girl*); Duffy and Lorenze; and Gladys and Alp Goulding (In *A Parisian Flirtation*) (*NYDM*, 26 August and 2 September 1914; Stockton newspaper clippings, scrapbook 1914, CPpR).

Rogers was at the Orpheum Theatre in San Jose, Calif., 4 and 5 September 1914 (*NYDM*, 26 August and 2 September 1914; *San Jose Mercury Herald* clipping, scrapbook 1914, CPpR).

2. The first Orpheum Theatre in Los Angeles opened on 31 December 1894. In 1903 Orpheum vaudeville moved into another theater on Spring Street, between Second and Third Streets. This theater was replaced by a new Orpheum that opened on 26 July 1911, where Rogers performed. This was Rogers's second appearance at the Los Angeles Orpheum, where he had previously appeared in August and September 1913. It was located at 624 South Broadway between Sixth and Seventh Streets. Planned by the architect G. Albert Lansburgh, the Orpheum featured a polychrome façade. It was situated on the ground floor of a five-story office building. Above the marquee were four figures in panels sculpted by Domingo Mora that symbolized music, song, comedy, and dance. The entrance featured imported marble, chandeliers, and wrought iron lamps. The interior had a large orchestra section, two cantilevered balconies, and thirty-nine boxes seating 2,000 people. Sight lines, stage design, indirect lighting, and ventilation were modern for their time. The entire project cost $350,000. The theater was managed by Clarence Drown, who was highly respected in his field by both performers and employees. The Orpheum's slogan was "The Standard of Vaudeville," and most of the leading names performed here, including Al Jolson, Nat Wills, Ethel Barrymore, W. C. Fields, Irene Franklin, Marie Lloyd, Eddie Foy, Fred Astaire, Eva Tanguay, Sarah Bernhardt, and the Marx Brothers. In 1918 Los Angeles had four big-time vaudeville houses: the Orpheum, Pantages (operated by Alexander Pantages's chain), Sullivan and Considine's Clunes Auditorium, and the Hippodrome, managed by Ackerman and Harris. But the Orpheum was considered the premier variety showplace. The Orpheum organization opened the Hill Street Theatre on 20 March 1922, and the Keith-Albee-Orpheum company built a new Orpheum Theatre with a seating capacity of 2,800, which opened on 15 February 1926 (*Orpheum Circuit of Theatres*; *Orpheum Circuit* 1925; Singer, "Vaudeville West," 120–21, 137–38, 141–83).

3. Appearing on the same playbill were most of the performers who had been on the California tour: Bertha Kalich and her company, The Trans-Atlantic Trio, The Gouldings, James T. Duffy and Mercedes Lorenze, Marie and Billy Hart, Wharry Lewis Quintette, and O'Brien Havel and Co. (playbill clipping, scrapbook 1914, CPpR). At one performance Rogers introduced Blanche Ring. On one clipping from the *Los Angeles Times* (9 September 1914) Rogers wrote, "Editorial in Los Angeles." The *Times* called Rogers "refreshing." "There is a cowboy down at the Orpheum with a real lariat, a smile that came from the fields and a war whoop that is music. He pre-

tends to be throwing a rope, but what he actually does is to give as fine a monologue as we have ever heard from the vaudeville stage" (clipping, scrapbook Ziegfeld Follies, CPpR). While in Los Angeles, Rogers went with the cowboy actor Frank Burns to a film studio in Edendale, where he watched Tom Mix perform stunts for a movie ("Movie Cowboys a Shock to Will Rogers," clipping, scrapbook 1914, CPpR).

Reviews from Salt Lake City Newspapers
28 September 1914
Salt Lake City, Utah

ORPHEUM.[1]

A better balanced bill has not been presented at the Orpheum since the opening of the season than the one which opened yesterday afternoon. There is a little bit of everything on the bill, with the exception of grand opera. The bill was made for laughing purposes. Will Rogers, the Oklahoma cowboy, who "learned to tie pretzels in lariats in Cincinnati," is a scream. The management does not give Mr. Rogers the full stage now—he has to work over the footlights. He uses a ladder in order to get around the small stage room and "inverts" his act. He gives an acceptable trick roping act, but the "jokes" which he writes into the part as he goes along caused the applause puncher back stage forcibly to punctuate the ribbon which tells Martin Beck how the audience likes the acts. . . .

Will Rogers, cowboy comedian, the only animal of his kind in captivity, convulsed the audience with his droll remarks. Rogers does some clever tricks with a rope, but the tricks are only a foil for his comedy. Rogers has to be seen and heard to be appreciated, and once seen and heard is only to want to go again and again. The stage hands say that the only thing about Rogers's act that stays the same is his repertoire of tricks. He just talks along telling joke after joke, until his audiences are so busy wiping tears from their eyes that they can hardly see the tricks he is performing. Rogers would be performing yet if last night's audience had had its way about the matter.

It would take downright fibbing to brag much about the new bill at the Orpheum. It has a few bright spots in it, but not enough.

There is but one way to judge and criticise variety shows. There is no standard for them, as there is on the legitimate stage. One must strike a good average for the circuit he is considering and make comparisons with that. It is impossible to keep from making comparisons with the previous week's bill. That is the natural thing, and it is the basis for the public's judging of nearly every vaudeville show.

The show that started yesterday can't stand such comparison. This doesn't mean that no one will like it. As a matter of fact, many may consider it much more entertaining than the previous week's program. There are those poor mortals who can't appreciate artistes like Bertha Kalich, or ballet dancing such as closed last week's bill.[2] They would consider the closing number this week much more to their liking. It is a knockabout tumbling act. You don't have to have any music, rhythm or poetry in your soul to understand what Gormley and Caffery, comedy acrobats, are doing this week.

Will Rogers, the Oklahoma cowboy, was the big hit with the Sunday matinee audience. His reception was the best proof that it isn't so much what you do as how you do it in vaudeville that counts. His act is practically the same as it was last year when he came here, but I enjoyed it every bit as much as I did before. He kept the audience chuckling every minute he was before the curtain. His incessant chatter is always amusing, and some of his tricks with the ropes are difficult and well done.[3]

PD. Printed in Salt Lake *Herald Republican, Tribune,* and *Evening Telegram,* 28 September 1914. Scrapbook 1914, CPpR.

1. After his engagement in Los Angeles, Rogers performed at the Spreckels Theatre in San Diego 20–25 September 1914. While there he went to Tijuana, Mexico, and sent a postcard to Will, Jr., with a bullfight picture of a matador piercing the bull's heart with a sword. Rogers next headed for Salt Lake City, where he appeared at the Orpheum the week of 27 September. The Salt Lake City Orpheum opened on 1 August 1913. It was located on the ground floor of a building at 46 West Second Street that had been designed by G. Albert Lansburgh in the Italian Renaissance style. The horseshoe-shaped auditorium had seating for 2,160 in four levels. It was later called the Capitol Theatre and used exclusively to show movies (Will Rogers to Billy Rogers, 23 September 1914, OkClaW; *NYDM,* 16 September and 23 September 1914; Frick and Ward, eds., *Directory of Historic American Theatres,* 255; *GHNTD,* 550).

2. Bertha Kalich (1874–1939) is considered one of the greatest actresses in the Yiddish theater. She starred in major European cities and New York City, and it is not surprising that some Salt Lake City audiences might not have appreciated her cosmopolitan artistry that blended both the Yiddish and English theater. By contrast, she received rave reviews in Los Angeles and San Francisco. Kalich was born in Lemberg (Lvov), Galicia, where she started her career. Soon she became a leading singer in the Jewish Theatre in Lemberg. Beginning in 1894, she starred in productions at the

Bucharest National Theatre in Romania. Anti-Semitism in Romania led her to immigrate to the United States in 1894. In New York she starred in Yiddish plays at the Thalia Theatre on the Lower East Side. Kalich performed in plays written by Abraham Goldfaden, who founded the Yiddish theater in Russia. She also played in Yiddish versions of classics and modern plays. Her greatest success was in Jacob Gordin's *Kreutzer Sonata* (1902), which she also performed on Broadway in 1906. She learned English, and from 1906 onward she appeared in several Broadway dramas. Kalich also appeared in movies, such as *Marta of the Lowlands* (1914) and *Slander* and *Ambition* (1916). Eye problems and surgery to prevent blindness eventually forced her to into semi-retirement. She made occasional appearances in plays until 1935 and performed at a benefit in 1939, shortly before her death. Called the Jewish Bernhardt, Kalich is said to have appeared in 125 roles in 7 languages ("Bertha Kalich—The Yiddish. Duse," *Theatre,* July 1905, 161–62; James, ed., *Notable American Women* 2:303–5; *NYT,* 19 April 1923; *OCAT,* 391; *VO,* 3:26 April 1939; *WhoThe,* 554; *WhScrn* 1:383; *WhThe,* 1324).

3. Most performers from earlier engagements went with Rogers to Salt Lake City: Billy and Marie Hart, The Trans-Atlantic Trio, James T. Duffy, and Mercedes Lorenze. The headline attraction was Eleanor Haber and her company in the playlet *The Office Lady.* Others were The Hess Sisters (Dancers) and Gormley and Caffery (Acrobats). While in Salt Lake City Rogers sent his wife, who was in Rogers, Ark., with the children, a postcard depicting the organ and choir at the Mormon Tabernacle. On the postcard he wrote, "Being with Clarks here reminded me of when we all came in here togeather" (To Mrs. Will Rogers, 26 September 1914, OkClaW). Rogers posed with Harry and Lillian Clarke, banjoists on the Orpheum Circuit, and other friends for a photograph taken on 27 February 1914. He also sent postcards postmarked 26 September 1914 to his mother-in-law, Will, Jr., and Mary (*Salt Lake Herald Republican,* 27 September 1914; *Salt Lake Tribune,* 27 September 1914; postcards, OkClaw).

Reviews from Kansas City Newspapers
26 October 1914
Kansas City, Mo.

From Salt Lake City, Rogers went on to perform in Denver and then traveled to the Midwest.[1] He appeared at Orpheum theaters in Lincoln and Omaha, Nebraska.[2] From Omaha he went to Kansas City, where, as usual, he received good reviews from local newspapers.

ORPHEUM—VAUDEVILLE.[3]

Although there are singers, a near-human chimpanzee and foreign dancers at the Orpheum this week, Will Rogers, plain Oklahoma cowboy, outshines them all.[4] Easily he is the big hit of the show. Rogers has been in Kansas City several times before, but his act this year is "bigger and better than ever." His personality is distinctly different and to him goes the honor of putting the "origin" in originality. Rogers has a rope act, but his wonderful rope whirling

Will Rogers with fellow vaudevillians, photographed while appearing at the Orpheum in Salt Lake City, September 1914. (*Left to right*) Harriet Keyes, James T. Dunfee, Lillian Clarke, Rogers, Josephine Dunfee, and Harry Clarke. Harry and Lillian Clarke, banjoists, Harriet Keyes, a singer, and Josephine Dunfee, a light opera singer, were on the official playbill with Rogers. *(OkClaW)*

becomes a side line when he starts his quips and jokes in his bashful, drawling voice. A pair of worn, and not fancy chaps, a blue shirt and an ordinary pair of trousers are his costume. The audience simply thundered its applause.

ORPHEUM–VAUDEVILLE.

Will Rogers, billed as the Oklahoma Cowboy, in a rope act, is a feature at the Orpheum this week. He does wonders in rope spinning but you get so much interested in his "patter" that you forget to watch the tricks, as he calls them. He is a monologuist disguised in chaps, and one of the best ever. One quip follows another in rapid succession, and his Western drawl is inimitable. After the third or fourth encore he remarks: "That's the way with these country boys; praise 'em a little and they'll work their fool heads off." The audience keeps Rogers working all the time.

PD. Printed in Kansas City *Post* and *Journal,* ca. 26 October 1914. Scrapbook 1914, CPpR.

1. Rogers played at the Denver Orpheum 4–10 October 1914. A rapidly growing manufacturing, mining, railroad-building, and agricultural center, Denver had a population of around 225,000 in 1908. The Denver Orpheum opened on 4 October 1903. It was on the ground floor of a small three-story building with a dome roof that contained a large clock. Below the dome was a cornice. The theater seated 2,040 people. On the playbill were the same performers: Eleanor Haber and her company; The Hess Sisters; The Trans-Atlantic Trio; Jimmy Duffy and Mercedes Lorenze; Gormley and Caffery; and Marie and Billy Hart. While playing in Denver, Rogers was initiated in the National Order of Cowboys ("Oklahoma Cowboy Heads Funny Orpheum Program," *Denver Express,* clipping, and unidentified clipping, scrapbook 1914, CPpR; *GHNTD,* 526; *Orpheum Circuit* 1925).
2. Rogers was at the Orpheum in Lincoln, Nebr., 11–17 October 1914. A major railroad hub, livestock market, and grain and agriculture center, Omaha attracted the Orpheum organization to build a theater to cater to a population of 200,000 in 1909. The theater seated 1,200 people. Rogers received reviews in the *Nebraska State Journal* and the *Lincoln Daily Star.* He performed at the Omaha Orpheum 18–24 October and received reviews in the *Omaha Bee* and the *Omaha World Herald* (*NYDM,* 7 October, 14 October, and 21 October 1914; *Orpheum Circuit of Theatres*; *GHNTD,* 537; clippings, scrapbook 1914, CPpR).
3. Rogers performed at the Kansas City Orpheum 26–31 October 1914. The Orpheum, which opened on 8 February 1898, was the third theater in the Orpheum chain. The theater seated 1,800 and was one of five variety theaters in the city. It was at this first Orpheum that Rogers performed. On 26 December 1914 the Orpheum opened a larger theater seating 2,220. In 1921 the Orpheum organization built a new theater, seating 3,000, called the Mainstreet Theatre, which offered a mixed bill of photoplays and vaudeville (*NYDM,* 21 and 28 October 1914; *GHNTD,* 536; *Orpheum Circuit* 1925; *Souvenir and Opening Program of the Orpheum's Circuit's New Orpheum Theatre*).

4. Also on the playbill were Harry Clarke and Lillian Clarke (banjoists); Mlle. Natalie and M. Ferrari; Josephine Dunfee; The Transatlantic Trio; Romeo the Great (Alfred Drowiskey's Educated Chimpanzee); Gertrude Clegg and Mortimer McRae (Comedy Cyclists); The Rose Valerio Sextet; and Orpheum travel pictures of Serbia, Austria, Italy, and Turkey (*Kansas City Post* and *Kansas City Journal*, 26 October 1914).

From Frank Stine
26 October 1914
Ochelata, Okla.

Ochelata Okla
OCT 26=14

Dear Will

Recieved your letter and also money order for $180^{00} which I will give credit on each note for $60^{00}[1]

I Was over to Chelsea Thursday   Stayed over night   found all Well   I guess you herd of my acident that I Recieved   I was Burnt the 2nd day of June have not done a days work Since. I am   Disabled in my Right arm and can not use it for Some time   So I have decided to go to Texas for this Winter and maby for good   I have Rented a little Place of 30 acr. I think I can make a living on it   I Will get a Car and take Every thing I got. one team 4 head of cows chickens and turkeys   So I Will very near have my living   I can not Work in the oil field for a year. So I can't Stand it that long

Johnie[2] was in Kansas City that last that I herd of him   if you hapen to see him tell him to Write me to Fort Worth Texas RFD#2   I Want to leave here Nov 2—   that Will be next monday. this [*illegible*] us all well   the children in School   Will close   Wishing you a Prosperous year   lots of love to you and Family from all the Stine Family

after this Week Write me at Fort Worth Texas RFD #2. Send me your future add. by—   return mail and I Will Write When I get there[3]

Frank

ALS, rc. OkClaW.

1. This is another payment by Rogers to his brother-in-law on the note Stine held as a result of Rogers buying his children's share of Clement Vann Rogers's property that had come to them through their deceased mother, May Rogers Yocum Stine (Frank Stine to Will Rogers, ca. 4 May 1914, above).

2. John Vann (Johnny) Yocum was Frank Stine's stepson. He lived in Dallas in the 1910s (see *PWR*, 1:175n.3, 453, 455, 553, 554–58, 569).

3. Attached to this letter was a receipt reading, "Ochelata Okla OCT. 26=1914 Received of Will Rogers $180.^{00} one hundred Dollars for Interest on notes from Sept 15=1914 to Sept 15=1915—Frank Stine Garde."

Vaudeville Act Performance Notes
ca. 30 October 1914
[New York, N.Y.?]

As these notes suggest, Rogers sometimes wrote his routine before appearing on stage. By his offhand manner, audiences still believed he was ad-libbing. New additions to his act included the use of props. He threw a rope from a stepladder and rode a uni-cycle, skipping a huge loop back and forth under it while balancing himself. If one of his tricks failed, he was prepared to joke about it. In a self-deprecating comic manner, Rogers ridiculed his act, calling it "rotten" and admitting that it "kinder drags right along here." As illustrated by his remarks about Theodore Roosevelt, he was beginning to joke about politics. He also planned jokes about other performers on the playbill.

Old Vaudeville Act.

Come on company and bring out the scenery. I used to be important enough to get the whole stage to work in but now they got me rooted down here in this little spot and by next year they will have me doing this out in the lobby,[1]

This is a rikerty old ladder you got here ill about break my neck trying [t]o elevate art.

If this thing falls ill light about the third row

Dont stand under it we will have hard luck enough anyway.

Thats all bring it back again tonight mabe earlier.

Gi I c[r?]abbed it ~~we~~ had it pretty near all out too well yhere aint much use doing it all over again just for that much,

My act is getting too big for this circuit anyway

Its a pretty good trick when i do it good.

I got it good the other night you should of been here then.

I dont hardly know what to do next there is not a great deal of inteligen[ce?] about this act any way I keep putting in a lot of stuff and most of it tu turns out to be rotten and i have to cut it out and i forget whwre i cut it out at.

YOU notice the act kinder drags right along here well I used to tell a Joke right in here and it got so it did not go so i cut it ouyt I used to tell a joke about Rosevelt but i dont tell it any more I wonder what ever become of him Well he was a good fellow when he had it. WEll some times they come back but not often

You know its hard to get ahold of a good joke nowadays ibeen on the bill with some of the best acts in vaudeville and have not got a good one yet

i thought i would get a good one here tonight but i have not herad one yet

That french gal knows a lot of good ones but they wont let me tell them

Ill get back here a little so a lot of actresses here can see this i wont call any names but that blonde that was just out here better go slip a comona on or she will catch cold, Worked that pretty good made my joke and trick come out even, every night, pretty soft for that guy if he ever gets sick and cant go on i come down

Got a new one here for you know a cowboy dont ride horses any more all the swell ones have automobiles igot one here dont go way ill be back in a min yes i got a one horned ford here this was my share of the profits it seats and unseats one person iwas out hunting one day and kicked over a log and two fords ran out and i roped this never mind covering it up isaw what it was, whats the matter mister wont she play, i can find every thing but the place you take the ashes out, No kidding i got one pretty good trick on this egg beat-er,here,[2] i could do better if i had something to lean agains[t] that was not so very good sometimes i get it better than that and sometimes worse that was about an average You know its only a matter of time till i break my neck on that thinganyway, pull some gag while jumping ask me quest

Got another little punk one here will try and ooze on to you dont have any idea you will fall for it i wouldent do this crazy thing but i got ajoke goes with it* will do it all over again i know a lot of you all were not paying attention this is an imitation of mr eddy foy[3] another great comedian there is only a few of us left, pretty little knot is it not, yes it is n

i have alittle german trick i will try thats a young one but its there

I thought some of you bar flies would recognize that between the war[4] and they have about put that trick on the bum

I got a new one here i been working on for some distance i tried it last week and spilled it all over the place, WAit a minute i havent got to it yet, you horned in with that music to soon[5]

I am going to get a moving picture of this trick and just stand and tell about it   IWillgeteven with the manager he will have to have some nrew shrubbery painted when ileave i am making my mark any way,

hot water bottle keep out of those bull rushes

Ive only got jokes enough for one misse s ive either got to practice or learn more jokes,

YOU know i am not supposed to go clear across with this thing coming

Any body thinksi am missing this thing on purpose has got another think

If i dont get this thing pretty soon i will have to givee out rain check

That was rotten you know i am a little bit handicapped up here the man dont even alow a fellow to cuss a little alittle when he misses out loud

Had no business coming back out here again should of let good enough alo

Thats the way with an old country boy brag on him a little and he will work his fool head off,

Give you an imitation of a friend of mine out home in oklahoma hes a yiddisher cowboy I know that will sound strange talking ▾About a yid▾[6]

Yes they got way out there too.

Cause cowboys dont get much money well this fellow is not doing so bad t that was three years ago and he ~~earns~~ owns the ranch how it was abig hog ranch,

You can tell thats a new one every time the orchestra laughs

TMS. OkClaW.

1. When he had performed his act with a horse, Rogers had used the full stage. Now that he was doing a single, or in vaudeville terms an act in one, he was assigned the front of the stage, often before the curtain. Most single acts and monologues performed there. One reviewer noted Rogers's trouble working in a narrow space: "He works under difficulties out in the runway before the curtain, but a step ladder and a one-seated bicycle raise him high enough to give the ropes fair latitude to swing" (*Syracuse Herald,* clipping, ca. 2–7 March 1914, scrapbook 1914, CPpR).

2. A reference to his unicycle.

3. Rogers performed an imitation of the comedian and acrobatic dancer Eddie Foy (1854–1928), a vaudeville and Broadway star. Born Edward or Edwin Fitzgerald in New York, the son of a tailor from Ireland, Foy had a distinct Irish accent and slurred way of speaking that Rogers imitated. After working his way up through minstrel shows, burlesque, and small-time variety, Foy became a vaudeville headliner noted for his eccentric costumes, imitations, and pantomime clowning. By 1912 Foy was doing an extremely popular vaudeville family act with his children, called Eddie Foy and the Seven Little Foys (Eddie Foy, Jr. [1905–83], became a Broadway and film star). Foy appeared in a series of Broadway musical comedies between 1901 and 1913. After World War I the act ended, and Foy returned to the stage as a single. On 16 February 1928 he died in Kansas City while performing at the Orpheum Theatre (*EV,* 188–91; *OCAT,* 272; *WhMuDr,* 1125; *WhoStg,* 178).

4. Hostilities between Germany and Austria-Hungary and the Allies (Britain, France, and Russia) had precipitated the beginning of World War I on 4 August 1914.

5. On cue the orchestra began to play.

6. For his encore, Rogers did his "Yiddisher cowboy" imitation, borrowing from the stereotyped ethnic humor that dominated early vaudeville comedy. According to Irving Howe, the caricature of the "stage Jew" and "Jew comic" became a staple of the American popular theater by the early 1900s. Audiences, he wrote, "seemed to need a few simple and unvarying traits by which to keep each group of 'foreigners' securely in mind, traits that would induce an uncomplicated recognition. And as for the comedians themselves . . . [t]heir humor gained some of its thrust from contempt" (Howe, *World of Our Fathers,* 403). Among the best known ethnic comics who parodied the Jewish immigrant figure were Joe Welch, Barney Bernard, and David Warfield (Distler, "Rise and Fall of the Racial Comics in American Vaudeville," 45–55,

158–176; Gilbert, *American Vaudeville*, 287–92). Rogers, with his "Yiddisher cowboy" gag, followed in the tradition of "Hebe" parts that used dialect and ethnic caricature for humorous effect. Howe argues that in general this "served as a sort of abrasive welcoming committee for the immigrants. Shrewd at mocking incongruities of manners, seldom inclined to venom though quite at home with disdain, they exploited the few, fixed traits that history or legend has assigned each culture. They arranged an initiation of hazing and caricature that assured the Swedes, the Germans, the Irish, and then the Jews that to be noticed, even if through the cruel lens of parody, meant to be accepted—up to a point" (402).

5. BROADWAY FOOTLIGHTS
November 1914–August 1915

Edward F. Albee, who operated the Keith Circuit, receiving a bronze tablet from the membership of the National Vaudeville Artists, a performers' organization, at the dedication of the new E. F. Albee Theatre in Brooklyn, 19 February 1925. (Left to right in front row) Harry Houdini, Fred Stone, Eddie Foy, Albee, Rogers, Leo Carillo. (Other members of the NVA are in the background.) Albee had great admiration for Rogers's show-business talent. *(NNMus)*

THE PERIOD FROM NOVEMBER 1914 TO AUGUST 1915 MARKED A DRAMATIC transformation in Rogers's career from the vaudeville stage to the footlights of Broadway. In November and December 1914 Rogers continued his tour of the Orpheum Circuit in the Midwest. In early January 1915 he joined the Keith Circuit and traveled throughout the South. He began the tour in Atlanta, Georgia, and concluded it in Richmond, Virginia, the first week of February, performing each week in a different southern city. During the second week of February Rogers made his second appearance at New York's Palace Theatre. After the Palace engagement he played the Keith Circuit in the Midwest and also made stops in Louisville, Washington, D.C., and Baltimore.

Returning to New York in April 1915, Rogers performed at the Victoria Theatre in a tribute to its manager Willie Hammerstein, who had died on 10 June 1914. The playbill featured Hammerstein's favorite acts. Hammerstein had been a fan of Rogers since his first appearance at the Victoria's Paradise Roof Garden in June 1905.[1] Rogers had performed at the Victoria Theatre and its Paradise Roof Garden many times after that. Rogers saved the playbill in his scrapbook and underlined the part where he is listed: "Who Always Made Willie Laugh On and Off the Stage."[2] His appearance that week was certainly a highlight of his vaudeville career.

The memorial program was the last week of vaudeville at the Victoria Theatre, for Willie Hammerstein's father, Oscar Hammerstein, had decided to sell the theater to the movie theater magnate S. L. (Roxy) Rothafel and his syndicate. At the time Hammerstein had other ambitions, which never reached fruition, but he was also very depressed over the loss of Willie and two other sons, Abe and Harry. Rothafel gutted most of the structure and built the Rialto, the first movie palace to open on Times Square (1916).[3]

The replacement of New York's grandest vaudeville showplace with a palatial movie theater symbolized vaudeville's loss of popularity to the movies, which by now reached an audience of millions. In the first decade of the twentieth century nickelodeons began to lure audiences and compete with vaudeville. Since 1896 big-time vaudeville had presented photoplays as part of the programming. With the advent of the full-length film in the mid-1910s, theaters began to offer programs that were an equal mix of movies and variety. Marcus Loew, who first owned nickelodeons, was a trailblazer who created a large circuit of small-time vaudeville and movie theaters.

San Francisco presents a poignant example of the popularity of the movies versus vaudeville. In 1909 50 percent of the city's theaters were vaudeville houses, including four major big-time circuit showplaces. By 1914 the number of vaudeville theaters had dwindled; meanwhile, there were thirty full-time motion-picture theaters. By February 1917 there were one hundred cinema theaters and only four vaudeville houses in San Francisco.[4] By 1920 the movies had clearly replaced vaudeville as America's favorite form of mass entertainment. This development continued unabated even though the Keith and Orpheum Circuits were still building and expanding theaters during this decade. Vaudeville and Broadway stars deserted the Great White Way for the limelight of Hollywood. In 1918 Rogers made *Laughing Bill Hyde,* his first film for the Goldwyn Pictures Corporation, and the next year he moved to California to perform in more Goldwyn films. Marcus Loew's theater chain was eventually used exclusively for movies, and his Metro Pictures Corporation merged to form Metro-Goldwyn-Mayer (MGM). In October 1928 the Keith-Albee-Orpheum Circuit (merged since 1927) combined with the Radio Corporation of America and the Film Booking Office to form Radio-Keith-Orpheum (RKO), a combination masterminded by Joseph P. Kennedy, father of the future president John F. Kennedy. Keith-Orpheum theaters, now RKO venues, became movie showplaces. The vaudeville circuits thus played a major role in the history of early film exhibition. Edward F. Albee, the tycoon who had ruled over a vaudeville empire, retired when he was forced out of the new company by Kennedy. "Didn't you know, Ed?" Kennedy said. "You're washed up, you're through."[5]

When he performed during the last week of variety entertainment at the Victoria Theatre, Rogers must have realized that vaudeville had already passed the peak of its popularity and was beginning to decline. After performing at Keith's theaters on the East Coast, he returned to New York City to be with his family. At this point he had reached an impasse in his career. He had been in vaudeville for ten years and had played just about every big-time variety theater in the country. His friend Fred Stone, a successful musical comedy star, encouraged him to remain in New York and to try Broadway.

Musical comedy was flourishing in New York. Although the influence of Viennese operetta was still evident in the works of Victor Herbert and Sigmund Romberg, other, innovative composers were experimenting with new musical forms and American subjects. One reason was an antipathy toward Germany and Austria due to the European war, which began in August 1914. Another was the emergence of a new group of musical comedy composers, such as Irving Berlin, whose *Watch Your Step* appeared on Broadway in 1914. At the Princess Theatre on Thirty-ninth Street near Broadway, Jerome Kern's early musical comedies were presented from 1915 to 1918. Kern's shows, such as *Nobody Home* (1915), *Very Good Eddie* (1915), *Oh, Boy!* (1917), and *Oh, Lady! Lady!!* (1918), created a new musical comedy form that integrated character development, believable situations, humor, and songs. The revue was another popular form which reached its zenith in Florenz Ziegfeld's *Follies* and the Shubert brothers' annual *Passing Show.* Rogers's talent was well suited to the popular Broadway revue that featured top-flight entertainers, chorus girls, flashy musical numbers, and spectacular scenery, and he would join the *Ziegfeld Follies* in 1916.[6]

While he waited for a role in a Broadway production, Rogers settled for the summer with his family near Freeport, Long Island. Freeport, in Nassau County, on the South Shore of Long Island, was one of several theatrical communities outside New York City and was popular with vaudevillians.[7] The little residential village derived its income from fishing and oyster harvesting, while the artist colony at Freeport represented a new trend in performers owning or renting summer homes. Leo Carillo might have been the first actor to settle there for the summer. A large number of theatrical people followed, among them Tommy Dugan, Frank Tinney, Mary Nolan, Max Hart, and Fred Stone. A Freeport attraction was the Lights Club, whose name stood for the Long Island Good Hearted Thespians' Society. Its clubhouse with a lighthouse was located on Long Island bay. Each July the club celebrated Christmas, since vaudevillians were on the road during the winter holiday season. On weekends during the summer the club presented shows performed by the local vaudevillians.[8]

On 18 July Rogers began a one-week engagement at the Palace Theatre. Two days later he received an offer from the producer, Lee Shubert, cofounder of the Shubert brothers' organization, to join the cast of a new musical comedy, *Hands Up.* Although a mediocre show with a cumbersome plot, *Hands Up* was a key event in Rogers's career.

On opening night Rogers performed "in one" near the end of the first act. The Shuberts wanted Rogers to appear for only a few minutes. But on opening night he exceeded his allotted time, perhaps because he was used to a longer vaudeville routine. Suddenly the lights went out on stage and Rogers, disgruntled, walked off. J. J. Shubert recalled: "I was back stage and I saw that there was only one thing for me to do: black him out so that the show could continue. I did so, but judge my surprise when the show did not go on. No, it did not. Instead there was a moment of confusion."[9] Fred Stone, who was in the audience, jumped up and yelled: "Don't let them do that to Will Rogers! Give the man a chance! It's a dirty trick!"[10] The audience agreed, gave Rogers an ovation, and he returned to perform additional rope tricks.

The following day New York newspapers publicized the story. The publicity helped Rogers obtain engagements at Florenz Ziegfeld's *Midnight Frolic* and the *Ziegfeld Follies*. Like the roping-the-escaped-steer story at Madison Square Garden in 1905, this event led to a new direction in his career, one that would bring him fame as America's favorite topical humorist (see *PWR*, 2:117–19, 119n.2).

Gene Buck, Florenz Ziegfeld's assistant, probably saw Rogers perform in *Hands Up*. Buck subsequently engaged Rogers for the *Midnight Frolic*, a popular late-night cabaret atop the New Amsterdam Theatre, where the *Ziegfeld Follies* played. On 23 August 1915 Rogers began performing his rope tricks mixed with humorous comments at the *Midnight Frolic* in the revue *Just Girls*. From September to November 1915 Rogers also appeared in Ned Wayburn's *Town Topics*, a musical revue at the Century Theatre. During the first half of 1916 Rogers performed often at the *Midnight Frolic*, where he gained a popular following. Here he began to expand and refine the topical humor he had begun in vaudeville with more jokes about politics and politicians. Rogers's success led to his engagement in July for the 1916 *Ziegfeld Follies*, in which he performed with Fanny Brice, W. C. Fields, and Bert Williams, all former vaudevillians.[11]

Vaudeville was truly a training ground for Will Rogers. Over a ten-year period he developed his persona as The Oklahoma Cowboy, an image that would mark his future career. By the time he left vaudeville he had mastered the style, mannerisms, idiosyncrasies, and trademarks associated with the Will Rogers of the 1920s and 1930s: the bashful grin, gum chewing, cowboy outfit, self-deprecating jokes, humorous comments about the audience and fellow performers, and even some gags about politicians. He had learned how to time his delivery, tell a joke, and win over his audience. Within a few years Rogers became the famous lampooner of politics and other aspects of the American scene. In the 1920s and 1930s he would undertake new careers as a newspaper columnist, film star, radio comedian, and popular speaker. The vaudeville years between 1905 and 1915 laid the groundwork for these achievements.

1. See *PWR*, 2:478–79 (Biographical Appendix entry for William Hammerstein).
2. See Victoria Theatre Playbill and Reviews, 26 April 1915, below.
3. *EV*, 226–27, 528–29; van Hoogstraten, *Lost Broadway Theatres*, 42.

4. Gagey, *San Francisco Stage*, 210–11.

5. *EV*, 281; see also Goodwin, *Fitzgeralds and the Kennedys*, 429–42; Gomery, *Shared Pleasures*, 36–38; Robinson, *From Peep Show to Palace*, 89–98.

6. Baral, *Revue*, 33–115; *OCAT*, 400–401, 559; Bordman, *American Musical Theatre*, 297–361.

7. Some biographers have claimed that in the summer of 1915 Rogers rented a house across the street from Fred Stone's home in Amityville, Long Island (actually Massapequa, although Amityville was the post office address; see Croy, *Our Will Rogers*, 134; Day, *Will Rogers*, 73; Rogers, *Will Rogers*, 125; Yagoda, *Will Rogers*, 131). Rogers listed his residence as Amityville on the birth certificate of James Blake Rogers (State of New York, Certificate and Record of Birth of James Blake Rogers, certificate no. 39778, 29 July 1915, OkClaW). In the summer of 1918 Rogers did rent a house near Stone's Chin-Chin ranch in East Massapequa (Amityville) on Clocks Boulevard, which had horse corrals and a polo field where Stone and Rogers played (home file, OkClaW; Stone, *Rolling Stone*, 139).

8. Grau, *Business Man in the Amusement World*, 297–98; Jo Coppola, "Success in Freeport," clipping, home file, OkClaW; Laurie, *Vaudeville*, 298–99; *WNGD*, 417).

9. "J. J. Shubert Tells Story of Will Rogers," *New York Sunday Mirror*, 29 July 1934, clipping, NNMoMA-FC. Another version was that Rogers missed a number of tricks because he lacked room in front of the curtain, and walked off in frustration. Hearing the ovation for Rogers, the stage director pushed him back on stage (see "Cowboy Rogers Turns Failure into Success," *New York Review*, clipping, *Ziegfeld Follies* scrapbook, CPpR). Betty Rogers wrote that Rogers was doing an encore when the lights went out and that the ovation prompted Shubert to go to Rogers's dressing room to convince him to return (*Will Rogers*, 127).

10. Stone, *Rolling Stone*, 170.

11. Wertheim, ed., *Will Rogers at the Ziegfeld Follies*, xvii, 3–9.

———

Article from the *Minneapolis Journal*
15 November 1914
Minneapolis, Minn.

The following article is significant for several reasons. It describes Rogers as a family man and tells how his son Will, Jr., grew up with lariats, spurs, and horses. Will and Betty Blake Rogers's other children, Mary and Jim, had similar experiences. In a self-deprecating tone, Rogers describes himself as a "regular bonehead" who went on the stage "because I never amounted to anything." Portraying himself as a simple cowboy with little schooling became a Rogers trademark. The article also shows Rogers's public image as the "bashful cowboy" and the extemporaneous wisecracker. An entertainer who constantly revised his act, Rogers talks about the cigarette-lasso trick he started to perform at this time.[1]

Out in Oklahoma there's a little chap, 3 years old, who is galloping around the room all day, tying knots in a tiny bit of rope, swinging it around his head and endeavoring to make it whirl. He hangs his head while he's doing it, and every once in a while he'll look up bashfully and say: "That ain't much of a trick." Nothing his parents can do will put an end to this ceaseless parading around the room, and so Will Rogers is certain that his boy is going to be a cow-puncher when he grows up, even if he doesn't equal his father's success on the stage. "He sleeps in his 'chaps' and his mother can't get them off," said the father. "He's a regular kid."

Will Rogers on the stage and Will Rogers off are the same person. Perhaps there is a little more seriousness about the Rogers of the dressing room than in the bashful cowboy who ducks his head at the end of every trick. Rogers knows the value of his own personality and his own individual kind of humor, but he is one of the most modest and likable persons one could meet. His clear eyes meet yours without embarrassment, and there is no evasion in his replies. He was a cowboy in Oklahoma for years before he went on the stage.

"Went on because I never amounted to anything," he says. "I'm a regular bonehead. Never could do anything. I can't think of a thing when I ain't on the stage. That's the way my jokes come. When circumstances arise, I think of the right thing to say. Of course, if it goes well, I may use it again.

"When I first started in vaudeville, I didn't do much the first three or four years. Thought every year would be my last. But I'm takin' it seriously now. You'll find me down at the theater every day at 12 practisin' my tricks. Sometimes I don't hardly know myself what I'm trying to do. Then I sit up here and practice on this old violin, and then I come back at 7 and study out more tricks. I've got one I'm goin' to try with a cigaret." Here Rogers illustrated a new feat getting the "makings," rolling and lighting a cigaret with his left hand, all the time whirling a rope with his right. "Funny part of it is," he said, "I had to learn to smoke to do it."

Musical Comedy is going to have a new star some day. Fred Stone says so. So do the critics. It is not dangerous to hazard that Will Rogers will be the star.

PD. *Minneapolis Journal,* 15 November 1914. Scrapbook 1914, CPpR.

1. From 8 to 14 November 1914 Rogers performed at the Minneapolis Orpheum Theatre, located on Seventh Street in the downtown commercial and shopping area. The theater opened on 22 October 1904 and was the sixth theater in the Orpheum chain. The theater had a capacity of 1,700 (*GHNTD*, 535). In response to the city's population growth, in 1921 the circuit built the Hennepin Orpheum, a larger theater seating nearly 3,000 and featuring vaudeville twice a day and photoplays. The first Orpheum was renamed the Seventh Street Theatre, and by the early 1920s it offered popularly priced continuous vaudeville and movies (*Orpheum Circuit* 1925).

The program, advertised as Standard Vaudeville, included the following acts: Paul Armstrong's *Woman Proposes,* a new one-act satire; Hayward, Stafford Co. (in *The Devil Outwitted*); Will Rogers (The Oklahoma Cowboy); McKay and Ardine (On Broadway); The Spinnette Quintette (A Novelty in Black and White); The Gouldings (A Paradise Flirtation); Kramer and Pattison (Physical Culturists Par Excellence); and Orpheum Travel Weekly (The World at Work and Play) (Orpheum Theatre playbill, *Minneapolis Journal,* 8 November 1914).

Reviews from Palace Theatre
ca. 8 February 1915
New York, N.Y.

After his stint in Minneapolis, Rogers went to Duluth and next to Winnipeg, Canada.[1] He continued his tour of the Midwest on the Orpheum Circuit with engagements in Wisconsin, Illinois, and Iowa.[2] In January he began a Keith Circuit tour of the South.[3] Then he returned to New York and made his second appearance at the Palace Theatre as part of an all-star bill that included Alla Nazimova, Ina Claire, and Pat Rooney and Marion Bent.[4] The New York critics praised Rogers's performance.

WILL ROGERS "ROPES" A HIT

Will Rogers, the cowboy, is always amusing. Rogers tells stories and offers incidental comments in a sheepish sort of informal way while he makes the lariat do all sorts of tricks. On a unicycle he jumps back and forth through a whirling lasso loop as easily as he ties a pretzel knot in rope end. Rogers dances, too, while manipulating the lasso, after remarking that he can "shake a very nifty hoof" himself.

❦

. . . Will Rogers, who chews gum, does fancy tricks with a rope an' kids himself an' the audience. It's my private opinion that Rogers is there as a' entertainer an' with some new stunts he is provin' that I know what I'm ravin' about. He opens now with a step ladder climbin' up ter the top ter spin a rope. When he gets up there he tells 'em that's his idear uv elevatin' the stage. His stuff is fast an' a unicycle is a feachure stunt fer a rope ac'.

❦

No. 7—Will Rogers expressed humorous unrest at his position in one but his ropes showed the benefit in their postgraduate course in obeying his dictates, and his jokes kept the laughs running all through his specialty. Rogers scored completely in every detail.

❦

WILL ROGERS, with a line of patter that got him over with much to spare, and a half dozen lariats, captured one of the laughing hits of the bill. It's a return engagement of Rogers at this house, and the way they applauded him showed what a big favorite he is.

PD. Printed in *New York Dramatic Mirror, New York Star, Billboard,* and *New York Clipper,* ca. 8 February 1915. Scrapbook A-2, OkClaW.[5]

1. Rogers performed at the Orpheum Theatre in Duluth, Minn., the week of 16 November 1914. He was advertised as The Oklahoma Cowboy. Also on the playbill were some of the performers he had appeared with in Minneapolis, as well as other vaudevillians: Hayward, Stafford Co. (in *The Devil Outwitted*); McKay and Ardine (On Broadway); Hickey Brothers (Acrobatic Dancers); Caliste Conant (Pianologue); Aileen Stanley (Personality Girl); Davis and Ramonelli (Trampolene Artists); Orpheum Symphony Orchestra; Orpheum Travel Weekly (In Burma, India, Egypt, and Scotland) (Duluth Orpheum playbill, week of 16 November 1914, scrapbook 1914, OkClaW).
From 22 to 28 November 1914 Rogers performed in Winnipeg, Manitoba, Canada. He received good reviews; one reporter wrote that in his spare time Rogers was reading Robert Service's poems of the Yukon and "can quote the longest of them by memory" ("Cowboy Joshes T. R.," *Winnipeg Tribune,* clipping, scrapbook 1914, CPpR; for Rogers's performance dates at Winnipeg see *NYDM,* 18 and 25 November, 1914).
2. Rogers performed at Milwaukee's Majestic Theatre from 29 November to 5 December 1914. An Orpheum Circuit theater, the Majestic had a capacity of 2,000 people. The theater was located on the ground floor of a multistory office building. It was the Orpheum's first theater in the city and opened on 24 August 1908. The the-

ater had a policy of two performances daily. In 1923 it switched to a policy of continuous vaudeville and photoplays with unreserved seats at popular prices. In response to
Milwaukee's population growth, in 1916 the circuit built the Palace Orpheum with a
seating capacity of 2,600. The new theater had a modern cooling and ventilation system that permitted it to be open all year. The Palace offered first-class vaudeville and
photoplays twice daily with reserved seating (*GHNTD*, 553; Milwaukee newspaper
clippings, scrapbook 1914, CPpR; *NYDM*, 25 November and 2 December 1914;
Orpheum Circuit 1925).

From Milwaukee, Rogers traveled to Chicago, where he performed at the
Orpheum's Majestic Theatre 6–12 December. The headliner on the program was the
famous comic singer Nora Bayes. Featured seventh on the playbill were Pat Rooney
and Marion Bent. Rogers, who had the fourth spot, poked fun at Rooney from the
wings during the latter's act and tried to lasso him, but instead Rooney dragged Rogers
to center stage with a rope. Rogers's act was fifteen minutes in one. Others on the program were McMahon and Chapelle, Waldemar Young and Jacobs, Brent Hayes, and
The Green Beetle (Chicago Majestic playbill and Chicago newspaper clippings, scrapbook 1914, CPpR; *NYDM*, 2 and 9 December 1914).

From Chicago Rogers probably next went to Cedar Rapids, Iowa, where he performed from about 13 to 19 December at the Majestic Theatre. The theater, managed
by Victor Hugo, seated 1,500. A reviewer wrote about the reception Rogers received:
"Will Rogers proved a riot, as he has in all the other big time theaters. He was called
back again and again; and every time he returned he had a new joke. Will stopped the
show for about five minutes. He finally had to refuse the calls of the audience, and as
a parting shout gave a western yell while on his way to the dressing room" ("Horrors,
First Act Stops Show and Rogers Is a Riot," clipping from Cedar Rapids [*Gazette?*],
scrapbook 1914, CPpR). Also on the program were Lennett and Wilson (Comedy
Horizontal Bar Experts); Maleta Monconi (Violin Virtuoso); Gertrude Van Dyke
(Singer); Kenney, Nobody, and Platt (Humorists Played by E. Bert, I. R. Nobody, and
E. Booth); Eddie Borden and Irene Shannon; and Dr. Nixon's Chinese Mystery
(*GHNTD*, 531; "Horrors, First Act Stops Show and Rogers Is a Riot," clipping from
Cedar Rapids [*Gazette?*], scrapbook 1914, CPpR).

Rogers probably performed at the Orpheum's Colonial Theatre in Davenport,
Iowa, between 21 and 26 December 1914. A clipping from *Billboard*, entitled
"California Frank's Wild West," in Rogers's scrapbook, reported that Rogers had
Christmas dinner in Davenport, Iowa, with the author of the news story. It mentioned
that Rogers had undergone an operation to remove a "large sliver in his thigh," from
an accident on stage at the Majestic Theatre in Cedar Rapids (scrapbook 1914,
CPpR). (According to the *New York Dramatic Mirror* of 16 and 23 December 1914,
Rogers was listed to perform at Cleveland's Hippodrome 21–26 December, but he was
on an Orpheum Circuit tour. The Hippodrome was a Keith theater, and he appeared
there the first week of March 1915.) The Columbia Theatre in Davenport opened in
1913 as the Orpheum Circuit's second venue in Iowa. It had a seating capacity of
1,350 and a two-performances-a-day policy (*Orpheum Circuit* 1925).

Rogers performed at Peoria's Majestic Theatre possibly between 27 December
1914 and 2 January 1915. A clipping from the *Peoria Journal* states that he was performing on a holiday-week bill, and another clipping reports that he was at a Majestic
Theatre over New Year's ("Big Audiences See Holiday Week Bill" and "Will Rogers
Can Make 'Em Laugh," scrapbook 1914, CPpR; see also *JCGHTG*, 155). On the
same scrapbook page is a clipping from the *Decatur Review* regarding Rogers's appearance at the Empress Theatre, an Orpheum-affiliated theater. The only time he could

have performed there would have been between 3 and 9 January 1915 ("Cowboy Act at the Empress," *Decatur Review,* scrapbook 1914, CPpR).

3. Rogers's first stop in his tour of the South was Atlanta, where he performed at the Forsyth Theatre 11–16 January 1915 (*NYDM,* 30 December 1914, 6 and 13 January 1915). Rogers, wrote one critic, wore "a faded blue shirt, a comic grin, an old pair of trousers and saddleworn chaps" (clipping, scrapbook A-2, OkClaW). A story in the *Atlanta Journal* reported that Rogers told baseball stories, including one about "Bonehead" Pete (scrapbook A-2, OkClaW). During the week Rogers met the Native American Charlie Wahoo, a well-known Carlisle athlete, and the two conversed about baseball. Rogers "ow[n]ed up to the fact that he is a Cherokee Indian" ("Little Chat in Club Room Brings Out Secrets of Actors," *Atlanta Journal,* clipping, scrapbook A-2, OkClaW). Also on the program were two comedy acts, Comfort and John King and Bertee Beaumont and Jack Arnold ("Keith Vaudeville," *Atlanta Constitution,* clipping, scrapbook A-2, OkClaW).

Rogers next performed at the Lyric Theatre in Birmingham, Ala., from 18 to 23 January. The Lyric had a capacity of 1,600, was affiliated with the UBO, and offered Keith vaudeville. It presented daily matinee (2:30 P.M., admission 25–35 cents) and evening performances (8:30 P.M., admission 25–75 cents). The program was as follows: Will Rogers (The Oklahoma Cowboy, Clever Comedian and World Famous Expert with Lariat); Mr. Hymack (The Chameleon Comedian, World's Greatest Quick Change Artist); Jack Tate's Co. (In *Motoring*); Bertee Beaumonte and Jack Arnold (Presenting *The Doctorine*); Marie and Billy Hart (Presenting Their Own Novelty Comedy Skit *The Circus Girl*); Sallie Fields (Excellent Singing Comedienne); DeLessio (Unique Novelty); and Pathe Weekly News Pictures, European War (*GHNTD,* 525; Lyric Theatre, Birmingham, Ala., playbill, scrapbook A-2, OkClaW).

Rogers performed at the Bijou Theatre in Savannah, Ga., 25–27 January. Affiliated with the UBO for bookings and managed by the Wells Amusement Company, the Bijou seated 1,200. He next went to Charleston, S.C., where he performed at the Victoria Theatre 28–30 January. From Charleston, Rogers traveled to Norfolk, Va., where he performed at the Academy Theatre 1–3 February. A Keith theater, the Academy seated 1,425. His last stop on his southern tour was at Richmond, Va., where he played at the Lyric Theatre 4–6 February. The Lyric seated 1,500 and was a Keith theater managed by C. G. Anderson (*NYDM,* 13, 20, and 27 January 1915, 3 February 1915; Norfolk and Richmond, Va., newspaper clippings, scrapbook A-2, OkClaW; *GHNTD,* 527, 551).

4. Rogers performed at the Palace Theatre 7–13 February 1915. One of the two headliners was the famous dramatic actress Alla Nazimova (1879–1945), who performed in the playlet *War Brides* (this was her third and last week at the Palace). Born in Yalta, Russia, in the Crimea, Nazimova studied music at the St. Petersburg Conservatory and method acting in Moscow under Konstantin Stanislavsy. She made her U.S. debut in 1905 in *The Chosen People* at the Herald Square Theatre in New York. Known for playing independent women on the Broadway stage, she starred in such plays as Ibsen's *Nora* and *Hedda Gabler.* She made her first appearance at the Palace in George Middleton's *Unknown Woman,* a one-act play that attacked New York's divorce laws. Her performance that week was canceled by Edward Albee when the New York Roman Catholic diocese complained about the play, though Albee still had to honor her five-week contract for $15,000. Nazimova's role in *War Brides* was her second appearance at the Palace. Written by Marion Craig Wentworth, the playlet was an antiwar and women's rights piece. Nazimova was such a success that she performed the playlet on tour with the Orpheum Circuit. This led to a film contract with

Lewis J. Selznick to do a movie based on the drama (1916). Nazimova appeared in more than twenty other films, from *Revelation* (1918) to *Since You Went Away* (1944). Her screen roles were stylized yet boldly innovative, and she was well respected by her colleagues in the film community. Nazimova made return engagements at the Palace Theatre in 1923, 1926, 1927, and 1928. She lived in Hollywood on Sunset Boulevard; her home became the Garden of Allah, the landmark apartment hotel where many celebrities resided, including F. Scott Fitzgerald (*NYDM*, 10 February 1915; *NYT*, 7 February 1915; *EV*, 368–70; *FilmEnc*, 996–97; *OCAT*, 501).

The other headliner was the musical comedy star Ina Claire (born Ina Fagan, 1892–1985), who sang songs, danced, and performed imitations. Born in Washington, D.C., she started in vaudeville in 1905 as a singing mimic, known for her imitation of the Scottish singer Harry Lauder. In 1911 she made her musical comedy debut in *Jumping Jupiter*, and that year she also played the lead in *The Quaker Girl*. After stage appearances on Broadway and in England, she joined the *Ziegfeld Follies* and performed in the 1915 and 1916 editions. In 1917 she received rave reviews for her role in *Polly with a Past*, which led to perhaps her biggest hit, *The Gold Diggers*, in 1919. She starred in many Broadway musicals in the 1920s and during this decade was recognized as the nation's top comedienne. From 1915 on she appeared in several films, but she never achieved the same success in film as on stage. Her Broadway roles in the 1930s and 1940s were not as well received as her earlier work. Her last part was in 1954 in T. S. Eliot's *Confidential Clerk*. She died in San Francisco (*FilmEnc*, 257; *NYT*, 8 February 1915; *OCAT*, 146–47; Ziegfeld and Ziegfeld, *Ziegfeld Touch*, 244, 289).

Rooney and Bent presented "Twenty Minutes of Pat and Marion." Others on the playbill were Marie Nordstrom (In *Bits of Actin*), Ralph Riggs and Katherine Witchie (In *Dance Divertissements*), Corradini's Menagerie, Kramer and Morton, and the Werner-Amoros Co. (*NYT*, 7 February 1915; Palace Theatre, New York, playbill, scrapbook A-2, OkClaW).

5. The newspaper articles appear as listed in the document source note.

Reviews from Keith's Theatre
ca. 22 March 1915
Louisville, Ky.

After performing at the Palace, Rogers resumed his Keith Circuit tour with perform-
ances in Rochester, New York; Toledo, Cleveland, and Columbus, Ohio; and
Indianapolis, Indiana.[1] He next went to Louisville, Kentucky, where he performed
on the same program with the illusionist Houdini.[2]

How is the bill at B. F. Keith's this week? Very nice, thank you. Will Rogers, the Oklahoma Cowboy, is on it and so are the three Leightons.[3] You remember them; they have been here before, but they have a new "act" this year, and it's very good. Just a dancing, singing and talking affair, but sufficient to show what they can do. One of them works in black face. Another is an eccentric character and he dances limberly. The other one is just a clean cut young man, who has a very pleasant voice. Their old favorite "Frankie and Johnnie," or

"You'll Miss Me, Hon," or whatever the thing is, came in for a round of applause again.

To get back to Will Rogers. You will remember him instantly. He throws ropes or twists them up like cowboys do when they are carrying on at "round-ups," politely called field days in the East, and he says many amusing things. The cleverest thing he does is to feed his "act" from the ones that have gone before him. This is mighty good advertising for the other "acts" and it makes his many times more entertaining to an alert audience.

The headline on the bill is Houdini, a self-liberator, who gets out of an invention of his own quickly and with evident ease. As he invented the thing, a combination of old-fashioned stocks, angle iron frames, grillage and plate glass, there is no reason why he should not know how to get out of it after he has been locked in securely. It is a good trick, because no one in the audience will know how it is done.[4] Another mystery presented is a needle trick. There is no need to describe it to you. Go and see it yourself. But don't try it. Before the trickster appears a series of motion pictures shows Houdini doing liberation feats done here in view of the audience by Hardeen or one with a similar name.

PLEASING BILL AT KEITH'S.

Furnishing Will Rogers with some of his brightest comedy, Houdini served a double purpose on this week's B. F. Keith's vaudeville bill. Unconsciously, of course, Houdini supplied the inimitable Rogers with his best lines but Rogers, always quick to take advantage of anything that offers, is deeply indebted to the self-liberator for his material and the audience owes a debt of gratitude to Rogers for discovering and emphasizing the egotistical absurdities of Houdini's self-assurance and self-sufficiency. Rogers, perhaps the most expert lariat athlete in captivity, added luster to a more or less acrobatic act, with a steady flow of original observations on Houdini in particular and things in general that made his recurrent visit welcome. Rogers and his act just refuse to grow old although they have been grown-up and full-sized for a long time. Houdini, bringing specialization to unheard-of degrees of specialization, secures headline salary for two tricks, both remarkable and mystifying. Atmosphere completes his effort at entertainment.

PD. Printed in *Louisville Courier-Journal* and *Louisville Times,* ca. 22 March 1915. Scrapbook 1914, CPpR.[5]

1. Rogers performed at the Grand Opera House in Rochester, 15–20 February 1915; at Keith's Theatre in Toledo, 22–27 February; at the Hippodrome Theatre in

Cleveland, 1–6 March; at Keith's Theatre in Columbus, 8–13 March; and at Keith's Theatre in Indianapolis, 15–20 March. At Cleveland's Hippodrome a Miss White (possibly Frances White, a singer and dancer) was the headliner, and on the program at Keith's Theatre in Columbus was Ethel Green, a singer of character songs (clippings from Toledo, Cleveland, and Columbus newspapers, scrapbook 1914, CPpR; *NYDM,* 10, 17, and 24 February and 3 March 1915).

2. Houdini was advertised as "The Elusive American" (see *PWR,* 2:486–88 [Biographical Appendix entry for Harry Houdini]). Rogers performed as The Oklahoma Cowboy at Keith's Theatre in Louisville, 21–27 March. Keith's was located at Fifth and Walnut Streets. It had a two-performances-a-day policy; matinees cost 10–25 cents. In addition to Rogers, Houdini, and The Three Leightons, the program included Lorraine and Dudley (In their New Comedy Sketch), Fritz Bruch and Sister (Cello and Violin Virtuosos), Helen Trix (Piano Song Whistleress), Meehan's Canines (Wonderful Leaping Hounds), Salores Trio (Sensational Aerial Artists), and Keithoscope (Selected Motion Pictures) (*NYDM,* 10 March 1915; B. F. Keith's Theatre, Louisville, playbill advertisement, *Louisville Times,* 20 December 1915).

3. Probably James Albert (Bert) Leighton (1877–1964), who with his brother Frank did a vaudeville act. Bert Leighton was a singer, composer, and author. As a songwriter, he collaborated with Boyd Bunch and Ren Shields. Leighton's songs included "Steamboat Bill," "Frankie and Johnny," "Ain't Dat a Shame," "Fare Thee, Honey, Fare Thee Well," and "I Got Mine" (*AmSCAP,* 431).

4. Houdini performed the Chinese Water Torture Cell.

5. The review in the *Louisville Times* was published on 22 March 1915.

Victoria Theatre Playbill and Reviews
26 April 1915
New York, N.Y.

From Louisville, Rogers traveled on the Keith Circuit to Pittsburgh, Cincinnati, Washington, D.C., and Baltimore.[1] Then he returned to New York City, where he performed at the Victoria Theatre in a program that honored the recently deceased Willie Hammerstein. The program featured Hammerstein's favorite acts, including Rogers.

WILLIE HAMMERSTEIN WEEK

Overture
GEO. MAY AND ORCHESTRA.

ALTHEA TWIN SISTERS
Singing and Dancing Duo.

HARRY BREEN[2]
Colonel of the Nuts—Always Made Willie Laugh in the Lobby.

O'BRIEN, HAVEL AND COMPANY[3]
Who Played for Willie When He Owned a Tent.

The Singing Truck.
SOLLY LEE[4]
Nature Made Him a Door Tender.
Willie Made Him an Actor.

EXPOSITION FOUR
Comedy and Music.
Who Willie Always Depended Upon to Make Good.

TIM—MCMAHON AND CHAPELLE—EDYTHE[5]
In Their Own Comedy, "Why Hubby Missed the Train."
Were on the First Bill of Vaudeville at the Victoria.

RUBY—NORTON AND LEE—SAMMY[6]
Late Features of "Firefly" and "Belle of Bond Street"
Singing and Dancing Novelty.
Whose First Engagement Here Resulted in Featured Contract with
Arthur Hammerstein's "Firefly" Co.

DAINTY MARIE
Assisted by MARGUERITE MEEKER
Covered by Willie in a Burlesque Show—Now a Standard Feature.

The Lassoer of the Bull.[7]
WILL ROGERS
Who Always Made Willie Laugh On and Off the Stage.

The Originator of Oriental Dances,
PRINCESS RADJAH
In Her Famous Cleopatra Dances.
[Saved] from Obscurity by Willie Hammerstein. His Exploitation and Her
Long Successful Engagement Here Paved the Way for Her
Present Standing and Prestige.

FRANK FOGARTY[8]
The Dublin Minstrel—Everybody's Favorite.
Always a Favorite of Willie's, Who First Made
Him a Headline Attraction.

BELL AND EVA
Comedy Trampoline.

HAMMERSTEIN'S
(Reviewed Monday Matinee, April 26.)

New York, April 26.—This is Willie's week at "The Corner," and almost every act on the bill is one that was either discovered or especially well liked by the late William Hammerstein. So well known are the acts on the bill that a review of the show can be little more than a tabulation.

No. 9—Will Rogers, "the lassoer of the bull," lassoed the entire house this afternoon, and stopped the show. He was the hit of the bill. Rogers has enlarged his act considerably, and it might almost be called a production now. He is using a step ladder and a unicycle in his act, in addition to his hat. Bill has also slipped in a couple of gags, thus improving an act that had already been accepted as pretty near perfect. Eighteen minutes, in one; six calls, two encores.

WILL ROGERS, who always made Willie laugh on and off the stage, went exceptionally "big." The big Westerner had the audience laughing continually at his bright wit. The rope tricks are done very unassumingly, nevertheless they are extremely difficult. His baseball story received many laughs.[9] He was forced to do two encores before they would allow him to go.

PD. Hammerstein playbill and unidentified clipping. Scrapbook A-2, OkClaW. *New York Clipper* clipping. Scrapbook 1914, CPpR.

1. Rogers performed at the Grand Opera House in Pittsburgh, 29 March–3 April 1915. At Keith's Theatre in Cincinnati, where he performed 5–10 April, Rogers shared top billing with the stage and film comedienne Trixie Friganza (1870–1955), who was known for her amusing imitations and costume changes. Rogers's engagement in Washington, D.C., 12–17 April, was at Keith's Theatre. Rogers's children,

Will, Jr., and Mary, were with him. "I try to sleep in the morning, but the children beg to feed the squirrels—and I just got to [do] as they ask," Rogers said to a reporter ("B. F. Keith's," clipping, scrapbook 1914, CPpR). Rogers performed at the Maryland Theatre in Baltimore, 19–24 April (*NYDM*, 17, 24, and 31 March and 7 April 1915; unidentified clipping and *Baltimore Sun* clipping, scrapbook 1914, CPpR; *EV*, 198–99).

2. Harry Breen was known for his comic monologue about Eastern European Jewish immigrants who lived on New York's Lower East Side, where he was born. Another Breen specialty was singing songs about people in the audience. One ditty went as follows: "There's a lady sitting over there / In the second row on the third chair / She has her hand up to her face / And the hat she has on is a disgrace" (Laurie, *Vaudeville*, 193).

3. O'Brien, Havel and Co. was a well-known act that performed skits with dancing and comedy. The company was headed by O'Brien Havel and had different members over the years. His son Arthur was at one time part of the act. There was also a Miss Valeska. Early in his career O'Brien Havel teamed with his wife, Clara Binns. They had two children. She died in 1906, and that year Effie K. Lawrence teamed with Havel. From around 1908 to 1911 the act was called O'Brien, Havel, and Kyle, and included Havel's son Arthur and the actress Bessie Kyle. O'Brien Havel was known for his eccentric dancing. One of the company's best sketches was *Tricks and Clicks*, written by Will Cressy. It was about work in an office with a typewriter and telephone. In 1914 the company performed another Cressy sketch entitled *Monday*, a comedy about vaudeville life (Locke env. 649, NN-L-RLC).

4. Solly Lee was a ticket taker and doorman at the Victoria Theatre for seven years. One day in 1913 Willie Hammerstein heard Lee humming a popular tune and let him perform at his theater. During his debut Lee sang three songs, "Alabama," "That Old Gal of Mine," and "I Want to Dance, Dance, Dance." Lee was such a success that he was held over for a second week. A singer, Lee was also known for his *kizotsky* dance (Locke env. 1144, NN-L-RLC).

5. The vaudeville team McMahon and Chappelle consisted of Tim McMahon (ca. 1863–1915) and his wife, Edythe Chappelle. They did their sketches in one instead of a full stage. Along with Chappelle, McMahon later produced girl acts for vaudeville, including The Pullman Porter Maids and The Sunflower Girl (Laurie, *Vaudeville*, 232–33; *VO*, 1:24 December 1915).

6. Sammy Lee (Samuel Levy, 1890–1968) was born in New York City. He began his dance career in Gus Edwards's children's revue. For six years he was teamed in vaudeville with Ruby Norton. Later he became a choreographer, staging shows such as *No, No, Nanette* (1925), *Show Boat* (1927), and *Rio Rita* (1927). He also choreographed many of Shirley Temple's dance sequences. During his career he had choreography contracts at Metro, Fox, and Paramount studios. He appeared as himself in the film *I Love You Wednesday* (1933). The actress Ruby Norton was born in Sheffield, England. Some of her stage roles were in *Belle of Bond Street* (1914), *First Frills* (1917), and *Nothing But Love* (1919) (*ABTB*, 582, 707; *OCAT*, 422; *VO*, 6:10 April 1968; *WhoHol*, 955; *WhScrn*, 2:271; *GRB*, 260).

7. Ten years after the event, Rogers was still remembered as the cowboy who had roped the escaped steer at the Madison Square Garden horse show. As this reference suggests, publicity from the event played a key role in his career.

8. Frank Fogarty (1875–1925) was born in Brooklyn, and as a boy was known for his knack in telling stories and singing. He began his professional life as a jewelry salesman, but soon went on the stage. He remained there for the next twenty-five years

until losing his voice at an appearance at the New York Hippodrome. He began as a small-time mimic, but then decided to approach a big-time vaudeville agent, and after an audition he performed at Keith's Theatre in Boston. He initially appeared as a single in a song-and-dance act and then did a two-man act. Later, he performed a single act again doing ethnic monologues, particularly Irish, for which he was named "The Dublin Minstrel" (*ABTB*, 379; *NotNAT*, 390; *NYDM*, 19 May 1914, 20; *NYT*, 7 April 1925; *VO*, 1:8 April 1925).

9. Rogers was an avid baseball fan and attended several World Series. He played baseball as a young man in the Claremore area and participated in games on the road like the one between performers at the Grand and Pantages theaters in Tacoma, Wash., in 1908. In 1914–15 Rogers began telling baseball stories in his routine. One was about "Bonehead Pete." A reporter in Atlanta wrote down the story while Rogers was appearing in the city in January 1915:

> As might be inferred from the moniker, Pete was several strokes above bogey in the think tank, and he could almost have been arrested for blocking traffic, when once he got on bases. But Pete could hit the ball. According to Rogers a large oak tree stood on the outskirts of right field in his home town park. Early one season Pete slammed a hard drive into that oak, but the ball bounded back and he was cut down at third. A month or so later, he whacked another that looked like a sure homer. But this one too hit the tree, bounded back, and Pete was caught at second. The next morning when the team turned out for morning practice, the manager discovered that Pete was already on hand and had all but cut the tree down. "What's going on here, Pete," he inquired. "What's the idea in cutting down that tree?" "Well, just this," replied Pete. "When I hit a home run I want to find it in the record books next winter, and there ain't a chance as long as that bloomin' tree is a-standing there." (*Atlanta Journal,* clipping, ca. 11–16 January 1915, scrapbook A-2, OkClaW)

Manager's Report, Keith's Philadelphia Theatre
10 May 1915
Philadelphia, Pa.

PHILADELPHIA SHOW

H. T. JORDAN   MAY 10, 1915.

HEARST SELIG PICTURES. Fairly interesting lot of pictures this week. All war pictures were eliminated owing to the feeling over the loss of the Lusitania.[1]

MYRL & DELMAR. 8 min. Two men working in a very pretty garden setting which they carry. Perform a series of very showy aerial and teeth tricks,[2] all new and very well done. A very pretty act and made good in the opening.

HENRY G. RUDOLF. 7 min. "The Vagrant Tenor." Man dressed as an Italian who sings grand opera and popular selections. Has a pleasing voice and was fairly well liked.

DARRELL & CONWAY.[3] 15 min. Their act remains about the same as they have been using the past two seasons except for a new opening which was funny and gets laughs. They still black up on the stage and finish with two songs, Miss Darrell changing to two striking costumes. Act scored nicely.

DOYLE & DIXON.[4] 19 min. These two boys have without doubt the classiest dancing act of its kind in vaudeville. Their dancing was a tremendous hit and their conversation-songs and bits of chatter also scored solidly. They work in evening clothes making an excellent appearance. An act that should be a hit on any bill.

REYNOLDS & DONEGAN.[5] 9 min. Their routine of fancy skating and dancing on rollers remains about the same as on former visits. The work is varied and finely executed and the picturesque costuming helps to make it a very showy act. They were accorded a liberal amount of applause.

WILL ROGERS. 19 min. His act in one is a sure fire on any bill. His handling of the ropes is made a big part of his act, but his dry humor keeps the audience in a roar of laughter from start to finish. He was one of the big applause hits of this bill and was forced to respond to two well deserved encores.

SAM MANN & CO.[6] 20 min. In "Lots and Lots of It." This sketch is a comedy drama written around the popular "Mutterzolb" stories which appeared in the Saturday Evening Post and were very widely read. It is a heart interest story with a bit of strong sentiment running through it and plenty of comedy lines to brighten it up. Mann gives an excellent character performance and has the support of a capable company. The sketch was very well liked and made a hit.

GRACE LA RUE.[7] 22 min. This well known musical comedy star is in vaudeville with one of the best singing turns we have seen in a long time. All her numbers are new, she sings them with splendid effect, introduces some attractive dancing and wears some wonderful gowns. This combination gives her an act that makes a great headline offering. She was a big hit here. Charles Gillen at the piano is a worthy asset to the act.

SIX WATER LILLIES. 10 min. A tank diving act with a very pretty picture stage setting and six girls in a series of diving feats. Very showy number and attracted a great deal of interest, holding the audience better than any closing act we have had for some time.

GENERAL REMARKS. This is a very good show from start to finish, plenty of variety, good singing and a liberal amount of comedy well distributed throughout the bill. As a special feature were shown, moving pictures of the Lusitania leaving New York on her last voyage. They followed the regular show and nearly every one waited for them.[8]

TD. KAC-IaU.

1. In 1914 Colonel William Selig, pioneer film producer, completed negotiations with the William Randolph Hearst news organization to produce a newsreel called the *Hearst-Selig News Pictorial.* This was the beginning of Hearst's involvement with newsreels, which lasted until 1968. The debut of the Hearst-Selig newsreel, on 28 February 1914, was advertised in *Moving Picture World* as "throbbing with live news interest in every foot of film . . . the vital dramatic features in the thrilling events that happen every week" (Fielding, *American Newsreel,* 87). Hearst and Selig also made a five-reel picture they called *A Wonderful Spectacular History of the World's Greatest War.* The advertisements promised a film "made on Gruesome Europe Battlefields and in the Blood-running, fighting trenches" (Mould, *American Newsfilm,* 36). Selig split from Hearst in December 1915 to join the *Chicago Tribune* in the production of the *Selig-Tribune.* Hearst then formed an alliance with the Pathé Company in 1917.

On 7 May 1915 the *Lusitania,* a 30,000-ton British Cunard liner, was attacked by a German U-boat and sunk. Some 1,200 men, women, and children died, including 128 Americans. The torpedo attack on the *Lusitania* was part of Germany's World War I blockade of all ships carrying contraband to Britain and France. Although the ocean liner was a passenger ship, and its sinking caused public shock and outrage, a release of its manifest fifty years later revealed that it was in fact carrying munitions. Within the context of the constraints placed on filming documentary footage during the war, the sinking of the *Lusitania* provided a boon for newsreel companies hungry for sensational material about the conflict. The 1915 disaster created an unprecedented new interest in preparedness organizations throughout the United States. The *Lusitania* footage was again used in the 1918 film entitled *The Kaiser, the Beast of Berlin,* as well as in the Committee of Public Information film *Pershing Crusaders* (1918). The sinking of the *Lusitania* was reenacted using a fictitious ship's name in the vehemently anti-German fiction film, *Civilization,* released in 1915 just months after the tragedy (Chambers, *Tyranny of Change,* 219–20; Fielding, *American Newsreel,* 85–88, 115–24; Isenberg, *War on Film,* 147; Mould, *American Newsfilm,* 36; Mould and Berg, "Fact and Fantasy in the Films of World War One," 52–53; Sugrue, "Newsreels," 11–12, 15–16; Ward, *Motion Picture Goes to War,* 35, 56, 95).

2. Teeth tricks were a form of aerial gymnastic work in which the performers would hang by their teeth from a wire, while performing various physical maneuvers.

3. Emily Darrell and Charlie Conway made up Darrell and Conway, a comedy, singing and dancing, blackface act. The act suddenly became very popular in 1915 for a sketch called *Behind the Scenes,* for which they blackened their faces as Conway played a minstrel man in a purple coat and white silk hat. A native of Portland, Ore., Darrell started in vaudeville around 1910. A reviewer described her as an eccentric comedienne who used her Boston terrier, Bijou, in the act. She performed in blackface and wore a wig in her sketches. She used a wardrobe trunk as an improvised dressing room on the stage for her costume changes. In 1917 Darrell teamed with a new partner, Billy Jackson. By 1919 she was doing a comedy single in vaudeville called *Late for Rehearsal.* The *Variety* reviewer wrote in 1919 about her performance at New York's Fifth Avenue Theatre: "Her routine, patter, and gags, containing some new corking puns, seem to be above the heads of the smaller time audiences. Miss Darrell enters in a semi-comedy make-up, explaining to the orchestra leader why she is late for rehearsal. The leader does straight for her, speaking a number of lines. Miss Darrell was formerly of Darrell and Conway. She now uses a pet bulldog in several trained bits. Miss Darrell must be blessed with a powerful voice. Her harsh shouting does not seem to augur well for its condition" (25 April 1919; see series 3, 356:167–76, NN-L-RLC).

4. James Doyle and Harland Dixon were song-and-dance men who performed tap dances with "a sort of comedy punctuation. They come with the charm of the unexpected so you are engrossed in watching the swing of agile limbs, the daring leaps and the marvelously high kicking—all accomplished with almost nonchalant ease" (clipping, *NYT,* n.d., scrapbook, series 3, 376:123–40, NN-L-RLC). Doyle and Dixon did minstrel and burlesque shows early in their career and in the 1910s were performing musical comedy and vaudeville. Harland Dixon was born in Toronto, Ontario, Canada, and lived there until he was nineteen. He moved to Buffalo, N.Y., where he worked as an elevator operator and took dancing lessons. He moved again, this time to Boston, and worked as a paper hanger while auditioning as a dancer. He obtained a position with Primrose and Dockstader's Minstrels. He left the minstrel troupe in Kansas City and began doing a single act on vaudeville. He returned to New York and performed in revues. Also a Canadian, James Doyle was born in Halifax, Nova Scotia, and began dancing professionally in 1905. He performed with Dockstader's Minstrels, where he met Dixon. The two formed a partnership and alternated seasons in vaudeville and in musical comedies. "Doyle and Dixon are already being sought for next season as Broadway stars and many vehicles have been written for their talents, as both are dancers, singers and actors," reported the *New York Dramatic Mirror* on 12 March 1913. Drawing on their minstrelsy experience, they did some numbers in blackface. In their main act they wore elegant top hats and tails, and were often compared in reviews to Montgomery and Stone. Between 1913 and 1917 they appeared in several musical comedies. They worked often for Charles Dillingham productions, and in 1916 they replaced Montgomery and Stone in the Dillingham show *Chin Chin* (*Theatre,* July 1917, clipping, scrapbook, series 3, 376:123–40, NN-L-RLC).

5. Earle Reynolds and Nellie Donegan were roller-skating experts who danced on skates in a husband-and-wife act. Known as Skater Reynolds, Earle had a single act as an ice skater in 1905–6, but he had difficulty establishing it. The *New York Telegraph* praised the novelty of his act, but said that was also its "chief handicap in obtaining a trial. Skating acts, as a rule, are in little demand, and Reynold's work, while very unusual, still comes within this class" (24 February 1906). Reynolds made the ice necessary for his act "himself with a gigantic machine of his own invention," hauling an ice machine and tank with him on the road. He was a hit as a skater in Anna Held's productions in New York in 1906, and in 1907 he added a partner, Bertha Doud Mack, to the vaudeville act. Reynolds reportedly taught Donegan, who was originally from Australia, how to skate. They shifted from ice skating to roller skating, thereby eliminating the need for an ice rink on the stage. In 1908 they were doing an act in which Donegan, "a wizard on wheels," did a buck-and-wing dance to the music of "Happy Days" and also skated while playing the banjo (*Variety,* 25 July 1908). Reynolds and Donegan were very popular in Great Britain, where they played an engagement at the Palace Theatre in London in 1909. So popular was this appearance that they obtained future contracts and were credited for starting a skating craze that swept England and the Continent in 1909–10. They were featured on the cover of *Variety* on 14 August 1909. Before becoming a celebrity in Europe, Donegan had taught skating to society women in New York and to members of the Metropolitan Opera, as part of the skating fad in the United States. Reynolds and Donegan did both modern and classic dances on skates, with Donegan making elaborate changes in costumes of sequins and furs in a nine-minute performance. They played the Orpheum Circuit in 1912 after appearing in France, Germany, and England. In 1914 they did a major international tour, including appearances in Australia, India, Singapore, China, Palestine, Egypt, and several European countries. Reynolds and Donegan had two

daughters, and by 1919 both were appearing in their parents' vaudeville act. The *New York Star* reported on 18 August 1920 that their act was topping the bills and "making one of the biggest hits made by any American act seen here in a long time." Reynolds and Donegan were still performing in 1942, when they did a command performance for the royal family at Buckingham Palace (*Billboard*, 23 February 1907; *New York Star*, 26 May and 18 August 1920; *New York Telegraph*, 24 February 1906, 20 August 1909, 6 October 1912, 14 May 1914; clipping file, NN-L-RLC).

6. On Sam Mann see Review from *Variety*, 6 May 1911, note 10, above.

7. Grace LaRue (1882–1956) was born in Kansas City, Mo. She began her stage career at age eleven in the Julia Marlowe Company. She started in vaudeville with the team Burke and LaRue. LaRue had numerous musical comedy appearances and was a featured singer in the first *Ziegfeld Follies* show of 1907. In 1913 she appeared at the Palace Theatre in London, where she performed her trademark song, "You Made Me Love You—I Didn't Want To Do It." In vaudeville she was in a short sketch called *The Record Breaker* (1912) at Poli's Theatre in Springfield, Mass. LaRue was primarily known as a singer and gave concerts. She appeared in several films from 1919 to 1940 (*ABTB*, 573; *CmpEnc*, 1071; "Just the Singing of a Song," *NYDM*, 16 December 1914, 18; Slide, *Vaudevillians*, 86; *VO*, 4:21 March 1956; *WhScrn*, 1:420; *WhoThe*, 843–44; *WhThe*, 1418).

8. On 11 May 1915 the *Philadelphia Telegraph* published an insightful review of the show and described Roger's performance: "Will Rogers, most skilful of lariat wielders, demonstrated his command of the rope and his fund of dry wit. His protests against playing his turn 'in one' and the difficulties he encountered in swinging rope in the narrow space allotted him added a touch of consciously unconscious humor" (clipping, series 3, 356:167–76, NN-L-RLC).

Manager's Report, Keith's Theatre
17 May 1915
Boston, Mass.

REPORT ON BOSTON SHOW FOR WEEK OF MAY 17–1915.
(R. G. Larsen.)

MOTION PICTURES OF THE BOSTON HIGH SCHOOL CREWS   14 minutes in one. Picture sheet. This is a special local picture of the high school boys of Greater Boston, whose crews compete on the Charles river this week for a trophy offered by Mr. Keith. An interesting local feature.

BOOTH AND LEANDER   13 minutes f.s. Garden. A very good bicycle act with some splendid comedy. A great opener.

HARRY AND EVA PUCK[1]   17 minutes in one and two. Olio and Palace Drops. Started off a bit slow, but worked up to a good finish. All right in this position.

MORAN AND WISER   16 minutes f.s. Wood. Hat jugglers. A great act of its kind. Full of novelty and plenty of good comedy. A hit.

LEW AND MOLLIE HUNTING   15 minutes in one. G.P. Drapery. Same act they have given us before, without a change of any kind. Going about as well as previously.

TAMEO KAJIYAMA[2]   18 minutes in one. Special Drop. This Jap has made quite a number of changes and improvements in his handwriting stunts since he played Boston before. Held the interest every minute. Closed strong.

WARD BROTHERS[3]   19 minutes in one. Street. Have some new material. A hit.

CAROLINA WRITE[4]   16 minutes f.s. C.D.F. Miss White is a Boston girl, and has sung here at the Opera House. Received a big hand at both performances, and her act went very well indeed. Has a good programme and a beautiful voice.

WILL ROGERS   17 minutes in one. Garden Drop. Rogers walked out after Miss White had scored a big hit, and simply walked away with the show. He kept the audience laughing every minute, and his lariat twirling got a big hand.

FIVE NIGHTONS   8 minutes f.s. Special Drop. A very pretty balancing act, with four men and one woman in white costumes. A good closer.

TD. KAC-IaU.

1. Eva Puck (1892–1979) and Harry Puck (1893–1964) were a brother-and-sister, song-and-dance act. Each continued on the stage after the breakup of their act. Eva Puck married a fellow performer, Sammy White, of the team Clayton and White, with whom she frequently appeared at the Palace Theatre. Their husband-and-wife act concerned a dancing instructor (White) tutoring an inept pupil (Puck) and resulted in a lampoon of grand opera and classical music. Eva Puck starred in *The Greenwich Follies of 1923* and, with White, in *The Melody Man* (1924). The first Rodgers and Hart production, *The Boyfriend* (1926), was written for Puck. She created the role of Effie in Jerome Kern's *Showboat* (1927). She appeared in a few Vitaphone shorts from the early sound era (*ABTB*, 765; *NYT*, 29 January 1964; Slide, *Vaudevillians*, 118–19; *VO*, 4:31 October 1979).

2. Tameo Kajiyama was an advocate of the "method" style of acting. He believed that subtle psychological nuance was necessary to produce a sophisticated, three-dimensional portrait on stage. In an article on the subject, he wrote that the audience "can really see beyond the surface of [the actor's] face" (Tameo Kajiyama, "Personality and Its Use in Vaudeville," *NYDM*, 31 December 1921, 1058).

3. The Ward Brothers were a dancing team of brothers and were awarded the Fox Medal, a medal for championship buck dancing established by the owner of the *Police Gazette* (Laurie, *Vaudeville*, 43–44).

4. Carolina White (Mrs. P. Longone) was born in Boston. She studied voice in Italy and made her debut as a soprano in Naples in a 1908 production of *Aida*. She appeared at other Italian opera venues and then returned to do a U.S. tour. She joined the Chicago Grand Opera Company, performing, among other roles, Minnie in a 1910 production of *The Girl of the Golden West* ("Carolina White, a Prima Donna of Personality and Preparedness," *Musical Courier*, 18 January 1917, 84; "Carolina

White, Soprano with the Chicago Grand Opera Company," *Musical Courier,* 28 December 1910, 1, 31).

From Lee Shubert
20 July 1915
New York, N.Y.

At the end of May Rogers returned to New York and with his family settled for the summer on Long Island. Tired from ten years in vaudeville and eager to try something else, he sought a new career on Broadway.[1] On 18 July 1915 Rogers began a one-week engagement at the Palace Theatre.[2] Two days later he received an offer from producer Lee Shubert, co-founder of the Shubert brothers' organization,[3] to join the cast of a new musical comedy, Hands Up.[4]

July 20, 1915

Mr. Will Rogers,

City.

My dear Sir:—

As per our conversation of to-day I wish to advise you that I hereby agree to engage you starting July 22nd, 1915. for fifteen (15) consecutive weeks in one of my New York productions to do your specialty at the salary of Three Hundred and Fifty ($350.) Dollars per week and I am to have a further option of twenty (20) weeks following the fifteen weeks which I will notify you of three weeks after your opening date.

_____L. S.

TL. 20 July 1915, NNSA.[5]

1. Needing money, Rogers might have performed under another name in small-time vaudeville theaters in the New York area at this time and did not want these engagements publicized (Rogers, *Will Rogers,* 126; Yagoda, *Will Rogers,* 181). Another reason for the lack of vaudeville appearances was that Rogers hit his head while learning to dive and for awhile was unable to rope (Rogers, *Will Rogers,* 125).

2. At the Palace Theatre Rogers performed on the same program with Fritzi Scheff (1879–1954), the headliner, called "The Brilliant Viennese Prima Donna." Scheff had appeared at the Metropolitan Opera House for three seasons starting in 1900. Afterward she did several Victor Herbert operettas on Broadway. In September 1913 she made her vaudeville debut at the Palace; her last appearance at the theater was in April 1930. In the 1940s she appeared in several Billy Rose productions. She died shortly after her appearance on television in *This Is Your Life* in 1954. Others on the Palace program were Adelaide and Hughes (America's Representative Dancers), James C. Morton and Frank F. Moore (famous Singing and Dancing Comedians), Courtney Sisters (Singing New Topical Songs), Avon Comedy Four (Presenting *The New Teacher*), Al and Fanny Stedman, Alf Loyal's Canines, and Mysteria (Supreme

European Sensation of the Century. Is it Illusion or Reality? Man or Magic?). Mysteria
was a European novelty "in which colored motion pictures are given in third dimen-
sion by a secret process of projection" (*NYT,* 18 and 20 July 1915; *EV,* 458–60).

    3. Lee (Levi) Shubert (1875–1953), Samuel Shubert (1877–1905), and Jacob J.
Shubert (1879–1963) grew up in Syracuse, N.Y. As youngsters, the brothers shined
shoes and sold newspapers. Sam Shubert began as a program boy at Syracuse's
Bastable Theatre, and five or six years later he became head of the box office at the
Wietang Theater. With his earnings he bought the rights to the Charles Hoyt play *A
Texas Steer* (1897). The production turned an enormous profit and marked the beginning of the Shuberts' career as producers. They soon acquired several theaters in
Syracuse, Utica, Troy, and Albany, N.Y. Then Sam and Lee Shubert procured leases
on three Broadway houses. The first star they signed was Richard Mansfield, who
brought them great success. By 1900 the Shuberts were producing traveling road
shows. By 1903 the Sam S. and Lee Shubert Corp. had begun to challenge the powerful Theatrical Syndicate, which then monopolized the legitimate theater industry.
The two organizations opposed one another in the areas of production, theater management and ownership, and booking. Unlike the syndicate, the Shuberts' organization was an independent, family-run business, but its founders were ambitious show-
men. By 1904 the Shubert Corp. had acquired fifty theaters. In 1905 Sam Shubert,
the spearhead of the organization, died in a train crash. As a tribute to him, the two
remaining Shubert brothers decided to continue the expansion, and by 1911 they
owned seventy-three theaters. In 1907 the Shubert brothers and their major business
rival Abraham Erlanger launched Advanced Vaudeville as a challenge to B. F. Keith's
UBO. The Shuberts supplied the theaters, but the effort failed and was sold to Keith;
the Shuberts agreed to stay out of vaudeville for ten years. Meanwhile they continued
to expand their chain of legitimate theaters. The Shubert chain in its heyday had theaters in almost every American city, but the principal houses, in New York City, were
the Princess, Shubert, and Winter Garden. The Winter Garden, located on Broadway
and Fiftieth Street, opened in 1911 and was one of the chain's largest and most elaborate theaters. The Winter Garden was known for extravagant shows that featured so-
called "girl" productions; some observers termed the shows "raw" (McNamara,
Shuberts of Broadway, 53). A popular annual event with Broadway audiences was the
Shuberts' annual revue called *The Passing Show* at the Winter Garden, which began in
1912. These revues featured well-known musical comedy performers and involved
spectacular stage effects. The Shuberts' New York theatrical empire was concentrated
on Forty-fourth and Forty-fifth streets, between Broadway and Eighth Avenue. The
Shuberts bought five theaters in this area during the 1910s and also built the Sam S.
Shubert Theatre, where Lee Shubert had his offices as well as his penthouse apartment.

    The Shubert theater chain reached its peak of success in the 1910s and 1920s. The
Great Depression of the 1930s and the World War II years, with the growing popularity of sound movies, caused financial losses for the theater industry, the Shuberts
included. In 1948 the Shuberts bought the leased land under the Plymouth,
Broadhurst, Booth, and Shubert theaters, and Shubert Alley, because they feared that
another company would buy the theaters and demolish them to build a motion-picture
complex.

    In 1953 Lee Shubert died in New York from a stroke. In 1955 the Supreme Court
found that the Shubert organization violated antitrust laws. J. J. Shubert was required
to stop booking and to sell several theaters. He died in New York after years of serious
illness. The Shubert Theatre, Booth Theatre, and Shubert Alley still exist as tributes to

the Shuberts' commitment to the American theater. In total the Shuberts produced 520 plays on Broadway (*ABTB*, 849; McNamara, *Shuberts of Broadway*, 5, 6–14, 33, 35, 41, 48–49, 81, 83, 96–97, 102, 113, 206, 212; *OCAT*, 623; *WhoStg*, 398).

4. J. J. Shubert claimed later that he was the brother who proposed Rogers for *Hands Up*. He felt that a scene near the finale needed improving and recommended Rogers. Lee Shubert opposed the idea and told his brother, "He's been in a couple of shows and hasn't gone over, I don't believe that he could do us any good." "No other suggestions were forthcoming, however, so we finally engaged him," said J. J. Shubert. "But it was with a distinct understanding that he should play a definite number of minutes and then stop" ("J. J. Shubert Tells Story of Will Rogers," clipping, *New York Sunday Mirror*, 29 July 1934, NNMoMa-FC).

Hands Up was originally to be produced by Lew Fields as his yearly summer show for the Shuberts. The plot revolved around a stolen necklace, and Fields planned to take a starring role as the detective. Lee Shubert loaned him $12,500 for the production. Fields hired Fanny Brice, her brother Lew Brice, Bobby North, and the dancers Maurice and Florence Walton. Fields bought several songs from Cole Porter, to strengthen what he saw as a weak score by E. Ray Goetz and Sigmund Romberg. Adding songs and film-clip prologues and giving the Waltons more time to dance made the show too long. The show previewed in New Haven on 7 June 1915. Fanny Brice received good reviews, but critics panned the cumbersome production. The road tryout the following week in Albany, N.Y., was likewise unsuccessful, and other previews were canceled. When Fields attempted to reshape the show for the New York opening, he ran into problems with the Shuberts over artistic decisions. Feeling that there were too many "Hebrew" comedians, J. J. Shubert fired Fanny and Lew Brice, although Fanny Brice replaced the ill Irene Franklin for two weeks in September when the show traveled to Philadelphia. As a result Fields decided to quit the show, and the production was taken over by the Shuberts themselves, who revised the cast, music, and book (Fields and Fields, *From the Bowery to Broadway*, 348–50, 355; Goldman, *Fanny Brice*, 73–75).

5. A representative of the Shubert organization drew a large wiggly line down the letter, and there are some numerals and other scribblings to the left of the signature. Filed with the letter is a memo, dated 23 July 1915, from Gertrude Bock to Mr. Helstein: "Please file the attached with Will Rogers contract. He is with the Hands Up Co." (NNSA).

Review of *Hands Up*
23 July 1915
New York, N.Y.

"THUMBS UP," SIGNAL FOR "HANDS UP,"[1]
First Musical Comedy of the Season
Music, Wit and Girls Please First Night Audience in
Forty-Fourth Street Theatre.[2]

FORTY-FOURTH STREET THEATRE.—

Hands Up, "musico-comico-filmo-melodrama"; book by Edgar Smith,[3] lyrics by E. Ray Goetz,[4] music by Mr. Goetz and Sigmund Romberg.[5]

Strong Arm Steve ....George Hassell[6]
Helene Fudge ....Miss Alice Dovey[7]
Percy Bonehead ....Artie Mehlinger
Mlle. Marcelle ....Miss Emilie Lee
Waltz King ....Maurice
La Belle Claire ....Miss Florence Walton
Ingersoll ....Alfred Latell
Simp Watson ....Bobbie North[8]
Fake Kennedy ....Ralph Herz[9]
Violet Lavender ....Miss Irene Franklin
Lindy...................................Miss Adele Jason[10]
Sergeant Murphy ....Peter Swift
Cowboy Will.............................Will Rogers
Mr. Need-in-time ....Burton Green[11]
Harry Lightfoot ....Donald Macdonald[12]
F. C. Centric ....A. Robbins

"Hands Up" is not a cue for thumbs down. Many first offerings of every new season are, but the musical review seen for the first time in the Forty-fourth Street Theatre last night—the first of the season of 1915–1916—revealed every indication of having arrived there to stay. Such music, such fast fun and such girls win approval without an effort.

Maurice and Miss Florence Walton spoke lines and sang songs for the first time on the stage, but they were only incidents in a cast of tried and true farceurs like Miss Irene Franklin, Ralph Herz, Miss Alice Dovey and George Hassell.

Edgar Smith, who was responsible for many laughs in the Weberfields [Joseph Weber and Lew Fields] frivolities of other days, obligingly has filled "Hands Up" with a lot of clever nonsense. Not since Lew Fields was a cab driver has an audience near Broadway laughed so boisterously as did that of last night at the scene in a dentist's office in which Ralph Herz, as the painless operator, and Miss Franklin, as his assistant, pounded the stout Mr. Hassell, who played the rôle of their writhing victim in the dental chair. Almost every one has suffered a similar experience in a modified form, and one touch of the buzzing drill makes the whole world kin.

Fortunately, "Hands Up" is devoid of plot. What there is of it involves the pursuit of a stolen necklace, with Mr. Herz as a burlesque detective and Mr. Hassell [*illegible*].

The "movies" are travestied in a big stage setting cut into separate scenes, in which the principals go through an old fashioned melodrama in true "movie" style, leaving nothing to the imagination.

Mr. Herz dons a score of disguises, Miss Alice Dovey sings with modest sureness and Miss Franklin is very much in evidence, her vaudeville act, with her husband, Burton Green, being incorporated in the second act. The music, by E. Ray Goetz and Sigmund Romberg, is effervescent, but many of the songs, especially Miss Dovey's "I'm Crazy Over You," can be heard several times, and the last time of hearing is the best. All of Miss Franklin's numbers were composed by Mr. Green. In the ball room scene of the last act, Maurice and Miss Walton interpolate a martial mazurka, one of the dances of Poland.

Alfred Latell was the best dog seen in many a dog day. A. Robbins imitated musical instruments in a droll manner. Bobby North was in black face. His voice, however, failed to get the real melody out of a swinging Hawaiian lullaby.

Another feature was Maurice's dancing double quartet, composed of Misses Anita Wood, Margaret Moll, Mary Newton and Margaret Meury, T. Sedgewick Draper, Frank Gillespie, Vincent Cassidy and Stuart Gilmore.

Will Rogers, cowboy, was on hand with a new series of lariat tricks. When he was trying to complete a difficult rope dance the lights were switched out and he was compelled to make way for a stage full of bathing girls. The audience resented this, and although the orchestra played several minutes the singing and dancing number had to be abandoned until Mr. Rogers had returned and completed the dance. Then there were shouts of applause. Five little girls, pupils of Maurice, danced with him in one number. They were recalled again and again.

As to the chorus, it may be said—anticipating the press agent—it was a riot of color, comeliness and cavorting! . . . .

PD. Unidentified clipping, ca. 23 July 1915. NNSA.

1. *Hands Up* concerns a film magnate with a plan to trick a famous amateur sleuth into appearing in a film. He sets up a sensational robbery and calls in the detective. All of this action, plus a slew of ensuing scenes in a prison, beach resort, and other places, is filmed by a hidden camera. Some film sequences were used as a prologue for the musical, and the style of performance was intended to lampoon movie detectives, as well as melodramatic acting and plotting from the movies. Each scene was intended to have a novel scenic effect, and many mimicked the visual styles of the movies. *Hands Up* also employed an unusually large number of young women in the chorus. In one scene, the stage is divided into six compartments, three stacked atop the other three. Each compartment displayed an aspect of the plot, as if six projectors were screening

six different films simultaneously. Contemporary reviewers liked this scene immensely, one calling it "a real eight-cylinder motor of laughs" (*New York American,* 23 July 1915, clipping, NNSA). Reviews of the production agreed that it was a good, lightweight piece, ideally suited for the summer season. One reviewer stated that while high-brow critics had disliked it, the public was giving it a good run, finding among other things that the frequent scene changes let the piece gather speed until it does "New York to Chicago in eighteen hours" (*New York American,* 23 July 1915, clipping, NNSA).

Maurice and Florence Walton were a big draw in their performance of numerous dance numbers, a lampoon of the dance craze for which they, along with Irene and Vernon Castle, were in large part responsible. They were counting on the production to launch them to fame in the way that *Watch Your Step* (1914) advanced the career of the Castles. The Castles, who attended the show, enjoyed it, but perhaps they were being graceful because critics agreed that Maurice and Florence Walton performed only passably well as actors (Bordman, *American Musical Theatre,* 297–98, 308, 313–14; *Hands Up,* clipping file, NNSA; Rogers, *Will Rogers,* 126–27; *Variety,* 30 July 1915).

2. The Forty-fourth Street Theatre was a Shubert-managed theater at 216 West Forty-fourth Street. In its twenty-four-year life span, the theater changed its name nine times. The auditorium seated 1,463, and sixteen chandeliers hung from the ceiling, a record number for that time. The balconies were shallow and set back against the wall, giving the theater a spacious air. The Shuberts named the theater Weber and Fields's Music Hall, in honor of the two legendary stage stars. The inaugural double-bill program on 21 November 1912 featured Weber and Fields's productions *Roly-Poly* and *Without the Law.* When Weber and Fields broke up in the months following, the Shuberts renamed the theater the Forty-fourth Street Theatre. In this period the theater presented musicals imported from England, classics, operettas, and spectaculars. During Prohibition the building housed a speakeasy in the basement called the Little Club. In 1928 the theater featured the Marx Brothers in *Animal Crackers.* In the 1930s it was known as the Nora Bayes Theatre and featured Federal Theatre projects and dance companies. In 1934 Gertrude Stein's opera *Four Saints in Three Acts* was performed there. In 1943 the building was purchased by the *New York Times* (which operated its annex nearby on Forty-third Street), and two years later it was demolished for an eleven-story extension of the *Times* newspaper plant (Henderson, *City and the Theatre,* 234; van Hoogstraten, *Lost Broadway Theatres,* 151–54).

3. Edgar McPhail Smith (1857–1938) was a librettist, lyricist, playwright, and actor. He began his career as an actor in *Julius Caesar* (1878) at Booth's Theatre in New York. He played in St. Louis for several years and wrote with Augustus Thomas the plays *Editha's Burglar* and *Combustion,* in which he also performed. In 1885–86 he was connected with the actress Patti Rosa and her company, and wrote the comedy *Love and Duty* for her. He then returned to New York, where he worked as a librettist at the Casino Theatre until 1892. Between 1899 and 1919 he wrote the libretto and lyrics for a show each year with the exception of 1914 (*AmSCAP,* 344; *CmpEnc,* 3:1769; *GRB,* 446–47; *NotNAT,* 465; *OCAT,* 630; *VO,* 2:9 March 1938; *WhoStg,* 404–05; *WhThe,* 4:2211; *WhoThe,* 939–40).

4. E. Ray Goetz (1886–1954) was principally a songwriter but also a producer and musical composer for the stage. He wrote many hit songs, among them, "For Me and My Gal," "Who'll Bring My Violets," and "Yaaka Hula Hickey-Dula." Other shows produced by Goetz, and containing many of his songs, were the *Ziegfeld Follies* (1907) and *George White's Scandals* (1922 and 1923). Most of his songwriting successes were

in the years before World War I; afterward he was principally occupied as a producer of plays for his wife, Irene Bodoni. His most successful years were 1928–30, when he produced *The Lady of the Orchids* (1928) and co-produced and co-wrote the music, along with Cole Porter, for *Paris* (1928), in which Bodoni starred. He also produced *Fifty Million French-Men* (1929–30) and *The New Yorkers* (1930), which included in the cast Jimmy Durante (*AmSCAP*, 135; *CmpEnc*, 973–74; *NotNAT*, 401; *NYT*, 14 June 1954; *OCAT*, 298).

5. Sigmund Romberg (1887–1951) was born in Hungary. Arriving in the United States in 1909, he first found employment in a pencil factory and also worked as a pianist in a Hungarian restaurant. By 1912 he was conducting the orchestra at Bustanoby's, one of New York's best restaurants, where he came up with a set of dance music for social dinner dancing, a new idea that made the restaurant even more popular. At the same time, he was composing American dance music. Romberg's next position was as a composer for the Shubert brothers. Within three years he wrote the music for seventeen productions. His most successful pieces were operettas, of which *Maytime* (1917) was the first. His next big successes were in the 1920s: *The Student Prince* (1924), *The Desert Song* (1926), and *My Maryland* (1927). By the 1930s Romberg's German-style operetta was no longer popular, although he continued to produce shows. He conducted an orchestra on his radio program, *An Evening with Romberg*, and composed several film scores (*AmSCAP*, 617–18; Bordman, *American Musical Theatre*, 308; *OCAT*, 586–87).

6. George Hassell (1881–1937) was an English actor born in Birmingham who came to the United States in 1906. An American manager discovered him performing on board a ship en route to Australia from South Africa, where Hassel had served in the Boer War for three years. Hassel appeared on Broadway for the Shubert organization for many years. His first screen appearance was in 1915 in a Lew Fields film called *Old Dutch*. He also appeared in *La Bohème* (1926) with Lillian Gish, *Becky Sharp* (1935), *Captain Blood* (1936), and others (*NotNAT*, 403; *WhoHol*, 710; *WhScrn*, 1:320; *VO*, 2:24 February 1937).

7. Alice Dovey (1885–1969) had a long career on Broadway beginning in 1903. In 1909–11 she appeared in New York in *A Stubborn Cinderella* (1909), *Old Dutch* (1909), *The Summer Widowers* (1910), and *The Pink Lady* (1911–13). She performed at the New Amsterdam in *Queen of the Movies* and *Papa's Darling*, both in 1914. In 1915 she appeared at the Princess Theatre in *Nobody Home* and *Very Good Eddie*. That same year she starred in a film for Famous Players-Lasky called *The Commanding Officer*, and in 1916 she starred in *The Romantic Journey* (*WhoHol*, 1:447; *WhoThe*, 2:695; *WhScrn*, 1:200).

8. Robert (Bobbie) North (1884–1976) performed on stage as an actor and dancer and also acted in film. His first performance as a stage professional was in 1896, but it was not until 1902 that he began performing in prominent theaters. Some of his best known Broadway shows were *Buster Brown* (1905), *Merry-Go-Round* (1908), *Just a Wife* (1910), *Hanky Panky* (1912), and *The Pleasure Seekers* (1913). He also produced Broadway musicals (*WhMuDr*, 238–39; *WhScrn*, 1:544).

9. Ralph Herz (1878–1921) was born in France and educated in England. His first stage appearance, at age twenty-three, was as an extra in *The School for Scandal* (1900) at the Haymarket Theatre in London. That same year he played in *Shock-headed Peter* and, in 1902, *Her Own Way* at the Garrick Theatre. In 1902 he came to the United States and joined Mrs. Patrick Campbell's theater company. He appeared at the Herald Square Theatre in *John Henry*. In 1905 he appeared in *Dolly Dollars* at New York's Knickerbocker Theatre and in 1907 in *The White Hen, Before and After,* and

Lola from Berlin. In 1908 he played the vaudeville summer circuit doing comedy impressions. In 1909–10 he performed at the New Amsterdam Theatre in *Madame Sherry,* and the following year at the Knickerbocker Theatre in *Dr. DeLuxe.* In 1912 he was in the cast of *The Charity Girl* and *Bachelors and Benedicts.* His career continued unabated until his death (*CmpEnc,* 1099–1100; *GRB,* 248; *NYDM,* 26 April 1911, 11 and 16 July 1921; *NYT,* 13 July 1921; *VO,* 1:15 July 1921; *WhMuDr,* 163–64; *WhoThe,* 304–05; *WhStg,* 235–36; *WhThe,* 2:1161).

10. Adele Jason was a singing comedienne, musician, and songwriter who gained considerable recognition beginning in 1916. A Californian, Jason lived near Santa Clara, where she owned a ten-acre fruit ranch. On stage she wore gorgeous gowns, and one of her catchy songs was "Wake Up America." In February 1917 she appeared in South Bend, Ind., in the Winter Garden Revue at the Orpheum. In 1918 she had a principal role in the *All Girl Revue,* a musical comedy composed of twenty-five women. She wrote the music and lyrics for the show as well as for four other, similar productions. In the revue Jason appeared in a minstrel comedy scene as the interlocutor (the master of ceremonies of a traditional minstrel show) with two blackface comediennes as the ends (the two comics, often called Tambo and Bones, who sat at each end of the semi-circle in a minstrel performance and exchanged jokes and comic replies with the interlocutor). The show toured for forty weeks across the country (Locke env. 814, NN-L-RLC).

11. The composer and pianist Burton Green (1874–1922) was the husband of Irene Franklin. While a pianist earning $75 a week at Tony Pastor's, Green met Franklin while she was performing at the theater. It was a turning point in his career. Beginning in 1907 Franklin and Green worked together, with Green playing the piano as Franklin sang. He composed music for her, including the song *Redhead,* which became her stage trademark. During her costume changes he would remain on stage doing solo numbers on the piano. Green and Franklin traveled overseas to entertain the troops during World War I (*NYC,* 22 November 1922, 30; *VO,* 1:24 November 1922).

12. The actor Donald Macdonald (1898–1959) was born in Texas, studied at the American Academy of the Dramatic Arts, and first appeared on stage in summer stock in Ottawa, Canada. His debut on Broadway came in 1913 in *When Dreams Come True.* He appeared in numerous successful productions in New York and London. In the 1920s and 1930s he performed as a supporting actor in films. In the 1950s he appeared on radio and television (*VO,* 5:16 December 1959; *WhoHol,* 2:1024; *WhScrn,* 1:461; *WhoThe,* 819; *WhThe,* 1564).

Clipping from Will Rogers's Scrapbook
ca. 26 July 1915
New York, N.Y.

James Blake Rogers, Will Rogers's second son and third child, was born on 25 July 1915.[1] Rogers was performing in Hands Up *at the time, and several newspapers published accounts of the birth.*

"It's the finest boy in the world, not counting my other children, that's what!" Rogers exclaimed. "I sure am lucky. Every time a baby comes I buy a pony."[2]

WILL ROGERS IS FOND PARENT FOR THE THIRD TIME
Cowboy Dancer Is Rejoicing in a New Son
at His Home in Freeport.

Will Rogers, the cowboy rope artist and dancer, who made such a hit on the opening night of "Hands Up" at the 44th Street Theatre, has another cause for rejoicing. Yesterday he became the father of a boy, the third child in the Rogers family. Mr. Rogers spends his summer at Freeport, and there he has a corral for his family and his horses. Unlike other parents, who put their newly born babes in cradles, Mr. Rogers buys a little pony every time a new child is born, and fixes up a saddle on the pony's back as a cradle for the baby. He believes in administering the open-air treatment to the little ones as soon as they are brought into the world, and every time he has an addition to his family he also adds one more pony to his stock.

PD. Unidentified clipping, ca. 26 July 1915. Scrapbook *Ziegfeld Follies*, CPpR.

1. According to the birth certificate, James Blake (Jim) Rogers was born in Manhattan at 629 Lexington Ave. It was the address of a brownstone, one of many on the street. One block north at 657 Lexington Ave. was the Babies Hospital. Possibly the attending physician, George E. Maurer, M.D., made a mistake in writing the address and Jim Rogers was born at the Babies Hospital, or the alternate address was used for lying-in patients (see State of New York, Certificate and Record of Birth of James Blake Rogers, certificate no. 39778, 29 July 1915, OkClaW; Lorraine Maier Hewins to Reba Collins, 12 July 1988, home file, OkClaW). Betty Blake Rogers's father was James Wyeth Blake (1845–82). See also Biographical Appendix entry, ROGERS, James Blake (Jim).

2. "Will Rogers Proud Papa for Third Time," clipping, scrapbook *Ziegfeld Follies*, CPpR. In another story, entitled "Will Rogers Rejoices," the reporter wrote: "There is every possibility that the stage in the near future will be graced by an act known as Will Rogers and the Several Little Rogers" (scrapbook *Ziegfeld Follies*, CPpR). Rogers put his children up on the saddles of ponies as soon as they were able to sit up, and thus they rode (at a walking pace, with adult assistance) while still in diapers, and before they could walk. He rode with infants in arms before the babies were able to sit, and they were riding on their own by age two. Riding and polo playing were an important part of the Rogers children's youth in New York and California.

Shubert Company Press Release
26 July 1915
New York, N.Y.

Rogers never finished his engagement at the Palace. On Thursday evening, 22 July, he performed at the Palace and in the opening of Hands Up. *When he arrived at the Palace Theatre on Friday afternoon for the matinee performance, the management notified him that his engagement had been canceled and another act had been hired in his place. Rogers's appearance in* Hands Up, *a Shubert production, obviously infuriated the Keith management. The Shubert and Keith organizations constantly fought one another over the former's attempt to enter the vaudeville business.*

Will Rogers, the cowboy dancer, monologist and rope artist, who scored such a tremendous hit at the opening of "Hands Up" at the 44th Street Theatre, on Thursday night, is now entirely out of vaudeville, and will confine his efforts in the future to appearing in "one" in big musical comedy productions, where his work is ideally adapted to "fill in," while a new scene is being set behind the drop in one that he uses.

The hit which Mr. Rogers scored in "Hands Up" was very distasteful to the managers of the Palace Theatre, at which house he was appearing the earlier part of the week, and when he arrived at the Palace Theatre on last Friday afternoon to go on for his act, he was informed by the management that he was not wanted and that another act had been secured to take his place. Mr. Rogers, therefore, gracefully retired to the confines of the 44th Street Theatre and its stage, on which he is nightly scoring as big an individual hit as any artist before the New York public today. He has added an imitation of Fred Stone and his lariat dance from "The Old Town," to his other rope tricks.

Mr. Rogers is not adverse to expressing his thanks to the management of the 44th Street Theatre and the "Hands Up" company, for the chance which he received on Thursday night to become famous over-night. He absolves the management of any blame in shutting the lights off a few seconds too early, and states that it was his own fault, as he had not given the proper music cues, and he is extremely grateful to the Messrs. Shubert and Mr. Harry J. Benrimo,[1] the stage director, who forced him to go before the curtain again and do his tricks over in the Bathing Scene, until he finally scored a victory.[2]

TD. NNSA.

1. Joseph Henry McAlpin (Harry) Benrimo (1874–1942) was an actor and playwright, as well as a stage director and producer. Professionally he was often known simply as Benrimo. He began his career as an actor in San Francisco, at age eighteen, and in 1895 joined Charles Frohman's Empire Theatre Co. As a stock player, Benrimo performed in supporting male roles in Shakespeare plays. Some notable stage appearances throughout his career were in *The Girl of the Golden West* (1905) and *The Great Divide* (1909). In 1912 he co-wrote the successful play *The Yellow Jacket*, which he claimed was based on a classic Chinese drama. He turned to Asian themes again in his 1917 play called *The Willow Tree*, set in Japan. In 1914 he began work as a director for the Shuberts. Throughout the 1920s he produced shows in London and New York (*ABTB*, 94; *NYT*, 27 March 1942; *OCAT*, 73; *OF*, 1:44; *WhThe*, 1:184; *WhoThe*, 298–99).

2. A reference to the incident when the lights went out during Rogers's opening-night act because the management felt his act had gone on too long. As the audience called for his return, the curtain went up on the next scene, a boardwalk bathing scene.

According to some accounts, Benrimo pushed Rogers back on stage when he heard the ovation for Rogers continuing.

Review of *Hands Up*
30 July 1915
New York, N.Y.

With his acerbic pen and perceptive insights, Sime Silverman, the founder and publisher of Variety, *wrote a review that found little to praise in* Hands Up. *Rogers luckily escaped Silverman's condemnation and was declared an "individual hit." Silverman knew a mediocre production when he saw one, and the show lasted only fifty-two performances. After several weeks in October on the road at the Lyric Theatre in Philadelphia, the show closed.*

HANDS UP.

It isn't long after the curtain goes up on this Shubert production at the 44th Street theatre before the majority of the audience believe the title is peculiarly appropriate.

The first act ran two hours Monday night. That's enough to ruin any musical comedy production. But the main whirlpool of the piece is that it appears to have been built for, around and to uplift Maurice and Walton, professional dancers, who look very well on a ballroom floor. They are featured in the billing and on the stage. A titter ran through the house when Maurice tried to take a high note. He and Florence Walton can dance in several styles, but they are not actors, yet, nor will this show make them that—nor singers. If the scheme was to incite comparison between two pairs of dancers, Mr. and Mrs. Castle and Maurice and Florence Walton, one can have a lot of inner pleasure while Maurice and Walton are on the stage, trying to imagine what would happen if the two couples were in the same show. This desire to become performers may be the best evidence the dance craze is wobbling badly.

"Hands Up" is an adapted play, its scheme or theme taken from a picture serial, one scene (and the best laugh maker of the evening, as far as laughs ever got) having been adapted from Conroy and Le Maire's "The Doctor Shop," and another (opening of the second act) being a liberal steal from "High life in Jail," a vaudeville act of some seasons ago. But the "High Life in Jail" thing has been done several times on Broadway since then in one guise or another, so it doesn't matter much. And it's the same about the teeth pulling affair.

Vaudeville in fact has contributed all there is and only what there is worth while in "Hands Up." Irene Franklin, looking prettily girlish, plays a role extremely well and with Burton Green at the piano, captured one of the large hits of the evening whilst singing a few of her songs, the audience compelling her to return for an encore. Will Rogers was another individual hit, with his lariat and talk, also from vaudeville, while Robbins, a Continental musical imitator, not receiving much attention while in vaudeville, did very well at the 44th Street, though misplaced in the running.

Then there was Artie Mehlinger, who can put over a rag and did so, while Bobby North, in blackface (entirely unsuited to him) had to struggle with a couple of rags during the evening, also singing a parody on "I'm Simply Crazy Over You," the musical hit of the score, the parody idea being a neat plan to repeat the melody, first sung straight by Mr. Mehlinger and Alice Dovey.

Ralph Herz was fearfully in wrong as Fake Kennedy, a detective of many silly disguises, even though they were so intended. Miss Dovey had little to do besides looking nice while playing opposite Mehlinger, and Emilie Lea, who certainly can dance in the high kicking way, was held down, as was also her cast partner, Ballard MacDonough. Adele Jason could hardly be detected, were it not for her brown make-up, and George Hassell, a big Englishman, who narrowly escaped making himself up as a red nose comic, was often heavily humorous in action and dialog.

There is nothing in this show for the London revue managers to worry over. The nearest to anything they want is "The Animated Screen" scene (also adapted from "The Telephone Tangle" in vaudeville). It is various sections on a double decked scene, lighted up to reveal different players in melodramatic bits. The only real scene of the production, and about the nearest approach to regular costuming, was the ballroom with the ballet at the finale of the second (and last) act. Just previously some chorus girls had reappeared in the same costumes they wore in a first act number.

Mr. Mehlinger had a good song, for this show, in "The Pirate Rag," the lyric explaining how two song writers had stolen the number from all of the best known rags. There may have been other good songs, but Maurice and Walton were singing several of them.

For looks the Shuberts have the best lot of dressed up homely Broadway chorus girls a $2 show has shown for years.

Edgar Smith wrote the book, E. Ray Goetz, the lyrics, and Mr. Goetz also composed the music, with S. Romberg. Benrimo staged the production and Jack Mason put on the dance ensembles, those that Maurice did not attend to. Of this lot, it can only be said it was a pity to waste the words and music on this show. Nothing in the staging stood out.

The "balloon" thing from "The Midnight Frolic" has been attempted in a crude manner, and this number was repeated for an encore, although there was not a sound from the front of the house after the song proper had concluded. Maurice in "The Best Little Sweethearts of All" had five little kidlets to draw the applause, especially the youngest two, a little blonde and brunet, with a couple of lines each to speak.

The young woman who tells about clothes under "With the Woman" in *Variety* opined Miss Walton's gowns in "Hands Up" should be worth looking at since Lady Duff Gordon designed them. Lady Duff, said she, is the only modiste in America at present who has or displays originality in creation of women's clothes; she is daring in her ideas, and more of that stuff women like. If the clothes worn by Miss Walton are a woman's idea of wonderful gowns, the Lord preserve us. When Miss Walton is not overdressed, her clothes look foolish, with the exception of the gown worn by her in the waltz. Miss Franklin literally "showed up" Miss Walton's million dollar wardrobe, though wearing sweetly simple gowns—that were becoming to her. And Miss Franklin's bathing costume may not have had Lady Duff working overtime on it, but it outprettied Miss Walton's. In fact, for Irene Franklin's debut as an-actress-with-a-part, "Hands Up" was as well built to display her qualifications, other than the singing of good songs, as it was to envelop Maurice and Walton with disaster. As the crowd was walking out the theatre a fellow just ahead, noting a girl who had been sitting in a box during the evening, remarked to the young woman with him: "See, that girl has a dress just like Florence Walton wore. She must be another professional dancer." He was right. She was—from Shanley's.

The book or plot of the piece runs with the rest—it's about a lost ruby Fake Kennedy is looking for, and in the end discovers he stole it himself. Which reminds that early in the performance Monday evening, Mr. Herz, telling how a poisoned arrow had been stopped by a "sterilized coat" worn by him, added, "If I had not worn the coat, I would have been killed and this play ended." A couple of people in front applauded the speech, and one continued the applause until an usher whispered to him.

"Hands Up" is very bad. The light house Monday evening that must have held quite some paper, indicated the big public outside the theatre knew of it. Neither does there seem to be any hope for the piece, although if the "Maurice and Walton" name has any value, this production should be sent on the road.

Sime.

PD. Printed in *Variety*, 30 July 1915.

To Lee Shubert
21 August 1915
New York, N.Y.

Rogers did not stay with Hands Up *during its entire run. Two days after he sent this receipt to Lee Shubert, Rogers made his debut at Florenz Ziegfeld's* Midnight Frolic *cabaret. He needed new material for his nightly appearances there, since many patrons attended regularly. Using more topical humor and jokes about politics from the daily newspapers, Rogers was a hit, and his success led to his engagement in the* Ziegfeld Follies *of 1916.[1]*

August 21, 1915.

RECEIVED from Mr. Lee Shubert, HANDS UP COMPANY, and the SHUBERT THEATRICAL COMPANY, THREE HUNDRED AND FIFTY DOLLARS ($350.00) in full for services rendered and I hereby release all of the above said parties from any and all claims of whatsoever name or nature.

. . .

Will Rogers

TDS, with autograph insertion. 21 August 1915, NNSA.

1. The *Midnight Frolic,* produced by Florenz Ziegfeld, Jr., was the first modern cabaret revue. It opened on 5 January 1915 in the nightclub roof cafe of the elegant New Amsterdam Theatre on Forty-second Street. The rooftop was transformed into an exotic environment by designers, and the *Frolic* was in many ways a form of experimental theater. Its lavish, stylish, stimulating acts featured showgirls and variety acts, with quick costume changes and spectacular set designs by the likes of Joseph Urban. Sophisticated patrons rode the elevator up to the cabaret, where they dined on delicious food and enjoyed cocktails and dancing to a live orchestra. Chorines in costume mingled with the guests on the dance floor and among the tables, dressed in gorgeous evening gowns, scanty outfits, elaborate headdresses, or in zany conceptual outfits, such as switchboards, clocks, or zeppelins, or simply with skirts made of inflated balloons. Book and lyrics for the *Frolic* were largely written by Ziegfeld's righthand man, the songwriter Gene Buck (1885–1957), who also scouted talent for the acts. Buck saw Rogers's comic routine in 1915, probably during Rogers's appearance in *Hands Up* at Broadway's Forty-Fourth Street Theatre, and he believed The Oklahoma Cowboy would make a hit in the *Frolic.* The result was the transition for Rogers from traveling on the vaudeville circuit to being a regular featured performer at home in New York.

Rogers made his debut with the *Frolic* as part of the second edition of the show, called *Just Girls,* which opened on 23 August 1915. He came out each night in his cowboy outfit and delivered a short monologue of jokes along with commentary on current events. A master of timing, he sparked his seemingly casual observations with rope tricks, sometimes using the chorus girls as targets of his lasso much as he had once used Teddy and Buck McKee. To keep his delivery fresh and new, Rogers purchased every edition of each day's New York newspapers and scoured them for material, using the headline news in his act. Ziegfeld was initially doubtful that Rogers's homespun

Broadway Footlights 397

humor would be appropriate amid the glitzy, expensive environment of the *Frolic,* but Rogers was a hit. As Rogers wrote in his gag book, "All these beautiful girls I am the contrast" (Wertheim, *Will Rogers at the Ziegfeld Follies,* 15). Rogers continued to perform with the *Frolic* intermittently between 1916 and 1919, and the show—which Rogers later called "Our world of 'make believe'"—remained highly successful as late-night entertainment until 1921, when Prohibition forced its closing (*LAT,* 25 July 1932). In 1922 Rogers toured with the *Frolic* stage show.

Most significantly for Rogers, his *Frolic* appearances led to a long-term affiliation with the *Follies.* Ziegfeld began the *Follies* as a variety revue featuring burlesque and showgirls in 1907. Starting in 1913, the shows were produced at the New Amsterdam Theatre in the heart of Times Square. The *Follies* proved to be popular entertainment for New Yorkers and out-of-towners, and the shows were produced annually through the 1920s. Like the *Frolic,* the *Follies* banked on adult fantasy, glamor, female sexuality, and spectacle. Rogers made his *Follies* debut in the *Ziegfeld Follies of 1916.* The show had opened on 12 June 1916 in the main auditorium of the New Amsterdam Theatre, but Ziegfeld felt it was overweighted with musical numbers, and he wanted to increase the comedy. Rogers was brought into the cast in July in an effort to remedy the imbalance. He performed in 1916 along with Fanny Brice, W. C. Fields, Ina Claire, Marion Davies, Justine Johnstone, Ann Pennington, and Bert Williams. Critical acclaim for Rogers was immediate, and he soon had star billing. Soon The Oklahoma Cowboy became known as The Cowboy Philosopher. Eddie Cantor joined Rogers, Fields, Williams, and Brice in the *Ziegfeld Follies of 1917,* and by the *Follies of 1918* Rogers, Cantor, Fields, and Williams were the comic mainstays of the show. Rogers was given a full scene in each show for his monologue and also appeared in comic sketches with other headliners. Rogers also starred in the *Follies* of 1922 and 1924, and in the following year he reunited with Fields in the *Follies of 1925.* That *Follies* show proved to be Rogers's swan song with the Ziegfeld enterprise. After he left it, he embarked on a nationwide lecture tour as a celebrity.

From that point on, Rogers concentrated on his journalism, radio, and film careers, but he occasionally made forays onto the stage in a tribute to his vaudeville and *Follies* beginnings. He had begun performing on radio and writing a weekly column for the McNaught Syndicate in 1922. The column and daily telegrams were syndicated in 1926, and carried by over five hundred newspapers nationwide. Rogers made his first silent film, *Laughing Bill Hyde,* in 1918 and moved to southern California to work for Samuel Goldwyn in Hollywood in 1919. He acted in two-reel comedies for Hal Roach in the summer of 1923, missing that year's *Follies.* In the latter part of the 1920s he appeared–without pay and for fun–in the *Cochran Revue of 1926* in London in July, and in December 1928 he filled in for the injured Fred Stone in the musical comedy *Three Cheers,* with Dorothy Stone. He appeared in Eugene O'Neill's *Ah, Wilderness!* in California in the spring of 1934. Building on the lampooning monologue style perfected in his vaudeville routines and his *Follies* appearances, he drew huge popular audiences with his radio talks in the early 1930s, most notably the Gulf Oil broadcasts made between 1933 and 1935. The *Follies,* meanwhile, were eclipsed by the movie industry, and the shows faded with the close of the Roaring Twenties, when Ziegfeld lost his fortune with the collapse of the stock market.

The trail that for Rogers began in Indian Territory, and wound through vaudeville and Broadway, ended in Hollywood. In the last six years of his life, from 1929 to 1935, Rogers starred in twenty-one films for the Fox Film Corporation. At the time of his death in a plane crash near Point Barrow, Alaska, on 15 August 1935, Rogers was the highest paid movie star in the United States. His love for his wife Betty Blake Rogers had proved to be steadfast and enduring. He was survived by her and their three remaining children.

In a eulogy for Ziegfeld prepared for the showman's funeral service in 1932, Rogers mused about what human beings know of divinity, and the relation of godliness to a show-business career. "Our profession of acting must be honorable and it must be necessary for it exists in every language and every race," he observed in his notes. "It's as old as life itself. Amusement must be necessary, for it's given to babes and children to laugh and to play. . . . In our life the curtain plays a great part, the curtain either rises or falls" (Notes for Tribute at Florenz Ziegfeld's Private Funeral Service," OkClaW; Wertheim, *Will Rogers at the Ziegfeld Follies*).

Biographical Appendix

Name Index

THE FOLLOWING INDIVIDUALS ARE PROFILED IN THE BIOGRAPHICAL APPENDIX.

Biographical Entries

The following alphabetical entries feature profiles of individuals named in this volume who were of particular significance to Rogers's family or career. For profiles of other persons significant to Rogers's personal life or career who appear in the documents in this volume but are not part of this volume's appendix, see also the appendices in other volumes of The Papers of Will Rogers.

BLAKE SIBLINGS. Betty Blake (1879–1944), daughter of James Wyeth Blake (1845–82) and Amelia J. Crowder (1845–1922), had eight siblings: John (1867–89); Cora (b. 1869); Anna (1871–1977?); Waite (1873–1976?); Theda (1875–1966); James, better known as Sandy (1877–1953); Virginia (1881–1975); and Zulika (1885–1929), a half-sister (daughter of Amelia Crowder and J. O. Boyd).

While Betty Blake was a child the Blake family lived in a small log and wood-frame house in Silver Springs, Arkansas, where her father, James Blake, operated a sawmill and gristmill. In 1882, at the age of thirty-seven, James Blake died, and the family moved from their home in Silver Springs to nearby Rogers, Arkansas. To make ends meet, Amelia Blake became a seamstress and her children began working for pay at early ages.

The family was prominent in Benton County affairs and was descended from Arkansas pioneers. The Blake family resided at 307 East Walnut Street in Rogers, a large, two-story white house. It was the site of considerable social activity. Betty Blake and Will Rogers held their wedding there, and Betty would often stay there with her children when her husband was performing in vaudeville. The Blake family attended the Congregational church. The Blake girls were locally renowned for their charm, gaiety, and accomplishments. As children, the girls performed in local plays and belonged to social groups such as the Plungers. The girls spent time with the Coin Harvey family, which included two handsome sons, in nearby Monte Ne, formerly Silver Springs, which Coin Harvey developed as a utopian resort. Betty Blake dated young Tom Harvey, and Zulika was Hal Harvey's favorite. Will Rogers was known to be jealous of Tom Harvey during his courtship of Betty.

Some of the Blake girls and their husbands worked for the railroad. The town of Rogers was founded in 1881 as a railroad town on the St. Louis and San Francisco (Frisco) railway line. It was named for Charles W. Rogers, vice president and general manager of the Frisco railroad (see *PWR*, 1:187n.2).

Born on 29 August 1867, John Blake was named for his uncle John Blake. He was a brakeman for the Frisco Railway Co. and died on 6 August 1889 as a result of a railroad accident at Purdy, Missouri. He was buried in Bentonville, Arkansas.

Cora Blake was born on 18 August 1869. She married Will Marshall, who worked for the railroad as a telegraph operator in Fort Gibson, Indian Territory. In 1900 she and her husband lived in Oolagah, Indian Territory, in three rooms in the train depot where Marshall was the railroad station agent. In the fall of 1900 Betty Blake stayed with them while recuperating from typhoid fever. One evening she was in the railroad station when Will Rogers arrived in town. She was at the ticket window when Rogers approached. "I looked at him and he looked at me, and before I could even ask his business, he turned on his heel and was gone without so much as saying a word," she wrote (Rogers, *Will Rogers*, 14). This was their first encounter. In 1922 the Marshalls were living in Lubbock, Texas. They had a daughter named Maxine who married and also lived in Lubbock.

Born on 23 August 1871, Anna Blake was a railroad telegraph operator in her youth as well as a clerk at Park's Dry Goods store. As a girl, Anna won a contest as the most graceful lady bicycle rider in Rogers. (Her sister Betty was also a contestant.) On 12 April 1899 she married Lee Adamson of Rogers; the wedding reception was held in the Blake home. At the time of their marriage Adamson was foreman of the construction workers on the Frisco railroad. He was also head of the railroad bridge crew in Rogers, and in March 1899 operated the wagon-spoke lathe at the town's new hub-and-spoke factory. Their first child died in infancy in 1900. In 1922 they were living in Dallas, Texas, and later they moved to Los Angeles, California. Adamson was the foreman on the Rogerses' Pacific Palisades ranch project when it was built and also laid out the roads there (see Telegram from L. H. Adamson, 18 May 1913, above). A skilled engineer, he executed the designs of the property that Rogers had drawn. Anna and Lee Adamson's son Richard worked with Betty Blake Rogers on her book *Will Rogers*.

Born on 9 February 1873, Waite or Waitie Blake (a daughter) was presumably named for General Stand Watie, principal chief of the Confederate Cherokees, under whom James Wyeth Blake had fought at the battle of Pea Ridge, Arkansas. (Will Rogers's father, Clement Vann Rogers, also served in

Watie's Regiment of Cherokee Mounted Rifles [see *PWR*, 1:47–48n.7, 538].)
Waite Blake married Arthur Ireland, a Frisco railroad car worker and mail
clerk, who was once stationed in Monett, Missouri. They moved to Los
Angeles. As caretaker on the Rogers Ranch, Ireland oversaw the avocado
orchard, cherimoya trees, and the vegetable garden. The Irelands had one son,
James Ireland (d. 1976).

Born on 19 January 1875, Theda Blake was named for her Aunt Theda
Crowder. Of all the sisters, she was considered the bulwark of the family. She
went by the nickname of Dick. She graduated from Rogers Academy in 1895
and worked as a public school teacher from 1896 to 1901. She also worked as
a sales clerk for the Stroud Mercantile Co. store in Rogers. She was a member of the Mas Luz Club, a literary club. In 1904 it was reorganized as a
women's study club. She helped found the Rogers Public Library and was
recording secretary for the Women's Progressive Club in 1920. She regularly
visited Will and Betty Blake Rogers when they lived in New York City and on
Long Island between 1911 and 1918. (Indeed, the Rogerses hosted other sisters and Betty's mother as well.) In 1931 she took a trip around the world. She
never married. Around 1922 she moved to Los Angeles, where she lived with
the Rogers family for many years, helping to raise the children, who adored
her. She accompanied the children on trips, as in the summer of 1932, when
she and Mary Rogers toured Europe together. Theda Blake also resided with
Mary Rogers when she was performing at a summer stock theater in
Skowhegan, Maine. She died in Beverly Hills in 1966. Betty Blake Rogers
dedicated her book *Will Rogers* to Theda Blake, her children's favorite Aunt
Dick.

Born on 14 February 1877, James K. (Sandy) Blake worked first as a
delivery boy for F. Z. Meeks grocery. He became a railroad agent at Nowata,
Indian Territory, and Jenny Lind, Arkansas. In 1903 he was transferred to Fort
Gibson, Indian Territory. In 1910 he married Josephine Meggs, and they had
a daughter named Ann. In 1922 the family was living in Fort Gibson,
Oklahoma, where Sandy Blake continued to work with the railroad. Later,
they moved to Beverly Hills, California, where Sandy Blake managed Will
Rogers's business and family affairs. Sandy and Josephine Blake were partic-
ularly helpful to Betty Blake Rogers after her husband died. Their daughter
Ann married a Mr. Campbell and lived in Houston, Tex. Sandy Blake died on
27 November 1952, after several years of ill heath.

Born on 16 August 1881, Virginia Blake graduated from the Rogers
Academy in 1899. She married B. W. Quisenberry, a local druggist. They
moved to Joplin, Missouri, in 1923, where her husband continued his drug

business. They had a daughter, Dixie Quisenberry, and two sons, Billy and Bruce. Dixie married a Mr. Evans and lived in Joplin. Bruce Quisenberry was a graduate of Rogers High School in 1922 and president of his class. After graduation, he studied law. In 1925 he went on a sixty-day Mediterranean cruise with his thirteen-year-old cousin, Will Rogers, Jr. In the mid-1920s, Bruce assisted Rogers in organizing his lecture tours and managed the day-to-day operations of the trips. He accompanied Rogers at each lecture stop. During a 1927 tour to raise money for victims of the Mississippi River flood, the two men spent seventy-five straight nights sleeping in a Pullman compartment; Rogers had the lower bunk, and Quisenberry the upper bunk. Later, Bruce moved to Chicago. Billy Quisenberry became a colonel in the U.S. Army. Virginia Quisenberry died in 1975.

Born on 28 November 1885, Zulika (or Zuleki) Blake was the daughter of Amelia Crowder Blake and I. O. Boyd, whom Amelia Blake married after the death of James Wyeth Blake in 1882. It was a short-lived marriage, and afterward Boyd left for Texas. Zulika was consequently raised as one of the Blake siblings and assumed the family name. In 1902 she attended the Rogers Academy and played on the school's first women's basketball team. In 1907 Zulika Blake married Everett Stroud (ca. 1884–1929), son of J. W. Stroud, a prominent Rogers merchant. Everett Stroud was killed in a hunting accident near Rogers in 1929. Zulika Blake and her family moved· to southern California in 1927. Her daughter Amelia (b. 1907) married Roger Dillingham on the patio of the Rogers Ranch. Amelia's second husband was Robert E. Steward, and they lived in San Clemente, California. Zulika and Theda Blake assisted Betty Blake Rogers when she opened the living room of the Rogers Ranch home for the benefit of the Red Cross and the Salvation Army during World War II. Zulika Blake Stroud died in 1969 (Betty Blake biographical material, RHM; Snelling, "One of the Blake Girls"; Sandmeier, "To the Docents [of] Will Rogers State Historical Park"; *WRFT*, 135).

BROOKS, Mary Amelia Rogers (1913–89). Movie and stage actress and second child of Will and Betty Blake Rogers, Mary Amelia Rogers was born in Rogers, Arkansas, on 18 May 1913. On that date her father was performing in vaudeville at the Majestic Theatre in Houston, Texas. Rogers got the news of the baby's birth via telegram (see Telegram from L. H. Adamson, 18 May 1913, above).

Mary Amelia Rogers was given her first name in honor of Will Rogers's mother, Mary America Schrimsher Rogers (1839–90); her middle name derived from Betty Blake Rogers's mother, Amelia Crowder Blake

(1845–1922). Mary Rogers spent her early years on Long Island, New York, where the Rogers family mainly lived until 1919. After Will Rogers signed with the Samuel Goldwyn studios, the Rogers family moved west and lived in several homes in the Los Angeles area. Mary Rogers's childhood in Beverly Hills and on the family ranch in Pacific Palisades had all the advantages the daughter of a movie star could expect. From attending a movie opening where she met Charlie Chaplin, Douglas Fairbanks, and Joan Crawford, to trips to Europe and a brief courtship by Howard Hughes, Mary Rogers lived a Hollywood childhood. She eventually followed in her father's footsteps and pursued an acting career both on the stage and in the movies.

Mary Rogers grew up, like her siblings, learning (at the age of two) how to ride Dopey, the family horse. As a girl she performed at horse shows with her family and at the Los Angeles National Horse Show, sitting astride her two brothers as they stood on their father's shoulders. Will Rogers, though somewhat of a workaholic and always on the go, always seemed to find time for his family. In August 1926, for example, Mary and her brother Jim, accompanied by Helen Maddy, a friend of the family, sailed to England to meet their father, who was performing in the *Cochran Revue* in London. Mary Rogers, who was then thirteen, kept a diary of her trip in which she wrote: "Daddy was waiting for us at the hotel. (We stopped at the Savoy hotel.) We were surely glad to see Daddy and he to see us. We then went up to our rooms and Daddy went to the theater because he had to go on in about twenty minutes. Daddy came back in about an hour and then we went down to dinner" ("My Trip Abroad, Mary's Diary, S.S. *Leviathan*, 1926," OkClaW). Will Rogers accompanied his wife and children to Hampton Court and Windsor Castle, and the family had dinner at the Cheshire Cheese. Mary went to see him in the *Cochran Revue*. "It was fair but Daddy was wonderful!" she wrote.

Mary Rogers and her father enjoyed a close relationship. In many ways, she was his favorite child. On her nineteenth birthday Will Rogers wrote: "You have ben a Dandy fine Girl, Sometimes we old one's dont see eye to eye with you Kids. But its us that dont stop to see your modern Viewpoint. Times change. But Human Nature dont, you are your Mama in a 1932 setting" (Will Rogers to "My Dear Daughter," undated [ca. 18 May 1932], OkClaW).

As she grew older, rather than pursue her father's equestrian interests, Mary Rogers turned her attention to a career in the theater. She attended the Beverly Hills Hotel School in 1927 and later the Marlborough School in Los Angeles. During the summer of 1932 she toured Europe with her favorite aunt, Theda Blake, known as Aunt Dick. After her tour she went to Sarah Lawrence College in Bronxville, New York, where she studied drama and music. She chose Sarah Lawrence, she said, "because it is so good musically and because it is near New York. I can go to school and have New York, too, with its concerts and theatres. . . . I don't know what I'll study except music. . . . Sometimes I think I want to go on the stage" (*New York World-Telegram*, 26 September 1932, NNMoMa-FC).

Mary Rogers attended college in 1932–33 for one year and returned to California to start her acting career. She felt that one year at college was enough. "If I'm going to do anything why put it off another year," she wrote her father from college (Mary Rogers to "Daddy dearest," postmarked 23 January 1933, OkClaW). According to press accounts at the time, she approached the Fox Movietone City studio and director David Butler for a supporting part in the movie, *My Weakness*. Not wanting to use her father's influence, she assumed the name Mary Howard and secured the part on her own merit. Will Rogers biographer Ben Yagoda states that Fox producer Winnie Sheehan suggested the part for Mary Rogers.

Within a few months after her initial success, Mary Rogers tested for the female lead in her father's new movie, *There's Always Tomorrow*. She failed to get the part. "The part is bigger than the usual girl's part in my pictures," Will Rogers said, "and Mary hadn't had enough experience. I didn't think so and she didn't either" ("'Nope, Mary's Not Quitting'—Will Rogers," unidentified clipping, 16 September 1933, Hearst Clippings File, CLSU). Mary Rogers subsequently turned to the stage and toured Canada in the spring of 1934 in Robert Sherwood's play, *Reunion in Vienna*. Her father was very supportive of her acting career. He encouraged her to keep at it even if it was difficult. "Now dont you worry, stay with em, and give em a little longer battle, you stick around there," he wrote. "Being and [an] actor, or actress' or being anything, is not just what its cracked up to be, you are going to get it on the chin time after time, and you would get it in any other 'racket', and I think you are pretty [']game' and I am proud of you" (Will Rogers to "Meme" [Mary Rogers], undated [ca. 1934], OkClaW).

In the summer of 1934 Mary Rogers joined a summer stock company, the Lakewood Players in Skowhegan, Maine, for the first of two seasons. Her father had encouraged her to try summer stock. "Now a stock company in one of those New England towns would be just the thing," Will Rogers wrote. "You see they play different parts every week, and sometimes you might get right good little parts, all depending on your ability, if you just went to New York and maby got in one show you might just have one or two little bits that you would have to do all summer. But its stock where you get the real training, hard work different show every week, not too large a town, great memory and acting training. You want a year of that, before you even start to tackle a New York even small part. Acting is experience, its not learned in a day" (Will Rogers to "My Dear Mary," undated [ca. January 1933], OkClaW).

In January 1935 Mary Rogers was performing at the National Theatre in Washington, D.C. Rogers wired her: "YOU GOT YOU OLD DADS GOOD WISHES SURE YOU ARE NERVOUS ALL GOOD ACTORS ARE NERVOUS" (telegram to Miss Mary Rogers, 14 January 1935, OkClaW). The following month Mary Rogers appeared on Broadway in a comedy called *On to Fortune*. She returned to Skowhegan the next summer and performed in a wide variety of plays, including Dorrance Davis's comedy *Apron Strings*, L. Lawrence Wever's musical farce *Little Jessie James,* and Eugene O'Neill's *Beyond the Horizon,* in which she played the part of Ruth. Afterward, Mary Rogers hoped she could "land a good part—then I can go out in the sails of that and get a better salary—writing my own ticket . . . in New York" (Mary Rogers to Will Rogers, Jr., ca. 1935, OkClaW).

Mary Rogers had made remarkable strides in her acting career when, in August 1935, she received the news of her father's death. She had just opened in a play, *Ceiling Zero,* with Humphrey Bogart, at the Skowhegan summer stock theater in Maine. She was playing the role, ironically, of a girl whose father dies in a plane crash. Her father had wanted to see her perform and he wired her: "I WILL BE UP TO SEE YOU BUT NOT TILL THE SNOW STARTS MELTING" (telegram to Miss Mary Rogers, 1 June 1935, OkClaW).

Rogers cabled his daughter again on 15 August 1935, the day his plane crashed at Point Barrow, Alaska, killing him and Wiley Post: "GREAT TRIP WISH YOU ALL WERE ALONG, HOWS YOUR ACTING, YOU AND MAMA WIRE ME ALL THE NEWS TO NOME. GOING TO POINT BARROW TODAY FURTHEREST POINT OF LAND NORTH ON WHOLE AMERICAN CONTINENT. LOTS OF LOVE, DONT WORRY. DAD" (telegram to Miss Mary Rogers, 15 August 1935, OkClaW). Humphrey Bogart heard the news that Rogers had been killed over the telephone from Alaska and rushed to the cottage where Mary Rogers and her mother were staying. Mary was not there, but Bogart broke the sad news to Betty Blake Rogers, who "doubled up for a minute as though I'd hit her." "Then she straightened up," recalled Bogart, and said, "'well, there's a lot of work to be done'." After Betty Blake Rogers told her daughter about the accident, "Mary seemed stunned," and all her companions could do after that was to "pat Mary on the shoulder and mumble our sorrow" (Bill Blowitz, "Notes from Humphrey Bogart," HCP-MoU). Mary Rogers immediately left the cast of the play, which had been open only one day.

After her father's death, Mary Rogers continued for a time to establish a career as an actress. She performed on stage and in November 1936 signed a long-term contract with Twentieth Century-Fox Film Corporation. Her acting career, however, came to an end shortly thereafter. "I decided," she wrote many years later, "I really didn't want to be an actress" (Mary Rogers to Mrs. [Reba] Collins, 1 February 1979, OkClaW). The shock of her father's death overwhelmed her, and she never completely recovered from the loss. When the family donated the Pacific Palisades ranch to the state of California, Mary Rogers "felt homeless and adrift" (Collins, "Will Rogers' Daughter Mary," 10). In January 1937 Twentieth Century-Fox granted her a leave of absence from her contract obligations. She never acted again.

Mary Rogers's married life was as evanescent as her acting career. In 1944 she announced her engagement to Victor Courtrier, Jr., a writer with RKO studios. Courtrier had earlier suffered a debilitating injury during World War II that left him an invalid. The marriage never took place. Six years later, on 28 September 1950, Rogers married Walter Brooks III. Brooks, heir to a banking fortune, was the grandson of Philadelphia society matron Mrs. E. T. Stotesbury. He was the son of Walter and Louise Cromwell Brooks; his mother later married General Douglas MacArthur.

Mary Rogers and Walter Brooks's courtship was apparently a precarious one, even, at least at one point, violent. A month before their wedding, Mary Rogers had her future husband arrested for hitting her during an argument. Their marriage lasted less than two years. In March 1952 Mary Rogers testified in divorce proceedings about her husband's excessive drinking and belligerence. She never remarried.

No longer working in the theater and no longer married, Mary Rogers spent most of the rest of her life abroad. She became part of the so-called jet set and lived at various times in Mexico, Italy, Spain, Morocco, and Greece. "I love to travel," she wrote in 1979, "and I speak several languages. I have been studying painting and writing poetry. My painting and poetry is not for commercial reasons but just for my own personal satisfaction and feeling of accomplishment. I am also a collector of antiques" (Mary Rogers to Mrs. [Reba] Collins, 1 February 1979, OkClaW). Interested in her business affairs, she spent much time also looking after her investments.

During the last years of her life Mary Rogers lived in an apartment in Los Angeles. She became ill with ovarian cancer and underwent surgery several times. She died on 13 December 1989 at St. John's Hospital in Santa Monica, California. She is interred beside her parents in the family sarcophagus at the Will Rogers Memorial in Claremore, Oklahoma (Collins, "Will Rogers' Daughter Mary," 10; Mary Rogers biographical clippings, CBevA, NNMoMa-FC, PP; Mary Rogers, Hearst Clippings File, CLSU; "Society,"

Rob Wagner's Beverly Hills Script, 15 June 1929, 26; Yagoda, *Will Rogers*, 149, 273, 314, 334).

BYERS, Chester (1892–1945). A well-known lariat artist, Chester Byers gained fame for his dexterity in trick and fancy rope spinning. He was born in Knoxville, Illinois, and moved to Mulhall, Oklahoma, at age three. This was where the Wild West showman Zack Mulhall lived, so it is perhaps natural that Byers decided to become a cowboy. Will Rogers, who was often in Mulhall, supposedly gave Byers lessons in roping. In 1905 the teenage Byers got a job as a roper with Pawnee Bill's show. However, he became ill and could not perform. Later that same year he joined a Buffalo chase organized by Zack Mulhall at the 101 Ranch. In 1907 he was a member of Lucille Mulhall's troupe in a show called Lucille Mulhall's Congress of Rough Riders. The following year he joined Pawnee Bill's show. Afterward, he traveled to California and joined a show at Lucky Baldwin's ranch in Los Angeles. In the city he met Fred Stone, who invited him to spend eight weeks improving Stone's roping technique. Soon after he joined the 101 Ranch Show. In 1914 he went to England with the show for the Anglo-American Exposition at Shepherd's Bush, London. Byers was the show's star roper; others included Guy Weadick and his wife Florence LaDue. Byers remained with the Miller Brothers' 101 Ranch until 1919. At the New York Stampede in 1916 he won the world championship in trick and fancy roping. After 1919 Byers decided to perform on his own rather than as part of a show. In the course of his career he traveled several times across the country performing in shows, as well as participating in events in South America and in England.

In 1928 Byers published the book *Roping: Trick and Fancy Rope Spinning*. Will Rogers wrote the foreword with tongue-in-cheek humor: "I doubt if the book will be any good, for it's on a subject. And all the books I ever read on subjects were written by men that dident know anything about the subject. . . . I would have had more confidence in it if he had picked out something he dident know anything about. Now Chet knows ropes, and Chet knows Roping, so it is liable to be awful uninteresting, and be contradicted by the 109 million that dont know roping. So Chet shows he dont know nothing about Authoring right there" (Byers, *Roping*, iv). Fred Stone also included a short introductory note, accompanied by four photographs of him roping. Elsie Janis, the vaudeville headliner, comic singer, and impersonator, contributed three pages on roping as well. "Don't expect to do Will Rogers' act the first week," she advised (Byers, *Roping*, xiv–xv). Byers's volume discusses how to perform a variety of lariat tricks, gives some biographical information, and provides a short review of the history of roping. Chapters deal with flat loops, vertical loops, stunts, and jumping in and out of a loop while it is spinning. Rogers is included among the list of male trick and fancy ropers, along with Vincente Oropeza, Guy Weadick, Jack Joyce, and many others. Byers's book is a classic on the art of roping.

In 1931 Rogers helped organize a tour to raise money for poor and unemployed people in Texas and Oklahoma devastated by the Great Depression and the Dust Bowl that swept the Southwest. The charity benefits were one-night stands at various Texas cities. Among the performers Rogers enlisted for the project was Chester Byers, who entertained with his lariat tricks. Considered among the best ropers of his time, Byers was elected to the National Cowboy Hall of Fame in Oklahoma City in 1969 (Byers, *Roping*; Clancy, *My Fifty Years in Rodeo*, 61; *TDW*, 15 and 22 February 1931; Porter, *Who's Who in Rodeo*, 36–37; Russell, *Wild West*, 83–94).

CANTOR, Eddie (1892–1964). Eddie Cantor was born Isadore Iskowitch, the son of Russian Jewish immigrant parents who lived on New York City's Lower East Side. Cantor's parents died when he was two, and he was raised by his maternal grandmother, Esther Kantowitz, who was sixty-two at the time she took him in. She was a hard-working woman who was seldom home, working long hours at several poorly paid jobs. At the age of fifteen, Cantor appeared in vaudeville as part of a song-and-dance team. He used the shortened, anglicized version of his grandmother's name at that time, having been enrolled in elementary school under the name Kantor.

As a child, Cantor received a near fatal blow to the forehead, which left a deep scar. Years later he whimsically wrote that such a scar might be "a stamp of eternal sadness," which the comedian always wears beneath his mask of makeup (Cantor, *My Life Is in Your Hands*, 20). Later he wrote: "Any wonder I used to hang myself from the street lamps to make kids laugh? We *had* to laugh to keep from crying, there was such poverty, such misery and disease. All the things that weren't good, we had" (Cantor, *Take My Life*, 13). For Cantor and many other talented children growing up on the Lower East Side, show business was a road out of the Jewish ghetto, a way to make money and join the American mainstream.

At the age of eight, Cantor entered a contest sponsored by the *New York Evening Journal* that offered a prize for the best letter to Santa Claus. Cantor wrote: "Dear Santa, I'm an orphan. . . . I live with my grandmother who is very poor. I have no warm clothes. I would like a pair of rubber boots, an overcoat, and a sled. That is all I want for Christmas" (Cantor, *Take My Life*, 14).

Cantor found companionship with older boys on the city's streets while he learned the latest songs. Life on the streets gave him ample opportunity to pick up the accents and mannerisms of the Lower East Side inhabitants. From the vendors in the Italian quarter, from the East European serving girls, and from his own Jewish community, Cantor learned and perfected accents and dialects. Later, as a mature performer, he performed a selection of well-known comedic songs with Jewish themes. He also became known for Jewish jokes. For example, he told a story about a Jewish aviator who could not cross the Atlantic like Lindbergh because he couldn't eat ham sandwiches as Lindbergh had done. Cantor also adopted blackface at times. His use of Jewish humor was based on the feeling that ethnic groups could live comfortably with their "otherness," and that the peculiarities of cultures, including his own, were fair game for laughter. He once stated: "When this kind of harmless humor was barred, it took half the fun out of show business" (*EV*, 84).

As a youth, Cantor was sent to a summer camp financed by the local welfare office. Located away from the city's bustle, Surprise Lake Camp was a paradise to him and his Lower East Side friends. Cantor was determined to stay on for more than a week and devised a scheme of performing recitals, songs, and dancing routines at the Saturday-night festivities. His hope was that the directors would keep him at the camp on the strength of his talent as an entertainer. One summer, he was able to stay on for seven weeks. When he grew up he became an active supporter of this camp, which was eventually named the Eddie Cantor Camp.

Back home on the city streets, Cantor returned to his usual routines of occasional public school attendance, petty theft of food from vendors and markets, girl chasing, and nighttime revelries with local gangs of boys. Cantor was lured by the culture of the street, and the attraction was intensified by the lack of structure in his home life. Drifting, often hungry, Cantor was humiliated by friends who refused to buy him a meal. In 1908 he appeared at an amateur night at Miner's Bowery Theatre for a dollar. His act was an unqualified success, and Cantor even won the manager's grand prize of a five-dollar bill.

Cantor had found his métier, and all that remained was for the world to discover it too. Driven by his budding ambition, and needing a way to support himself, he went to work as a singing waiter at Coney Island. There he had to know every song a customer would request, and frequently had to make up a rendition that would sufficiently amuse the customers. The pianist was Jimmy Durante, a versatile performer of whom Cantor wrote: "With him at the piano I could have shouted, 'Encyclopedia Britannica!' and he'd have said, 'O.K!' and set a tune to that too" (Cantor, *My Life Is in Your Hands*, 100).

After a series of minor performing jobs, Cantor appeared in Gus Edwards's Kid Kabaret. The opportunity to join Edwards's troupe of child performers was Cantor's first real break. Edwards was a successful songwriter who specialized in producing children's vaudeville shows. Kid Kabaret was a first-class vaudeville act involving a number of youngsters who went on to make big names on the stage. Among them was George Jessel, who became a lifelong friend of Cantor's.

While playing for Edwards on the Orpheum Circuit, Cantor met Will Rogers, a man he idolized from the start. Cantor's first encounter with Rogers was in 1913 in Winnipeg, Canada. Cantor later remembered the meeting with a great deal of feeling. He wrote: "Twenty-eight years ago, I met an actor whose friendship is one of the most cherished memories of my life. . . . We, of the Gus Edwards troupe, would stand behind the wings and watch this tall, unknown Westerner, who was always grinning and chewing gum, do the most astounding rope tricks with very little effort. Such was my first glimpse of the Great American. . . . He was the finest man I've ever known" (Cantor, statement attached to photograph of Rogers roping Cantor on the Orpheum Circuit, 13 June 1940, OkClaW). On the Orpheum tour Rogers supposedly suggested to Cantor to tone down his act and make it more subtle. Others believe that Rogers recommended Eddie Cantor to Florenz Ziegfeld for a role in his *Follies*.

Some insight into Cantor's worship of Will Rogers may be drawn from a story Cantor told about his first performance on stage at an amateur event. Cantor winced when his name was announced as "Edward Cantor." While the name was far more mainstream than his birth name, Cantor apparently felt that it still was not American enough. He wrote: "There was a loud derisive laugh from the audience. . . . Any man whose name wasn't John, Jim, or Harry had no right to live" (Cantor, *My Life Is in Your Hands*, 81). Cantor's desire to conceal his Jewishness and to Americanize himself explains his avid interest in Will Rogers both as a person and as a symbol of America. Cantor once described Rogers as "Mr. American Citizen himself" (Cantor, *Take My Life*, 115).

Both Cantor and Rogers participated in the *Ziegfeld Follies* of 1917 and 1918, and it was during this time that they became good friends. Rogers, Cantor, and W. C. Fields were the three leading comedians of the *Follies*, and everyone from Ziegfeld to fellow cast members recognized how closely they were bonded. Remembering those days in 1956, twenty-one years after Rogers's death, Cantor wrote: "Will Rogers, W. C. Fields and I were such pals, the rest of the company referred to us as 'The Three Musketeers.' It reached a point where we were ready to 'lay down our laughs' for one another (the acid test for comedians)" (Cantor, "Durable Quips of Will Rogers," clipping [ca. 1956], personality file, PP).

Cantor wrote several books about his years in show business, and memories of Rogers figure prominently in these memoirs. Rogers wrote the foreword, entitled "Warnings," to Cantor's 1928 autobiography, *My Life Is in Your Hands*. "When I first met Eddie," Rogers wrote, "neither of us knew whether Ziegfeld had a "Follies" or whether he was maby a Livery stable keeper. I liked him as a kid, right from the start. . . . There is a lot of sentiment about Eddie, and a lot of fine qualities" (*My Life Is in Your Hands*, xii–xiii).

Prior to his friendship with Rogers, Cantor's sole ambition was to be rich and famous. It was Rogers who taught him to take "pride in being a working member of the United States of America" (Cantor, *Take My Life*, 104). Rogers probably inspired Cantor to devote himself to humanitarian efforts after his retirement from the stage. Cantor wrote: "Rogers was my grammar school, high school, and college. He taught me that the world doesn't end at the stage door and that politics are every man's business, actors not excluded. He kept on giving me an education as long as he lived; and since his death his writings are still my source book" (Cantor, *Take My Life*, 104–5).

Rogers was interested in Cantor's Jewish background and often accompanied him to kosher restaurants while they were on the road. On one occasion Rogers was the toastmaster at a Friars Club event to "roast" Cantor, and he delivered his talk imitating Cantor's "Yiddish" inflections. Rogers described Cantor as "a little boy in de Gus Edwards act, a little skiny Jew, vas he funny, vas he pop eyed? He black 'em up de face and he jump around so fast de audience couldn't hit him. . . . And I see him in de big fine pictures, vot fun, and I hear him over de radio, and ven he sing, 'One Hour Vit You,' and finish, I turn off the radio and I am happy, and I feel so happy. It's my little Jewish friend" (Rogers, "Speech at Dinner for Eddie Cantor," typed manuscript, OkClaW).

Cantor's appearance in the *Ziegfeld Follies* was the turning point of his career. Although Cantor and Ziegfeld argued over the former's participation in the 1919 Actors' Equity strike, their differences were resolved, and Cantor starred on stage in Ziegfeld's *Kid Boots* (1923) and *Whoopee!* (1928), both Broadway successes. Cantor began his film career in 1926 and made a film version of *Whoopee!* in 1930, by which time he was earning half a million dollars a year in films. Most of his films were musical comedies made for Samuel Goldwyn. In 1953 Cantor's life story was made into the film *The Eddie Cantor Story*.

Cantor began his successful radio career in 1931 with an appearance in Rudy Vallee's *Fleischmann Hour*. Later that year he starred on *The Chase and Sanborn Hour*, and made it one of the most popular shows of the early 1930s. On that program, Cantor urged his studio audiences to cheer and applaud loudly, rather than maintaining a strict silence as studio audiences had in the past. In 1944 Cantor raised $40 million for war bonds during a twenty-four-hour radio marathon. When Cantor's radio career ended in 1949, he began working in television, but was stricken with a heart attack from which he never completely recovered.

Cantor enjoyed tremendous popularity, particularly in his later career; he was known as a humanitarian as well as a favorite performer. He helped create the March of Dimes and took a vital interest in Jewish affairs. In 1964, just before Cantor died, President Lyndon B. Johnson awarded him the U.S. Service Medal for his humanitarian efforts (Cantor, *My Life Is in Your Hands*, 15–23, 34–37, 77–88, 99–101, 129–35; Cantor, *Take My Life*, 13–14, 104–5, 115; *DAB*, suppl. 7:106; Dunning, *Tune In Yesterday*, 179; *EV*, 83–86; Howe, *World of Our Fathers*, 404; Slide, *Vaudevillians*, 23; Wertheim, ed., *Will Rogers at the Ziegfeld Follies*, 175–91; Ziegfeld and Ziegfeld, *Ziegfeld Touch*, 289).

CASEY, Pat (1875–1962). Born in Springfield, Massachusetts, Pat Casey was a well-known talent agent, theater executive, and labor negotiator. Casey was one of Will Rogers's agents during his vaudeville years. At age fifteen he began work selling peanuts and candy at baseball games. Later he became assistant manager of a twenty-wagon traveling circus called Tucker's Giant Shows. The rigors of playing small towns in New England proved to be Casey's initiation into show business. "I wouldn't trade my circus experience for a million dollars," he recalled. "You couldn't buy it for that amount" (*Variety*, 14 December 1908).

Casey next worked for small theaters in his hometown of Springfield, first for the old Parlor Theatre and then as treasurer and manager of the Gilmore Theatre. In Springfield, he worked for P. F. Shea as a manager of Shea's vaudeville theaters. Casey reportedly once managed a roof show for F. W. Woolworth. Upon the death of his parents in 1895, Casey relocated to New York City. In the spring of 1896 he began work in the William Morris office. When Morris became the principal booking agent for Marc Klaw and Abraham Erlanger's Advanced Vaudeville in 1907, Erlanger developed a decided liking for Casey.

After the sudden demise of Advanced Vaudeville in late 1907, Casey resigned from his position in the Morris agency. He played an important role in transferring many vaudeville acts from Advanced Vaudeville to the UBO. A columnist wrote at the time: "'Pat' has been the haven sought by disgruntled artists. . . . His handling of the situation secured for him the confidence of the managers, both in the United offices and the Klaw and Erlanger headquarters." Sensing that this was an opportune time to go into business for himself, Casey started his own agency, which officially opened on 1 April 1908. Casey took out full-page advertisements in *Variety* stating that, beginning on 27 April, his offices would be located in the St. James Building on Broadway and Twenty-sixth Street. To attract clients, the agency advertised, "No Act too Big; No Act too Small. I Shall Make the Pat Casey Agency the Biggest in the World" (*Variety*, 28 March 1908). The move to start his own agency was not a surprise to the industry. *Variety* speculated, with reference to Casey's large physical size, that "'Pat' will not 'tie up' with anybody. He is too big and requires too much room for himself" (18 January 1908).

Robert Grau described Casey as follows: "He has a very large face, and when a smile illuminates it, one feels that it comes from the heart. Mr. Casey does not drink or smoke, but he has a splendid appetite, and there are two things he can do to perfection, laugh and—swear! However, his earnings even under the conditions stated, are not less than $40,000 a year" (Grau, *Business Man in the Amusement World*, 91–92).

By the end of 1908 *Variety* was declaring that Casey "had made himself and his agency a power in vaudeville" (14 September 1908). Casey became a dominant presence on the Broadway scene. The Casey Agency was the eastern representative for the Pantages Circuit in the West. A bachelor, Casey lived alone in a nine-room apartment in Manhattan where he hosted lavish dinner parties. Casey's clients included many stage stars, including Phil Baker, Ted Lewis, and Will Rogers.

In December 1908 Casey replaced Mort Shea as Rogers's agent. He promptly secured a series of vaudeville engagements with the Western Vaudeville Managers' Association and its major theaters, the Orpheum Circuit, for the winter and spring of 1909 (vaudeville contracts, 14 December 1908, OkClaW). Performing his lariat/horse act with his assistant Buck McKee and earning $300 a week, Rogers opened his western tour at the American Theatre in St. Louis on 28 December 1908. He next traveled to Memphis, where he performed at the Orpheum, beginning the week of 4 January 1909. The tour took him to the South, where he opened in New Orleans on 11 January 1909. In the Midwest he appeared at theaters in Omaha, Minneapolis, and Kansas City. In the spring he traveled west, with stops in Butte, Seattle, Portland, San Francisco, and other towns. Casey probably represented Rogers until 1911, when Max Hart became his agent.

In an interview with *Variety*, Casey discussed his policies as an agent, the middleman between the performer and the theater manager. He noted that he got engagements for about 400 acts a year and kept extensive records on each act. "I do not, except in rare instances, accept acts to book which I have not seen, nor will I . . . take an act to place at a larger salary than I think that act can secure," he said. Casey believed it was important to gain the confidence of theater managers who would then rely on the agent as a supplier of acts (*Variety*, 11 December 1909).

Casey continued his agency business in 1909. In that year he also headed a small-time vaudeville circuit, called the Metropolitan Vaudeville Exchange, with his brother Dan and Joe Wood as partners. In 1913 he was named general manager of the Protective Amusement Co., a film company headed by Klaw and Erlanger and A. H. Woods, a theatrical producer. In alliance with the Biograph Co., the New York–based company with offices at 1493 Broadway intended to produce 104 films of well-known plays annually. The Klaw and Erlanger and Biograph combination, however, produced only twenty-six films. The company was beset by box-office losses, exacerbated by high admission prices, technical and distribution problems, and outdated plays that did not transfer well to the screen. Consequently, the company disbanded at the end of 1914.

In 1914 the Pat Casey Agency was still active, with offices in the Putnam Building at 1493 Broadway. But in 1916 Casey closed his agency and became an executive for the Vaudeville Managers' Protective Association (VMPA), a trade organization formed in 1911 that was controlled by the Keith-Albee interests. He remained at the VMPA for six years, witnessing, among other events, the 1916–17 White Rats strike by actors against the managers' company union, the National Vaudeville Artists, Inc. Casey testified before the Federal Trade Commission (FTC) in 1919 that the unsuccessful strike had cost the managers $2 million. Defending the blacklisting of performers who signed with the White Rats, Casey told the FTC that the banned actors "were irresponsible, and could not be depended upon to fill any contracts that they made or might enter into" (Snyder, *Voice of the City*, 77–78). Casey had many friends in the Keith-Albee organization, especially John J. Murdock, executive manager of the UBO and a prominent behind-the-scenes figure in the Keith-Albee vaudeville empire.

Although a Keith-Albee executive, Casey remained a close friend of Sime Silverman, the founder of *Variety* and a staunch opponent of Albee's control of vaudeville. Silverman addressed many open letters and editorials to Casey, and criticized him in a humorous vein for his association with Albee: "Patsy, are you going to keep on being a chump? Or are you coming over? Please come over, dear" (Stoddart, *Lord Broadway*, 376). Sime's favorite phrase "Come on over, Pat" became an inside joke among vaudevillians. Casey's friendship with Silverman placed him in an awkward spot when in the mid-1920s Albee banned all *Variety* representatives, and even copies of the paper, from his theaters and offices. Albee was particularly irked by the publication's persistence in pointing out the imminent decline of vaudeville. Casey supposedly arranged a temporary truce between Albee and Silverman, but the disagreements between the two were really never resolved. Casey and the entertainer George Jessel were the two eulogists at Silverman's funeral in 1933.

In 1926 Casey joined the Association of Motion Picture Producers as chairman of the producers' labor committee. He retired in 1947 but continued as a consultant to the association until 1952. When he died at the age of eighty-seven in 1962, Casey was praised in *Variety* for his skills and his training of many agents and managers: "He was a deft negotiator, a go-between and private emissary for innumerable individuals, organizations and trade causes" (*VO*, 5:14 February 1962; "Casey Agency Will Incorporate," *Variety*, 4 April 1908, 3; *EV*, 89–90, 361–62, 466–67; "Flood of Small Time Gives One New Agency 50 Weeks," *Variety*, 29 May 1909, 3; Gilbert, *American Vaudeville*, 391; Grau, *Business Man in the Amusement World*, 91–92, 94; Grau, *Forty Years Observation of Music and the Drama*, 35; "History of Pat Casey," *Variety*, 14 December 1908, 45, 75; Laurie, *Vaudeville*, 241–42; Niver, *Klaw and Erlanger Present Famous Plays in Pictures*, 34–52, 171–75; "Pat Casey Agency," *Variety*, 21 March 1908, 3; "'Pat' Casey Leaves Morris," *Variety*, 7 December 1907, 2; *NYT*, 8 February 1962, 31; Spitzer, *Palace*, 84–85; Stoddart, *Lord Broadway*, 122, 232, 376–77).

CASTLE, Vernon (1887–1918) and Irene (1893–1969). The names of Irene and Vernon Castle are synonymous with elegant and refined ballroom dancing. The Castles became popular at the height of the pre–World War I dance craze, which had men and women of all ages and social stations dancing. Their contribution was not only in their style of dancing but in their presentation of a model the middle and upper classes could accept.

Irene Castle was raised by parents with a taste for the daring and unusual. Her mother, Annie Elroy Thomas, was reportedly the first woman in the United States to go aloft in a balloon. Her father, Hubert Townsend Foote, was a medical doctor with a passion for homeopathy. Young Irene had an idyllic childhood, replete with summer bicycling trips from New York City to Coney Island, stopping at little restaurants and lemonade stands en route. Her father died of tuberculosis when Irene was still a young woman. The event prompted her family to support her desire to be on the stage. They saw it as a means for her to support herself.

Vernon Castle was born Vernon Blythe in Norwich, England. He took the stage name Castle because it evoked Windsor Castle, and was easy to pronounce and remember. He graduated from Birmingham University with a degree in engineering. Afterward he traveled to the United States, where he went on the stage as a comedian. A typical act featured Castle playing a gentleman called Souseberry Lushmore who had had too much to drink. A Boston paper declared that Castle exhibited gentlemanly qualities in his humor: "For his humor he may descend to climbing upon chairs or ladders and falling to the floor, but he does not call in the risque to get his laughs" (Castle, *Castles in the Air*, 37).

In 1910 Vernon Castle met Irene Foote at a rowing club, and they became good friends. Castle helped her get a role in a Lew Fields show. Soon the two became romantically involved and decided to marry. Not long after their wedding, the couple traveled to Paris to perform comedy as a team. Vernon Castle was twenty-three and Irene was seventeen. They were accompanied by Walter Ash, who worked as a domestic servant for Irene's family. When their act failed, they were prevented from starving by the efforts of Ash, who earned money playing dice with the building concierge. In desperation they turned to dancing and became an enormous success.

When they returned to the United States in 1912, they were an immediate hit. At one point they worked for restaurateur Louis Martin at the New York City Cafe de l'Opera for $300 a week. This club was known as a "bottle and bird" club. Guests ate pheasant under glass and drank champagne. The club had a small dance floor on which the Castles would perform at midnight, and afterward they danced with the guests. One of their most famous dances was called The Castle Walk, featuring a step much like a skip. It was a huge sensation, and Vernon was occupied throughout the day giving lessons on the new step, a service for which he charged a dollar a minute.

In New York City the Castles performed at elegant cabarets that catered to wealthy patrons desiring an exotic night on the town. Cabaret audiences were drawn from the upper classes and Fifth Avenue socialites in unprecedented numbers. Among their favorite performers were Irene and Vernon Castle. One columnist wrote: "The Avenue is invading the Broadway dance palaces and there are so many invaders in the army from 'the Avenue' that recently society journals have taken notice of the fact" (Erenberg, *Steppin' Out*, 161). The Castles gave private dancing lessons to Millicent Willson Hearst, wife of

William Randolph Hearst, and others prominent in blue-ribbon circles. They were frequent guests at dinner-and-dance parties at Hearst's Clarendon residence on 86th Street and Riverside Drive in New York. The Castles' popularity led to several Broadway roles. Their biggest stage success was the Irving Berlin musical *Watch Your Step* (1914) at the New Amsterdam Theatre. The Castles developed a style of dancing that was both creative and respectable. Before the Castles popular dancing had been frowned upon by high society for its association with concert saloons, beer halls, and burlesque entertainment. The Castles' dance style was athletic and vigorous—the grace coming from the precise execution of the movements rather than from a sensuality that would have been perceived as threatening. Irene Castle described their contribution to the art of dance: "We were clean-cut; we were married and when we danced there was nothing suggestive about it. We made dancing look like the fun it was" (Castle, *Castles in the Air*, 86). The Castles cooperated with society matrons in establishing Castle House, an uplifting locale where children could learn to dance without being exposed to questionable elements. The censorship against dancing exerted by conservatives was curtailed when the *Ladies Home Journal*, considered to be the final arbiter of manners and behavior, published photos of the Castles dancing, along with diagrams of the steps. In 1914 the pair published *Modern Dancing*, a book that elaborated on their socially acceptable style.

The Castles created a white, middle- and upper-class, sanitized style of dancing, one that contrasted sharply with the sensual, expressive physicality of dance found in working-class dance halls and African American clubs and parties. Instead of joy and abandonment, the Castles emphasized constraint and control. They counseled couples to stand far enough apart to dance gracefully, and minimized the movement of hips, arms, and shoulders. Their ballroom style emphasized the woman following her male partner, who should lay his hand lightly against her back, touching her only with the wrist and fingertips. Irene Castle's upper-class origins and her husband's British accent reinforced their respectability and propriety for middle- and upper-class society. An editorial in the *Christian Science Monitor* after Vernon Castle's death summed up the couple's impact on dance reform: "The Castles showed and taught people of two continents how modern dances ought to be danced. They eliminated vulgarity and replaced it with refinement. . . . Dancing was running down to the depths when they first came upon the scene, and before the war separated them, they had reversed the current" (quoted in Castle, "My Memories of Vernon Castle," *Everybody's Magazine*, March 1919, 41).

Irene Castle was also a champion of exercise for women through dance and was a strong example of the new twentieth-century woman. She was among the first to bob her hair, in what was called the "Castle clip," a style that paved the way for the flapper styles of the 1920s. She was regularly featured in women's fashion pages in youthful gowns, without corset or frills, that emphasized her willowy figure. She also was associated with freer clothes and new underwear designs.

The Castles were among the first public figures to achieve what would be called later "the companionate marriage," in which the two partners are not only lovers but equal friends in the relationship. Throughout their marriage, Irene Castle was greatly concerned that her husband was squandering their money on frivolous purchases, loans, and gifts to friends. Finally, they decided to split their income fifty-fifty, with each taking charge of half. To boost their income, they would periodically appear in vaudeville, although they preferred the legitimate stage. In vaudeville, they were shocked by the cruelty to animals in the animal acts and bought many dogs, monkeys, and even bears from their owners. They finally decided to make it a condition of their contracts that no animal acts would appear on the bill with them.

At the height of their popularity in 1914, Vernon Castle joined the Royal Air Force to participate in World War I. He served two years in Europe and flew over 160 flights over the enemy lines. The Castles made their last appearance together at a British Recruiting Benefit performance held at New York's Hippodrome. In 1918 Vernon Castle was serving as a flight instructor for Canadian Air Force pilots when he was killed in a training exercise near Fort Worth, Texas. Among his belongings at the camp was a set of drums—he was an inveterate drummer who often amused the fliers with concerts—and a copy of the five-reel film *The Whirl of Life* (1915), which was about the Castles. He was very popular at the camp and performed stunts in the air that held the soldiers spellbound.

The film *The Whirl of Life*, written by Vernon Castle, was based upon the story of their lives, but it also contained many melodramatic elements. When a stockbroker falls in love with Irene, he takes her to the beach where she meets Vernon and elopes. The rejected suitor kidnaps Irene to prevent the Castles from opening a nightclub. Vernon finds her, and they leap off a cliff into the sea, swimming ashore just in time to perform at their nightclub's opening and make it a success.

Will Rogers performed on the same program with the Castles in vaudeville. They appeared on the same stage the week of 19 January 1914 at

Hammerstein's Victoria Theatre. The Castles were the headliners, advertised as "America's Foremost Interpreters of Modern Dances" (clipping, scrapbook A-3, OkClaW). The Castles and Rogers developed a close association. Rogers wrote a eulogy for Vernon Castle that was published in the *Chicago Sunday Tribune* of 17 February 1918 under the headline "'A Regular Guy,' 'Pal' Cites Examples of Vernon Castle's Nerve." Rogers wrote that although Castle was a dancer, "I'll tell the world he was game." Rogers cited numerous physical exploits performed by Castle, such as riding horses, driving fast cars, and doing stunts on horseback. Castle liked playing polo, and he and Rogers played together on numerous occasions, along with Frank Tinney and Fred Stone, on a deserted field on Long Island near the Castles' home in Manhasset. Rogers sometimes described these games during his *Midnight Frolic* nightclub routine. Once when the Castles attended the *Midnight Frolic* on top of the New Amsterdam Theatre, Rogers went into the audience and shook Vernon's hand saying, in reference to his service abroad: "Ladies and gentlemen, here's one tea hound that went out and made good" (clipping, scrapbook *Ziegfeld Follies*, CPpR). Rogers's folksy humor was much admired by Irene Castle. She wrote that she liked his "special ease on the stage and an immediate communication with the audience" (Castle, *Castles in the Air*, 134).

Irene Castle remarried three times following Vernon Castle's death. She returned once to vaudeville with a dancing partner in an appearance that was considered to be unsuccessful. In later life, she lived in Arkansas and Chicago. She was an avid animal-rights activist, who was opposed to vivisection. She made seventeen feature films between 1916 and 1922, and also appeared in a ten-episode serial called *Patria*, produced by Pathé and Hearst's International Film Service in 1916 and shown between 1916 and 1917. *Patria* showed the influence of Hearst and the war. Basically a preparedness film, it contained anti-Mexican and anti-Japanese content. It became embroiled in controversy, which forced its re-editing and rescreening in 1917. Hearst, meanwhile, loyally promoted Castle at the same time that he was aiding the career of Marion Davies. The Castle story was presented as an RKO feature called *The Story of Vernon and Irene Castle* (1939), starring, fittingly, Fred Astaire and Ginger Rogers (Castle, *Castles in the Air*; Castle, "My Memories of Vernon Castle"; Cook, "Irene Castle Watches Her Step"; "Dancer + Air Bird + Hero = Death," *Chicago Daily Tribune*, 16 February 1918; Erenberg, *Steppin' Out*, 159–64; *EV*, 90–91; Nawsaw, *The Chief*, 230, 237, 256, 261, 579; Samuels and Samuels, *Once upon a Stage* 251–53; *VO*, 1:22 November 1918, and 7:29 January 1969).

HART, Max (1874–1950). The agent Max Hart played a pivotal role in Rogers's career at the time when he changed his vaudeville routine to a single act without a horse and assistant. Born in Chicago, Hart's real name was Max Numkovsy. He started in show business by managing road tab shows (traveling tabloid musical comedies). Later he became the manager of a vaudeville office, at a salary of $8 per week. When he had learned enough about the business to feel confident, he went into the theatrical agency business by himself. Considered a leading vaudeville agent for his time, Hart managed a large number of stars in addition to Will Rogers. He was also known for bringing an antitrust suit against the Keith-Albee vaudeville monopoly.

Only anecdotes explain how Hart and Rogers became acquainted. One story is that Hart saw Rogers performing at New York's Fifth Avenue Theatre. If so, it was during his engagement the week of 6 March 1911, which featured Will Rogers and Co., the small Wild West show Rogers had organized. Hart claimed that he advised Rogers to discontinue using a horse on stage and instead encouraged him to do a humorous monologue with rope tricks. Although Hart's assertion cannot be proven, Rogers first performed his single act approximately two months after his appearance at the Fifth Avenue Theatre. The premiere of his new solo routine took place at Hammerstein's Victoria Theatre, the week of 1 May 1911.

A born salesman and promoter with a flair for publicity, Hart was the perfect agent to boost Rogers's career and to help change the nature of his act. The aggressive Hart, according to *Variety*, "knocked over anybody that stood in his way" (*VO*, 4:24 May 1950). Hart probably originated Rogers's new epithet, one that would be associated with him throughout his career—The Oklahoma Cowboy. Hart got Rogers an appearance as a single act at Chicago's Majestic Theatre the week of 12 June 1911. On the playbill Rogers was advertised as The Droll Oklahoma Cowboy. Rogers was so successful that he was held over for a second week. Taking advantage of this success, Hart published a large advertisement in a Chicago newspaper highlighting The Oklahoma Cowboy's rave reviews. Splashed across the ad in bold letters was the slogan "WILL ROGERS IN HIS NEW SINGLE OFFERING, ALL ALONE, NO HORSE." A self-promoter as well, the agent put at the bottom of the ad "DIRECTION, Max Hart" (Clipping from Will Rogers's Scrapbook, ca. 19 June 1911, above).

Hart helped expand Rogers's routine and in so doing opened up new opportunities for the entertainer. For one thing, he knew that Rogers's talent should not be confined to vaudeville. He undoubtedly had something to do with Rogers's appearance in *The Wall Street Girl* in 1912. This was Rogers's first engagement on the Broadway stage, and the exposure to a different audience than vaudeville boosted his career. The favorable reviews Rogers received in *The Wall Street Girl* led Hart again to purchase newspaper advertising space, which highlighted both his client's success and his personal direction.

Just how long Hart was Will Rogers's theatrical agent is difficult to ascertain. He appears to have had no role in Rogers's film career. Rogers probably relied on Hart, who had his office in New York City, to find him Broadway engagements when he needed them. The two seem to have kept in touch over the years. In 1921 Hart negotiated a lucrative contract for Rogers at $3,000 a week to appear in Advanced Vaudeville shows produced by Lee and J. J. Shubert. When Rogers underwent surgery for gallstones in 1927, Hart wired: "My prayers every night to one of my best friends to get well soon to bring joy and laughs to the world" (Max Hart to Mrs. Will Rogers, 21 June 1927, OkClaW; see also Hart's telegram to Rogers wishing him success in *Three Cheers*, 1 October 1928, OkClaW).

Hart was known for having a superior eye for talent, and house managers would take acts recommended by him, sight unseen. He had an uncanny ability to get his vaudevillians a better position on the playbill and to reinvent his acts so that they would get larger salaries. A power at one time in the vaudeville industry, Hart was said to have so many headliners that he could threaten to ruin theater operators if they did not meet his salary demands.

Hart's famous clients included Buster Keaton, Eddie Cantor, W. C. Fields, Frank Tinney, Fred Stone, Blossom Seeley, Bert Williams, and Fanny Brice, among others. Hart helped Fanny Brice in her career when he got her a big-time vaudeville date at Hammerstein's Victoria Theatre on 22 April 1912. Hart was Brice's agent sporadically for the next two years. As he had done for Rogers, Hart promoted Brice by buying advertising space; he placed ads for her in the 25 December 1914 issue of *Variety* and the 16 December 1914 issue of the *New York Dramatic Mirror*. Hart discovered the blackface comedian Frank Tinney performing in Texas at $50 a week. Hart signed Tinney, and soon he was making over $1,000 weekly at Hammerstein's Victoria. In the 1910s blackface comedians were sure-fire successes, Hart believed, and in 1917 he urged his client George Jessel, then a vaudevillian, to change his name and to wear blackface makeup. In this case, Jessel refused and left Hart.

Hart also played an influential role in Eddie Cantor's career. In 1914 Cantor was a blackface dialect and imitation comedian. Hart got him a straight-man partner named Al Lee, and the two toured vaudeville houses around the country. In 1916 Hart helped Cantor obtain his first job with Ziegfeld's *Midnight Frolic* and with the 1917 *Follies,* important steps in

Cantor's rise to stardom. Hart handled Cantor until he went to Hollywood, but Cantor said that out of loyalty he kept Hart on his payroll for twenty-two years.

For a short time Hart had under contract, before their film careers, Roscoe (Fatty) Arbuckle and Buster Keaton. He lost them both to the silent-movie business. Arbuckle left him when another agent, Lou Anger, got him a lucrative film contract with the Joseph Schenck organization. For Buster Keaton, Hart obtained a comic part in the Shubert brothers' musical comedy revue *The Passing Show* in 1917. Shortly afterward Keaton visited Arbuckle at a film studio where the latter was doing a movie. Keaton was so taken with the studio, the camera, and the cutting room, as well as film's comic potential, that he left Hart and signed with Joseph Schenck.

By 1920 Hart had lost some of his star clients. For those Hart had left, he had trouble finding bookings. He blamed the difficulty on the oligopoly (the Keith-Albee and Orpheum Circuits) that controlled vaudeville. The result, he believed, was a stranglehold on both the agent and the performer. In 1921 Hart sued Keith-Albee, which controlled the Vaudeville Exchange and the Orpheum Circuit, as well as Excelsior and Vaudeville Collection Agencies, for violation of the 1890 Sherman Anti-trust Act. Hart charged that the vaudeville combine was stifling competition and preventing performers from appearing in Keith and Orpheum theaters unless they scheduled performances through their booking agencies. He sued for $5 million in damages and hired Martin Littleton, a well-known attorney, to argue his case. The suit lasted five years and was dismissed by federal judge Augustus Hand on the grounds that the Keith-Albee organization was not engaged in interstate commerce within the strict interpretation of antitrust laws. Hart's attorney appealed to the Supreme Court, but on 23 November 1926 the judges decided not to review the case. Large legal fees and the loss of more stars during the suit ruined Hart financially.

The suit was only one of several problems that afflicted Hart. His divorce from his first wife, Madge Fox (known in vaudeville circles as The Flip Flop Girl), contributed to his financial problems. To avoid making large alimony payments, Hart denied that certain big-name acts were represented by him. He was correct—performers took the opportunity to leave him for better contracts elsewhere. Later, he married Adele Hoppe and moved to Hollywood for a time. He then returned to New York, where he was associated with Al Grossman, the theatrical agent.

Sick and practically penniless at the end of his life, Hart got help from a few staunch vaudeville friends who sponsored yearly trips for him to Hot

Springs, Arkansas. When Hart died in Brooklyn's Jewish Sanitarium and Hospital for Chronic Diseases at the age of seventy-six, he was eulogized as a "model agent" and "a product of his particular era" (*VO*, 4:24 May 1950; Cantor, *My Life Is in Your Hands*, 152–53; Cantor, *Take My Life*, 96–103; *EV*, 504; Gilbert, *American Vaudeville*, 238–39, 280–81, 303; Goldman, *Fanny Brice*, 57, 69–70; Grossman, *Funny Woman*, 83; Jessel, *So Help Me*, 42–43; Meade, *Buster Keaton*, 56–58, 61, 63–64; *NYT*, 11 August 1918 and 24 May 1950; Spitzer, *Palace*, 130; *Variety*, 21 October 1921; Yagoda, *Will Rogers*, 92, 124, 126, 130, 187, 241).

LaDue, Florence (1883–1951). Champion fancy roper and trick rider, Florence LaDue (sometimes spelled and publicized as Flores or Florence La Due) was born Florence Bensel in Montevideo, Minnesota. Her grandfather was a government agent for a Sioux reservation, and she was raised on the reservation. Her parents were Mr. and Mrs. C. D. Bensel. She began her rodeo career in 1905 working for the Wild West show promoter Frederick Cummins. In 1910 LaDue was among a group of skilled cowgirls hired by Will Rogers when he produced his own Wild West show for vaudeville and outdoor arenas. Rogers's show failed due to mismanagement and financial losses.

A superb roper and rider, LaDue won many competitions and championships. Her contests with her main rival Lucille Mulhall drew considerable publicity. In 1912 LaDue narrowly beat Mulhall in a championship trick roping event at the first Calgary Stampede. At the 1913 Winnipeg Stampede she again beat Mulhall in roping and trick riding contests. LaDue was a featured performer (act no. 23) in the Winnipeg Stampede program of 12 August 1913. In all, she won the world championship for women ropers three times. She retired from riding and roping contests as the undefeated champion in 1916 after beating Mulhall in fancy roping at the New York City Stampede. She continued, however, to display her skill with the lariat. As late as 1919, for example, she appeared in the Calgary Stampede.

LaDue participated frequently in the Miller Brothers' 101 Ranch Real Wild West Show. In May 1914 she performed with the Miller show as a fancy roper at New York's Madison Square Garden. For its time, the show with 276 mounted riders, as well as 50 Mexican soldiers and 8 Mexican fancy ropers, was one of the largest and most spectacular western extravaganzas. In the same show were the champion fancy ropers Chester Byers and Tommie Kirnan. The show also traveled to Europe.

On 17 November 1906 in Memphis, Tennessee, LaDue married Guy Weadick, organizer and promoter of the stampedes in Calgary and Winnipeg (see Biographical Appendix entry WEADICK, Guy). They met in Chicago where LaDue was participating in Cummins's Wild West Show and Indian Congress. Weadick was likewise a talented rider and roper, and the two appeared as a team in Wild West performances. Among their first performances together was a role in *Billy the Kid* with Joseph Santley. In his column, "Here and There," for *Billboard*, Guy Weadick called the performances of LaDue and the other ropers in the 101 Ranch shows "nothing short of marvelous and seems to go bigger at every performance" (16 May 1914).

In addition to appearing in rodeo and Wild West shows, Weadick and LaDue performed in vaudeville as a successful team. In 1908 LaDue had been a member of John P. Kirk's Elite Vaudeville Co. doing a single roping act. She and Weadick formed a cowboy-and-cowgirl, twelve-minute vaudeville act called Wild West Stunts (at other times called Weadick and LaDue). A newspaper account of the time described LaDue: "The woman of the team is very small, very dark complexioned and very wiry. She rides a horse like an Indian, and spins the lariat with a skill that draws forth frequent applause." According to the reporter, their act was a big hit: "The man [Weadick] tied the woman [LaDue] up completely by circling her legs, arms, and head with the coils, and the act was finished when the woman spun a lariat from horseback. The couple do quite a little talking, which gets across nicely" ("Weadick and LaDue," GWP-GA). They played on the Keith-Albee, Orpheum, and Pantages Circuits as one of several such acts in vaudeville (others were Clinton and Beatrice, The Chamberlains, The Shephards, Jack and Violet Kelly, and Shield and Rogers [no relation to Will]). Weadick and LaDue made a European tour in the spring of 1911, sailing second-class on the White Star liner S.S. *Laurentic*. They performed in Glasgow, London, and Paris to good reviews. Weadick appears to have also organized a Wild West show act called The Stampede, which, according to Joe Laurie, Jr., "was the first rodeo in vaudeville" (*Vaudeville*, 165). LaDue probably also participated in this act.

From 1920 to 1947 LaDue and Weadick made their home at The Stampede (T. S.) Ranch at High River near Calgary, Alberta, Canada. There they operated a large working ranch that let them express their love of horses and the outdoor life. In 1948 they sold the ranch due to the severity of the Canadian winters and LaDue's failing health. In 1950 LaDue and Weadick moved to Phoenix, Arizona, hoping the change would improve her health. A year later she died from heart failure. LaDue was buried in High River; her funeral was attended by friends, cowboys, cowgirls, and neighbors, both Anglo and Indian (biographical material, GWP-GA; *Billboard*, 29 December 1934; Clancy, *My Fifty Years in Rodeo*, 62; Croy, *Our Will Rogers*, 125–27; "Florence

Weadick Passes On," *Hoofs and Horns*, November 1951, 16; Laurie, *Vaudeville*, 22, 36, 165; LeCompte, *Cowgirls of the Rodeo*, 51–53, 63, 172; Riske, *Those Magnificent Cowgirls*, 40, 53; Roach, *Cowgirls*, 89, 92; Stansbury, *Lucille Mulhall*, 131, 133, 135, 153).

RING, Blanche (1877–1961). A Broadway musical comedy singer and vaudeville star, Blanche Ring was one of the big names in popular theater during the first two decades of the twentieth century. Will Rogers performed with her in *The Wall Street Girl* in 1912. Born in Boston, Ring came from a long line of theatrical performers. Four generations of her English-Irish-Scottish family had been Shakespearean actors. Her great-grandfather, Charles Fisher, had traveled throughout the eastern United States with a theatrical caravan. Her grandfather, James (Jimmy) Ring, was a member of the Boston Museum's stock company for thirty years.

At age fifteen, Blanche Ring appeared in small parts with her grandfather's company, and soon performed with her sisters Julie and Frances in a song-and-dance act. Both her sisters were on the stage, but they never became Broadway stars. Ring first gained recognition when she performed in *The Defender*, a musical comedy that opened on 3 July 1902 at the Herald Square Theatre. In this production Ring sang her first hit, "In the Good Old Summertime."

When performing in vaudeville, Ring was noted for getting the audience to sing along with her, a novelty at this time. She began this innovation with her appearance in *The Defender*. Ring later recalled the singalong when she sang "In the Good Old Summertime": "There were about twenty boys who used to come to the theatre every night and who always sang the chorus with me" (Patterson, "When Blanche Ring Smiles," 198).

Ring's delivery was as important as her material. A contemporary reviewer wrote: "Blanche Ring is one of vaudeville's heartiest smiles. She is radiant with this element. Few singing actresses know how to put a song over better than she" (quoted in *EV*, 419). She delivered her numbers in an Irish brogue, and would also perform short character sketches between songs.

Ring found vaudeville an excellent medium for her comedic talent. In 1909 she wrote: "The vaudeville stage . . . for a comedian . . . is an excellent school, and there are few of the younger comedians of the present day who were not schooled in vaudeville" (*Variety*, 11 December 1909). Comedy and laughter were at the heart of Ring's success. When asked what was her secret, Ring replied: "The charm is in the audience, in this great American public that wants to laugh." For Ring, the secret was in enjoying her work, and in communicating her pleasure to the audience: "Just get your song and sing it; sing it hard" (Ring, "How to Put 'Em Across," 45).

After achieving stardom in 1902 with *The Defenders*, Ring appeared in 1903 in *The Jewel of Asia* and *The Jersey Lily*. That same year she also made her London debut at the Palace Theatre. In 1906 Ring did *About Town*, followed by a tour with Joe Weber in his production of *The Merry Widow* (1908). In 1909 she appeared in *The Yankee Girl*, directed by Lew Fields (she also starred in the film version in 1915). In *Midnight Sons* (1909), she sang her second most remembered tune, "I've Got Rings on My Fingers." Other songs she made famous were "Come, Josephine, in My Flying Machine," "Waltz Me Around Again, Willie," "Bedelia," "The Belle of Avenue A," and "Yip-I-Addy-I-Ay." In 1913 she starred in *When Claudia Smiles*, and she was featured in the revue, *The Passing Show of 1919*. In the latter she appeared with her husband Charles Winninger, both doing impersonations. In total, Ring appeared in twenty-four musicals between 1902 and 1938.

Ring had a brief career in films. In 1926 she appeared in *It's the Old Army Game* with W. C. Fields. Her third film was *If I Had My Way* (1940), a film with Bing Crosby in which Ring had a cameo role. Ring never liked the restrictions on her comedic style imposed by the medium of film. In 1916 she said of her film *The Yankee Girl* that she disliked the work and only did it because she needed the money after a period of lavish spending.

Ring played a pivotal role in Will Rogers's career when he appeared with her in the Broadway musical *The Wall Street Girl* in 1912. In an interview, Ring stated: "I put him in the business" (Blanche Ring oral history interview, Oral History Collection, NNC, 8). Her statement was a little exaggerated, because Rogers had already made a name for himself in vaudeville. Ring recalled that she was in *The Yankee Girl* in Texas when she saw Rogers on the vaudeville stage. She arranged for him to appear in *The Wall Street Girl* delivering humorous comments and spinning the lariat. Ring recalled that at first Rogers was very shy, but she encouraged him to relax on the stage. She said that Rogers used to call her his "first boss." Although she often exaggerated her importance in Roger's career, it is true that *The Wall Street Girl* gave Rogers valuable exposure to a Broadway audience.

Rogers liked to talk about the fiddle he played backstage during the time he was in *The Wall Street Girl*. Ring, he wrote, "stood it as long as she could. Finally she sent word, 'Will, you can stay, but that Agony Box you are scraping on must vacate.' Blake just about wrecked my musical future" ("Rogers Takes a Look at Elinora, Mellie, Nick, and Congress," weekly article ms., published 26 and 27 December 1925, OkClaW).

Ring was married four times, to Walter F. MacNichol, James Walker, Jr., Frederick Edward McKay, and Charles Winninger. After her third marriage, Ring wrote an article in 1913 called "The Great American Husband" for *Green Book Magazine*. She advised American men to either marry their housekeepers or become more liberal in their thinking about the role of a modern wife.

Probably the last time Rogers saw Ring was in the winter of 1935 at the Actors' Fund Benefit at New York's New Amsterdam Theatre. "She did look great," wrote Rogers (*TDM*, 3 February 1935). But by this time Ring's heyday was over. She did very little performing after 1938. Largely forgotten by the public, Blanche Ring died at the age of eighty-nine in Santa Monica, California. She was survived by a son from her first marriage (Blanche Ring biography file, CLAc; Blanche Ring interview, Oral History Collection, NNC; *EV*, 419–20; Mantle and Sherwood, eds., *Best Plays of 1899–1909*, 413; *NYT*, 15 January 1961; *OCAT*, 579; Patterson, "When Blanche Ring Smiles," 198; Ring, "Great American Husband"; Ring, "How to Put 'Em Across"; Rodgers, "Pursued by Songs," 1102–4; Slide, *Vaudevillians*, 121–22; Taylor, "Blanche Ring Rites Draw Oldtimers," *Citizen-News*, 16 January 1961; *Variety*, 11 December 1909).

ROGERS, James Blake (Jim or Jimmy) (1915–2000). Jim Rogers was born on 25 July 1915 in New York City, at 629 Lexington Avenue or perhaps at a nearby Babies Hospital. He was named after his maternal grandfather, James Wyeth Blake (1845–82). At the time Jim Rogers was born, the family was living on Long Island for the summer and Will Rogers was performing in the Broadway musical *Hands Up*. New York newspapers printed stories about Rogers being a proud father for the third time. On the occasion of Jim's birth Rogers, as was his habit, bought a pony for the child. His idea was that each new baby should have a cradle strapped on the pony's back like a saddle to allow them to take fresh air, while learning the horse's walking gait. Rogers related in one of his *Hands Up* appearances that the new baby had said "howdy" soon after birth.

Between 1915 and 1919 Jim Rogers lived with his family in a rented house in Forest Hills in the New York borough of Queens, at 5 Russell Place. When he was old enough, his father took him and the other children to a nearby site to practice roping. Summers were spent in rented houses in Amityville, Long Island, near Fred Stone's ranch. By the age of two, Jim Rogers was a rider with the Rogers gang, along with four-year-old sister Mary and six-year-old brother Bill. The Rogers gang went for long horseback rides on the Long Island beaches. Each child had his or her own pony, silver-mounted saddle, and bridle. A picture of the Rogers gang shows Jim, then around two and a half, riding like his older siblings without holding on to the saddle horn. "None of these kids pull leather when they ride, you can sure bet," said Rogers ("'The Rogers Gang' Have Great Sport," unidentified clipping, scrapbook 20, OkClaW).

After Rogers decided to work in films, the family moved to Los Angeles in 1919. They lived first on West Adams Street and by 1920 resided at 111 South Van Ness Avenue, near downtown and the Hancock Park area. Here, on 17 June 1920, Jim Rogers's younger brother Fred (b. 15 July 1918) died from diphtheria. Jim Rogers and his brother Will, Jr., also became ill but recovered. Fred Rogers's death was a tragedy for the entire family, a painful ordeal that Will and Betty Blake Rogers and the children rarely talked about later in their lives.

Jim Rogers had an idyllic childhood on the Beverly Hills estate that Rogers purchased. "From the very beginning, my childhood was a happy one," he said. "I guess we moved around the country more than most people, but we didn't mind that" (Albert, "The Rogers 'Carry On'," 10). The family resided in Beverly Hills beginning in 1921. The eleven-acre estate at 925 North Beverly Drive (located behind the Beverly Hills Hotel) contained a large swimming pool. The children would go down a slippery slide into the pool. "Bill is nine, Mary seven, and Jim five, and they can all ride and swim like experts," said Rogers at the time. "Charlie Aldrich, an old cowpuncher pal of mine, acts as a nurse to them, and what he can't teach 'em ain't worth knowing" ("An Ideal Home, Will Rogers at His Beverly Hills Estate," unidentified clipping, 13 August 1921, scrapbook 20, OkClaW). The estate also had horse barns and a large garden. Rogers and his children rode on the Beverly Hills riding trail that went down what is now Sunset Boulevard.

Rogers, however, wanted a larger place with open grounds away from Beverly Hills, which he felt was too crowded. On 29 January 1925 Rogers made an agreement to buy the land that would become the Rogers Ranch. He purchased the initial 159.721 acres from Alphonzo Bell's Los Angeles Mountain Park Co. for $2,000 an acre. (Bell's company owned some 22,000 acres in the Santa Monica Mountains, and he developed the wealthy area known as Bel-Air.) Rogers bought a large spread of undeveloped land in Pacific Palisades, located in the Rustic Canyon area off Beverly (later Sunset) Boulevard. During the following years he bought adjacent land from Bell's company, so that eventually his holdings totaled around 350 acres. Formal ownership came when the grant deed was filed on 20 February 1928. The entire area became the Rogers Ranch, now a California state park.

Construction began in 1926, and over the next few years barns, stables, and a house were built. Here Rogers and his children could freely ride, rope, and play polo. Before the main house was constructed, Rogers and the children would ride their horses on nearby trails that wind around the Santa Monica Mountains. Often they rode over from their Beverly Hills home for a picnic on the property. Jim Rogers sometimes rode down to the ocean and took a swim. At first there was a cottage where the family could stay, as well as a temporary barn and stables. In 1928–29 the family moved into their newly built home. Pieces of a large barn, purchased in the San Fernando Valley, were transported and reconstructed into a building with two wings separated by a tall rotunda. The new barn had plenty of stables for their horses. Cattle grazed around the acreage, and some served as targets of roping for the children. A pet calf called Sarah was allowed to roam around the house. Jim and his brothers had fun roping calves in a specially constructed roping corral. Roping was often an after-dinner activity, and each of the children had his or her own lasso. There was also a roping chute on the polo field. Jim Rogers eventually had his own room, which had a separate stairway entrance. A golf course was laid out on the front lawn and the surrounding grounds. Family barbecues and larger events for guests were held on the patio.

Jim Rogers was the child who loved the ranch life best. He was always outdoors riding and roping. When the polo field was finished, he played polo frequently. He participated in the Sunday polo matches against Hollywood celebrities. Will Rogers told the story of the time twelve-year-old Jim was shouting playing instructions to screenwriter Agnes Johnson on the polo field, calling her Aggie. His mother told him that it was not polite to call her by her first name or by a nickname. Jim replied: "Well when you are going so fast and you want her to leave the ball, you haven't got time to say a lot of names. I can't holler 'Leave it Mrs. Agnes Johnson Dazey!' The game would be over by then" (*TDW*, 12 May 1935). By 1931 Jim was recognized as an expert polo player and that year participated in a match between the Reds (Hal Roach, Snowy Baker, and others) and the Blues (Jim Rogers, David Wyte, and others) at the Uplifters Club. During the summer of 1932 he taught polo classes at the Cowboy College at the Circle Bar Ranch in Texas.

Jim's love of the western life created a special bond between him and his father. While on the road his father wrote him about plans he had for the ranch: "We will have alot of roping this summer, Fancy and Calf and Goats. We will get us some Goats and keep em up in a small pen all the time." Sometimes his father gave him instructions regarding ongoing improvements and landscaping to be done at the Rogers Ranch: "Jim I wish you would look after some things down there at the Ranch for me. Get em to build the back part on the big barn, Uncle Lee [Adamson] will know what we had talked of, Get those Logs put around the outside of the east hill, Then if they have time move the old Stables, and fix up a Bunk House out of part of the old one, Now see what luck you can have on this" (Will Rogers to Jim Rogers, ca. 30 December 1928, OkClaW). Growing up on the Rogers Ranch gave Jim Rogers his lifelong love of ranch life. The lad worshiped his father: "I worshipped Dad, but not because of his achievements. To the world he might be a great humorist or a wonderful actor, but to me, it was just my dad. I admired him tremendously because of the kind of life he lived and because of the kind of human being he was" (Albert, "The Rogers 'Carry On'," 3).

During Jim Rogers's youth there were also trips to Europe, Hawaii, the Grand Canyon, and other places. Friends included Fred Stone's children, Patricia Ziegfeld (daughter of Florence Ziegfeld), and many others. Jim liked to listen to his father on the radio. He wrote his sister Mary: "I am so glad Dad changed his time on the radio so now I can listen to his talks" (Jim Rogers to Mary Rogers, n.d, OkClaW).

Jim Rogers appeared as a child actor in several of his father's films, using the name Jimmy Rogers. His first film was *Jes' Call Me Jim* (1920), a Goldwyn Pictures release. Jim, age four, played Harry Benedict, whose father, Paul Benedict, is being held in the county asylum on false charges. While he is imprisoned, Harry is taken care of by Miss Butterworth, a milliner, played by Irene Rich. During the shooting, Jim came down with measles and the filming had to be delayed. While appearing in *Jes' Call Me Jim*, Jim spoiled a scene that had been meticulously set around a dog called Seldom, by reciting spontaneously, just as the scene was to be shot: "Whoa, little Seldom, whoa little pup; He can sit up on his hind legs if you hold his front ones up." All those present burst out laughing. The same reporter noted that "he has several very piquant, but not necessarily exhausting bits to rehearse on the studio lot, and the rest of the time he goes to school and plays with the 'gang' like any other regular feller" ("Little Trips to Los Angeles Studio," unidentified clipping, scrapbook 20, OkClaW).

That same year Jim Rogers played Billy Gardner in *The Strange Boarder* (1920). Will Rogers played his father, Sam Gardner, an Arizona rancher who promises his dying wife that he will give his son a good education. With his son, he goes to Chicago where he is robbed of his money and arrested for murder. He is finally released and finds a new romance with Jane Ingraham, played by Irene Rich.

Years later, in 1971, Irene Rich was interviewed by Bryan and Frances

Sterling. She recalled one scene she did with Jim Rogers: "I'm holding little Jimmy in my arms? Well, when the scene was being taken, with me facing the camera and Jimmy in my arms, at right angle to it, his little hand behind my back was inside my dress, going up and down on my spine. Now, don't you think I didn't have a hard time doing that scene. I still remember little Jimmy. He was a sweet, cuddly little kid" (Sterling and Sterling, *Will Rogers in Hollywood*, 26).

In 1921 Jim Rogers appeared in the Goldwyn film *Doubling for Romeo* as Jimmie Jones, a child screen star. He helps country yokel Sam Cody (played by Will Rogers) find a job in the movies, and the fellow proceeds to make a fool of himself in amusing scenes that parody Hollywood leading men. This film was followed by *Fruits of Faith* (1922), produced by Will Rogers, in which Rogers played a child found in the desert by the tramp Larry (Will Rogers) who takes care of the youngster. Larry marries a woman, played by Irene Rich, but suddenly the child's father appears and wants his son back. Realizing how much his son likes his new parents, the father agrees that he can stay with them.

Jim Rogers also had parts in two family films. *One Day in 365* (1922), a Rogers production that was never released, starred the whole family as they went about a typical day in Beverly Hills. Jim Rogers also was in *Reeling Down the Rhine with Will Rogers* (1928), a travelogue with his father and mother. These films underscored Will Rogers's role as a family man. Indeed, photographs of the family in domestic scenes were printed frequently in newspapers. The presence of Jim Rogers in these photographs and in his father's films emphasized the family values associated with Will Rogers.

In the fall of 1931 Jim attended the New Mexico Military Institute at Roswell. At this time his brother, Will, Jr., was at Stanford University. Their father wrote about the departure of the two boys in his Daily Telegram: "Early in the autumn, Mrs. Rogers and I sent two sons away supposedly to schools. (We got tired trying to get 'em up in the morning.) One went north, here in this State; another to New Mexico. Since then we have received no word or letter. We have looked in every football team all over the country. Guess they couldn't make the teams, knew their education was a failure and kept right on going. Any news from any source will be welcome. I am flying to Mexico City today. The big one [Will, Jr.] spoke Spanish, so maybe he is there. The little one [Jim] didn't even speak English, but he loved chili and hot tamales, so he may be there, too" ("Mr. Rogers Is Out to Round Up 2 Strays from the Home Corral," *NYT*, 2 November 1931).

Jim Rogers next attended the Webb School in Claremont, California, a boys' preparatory boarding school, founded by Thompson Webb, that had a fine academic reputation. The school, nestled below the San Gabriel Mountains, was located in what was then a rustic area with much room for riding and other sports. On the occasion of his son's graduation, Rogers sent a telegram to the entire senior class: "THEY TELL ME YOU BOYS ARE GRADUAT-ING OUT THERE AT WEBB WELL YOU ARE MAKING AN AWFUL MISTAKE YOU WILL NEVER FIND A BETTER SCHOOL YOU CAN SCATTER TO THE FOUR WINDS AND YOU WONT FIND ANOTHER MR WEBB I KNOW IF YOU ARE GRADUATING YOU HAVENT GOT MUCH TIME TO BE MESSING AROUND WITH CONGRATULATIONS AND ADDRESSES ITS GETTING HOT IN THOSE LEMON ORCHARDS IF YOU CANT GO TO COLLEGE DONT FEEL BAD MR WEBB HAS GIVEN YOU ENOUGH RIGHT THERE THAT IF ITS IN YOU YOU CAN BAT AGAINST WORLD PITCHING RIGHT NOW YOU ARE A FULL FLEDGED CITIZEN OF THESE UNITED STATES COURSE IF YOU LIKE FOOT-BALL WELL ENOUGH TO PLAY IT FOUR YEARS PROFESSIONALLY AT COLLEGE WHY GO AHEAD GOOD LUCK TO YOU WILL ROGERS" (To the Webb School Graduating Class, TG, 13 June 1934, original at Webb School). Jim Rogers attended Pomona College in Claremont, California, for one year following his gradua-tion from Webb. After his father died in the summer of 1935, he decided not to return to college in the fall.

On 28 March 1938 Jim Rogers married Marguerite Astrea Kemmler (1917–87). They had met at the Riviera Country Club a few years before their wedding. Born in New York City, Astrea (the name she preferred) came from a socially prominent family. She was the daughter of Charles William Kemmler, whose parents were from Stuttgart, Germany, and Marguerite Drake, from Tucson, Arizona. Astrea Kemmler graduated from the Marlborough private school and studied at Heidelberg, Germany. The wed-ding was a gala social event with prenuptial parties that included a dinner dance at the famous nightclub, the Cocoanut Grove. The ceremony was held at St. John's Episcopal Church with Mary Rogers as the maid of honor and Patricia Ziegfeld as one of the bridesmaids. The reception with over three hun-dred invited guests was held in the French Room at the Town House. For their honeymoon the couple drove to Sun Valley, Idaho, and on to Oklahoma where they visited relatives.

The couple first made their home on their 15,000-acre Jalama Ranch near Lompoc, California. With his partner, Edward Vail, Jim Rogers oversaw 2,500 head of Hereford cattle. Although his wife had little outdoor experience, she was active on their ranch. Besides running the household, she sometimes par-ticipated with her husband in roundups and team roping events at rodeos. In the 1940s Jim Rogers appears to have had a small movie career performing in comedy Westerns. On 11 October 1941 gossip columnist Louella Parsons reported that he had signed a contract with Hal Roach. Rogers appeared in a movie with Noah Beery, Jr., based on a magazine story called "Dudes Are Pretty People." Production seems to have halted temporarily when Rogers suffered a serious eye injury while fixing a motorboat. Chips from a metal screw pierced his eye, were removed, and the eye bandaged. For two months he was bedridden until the bandage was removed. Fortunately, his eyesight was not impaired.

Another Hal Roach movie that Jim Rogers did with Beery was *Calaboose* (1943). He also had a leading role in the 1943 Roach film *Prairie Chickens*. At one time he was considered for a role as his father in a film based on his mother's memoir, *Will Rogers* (1941). But he wasn't interested. "I couldn't possibly enjoy making a picture in which I was supposed to mimic Dad," he said. "I'm not a good enough actor for the part" (Albert, "The Rogers 'Carry On'," 3). His brother, Will, Jr., did play the part in *The Story of Will Rogers* (1952). Jim Rogers played a cowboy in three Hopalong Cassidy films. In February 1943 it was reported that he had signed with Harry Sherman to play William Boyd's sidekick in the Hopalong Cassidy film series, but Sherman ended the series that year.

For a time Jim Rogers was associate editor of the *Beverly Hills Citizen* newspaper, first working with brother Bill, and then by himself when his brother left the paper in 1942 to go to Washington as a member of Congress from California (he later enlisted in the army). Jim Rogers contributed a column similar in style to the homespun wisdom that had made his father famous. He also occasionally supported political candidates in his signed editorials. In the presidential election of 1944 he endorsed the Republican candidate Thomas E. Dewey for president, to the astonishment of his brother Will, Jr., who backed the Democratic incumbent, President Roosevelt. Will, Jr., then stationed in Holland, was furious about the endorsement. Jim Rogers replied that the *Citizen* was a Republican paper and as acting chief editor he had made the decision and signed the editorial. "I made the decision to indorse Dewey and signed my name to the editorial," he said. "It is unfortunate there have been any insinuations that Bill indorsed Dewey" (Carl Greenberg, "Rogers Paper Family Owned," Jim Rogers biographical material, Hearst Clipping File, CLSU). In April 1945 Jim Rogers left the paper to join the Marines at Camp Pendleton, California. He served as a writer-correspondent and made U.S. Army training films with actor Rod Cameron.

In March 1941 Jim Rogers secured title to a 9,220-acre ranch, the Rancho Jesus Maria, north of Santa Barbara, for about $130,000. The ranch was located at Bear Mountain, part of the Tehachapi Mountains, near Bakersfield, in

Kern County, California. There he operated a successful cattle business, with a cow-breeding herd of over one thousand head. In the Rogerses' spacious and lovely home were paintings and sculpture by Charles Russell. The Rogerses lived there until they moved to Bakersfield. Jim and Astrea Rogers had three children: James Kemmler (Kem) Rogers (b. 1939), Charles Edward (Chuck) Rogers (b. 1941), and Astrea Elizabeth (Betty) Rogers Brandon (b. 1943). Jim and Astrea Rogers made many trips over the years to the Will Rogers Memorial in Claremore, Oklahoma, and attended Will Rogers Birthday celebrations hosted by the Pocahontas Club. After a lingering illness, Astrea Rogers died on 19 November 1987 in Bakersfield. Jim Rogers continued to live in Bakersfield near his daughter Betty and her family. He helped preserve his father's legacy by serving as a member of the Will Rogers Memorial Commission and as a consultant to the Will Rogers State Historic Park in Pacific Palisades, California, and by attending many functions associated with his father. He died of cancer on 28 April 2000, at the age of eighty-four. He was survived by his second wife, Judith Braun, his three children, six grandchildren, and eleven great-grandchildren (Albert, "The Rogers 'Carry On'," 3, 10; California State Board of Health Standard Certificate of Death, Fred Rogers, filed 19 June 1920, OkClaW; Collins, *Roping Will Rogers Family Tree*, 32, 135; Dunn, "History of the Will Rogers Ranch and State Historic Park in California"; *FilmEnc*, 158–59; "Historical Data—Will Rogers Ranch"; *LAT*, 30 April 2000, B5; *NYT*, 3 May 2000, A29; Jim Rogers biographical material, Hearst Clipping File, CLSU; Rollins, *Will Rogers*, 46, 175, 177, 180, 182, 193, 258; Sterling and Sterling, *Will Rogers in Hollywood*, 24–28, 49–50, 171; Will Rogers biographical file, unidentified clipping, ca. 1920, NNMoMa-FC; Yagoda, *Will Rogers*, 207–8; Randy Young, "Time Line of Ranch," unpublished ms. in possession of author).

Rogers, Mary Amelia. See BROOKS, Mary Amelia Rogers.

ROGERS, William Vann (Will, Jr., or Bill) (1911–93). Will and Betty Blake Rogers's first child, Will, Jr., or Bill, became a newspaper publisher, reporter, Democratic politician, member of Congress, war hero, Indian activist, and actor in film, television, and radio. He was born on 20 October 1911 at a nursing home in New York City (see Notice of Birth of Will Rogers, Jr., ca. 20 October 1911, above). At the time his parents were living at 551 West 113th Street and his father was performing in vaudeville. Will, Jr., spent the first few years of his life primarily in New York, but often he and his mother would stay at Amelia Blake's house in Rogers, Arkansas. Between 1915 and 1919 the

Rogerses lived primarily in the Forest Hills section of Queens in New York City, at 5 Russell Place. Summers were spent at Freeport and Amityville, Long Island.

In many ways Will, Jr., had an idyllic childhood. He grew up in his family's homes in Los Angeles and Beverly Hills, and finally on the Rogers Ranch in Pacific Palisades. During his school years Rogers attended the Culver Military Academy in Culver, Indiana, and Beverly Hills High School. He played polo, participated in the school theater, and competed in oratorical contests. He was a talented polo player, a game he and his father loved, and also a debater. At age seventeen he was seen as a coming polo star. In 1925 he went on a long cruise through the Panama Canal and across the Atlantic to Europe with his cousin Bruce Quisenberry. In the spring of 1926 he accompanied his father to England, France, and Italy as he was writing articles on European life and politics for the *Saturday Evening Post,* material that resulted in his *Letters of a Self-Made Diplomat to His President* (1926).

After graduating from high school in 1931, Will, Jr., took up, like his father, an interest in journalism. He worked for six months at the Fort Worth, Texas, *Star Telegram,* earning admiration for his talents from the newspaper staff and its publisher Amon Carter, a good friend of his father. At the end of his internship at the paper his father telegrammed Carter that "I have a distant son that used to be in Texas somewhere he cant write so we figured he must be on the Fort Worth Star Telegram." Carter answered that "Your distant son comes by his not writing honestly like father like son" (Will Rogers to Amon Carter, 6 July 1931, and Amon Carter to Will Rogers, 7 July 1931, Will Rogers subject file, TxFACM). When he cabled, Will Rogers had not yet received a letter that Carter had written two days before, praising his son for his diligence and industry. "I think [he] has acquired as much information about the newspaper business in the time as anyone possibly could have absorbed. He has made lots of friends and I am sure . . . that neither you nor Mrs. Rogers will have any occasion to worry about Bill. He has a keen mind, exceedingly friendly attitude, plenty of courage and an ambition to succeed as Bill Rogers on his own merit and not merely as the son of Will Rogers" (Amon Carter to Will Rogers, 5 July 1931, Will Rogers subject file, TxFACM). Amon Carter kept in touch with Will, Jr., and was later instrumental in helping him and his family deal with arrangements following Will Rogers's death in 1935.

After his stint in Texas, Will, Jr., entered Stanford University. At the end of his first year he left Stanford and transferred to the University of Arizona to play on its first-rate polo team. Unfortunately, he, in his own words, "damn near flunked out and went down to Nogales, Mexico and got drunk and misbehaved" (*People Magazine*, 26 November 1979, 97). He then returned to Stanford.

Will, Jr., majored in philosophy at Stanford and excelled in sports and debating. He set a 100-yard backstroke swimming record, while also making captain of the polo team. As a member of the debating team, he participated in the first transoceanic radio debate in 1933 with Cambridge University. He won the Pacific Forensic League Conference speaking contest and, along with a partner, won the Western Conference Debate Championship. His most significant work for his future, however, was as a journalist. Not only was he the editor of the *Stanford Daily*, but also he started his own off-campus weekly news magazine. While working on the *Stanford Daily* he met Collier Connell, his future wife.

Once while at college Will, Jr., had forgotten to pay a woman who had done his laundry. She wrote Will Rogers asking if he could pay her. His son's negligence bothered Rogers, and in a scolding tone he wrote him: "Now you can just kinder imagine my humiliation at a thing like that, there is lots and lots of things that I dont want you children to do, lots of em you will abide by and some you wont, but to ever tell anybody a lie, or to not promptly pay your debts is two things I feel that I have a right to demand, a great deal of it is carelessness . . . which grows into habit, but you break yourself right now, at Tucson you had a bit of the same thing, now these are not accidents, dont you ever buy anything you cant pay for, and pay for it the minute you buy it, I dont want a bill of any description following you, so you get busy and rack your brain of any obligation and go and pay em immediately, and you apologise to this woman, nothing is as 'honery' as that trait" (copy of Will Rogers to Bill, n.d., letterhead, Will Rogers, Beverly Hills, Calif., J. B. Milam Collection, OkClaW).

Will, Jr., graduated from Stanford in the middle of the Great Depression in 1935. Returning to southern California, he found work, with a little help from his father, as an engine-room swabber aboard the Standard Oil tanker *H. M. Storey*. But while aboard the tanker waiting to cast off for the Philippines, he was brought on deck by a company official to his waiting cousin, Mary Ireland, who had news of his father's death. "Stunned as though struck," said a newspaper, "young Will took the blow dry eyed and rode silent to his ranch home with his cousin" ("Death News Shocks Will Junior," unidentified clipping, Will Rogers, Jr., biographical material, Hearst Clipping Collection, CLSU).

For Will, Jr., the decade following his father's death was the toughest of his life. He survived, he said, by learning "to roll with it" and in the process accomplished a great deal (*People Magazine*, 26 November 1979, 97). Lurking behind him throughout his life was his father's shadow—not only the memory of his father, whom he loved, but the difficulty of living up to his father's name. He inherited both the name and all that it meant, but also the burden of being always compared to his father. Fortunately, he had his own skills that would bring him a different type of fame.

In 1935 Will, Jr., started a career in journalism that would occupy a period of his life in which he married, served a term in Congress, and fought heroically in World War II. He also championed liberal causes and was a voice of conscience in Congress for European Jewry during the war. One could say that he inherited his father's defense of the underdog and the dispossessed during hard times.

After his father's death, Will, Jr., invested part of his inheritance in a newspaper, the *Beverly Hills Citizen*. It was jointly owned by him, his brother Jim Rogers, and his sister Mary Rogers. As its publisher for eighteen years, he built the *Citizen* into one of the largest weeklies in the West. In Los Angeles the *Citizen* was a voice of liberalism, supportive of President Roosevelt's New Deal policies in the 1930s. Liberal in its outlook, the *Citizen* had a broad readership; its writings were fresh and first-rate. Moreover, it offered an alternative to the Hearst-controlled *Los Angeles Examiner* and the Chandler-controlled *Los Angeles Times*. This experience established Will, Jr., as a businessman in the Los Angeles area and added substantively to his future political prospects.

In 1938 Will, Jr., temporarily left the offices of the *Citizen* to cover the Spanish Civil War as a reporter for the McNaught Syndicate. During this trip he toured both Europe and parts of Asia and returned convinced that Japan's aggression had to be met with some resistance. Urging an embargo on goods to Japan, he soon entered into Democratic Party politics in California.

Will, Jr.'s first political appointment came in 1941 when Governor Colbert Olson placed him on the California Maritime Commission. Shortly thereafter, he ran for southern California's 16th Congressional District seat as a Democrat. His bid for office was unusual. Having enlisted in the U.S. Army just before the race, he served during the entire campaign as a second lieutenant in Texas. In the election of November 1942 he defeated the Republican incumbent Leland M. Ford and, placed on army inactive status, took office.

As Will, Jr., entered the House of Representatives, he claimed to have no specific legislative agenda in mind except to educate the public on the war. He quickly developed a liberal reputation. In his first speech in the House, Representative Rogers attacked the Texas Democrat Martin Dies for his work as chairman of the House Committee on Un-American Activities (HUAC) and called for the abolishment of HUAC. Six months later he claimed that partisan wrangling in a nearly equally divided Congress had "sent crashing down many of the great social gains of the past ten years" (*Current Biography*, December 1953, 27). He supported a liberal program by voting against an antistrike measure and for an anti–poll tax bill and a veterans bonus bill. He also gained a seat on the important House Foreign Affairs Committee and subsequently called for more aid to China to fend off the Japanese.

Representative Rogers was particularly concerned about the growing threat to Jews in Nazi Germany and Eastern Europe. He became an active member of the Bergson group, a circle of legislators who called for action to aid European Jewry. In August 1943 he undertook, at his own expense, a seven-week unofficial mission to England as a representative at the conference of the Emergency Committee to Save the Jewish People. He was the keynote speaker at the conference's opening session. When he returned to the United States, he called on the State Department to establish an agency to deal with the Jewish refugee problem. He introduced legislation in the House of Representatives to set up a rescue agency. "I just did what anybody would have done," he said. "I did very much want the United States as a country and as a nation to . . . protest and to stand for the rescue of these people when it could be done" (*America and the Holocaust*). His actions pushed President Roosevelt to issue Executive Order 9417 in January 1944, which established the War Refugee Board. This board played a role in saving 200,000 Jews. Will, Jr., continued his support for European Jews after the war. He became cochairman of the American League for a Free Palestine and called on President Truman in 1946 to insist that Britain and the United States allow 100,000 Jews to enter Palestine.

As the war continued, and his term neared its end, Will, Jr., resigned from Congress and rejoined the U.S. Army. On 25 May 1944 he left the House of Representatives in the belief that he could better serve his country in uniform. His conscience, he claimed, dictated that he should not seek reelection.

Will, Jr., served as a platoon leader in a reconnaissance company of the 814th Tank Destroyer Battalion attached to the Seventh Armored Division. His unit landed in France a month after D-Day, and he saw action at Le Mans, Verdun, and Metz. On 18 February 1945 he was promoted to first lieutenant and received the Bronze Star for heroism in the Battle of the Bulge. During the battle he led a patrol against a German force that threatened to cut off part of the division's withdrawal from St. Vith.

On 9 April 1945, the last week of the war, Will, Jr., was hit in the knee by shrapnel during the Battle of the Ruhr. He spent three months in hospitals in

England and France, and had three operations to remove all the debris. He received the Purple Heart for his injuries. After the war he spoke out for wounded veterans and called on the federal government to increase its financial support for soldiers who had sacrificed so much for America's victory.

When he returned home to California, Will, Jr., reentered politics. In 1946 he received the Democratic Party's nomination to run for the U.S. Senate from his home state. He campaigned amid escalating Cold War tensions. Although he had previously called for a "close and lasting" alliance with Russia as the only alternative to a third world war, he also positioned himself squarely against Henry Wallace and "appeasement" of the Soviet Union ("Will Rogers Jr. for Alliance," unidentified article, 21 September 1943, Will Rogers, Jr., biographical material, Hearst Clippings Collection, CLSU). He was pressured to announce his opposition to communists and communist sympathizers. The Teamsters, who along with the rest of the American Federation of Labor, had announced their support of his candidacy, threatened to withdraw their support because of his association with James Roosevelt (President Roosevelt's son) and his purported ties with communists. But Will, Jr.'s efforts to please both his supporters and his critics came to naught. He lost to the Republican William Knowland, a staunch anticommunist. In the same 1946 California election, Richard Nixon was elected to Congress using a successful red-baiting campaign against Helen Gahagan Douglas. Douglas was an early casualty of what would be called McCarthyism in the 1950s.

Will, Jr., remained active in Democratic politics despite his election loss. In 1948 he served as a California delegate pledged to Harry Truman at the Democratic convention and managed Truman's southern California presidential campaign. He also used his high public profile to condemn communist influence in the Democratic Party. "Real Communists and real Democrats do not mix," he asserted, "a fact that the Communists well recognize by excluding democratic processes. It is a fact all Americans should recognize by barring members of the Communist Party from the membership of any democratically run organization" (unidentified article, 24 March 1948, Will Rogers, Jr., biographical material, Hearst Clippings Collection, CLSU). He resigned from the American Veterans Committee, claiming it was a communist front organization, and later condemned communist infiltration in the California Democratic Party. In other ways, he continued his support of a liberal agenda, defended the labor movement, and opposed an anti-union, right-to-work proposition in 1958. Two years later he co-chaired the campaign speakers' bureau of the Southern California Kennedy for President Committee.

Besides his political work in the Democratic Party, Will, Jr., had long been involved with American Indian affairs. In 1948, in a speech before the National Congress of American Indians, he criticized the Department of Interior's Indian Service. He condemned the dearth of Indian educational facilities, particularly for Navajos, and proposed the complete reorganization of the Indian Service. He called for making Native Americans part of the American system rather than wards of the state and listed a three-point program: first, the appointment of an Indian commissioner sympathetic to the Indians' problems; second, an order by Congress withdrawing Indians from wardship status without loss of tribal property rights; and third, the enactment of the Navajo Rehabilitation Program, which would set up reservation industries to use local raw materials and then educate Native Americans for employment. He argued that Indian youngsters should be educated in white schools where they could learn the language and attitudes of white society as well as employment skills. The National Congress of American Indians showed its support by endorsing him for the post of U.S. Indian commissioner. In 1949 he assumed the presidency of the Congress's affiliate, the American Restitution and Righting of Old Wrongs, Inc.

During the winter of 1948–49 terrible weather conditions caused tremendous suffering among the Navajo Indians in the West, and Will, Jr., made a special effort to bring them assistance. "Their plight is desperate," he argued. "Besides dire need many of them are stricken with pneumonia, frostbite, burst eardrums, snow blindness and other illnesses" ("Will Rogers Jr. Pleads for Aid at Once to Starving Navajos," unidentified article, 20 February 1949, Will Rogers, Jr., biographical material, Hearst Clippings Collection, CLSU). He then spearheaded a $100,000 emergency campaign with the Save-the-Children Federation and chaired the federation's Indian Committee.

At this point Will, Jr., and his wife Collier Connell adopted a ten-year-old Navajo boy named Shazzi Endischae (b. 1938), whom they renamed Clem Adair after Will, Jr.'s paternal grandfather, Clement Vann Rogers, and family friend William Penn Adair. On 26 May 1941 Will, Jr., had married Connell, whom he had met while editing the *Stanford Daily*. Connell was born in Tularosa, New Mexico, and educated at Smith College and Stanford. Her father, a Harvard-trained lawyer, moved to the Southwest to take up ranching. Her mother was a schoolteacher from Omaha, Nebraska. Possibly because of Collier's left-wing politics and ardent interest in cultural rights issues, the Rogers family disapproved of her. Nevertheless, the marriage was long lasting. Besides Clem Adair, the couple had another son, Carl Connell (b. 1952).

Will, Jr.'s work with American Indians continued, and in 1960 president-elect Kennedy considered him for the post of commissioner of the Bureau of Information of Indian Affairs. He had to wait, however, until 1967, when Stewart Udall, then secretary of the interior, appointed him special assistant to the commissioner. Will, Jr., then relocated to Washington, D.C., and stayed in this new position for two years. In 1969 he resigned to continue as a part-time consultant for the bureau. Undoubtedly, his commitment to Native American rights and affairs stemmed partly from his interest in the Cherokee heritage he inherited from the Rogers family.

In addition to Will, Jr.'s involvement in Indian matters, politics, and journalism, he was a movie, television, and radio actor. He began his "theatrical" activities as a twelve-year-old playwright when he won David Belasco's Little Theatre tournament for his play *Judge Lynch* in 1924. Twenty-seven years later he starred in his first motion picture, *The Story of Will Rogers.* Warner Brothers had been interested in making this movie, based on Betty Blake Rogers's book, since 1941. After five years and a long search for the lead man, a cast was chosen with Will, Jr., in the role of his father. Will, Jr.'s work on his newspaper and in politics interfered with the making of the movie, and production, delayed for three years, did not begin until 1951. Taking a three-month leave of absence from his paper, Rogers practiced the trick roping his father had taught him as a boy and readied himself to play opposite Jane Wyman as his mother.

The filming of the picture went well, and *The Story of Will Rogers* was a commercial success. Will, Jr., however, thought he was not prepared for an acting career. "I'll go back to my newspaper and my politics," he said. "You know, I never spoke any lines, not even 'shut the door, open the window,' until I played my father. I hadn't even been in plays at college" ("Louella O. Parsons in Hollywood," unidentified article, Will Rogers, Jr., clipping file, NN-L-BRTC). Despite his apparent resolve, he did not return to newspaper work for long. He soon signed with Screen Gems to star in a Ford Television Theater production, *Life, Liberty and Orin Dooley*, the story of a Korean War veteran. He followed this with a second picture in 1954 for Warner Brothers, *The Boy from Oklahoma*, along with *Look for the Silver Lining* and *The Eddie Cantor Story*. He also played in *Gift of the Devil*, on the ABC television network, and in *A Mule for Santa Fe*, on CBS.

Will, Jr., worked in radio as well as television. In the early 1950s he signed a contract with the CBS radio network to perform in *Rogers of the Gazette*. In this series he played the editor of a small-town weekly newspaper. He found radio a more congenial environment than television. "Radio is so much easier," he said. "Television needs a dramatic sock, but radio is milder, an I just happen to be a mild-mannered fellow." An editor of a small weekly newspaper was also the perfect role for him. "I'm not an actor. I can't do anything outside of my own character, so I just try to be natural and not act. Any role I play in has to be tailor-made or it sounds phony" (Val Adams, "He Just Does What Comes Naturally," unidentified article, Will Rogers, Jr., clipping file, NN-L-BRTC). On 26 June 1953 he narrated the one-hour radio program *38th Parallel—USA* and in later years two documentaries, one on Geronimo and one on Arizona ghost towns.

Will, Jr., dabbled in other performance roles over the years. He had a brief stage career in 1954 when he played the small-town newspaper publisher in Eugene O'Neill's *Ah, Wilderness!* at the Pasadena Playhouse. He also appeared on television as the anchor for CBS's *Good Morning* show in 1957–58 and in commercials for Grape Nuts cereal, Washington state apples, and Massey-Ferguson tractors.

Throughout his life Will, Jr., sought his own place and recognition in the world apart from his father. Yet after publishing a newspaper (he sold the *Beverly Hills Citizen* in 1954), serving in Congress, and fighting heroically in war, he still believed he had not accomplished much. His father's reputation apparently overshadowed and repeatedly dwarfed his many accomplishments. "If anything ever turned me off Will Rogers it was the way that people approached me for the first 10 or 15 years after his death," he recalled. "I heard I would never be the man my father was. I was told I had to behave, be polite, never raise hell, because—oh God!—that would destroy the name. My younger brother Jim had no compunction. But I had the name" (*People Magazine*, 26 November 1979, 97). Years earlier he told a reporter that he planned on dropping the junior from his name "just as soon as I can" (*Dallas Morning News*, 30 June 1946, Will Rogers clipping file, NN-L-BRTC).

In 1959 Governor Edmund Brown appointed Will, Jr., to a four-year term as a California state park commissioner, and within a year the commission elected him chairman. His service on the commission was cut short, though, when in 1961 he was arrested and tried on a morals charge. While driving on U.S. Highway 101 near the city of Encinitas, California, Will, Jr., had allegedly exposed himself to passing motorists. At the time he said he felt "out of his mind from overwork and on the verge of a nervous breakdown" ("Fate of Rogers Jr. Put in Hands of Jury," unidentified article, 18 August 1961, Will Rogers, Jr., biographical material, Hearst Clipping Collection, CLSU). Charged with lewd and dissolute conduct, he was vindicated in court when a jury found him innocent.

Comparison with the famous Will Rogers and the challenge of living up to his father's reputation haunted Will, Jr., all his life. Curiously, in some degree he replicated his father's own experiences. His father had written front-page, weekly and daily newspaper columns for years, and Will, Jr., chose a career in journalism. His major acting debut was as his father in *The Story of Will Rogers*, and his one major stage appearance was in the same role his father had played in Eugene O'Neill's *Ah, Wilderness!* When a friend suggested that he never had the hunger to build a film career, he answered, "Maybe not, but the old man had already reached the top so there was no way I could ever beat that. Why try?" (Collins, "Fond Farewell").

Will, Jr., remained active, operating a real estate business in Beverly Hills and managing the family's investments and his father's copyrights. He represented his family at his father's centennial birthday celebrations in New York, California, and Oklahoma. He was active as a member of the Will Rogers Memorial Commission that oversaw his father's museum in Claremore, Oklahoma. He took great interest in the work of scholars who wrote about his father, often making himself available to authors who wanted to make sure their facts were correct. He also taped his father's old movies and radio broadcasts in order to preserve them for later use. At the time of his death he had just finished narrating a new version of his father's 1922 movie, *The Roping Fool*.

Will, Jr., lived the last years of his life in Tubac, Arizona. Collier Rogers had selected this site for a home when she found it congenial to her health. She suffered for a long time from a debilitating case of tuberculosis and died in 1976. When Will, Jr., reached his early eighties, he was in ill health and in considerable pain. He had suffered from two strokes, the after-effects of hip-implant surgery, and disability from his old war wound to his knee. The strokes had resulted in some memory loss. On 9 July 1993 he drove his car to the outskirts of Tubac. He was found there, dead, the next day, his death the result of a self-inflicted gunshot wound to the head. William Vann Rogers was eighty-one years old (Collins, "Fond Farewell"; *Current Biography*, September 1993, 59; *LAT*, 11 July 1993; *NYT*, 10 May 1924 and 11 July 1993; Will Rogers, Jr., biographical file, PP; Will Rogers, Jr., biographical material, Hearst Clippings Collection, CLSU; Will Rogers, Jr., subject file, NNMoMa–FC; Will Rogers, Jr., clipping file, NN-L-BRTC; Yagoda, *Will Rogers*, 130–31, 272–73, 313–14, 326).

SILVERMAN, Sime J. (1873–1932). As the founder and owner of the trade paper *Variety*, Sime Silverman became the best known theatrical publisher of his era. Born in Cortland, New York, and raised in Syracuse, New York, he was the son of Rachel Ganz and George Silverman. Although he did not come from a theatrical family, his mother, a native of Bristol, England, had a passion for music, which she passed on to her son. As a young man Silverman worked for his father's business, the Financial Security Co., which had several theatrical clients who interested Silverman in show business. He soon felt compelled to find theatrical work in New York City. In 1899 he began work as a vaudeville critic for George Graham Rice's *Daily American*, an entertainment and horse-racing publication, for which he wrote a column called "The Man in the Third Row." When the paper folded, he replaced the critic Epes W. Sargent on the *New York Morning Telegraph*, a similar publication, for which he wrote under the pseudonym Robert Spear. Legend has it that he was soon fired for writing a very critical review of a vaudeville performance by Radford and Winebuster, called "Two-Man Comedy Knockabout Turn." Angry about Sime's remarks, the vaudeville team canceled their advertising with the paper. Sime recalled that the editor "said I was incompetent and I knew how terribly true that was. He added that I was the worst ever, and I agreed with him" (Stoddart, *Lord Broadway*, 76).

Losing this job proved to be the impetus for starting his own entertainment trade paper, *Variety*, a weekly whose first issue appeared on 16 December 1905. Independent in style and tone, in its premiere issue *Variety* editorialized that it would be devoted to fairness and opposed to censorship of any kind. It became notorious for its honest reviews and attacks on what the paper called "lousy" shows. The first issue, a mere sixteen pages long and selling for 5 cents a copy, was written by a staff of three people, John J. O'Connor, Al Greason, and Silverman. It sold only 320 copies—a modest start for what became the nation's leading show-business trade paper, still in existence today. Silverman rented a one-room office in the Knickerbocker Building at Broadway and Thirty-eighth Street. The struggling enterprise was financially unstable, and *Variety* assets were attached for failure to pay its bills. The weekly was saved by substantial loans of approximately $30,000 by its printer C. J. O'Brien. By the end of its first year, *Variety* was outselling its rivals, the *New York Clipper* and *Billboard*, but still was not profitable.

As its name implies, *Variety* was at first primarily devoted to vaudeville and called itself "The Vaudeville Paper!" (advertisement, *NYDM*, 16 December 1905). Through its reviews and features, *Variety* had an important impact on the development of vaudeville. Iconoclastic in tone, it attacked monopolistic practices in vaudeville theater management and booking, and defended independent vaudeville and the rights of performers. *Variety* also devoted space to the legitimate theater and printed reviews on burlesque, minstrel shows, Broadway productions, circuses, fairs, and other outdoor amusements. As motion pictures developed as a commercial medium and vaudeville declined, *Variety* began to devote more space to films.

In the pages of *Variety*, Silverman fought the vaudeville managers' trust, headed by B. F. Keith and Edward Albee, and its control of bookings. Articles denounced Keith and Albee's opposition to the White Rats, an independent artists' union. From February to June 1906 Silverman wrote a series of editorials in *Variety* entitled "Why the Vaudeville Artists of America Should Organize," in support of the White Rats. Fiercely independent, like his friend the agent William Morris, Silverman attacked the monopolistic practices of the Keith-Albee empire. His good friend John J. Murdock, a Keith-Albee executive, supplied Silverman with inside information regarding its monopoly of the vaudeville field. Through the efforts of Murdock, a meeting was held between Albee and Silverman in the fall of 1904 and a temporary truce arranged.

The truce did not last long. Angry about the stand taken by *Variety* and the staff's consistent panning of Keith Circuit acts, Albee threatened to drive Silverman out of business. Silverman resisted, and the quarrel intensified between 1910 and 1914. In retaliation, Albee ordered his performers and music publishers to cancel their advertising in *Variety*, and in 1913 the paper was banned in Keith-Albee offices. In addition, Albee stole key *Variety* staff members with offers of lucrative agent franchises. The feud almost bankrupted the paper, and Silverman had to seek loans to keep the paper alive.

The weekly *Variety* became noted for its lively writing style, and Silverman hired the best dramatic critics in New York. Silverman himself was among its most outspoken reviewers, but it also had a staff of excellent critics, including Epes W. Sargent (pen name Chicot) and Alfred Rushford Greason (pen name Rush). Silverman had little regard for proper grammar, and he instructed writers to use the "hip" slang of Broadway and Tin Pan Alley. An example of this style is the following: "With Monday of this week, the outlook was rain for the proposition, and a dull vaudeville sky hovered around until Wednesday, when the sun commenced to peek through again" (*Variety*, 3 September 1910). When the stock market crashed in 1929, *Variety* headlined "WALL ST. LAYS AN EGG" (*NYT*, 23 September 1933). *Variety* writers had their own ingenious idioms and pet expressions, such as statements that an actor "wowed" or "panicked" an audience, and they coined such slang terms as *nuts, palooka,* and *scram.* Another of Silverman's innovations was the "new acts" column that kept readers current on up-and-coming performers, as well as new material being performed by established vaudevillians.

Silverman was a personal friend of many show people, including Will Rogers. Around 1910 the editor asked Rogers to write an autobiographical piece about how he had entered show business. Rogers began, "Sime asked me how I got into show business and why I stayed." Rogers never finished the reminiscence (see Excerpt from Unpublished Autobiography, ca. late 1910, above). In a review of *Hands Up*, Sime called Rogers an "individual hit" but panned the show: "The first act ran two hours . . . that's enough to ruin any musical comedy production" (see Review of *Hands Up*, 30 July 1915, above). Sime usually gave Rogers good reviews.

By the 1920s *Variety* was a power in the entertainment industry. William Randolph Hearst once offered over a million dollars to buy the paper. Sime eventually supported Albee's company union and opposed the White Rats because he did not like their leader, Harry Mountford. Silverman acquired his show-business rival, the *New York Clipper*, in 1922 and published it separately until 1924, when it was partially absorbed by *Variety*. He also originated the *Times Square Daily*, a gossip paper, and began a daily issue of *Variety* in Hollywood on 6 September 1933.

Silverman became a commanding presence on the New York theatrical scene, leading Mayor James J. Walker to suggest that Broadway's focal point be renamed "Sime's Square." In 1898 Silverman married Hattie Freeman, who for a time wrote a women's column for *Variety* under the pen name Skirt. They were the parents of two daughters and a son. When Silverman died unexpectedly in Los Angeles at age sixty from a lung hemorrhage, he left 51 percent interest in *Variety* to his wife and children. His son, Syd, who as a young boy wrote a children's column in *Variety* using the name Skigie, assumed the editorship. The remaining 49 percent interest in the paper went to his favorite loyal employees, making them part owners.

At the time of Silverman's death, *Variety* had become a theatrical institution with a staff of 225, and its issues were often over 100 pages long. *Variety* featured its founder's obituary on the editorial page, written by Jack Lait. Sime, he wrote, would have said about his obituary: "Aw, stick it back in the obit department—for the record." But "his boys think it rates editorial-page position. In this sheet or any other, when the biggest, bravest heart on Broadway stopped, it was a big story. Show business knows that. And *Variety* has always been edited for show business" (*VO*, 2:26 September 1933; *DAB*, 9:167–68; *EV*, 466–67, 524–25; Gilbert, *American Vaudeville*, 373–82; Laurie, *Vaudeville*, 312–13, 352; *NYT*, 23 September 1933; *OCAT*, 625; Staples, *Male-Female Comedy Teams in American Vaudeville*, 121; Stoddart, *Lord Broadway*).

STONE, Val Andrew (Fred) (1873–1959). Fred Stone was born in a log cabin near Valmont, Colorado. His family had gone west some years before in a schooner as part of a wagon train. His father named him Val, but his grandmother changed his name to Frederick. His father was a traveling barber, which meant that the family moved frequently. When Stone was eleven, the family was living in Wellington, Kansas, where as a boy he enjoyed climbing telegraph poles. When the W. W. Cole Circus came to town, he did stunts for the performers. At age ten he saw the Walter Kirby Circus, a traveling 10-cent show, which inspired him to practice tightrope walking in his backyard. He soon excelled at a wide variety of tricks and was hired by Kirby's circus to perform as "Mlle. Amy d'Arcy, the Human Doll." A few years later, after the family had moved to Topeka, Kansas, Stone and his younger brother Ed appeared for several weeks with the D'Arby and O'Brien Circus. In the circus Fred Stone was noted for his athletic feats (later he boxed champion James J. Corbett at benefit performances, excelled at rough riding, and acquired the skills of a professional ice skater).

In 1887 Stone met David Craig (Dave) Montgomery, who was then working as a clerk in a railroad office. He was playing the Seckett Circuit of dime museums in St. Joseph, Missouri. Neither knew that eight years later they would begin a partnership that would last until Montgomery's death in 1917. In 1895 Stone was performing in Galveston, Texas, where he met Montgomery again. Montgomery asked him to team up with him in a blackface, two-man minstrel act. Their first successful show together was with Billy Rice's Minstrels in Chicago. From there they moved to a seedy Bowery theater in New York. Finally, they got the opportunity they were looking for. In 1901 they were hired by the theater producer Charles Frohman for the musical comedy *The Girl from Up There*.

The play that made them famous was the musical *The Wizard of Oz* in 1903. Stone played the Scarecrow, while Montgomery took the role of the Tin Woodsman. Stone opened the show hanging on a pole, as if in the middle of a cornfield. Sometimes the show's opening was delayed slightly backstage, and Stone found his limbs going to sleep in this uncomfortable position. His costume was stuffed with straw, a bale of straw being delivered to his dressing room before each performance. His role consisted largely of dancing. Publicity stories commented that he danced a distance equal to that between San Francisco and New York City throughout the run of the show. Stone and Montgomery gave up the chance of a twenty-week run at the London Hippodrome. Montgomery urged Stone that they remain in London, but Stone felt that he belonged in the United States, and they crossed the Atlantic to open the show in Chicago. The production eventually moved to the Majestic Theater on Columbus Circle in New York.

In the cast of *The Wizard of Oz* was the actress Allene Crater. Stone and Crater had met briefly in Denver, and Stone was delighted to discover that she had joined the company. At a party for the cast given by Montgomery and Stone while they were playing in Boston, Stone and Crater began the love affair that culminated in their marriage in 1904.

Montgomery and Stone were featured in other musical comedies that were really vehicles for their versatile talents. In these shows the two became known for their many funny disguises that allowed them to perform a variety of characters. In *The Red Mill* (1906) Stone was able to display his acrobatic skill. He fell backward down an eighteen-foot ladder and rescued a woman prisoner from the top of a windmill while he swung down a mill runner. Stone and Montgomery played show-business vagabonds in *The Old Town* (1912), a hit show in which they sang the popular "Travel, Travel Little Star." In this show Stone performed a lariat dance, jumping in and out of a rope. Rogers taught him the stunt, as well as other rope tricks. Rogers mimicked Stone's dance in his Oklahoma Cowboy vaudeville single at this time. In October 1912 Montgomery and Stone opened in Victor Herbert's musical play *The Lady of the Slipper.* In the show Stone performed a dance on hidden trampolines called "The Punch Bowl Guide." At the surprise conclusion of the second act, Stone and Montgomery did a zany sequence of marches, songs, and dances: an Indian war dance, the Marseillaise, a highland fling, "Pop Goes the Weasel," and an eccentric rendition of "Dixie."

The culmination of their musical comedy successes was *Chin-Chin* (1915), a tour de force that gave them the opportunity to display their comic skills. In the production they changed characters several times as the picaresque tale based on Aladdin demanded. This allowed them to perform innovative acrobatic dancing and clowning in their various roles. Stone, for example, imitated Paderewski and performed a horse-riding stunt in drag as Madame Falloffski. The show was a potpourri of exaggerated dances, chorines, novelties, ludicrous puns, and one-liners. With his inventive dances, acrobatic feats, pleasant singing voice, and inane gags, Stone was a unique talent on the Broadway stage. He once confided to Will Rogers: "It's nothing to get to the top, but darned if it don't keep you hustling to stay there" (unidentified clipping, scrapbook A-2, OkClaW). While on the road with *Chin-Chin,* Dave Montgomery fell increasingly ill. He was hospitalized, lapsed into a coma, and died in 1917. Stone never had another partner. He launched his individual career, taking leading roles in Broadway productions.

Stone and Rogers became great friends and shared a love of roping and the West. One could venture to state that Stone was Rogers's closest friend. Rogers named his youngest son, Fred Rogers (1918–1920), after Stone (young Fred died tragically from diphtheria in Los Angeles; see Biographical Appendix entry ROGERS, James Blake, above). Rogers liked Stone because he had no pretenses and was a down-to-earth person. Rogers once wrote: "You can practice and learn stunts—you got to be born a regular guy" (Rogers, "About Fred Stone," Will Rogers Autobiographical Notes, OkClaW). Much like Rogers, Stone was a proficient roper who could lasso three horses with one loop and do tricks he called Butterflies. He was a good friend of Annie Oakley, whom he had known since his circus days, and Oakley taught his daughter, Dorothy, how to shoot. A rodeo fan, Stone originated the idea of the New York Stampede in 1916.

On several occasions Stone saw Rogers perform his vaudeville routine. During the week of 16 February 1914 both were in Columbus, Ohio. Stone was performing in *The Lady of the Slipper*, while Rogers was appearing at Keith's Theater. Seeing Stone in the audience, Rogers yanked him to the stage by lassoing him in his box. Removing his coat, Stone performed some lariat tricks and danced (Keith's Theatre, Columbus, Ohio, clippings, scrapbook A-3, OkClaW).

Between 1915 and 1919 Rogers and Stone sometimes lived near each other. This was a crucial period in Rogers's career as he left vaudeville for the Broadway stage. With Rogers's vaudeville career at a standstill, Stone encouraged him to find roles in Broadway productions. Rogers did find a part in *Hands Up*, and his success led to other opportunities on the Great White Way. From 1915 to 1919 Rogers was in the *Ziegfeld Follies*, performing at Broadway's New Amsterdam Theatre and its rooftop cabaret, the *Midnight Frolic*.

During this time Rogers and his family were frequent visitors to Stone's forty-three-acre Long Island estate, called Chin-Chin Ranch, in the Massapequa-Amityville area. The grounds contained a polo field, corrals, horses, buffalo barns, and a log cabin. In the summer of 1915 the Rogers family rented a house near the Amityville ranch. The Stones also had a home in Forest Hills in the New York City borough of Queens. The Rogers family lived at 5 Russell Place in Forest Hills beginning in 1915 and possibly until 1919. In the summer of 1918 they rented a three-story house on Clock's Boulevard very near Stone's estate. Once Stone greeted Rogers at the Amityville train station with an old stagecoach drawn by four horses. Rogers played polo frequently on Stone's property, and the two enjoyed doing roping stunts together. Other visitors to the Stone ranch included Annie Oakley, Vernon Castle,

Frank Tinney, Leo Carillo, and the vaudevillians who lived in the nearby artist colony of Freeport. When Rogers went to Hollywood in 1919 to act in films for Samuel Goldwyn, the Rogers family moved in with the Stones while he was away. Rogers's first film, *Laughing Bill Hyde* (1918), filmed in New Jersey, was based on a novel by the popular writer Rex Beach, who was Stone's brother-in-law and a frequent visitor to the Stone ranch.

The Stones's life on the ranch with their daughters Dorothy, Paula, and Carol revolved around riding, theatrical games, and elaborate make-believe. The three Stone children and three of the Rogers children all learned to ride a pony there. In addition, the six children all participated in Wild West shows on Long Island. The Stone girls grew up in the world of the theater, and all acted on the stage. Of them all, Dorothy Stone had the most successful acting career. Though their parents had intended that life in the country would keep the girls away from the lure of the theater, the parents and their friends, such as Rogers, inadvertently brought the theater to the ranch.

Later the Stones and Rogerses got together in Hollywood. At his Pacific Palisades ranch Rogers had a golf course where Stone frequently played. Rogers, who was not a golfer, would caddy for Stone on the course, which consisted of steep inclines and other difficult traps. Betty Blake Rogers recalled that the two could never sit still at dinner and always had to be doing something. Sometimes they roped between courses. She remembered why their friendship developed: "Both of them lived eventful and adventurous lives. They were both outdoor men and always kept themselves in trim as trained athletes do. Fred was already an expert roper and he loved the twirling of the lasso as much as Will did" (Rogers, *Will Rogers*, 113).

Stone and Rogers were also both aviation enthusiasts. Stone flew between his work in Manhattan and his ranch on Long Island. Although he never piloted a plane himself, Rogers flew for pleasure and speed, and also out of a desire to popularize aviation. In 1928 Stone suffered a disastrous crash in his plane named "Done Walking," and at the time fretted that he might have "hurt aviation." Said one reporter: "Tonight, the funny man, the gay dancer, whose grinning jokes made one's side split, lies here in the hospital, his legs fractured, his jaw broken. . . . He may never return to the stage" (Clark, "They Said He'd Never Dance Again," 50). Rogers visited Stone in his hospital room, and true to form, told jokes in hopes of aiding his recovery.

Since Stone was unable to perform in the play *Three Cheers* (1928), Rogers replaced him in the lead role. Stone was to have begun rehearsal the week of his accident. Stone's mind was eased by the thought that the ninety or so performers in the show would not be unemployed and that the backers would not go bankrupt. Stone wired Rogers to express his thanks: "Bill, come up and see me. . . . I'm in a production of my own called Plaster of Paris. In fact, I'm the only one in the cast (Stone, *Rolling Stone*, 237). Rogers replied: "I will be right up, Fred, cause I have to make a picture called *They Had to See Paris First* (Stone, *Rolling Stone*, 237). Nonetheless, missing the show was a disappointment to Stone, for it would have been a chance to co-star with his daughter Dorothy.

Discharged after months in the hospital, Stone wanted to go home by plane, but his wife objected. He undertook a recovery regime in Florida, exercising outdoors and slowly bringing flexibility and strength back to the mended bones and tendons. He thought of the recovery process as if he were preparing for a play: "When I learn something for the stage. . . . I break it into parts, and learn one part, then another. . . . So it was second nature to figure on getting back in shape along the same lines, and I was sure it was just another case of practice, practice, practice" (Clark, "They Said He'd Never Dance Again," 50).

Stone had a long and fairly successful Broadway stage career in the 1920s and 1930s. He appeared in *Tip-Top* (1920), *Stepping Stones* (1923) with his daughters, *Criss-Cross* (1926), *Ripples* (1930), *Smiling Faces* (1932), *Jayhawker* (1934), and *Lightnin'* (1938). His last stage appearance was in 1945 in *You Can't Take It with You*. But these shows never lived up to his early musical comedies with Dave Montgomery.

After Montgomery's death in 1917, Stone appeared in a film called *Under the Top* (1918) for Jesse Lasky. Stone's film career, however, never matched his Broadway appearances. He ended up playing a series of character roles in films. These included roles in *Broadway after Dark* (1924), *Smiling Faces* (1932), *Alice Adams* (1935), and *The Trail of the Lonesome Pine* (1936).

Off stage, Stone was active in the union movement on behalf of vaudeville actors. In 1900 Stone and Montgomery, as well as six other performers, established the actors' union, the Grand Order of White Rats (the White Rats of America). Functioning as a vaudeville fraternal order as well as a union representing performers' rights in dealing with management, the Rats opposed monopolistic practices and booking policies in the vaudeville industry, chiefly by the UBO, the Vaudeville Managers' Protective Association (VMPA), and the Keith-Albee organization.

As a White Rat, Stone supported better salaries, lower booking commissions (paid by artists to agents), greater artistic control over the content of acts (in part, a censorship issue), fair contracts, and better regular working conditions for vaudevillians. The White Rats also protested certain house rules set by managers, such as rules that required performers to punch time clocks or held them from leaving the theater for the remainder of shows, even if their own act was completed. These restrictions hampered artists who wanted to appear at more than one theater in a given night and helped managers monopolize talent that otherwise could have gone to competing venues. Another major issue was the power of managers to cancel acts at will. The White Rats organized a strike protesting these types of policies in 1901. In 1910 the group merged with the militant International Actors' Union under the name of the White Rats Actors' Union of America and represented stage entertainers as an affiliate of the American Federation of Labor (AFL). The union staged walk-outs in Chicago and California to protest cancellation of shows and other unfair labor practices.

In the initial stages, the White Rats was an all-male, all-white fraternity, with secret initiation rites. Over time it came to include African American male members, and it formed a female auxiliary, the Associated Actresses of America (AAA). Although Will Rogers was a close friend and supporter of many White Rats activists, it is not known if he actually became an initiate in the fraternity or was simply an honorary member (see *PWR*, 2:387n.3, 456–57). Consequences of active membership could be dire, as some agents and managers canceled or refused to book known Rats. For a time Stone was blacklisted by the Keith Circuit for his membership.

In 1916–17, as the White Rats worked toward a general strike by perform-ers in the industry, focusing on a dispute in Rogers's home state of Oklahoma, Stone served as president of the rival, pro-VMPA, National Vaudeville Artists Association (NVA), a company union created by Edward F. Albee in 1916. The NVA helped maintain the VMPA blacklist barring those who supported a boycott of nonunion theaters from working and effectively excluding White Rats from appearing in theaters that booked through the UBO. Although the picketing of theaters continued, the boycott was soon broken as artists were forced back to work. The strike failed, and the White Rats called an official end to it in April 1917. In 1919–20 the White Rats challenged Edward F. Albee's control over vaudeville bookings in hearings before the Federal Trade Commission (the commission ruled in Albee's favor). Rogers's friend Pat Rooney was among those who testified in the hearings. After losing the bid with commission, the Rats sold their New York clubhouse to Albee, and it was turned over for use by the NVA. By 1923 the White Rats of America was defunct. Stone's career, meanwhile, prospered.

Stone died of a heart attack at his home in Los Angeles. He was survived by his three daughters. In a weekly article in 1923, Rogers wrote a fitting epitaph: "He is the best loved actor on the Stage today. He plays to the highest type audience of any Musical Show. He is the only Musical comedy comedian that has matinees packed with children, for none of our other Musical Comedy Comedians has ever been able to please the children and the grown ups too. He is as great a pantomimist on the stage as Chaplin is on the screen" ("Application by White Rats," 5; "We Need More Fred Stones," weekly article ms., published on 11 March 1923, OkClaW; Clark, "They Said He'd Never Dance Again," 50; DeFoe, "Fred Stone, Expert Clown," 1003–11; *EV*, 479; Kibler, *Rank Ladies*, 171–98; Fred Stone file, NNMus; Fred Stone biographical file, CSf-PALM; *Los Angeles Examiner*, 15 August 1930; Mordden, *Broadway Babies*, 59–62; Mullett, "Climbing a Greased Pole Was Fred Stone's First Triumph," 19, 133–39; *NYDM*, 21 July 1900, 26 January and 16 February 1901; *NYT*, 16 June 1911, 3 January 1915; Mayme Ober Peak, "Mrs. Fred Stone Tells of Rogers Family Friendship," Will Rogers Personality File, PP; Rogers, "About Fred Stone," Will Rogers Autobiographical Notes, OkClaW; Rogers, *Will Rogers*, 112–14; Slide, *Vaudevillians*, 143–44; Stone, "A Clown Who Built a Skyscraper with Laughs," 32–34, 88–95; Stone, "Stone Recalls Rogers's First Visit with Him," *New Bedford-Standard Times*, 18 August 1935, HTC-MH; Stone, *Rolling Stone*, 129–30, 133–36, 224–25, 237; "Time Clock on Performers," 1; "Triple Victory for the White Rats," 22; "Two More Victories," 9; *Variety*, 18 June 1910, 5; 18 August 1916, 14; 3 November 1916, 6; *VO*, 5:11 March 1959; "White Rats Strike," 4; *WRB*).

WEADICK, Guy (1885–1953). Guy Weadick was born on 23 February to Irish parents in Rochester, New York. At age twenty he went to Wyoming where he learned to rope, ride, and master other cowboy skills. By 1905 Weadick had met Bill Pickett, the famous African American bulldogger, and he became Pickett's promoter in Wild West performances. They worked their way across the prairies to Winnipeg, Canada, until a gang of rustlers stole their horses and escaped across the U.S. border with them. They performed with the Miller Brothers' 101 Ranch Show beginning in 1908, the show's first year on the road. During the winter Weadick appeared on the vaudeville stage performing an act called Roping and Gab, a mixture of rope tricks and patter that resembled Will Rogers's stage routine. In 1906 Weadick met and married Florence LaDue, a well-known trick roper and cowgirl. For a time the two performed together in Wild West shows and vaudeville (see Biographical Appendix entry, LaDue, Florence).

In Wild West shows Weadick was known as Cheyenne Bill, a name that top bronco rider Jim Gabriel also began to use, some years after Weadick. In late

1909 Weadick attempted to differentiate himself from a rodeo outfit run by Jim Gabriel under the name Cheyenne Bill. He wrote a short piece in *Billboard* in January 1909 regarding the origin of the name.

Weadick wrote a column on Wild West shows for *Billboard* magazine, perhaps the first of its kind. His involvement with *Billboard* continued for decades. For the magazine's fortieth anniversary, Weadick wrote a column that praised the staff for recognizing rodeo and Wild West shows as important performance art forms unique to America. Around 1923 Weadick began writing a two-volume work called "Cowboys I Have Known." He pursued this project throughout his lifetime, but never completed it.

Having a mutual love of the cowboy life and many experiences in common, Weadick and Rogers were friends for thirty years. Their paths often crossed on the vaudeville circuit, at stampedes, and in Wild West shows. While Weadick was on the road as a vaudeville lariat performer, he sometimes sent postcards to Rogers. In his *Billboard* column he frequently mentioned Rogers and once noted the death of Rogers's father, Clement Vann Rogers. In one column, entitled "That Ropin' Rogers Kid," Weadick wrote about the origins of Rogers's career. He discussed Rogers's performances at the 1904 St. Louis World Fair, the Wintergarten Theatre in Berlin, and Hammerstein's Victoria Theatre. Both Weadick and Rogers were friendly with the artist Charles M. Russell. Weadick also published an article on Rogers in the February 1935 issue of *West* magazine. When Rogers died in a plane crash in 1935, Weadick was informed at his ranch in Calgary, Canada. "It's a great shock," said Weadick. "He was a great fellow" (*NYT*, 17 August 1935). The two had planned to meet in Alberta, Canada, in the near future.

Weadick was an innovator in organizing Frontier Day celebrations called stampedes and a leader in the development of large-scale Wild West shows that were the genesis of professional rodeos. These events drew on the vogue of the West that was sweeping the nation, the romanticization of the cowboy, and nostalgia for the old West. With the financial aid of four wealthy Canadian cattle owners, he produced the first Calgary Stampede in 1912. This inaugural stampede celebrated the frontier with parades, Wild West shows, and roping and riding competitions that drew skilled cowboys and cowgirls from the United States, Canada, and Mexico. After a hiatus during the World War I years from 1914 to 1918, the Calgary Stampede resumed in 1919. A financial success, this 1919 Stampede featured exciting competitions and offered large purses in prize money that attracted the best cowpunchers in the United States and Canada. Beginning in 1923 the Calgary Stampede became an annual celebration, and Weadick managed the event until 1932.

Two other events Weadick staged were the 1913 Winnipeg Stampede, for which Rogers wrote his article "Various Styles of Roping," published in the official program (see Article by Will Rogers from *The Stampede*, 9–16 August 1913, above). Another ambitious undertaking was the 1916 New York Stampede at the Sheepshead Bay Raceway. Rogers described the activities in two articles for the *New York American*. The New York Stampede helped publicize the sport of rodeo in the New York area, and its popularity eventually led to the holding of rodeo world championships at Madison Square Garden.

In 1920 Weadick bought a ranch in High River, near Calgary, called The Stampede Ranch or T. S. In the 1930s he transformed it into a dude ranch and once hosted the prince of Wales there. In 1950 LaDue and Weadick moved to Phoenix, Arizona, and sold their ranch. When they left Calgary, friends and neighbors presented them with going-away presents that included a check for $10,000, a gold cigarette case and watch, and red roses. The local Blackfoot Native Americans gave gifts of beadwork and exquisite handicrafts. A friend, A. L. Smith, at the presentation ceremony called Weadick the "Will Rogers of Alberta" ("$10,000 Check Was Gift from Alberta Friends to Weadicks," *Montevideo News*, 17 August 1950, GWP-GA). After LaDue died in 1951, Weadick married a lifelong friend, Dorothy Mullins, also a Wild West performer. Weadick died in 1953. He was posthumously inducted into the National Cowboy Hall of Fame in 1976 and the Canadian Rodeo Hall of Fame in 1982 (Armstrong, "Guy Who Started the Stampede," 6; *Billboard*, 23 January and 18 December 1909, 22 January 1910, 22 April, 4 November, and 18 November 1911, 24 August 1935); Guy Weadick biographical material, GWP-GA, OkNCHOF; Dippie, *Charles M. Russell, Word Painter*, 135, 279, 319, 323, 374; "Guy Weadick Traveled Rocky Trail before Hitting Pay Dirt in 1912," 24; Hanes, *Bill Pickett, Bulldogger*, 54; Kennedy, *Calgary Stampede Story*, 21, 25, 28–29, 49; LeCompte, *Cowgirls of the Rodeo*, 52; Porter, *Who's Who in Rodeo*, 136–37; Russell, *Wild West*, 82–83, 105–6; Weadick, "That Ropin' Rogers Kid," 6, unidentified clipping, NNMoMA-FC).

WINTER, Winona (1888?–1940). The actress, singer, and ventriloquist Winona Winter was born in Huntsville, Alabama. She was the daughter of Banks Winter (1855–1936), the minstrel-song writer and composer, and his wife (d. 1922, unnamed in sources located regarding the family). Banks Winter was known for his "silver" tenor voice, and it was said that without him "no minstrel grand circle was considered complete. He sang with most of the leading minstrel shows in his day and had toured with Chauncey Olcott and for Charles Frohman at a time when Frohman was regarded as one of the top minstrel men" (*VO*, 2:16 December 1936). He is best known for his ballad "White Wings."

Winona Winter attended Boston High School. She began acting earlier, at age seven, and made her stage debut in Detroit with a company doing *The Little Tycoon*. Her father staged a comeback ca. 1906, primarily to introduce Winona Winter into vaudeville. Invariably praised for her great beauty, she was a hit in vaudeville theaters in the United States and then in London, where she headlined in big-time music halls. She was hired by producer Charles Frohman to appear in his musical comedy company in the summer of 1906, and she was featured as Lady Agnes Congress in his *Little Cherub*, a three-act comedy by Owen Hall, with music by Ivan Caryll. She played in the U.S. production of *The Little Cherub* with James Blakely at the Criterion Theatre, New York, in the 1906 and 1907 seasons. In 1910 she was playing the role of Constance Harvey in *He Came from Milwaukee*, a musical comedy in two acts by Mark Swan, with music by Ben M. Jerome and others and lyrics by Edward Madden. She received high praise for her performance in the role at the Casino Theatre. After commenting on the beauty of the female cast members in the comedy, the *New York Times* singled out Winter: "It is doubtful . . . if there is in this country another singing soubrette with as much general ability and absolutely no affectations as Miss Winona Winter, who used to ventriloquize in vaudeville. She acts charmingly, sings very sweetly, and always with such delightful diction that not a word of her songs is lost. One of the numbers, 'The Sentimental Moon,' is a particularly pleasing number" (*NYT Theater Reviews*, 22 September 1910).

In 1911 Winona Winter did *The Fascinating Widow* at the Liberty Theatre with the famous female impersonator from vaudeville, Julian Eltinge. She played the role of Margaret Leffingwell in the three-act musical comedy, which featured music by Otto Hauerbach. A conservative reviewer stated that "once over the initial unpleasantness of the idea of female impersonation, which is not easy for people of delicate sensibilities, there is nothing especially displeasing about Mr. Eltinge's efforts at femininity. He looks remarkably well in women's togs, manages to affect the gait and voice and manner of some members of the sex, and . . . [is] applauded as either highly humorous or amazingly audacious" (*NYT Theater Reviews*, 12 September 1911). Eltinge played a male suitor to Winter who chose to disguise himself as a woman in order to be near the woman he loved, after her parents initially disapproved of his advances.

Rogers appeared on the bill with Winona Winter at the Majestic Theatre in Chicago in 1912, when Clement Vann Rogers came to see his son perform, and the two periodically performed together on the same programs over the years. Will and Betty Blake Rogers became good friends with Winter and her parents. In 1909 Banks Winter bought a flat in Hyde Park, outside Chicago. He wrote warmly to Will Rogers from Winona Winter's engagement at the La Salle Theater in March 1909. He enclosed a formal printed announcement of Mort Singer's "latest La Salle Theatre success, 'The Golden Girl,' by Adams, Hough, & Howard, A West Point Musical Comdedy" with headliners Harry Tighe and Winona Winter. He addressed the letter to "Will Rogers, "The Cowboy and the Lady" (a reference to Betty Blake Rogers) at the Orpheum Theatre in Seattle, Washington (Banks Winter to Will Rogers, with enclosure, 14 March 1909, OkClaW). Betty Blake Rogers received a letter from a Clara Winter (perhaps Winona Winter's mother, or else a sister) written from Chicago in February 1909 that sent news of Winona Winter's work and heart-felt thanks for all the support and friendship Will and Betty Blake Rogers had given Winona ("these little kind attentions from those you love, make life worth while") (Clara Winter to Mrs. Will Rogers, c/o Orpheum Theatre, Minneapolis, Minn., 15 February 1909, OkClaW). Winona Winter's mother died in 1922. The *Variety Obituaries* listing for 20 October 1922 reported that "the wife of Banks Winter and mother of Winona Winter died Oct. 13 of heart failure at the Battle Creek (Mich.) Sanitarium" (*VO*, 1:20 October 1922).

Winona Winter and the Rogerses socialized when their schedules permitted, and she and Rogers did benefit work together when both were working in New York. She was still doing musical comedy work in 1921, when she appeared in *The Broadway Whirl*. Like Rogers, Winter successfully made the transition from vaudeville to legitimate stage work to film. She was a supporting actress in silent films, including John Barrymore's *Man From Mexico* (1914). Winter married sports statistician Norman Leopold Sper (ca. 1896–1955), and they had one son, Norman Sper, Jr. Sper was from Brooklyn and worked briefly as a journalist after World War I. He went into publicity work for celebrities,and met Winter when she was working on stage. Their son became a national college diving champion as a student at the University of North Carolina, where he majored in theater arts. The elder Norman Sper became a director and producer of football features for television and was assisted in his successful *Football This Week* show by his son. Winona Winter died in Hollywood, California, on 27 April 1940. Sper remarried after her death. He died of a cerebral hemorrhage in Hollywood on 26 January 1955 (*EV*, 526; *NYT Theater Reviews*, 7 August 1906; Kibler, *Rank Ladies*, 33; Laurie, *Vaudeville*, 116; Mantle and Sherwood, eds. *Best Plays of 1899–1909*, 516; *Theatre Magazine*, 24 [November 1921], 303; *VO*, 3:8 May 1940, 4:9 February 1955; *WhoHolly*, 1839; *Who Stg*, 457).

Bibliography

THE SOURCES USED IN THIS VOLUME ARE LISTED IN THREE CATEGORIES: BOOKS, articles and chapters in anthologies, and unpublished and miscellaneous sources. Titles given in quotation marks in the document endnotes and in the Biographical Appendix entries may be found either in the "articles and chapters" section or among the "unpublished and miscellaneous sources." See also the list of symbols and abbreviations in the front matter of the volume.

BOOKS

Allen, Michael. *Rodeo Cowboys in the North American Imagination.* Reno: University of Nevada Press, 1998.

Allen, Robert C. *Horrible Prettiness: Burlesque and American Culture.* Chapel Hill: University of North Carolina Press, 1991.

———. *Vaudeville and Film, 1895–1915: A Study in Media Interaction.* New York: Arno Press, 1980.

Anderson, Donald F. *William Howard Taft: A Conservative's Conception of the Presidency.* Ithaca, N.Y.: Cornell University Press, 1973.

Anderson, Judith Icke. *William Howard Taft: An Intimate History.* New York: W. W. Norton, 1981.

Arpad, Joseph J., and Kenneth R. Lincoln. *Buffalo Bill's Wild West.* Palmer Lake, Colo.: Filter Press, 1971.

Ashby, LeRoy. *William Jennings Bryan: Champion of Democracy.* Boston: Twayne Publishers, 1987.

Auster, Albert. *Actresses and Suffragists: Women in the American Theater, 1880–1920.* New York: Praeger, 1984.

Baker, Paul R. *Richard Morris Hunt.* Cambridge, Mass.: MIT Press, 1980.

Balio, Tino, ed. *The American Film Industry.* Madison: University of Wisconsin Press, 1985.

Baral, Robert. *Revue: The Great Broadway Period.* New York: Fleet Press, 1962.

Beautiful Daring Western Girls: Women of the Wild West Shows. Cody, Wyo.: Buffalo Bill Historical Center, n.d.

Berg, A. Scott. *Goldwyn: A Biography.* New York: Alfred A. Knopf, 1989.

Bergan, Ronald. *The Great Theatres of London: An Illustrated Companion.* London: Admiral, 1987.

Bernheim, Alfred L. *The Business of the Theatre.* New York: Actors' Equity Association, 1932.

Berson, Misha. *The San Francisco Stage: From Golden Spike to Great Earthquake, 1869–1906.* San Francisco: San Francisco Performing Arts Library and Museum Series 4, February 1992.

Birkmire, John H. *The Planning and Construction of American Theatres.* New York: John Wiley and Sons, 1906.

Blesh, Rudi. *Keaton.* New York: Macmillan, 1966.

Bogle, Donald. *Toms, Coons, Mulattoes, Mammies, and Bucks: An Interpretive History of Blacks in American Films.* New York: Viking Press, 1973.

Bordman, Gerald. *American Musical Theatre: A Chronicle.* New York: Oxford University Press, 1992.

_____. *Jerome Kern: His Life and Music.* New York: Oxford University Press, 1980.

Bowser, Eileen. *The Transformation of Cinema 1907–1915.* New York: Charles Scribner's Sons, 1990.

Bright, Brenda Jo, and Liza Bakewell, eds. *Looking High and Low: Art and Cultural Identity.* Tucson: University of Arizona Press, 1995.

Brooks, Tim, and Earle Marsh. *The Complete Directory to Prime Time Network TV Shows: 1946–Present.* New York: Ballantine Books, 1979.

Brown, T. Allston. *A History of the New York Stage: From the First Performance in 1732 to 1901.* 3 vols. New York: Dodd, Mead, 1903.

Bryan, William Jennings, with Mary Baird Bryan. *The Memoirs of William Jennings Bryan.* Philadelphia: John C. Winston Co., 1925.

Bryan, William Jennings, with Mary Baird Bryan. *Speeches of William Jennings Bryan.* New York: Funk and Wagnalls, 1909.

Busby, Roy. *British Music Hall: An Illustrated Who's Who From 1850 to the Present Day.* London: Paul Elek, 1976.

Butsch, Richard, ed. *For Fun and Profit: The Transformation of Leisure into Consumption.* Philadelphia: Temple University Press, 1990.

Byers, Chester. *Roping: Trick and Fancy Rope Spinning.* New York: G. P. Putnam's Sons, 1928.

Caffin, Caroline. *Vaudeville.* New York: M. Kennerley, 1914.

Cantor, Eddie. *As I Remember Them.* New York: Duell, Sloan and Pearce, 1963.

_____. *My Life Is in Your Hands.* New York: Blue Ribbon Books, 1932.

Cantor, Eddie, with Jane Kesner Ardmore. *Take My Life.* Garden City, N.Y.: Doubleday, 1957.

Castle, Irene. *Castles in the Air.* Garden City, New York: Doubleday, 1958.

Ceram, C. W. *Archaeology of the Cinema.* London: Thames and Hudson, 1965.

Chambers, John Whiteclay. *The Tyranny of Change: America in the Progressive Era, 1890–1920.* New York: St. Martin's Press, 1992.

Chaplin, Charles. *My Autobiography.* New York: Simon and Schuster, 1964.

Chapman, John, and Garrison P. Sherwood, eds. *The Best Plays of 1894–1899.* New York: Dodd, Mead, 1955.

Charters, Ann. *Nobody: The Story of Bert Williams.* London: Macmillan, 1970.

Chauncey, George. *Gay New York: Gender, Urban Culture, and the Making of the Gay Male World, 1890–1940.* New York: Basic Books, 1994.

Clancy, Foghorn. *My Fifty Years in Rodeo: Living with Cowboys, Horses and Danger.* San Antonio, Tex.: Naylor, 1952.

Cobble, Dorothy Sue. *Dishing It Out: Waitresses and Their Unions in the Twentieth Century.* Urbana: University of Illinois Press, 1991.

Cohan, George M. *Twenty Years on Broadway and the Years It Took to Get There: The*

True Story of a Trouper's Life from the Cradle to the "Closed Shop." New York: Harper and Brothers, 1924.

Cohen, Richard M., and David S. Neft. *The World Series: Complete Play-by-Play of Every Game, 1903–85.* New York: Macmillan and Collier Books, 1986.

Cohen-Stratyner, Barbara. *Ned Wayburn and the Dance Routine: From Vaudeville to the Ziegfeld Follies.* N.p.: Society of Dance History Scholars, 1996.

Cohen-Stratyner, Barbara, ed. *Popular Music, 1900–1919.* Detroit, Mich.: Gale Research, 1988.

Collings, Ellsworth. *The Old Home Ranch: Birthplace of Will Rogers.* 2d ed. Claremore, Okla.: Will Rogers Memorial, 1982.

Collins, Reba. *Will Rogers: Courtship and Correspondence, 1900–1915.* Oklahoma City: Neighbors and Quaid, 1992.

Collins, Reba, ed. *Roping Will Rogers Family Tree.* Claremore, Okla.: Will Rogers Heritage Press, 1982.

Cooper, Gail. *Air-conditioning America: Engineers and the Controlled Environment, 1900–1960.* Baltimore: Johns Hopkins University Press, 1998.

Craig, Warren. *Sweet and Lowdown: America's Popular Song Writers.* Metuchen, N.J.: Scarecrow Press, 1978.

Cressy, Will M. *Continuous Vaudeville.* Boston: Richard G. Badger, 1914.

Croy, Homer. *Our Will Rogers.* New York: Duell, Sloan and Pearce. Boston: Little, Brown, 1953.

Davies, Acton. *Maude Adams.* New York: F. A. Stokes, 1901.

Davies, Marion, Pamela Pfau, and Kenneth S. Marx, eds. *The Times We Had.* Indianapolis: Bobbs-Merrill, 1975.

Davis, Tracy C. *Actresses as Working Women.* London: Routledge, 1991.

Day, Donald. *Will Rogers: A Biography.* New York: David McKay, 1962.

Day, Donald, ed. *The Autobiography of Will Rogers.* Boston: Houghton Mifflin, 1949. Reprinted., New York: AMS Press, 1979.

DeGregorio, William A. *The Complete Book of U.S. Presidents.* 2d ed. New York: Dembner Books, 1989.

Delehanty, Randolph. *Walks and Tours in the Golden Gate City San Francisco.* New York: Dial Press, 1980.

Dennett, Andrea Stulman. *Weird and Wonderful: The Dime Museum in American Culture.* New York: New York University Press, 1997.

Dennison, Sam. *Scandalize My Name: Black Imagery in American Popular Music.* New York: Garland, 1982.

DiMeglio, John E. *Vaudeville U.S.A.* Bowling Green, Ohio: Bowling Green University Popular Press, 1973.

Dippie, Brian W., ed. *Charles M. Russell, Word Painter: Letters 1887–1926.* Fort Worth, Tex.: Amon Carter Museum, 1993.

Dizikes, John. *Opera in America: A Cultural History.* New Haven: Yale University Press, 1993.

Downing, Antoinette F., and Vincent J. Scully, Jr. *The Architectural Heritage of Newport, Rhode Island, 1640–1915.* 2d rev. ed. New York: Clarkson N. Potter, 1967.

Dunning, John. *Tune In Yesterday: The Ultimate Encyclopedia of Old-Time Radio.* Englewood Cliffs, N.J.: 1976.

DuPriest, Maude Ward, Jennie May Bard, and Anna Foreman Graham. *Cherokee Recollections: The Story of the Indian Women's Pocahontas Club and Its Members in the Cherokee Nation and Oklahoma Beginning in 1899.* Stillwater, Okla.: Thales Microuniversity Press, 1976.

Elliott, Eugene Clinton. *A History of Variety-Vaudeville in Seattle: From the Beginning to 1914.* Edited by Glenn Hughes. University of Washington Publications in Drama 1. Seattle: University of Washington Press, 1944.

Erenberg, Lewis A. *Steppin' Out: New York Nightlife and the Transformation of American Culture, 1890–1930.* Chicago: University of Chicago Press, 1981.

Ewen, David. *American Songwriters.* New York: H. W. Wilson, 1987.

Ewen, David, ed. *American Popular Composers: From Revolutionary Times to the Present.* New York: H. W. Wilson, 1962.

Fall, Thomas. *Jim Thorpe.* New York: Crowell, 1970.

Fell, John, ed. *Film before Griffith.* Berkeley: University of California Press, 1983.

Felstead, Theodore S. *Stars Who Made the Halls: A Hundred Years of English Humour, Harmony and Hilarity.* London: T. Werner Laurie, 1946.

Fielding, Raymond. *The American Newsreel, 1911–1967.* Norman: University of Oklahoma Press, 1972.

Fields, Armond, and L. Marc Fields. *From the Bowery to Broadway: Lew Fields and the Roots of American Popular Theater.* New York: Oxford University Press, 1993.

Fisher, James. *Al Jolson: A Bio-Bibliography.* Westport, Conn.: Greenwood Press, 1994.

Foster, William Trufant. *Vaudeville and Motion Picture Shows: A Study of Theaters in Portland, Oregon.* Portland: Reed College, 1914.

Fox, Charles Donald. *Famous Film Folk: A Gallery of Life Portraits and Biographies.* New York: George H. Doran, 1925.

Franklin, Joe. *Joe Franklin's Encyclopedia of Comedians.* Secaucus, N.J.: Citadel Press, 1979.

Fredriksson, Kristine. *American Rodeo: From Buffalo Bill to Big Business.* College Station, Tex.: Texas A&M University Press, 1985.

Freedland, Michael. *Jolson.* New York: Stein and Day, 1972.

Frick, John W. *New York's First Theatrical Center: The Rialto at Union Square.* Ann Arbor, Mich.: UMI Research Press, 1985.

Frick, John Ward, and Carlton Gray, eds. *Directory of Historic American Theatres.* New York: Greenwood Press, 1987.

Frohman, Charles. *The Maude Adams Book.* New York: C. Frohman, 1909.

Furia, Philip. *The Poets of Tin Pan Alley: A History of America's Great Lyricists.* New York: Oxford University Press, 1990.

Gaenzl, Kurt, ed. *Encyclopedia of the Musical Theatre.* 2 vols. New York: Schirmer Books, 1994.

Gagey, Edmond M. *The San Francisco Stage: A History.* New York: Columbia University Press, 1950.

Gammond, Peter. *The Oxford Companion to Popular Music.* Oxford: Oxford University Press, 1991.

George-Graves, Nadine. *The Royalty of Negro Vaudeville: The Whitman Sisters and the Negotiation of Race, Gender, and Class in African-American Theater, 1900–1940.* New York: St. Martin's Press, 2000.

Gilbert, Douglas. *American Vaudeville: Its Life and Times.* New York: Whittlesly House, 1940.

Gilkeson, John S., Jr. *Middle-Class Providence, 1820–1940.* Princeton: Princeton University Press, 1986.

Glad, Paul W. *The Trumpet Soundeth: William Jennings Bryan and His Democracy, 1896–1912.* Lincoln: University of Nebraska Press, 1960.

Glazer, Irvin R. *Philadelphia Theaters: A Pictorial Architectural History.* Philadelphia: The Athenaeum of Philadelphia and Dover Publications, 1994.

_____. *Philadelphia Theatres, A–Z: A Comprehensive, Descriptive Record of 813 Theatres Constructed since 1724.* Westport, Conn.: Greenwood Press, 1986.

Glyn, Elinor. *Three Weeks.* 1907. Reprint. London: Duckworth, 1974.

Goble, Danney. *Progressive Oklahoma.* Norman: University of Oklahoma Press, 1980.

Golden, George Fuller. *My Lady Vaudeville and Her White Rats.* New York: Broadway Publishing, 1909.

Goldman, Herbert G. *Fanny Brice: The Original Funny Girl.* New York: Oxford University Press, 1992.

_____. *Jolson: The Legend Comes to Life.* New York: Oxford University Press, 1988.

Gomery, Douglas. *Shared Pleasures: A History of Movie Presentation in the United States.* Madison: University of Wisconsin Press, 1992.

Goodwin, Doris Kearns. *The Fitzgeralds and the Kennedys.* New York: St. Martin's Press, 1987.

Grau, Robert. *The Business Man in the Amusement World: A Volume of Progress in the Field of the Theatre.* New York: Broadway Publishing, 1910.

_____. *Forty Years Observation of Music and the Drama.* New York: Broadway Publishing, 1909.

_____. *The Stage in the Twentieth Century.* 1912. Reprint. New York: Benjamin Blom, 1969.

Green, Abel, and Joe Laurie, Jr. *Show Biz: From Vaude to Video.* New York: Henry Holt, 1951.

Green, Stanley. *Encyclopaedia of the Musical Theatre.* New York: Dodd, Mead, 1976.

Grossman, Barbara. *Funny Woman: The Life and Times of Fanny Brice.* Bloomington: Indiana University Press, 1991; Midland Book, 1992.

Gubar, Susan. *Racechanges: White Skin, Black Face in America.* New York: Oxford University Press, 1997.

Günter, Ernst. *Geschichte des Variétés.* Berlin: Henschelverlag, 1981.

Guiles, Fred Lawrence. *Marion Davies.* New York: Bantam Books, 1972.

Gurock, Jeffrey S. *When Harlem Was Jewish: 1870–1930.* New York: Columbia University Press, 1979.

Halliwell, Leslie. *Leslie Halliwell's Film Guide.* 7th ed. New York: Harper and Row, 1989.

Hampton, Benjamin B. *History of the American Film Industry.* New York: Dover, 1970.

Hanes, Col. Bailey C. *Bill Pickett, Bulldogger.* Norman: University of Oklahoma Press, 1977.

Harding, Alfred. *The Revolt of the Actors.* New York: William Morrow, 1929.

Hart, James D. *The Oxford Companion to American Literature.* 4th ed. New York: Oxford University Press, 1965.

Hartnoll, Phyllis, ed. *The Oxford Companion to the Theatre.* 3d ed. London: Oxford University Press, 1967.

Henderson, Mary C. *The City and the Theatre: New York Playhouses from Bowling Green to Times Square.* Clifton, N.J.: James T. White, 1973.

Herbert, Ian, ed. *Who's Who in the Theatre.* 17th ed. Detroit: Gale Research, 1977.

Herman, Hal C., ed. *How I Broke into the Movies: Signed Autobiographies by Sixty Famous Screen Stars.* Hollywood, Calif.: H. C. Herman, 1929.

Herrick, Howard, ed. *Who's Who in Vaudeville 1911.* New York: Dupree and Pope, 1911.

Herrick, Robert. *Together.* New York: Macmillan, 1908.

Hickok, Ralph. *A Who's Who of Sports Champions: Their Stories and Records.* Boston: Houghton Mifflin, 1995.

Hitchcock, H. Wiley, and Stanley Sadie, eds. *The New Grove Dictionary of American Music.* 4 vols. London: Macmillan Press, 1986.

Holand, Charlie, comp. *Strange Feats and Clever Turns: Remarkable Specialty Acts in Variety, Vaudeville, and Sideshows at the Turn of the 20th Century as Seen by Their Contemporaries.* London: Holland and Palmer, 1998.

Houdini, Harry. *A Magician among the Spirits.* New York: Harper and Brothers, 1924.

Howard, Diana. *London Theatres and Music Halls, 1850–1950.* London: Library Associates, 1970.

Howe, Irving. *World of Our Fathers.* New York: Harcourt Brace and Jovanovich, 1976.

Isenberg, Michael T. *War on Film: The American Cinema and World War I, 1914–1941.* London: Associated University Presses, 1981.

Isman, Felix. *Weber and Fields: Their Tribulations, Triumphs and Their Associates.* New York: Boni and Liveright, 1924.

James, Edward T., ed. *Notable American Women, 1607–1950.* 3 vols. Cambridge, Mass.: Belknap Press, Harvard University Press, 1971.

Jelavich, Peter. *Berlin Cabaret.* Cambridge, Mass.: Harvard University Press, 1993.

Jenkins, Henry. *What Made Pistachio Nuts?: Early Sound Film and the Vaudeville Aesthetic.* New York: Columbia University Press, 1992.

Jessel, George. *Elegy in Manhattan.* New York: Holt, Rinehart and Winston, 1961.

———. *So Help Me: The Autobiography of George Jessel.* New York: Random House, 1943.

Jessel, George, with John Austin. *The World I Lived In.* Chicago: Henry Regnery, 1975.

Johnson, Stephen Burge. *The Roof Gardens of Broadway Theatres, 1883–1942.* Ann Arbor: University of Michigan Press, 1985.

Jordan, Teresa. *Cowgirls: Women of the American West.* Garden City, N.Y.: Anchor Press, 1982.

Kasson, John. *Amusing the Millions: Coney Island at the Turn of the Century.* New York: Hill and Wang, 1978.

Katchmer, George A. *Eighty Silent Film Stars: Biographies and Filmographies of the Obscure to the Well Known.* Jefferson, N.C.: McFarland, 1991.

Keaton, Buster. *My Wonderful World of Slapstick.* Garden City, N.Y.: Doubleday, 1960.

Kennedy, Fred. *The Calgary Stampede Story.* Canada: T. Edwards Thonger, 1952.

Ketchum, Richard M. *Will Rogers: The Man and His Times.* New York: American Heritage and Simon and Schuster, 1973.

Kibler, M. Alison. *Rank Ladies: Gender and Cultural Hierarchy in American Vaudeville.* Chapel Hill: University of North Carolina Press, 1999.

Kinkle, Roger D. *The Complete Encyclopedia of Popular Music and Jazz, 1900–1950.* 4 vols. New Rochelle, N.Y.: Arlington House, 1974.

Lardner, John. *White Hopes and Other Tigers.* Philadelphia: J. B. Lippincott, 1951.

Lasky, Betty. *RKO: The Biggest Little Major of Them All.* Santa Monica, Calif.: Roundtable Publishing, 1989.

Laurie, Joseph, Jr. *Vaudeville: From Honky-tonks to the Palace.* New York: Henry Holt, 1953.

Lax, Roger, and Frederick Smith. *The Great Song Thesaurus.* 2d ed. New York: Oxford University Press, 1989.

Leavitt, Michael Bennett. *Fifty Years in Theatrical Management.* New York: Broadway Publishing, 1912.

LeCompte, Mary Lou. *Cowgirls of the Rodeo: Pioneer Professional Athletes.* Urbana: University of Illinois Press, 1993.

Levine, Lawrence. *Highbrow/Lowbrow: The Emergence of Cultural Hierarchy in America.* Cambridge, Mass.: Harvard University Press, 1988.

Lloyd, Herbert. *Vaudeville Trails thru the West: "By One Who Knows."* San Francisco: San Franciso Publishing and Advertising, 1919.

Lockwood, Charles. *Manhattan Moves Uptown: An Illustrated History.* Boston: Houghton Mifflin, 1976.

Lost Theatres of London. East Kilbride, Scotland: Thomson Litho, 1976.

Lott, Eric. *Love and Theft: Blackface Minstrelsy and the American Working Class.* New York: Oxford University Press, 1993.

Mander, Raymond, and Joe Mitchenson. *British Music Halls.* Rev. ed. London: Gentry Books, 1974.

Mantle, Burns, and Garrison Sherwood, eds. *The Best Plays of 1899–1909 and the Year Book of the Drama in America.* Reprint, New York: Dodd, Mead, 1944.

Mantle, Burns, and Garrison Sherwood, eds. *The Best Plays of 1909–1919 and the Year Book of the Drama in America.* New York: Dodd, Mead, 1933.

Marquis, Arnold. *A Guide to America's Indians: Ceremonials, Reservations, and Museums.* Norman: University of Oklahoma Press, 1974.

Marston, William Moulton, and John Henry Feller. *F. F. Proctor: Vaudeville Pioneer.* New York: Richard R. Smith, 1943.

Martin, Linda, and Kerry Segrave. *Women in Comedy.* Secaucus, N.J.: Citadel Press, 1986.

Mast, Gerald. *Can't Help Singin': The American Musical on Stage and Screen.* Woodstock, N.Y.: Overlook Press, 1987.

Mates, Julian. *America's Musical Stage: Two Hundred Years of Musical Stage.* Westport, Conn.: Greenwood Press, 1985.

May, Lary. *Screening Out the Past: The Birth of Mass Culture and the Motion Picture Industry.* New York: Oxford University Press, 1980.

McArthur, Benjamin. *Actors and American Culture, 1880–1920.* Philadelphia: Temple University Press, 1984.

McCabe, John. *George M. Cohan: The Man Who Owned Broadway.* Garden City, N.Y.: Doubleday, 1973.

McCallum, John D. *The World Heavyweight Boxing Championship.* Radnor, Pa.: Chilton Book, 1974.

McKelvey, Blake. *Rochester, the Quest for Quality: 1890–1925.* Cambridge, Mass.: Harvard University Press, 1956.

McLanathan, Richard. *The American Tradition in the Arts.* New York: Harcourt, Brace and World, 1968.

McLean, Albert F., Jr. *American Vaudeville as Ritual.* Lexington: University of Kentucky Press, 1965.

McNamara, Brooks. *The Shuberts of Broadway: A History Drawn from the Collections of the Shubert Archive.* New York: Oxford University Press, 1990.

McNeil, Alex. *Total Television: A Comprehensive Guide to Programming from 1948 to 1980.* New York: Penguin Books, 1980.

Meade, Marion. *Buster Keaton: Cut to the Chase.* New York: Harper Collins, 1995.

Menke, Frank G. *The Encyclopedia of Sports.* 5th rev. ed. Revisions by Suzanne Treat. South Brunswick, N.J.: A. S. Barnes, 1975.

Mix, Olive Stokes, with Eric Heath. *The Fabulous Tom Mix.* Englewood Cliffs, N.J.: Prentice-Hall, 1957.

Mix, Paul E. *The Life and Legend of Tom Mix.* London: Thomas Yoseloff; South Brunswick, N.J.: A. S. Barnes, 1972.

Mix, Tom. *West of Yesterday.* Los Angeles: Times-Mirror Press, 1923.

Mordden, Ethan. *Broadway Babies: The People Who Made the American Musical.* New York: Oxford University Press, 1983.

Morehouse, Ward. *George M. Cohan: Prince of the American Theater.* New York: J. B. Lippincott, 1943.

Morris, Juddi. *The Harvey Girls: The Women Who Civilized the West.* New York: Walker, 1994.

Moses, L. G. *Wild West Shows and the Images of American Indians, 1883–1933.* Albuquerque: University of New Mexico Press, 1996.

Mould, David H. *American Newsfilm 1914–1919: The Underexposed War.* New York: Garland Publishing, 1983.

Muscatine, Doris. *Old San Francisco: The Biography of a City from Early Days to the Earthquake.* New York: G. P. Putnam's Sons, 1975.

Musser, Charles. *Before the Nickelodeon: Edwin S. Porter and the Edison Manufacturing Company.* Berkeley: University of California Press, 1991.

———. *The Emergence of Cinema: The American Screen to 1907.* New York: Charles Scribner's Sons, 1990.

Musser, Charles, with Carol Nelson. *High-class Moving Pictures.* Princeton, N.J.: Princeton University Press, 1991.

Nawsaw, David. *The Chief: The Life of William Randolph Hearst.* Boston: Houghton Mifflin, 2000.

Nawsaw, David. *Going Out: The Rise and Fall of Public Amusements.* New York: Basic Books, 1993.

Niver, Kemp R. *Biograph Bulletins 1896–1908.* Edited by Bebe Bergsten. Los Angeles: Locare Research Group, 1971.

———. *D. W. Griffith, His Biograph Films in Perspective.* Edited by Bebe Bergsten. Los Angeles: John D. Roche, 1974.

_____. *Early Motion Pictures.* Edited by Bebe Bergsten. Washington, D.C.: Library of Congress, 1985.

_____. *Klaw and Erlanger Present Famous Plays in Pictures.* Edited by Bebe Bergsten. Los Angeles: Local Research Group, 1976.

Nye, Russell. *The Unembarrassed Muse: The Popular Arts in America.* New York: Dial Press, 1971.

Oberfirst, Robert. *Al Jolson: You Ain't Heard Nothing Yet.* San Diego, Calif.: A. S. Barnes, 1980.

Odell, George C. D. *Annals of the New York Stage.* 15 vols. New York: Columbia University Press, 1927–49.

Oldham, Gabriella. *Keaton's Silent Shorts: Beyond the Laughter.* Carbondale: Southern Illinois University Press, 1996.

Orpheum Circuit of Theatres. New York: Orpheum Theatre and Realty, 1909.

Page, Brett. *Writing for Vaudeville.* Springfield, Mass.: Home Correspondence School, 1915.

Patterson, Joseph Medill. *A Little Brother of the Rich.* Chicago: Reilly and Britton, 1908.

Payne, Darwin. *Owen Wister: Chronicler of the West, Gentleman of the East.* Dallas, Tex.: Southern Methodist University Press, 1985.

Payne, William Howard, and Jake G. Lyons, eds. *Folks Say of Will Rogers: A Memorial Anecdotage.* New York: G. P. Putnam's Sons, 1936.

Peiss, Kathy. *Cheap Amusements: Working Women and Leisure in Turn-of-the-Century New York.* Philadelphia: Temple University Press, 1986.

Pickard, Roy. *A Companion to the Movies.* London: Lutterworth Press, 1972.

Poling-Kempes, Lesley. *The Harvey Girls: Women Who Opened the West.* New York: Paragon House, 1989.

Porter, Willard H. *Who's Who in Rodeo.* Oklahoma City: Powder River Book, n.d. [ca. 1982–83].

Purdy, Helen Throop. *San Francisco As It Was, As It Is and How to See It.* San Francisco: Paul Elder, 1912.

Rabinovitz, Lauren. *For the Love of Pleasure: Women, Movies, and Culture in Turn-of-the-Century Chicago.* New Brunswick, N.J.: Rutgers University Press, 1998.

Read, Jack. *Empires, Hippodromes and Palaces.* London: Alderman Press, 1985.

Reed, Langford, and Hetty Spiers. *Who's Who in Filmland.* 3d ed. London: Chapman and Hall, 1931.

Renton, Edward. *Vaudeville Theatre: Building, Operation, Management.* New York: Gotham Press, 1918.

Report of the State Recreational Inquiry Committee. California State Printing Office, 28 September 1914.

Riske, Milt. *Those Magnificent Cowgirls: A History of the Rodeo Cowgirl.* Cheyenne: Wyoming Publishing, 1983.

Ritter, Lawrence. *Lost Ballparks.* New York: Penguin Books, 1994.

Roach, Joyce Gibson. *The Cowgirls.* Denton: University of North Texas Press, 1990.

Robbins, Phyllis. *Maude Adams, An Intimate Portrait.* New York: Putnam, 1956.

Robinson, Alice M., Vera Mowry Roberts, and Milly S. Barranger. *Notable Women in the American Theatre.* Westport, Conn.: Greenwood Press, 1989.

Robinson, David. *Buster Keaton.* London: Secker and Warburg with the British Film Institute, 1969.

_____. *From Peep Show to Palace: The Birth of American Film.* New York: Columbia University Press, 1996.

Rogal, Samuel J. *A Chronological Outline of American Literature.* New York: Greenwood Press, 1987.

Rogers, Betty. *Will Rogers: His Wife's Story.* 1941. New ed. Norman: University of Oklahoma Press, 1989.

Rollins, Peter C. *Will Rogers: A Bio-Bibliography.* Westport, Conn.: Greenwood Press, 1984.

Rose, Al, and Edmond Souchon. *New Orleans Jazz Family Album.* Baton Rouge: Louisiana State University Press, 1967.

Rose, Frank. *The Agency: William Morris and the Hidden History of Show Business.* New York: Harper Business, 1995.

Rosenthal, Harold, and John Warrack. *Concise Oxford Dictionary of Opera.* 2d ed. New York: Oxford University Press, 1979.

Rosenzweig, Roy. *Eight Hours for What We Will: Workers and Leisure in an Industrial City, 1870-1920.* New York: Cambridge University Press, 1983.

Rowe, Kathleen. *The Unruly Woman: Gender and the Genres of Laughter.* Austin: University of Texas Press, 1995.

Rowland, Mabel, ed. *Bert Williams: Son of Laughter.* New York: English Crafters, 1923.

Russell, Charles M. *Good Medicine: The Illustrated Letters of Charles M. Russell.* Garden City, N.Y.: Doubleday, 1929.

_____. *Trails Plowed Under.* Garden City, N.Y: Doubleday, Doran, 1944.

Russell, Don. *Lives and Legends of Buffalo Bill.* Norman: University of Oklahoma Press, 1960.

_____. *The Wild West: A History of the Wild West Shows.* Fort Worth, Tex.: Amon Carter Museum of Western Art, 1970.

Sampson, Henry T. *Blacks in Blackface: A Source Book on Early Black Musical Shows.* Metuchen, N.J.: Scarecrow Press, 1980.

_____. *The Ghost Walks: A Chronological History of Blacks in Show Business, 1865–1910.* Metuchen, N.J.: Scarecrow Press, 1988.

Samuels, Charles, and Louise Samuels. *Once upon a Stage.* New York: Dodd Mead, 1974.

Schoor, Gene, and Henry Gilfond. *The Jim Thorpe Story: America's Greatest Athlete.* New York: Messner, 1951.

Schuster, Mel. *Motion Picture Performers.* Suppl. 1. Metuchen, N.J.: Scarecrow Press, 1976.

Sell, Henry Blackman, and Victor Weybright. *Buffalo Bill and the Wild West.* New York: Oxford University Press, 1955.

Sheean, Vincent. *Oscar Hammerstein I: The Life and Exploits of an Impresario.* New York: Simon and Schuster, 1956.

Short, Ernest. *Fifty Years of Vaudeville.* London: Eyre and Spottiswoode, 1946.

Simon, Louis M. *A History of the Actors' Fund of America.* New York: Theatre Arts Books, 1972.

Sklar, Robert. *Movie-made America.* New York: Random House, 1975.

Slide, Anthony. *The Big V: A History of the Vitagraph Company.* Metuchen, N.J.: Scarecrow Press, 1976.

_____. *The Vaudevillians: A Dictionary of Vaudeville Performers.* Westport, Conn.: Arlington House, 1981.

Slide, Anthony, ed. *Selected Vaudeville Criticism.* Metuchen, N.J.: Scarecrow Press, 1988.

Slout, William L. *Theatre in a Tent.* Bowling Green, Ohio: Bowling Green University Popular Press, 1972.

Slout, William L., ed. *Broadway below the Sidewalk: Concert Saloons of Old New York.* San Bernardino, Calif.: Borgo Press, 1994.

Smallwood, James M., and Steven K. Gragert, eds. *The Coolidge Years: 1925–27,* vol. 2 of *Will Rogers' Weekly Articles.* The Writings of Will Rogers, 3d ser. Stillwater: Oklahoma State University Press, 1980.

Smith, Bill. *The Vaudevillians.* New York: Macmillan, 1976.

Smith, Eric Ledell. *Bert Williams: A Biography of the Pioneer Black Comedian.* New York: McFarland, 1992.

Snyder, K. Alan. *Defining Noah Webster: Mind and Morals in the Early Republic.* Lanham, Md.: University Press of America, 1990.

Snyder, Robert W. *The Voice of the City: Vaudeville and Popular Culture in New York.* New York: Oxford University Press, 1989.

Sobel, Bernard. *A Pictorial History of Burlesque.* New York: Putnam, 1956.

Spitzer, Marian. *The Palace.* New York: Atheneum, 1969.

Springer, John, and Jack Hamilton. *They Had Faces Then.* Secaucus, N.J.: Citadel Press, 1974.

Stange, G. Robert, ed. *The Poetical Works of Tennyson.* Boston: Houghton Mifflin, 1974.

Stansbury, Kathryn. *Lucille Mulhall: Her Family, Her Life, Her Times.* 1985. 2d rev. ed. Mulhall, Okla.: Homestead Heirlooms Publishing, 1992.

Staples, Shirley. *Male-Female Comedy Teams in American Vaudeville, 1865-1932.* Ann Arbor, Mich.: UMI Research Press, 1984.

Starr, Emmet. *History of the Cherokee Indians and Their Legends and Folk Lore.* 1921. Reprint. New York: Kraus Reprint, 1969.

Steckbeck, John S. *Fabulous Redmen: The Carlisle Indians and Their Famous Football Teams.* Harrisburg, Pa.: J. Horace McFarland, 1951.

Stein, Charles W., ed. *American Vaudeville As Seen by Its Contemporaries.* New York: Da Capo Press, 1984.

Sterling, Bryan, and Frances N. Sterling, eds. *Will Rogers in Hollywood.* New York: Crown, 1984.

Stern, Robert A. M., Gregory Gilmartin, and John Montague Massengale. *New York 1900: Metropolitan Architecture and Urbanism, 1890–1915.* New York: Rizzoli International Publications, 1983.

Stoddart, Dayton. *Lord Broadway: Variety's Sime.* New York: Wilfred Funk, 1941.

Stone, Fred. *Rolling Stone.* New York: McGraw-Hill, 1945.

Sturtevant, William C., gen. ed. *Handbook of North American Indians.* Vol. 10: *Southwest.* Edited by Alfonso Ortiz. Washington, D.C.: Smithsonian Institution, 1983.

Sunday, William E., Marcel M. DuPriest, Marilee Brenhardt, and Quannah Archer Chu-lee-wah. *Gah Dah Gwa Stee.* Pryor, Okla.: Byron Smith, 1953.

S. Z. Poli's Theatrical Enterprises. [Booklet, ca. 1908.] Reprint. Notre Dame, Ind.: Theatre Historical Society, 1978.

Taylor, William R., ed. *Inventing Times Square: Commerce and Culture at the Crossroads of the World.* New York: Russell Sage Foundation, 1991.

Toll, Robert C. *Blacking Up: The Minstrel Show in Nineteenth-century America.* New York: Oxford University Press, 1974.

_____. *The Entertainment Machine: American Show Business in the Twentieth Century.* New York: Oxford University Press, 1982.

_____. *On with the Show! The First Century of Show Business in America.* New York: Oxford University Press, 1976.

Toole-Stott, R. *The Circus and Allied Arts.* 4 vols. Derby, England: Harpurt, 1962.

Traub, Hamilton, ed. *The American Literary Yearbook.* Vol. 1: 1919. Henning, Minn.: Paul Traub Publishers, 1919. Reprint. Detroit: Gale Research, 1968.

Tuchman, Barbara W. *The Proud Tower: A Portrait of the World before the War: 1890–1914.* New York: Macmillan, 1966; Bantam Books, 1967.

Tucker, Sophie, with Dorothy Giles. *Some of These Days: The Autobiography of Sophie Tucker.* Garden City, N.Y.: Doubleday, Doran, 1945.

Van Hoogstraten, Nicholas. *Lost Broadway Theatres.* Princeton, N.J.: Princeton Architectural Press, 1991.

Vaudeville Managers' Protective Association, 1912 Yearbook. Chicago: General Publicity Service, 1912.

Vaudeville Year Book, 1913. Chicago: Western Vaudeville Managers' Association, 1913.

Waller, Charles. *Magical Nights at the Theatre: A Chronicle.* Melbourne: Gerald Taylor, 1980.

Ward, Larry Wayne. *The Motion Picture Goes to War: The U.S. Government Film Effort during World War I.* Ann Arbor, Mich.: UMI Research Press, 1985.

Wardell, Morris L. *A Political History of the Cherokee Nation, 1838–1902.* Norman: University of Oklahoma Press, 1938.

Waterhouse, Richard. *From Minstrel Show to Vaudeville: The Australian Popular Stage, 1788-1914.* New South Wales: New South Wales University Press, 1990.

Waters, T. A. *The Encyclopedia of Magic and Magicians.* New York and Oxford: Facts on File Publications, 1988.

Wearing, J. P. *American and British Theatrical Biography.* Metuchen, N.J.: Scarecrow Press, 1979.

Weeks, Philip. *Farewell, My Nation: The American Indian and the United States, 1820-1890.* Washington Heights, Ill.: Harlan Davidson, 1990.

Wertheim, Arthur Frank, ed. *Will Rogers at the Ziegfeld Follies.* Norman: University of Oklahoma Press, 1992.

Wesser, Robert F. *A Response to Progressivism: The Democratic Party and New York Politics: 1902-18.* New York: New York University Press, 1986.

Westermeier, Clifford P. *Man, Beast, Dust: The Story of Rodeo.* N.p.: World Press, 1947.

Wheeler, Robert W. *Jim Thorpe, World's Greatest Athlete.* Rev. ed. Norman: University of Oklahoma Press, 1979.

White, G. Edward. *The Eastern Establishment and the Western Experience: The West of Frederic Remington, Theodore Roosevelt, and Owen Wister*. New Haven: Yale University Press, 1968.

Wilmeth, Don B. *Variety Entertainment and Outdoor Amusements*. Westport, Conn.: Greenwood Press, 1982.

Wilmut, Roger. *Kindly Leave the Stage!: The Story of Variety, 1919–1960*. London: Methuen, 1989.

Wister, Owen. *The Virginian: A Horseman of the Plains*. New York: Macmillan, 1902.

Woll, Allen. *Black Musical Theatre: From Coontown to Dreamgirls*. Baton Rouge: Louisiana State University Press, 1989.

_____. *Dictionary of the Black Theatre: Broadway, Off- Broadway, and Selected Harlem Theatre*. Westport, Conn.: Greenwood Press, 1983.

Yagoda, Ben. *Will Rogers: A Biography*. New York: Alfred A. Knopf, 1993.

Young, William C. *Documents of American Theater History*. 2 vols. Chicago: American Library Association, 1973.

_____. *Famous Actors and Actresses on the American Stage*. New York: R. R. Bowker, 1975.

Zeidman, Irving. *The American Burlesque Show*. New York: Hawthorn, 1967.

Zellers, Parker. *Tony Pastor: Dean of the Vaudeville Stage*. Ypsilanti, Mich.: Eastern Michigan University Press, 1971.

Ziegfeld, Richard, and Paulette Ziegfeld. *The Ziegfeld Touch: The Life and Times of Florenz Ziegfeld, Jr.* New York: Harry N. Abrams, 1993.

ARTICLES AND CHAPTERS IN ANTHOLOGIES

Acton, Mildred Mulhall. "The Original Cowgirl." *Ranchman*, February 1942, 6–7.

Adler, Dankmar. "Chicago Auditorium." *Architectural Record* 1 (July 1891–92): 415–34.

Albert, Dora. "The Rogers 'Carry On'." *Rexall Magazine*, June 1943, 3, 10.

Allen, Jeanne Thomas. "Copyright and Early Theater, Vaudeville, and Film Competition." In *Film before Griffth*, edited by John Fell, 176–87. Berkeley: University of California Press, 1983.

Allen, Robert C. "B. F. Keith and the Origins of American Vaudeville." *Theatre Survey* 21 (November 1980): 105–15.

_____. "Contra the Chaser Theory." In *Film before Griffth*, edited by John Fell, 105–15. Berkeley: University of California Press, 1983.

"Application by White Rats Made to Federation of Labor." *Variety* (24 September 1910): 5.

Armstrong, Jerry. "The Guy Who Started the Stampede." *Western Horseman* 24 (August 1959): 6–7, 62–65.

Bagley, Harry B. "Riding, Roping and Trouping with Will Rogers: Buck McKee Was Boyhood Pal and Vaudeville Partner of Famous Humorist." *Sacramento Bee*, magazine section, 18 January 1941, 3.

Bayes, Nora. "After the Play." *New Republic*, 4 June 1918, 297.

_____. "Why People Enjoy Crying in a Theater." *American Magazine*, April 1918, 33–35.

Berkery, Denny. "Tompkins Wild West Show 1913–17: A Supplement." *Bandwagon*, May–June 1971, 30–31.

"B. F. Keith's Memorial Theatre." *Marquee*, Spring 1983, 1–31.

Bird, Carol. "May Vokes." *Theatre Magazine* 36 (October 1922): 241.

Blathwayt, Raymond. "The Control of a Great Music-Hall: Mr. Alfred Butt and the Palace Theatre." *World's Work* (London) 17 (February 1911): 248–53.

Botkin, Sam L. "Indian Missions of the Episcopal Church in Oklahoma." *Chronicles of Oklahoma* 36 (Spring 1958): 40–47.

Bradbury, Joseph T. "Tom Mix Circus 1936 Coast to Coast Tour." *Bandwagon*, April–May 1952, 5–8.

_____. "Tompkins Wild West Show, 1913–1917." *Bandwagon*, March–April 1971, 4–15.

_____. "Tompkins Wild West Show 1913-17, Supplement." *Bandwagon*, May–June 1971, 30–31.

_____. "Tompkins Wild West Show, Supplement 2." *Bandwagon*, November–December 1971, 26–28.

Brenneman, Lyman. "A Look Backstage at the Hippodrome." *Marquee*, Spring 1973, 8–9.

Brown, A. Ten Eyck. "The Forsyth Theater and Office Building, Atlanta, Ga." *American Architect* 96 (18 August 1909): 63–66.

Cantor, Eddie. "Bert Williams—The Best Teacher I Ever Had." *Ebony*, June 1958, 103–6.

Cary, P. "From the Old Frontier to Film." *Wild West* 7 (October 1994) 42–48.

Castle, Irene. "My Memories of Vernon Castle." *Everybody's Magazine*, December 1918, 36–41; January 1919, 38–42; February 1919, 50–55; March 1919, 39–42.

Chavanne, Paul J. "The Boston Orpheum." *Marquee*, Fall 1972, 19– 21.

Clancy, Foghorn. "Memory Trail." *Hoofs and Horns*, May 1942, n.p.

Clark, Neil M. "They Said He'd Never Dance Again." *American Magazine*, May 1931, 50.

Clinton, Fred S. "The Indian Territory Medical Association." *Chronicles of Oklahoma* 26 (1948): 23–55.

Collins, Reba. "A Fond Farewell: 'Love, Reba.'" *Will Rogers Roundup*, October 1993, 2.

_____. "Will Rogers' Daughter Mary: A Storied Life." *Oologah Lake Leader*, 4 January 1990, 10.

"Colonial Theatre Sixty-Fifth Street Blvd." *Architecture and Building* 30 (1890): n.p.

Conover, Richard E. "The Sells Brothers Bandchariot and Their 50-Cage Menagerie." *Bandwagon*, May–June 1966, 14–15.

Cooke, Louis E. "Walter F. Main: America's Best Railroad Shows." *Bandwagon*, July–August 1967, 3–8.

Copley, Frank B. "The Story of a Great Vaudeville Manager." *American Magazine*, December 1922, 46–47, 152–55.

Cox, James A. "Fred Harvey, the Righteous Restaurateur." *Smithsonian*, September 1987, 130–39.

Crane, Warren Eugene. "Alexander Pantages." *System: The Magazine of Business* 37 (March 1920): 501–3.

Cronican, Frank. "Hip, Hip, Hippodrome!" *Marquee*, Fall 1972, 3–5.

"Cummins' Real Wild West Show." *Banner Line,* 15 April 1954, 5.

"Cummins' Wild West Show." *Bandwagon,* July–August 1962, 4.

Czitrom, Daniel. "Underworlds and Underdogs: Big Tim Sullivan and Metropolitan Politics in New York, 1889–1913." *Journal of American History* 78 (September 1991): 536-58.

Davis, Hartley. "The Business Side of Vaudeville." *Everybody's Magazine,* October 1907, 527–37.

Davis, Norris N. "Al Latell Leads a Dog's Life–But He Likes It." *American Magazine,* April 1924, 68–69.

DeFoe, L. V. "Fred Stone, Expert Clown." *Green Book Magazine,* June 1915, 1003-11.

DiMaggio, Paul. "Cultural Boundaries and Structural Change: The Extension of the High Culture Model to Theater, Opera, and the Dance, 1900–1940." In *Cultivating Differences: Symbolic Boundaries and the Making of Inequality,* edited by Michele Lamont and Marcel Fournier, 21–57. Chicago: University of Chicago Press, 1992.

Dormon, James. "American Popular Culture and the New Immigrant Ethnics: The Vaudeville Stage and the Process of Ethnic Ascription." *American Studies* 36, no. 2 (1991): 179–93.

Dresser, Louise. "My Friend, Will Rogers." *Screen Book,* June 1934, 40, 72.

Eaton, Walter Prichard. "The Wizards of Vaudeville." *McClure's Magazine,* September 1923, 43–49.

Eltinge, Julian. "How I Portray a Woman on the Stage." *Theatre Magazine* 150 (August 1913): ix, 56, 58.

Everson, William K. "Songs of Innocence." *Sight and Sound* 2 (December 1992): 63.

Fausett, Jessie. "The Symbolism of Bert Williams." *Crisis,* 24 May 1922, 12–15.

Ferguson, Blanche. "Black Skin, Black Mask: The Inconvenient Grace of Bert Williams." *American Visions* 7 (June–July 1992): 14–16, 18.

Fiedler, Leslie. "The Legend." In *Buffalo Bill and the Wild West,* 84–95. New York: Brooklyn Museum; Museum of Art, Carnegie Institute; and Buffalo Bill Historical Center, 1981.

Fogarty, Frank. "Frank Fogarty Talks on the Grin as an Asset." *New York Dramatic Mirror,* 27 May 1914, 20.

"A Foot in Each World." *True West,* May–June 1979, 26–27, 46.

Fowler, Andrew C. "Hippodromes." *Marquee,* Fall 1993, 4–28.

Fox, Richard W. "The Discipline of Amusement." In *Inventing Times Square,* edited by William R. Taylor, 83–98. New York: Russell Sage Foundation, 1991.

Franklin, Irene. "Back from the Trenches." *Theatre Magazine,* December 1918, 336.

_____. "Making Songs Tell a Story." *New York Dramatic Mirror,* 16 December 1914, 19.

_____. "Mike-Wise." *Theatre Magazine,* July 1929, 26.

Fulton, A. R. "The Machine." In *The American Film Industry,* edited by Tino Balio, 27–42. Madison: University of Wisconsin Press, 1985.

Gabriel, Jim. "Frontier Celebration Events." *Billboard,* 10 September 1910, 20.

Glazer, Irvin R. "The Metropolitan Opera House—Philadelphia." *Marquee,* Summer 1979, 3–15.

Glenn, Susan. "'Give an Imitation of Me': Vaudeville Mimics and the Play of Self." *American Quarterly* 50, no. 1 (March 1998): 47–76.

Grau, Robert. "A Napoleon of the Vaudeville World." *Theatre Magazine* 116 (October 1910): 117.

Gray, Christopher. "The Ghost behind a Huge Sign." *New York Times,* 29 January 1989.

"Guy Weadick Travelled Rocky Trail before Hitting Pay Dirt in 1912." *Calgary Herald,* 9 July 1949, 24, 31.

Hancock, La Touche. "Some Humor of Some Humorists." *Bookman* 16 (September 1902): 15–22.

Hardy, Camille. "Flashes of Flamenco: The American Debuts of Carmencita and Otero." *Arabesque: A Magazine of International Dance* 9 (May–June 1983): 16–23.

Hartung, A. N. "James H. Minnick." *Back in the Saddle,* May 1948, 13, 30.

Havig, Alan. "The Commercial Amusement Audience in Early 20th-Century American Cities." *Journal of American Culture* 5 (Spring 1982): 1–19.

Headley, Robert K., Jr. "Source Records for Theater History." *Marquee,* Winter 1969, 9–12.

_____. "The Theatres of Milwaukee . . . A Brief Theater Reconnaissance of Milwaukee." *Marquee,* Winter 1971, 3–12.

Helgesen, Terry. "B. Marcus Priteca, 1890–1971: The Last of the Giants." *Marquee,* Spring 1972, 3–12.

Henderson, Sam. "Show Biz Western Style." *Wild West,* October 1994, 34–40, 72.

Hendricks, Gordon. "The History of the Kinetescope." In *The American Film Industry,* edited by Tino Balio, 43–56. Madison: University of Wisconsin Press, 1985.

Hendrix, John M. "He Put Will Rogers on the Stage." *West Texas Today,* March 1936, 14, 28.

_____. "Mis' Minnick and Jim." *Hoof and Horns* 5 (February 1936): 12, 26.

Hinkle, Milt. "Memoirs of My Rodeo Days." *Real West,* September 1968, 35–37.

_____. "The Way a Wild West Show Operated." *Frontier Times,* February–March 1969, 20–23, 50–52.

Hodin, Mark. "Class, Consumption, and Ethnic Performance in Vaudeville." *Prospects* 22 (1997): 193–221.

"Ideas about Husbands." *Green Book Magazine* 10 (August 1913): 210–14.

Judson, William. "The Movies." In *Buffalo Bill and the Wild West,* 68–83. New York: Brooklyn Museum; Museum of Art, Carnegie Institute; and Buffalo Bill Historical Center, 1981.

Kahn, Ely J. "Ziegfeld Theatre." *Architectural Record* 61 (May 1927): 385–93.

Kajiyama, Tameo. "Personality and Its Use in Vaudeville." *New York Dramatic Mirror,* 31 December 1921, 1058.

"Keith Palace Theater, Cleveland, Ohio." *Architecture and Building* (May 1923): 110–11.

Kibler, M. Alison. "Nothing Succeeds Like Excess: Lillian Shaw's Comedy and Sexuality on the Keith Vaudeville Circuit." In *Performing Gender and Comedy,* edited by Shannon Hengen, 59–80. Amsterdam: Gordon and Breach, 1998.

_____. "Rank Ladies, Ladies of Rank: The Elinore Sisters in Vaudeville." *American Studies* 38 (Spring 1997): 97–116.

King, Donald C. "From Museum to Multi-Cinema." *Marquee,* Summer 1974, 5–10, 15.

_____. "Keith-Albee et al. . . ." *Marquee,* Summer 1975, 3–10.

_____. "New York's Oldest Existing Theatre—The Union Square." *Marquee,* Spring 1974, 48.

_____. "Sylvester Z. Poli Story: From Wax to Riches." *Marquee,* Spring 1979, 11–18.

Koger, Alicia Kae. "Harrigan's Theatre." *Marquee,* Winter 1983, 16–18.

Krasner, David. "Rewriting the Body: Aida Overton Walker and the Social Formation of Cakewalking." *Theatre Survey* 37 (November 1996): 66–92.

LaLanne, Bruce. "Hippodrome Memories." *Marquee,* Summer 1983, 14–16.

Lamar, Howard R. "The Cowboys." In *Buffalo Bill and the Wild West,* 57–67. New York: Brooklyn Museum; Museum of Art, Carnegie Institute; and Buffalo Bill Historical Center, 1981.

Lansburgh, G. Albert. "Some Novel Features of a Strictly Fire-proof Theater Building." *Architect and Engineer of California, Pacific Coast States* 17 (June 1909): 37–41.

LaRue, Grace. "Just the Singing of a Song." *New York Dramatic Mirror,* 16 December 1914, 18.

Lasser, Michael. "The Glorifier: Florenz Ziegfeld and the Creation of the American Showgirl." *American Scholar* (Summer 1994): 441–48.

Laurie, Joe, Jr. "Vaudeville Dead? It's Never Been." *New York Times Magazine,* 14 October 1951, 25, 67, 70–71.

_____. "Vaudeville's Ideal Bill." *New York Times Magazine,* 15 May 1949, 24–25.

Lazzara, Robert L. "Orpheum Theatre, San Franciso California." *Marquee,* Fall 1983, 16–17.

Levin, Steven. "San Francisco Story: From the Fire to the Fair." *Marquee,* Winter 1975, 3–9.

Loney, Glenn. "Denishawn in Vaudeville and Beyond." In *Musical Theatre in America: Papers and Proceedings of the Conference on the Musical Theatre in America,* edited by Glenn Loney, 179–85. Westport, Conn.: Greenwood Press, 1984.

_____. "Theatres of 42nd Street." *Marquee,* Fall 1977, 15–16.

Manning, Fowler. "The Part Our Field Representatives Are Playing." *Winchester Record* 1 (22 November 1918): 1–4.

Marquis, Arnold. "Will and Charlie." *Frontier Times* 41 (June–July 1967): 6–9, 47–49.

_____. "Will Rogers and His Horses." Part 1. *Western Horseman* 28 (February 1963): 28–30, 71–73.

Martin, George. "The Wit of Will Rogers: The Story of a Cowboy Who Has Become a Famous Comedian." *American Magazine,* November 1919, 34–35, 106–10.

McCall, John Clark, Jr. "Loew's Grand, Atlanta, Georgia." *Marquee,* Summer 1977, 11–13.

McLean, Albert F. "Genesis of Vaudeville: Two Letters from B. F. Keith." *Theatre Survey* 1 (1960): 82–95.

_____. "U.S. Vaudeville and the Urban Comics." *Theatre Quarterly* 1 (October–December 1971): 47–52.

McSpadden, Herb. "Horses and Horse Collars." *Ranchman,* November 1942, 11–12.

Meacham, Jon. "What Will Rogers Could Teach Rush Limbaugh." *Washington Monthly,* January–February 1994, 16–22.

Mensel, Robert E. "'Kodakers Lying in Wait': Amateur Photography and the Right of Privacy in New York, 1885–1915." *American Quarterly* 43 (March 1991): 24–30.

Meserve, John Barlett. "Trinity Episcopal Church, Tulsa." *Chronicles of Oklahoma* 17 (September 1939): 269–73.

Miller, Michael. "Proctor's Fifty-eighth Street Theatre." *Marquee,* Summer 1973, 7–15.

Mintz, Lawrence E. "Humor and Ethnic Stereotypes in Vaudeville and Burlesque." *MELUS* 21 (winter 1996): 19.

Mitchell, George, and William K. Everson. "Tom Mix." *Films in Review* 8 (October 1957): 387–97.

Moorcock, Michael. "Songs of Innocence." *Sight and Sound* 2 (October 1992): 36–37.

Morgan, J. H. "New York Hippodrome." *Architects and Builders Magazine* 37 (August 1905): 490–99.

Morrison, William. "Oscar Hammerstein I: The Man Who Invented Times Square." *Marquee,* Winter 1983, 3–15.

_____. "Oscar Hammerstein I, Part II: Impresario in Excelsis." *Marquee,* Summer 1984, 17–23.

Mould, David H., and Charles M. Berg. "Fact and Fantasy in the Films of World War One." *Film and History* 14 (September 1984): 50–60.

"Movie Theatre History in Wisconsin." *Marquee,* Fall 1980, 3, 6, 7.

Mullett, Mary B. "Climbing a Greased Pole Was Fred Stone's First Triumph." *American Magazine,* December 1926, 19, 132–39.

Newman, Richard. "The Lincoln Theatre: Once a Carnival of Merrymaking." *American Visions* 6, no. 4 (August 1991): 29–33.

Oberdeck, Kathryn. "Contested Cultures of American Refinement: Theatrical Manager Sylvester Poli, His Audiences, and the Vaudeville Industry, 1890–1920." *Radical History Review* 66 (1996): 40–91.

O'Connor, Patrick J. "Vaudeville Venues in Kansas." *Journal of the West* 32, no. 1 (January 1993): 46–53.

Patterson, Ada. "I Am Thirty-six and Proud of It." *Green Book Magazine* 13 (January 1916): 161–68.

_____. "When Blanche Ring Smiles." *Theatre Magazine* 19 (April 1914): 198.

"Personal." *New York Dramatic Mirror,* 7 May 1913, 7.

"Photo Record of the Poli Empire." *Marquee,* Spring 1979, 19–28.

Reynolds, Chang. "101 Ranch Wild West Show." *Bandwagon,* January–February 1969, 4–21.

"Riding, Roping and Trouping with Will Rogers." *Sacramento Bee,* magazine section, 18 January 1941, 3.

Ring, Blanche. "The Great American Husband." *Green Book Magazine* 10 (August 1913): 210–14.

_____. "How to Put 'Em Across." *Green Book Magazine* 9 (July 1912): 45- 49.

Robinson, C. O. "Tom Mix Was My Boss." *Frontier Times* 43 (1969): 18–20, 42–43.

Robinson, Jack. "Brooklyn's Magnificent Ruin: The Bushwick." *Marquee,* Winter 1986, 22–23.

_____. "8 Big Acts—A Glance Backwards." *Marquee,* Winter 1977, 3–10.

_____. "Fourteenth Street, Cradle of American Vaudeville." *Marquee,* Winter 1983, 19–20.

_____. "A Stroll through Harlem." *Marquee,* Summer 1981, 10–12.

Rodgers, John J. "Pursued by Songs." *Green Book Magazine* 13 (June 1916): 1102–6.

"Roof Gardens Open the Summer Season." *Theatre Magazine* 53 (July 1905): 158–59.

Roth, Barbara Williams. "101 Ranch Wild West Show." *Chronicles of Oklahoma* 43 (Winter 1965–66): 416-31.

Russell, Don. "The Golden Age of Wild West Shows." *Bandwagon,* September–October 1971, 21–27.

Safer, Karen J. "The Functions of Decoration in the American Movie Palace." *Marquee,* Spring 1982, 3–7.

Schallert, Elza. "Louise Dresser: Tribute on Birthday." *Los Angeles Times,* 2 March 1959, 1, 30.

Senelick, Laurence. "Variety into Vaudeville: The Process Observed in Two Manuscript Gagbooks." *Theatre Survey* 19 (1978): 1–15.

Shteir, Rachel B. "The Vaudeville Mirror." *American Theatre* 9, no. 5 (September 1992): 12–18.

Singer, Ben. "Early Home Cinema and the Edison Home Projecting Kinetoscope." *Film History: An International Journal* 2 (1988): 37–70.

Singer, Stan. "Vaudeville in Los Angeles, 1910–1926: Theaters, Management, and the Orpheum." *Pacific Historical Review* 61, no. 1 (February 1992): 103–14.

Slotkin, Richard. "The Wild West." In *Buffalo Bill and the Wild West,* 27–44. New York: Brooklyn Museum; Museum of Art, Carnegie Institute; and Buffalo Bill Historical Center, 1981.

"Special Anniversary Issue: The Roxy Theatre." *Marquee,* Winter 1979, 1–28.

Sprague, Stuart Seely. "Meet Me in St. Louis on the Ten-Million- Dollar Pike." *Missouri Historical Society Bulletin* 32 (October 1975): 26–32.

Spring, Agnes Wright. "Horseman Extraordinary." *Western Horseman,* November 1949, 14–15, 32, 34, 36–37.

Stainton, Walter H. "Irene Castle." *Films in Review* 16 (1965): 347–55.

Stewart-Gordon, James. "Houdini, The Man No Lock Could Hold." *Reader's Digest,* February 1976, 151–55.

Stone, Fred. "A Clown Who Built a Skyscraper with Laughs." *American Magazine,* October 1917, 32–34, 88–95.

Sturtevant, C. G. "A Famous Circus Fan." *The Whitetops,* November 1936, 3–4.

Sugrue, Thomas. "The Newsreels." *Scribner's Magazine,* April 1937, 9–32.

"Texas, Houston." *Marquee,* Winter 1978, 12.

"Time Clock on Performers." *The Player* (24 December 1909): 1.

Todd, Robert B. "The Organization of Professional Theatre in Vancouver, 1886–1914." *BC Studies* 44 (Winter 1979–80): 3–24.

Tompkins, Charles H. "Gabriel Brothers Wild West." *Westerners Brand Book* 13 (October 1956): 64.

———. "My Association with Will Rogers." *Old Trail Drivers Convention,* October 1953 (Will Rogers Memorial Edition), 7–12.

"Triple Victory for the White Rats." *The Player* (31 March 1911): 22.

"Two More Victories." *The Player* (19 May 1911): 9.

"Vaudeville." *Variety* (11 November 1925): 19.

Ver Halen, Charles J. "Young Buffalo Wild West." *Billboard,* 6 May 1911, 5.

Walton, Florence. "The Most Striking Episode in My Life." *Theatre Magazine* 29 (January 1919): 14.

Washington, Booker T. "Interesting People: Bert Williams." *American Magazine,* September 1910, 600–601, 603–4.

Weadick, Guy. "Here and There." *Billboard,* 18 February 1911, 20; 25 February 1911, 24; 8 April 1911, 31; 13 January 1912, 23.

West, Magda Frances. "The Manns and Their Mountains." *Green Book Magazine* 10 (February 1913): 321–28.

"When You Coming Back." *Los Angeles Magazine,* October 1979, 82–92.

White, Jack R. "Houdini and His Movies." *Classic Film Collector* 2 (Winter 1970): 46–47.

"White Rats to Admit Women." *New York Dramatic Mirror,* 26 January 1901, 18.

"The White Rats of America." *New York Dramatic Mirror,* 21 July 1900, 7.

"White Rats News." *Variety* (18 August 1916): 14.

"White Rats Strike." *The Player* (9 February 1917): 4.

"White Rats and Unionists." *Variety* (18 June 1910): 5.

"The White Rats Win Their Point." *New York Dramatic Mirror,* 16 February 1901, 20.

"William Morris: Dean of the Golden Age of Vaudeville." *Billboard* 106 (1 November 1994): 32.

Williams, Bert. "The Comic Side of Trouble." *American Magazine,* January 1918, 33–34, 58.

Williams, Percy G. "Vaudeville and Vaudevillians." In *The Saturday Evening Post Reflections of a Decade, 1901–1910,* 45–47. Indianapolis: Curtis Publishing, 1980.

Williams, Robert L. "Tams Bixby (1855–1922)." *Chronicles of Oklahoma* 39 (September 1941): 205–12.

Wolf, Rennold. "The Greatest Comedian on the American Stage." *Green Book Magazine* 9 (June 1912): 1173–84.

————. "Nora Bayes, an Expert in Songs and Matrimony." *Green Book Magazine* 11 (April 1914): 571–80.

Woods, Leigh. "The Golden Calf: Noted English Actresses in American Vaudeville, 1904–16." *Journal of American Culture* 15, no. 3 (fall 1992): 61–72.

————. "Sarah Bernhardt and the Refining of American Vaudeville." *Theatre Research International* 18, no. 1 (spring 1993): 16–25.

————. "Two-a-day Redemptions and Truncated Camiles." *New Theatre Quarterly* 10, no. 37 (February 1994): 11–24.

Woodward, R. T. "The Continuous Performance." *Illustrated American,* 4 November 1898, 358–59.

Woolf, S. J. "Gus Edwards's Academy." *New York Times Magazine,* 23 March 1941, 12, 19.

Zellers, Parker. "The Cradle of Variety: The Concert Saloon." *Educational Theatre Journal* 20 (December 1968): 578–85.

UNPUBLISHED AND MISCELLANEOUS SOURCES

America and the Holocaust: Deceit and Destruction. Public Broadcasting System, 1993. Videocassette.

Connors, Timothy D. "American Vaudeville Managers: Their Organization and Influence." Ph.D. diss., University of Kansas, 1981.

Cook, Susan C. "Irene Castle Watches Her Step: Dance, Music, and Dangerous Pleasures." Paper presented at the American Studies Association Annual Conference, Nashville, Tenn., October 1994.

Distler, Paul. "The Rise and Fall of the Racial Comics in American Vaudeville." Ph.D. diss., Tulane University, 1963.

Dunn, Jonathan Alexander. "A History of the Will Rogers Ranch and State Historic Park in California." Master's thesis, University of Southern California, 1986.

Fisch, Martha. Oral history sessions on the Mulhall family history. Conducted with Barbara Bair of the Will Rogers Papers Project. Guthrie, Okla., January 1994. WRPP.

Gustafson, Antoinette McCloskey. "The Image of the West in American Popular Performance." Ph.D. diss., New York University, 1988.

"Historical Data—Will Rogers Ranch." Unpublished ms., ca. 1940. CPpR.

Jewell, Richard Brownell. "A History of RKO Radio Pictures, Incorporated, 1928–1942." Ph.D. diss., University of Southern California, 1978.

Keith, Harold. "Clem Rogers and His Influence on Oklahoma History." Master's thesis, University of Oklahoma, 1938.

Knapp, Margaret May. "A Historical Study of the Legitimate Playhouses on West Forty-second Street between Seventh and Eighth Avenues in New York City." Ph.D. diss., City University of New York, 1982.

Koch, Iris. "Zack Mulhall, His Family, and the Mulhall Wild West Show." Master's thesis, Oklahoma Agricultural and Mechanical College, 1940.

Mickols, Robert Anthony. "The Boss of the Bowery: The Life and Times of Big Tim Sullivan." Master's thesis, University of California, Santa Barbara, 1957.

Mudd, A. I. "History of Polite Vaudeville in Washington, D.C." Copy, NN-L-BRTC.

[Mulhall], Georgia Smith Casey. Scrapbook of newspaper clippings and photographic albums of the Mulhall Wild West Show and Mulhall Family [ca. 1904–1910]. Original, MFC; microfilm, OkHi.

Oberdeck, Kathryn. "Labor's Vicar and the Variety Show: Popular Theater, Popular Religion, and Cultural Class Conflict in Turn-of-the-Century America." Ph.D. diss., Yale University, 1991.

Orpheum Circuit 1925. Pamphlet. Copy, Illinois State University, Special Collections, Milner Library.

Riley, Robert. *Coin Harvey and Monte Ne.* N.p.: n.p., n.d. Booklet, RHM.

Sandmeier, Emil. "To the Docents [of] Will Rogers State Historical Park." Unpublished ms., Emil Sandmeier private papers, Pacific Palisades, Calif.; copy, WRPP.

Singer, Stanford P. "Vaudeville West: To Los Angeles and the Final Stages of Vaudeville." Ph.D. diss., University of California, Los Angeles, 1987.

Snelling, Lois. "One of the Blake Girls: The Story of Betty Blake (Mrs. Will Rogers) and Her Benton County Family." Ca. 1977. TMS. OkClaW.

Snyder, Frederick Edward. "American Vaudeville—Theatre in a Package: The Origins of Mass Entertainment." Ph.D. diss., Yale University, 1970.

Souvenir and Opening Program of the Orpheum Circuit's New Orpheum Theatre. Sioux City, Iowa, 19 December 1927.

Summer Days and Nights in New York. Pamphlet. N.p.: n.p., n.d. [1898]. Copy, New York Public Library.

Index of Performers and Acts

This index lists performers and acts (including those from vaudeville, burlesque, music hall, musical comedy, and variety) mentioned or referenced in this volume in connection with Will Rogers's stage career.

Stage performers who were personal friends of Rogers are listed in the General Index (and indicated herein by cross-references). For Wild West performers and shows, Broadway and Off-Broadway productions, musicals, and various vaudeville-variety plays, sketches, and stock companies, see the General Index.

References to notes that provide primary biographical information about an individual or act are preceded by an asterisk (*). References to illustrations are printed in **boldface** type.

General Index

References to illustrations are printed in **boldface** type.

References to notes that provide primary biographical information about an individual or historical background about a theater are preceded by an asterisk (*).

For page numbers of correspondence between given individuals and Will Rogers, see Documents list in the preliminary matter of the volume (*ix–xii*).

For Will Rogers's vaudeville, Wild West, and theater itineraries for the time period covered by this volume, including the particular theaters and cities where he appeared, consult the Chronology in the preliminary matter of the volume (9–28). The Chronology and Documents lists may also be used as guides to help locate particular documents of interest within the volume by date or time period.